The Best of Creative Computing
Volume 1

ORDERING INFORMATION

Additional copies of *The Best of Creative Computing — Volume 1* are available direct from the publisher for $8.95 plus $1.00 postage and handling (USA) or $2.00 (foreign).

Subscriptions to *Creative Computing* magazine are available for $8.00 per year (paid in advance) in the U.S. Foreign subscriptions are $12.00 surface or $20.00 air mail. A subscription form is bound in the back.

Creative Computing Press
P.O. Box 789-M
Morristown, N. J. 07960

DEBERNY

The Best of

creative computing

Volume 1   Edited by David H. Ahl

Creative Computing Press

Morristown, New Jersey

**OTHER BOOKS
BY DAVID H. AHL**

101 BASIC Computer Games
Understanding Mathematics and Logic Using BASIC Computer Games
Getting Started in Classroom Computing

BY CREATIVE COMPUTING PRESS

Artist and Computer
Amazing, Thrilling, Fantastic Computer Stories
The Colossal Computer Cartoon Book
The Best of Creative Computing — Vols. 1 and 2
The Best of Byte — Vol. 1

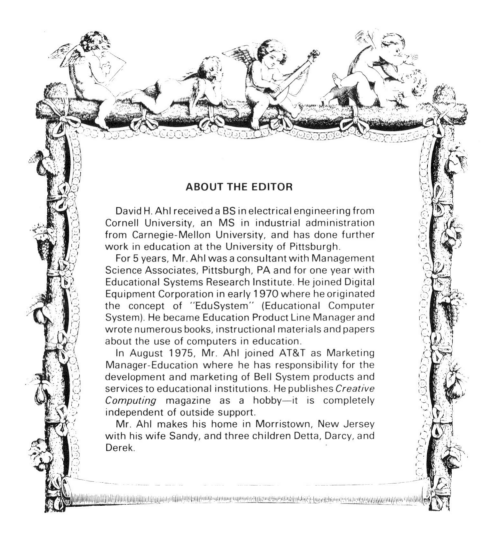

ABOUT THE EDITOR

David H. Ahl received a BS in electrical engineering from Cornell University, an MS in industrial administration from Carnegie-Mellon University, and has done further work in education at the University of Pittsburgh.

For 5 years, Mr. Ahl was a consultant with Management Science Associates, Pittsburgh, PA and for one year with Educational Systems Research Institute. He joined Digital Equipment Corporation in early 1970 where he originated the concept of "EduSystem" (Educational Computer System). He became Education Product Line Manager and wrote numerous books, instructional materials and papers about the use of computers in education.

In August 1975, Mr. Ahl joined AT&T as Marketing Manager-Education where he has responsibility for the development and marketing of Bell System products and services to educational institutions. He publishes *Creative Computing* magazine as a hobby—it is completely independent of outside support.

Mr. Ahl makes his home in Morristown, New Jersey with his wife Sandy, and three children Detta, Darcy, and Derek.

First Printing   January 1976

Second Printing   July 1977

ISBN 0-916688-01-1
Library of Congress Catalog Card Number: 76-438
Printed in the United States of America

Preface to the 2nd Edition

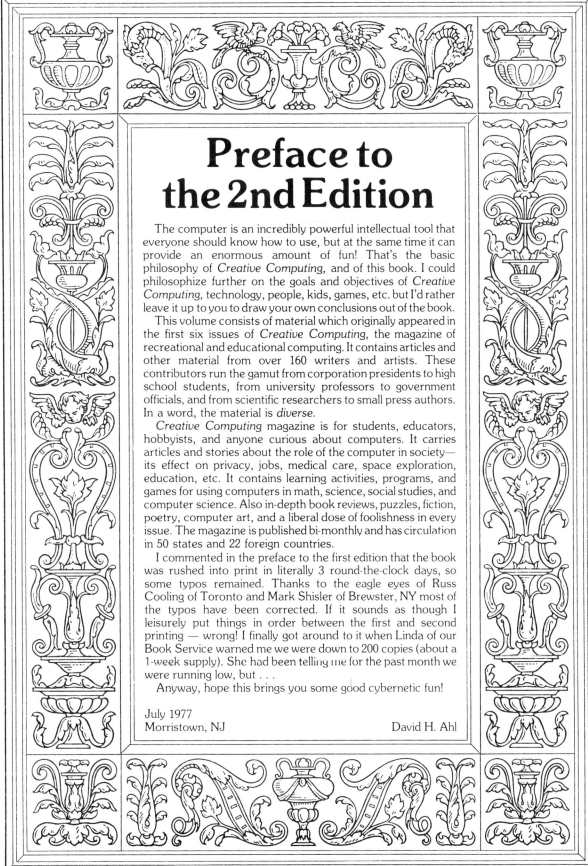

The computer is an incredibly powerful intellectual tool that everyone should know how to use, but at the same time it can provide an enormous amount of fun! That's the basic philosophy of *Creative Computing,* and of this book. I could philosophize further on the goals and objectives of *Creative Computing,* technology, people, kids, games, etc. but I'd rather leave it up to you to draw your own conclusions out of the book.

This volume consists of material which originally appeared in the first six issues of *Creative Computing,* the magazine of recreational and educational computing. It contains articles and other material from over 160 writers and artists. These contributors run the gamut from corporation presidents to high school students, from university professors to government officials, and from scientific researchers to small press authors. In a word, the material is *diverse.*

Creative Computing magazine is for students, educators, hobbyists, and anyone curious about computers. It carries articles and stories about the role of the computer in society—its effect on privacy, jobs, medical care, space exploration, education, etc. It contains learning activities, programs, and games for using computers in math, science, social studies, and computer science. Also in-depth book reviews, puzzles, fiction, poetry, computer art, and a liberal dose of foolishness in every issue. The magazine is published bi-monthly and has circulation in 50 states and 22 foreign countries.

I commented in the preface to the first edition that the book was rushed into print in literally 3 round-the-clock days, so some typos remained. Thanks to the eagle eyes of Russ Cooling of Toronto and Mark Shisler of Brewster, NY most of the typos have been corrected. If it sounds as though I leisurely put things in order between the first and second printing — wrong! I finally got around to it when Linda of our Book Service warned me we were down to 200 copies (about a 1-week supply). She had been telling me for the past month we were running low, but . . .

Anyway, hope this brings you some good cybernetic fun!

July 1977
Morristown, NJ

David H. Ahl

ACKNOWLEDGEMENTS

The articles, stories, programs, and graphics in this volume were assembled from a wide variety of sources. Most are noted on the contribution, however, the following people also contributed. Inevitably, I have overlooked someone, for which I apologize in advance. — DHA.

Writers and Editors
Eleanor Corr, Keystone Jr. College, PA
Steve Gray, Darien, CT
Susan Hastings, Florham Park, NJ
Tom R. Kibler, Georgia State Univ., GA
Walter Koetke, Lexington High School, MA
Peter Kugel, Boston College, MA
John Lees, University of Missouri
Bob McElwain, Sylmar High School, CA
A. Kent Morton, Dartmouth College, NH
Trish Todd, Brown University, RI
Lynn Yarbrough, Lexington, MA

Art and Graphics
George Beker, Stratford, CT
Kimberly Collins, University of New Hampshire
Will Eisner (from the book ''Incredible Facts, Amazing Statistics, and Monumental Trivia'')
Craig Johnson, Ravenna, OH
Ed Manning, Stratford, CT
Carol Rasmussen, Concord High School, MA
Jeanne S. Roberts, Lincoln, MA

Business Staff
Jane Fletcher, Stow, MA
Andree Stone, Concord, MA
Josie Task, Morris Plains, NJ
Carol Tick, Bernardsville, NJ

Encouragement and Understanding
Sandy Ahl

COVERS

The Best of Creative Computing
   Computer Picture of Mr. Spock by Sam Harbison, Carnegie-Mellon University (formerly Princeton Univ.). A negative (of a TV image) was converted to computer-readable form by a scanning digital densitometer. A computer program then translated the 255 optical density values to single or overstruck line printer characters.

Nov/Dec 1974, Vol. 1, No. 1.
   A photographic study by Lisa Sheble, a teacher of art and photography at the Spence School, New York. Kary Heuston is using the terminal while Janet Chaplan looks on.

Jan/Feb 1975, Vol. 1, No. 2.
   ''Inner City Variation No. II'' by Ruth Leavitt is one of a series exploring plastic deformation of three-dimensional projected objects. It was produced by an interactive Fortran IV program outputting onto microfilm.

Mar/Apr 1975, Vol. 1, No. 3.
   ''The Dawn of Creative Computing'' by Katy Owens was programmed in Fortran and then produced off line on a CalComp 563 31'' plotter. Katy, at Ball State University, was assisted by Tom Huston of Computra.

May/Jun 1975, Vol. 1, No. 4.
   ''Lost World'' is by Marilyn Clark of the University of California, San Francisco. The original medium is charcoal.

Sep/Oct 1975, Vol. 1, No. 5.
   ''Young Thinker'' was done by an anonymous programmer in a contest sponsored by California Computer Products, Inc. It was plotted on a CalComp 502 plotter with a step size of .01 inches.

Nov/Dec 1975, Vol. 1, No. 6.
   Craig Johnson of Ravenna, Ohio calls his Moire face a ''poor man's approach to computer graphics.'' He feels the use of Moires in design is ''sort of like painting with pure mathematics.''

Volume 1, Number 1

Volume 1, Number 2

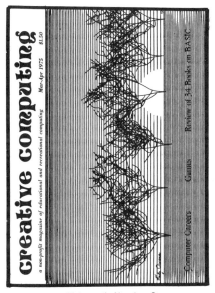

Volume 1, Number 3

Volume

1

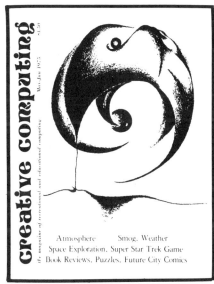

Volume 1, Number 4

Volume 1, Number 5

Volume 1, Number 6

Table of Contents

Articles and Commentary

SONIC BOOM

CREATIVE COMPUTING
Editorial

Birth of a Magazine

Early in my days as Education Marketing Manager at Digital Equipment Corporation, it became apparent that DEC was not communicating very well with its educational users and communication among users was virtually nonexistent. Consequently, I started *EDU* to act as a communication vehicle between DEC, its users, and prospective users. The first issue of *EDU* appeared in the Spring of 1971.

Over the years *EDU* flourished and grew into a 48-plus page magazine. However, there were certain aspects of educational computing which *EDU* could not satisfactorily address. In particular, school users, both college and elementary/secondary, need far more classroom activities, exercises, problems, and ideas than are available in textbooks and other magazines. Also, there ought to be a discussion of the social aspect of the computer, its effect on jobs, medical care, privacy, and the like. Furthermore, what about the user of non-DEC computers? Clearly to be responsive to these needs another vehicle was needed. Thus, *Creative Computing* was born, at least as an idea.

Since *Creative Computing* was intended to be responsive to the entire educational computing-using community and also schools who wished to expose their students to computer technology but could not afford the hardware, I reasoned that the National Science Foundation ought to be willing to provide some funding. My ideas were met with a great deal of encouragement, however, when it came to actually allocating some dollars I got passed from one office to another and eventually out the door.

NIE and OE were also very optimistic at first, but came up with no funds, even with some minor prodding from Senator Edward Brooke who was very helpful to us. Since I had prepared a rather extensive (and expensive!) proposal for the NSF, I decided to rework it slightly and approach various philanthropic foundations that were interested in education and technology. I ultimately submitted various versions of the proposal to 36 foundations. Twenty-eight sent a standard form letter refusal usually with a paragraph encouraging us to continue even though they couldn't help us financially. Two even sent the proposal back in case we wanted to use it elsewhere (that was, in fact, a very nice gesture since each proposal cost about $3.50 to print). Four foundations sent letters which indicated that someone had actually read more than just the abstract, however, still no money. And four foundations didn't reply at all (including two big, well-known ones that put out lots of glossy PR about the wonderful job they're doing).

Concurrent with the funding requests to foundations, I was also contacting various educational leaders to secure their endorsement of *Creative Computing* for other funding requests in the future. Out of 36 educators contacted, 33 endorsed the objectives of *Creative Computing* and allowed us the use of their signature on funding proposals. Armed with this additional high-powered ammunition, I printed more proposals (Variety 3) aimed at industry (makers of computers, peripherals, textbooks, etc.). One hundred and six companies were contacted. I'm afraid that activity lowered my rather high opinion of U. S. industry by several giant steps. Of the 106 companies, only seven bothered to reply at all! With the exception of three companies, the responses were negative.

I felt that three companies were not a broad enough base to put together a sponsorship program for *Creative Computing*, hence I decided to gut it alone on a shoestring out of my own pocket. (The three companies did render aid in various ways — advertising, mailing flyers, etc., and they deserve recognition: Educomp Corp., Hartford, CT; Hewlett-Packard, Cupertino, CA; and Computra, Munice, IN). However, most of the money and effort to print, address, and mail the initial 11,000 flyers came from me along with a handful of hired and voluntary high school helpers.

Response to the flyers was excellent; about 850 people subscribed before we even published an issue. However, about two-thirds of them asked to be billed (or invoiced). Imagine doing that by hand — which I did along with Andree Stone in Concord, MA. Ugh!

Between July and September 1974 was a busy time to say the least. Some of the concurrent activities going on included: writing 150 companies seeking advertising (2 responded), distributing flyers at 6 conferences (a waste of time — people take them and toss them in one continuous motion), preparing a subscription poster, preparing and mailing four different press releases to 224 other magazines (printed eventually by 19), purchasing mailing lists, contacting writers, artists, reviewers, and contributors, editing the first issue, finding and getting price quotes from typesetters, getting illustrations for articles, finding and getting quotes from printers, laying out the magazine, and answering on the average of 30 letters a week. All this while I was selling a house in Concord, Massachusetts, arranging for a move, purchasing a house in Morristown, N. J., moving, getting settled, finding schools for my kids, and learning the ropes of my new position as Marketing Manager-Education with AT&T. Whew! Disaster and/or divorce loomed nearer with every minute of every day.

Out of the scores of well-meaning volunteers (most of whom never seemed to have time when it was actually needed), three people emerged to do a bang-up editorial job on their respective sections. A. Kent Morton at Dartmouth edited the higher education section, Lynn Yarbrough coordinated and edited the reviews, and Walt Koetke of Lexington High School prepared the problems section. These people continue to be the nucleus of the editorial staff. Of course, many writers, artists, and other people contribute to the success of each issue.

October 7, 1974, the first issue rolled off the presses. Forty-three cartons, 52 pounds each — 8,000 copies. One basement plus family room full. Junior high school kids in the house around the clock. Label on each magazine, rubber stamped "ATTN: so and so", "Dear Comp. Center Director" or Librarian or — letter inserted, keep them in zip code order (ha!), sort again, tie into bundles, cart to the post office (oh for a large truck!), weigh, and mail.

Did it do the job? So far the world seems to like *Creative Computing*. Subscriptions keep coming in every day. Letters pile up and periodically get answered. The catastrophic disaster period seems to be ebbing away (although my wife hasn't noticed), and the magazine seems to have an established base of readers and contributors. Financially, an end to the descent into the red ink seems to be in sight and, if subscribers continue to join, the black ink can't be too far away.

Obviously, this is an unfinished story. Its ultimate conclusion will depend on people — contributors and readers. Perhaps I'll write the last chapter in three years or thirty years or never. Watch these pages!

David H. Ahl

> "The reasonable man adapts himself to the world; the unreasonable man persists in trying to adapt the world to himself. Therefore, all progress depends upon the unreasonable man."
>
> G. B. Shaw

A Computer in the Classroom?

A very large part of the General Public is probably not aware of the need for a computer in the classroom. The "successful" adult says, "What's all the fuss about? I got educated the old way. I learned a lot. I had some tough teachers and they made me toe the mark. I must say I've done well in life. Why do today's children have to be taught differently?" The "unsuccessful" adult says, "I was never any good in school — I just wasn't a brain. I was too dumb to get the stuff the way all the smart kids did. I never knew what it was all about. But that doesn't mean they should teach school for kids like me. There probably aren't many like me." Neither believes that a change is needed because neither believes what the more perceptive teachers know: that a very large proportion of math and science students "don't really know what it's all about."

Much that is reported in CREATIVE COMPUTING will be familiar to many members of the school science community. It should be. To find otherwise would be to find that they were insensitive to their surroundings. Why does it need to be said again? The ambience is not static. The atmosphere in which it is said today is not the atmosphere in which John Dewey spoke, in which Sputnik took flight, in which PSSC entered the schools. We urge a renewed awareness of familiar needs in today's ambience and an awareness of new needs arising from the pressures of today.

It is hoped that CREATIVE COMPUTING will focus attention on these needs, sharpen our awareness of them, and result in action.

Dave Ahl

Is Breaking Into A Timesharing System A Crime?

Is it a crime to practise the art of attempting to defeat the software security of a time-sharing computer? There are several cases that we should consider here: in the first case the user is solely concerned with demonstrating that the software is not secure and once he has done this he delights in revealing the circumstances to his computer centre (and probably suggests what they should do to avoid such breaches of security in the future.) Secondly a user may simply abandon all interest as soon as he has achieved his object but fails to tell anyone and fails to keep secure the knowledge that he has gained. In the third case we consider a user who deliberately breaks the security of a system so that he can vandalise data belonging to other users and finally we must consider the case of the user who gains illegal access to data for personal gain.

In an educational environment we must consider these cases in the same way that we might consider the case of a boy who attempts to defeat the combination lock on someone else's bicycle. Any boy who behaves like this is certainly foolish for his motives are almost certain to be misunderstood by anyone in authority who catches him. But we must not make crimes where none exist for in all probability the motivation is the intellectual challenge not the thought of subsequent gain. How then ought we to advise our students on this issue?

It seems to me that we should not attempt to dissuade our students from practising this art, for we shall not succeed in stopping all cases only those that are least harmful to the system. The student in the first category might well be of benefit to users generally(although the computer centre may not think so for undoubtedly he makes more work for them). The student who commits acts of vandalism on the other hand is a public nuisance and will probably be recognised as such by his colleagues who simply want to use the system. Admittedly any kind of vandalism can sometimes be classified as a "joke". But here the general rule that, once is folly, twice is a nuisance and three times is wicked, holds good.

It is going to be counterproductive to take these so-called jokes too seriously since in all probability scolding will simply make it seem more funny. Breaking the security of the system for material gain in practice is unlikely to happen for it is difficult to see what a student could hope to gain by it. Although theoretically a teacher might leave a confidential examination question on the system, in practice he would be very unlikely and somewhat foolish to do so. There can be very little to be gained from illegal access to the system since legal access must and should be so easy so that although any lack of security in an educational time-sharing system must worry people, there is probably little likelihood of any great harm being done provided we keep a sense of proportion.

Of course it should be impossible for any student to succeed in breaching the security barrier and as time passes we shall probably find that it is virtually impossible to succeed. Is attempting to defeat the manufacturers security software a waste of computing resources? That is another matter entirely and one perhaps we could discuss on a future occasion. Has anyone any views?

In Hatfield, the Computer Centre at the Polytechnic is well aware of these problems and, like many educational services, is short of resources to cope with them. Maybe they should be protected from the onslaught of students who always seem to have a desire to take things to pieces to see how they work. We talk about teaching the social implications of computers and perhaps lesson time spent on this issue and related topics might help to give students a better appreciation of all the problems.

W. Tagg

Reprinted with permission from *Advisory Unit for Computer Based Education Bulletin*, Hatfield, Hertfordshire, England.

Dear Editor:

As the former Systems Programmer for the Long Island Regional Instructional Computer Services (LIRICS) I am well aware of the problem of students compromising software security. (Editorial, Jan-Feb 1975) At LIRICS we had to deal with all three types of security breachers described by Mr. Tagg in over 60 school districts.

Students who discovered ways to breach system security and reported it to me without using it were thanked. Such students saved many man-hours of blind searching which would have been required had a malicious user discovered the problem.

Students that discovered but did not use or report problems were ignored since we could not track them down anyway.

Students who used holes in the software security to disrupt our operation in any manner were attacked from two directions. Management attacked with a seek and destroy type inquiry while software people attacked with rigged controls and monitoring.

We believe our method of dealing with these students was successful. I would suggest that educational institutions encourage experimentation but attack malicious students with a determined and sneaky software specialist.

Harold R. Berenson
Syosset, New York

"The computer is incredibly fast, accurate, and stupid. Man is unbelievably slow, inaccurate, and brilliant. The marriage of the two is a force beyond calculation."

Leo Cherne

Where Are We Going?

One evening last July, I was lying on my back on the esplanade next to the Charles River. The strains of a Mozart piano concerto by the Boston Pops filled the air. The night was particularly clear and the stars in the moonless sky were glittering like diamonds on a piece of black velvet. Counting the stars that could be seen with the naked eye in even one small sector of the sky would have been an absolute impossibility.

The entire vista recalled to mind a statement from the Project Cyclops* report. It stated that scores of other intelligent races are radiating communication signals that can be received on Earth. This should come as no surprise. Given the incredibly vast numbers of galaxy clusters, galaxies, stars and solar systems, the probability of other races of superior intelligence or in a considerably advanced evolutionary state to humans is literally astronomical.

Entering the realm of speculation, it is quite possible that we on Earth have been observed by another race and ignored much as you or I might view a slug or an ant. The number of cells in the brain of a slug indicate that it has virtually no intelligence whatsoever and who in their right mind would want to communicate with such a hideous, slimy creature anyway? Is there any reason to believe that we humans haven't been examined by some extraterrestrial race (the Bermuda Triangle disappearances?) and then been discarded as too barbaric and dumb to communicate with and too revolting and ugly to worry about anyway?

Consider the human species for a moment. Over the some odd thousand years of recorded history, the human race has made enormous gains in technology. No question

about that. It's curious, however, that there have been virtually no corresponding gains in interpersonal relationships. Nations still war with one another as do states, neighbors, and husbands and wives.

To an extraterrestrial, our advanced technology probably looks like cute little toys for the human ants to play with. But fundamentally, all the technology of the past 2000 years hasn't altered the native intelligence and conduct of the species one iota. We still war with one another and lash out at those closest to us. Will computers help? What can we expect from our association with these logical companions? I have to believe that computers give us more potential to extend our intellect than we've ever had before. However, if we take history into account, I can't be overly sanguine about the outcome.

If there's a message in all of this I guess it's got to be: "STOP and THINK for a minute. What are the goals of the human race? Where should we be going as a species? Are you, you personally, contributing to that goal? In the 24 hours just past, what percentage of the time were you really using your intelligence to the fullest and what percentage were you a human ant responding to the myriad pressures of job, family, school, or society? Why not take 10 minutes a week (one-tenth of one percent of the time in a week) to ponder humankind on a galactic scale? You might be surprised at the outcome!"

David Ahl

*Project Cyclops was an intensive 3-month study at Stanford to recommend an approach to search for extraterrestrial life.

An aluminum plate was placed aboard the spacecraft "Pioneer 10" launched in March 1972. On it is etched a message designed to tell any interstellar finder that there is intelligent life on this planet. "Pioneer 10" is destined to fly-by Jupiter and continue into outer space. Earth scientists are hoping this will bring some response one day.

What's Wrong With the Little Red Schoolhouse?

I have a couple of observations on education and learning:

1. Kids learn best from other kids, probably outside of school. Some of the best learning probably occurs in the street!

2. Although textbooks are written by the best minds and are cram full of enlightened information of allegedly great worth and importance, they never get stolen.

3. Kids spend a fantastic amount of time in front of the boob tube. Indeed, at the time of entering first grade, the average child has spent more time with the TV than with both of his parents.

4. Motivation is much more important than teaching method or style of delivery.

5. Kids don't respect people who talk down to them, try to use their slang without knowing what it means or who are in any way artificial or self-important.

6. Kids' minds are unencumbered by constraints of what can and can't be done. Kids will try just about anything.

7. Learning by discovery, doing, or manipulating sticks with you far better than learning by reading about it.

8. Learning to learn is infinitely more important than learning facts and data.

9. Isaac Asimov, Herbert Simon, Marshall McLuhan, and Herman Kahn will have more impact on the future than all the textbooks in print.

10. Computers are the most powerful tool man has ever invented and the most awesome responsibility he has ever faced.

11. Education has become relatively less efficient than practically any other aspect of our economic or social development.

What does all this mean? In short, it means that the little red schoolhouse which we hold so dear to our hearts is no longer satisfactory. Not only just unsatisfactory, but in urgent need of change. No longer can we rely upon the teaching approaches of yesterday; in fact, we can't even rely upon the ones of today. Half of the piecemeal, one-at-a-time changes we're making in the educational process are out of date before they're even implemented widely.

Compounding the slowness of educational innovation is the fact that many of the new systems introduced over the last 20 years using the latest technology have fallen flat on their faces. This is true of things like teaching machines, drill-and-practice CAI, language labs, closed-circuit TV, and perhaps now even the "new math." These shortcomings and failures have given the traditionalists all kinds of ammunition to shoot down other new things on the horizon and, indeed, have imbued nearly every educator with a hearty skepticism for educational technology.

Those educators who have revolted against drill-and-practice PI and CAI believe that getting a pile of data into a kid's head is not as important as teaching underlying structure and modes of self-learning. Challenging and stimulating students, and then providing them with an information-rich environment in which they can seek their own solutions, is seen as a better way to teach. On the other hand, opponents of these new ideas fear that free-form education will result in gaps in the basic knowledge considered essential in conventional education.

Determining who is right and who is wrong is probably not very productive, although many researchers are engaged in that happy pursuit. More to the point, when one looks more deeply, it's not clear that all the technological innovations did fail. Some of them undoubtedly did. However, what's much more evident is that we probably don't know how to measure the results. Or going one step deeper, it's not at all clear that we have even established meaningful objectives.

Objectives must be broadly stated and must not only be relevant to the world of today but to the world of the future. Knowledge is changing and advancing so rapidly that we must expect objectives to change, or conversely, be formulated in a broad enough fashion to keep up with technological advances. The Mager-style behavioral objectives don't begin to meet the need. Education today needs more than small behavioral steps. It needs objectives that are dynamic and can be expected to change over time; objectives that are stated in an entirely new way.

Objectives must be devised to lead young minds through an imaginative exploration of the jungle of political, social, psychological, and ethical issues that will confront them as adults. What is the objective which will foster decision-making ability under uncertainty? What are the objectives which elucidate the ways in which technology and values will interact in the world of tomorrow? How does one measure whether one has learned to learn? I'm not saying these objectives are impossible to devise. Indeed, these are the kinds of things that education must focus on, and these are the objectives that must be devised.

And while educational objectives must change and grow, so must its methods. One-third of the observations stated at the outset say, in one way or another, that the medium really is the message. Today, learning to read from a book can be substantially enhanced with the "Electric Company" on TV and with Moore's

Talking Typewriter. For some aspects of education today the book is hardly an acceptable alternative at all; yet for other aspects, it's still the best approach.

For example, learning to fly an airplane is best done on a flight simulator. Learning to create a movie is best done by actually creating one. Learning about political action is best done by observing and participating. Learning about resource management and resource utilization is best done by manipulating computer simulation models. Learning a logical approach to problem solving is best done by breaking a real problem down into manageable pieces, flowcharting it, and programming it for a computer. Learning an appreciation for literature is best done by reading books.

So, in addition to broad, dynamic objectives, education also needs some new methods. Not one to the exclusion of others, but a whole potpourri of techniques. Things like peer teaching, computer games and simulations, free learning environments and piles of motivation. Motivation is strongest when it comes from real involvement and genuine accomplishment. We have to let kids work with real tools on real problems, not a bunch of contrived textbook situations. We have to give kids tools far more powerful than we think they can possibly use. The results will be unbelievable!

David H. Ahl

Reprinted with permission from *EDU* No. 10 published by Digital Equipment Corp.

How to Cope With Your Computer

Susan S. Most
Cape Elizabeth High School, ME

It cannot think. It's just a big metal box with a mess of wires inside and a myriad of lights continually flashing on and off. Ingenious device that it is, that box is capable of solving infinitely complicated problems in less time than one's lips can say "computerman". Alas, but if you don't know how to operate it, you might as well take it to the dump.

One cannot imagine the sheer frustration a person feels when faced with the task of operating a computer for the first time. You're standing in a room where people look disgustingly productive with yards of yellow paper spewing from their teletypes. A continuous clicking, clicking noise comes at your ears in such an important and official manner that you shiver a bit at the idea that perhaps someday you might be in charge of one of these "things". Your feeling of impending importance is burst like the rush of air from a pin-pricked balloon.

You can't even read what it prints, to say nothing of telling it what to do. Bits of incomprehensible brilliance flow forth each fraction of a second as the carriage on the teletype races back and forth; and the lights on the front panel merrily wink at your ignorance.

It's not a question of just saying in plain English what fantastic chore you want it to perform — this "box" doesn't understand plain English. Since the box really has no "brain" inside — only wires; the operator must learn "the tongue" that it does understand. This code includes such startlingly clear terms as TAD, DCA, JMS, etc., and those are cinchy compared to 7402

and, how's this — ready: 111 000 010 101. Imagine a number like that meaning something to anybody. Ridiculous, you think? Well, to the box it's crystal clear. That is, of course, assuming you're using a computer that understands that language. To add another fly to the ointment, there are many languages which are not interchangeable with machines designed by other companies.

The most helpful tool to the harried individual attempting to coexist with a computer is a diagram called a "flowchart". It's not a plumber's helper nor a sea captain's guide. Rather, a flowchart is a way to clarify on paper exactly what sequence of calculations you want the computer to carry out. At the same time it helps you chart your train of thought, assuming of course there is some flow to your ideas.

Once the flowchart has been written, don't think telling the computer to follow it will be a cinch — that's the hardest part. Being a brainless genius, the computer must be told exactly, in the correct order, what to do. Coding is not the language of martians, but an analyst's shorthand — usually the initials of processes one wants the computer to do.

Yet understanding a code and having written a flowchart still cannot guarantee success. Writing a program containing all the operations to get the correct answer can cause such frustration that one could be driven to his nearest analyst — in psychoanalysis, that is. This novice programmer nearly climbed a flagpole trying to think "like the box". Take heart, however, eventually you win.

Recent Trends in Mathematics Curriculum Research

Marogt Critchfield
Project Solo,
University of Pittsburgh 15260

Mathematics curriculum reform in the last 10 years (1964-74) cannot be as neatly characterized as that of the decade which preceded it. The years 1954-64 saw the rise of a 'glamour movement,' the 'new mathematics,' which markedly changed the subject matter of school mathematics. The principal mechanism used to effect these changes was textbook writing. The change was accomplished with unusual swiftness and a good deal of publicity. A number of different research projects were involved, and yet there appears to have been unanimity regarding the changes needed and the topics to be incorporated. It is this period of research which most strongly influences school practice today, and which is subject to the greatest scrutiny.

By contrast, the ten years of research 1964-74 have not yet had a widespread influence on actual school practice. Also, the unanimity of the earlier period appears to have dissipated considerably during the second. (I suspect that a deeper analysis of the earlier period might reveal more diversity, as well.) There are a number of developing trends in the period 1964-74; I will discuss three of these, which I consider most important.

First, there appears to be a change in the attitude of professional educators toward curriculum research. I consider this to be as important as the development of any new movement. Evidence of this can be seen in a booklet put out by the National Council of Teachers of Mathematics in 1968 [14]. In contrast to a previous booklet with similar cover design and similar title put out in 1961 [13], this collection of articles is generally cooler and contains more diverse viewpoints. While calling for still more changes in the curriculum (and for much the same reasons as the earlier book), it does so only after having described the problems as having many different facets. It calls for greater care on the part of school decision makers in choosing from the available curriculum projects.

> "They should not accept change simply because it is the current fad, nor should they assume it is successful simply because it is new."

Some of the most prominent topics of the new math — sets, non-decimal number bases, and axiomatics come in for criticism, although no blanket condemnation is expressed:

> "it will become increasingly necessary, however, for educators to make value judgments as to which topics must be stressed heavily for which children."

Significantly, I think, the pamphlet encourages local district curriculum development, which it felt had gone into a decline with the emergence of large-scale, national curriculum projects.

> "Some local directors of curriculum apparently have decided that the period of curriculum-making at the school or district level was over and that the challenge now was to select the best program available that had been developed by the 'experts' . . . the 'best' may consist of a selection of useful topics from several programs."

This second booklet spotlights the provocative curriculum suggestions of the Cambridge Conference on School Mathematics (CCSM) at the very front. (CCSM will be the second major trend discussed here.) However, the authors of this pamphlet appear to find many problems that are not helped by CCSM and the controversy it sparked.

By 1973, this cooler attitude seems to have 'congealed'. The report of an NSF sponsored conference that summer, made the following statements [17] :

> "There is a substantial lack of trust and communication between the mathematics education community in the universities and that in the schools. Efforts need to be instigated to re-establish cooperation."

> "At the present time, there seems to be no clear consensus with regard to the mathematics which should be taught in K-12 and there is an urgent need for a program which will examine societal needs and delineate the goals of mathematics education with sufficient authority to provide a broadly acceptable base for curriculum development."

The second important trend of research activity is what I term a continuation and intensification of the spirit of 'new math.' The Cambridge Conference on School Mathematics (CCSM) held its first meeting in June, 1963. It was a brainstorming session, not a textbook writing one, but its recommendations fit into the category of wanting "more and better mathematics" in schools. Further, many of the old 'new math' approaches and topics, if not their current implementation, were re-affirmed in its recommendations. CCSM produced *Goals for School Mathematics* in 1964 [2] and went on to write two more documents, *Goals for Mathematical Education of Elementary Teachers,* 1966 [3] and *Goals for the Correlation of Elementary Science and Mathematics,* 1969 [4], as well as experimental units embodying their goals.

CCSM's goals, although accompanied by warnings that they were tentative and not to be used as a blueprint, were an audacious challenge by intellectuals to the schools and curriculum developers.

> ". . . thirteen years of mathematics in grades K to 12 should [give] a level of training comparable to three years of top-level college training today; . . . two years of calculus, and one semester each of modern algebra and probability theory." [2]

> "We propose to gain three years through a new organization of the subject matter and the virtual total abandonment of drill for drill's sake, . . ." [2]

Some of the other features mentioned in CCSM's 1963 report were:

(1) ". . . the parallel development of geometry and arithmetic (or algebra in later years) from kindergarten on."

(2) ". . . structure of the real number system and the basic ideas of geometry both synthetic and analytic . . . considerable attention . . . to inequalities in the earliest grades."

(3) "'spiral' curriculum which repeatedly returns to each topic, always expanding it and showing more connections with other topics."

(4) "(K-6) should be understandable by virtually all students; it should lead to a level of competence well above that of the general population today."

(5) ". . . for those who take mathematics only a few years after grade school . . . an elementary feeling for probability and statistics . . . [and] . . . a nodding acquaintance with the calculus."

The 1969 book [4] contains some interesting thoughts about the mathematics and science curricula in general, which reveal a fuller development of CCSM's point of view:

"Science and mathematics, by their inherent simplicity in comparison to most areas of knowledge, lend themselves to the development in children of attitudes of lifelong and general value. . . . They include (in no order of priority) a conviction that through analysis and synthesis comes understanding; a belief that quantitative measure adds dimensions to one's understanding that are always difficult and sometimes impossible to achieve by other means; a tolerance that permits consideration of all reasonable testable hypotheses which are consistant with available evidence; a healthy skepticism even toward conclusions supported by existing evidence; an optimism based on the belief that nothing is unknowable while much remains unknown; and finally, a belief that to understand, while indeed a means to power, is to enjoy and is therefore an end in itself."

"In his school experience with science, a child can make his own observations and organize them, then make his own predictions and check them. Thus he can directly appreciate the power of the scientific style of thought."

"We do not want these experiments to be done occasionally as a sort of special treat, . . . but sufficiently often that the thought patterns that underlie the world of science will be habitual, if rudimentary, in every school graduate."

"A primary message of education should, we believe, be that thinking is worthwhile. Unfortunately, education has often been directed away from the imaginative and creative toward uninteresting, rote attention to details."

"Each child must be convinced that *his* thinking is worthwhile."

This is very exciting intellectual stuff: it's wise and idealistic in the best sense of that word. Reading it, one almost forgets two important things: (1) In spite of a clear intention to the contrary, these goals put pressure on researchers and schools to focus attention on still more new topics and new courses and away from such perennial problems as student motivation, teacher's job satisfaction, and the real need for students to acquire essential skills in an acceptable length of time. (2) The mathematicians and scientists who have come together as CCSM conferrees seem to have only a very hazy notion of what the non-mathematics-using citizen needs:

". . .difficult and important decisions are better made by people used to connecting reality with rationality . . . . through the vital process of constructing simplified conceptual models for real world objects and interactions . . . . There are severe limitations on a quantitative approach in a real life situation; but it seems better to go as far as one can with that approach than to abandon decisions to guess or superstition."

"Environmental pollution, for example, is among the most critical problems of our times. Its solution will require the active cooperation of every individual. We will not get this cooperation until every citizen understands the problem well enough to feel the importance of his own role in the solution."

In our highly organized and specialized society, I wonder whether the ability of an individual to make "simplified conceptual models" will contribute directly to his role in decision making. Also, is it realistic to imply that a process which has "severe limitations" in the hands of professionals will survive in a classroom setting lacking any but the most primitive tools for computation and analysis?

One curriculum project has grown directly out of CCSM's efforts --Unified Science and Mathematics for Elementary Schools (USMES), and another has dedicated itself to implementing CCSM's goals-- Comprehensive School Mathematics Program (CSMP). However, there is not the boundless enthusiasm of old, nor the move to make swift changes in schools. Many researchers simply do not believe that the acceleration proposed is compatible with growth in understanding and enjoyment, especially at the elementary level. Burt Kaufman, Director of CSMP, an advocate of CCSM's goals, is cautious:

"We've simply torn down the entire curriculum and rebuilt it from scratch. It could have a very big impact if the public is ready for it but it is going to be more difficult for the teacher." [12]

The third major trend in the 1964-74 period is a very different kind of phenomenon. It has some, but not all, of the aspects of a new 'glamour movement' --computers in education. (While not strictly a development in mathematics, computing has impinged more on the mathematics curriculum than other subject areas for complex reasons, some social, some technical.) Before 1964, pioneering research in computer-assisted instruction by Bitzer at the University of Illinois and Suppes at Stanford gave rise to high hopes and some inflated statements:

"the kind of individualized instruction once possible only for a few members of the aristocracy can be made available to all students at all levels of ability." [Suppes, 1]

In the period since, and at the present, a good deal of research has been undertaken regarding not only computer-assisted instruction but a variety of other computer uses in education. An idea of the growth of research in computing can be gotten from Figure 1. This is a chart of some major mathematics curriculum (and related) projects, selected mainly from [10] and [15]. It is not exhaustive, but should encompass most projects mentioned in widely read journals. Computer manufacturers have actively promoted their products to schools for both educational and administrative purposes. All this would point to a new educational panacea destined to fade or be absorbed without any deep effect. However, at least two features of this trend definitely set it apart from those have come (and gone) before it.

First, the adoption of computers in schools is taking place independently as well as with funded research activity. The American Institutes for Research Survey [5] * figures of secondary schools using computers for educational or instructional (not administrative) purposes are:

1965------- 2%
1970-------13%.

Even though these figures must be considered very approximate, this growth cannot be accounted for by research programs.

*A new survey is scheduled for release in 1975.

10

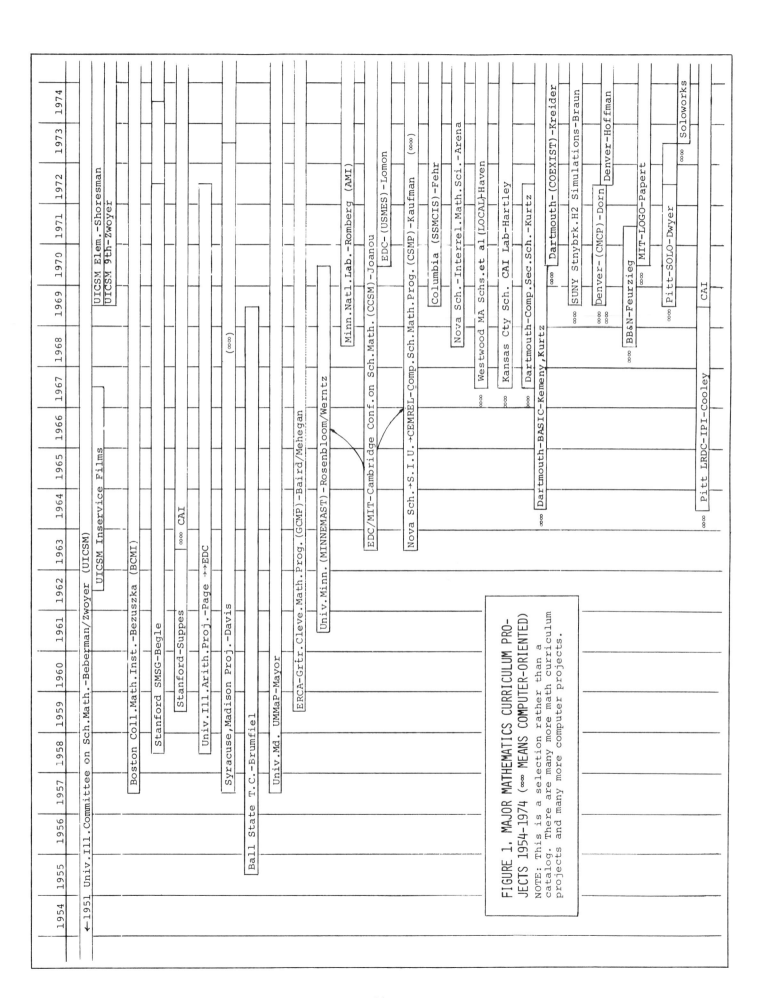

FIGURE 1. MAJOR MATHEMATICS CURRICULUM PRO-
JECTS 1954-1974 (∞∞ MEANS COMPUTER-ORIENTED)

NOTE: This is a selection rather than a
catalog. There are many more math curriculum
projects and many more computer projects.

Secondly, computers are profoundly *unlike* any other technical or curricular innovation that has invaded schools before. A computer can best be thought of as a machine that can transform itself into any other machine--that is, it can carry out any procedure that can be fully described to it. Therefore, it can be a medium of instruction, a lunar lander, a game player, a mathematical formula cruncher, an ecological system, and so on, ad infinitum. One writer likens the potential effects of the computer on education (and on society) to the effect that would be produced by the sudden introduction of writing and the printing press on a civilization that had developed without them [11]. Furthermore the kinds of 'machines' that a computer can be instructed to imitate range from extremely simple to extremely complex, offering the potential of a continuum of experiences for students (Figures 2 and 3)

```
GUESS    05:05 PM        19-OCT-74
5 RANDOMIZE
7 X=INT (RND*25)
10 PRINT " PICK A NUMBER FROM 0 TO 25 "
20 INPUT A
25 IF A >25 THEN PRINT" NUMBER TO LARGE-- TRY AGAIN": GOTO 10
27 IF A <0 THEN PRINT" NUMBER TOO SMALL--TRY AGAIN!":GOTO 10
30 PRINT " YOU PICKED "A"!"
35 PRINT" THE COMPUTER PICKED "X" !"
40 PRINT " YOU MISSED BY "ABS(X-A)" !"
45 IF ABS(X-A)=0 THEN PRINT" YOU WON !!!!! "
47 IF ABS(X-A)<>0 THEN PRINT" YOU LOST!!"
50 INPUT "DO YOU WANT TO TRY AGAIN !";C$
60 IF LEFT(C$,1)="Y" THEN PRINT" AGAIN!" : GOTO 7
70 IF LEFT(C$,1)="N" THEN PRINT "THAT'S ALL!" :GOTO 90
80 IF LEFT(C$,1)<>"Y" OR LEFT(C$,1)<>"N" THEN PRINT "WHAT--
NOT IN CORRECT FORM--PLEASE RETYPE?????": GOTO 50
90 PRINT" BYE!!!"
100 END

READY

RUN
GUESS    05:06 PM        19-OCT-74
 PICK A NUMBER FROM 0 TO 25
? 5
 YOU PICKED  5 !
 THE COMPUTER PICKED  20  !
 YOU MISSED BY  15 !
 YOU LOST!!
DO YOU WANT TO TRY AGAIN !? Y
 AGAIN!
 PICK A NUMBER FROM 0 TO 25
? 0
 YOU PICKED  0 !
 THE COMPUTER PICKED  19  !
 YOU MISSED BY  19 !
 YOU LOST!!

DO YOU WANT TO TRY AGAIN !? H
WHAT-- INPUT DATA  NOT IN CORRECT FORM--PLEASE RETYPE?????
DO YOU WANT TO TRY AGAIN !? Y
 AGAIN!
 PICK A NUMBER FROM 0 TO 25
? 228
 NUMBER TO LARGE-- TRY AGAIN
 PICK A NUMBER FROM 0 TO 25
? -1
 NUMBER TOO SMALL--TRY AGAIN!
 PICK A NUMBER FROM 0 TO 25
? 5
 YOU PICKED  5 !
 THE COMPUTER PICKED  12  !
 YOU MISSED BY  7 !
 YOU LOST!!
DO YOU WANT TO TRY AGAIN !? Y
 AGAIN!
 PICK A NUMBER FROM 0 TO 25
? 7
 YOU PICKED  7 !
 THE COMPUTER PICKED  7  !
 YOU MISSED BY  0 !
 YOU WON !!!!!
```

FIGURE 2. Listing and run of a program, GUESS, by a beginner (Danny Cohen, Age 10).

FIGURE 3. A run of a program by an advanced student is not shown. For an example of such a run, please refer to SUPER STAR TREK found elsewhere in this issue.

Research in educational computing today encompasses a variety of approaches and the interchange of ideas is enlivened by a sharp philosophic disagreement between those researchers who believe, with Suppes, that "the truly revolutionary function of computers in education . . . lies in the novel area of computer-assisted instruction" [1], and those who believe, with Luehrmann, that "computing constitutes a new and fundamental intellectual resource. To use that resource as a mere delivery system for instruction, but not to give a student instruction in how he might use the resource himself, has been the chief failure of the CAI effort." [11], or even more strongly,

"... education may have caught a tiger by the tail. It comes in the form of an activity called ... 'solo mode' computing. Such use of computers (as the tiger image suggests) often exhibits an unexpected raw power for eliciting complex learning behaviors in all kinds of students." [7]

A taxonomy of educational computing is useful for understanding the implications of this research. The following is adapted from [8] and is intended to clarify the relationships between the types of educational computing.

COMPUTER-ACTIVATED LEARNING SCHEMA

A. DUAL MODE COMPUTING

The constraints on the learner are (primarily) pedagogically determined--the CAI lesson or other program flows from the program author's concept of how the student must proceed in learning the subject matter.

Minor skills required of the student.

Major design skills required of the program author.

I. DUAL, AUTHOR-DIRECTED COMPUTING
--Drill and Practice } term CAI used most often
--Tutorials } here
--Diagnostic Testing
--Computer-Managed Instruction (CMI)[1]

II. DUAL, LEARNER-DIRECTED COMPUTING
--Simulations
--Games
--Information Retrieval
--Tutorials (sophisticated branching)[2]
--Dialogue[2]

B. SOLO MODE COMPUTING

The constraints on the learner are (primarily) reality-determined--the student explores areas of the subject matter within the bounds of the computer system and his own imagination.

Increasing programming skills are required of students.[3]

Major guidance and some computing skills required of the teacher.

III. SOLO, HANDS-ON COMPUTING (SOMETIMES CALLED ALGORITHMIC OR PROBLEM SOLVING COMPUTING)
--Writing programs, debugging them, running them.

IV. SOLO, LEARNER-ORGANIZED COMPUTING
--Model Building (may include writing I, II, or III).
    A higher level of student responsibility is indicated here; programs are used by others.

All of these types of computing are currently being researched and their emergence as integral parts of the newer mathematics education curricula lies in the near future. A recent conference on the K-12 mathematics curriculum gave the following recommendations regarding computing: [17]

"1. The computer should be an important part of any future curriculum efforts.

2. Emphasis should be placed on using the computer to involve students in problem solving activities. Computer use for drill and practice on computational skills should receive less attention.

3. Certain readiness concepts about the use of computers should be included in the elementary grades (1-6). These should involve the use of calculators and an exposure to algorithmic approaches.

4. In grade seven, students should be taught a programming language which is appropriate for the level of students involved. In this grade students should become familiar with information processing and the computer should be used as an integral part of the mathematics course.

5. The mathematics curriculum in grades 7-12 should be studied and revised in order to make optimal use of the computer as a tool in mathematics courses.

6. A one semester computer science course should be offered in grade 12 which may be selected as an option.

7. Societal uses and implications of the computer should be studied at some point in the school program, possibly in the 10th or 11th grade. The writing of modules on this subject that can be inserted in a social studies course is encouraged. Another possibility might be the development of a course 'Mathematics and the Computer in Society'.

8. There should be continued funding of efforts to investigate uses of the computer in a variety of instructional modes until more data are available regarding the value of these modes. Funded projects which explore the potential of different uses of the computer in education are encouraged.

9. If computers are to be systematically employed in the above ways in the schools, then the implications of this for widespread computer-access and teacher education should be effectively faced, spelled-out, and dealt with."

All these suggestions seem good and worthwhile. In fact, many of the original thoughts of the 'old' new math writers and 'new' 'new math' writers seem good and worthwhile. But the problems of their actual implementation in school are complex. The notion that such ideas can be packaged into infallible, teacher-proof forms, such as texts or CAI programs becomes more and more ridiculous.

If one impression can be derived from the history of mathematics curriculum research of the last twenty years it is that reform of curriculum (that is, the relatively tangible books, lists of topics, courses, and materials that codify and justify much of school life) must be related to more subtle and far reaching reforms. There must be conscious attention paid to the social relations that form the substructure of school life.* Such research is difficult to carry out, but the researcher involved in these reforms should, as a minimum, engage in face-to-face contacts with teachers at

---

[1] Computing as a research tool for developing and testing theories of learning and instruction is related to this type of computing. It is not part of this taxonomy because it does not exist at the level of on-going teaching-learning activities.

[2] Real "dialogue" is still more promise than fact. Research in this area is better characterized as part of "artificial intelligence" than education.

[3] Two books which emphasize the step-by-step build-up of programming skills needed for solo mode computing are [6] and [9].

all stages of their development, teachers of teachers, professional scholars whose specialty is education, and professional scholars in the disciplines to which the curriculum must be connected. These contacts should influence every stage of the innovation.

*Required reading for anyone engaged in making changes in schools should be Seymour Sarason's *The Culture of the School and the Problem of Change.* [16]

BIBLIOGRAPHY

1. Atkinson, Richard C. and H. A. Wilson, Eds. *Computer-Assisted Instruction, A Book of Readings,* Academic Press, 1969.
2. Cambridge Conference on School Mathematics. *Goals for School Mathematics,* (Educational Services Incorporated) Houghton Mifflin Co., Boston, 1967
3. -----. *Goals for Mathematical Education of Elementary School Teachers,* (Education Development Center, Inc.) Houghton Mifflin Co., Boston, 1967.
4. -----. *Goals for the Correlation of Elementary Science and Mathematics,* (Education Development Center, Inc.) Houghton Mifflin Co., Boston, 1969.
5. Darby, C. A., Jr. et al. *Survey of Computing Activities in Secondary Schools,* American Institutes for Research, Silver Springs, Md., October, 1970.
6. Dwyer, T. A. *A Guided Tour of Computer Programming in BASIC,* Houghton Mifflin Co., Boston, 1974.
7. Dwyer, T. A. "The Significance of Solo-Mode Computing for Curriculum Design," *EDU--Issue No. 13:* Fall, 1974. (Education Products Group, Digital Equipment Corp., Maynard, Mass. 01754)
8. Dwyer, T. A. and M. Critchfield. "CATALYST: CAI in a General Time-Sharing Environment," *EDUCOM Bulletin* (Winter, 1970).
9. Dwyer, T. A. and M. Critchfield, *A Computer Resource Book--Algebra,* Boston, Houghton Mifflin Co., 1975.
10. Lockard, J. David, Ed. *Seventh and Eighth Reports of the International Clearinghouse on Science and Mathematics Curricular Developments (1970, 1972),* (American Association for the Advancement of Science, Washington, D. C.) Science Teaching Center, Univ. of Md., College Park, Md.
11. Luehrmann, Arthur W. "Should the Computer Teach the Student or Vice Versa," *Proceedings of the Spring Joint Computer Conference,* Amer. Fed. of Info. Processing Societies, 1972.
12. Martin, Richard. "Sum & Substance," *Wall Street Journal,* May 31, 1973.
13. National Council of Teachers of Mathematics (Regional Orientation Conference). *The Revolution in School Mathematics, A Challenge for Administrators and Teachers,* 1961.
14. National Council of Teachers of Mathematics, *The Continuing Revolution in Mathematics,* 1968.
15. National Science Foundation. *Education Programs in Mathematics for Elementary and Secondary Schools,* April, 1974.
16. Sarason, Seymour B., *The Culture of the School and the Problem of Change,* Allyn and Bacon, Inc., Boston, 1971.
17. Springer, George (Dir.). *Report of the Conference on the K-12 Mathematics Curriculum (NSF), June 1973,* Mathematics Education Development Center, Indiana Univ., Bloomington, In. 47401.

Did You Ever Talk With A Computer?

AIP/360 — PLEASE SIGN ON: 16

TERMINAL N SIGNED ON, 02/15/71

UNFORMATTED MODE

AIP/360 — PLEASE SIGN ON: 16

TERMINAL N SIGNED ON, 02/15/71

UNFORMATTED MODE
clear

CLEARED ONE MESSAGE WAITING

SIGNAL WHEN READY
ready

WOULD YOU LIKE TO STUDY SCIENCE?
I don't know.

THAT IS A GOOD ANSWER. THINK AGAIN. WOULD YOU LIKE TO STUDY SCIENCE?
what for?

YOU HAVE GIVEN IT A LITTLE THOUGHT. SOCIETY NEEDS PEOPLE LIKE YOU.
what for?

SOCIETY NEEDS TO MAKE BETTER USE OF ITS NEW TECHNOLOGY. DO YOU LIKE PHYSICS?
I don't know — what's physics?

PHYSICS IS CONCERNED WITH THE PROPERTIES OF MATTER AND THE LAWS WHICH DESCRIBE ITS BEHAVIOR.
what's that got to do with me?

ILLEGAL ENTRY. LINE CANCELLED. TRY ANOTHER RESPONSE.
why should I know about science?

SCIENCE IS INTERESTING. IT HELPS US TO UNDERSTAND THE WORLD IN WHICH WE LIVE.

CITALA
An Exploration of Instructional Computing in a Two-year College

David Howard
Bruce Corliss
Delta College
and
Karl L. Zinn
University of Michigan

This report on Project CITALA was adapted by Diann Bradarich from an article in the ON-LINE newsletter. A lengthier manuscript is available from Gene Arnold, Delta College, University Center, Michigan 48710 or Karl Zinn, Center for Research on Learning and Teaching, 109 E. Madison, Ann Arbor, Michigan 48104.

Realizing the potential impact of academic computing, Delta College in University Center, Michigan initiated an institutional study to investigate the use of the computer as an instructional tool in the community college. During the spring of 1973 a faculty seminar on instructional use of computers developed the nucleus for the Delta College staff team which conducted Project CITALA (Computers in Teaching and Learning Activities).

From the outset, the Project was largely faculty-oriented. Althouth the basic responsibility for the Project rested with the President, who provided general direction, the daily planning and development were the responsibility of the Team. All decisions regarding methods of procedure, institutions to be visited, consultants, and other details regarding the specific direction of the Project were made by the Team members.

The basic philosophy governing formation of the Team and its subsequent activity was inspired by the college's own *Institutional Profile* as of 1972. As a student-centered institution, Delta College bases future action on answers to the question: "What is best for the student?" The college seeks to provide educational services that prepare students for immediate employment and, certainly, experience with computers is becoming an increasingly valuable skill. Delta is committed to experimentation and research in areas which facilitate learning; thus, the decision to explore computing was a logical conclusion.

Domain for the Study

The Project Team concentrated on possible expansion of computer facilities as support tools and investigated feasible applications for Delta College. CITALA staff soon recognized that instructional uses of computers divide naturally into two areas — instruction *about* and instruction *with* computers. In instruction *about* computers, the machine is the subject of the study; it is not substituting for or replacing some other device, and it cannot be replaced itself. In instruction *with* the computer, however, the machine is a tool of instruction used when it offers some instructional advantage.

Delta's present equipment configuration is primarily designed for and used for instruction *about* computers and does not lend itself well to an expanded program of instruction *with* computers. Of course, instruction *about* computers is by far the greatest proportion of instructional use of the computer in education today, and the vocational training provided at Delta will continue to be considered. At the same time, however, exciting things are happening in the area of instruction *with* computers, and the activities of the Project Team were focused primarily in this direction.

Goals and Procedures

CITALA staff members engaged in extensive and varied activities directed towards the implementation of ten specific objectives: investigate many examples; visit key locations; collect information; collect materials organized by discipline; plan implementation; determine methods for faculty involvement; determine time sequence for expansion; design in-service programs; determine necessary expertise; and locate experts for advice. The major activities can be classified into several categories: identification of resources; use of consultants; trial computer use; and data collection from site visits.

Team members spent several days familiarizing themselves with project objectives and present facilities and programs at Delta. From the exchange of ideas emerged several valuable techniques designed to encourage effective operation as a team. A library file housing all material gathered on visits and through correspondence was maintained for the general information of all members. A checklist developed by the team assisted members in gathering pertinent data during visits to other colleges. Regularly scheduled meetings aided members in planning and sharing the analysis of their activities.

After the preliminaries of orientation, serious investigation began. Invitations to visit the campus were extended to consultants in instructional computing. Karl Zinn, who earlier directed the faculty seminar, visited Delta several times to help with planning, resources the preparation of reports. A team of experts from the University of Illinois spent two days at Delta demonstrating the PLATO terminal. In addition, conversations were held with a number of other experts from across the country, several of whom have since visited the Delta campus.

Through the cooperation of Project EXTEND (funded by Exxon Education Foundation) at the University of Michigan, a portable terminal was available on campus throughout the Project for use of computers at Michigan State University, the University of Michigan, and Dartmouth College. Team members and other interested persons gained experience in using the terminal and tested various educational programs that are stored in the computers at the three different institutions.

The last and perhaps most crucial activity focused on the collection of data from colleges visited by the Project Team. The highly worthwhile activity provided an opportunity to see new approaches in action as well as to establish contacts for long range developments in instructional computing.

Visits to Colleges Using
Computers in Instruction

In order to select educational institutions for visitation, several criteria were established. First, the school had to be actively engaged in instructional computing; the Team wanted to see an operating system as opposed to a description existing only on paper. Second, an institution chosen for a visit needed to be involved in computing activities relevant to community colleges. Conceivably, the system could be applied at Delta. Three visitation sites received major attention, each meeting these criteria: Golden West Community College in the Los Angeles area, Dartmouth College in Hanover, New Hampshire, and the University of Illinois in Urbana, Illinois. Other sites visited, usually in connection with conferences held there, included: Cuyahoga Community College, Cleveland; University of North Dakota, Grand Forks; three Chicago City Colleges (Malcolm-X, Wright and Kennedy-King); and the University of California at Irvine.

In each visitation, the specific purposes varied. Golden West was viewed primarily as an example of a community college actively involved with instructional uses of computers. Naturally, the Team was interested in seeing what they were doing, what their experiences were, and what success they were having with instructional computing. While in the area, the Team made a visit to the University of California at Irvine to talk with Alfred Bork who employs the computer in teaching physics.

The visits to Dartmouth College and the PLATO project at the University of Illinois had a somewhat different purpose. While the Team was interested in experiences, successes and failures as at Golden West, attention was also devoted to exploring the possibilities of either connecting to or importing these systems at Delta. In connection with the PLATO project, the related visits to three campuses of the Chicago City College system were important since a number of PLATO terminals are being installed to make use of the central system in Urbana. Extensive plans are underway to use the PLATO system with community college students there and at Parkland College in Urbana.

Implications for Delta College

Area employers interviewing Delta students ask about experience with computers. Delta has a responsibility to its students to provide the opportunity for each student to say: "Yes, and it did these things for me," relating specific advantages of the computer as a tool for learning and for professional work. Delta College has a strong commitment to its students as individuals coming from diverse backgrounds with a variety of educational and vocational goals. The ultimate test of expanded use of the computer is found in the answers to the question: "What are the advantages to the student?" After extensive observation at many other sites, CITALA staff put forth a number of advantages to the student exposed to instructional computing.

Greater individualization of instruction can be achieved. Each student has a program tailor-made for his own needs. The use of self-paced learning can be increased

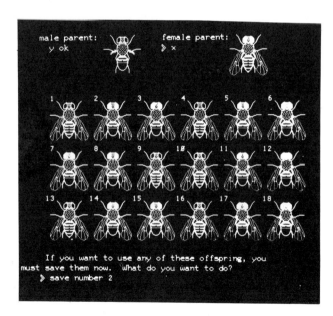

Biology via PLATO terminal. The characteristics of offspring are shown in a fruit fly genetics experiment.

since each student proceeds through course materials and individual lessons as rapidly or slowly as he feels is appropriate. More individual student remediation is available, particularly where drill and practice are needed. In additional to the obvious advantages of individualized attention, students are exposed to simulations and problem-solving situations. Simulations enable students to interact with concepts and situations that otherwise must be dealt with as abstractions rather than as real-world phenomenon. As a high-speed calculating machine, the computer facilitates student problem solving, permitting direct interaction with problems of a type and size encountered in real life situations. By no longer being limited to exercise problems of pencil and paper solution, the student and instructor can use the computer as an aid in solving a wider range of problems. Students can manipulate large amounts of data rapidly, thus being able to experiment with these data in ways formerly not available.

Students can fail without embarrassment; as a consequence students who have particular learning difficulties can interact with a computer at a terminal, while they would not be willing to admit a learning problem to an instructor or counselor.

However, such benefits for the student are impossible without quality instructional materials and a computer system with certain physical characteristics critical to success:

    a. terminals must be easily accessible for both student and faculty use;

    b. terminals should be easy to operate, with clearly-labeled keyboards and instructions for use;

    c. lessons and programs should be easy to understand;

    d. the system should have a library of instructional programs available for student and faculty use;

    e. the system should have an easily-learned, user-oriented language for authors of programs;

    f. the system should lend itself well to both problem solving and computer-assisted instruction uses;

    g. the system needs, in addition to computing power and text processing, the ability to display graphs or drawings and project other visuals (slide and/or microfiche).

The full report discusses alternative means of providing these capabilities: the MERIT Computer Network (or one of its host computing centers); the Dartmouth Time Sharing System; the PLATO IV System; a commercial time-sharing service with special educational rates; and an expanded IBM 360/40 (Delta's present system). Other possibilities were considered but with less detail: a stand alone minicomputer; a different on-site computer system; a split system with one medium size computer for administration and another for instruction.

Expanding Instructional Uses

The Project Team realized that students, faculty, and staff of Delta College needed experience with the computer as an instructional tool. Thus, conclusions at the close of the investigation were quite positive. The Team recommended implementing a three-year, pilot project designed to expand instructional computing at Delta. The final report spelled out a plan that included immediately leasing four ports on the Dartmouth Time Sharing System, leasing six terminals for use on the Dartmouth System or elsewhere, and ordering four PLATO IV terminals. Under the supervision of a Project Director, the Delta staff would develop and implement in-service training programs and incentives to encourage faculty involvement in using the computer as a teaching tool. The final stages of the pilot project would concentrate on evaluative measures.

The rationale for the recommendations may be of more interest than the details. Students, faculty, and staff of Delta College need experience with the computer as an instructional tool. The best way to acquire this experience seems to be to lease time on an educational time sharing system with extensive educational software available and appropriate for college use. Among the various alternatives, only the Dartmouth and PLATO systems have extensive software for community colleges; the Dartmouth System was immediately available.

The crucial questions regarding remote computing relate to timing. Today university computing centers provide rich resources for a wide range of users; however, they tend to charge more for the most straightforward kinds of instructional computing than a small computer dedicated to the purpose. Eventually the rates charged by university computing centers will come down, especially as the universities provide special computing systems or means of access for just these limited kinds of computing on their own campuses.

The capabilities of small computers are increasing while costs continue to go down. Today one can get a "personal" computer for under $4,000 but not very much interesting software is available with it and storage of large files of data and programs is inconvenient. In a few years the cost of such a personal computer will drop to below $1,000 and the capabilities will increase markedly at least in special areas of use for which vendors anticipate large markets. These individual computers and small clusters of terminals on slightly larger machines will provide an important part of instructional computing on college campuses.

A prediction about the mixture of networks and mini-computers in the next ten years is further complicated by difficulties in predicting communication costs. Service networks designed for communications between users and their computers, and perhaps non-profit organizations serving educational institutions, will make reliable and low-cost communications available just for the purpose of access to networks. Until this happens, a college like Delta is rather "distant" in communication dollars from the serviceable networks.

Since the relations among cost, software, storage and communications will shift in the next five to ten years, the future is difficult to judge. Delta would like to develop multiple sources of computing: a college facility for moderate-sized problems; occasional minicomputers for departments, special courses, or other situations in which some cost-saving can be achieved; and telephone access to large computers for problems requiring special software systems or a large data base. At the same time, programs and data should be able to migrate from one system to another, so that the specialized data base at a university can be moved to the local computer when execution locally will be more economical. The software developed on the local computer for instruction might later be programmed into the minicomputer for more economical execution with students in a given unit of the college.

The sharing of materials, programs, and ideas with other authors, programmers, and users will be of considerable value. Because both the Dartmouth and PLATO systems serve networks of users similar to Delta College, the opportunities for sharing with other users in the network are much greater than for "stand-alone" and commercial time-sharing systems.

In short, the rationale behind Team recommendations relies on the assumption that instructional uses of computing are evolving rapidly and Delta will benefit from experimenting with various innovations in equipment, software and applications.

The participants in Project CITALA were Doug Anderson, M. Gene Arnold, Mark Baldwin, Darrell Berry, Bruce Corliss, Robert DeVinney (Chairman), Gayle Hanna, David Howard, John Kostoff, Craig McClain, Dennis McNeal, and Betsy Smith.

Decision-Making

Nay, lad! *Deciding's* not your ploy,
For that's a risky game.
It's *making a decision*
That's your surest road to fame.

Decide means *to take action,*
And that might rock the boat,
And you act and don't succeed,
Small chance you'll stay afloat.

But . . . *making a decision.*
Ah! *That's* the way to swing.
It keeps the masses happy
And doesn't change a thing.

So get yourself a task force
Well-skilled in all the arts
And call them all together
And watch them flip their charts.

For Jack says no and Jim says yes
And Billy says perhaps
And Chester asks good questions
. . . When he isn't taking naps.

And Bertram, chomping his cigar,
Is chock full of statistics,
While Waldemar, who smokes a pipe,
Is famed for his heuristics.

"The figures prove. . . ," "The model says . . ."
"The forecast bears me out."
"The complex simplex program
Shows I'm right without a doubt."

Let's tiptoe out and close the door
And let them stew a while.
No fear that they'll do something rash,
For *doing's* not their style.

Reality's an untamed beast
That's difficult to master,
But models are quite docile
And give you answers faster.

So build yourself a model
To glorify your name.
Then get yourself a task force
And learn to play the game.

—J. C. L. Guest

EXPER SIM: *Experimental Simulation*

by Dana B. Main
University of Michigan

EXPER SIM (Experimental Simulation) is a *system* for teaching research design through computer simulation. It includes not only a set of computer programs and accompanying written materials for student and faculty use, but a classroom pedagogy designed to emphasize the learning of research strategies in the context of a simulated scientific community.

EXPER SIM has been developed for the student *and* instructor who are naive in the use of computers and who do not know how to program.

It is appropriate for any undergraduate course concerned with research questions and analyzing empirical results from experiments addressing such questions. Although the system was conceived and developed within a behavioral science context, it also claims applicability to biological, physical and political science.

Written Materials that Accompany the Program

The student receives a written description of a particular problem area and a list of variables that he can manipulate in experiments. He is given the range of possible values of the manipulable variables, which may be numeric or key words. He is informed of the possible dependent variable allowed in the model. He is further informed of the default value of each manipulable variable should he choose to ignore it in any particular experiment. The default value may be constant from one execution to the next, or it may be randomly selected from the set of possible values.

Accompanying these materials is a student's guide for using the Michigan Experiment Simulation Supervisor (MESS). All models in the library are controlled by a large supervisory program that handles communication between the student and the computer. Once the student learns to use the supervisor commands he can easily explore other models based on quite different subject matter.

Use of LESS for Smaller Computers

For smaller computers with a minimum of 8K storage the Louisville Experiment Simulation Supervisor (LESS), written by Arthur Cromer, may be implemented rather than the Michigan (MESS) programs. They both, in time, will contain the same library of data-generating models. The difference in the two programs lies in the size of the supervisor managing the libraries. MESS has more flexibility, allows names of variables, permits abbreviations and accepts considerable misspelling. LESS, because it is designed for smaller computers, is more restrictive but still very easy for students to use.

Input: Experimental Designs

A student designs an experiment by specifying 1) the number of experimental groups in his design, 2) for each group, the values of the manipulable variables and the name(s) of the dependent variable(s), and 3) the number of subjects (within a specified range) for each group. (It is also possible for a model to contain the capability of repeated measures. If so, then the number of measures on a subject can be specified.)

Output: Experimental Results

This information is submitted to the computer and serves as commands to a data-generating model. The student's output are values of the specified dependent variable(s) which can be plausibly interpreted as raw data. All data-generating models in the MESS library are probabilistic; therefore, the very same design generates different values of the dependent variable.

Depending on his research goal the student generates hypotheses, designs experiments, summarizes results, and explores relationships between manipulable variables as well as functional relationships among different dependent variables. He gets into problems of scaling and is motivated to acquire some statistical skills in order to make inferences about the underlying model generating the data. He is encouraged to report his findings in terms of support or refutation of possible theories.

Operationalizing New Variables

Sometimes a student may be informed of only a subset of the manipulable variables and of all, some, or none of their possible values. He may also be informed of only a subset of possible dependent variables utilized by the data-generating model. He is made aware, either initially or later, of one or more X-variables which may affect his results. The concept of X-variables in instructional simulations was first suggested to us by Richard Johnson in 1972 and was developed for classroom use by Cromer and Thurmond at the University of Louisville (reported in the *Proceedings of the 1972 Conference on Computers in Undergraduate Curricula*). In Cromer and Thurmond's instructional models the student is provided with a complete set of variables, less one: the X-variable. Information gained from runs on the other variables may or may not lead the student to infer the X-variable. If he does, the instructor provides him with a computer command that causes the X-variable to contribute to the values of the data in subsequent runs. If the student has not correctly inferred the appropriate variable, but some other implausible or

more

impossible alternative, the instructor may give him a command that makes no systematic contributions to subsequent data values.

The Pedagogy: a Simulated Scientific Community

The classroom structure of the course is that of a scientific community where each student plays the role of an individual researcher. The student participates in activities designed to parallel those of a scientist in a real community. For example, the student is directed toward a particular problem area. He becomes familiar with at least some of the literature in that area and examines current theories and research bearing on it. He is acquainted with some of the costs associated with conducting research in that field, and he is informed of the resources available to him. These resources, usually in the form of points, are designed to parallel those known to exist in the real world. He proposes research that he would like to conduct, bringing to bear what he is learning about the subject matter, research design principles and his available resources. He designs a research program, not merely isolated experiments. He argues for his research strategy articulating how he believes such a strategy will accomplish his stated research goals. Upon receiving his "contract", he proceeds to implement his strategy by conducting the experiments he has proposed. He updates his knowledge about the area by re-examining or modifying later experiments, based on what he has learned from his own research and other "scientists" in his "community". He communicates his updated knowledge to the rest of the "community" in the form of research reports written in a format acceptable for publication, through formal presentation at "conventions" and through informal bull sessions with other members of the community. In this communication, he not only articulates his research goal, hypotheses tested, and experimental designs, but his method of data analysis and his conclusions. On the basis of updated knowledge, he plans his next experiments, taking into account the costs of such experiments, and the cycle is repeated. One of his final scientific communications may be a review paper that summarizes the state of knowledge of his scientific community in a particular area. It may be a report to a sponsor. Within a two-month period he will have designed and analyzed the results of about ten experiments that he himself has conducted on several problem areas.

The simulated scientific community is facilitated by the use of computer data-generating models. The student rehearses all of the major roles of the scientist except the very time-consuming and expensive data collection step. (Even this step can be included in some problems and in some sessions of the course, but the simulation does not depend on its inclusion.) This process is summarized below:

Sequence of Student Activities in Simulated Scientific Community

1. Orientation to the Scientific Community
   a) Activities involved in participating in the scientific community.
   b) Familiarity and experience with the computer in terms of running EXPER SIM experiments.
   c) Discussion of issues and problems associated with the particular model in the library that will be used.
   d) Explanation of simulated costs and budget.
2. Students submit a proposal of their research plan for approval by the instructor.
3. Upon approval of research plan, students submit their first design to the computer and write a short report that will either be posted or dittoed for all class members. If the latter, then it may be viewed as Vol. 1 of a journal for which the students can select a name and formulate editorial policy.
4. Students, now working individually and in collaboration with other students, submit the next design to the computer. It should be based on what has been learned from the first set of experiments. This report goes into Vol. 2.

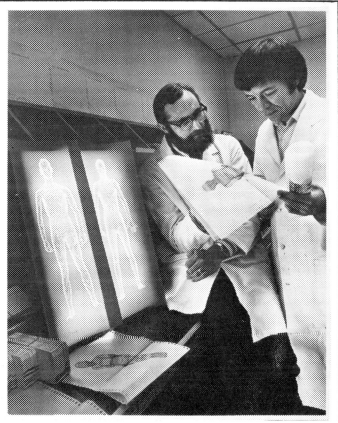

COMPUTERS IN MEDICAL RESEARCH
Scientists at the Texas Institute for Rehabilitation and Research in Houston are using computer produced three-dimensional measurements to study medical applications ranging from deformities in children to weight loss in astronauts. Dr. R. E. Herron, left, Director of the Institute's Biostereometrics Laboratory and Professor Jaime R. Cuzzi, study contour maps of the body which can be produced in other ways such as a graph showing how body volume is distributed from head to foot and cross sections or slices of the body. (Photo IBM)

5. Students design a third experiment based on knowledge gained previously and within the resources of their budget. The report on this design goes into Vol. 3.

6. Students review the "literature" generated in their class and write a review paper. The paper not only discusses their own research, but that conducted by other classmates.

7. An optional exercise is to have students write a report to their sponsor justifying their own research and the expenditure for that information. This may be reserved for students who have overspent their "budgets" or who have conducted a series of disjointed or trivial experiments which the instructor believes needs to be rationalized.

Building New Models

Both MESS and LESS have been written so that new models can be added to the library by writing FORTRAN subroutines to operate with the supervisor or management program. In other words, a professor or advanced student can write his own model as a FORTRAN subroutine for the supervisor program. He need not concern himself with the programming required to interface the student with the data-generating model.

For instructors or students who do not program or do not wish to commit themselves to a programming task, it is possible to develop and build new models for the library making use of the Simulation Writer Interactive Program (SWIP) written by Robert Stout and developed at the University of Michigan. For smaller computers, LESS has features that would enable the building of certain kinds of models. Both are possible in the interactive mode.

The development of SWIP and the LESS programs makes it possible to add models to the library that are concerned with physics, chemistry, biology, medical sciences, and engineering as well as psychology, sociology, economics, education, and political science.

Such models can be used in methodology and statistics courses as well as specific content courses where it is desirable to teach students by way of a method of inquiry.

Costs

The cost of using MESS and LESS once they are implemented is very small compared to the cost of maintaining a traditional laboratory course.

The programs are designed for batch processing (requiring the use of a keypunch or equivalent) as well as interactive processing (requiring the use of a teletype or other user terminal). At the University of Michigan both methods are used simultaneously in the psychology course. (A sample batch run follows this article.) The parameters of an experiment can be conveyed to the computer on about a dozen cards, many of which can be used over and over again. In the interactive mode the student is prompted for the input required, and error messages are immediately available. The cost of batch processing student experiments is usually many times cheaper than the interactive mode. Its disadvantages are a longer turn-around time and delayed access to error messages. Although the interactive mode is more expensive, the student obtains "results" from his experiment more quickly. Even with this more expensive mode, a budget of $7.00 to $10.00 per student has been sufficient for a given term. Cost figures on SWIP will be available soon.

The programs can be obtained for a nominal fee. For information on MESS and SWIP write: Dr. Dana B. Main, 3435 Mason Hall, Department of Psychology, University of Michigan, Ann Arbor, Michigan 48104. For information on LESS write: Dr. Arthur Cromer, Computing Center, University of Louisville, Louisville, Kentucky 40208.

Acknowledgement

EXPER SIM was developed in conjunction with the center for Research on Learning and Teaching at the University of Michigan with support from the Exxon Education Foundation.
[Ed. note: the IMPACT Program of the Exxon Education Foundation has selected EXPER SIM as a tried and effective innovation for which adoptions are encouraged. IMPACT provides modest grants to potential adopters of EXPER SIM (and other items on their adoption "menu") on the basis of proposals received. Contact Ms Caryn Korshin at the Exxon Education Foundation for further details.]

```
MICHIGAN EXPERIMENTAL SIMULATION SUPERVISOR
         VERSION 3-SB   JANUARY, 1973
```
These lines give program title and authors' credits.

```
IMPRINTING SIMULATION
D. W. RAJECKI, FALL, 1970
MODIFIED BY BOB STOUT, AUGUST, 1972

ENTER SUPERVISOR COMMAND
>>EXPT
```
(d) Here the program asks for instructions. Card (d) is printed, which tells the program to begin an experiment.

```
ENTER EXPERIMENT TO LINE
A. EINSTEIN SECT. 029 TARG-ARO EXPT
```
(e) The program asks for an identification line and card (e) is printed.

```
ENTER NO. OF EXPERIMENTAL CONDITIONS
```
(f) 4 — This experiment is to have four conditions, as indicated on card (f).

```
DEFINE EXPERIMENTAL CONDITION(S)
TARG=CYL, HEN   ARO=3,5 WALK=mat
@END
```
(g) The program asks for experimental condition definitions. Cards (g) and (h) are printed.

```
4 CONDITION(S) DEFINED
```
(h) The program agrees that four conditions have been defined.

```
THE FOLLOWING VARIABLE SETTINGS ARE CONSTANT ACROSS ALL CONDITIONS:
        REARING=SOCIAL      INDUCT=MECH
        AGE=RANDOM          WALK=MATCHED
        TEST=1.000
```
The program states which variables are to remain constant across all the four conditions. Note that the variables—REARING, INDUCT, and AGE—have been set to their default values.

```
VARIABLE SETTINGS FOR CONDITION A
        TARGET=CYLINDER
        AROUSAL=3.000
```
Each condition is defined. Note that the variable TARGET alternates first between CYLINDER and HEN, then the variable AROUSAL alternates between 3 and 5.

```
VARIABLE SETTINGS FOR CONDITION B
        TARGET=HEN
        AROUSAL=3.000

VARIABLE SETTINGS FOR CONDITION C
        TARGET=CYLINDER
        AROUSAL=5.000

VARIABLE SETTINGS FOR CONDITION D
        TARGET=HEN
        AROUSAL=5.000
```

```
ENTER NO. OF SUBJECTS IN EACH GROUP
```
(i) 15 — The program asks for the number of subjects to be run in each condition, and then prints card (i).

```
A. EINSTEIN SECT. 029 TARG-ARO EXPT
16:59.08 APR 23, 1973
GROUP NUMBER 1
CONDITION(S): A
NUMBER OF SUBJECTS: 15

        TEST1   SCORES
        2.00    2.80    0.600   1.30    1.30
        0.500   0.700   3.70    1.70    2.50
        1.10    0.900   1.40    6.40    5.20
```
The experimental simulation begins: the first line is the identification line, then comes the time and date of the experiment. Group Number 1 is to be run under condition A and has 15 subjects.

The score for each subject is printed out.

```
NO. OF SS WITH COMPLETE DATA: 15

VARIABLE: TEST1
MEAN: 2.140
VARIANCE: 3.031
STD. DEVIATION: 1.741
```
The scores are analyzed and the statistics are printed out.

The output for conditions B-D follows the same format as the output for condition A.

```
A. EINSTEIN SECT. 029 TARG-ARO EXPT
16:59.09 APR 23, 1973
GROUP NUMBER 2
CONDITION(S): B
NUMBER OF SUBJECTS: 15

        TEST1   SCORES
        4.30    1.50    3.30    1.50    3.10
        0.700   1.90    4.00    4.00    0.200
        5.10    0.0     0.600   1.50    2.60

NO. OF SS WITH COMPLETE DATA: 15

VARIABLE: TEST1
MEAN: 2.287
VARIANCE: 2.613
STD. DEVIATION: 1.616
```

```
A. EINSTEIN SECT. 029 TARG-ARO EXPT
16:59.09 APR 23, 1973
GROUP NUMBER 3
CONDITION(S): C
NUMBER OF SUBJECTS: 15

        TEST1   SCORES
        6.90    12.6    7.60    1.20    9.00
        10.7    7.50    1.20    7.50    9.50
        6.50    1.90    0.900   1.30    10.3

NO. OF SS WITH COMPLETE DATA: 15

VARIABLE: TEST1
MEAN: 6.307
VARIANCE: 15.93
STD. DEVIATION: 3.992
```

```
A. EINSTEIN SECT. 029 TARG-ARO EXPT
16:59.09 APR 23, 1973
GROUP NUMBER 4
CONDITION(S): D
NUMBER OF SUBJECTS: 15

        TEST1   SCORES
        7.20    8.40    7.40    0.800   8.10
        9.90    12.7    7.50    1.10    0.600
        8.40    0.0     12.0    0.0     7.50

NO. OF SS WITH COMPLETE DATA: 15

VARIABLE: TEST1
MEAN: 6.107
VARIANCE: 19.43
STD. DEVIATION: 4.408

EXPERIMENT COMPLETED.
```
Notification of completion of the experiment. The user knows that all went well with this run.

```
(j) ENTER SUPERVISOR COMMAND
    >>STOP

        NUMBER OF EXPERIMENTAL RUNS      1
        NUMBER OF GROUPS SIMULATED       4

    $SOURCE PREVIOUS
(k) $SIGNOFF
```
The program asks for another simulation supervisor command. Card (j) is printed and the program tallies the number of experiments and groups simulated.

The user signs off with card (k) and MTS prints out the signoff statistics.

```
****  ON AT 16:59.48      04-23-73
****  OFF AT 16:59.18     04-23-73
****  ELAPSED TIME            .483 MIN.
****  CPU TIME USED         4.441 SEC.          $.35
****  CPU STOR VMI          1.816 PAGE-MIN.     $.09
****  WAIT STOR VMI          .162 PAGE-HR.
****  CARDS READ              20
****  LINES PRINTED          227                $.02
****  PAGES PRINTED           11                $.10
****  DRUM READS             114                $.04
****  APPROX. COST OF THIS RUN IS   $.58
```

Monty Python meets Monte Cristo

or

French Disconnection

Robert P. Taylor
Teachers College, Columbia University

A final panel discussion at 5 p.m. on Friday, September 5th (a session unfortunately not recorded in the two-volume proceedings) really summarized the essence of the IFIP 2nd WORLD CONFERENCE ON COMPUTERS IN EDUCATION (WCCE II). I will therefore emphasize that session in this report and leave to other reporters the task of issuing a more academic, comprehensive summary of the conference.

The first panelist, an Englishman, suggested that at WCCE II he had discovered where Monty Python's creators got their inspiration. He believed they must certainly have attended some earlier, unrecorded IFIP conference in Marseille. Such wildly surrealistic arrangements as those at WCCE II, he maintained, were simply too much like Monty Python skits for one to assume anything but that Monty's creators had been through a similar conference: no water, electricity, or food initially available at the Luminy campus accommodation when hundreds of delegates began arriving on Sunday night; transport to meeting site in busses which broke down only to move when the drivers got out to see what was wrong; transparency projectors which either didn't project or which shocked those who tried to adjust them; mandates against reading papers from the podium even for the first meeting though no one could possibly have had time to familiarize himself with the papers being presented; galas and receptions of questionable distinction; ostensibly spectacular outings to what turned out to be quite insignificant spots; heavy rains in a city normally noted for its dry climate; and so on. Some attendees, the Englishman noted, might mistake this stupendous accumulation of the bizarre as chance, but no keen follower of Monty Python could make such a mistake. The parallel between such an accumulation at WCCE II and the well-planned chaos which is standard fare on Monty Python's Flying Circus is too striking to be overlooked. "To have thus discovered the roots of dear old Monty," he concluded, "... ah, that alone made this a conference I shall not soon forget."

The next panelist at this end-all session, an American expert on computer-generated animation, interpreted the whole thing cinematically. He maintained that WCCE II should have been filmed and distributed — as *French Disconnection*! The American then elaborated on the parallels and contrasts between such a film and the currently popular *French Connection II*. He stressed three obvious parallels in the two dramas — (1) the Marseille setting; (2) the odd reception accorded the visiting hero(es); and (3) the scenes of wasteful chaos with which each drama begins. He claimed that significant contrasts were just as striking and numerous. As illustration he commented briefly on (1) torture of the hero(es) and (2) dramatic climax. He noted that while torture was intense and centered on a single victim in *French Connection II*, torture was mild and distributed across hundreds in *French Disconnection*. About climax, he had this to say: "French Connection II had a terrific climax — the shooting right at the end, while this thing ... why this thing just petered out, dried up. There wasn't any climax at all!"

The final panelist*, a European with a slightly German accent, focused attention on the classics. Recalling *le Compte de Monte Cristo*, this panelist had, the evening before, paid a visit to le chateau d'If, the island prison which Dumas had used for the setting of *Monte Cristo*. Upon completing that visit, she said she sensed that our hosts for WCCE II had made an enormous *faux pas*: they had chosen the wrong site for delegate housing. Upon sailing back to Marseille from the visit, she realized that the stout towers and rocky cliffs of the prison island would have made a far more classic (and remote and inaccessible)

accommodation than the Luminy campus chosen by the conference organizers. "Why," she pointed out, "one could actually *walk* in from Luminy if one were really desperate. It's a mere ten or twelve kilometers. But the chateau d'If, well ... one can't walk in from there, can one?"

On this point, one of greater clarity than many points made at WCCE II, the final panel session ended. The panelists gathered up their baggage, left the lobby, and labored down the winding drive to catch a special IFIPS chartered bus for the Gare St. Charles. They boarded the first bus at the bottom of the drive, then disembarked and entered a second bus. (The first one was probably going back to Luminy.) Eventually the second bus pulled away and disappeared up the road in the direction of the train station. If it was anything like the other IFIPS busses at WCCE II, those panelists missed their train. The bus either broke down or went to the wrong place.

Does my presentation of this final panel session imply this was a bad conference? No, merely that there were some real problems. Once one gets beyond some of the unique flaws of WCCE II (and humor helps), one sees that it probably wasn't such a bad conference after all (it had to be good ... why else would I have spent so much to go). There were over 1000 attendees representing both developed and developing countries around the world and over 150 papers (rather completely presented in the proceedings), covering a wide range of topics with a wide range of sophistication. One learned (or relearned) that some of the problems one thinks are unique to one's own shop (or city or country) are really rather universal problems inevitably tied to the rapid growth of computing and education for computing: there is still no perfect way to teach programming; no ideal language has yet been discovered; a gap exists world-wide between academic or scientific computing and data processing; and everyone everywhere is beginning to face the computing literacy problem confronting the masses.

Probably no one during the conference digested even a quarter of what was presented or what was written in the proceedings. Perhaps few attendees will do so even after returning home. Some papers will probably never be read or looked at again and many will be only glanced at. A select few, though, will certainly be read carefully by many people in various countries. The substance of those papers and the experience of meeting so many people with common interest in the present and future of computers in education merged to make WCCE II a rare experience.

Was it really unforgettable? Certainly. Was it worth it? Who can say — for some, definitely; for others, possibly; for still others, probably not. Would the average attendee go again knowing beforehand exactly what it would be like? Who can say? I think I would.

(This report is appearing simultaneously in *SIGCUE Bulletin*.)

---

*A fourth panelist was invited but did not attend because his bus went to the wrong place. The following is a summary of his comments.

Getting there is half the fun! The conference started on September 1, thereby forcing peoply to fly to France in August while peak fares were still in effect. A one-day later starting date could have saved the U. S. attendees some *$30,000* in air fares. Participants were promised a 20% reduction on their return railroad trip if they flew into a city other than Marseilles (I came by way of Frankfurt). However, this discount was actually a myth due to the incorrect translation of instructions for its use into English.

But once there, the fun continued. Conference lunches

IFIP 2ème Conférence Internationale
" INFORMATIQUE et ENSEIGNEMENT "

An Interview with J. Hebenstreit, Conference Chairman

HEBENSTREIT. We observe that the great majority of papers look at computers as a replacement for current teaching methods. This is valuable in that the methodology of informatics may cause us to re-analyze what teaching and learning is and what it should be. *We cannot continue to teach the way we have been and are currently.* How can we expect children to continue to memorize in light of the information explosion? The accumulated knowledge of humanity is doubling every 13 years. There is an upper limit to the time an individual can spend in learning and also to the speed of learning. But the amount of knowledge has no upper limit. What then, is the solution?

The best approach appears to be to give the individual a model of his environment, or a portion of it; and then train people to extend and build their own models. These models, or simulations are not meant to teach model-building, but rather other subjects. We see a definite trend toward more papers in this area. Computers are being used less in a mechanical sense and more to affect the pedagogy of teaching and learning.

I want to emphasize a very important point: the way to use the computer, when to use it, and how to use it is the responsibility of the teacher. Solely. Totally. This is never the responsibility of the computer scientist.

QUESTION. What about teacher resistance to computers?

HEBENSTREIT. Unfortunately teaching is not only a profession but a bureaucracy. The attitude is, "I've got enough problems. Don't bother me with new things". However, the learning of nearby, non-threatening disciplines introduces interdisciplinary learning and it seems to work. In other words, "I can use a computer model to illustrate my point nicely, but I'd like to really know how it works (statistics, etc.) and I'd like to be able to modify and extend it (programming, data structure, etc.).

QUESTION. What's coming?

HEBENSTREIT. Cheap, off-line devices. Telecommunications costs are high and will remain so, hence microprocessors and MOS technology will be the heart of educational computers in the near future (5—10 years). While generally stand-alone, from time to time these devices may be connected to large computers or data banks.

QUESTION. When is the next world Computers in Education Conference?

HEBENSTREIT. Probably 1981. As of this time no country or sponsoring organization has been selected. We're seeking volunteers. It's quite a massive job — this conference had over 1,000 attendees from 50 countries.

Conference attendees discuss a report with Arnold Krotokin at the World Computers in Education Conference.

CONFERENCE REPORTS

The official 2-volume (over 1000 pages) IFIP World Computers in Education Conference Proceedings were published by North Holland/American Elsevier, 52 Vanderbilt Ave., New York, NY 10017. Price unknown (probably high).

. A computerized data base of authors, subjects and keywords from the papers has been prepared by Phil Barker. A report of this (Report 7504) and an excerpt from the report are available from P. G. Barker, Dept. of Computing, University of Durham, Science Labs, South Road, Durham DH1 3LE, England.

Robert Taylor, Alfred Bork, and Arthur Luehrmann discuss an important point at the IFIP 2nd World Computers in Education Conference in Marseilles, France, September 2, 1975.

Monty Python footnote con't.
were outrageously priced at $5.00 each and required waiting in a queue for 15 to 60 minutes just to get in. The "gala evening" was a gala ripoff costing $22.50 per person; this buffet/folkloric festival 1) was held in a gravel pit mislabeled a garden, 2) ran out of beef and shellfish but had plenty of thick crusted, soggy pizza, 3) had a display of singing and dancing which could be seen only by those who shoved their way to the front row, 4) had no chairs or place to sit, save on the gravel, and 5) was typical of the local arrangements in general.

One must sincerely hope that future conferences would not be organized by sadists, held at a school with no interest in the subject (Faculty of Medicine), in a city with little interest in visitors (Marseilles). Why, Big Apple (Fun City) would even be better!

The Parable of the Horse

Being a diversion intended to produce a few horse laughs and perhaps some horse sense on a subject that has already fertilized too many fields.

by
John M. Nevison

Author note:
The author has wrangled programs of his own for many years. He has served as a shipping clerk for Project Conduit at the Kiewit Computation Center of Dartmouth College. Presently he is engaged in some private ranching on forest watershed models. Copyright 1974 by John M. Nevison.

The Parable

There was a farmer who caught a wild horse. He put the animal to work, enlarged his farm and called it a ranch. The idea caught on and soon everyone was after horses to help with their work. Horsemanship developed apace. The wrangler was born. Horse trading flourished. So did stealing.

After the railroads came, horses were shipped from one range to another. Ranchers benefitted from the increase of good animals. And the many regions prospered as the artistry of their breeding and the skill of their training improved the quality of their stock.

The Animal

Bad tempered programs kick even their own handlers.

A computer program has much in common with a wild horse. It is temperamental; docile one moment and vicious the next. With good training it will return a lifetime of hard work. It usually performs well for only one person. And like all living things, it eventually grows old and dies.

Programs and horses exhibit a similar variety. There are frisky colts, hard racing two-year-olds, even tempered mares, ornery stallions, heavy hooved plow-horses, high stepping trotters, quick turning quarter-horses, and broken down nags.

The Home Range

A professional who uses a computer program without knowing how to write one is like a rancher who has never ridden a horse: he may succeed, but he does so under a severe handicap.

Often a skilled academic will train a string of programs to cover his range. How he uses a program will vary with the geography of his subject, the landscape of his students and the weather of his research. Different animals are appropriate to different tasks on a constantly changing range.

A teacher who has learned how to ride a program uses it with discrimination. He knows what it does best, what its limits are, and how to use it most efficiently. Further, like the rancher who knows how to ride, he can manage with skill the wranglers in his employ.

The program wrangler often adapts a preexisting program to his own use. Even the most docile of programs will kick and buck when a new wrangler begins to work with it. Very few programs are well mannered enough to work for someone other than their master. Not surprisingly, a wrangler learns to examine what he wants to do and voids difficult retraining by breeding his own program.

To get his ranch work done the professional is constantly deciding whether to have his cowboys breed a horse suitable to the task or import one from another range and train it to the local tasks. The decision depends heavily on the size of the program.

The Size of the Beast

A nag is a nag.

All kinds of programs come in one of three sizes: large, small, or middle. Large ones are those that take months of a programmer's time or tens of millions of bytes of storage on a computer. Small ones are those less than ten lines long. The middle size ones are those left in between.

A very large program is cumbersome enough to move and store that a telephone connection to the source often costs less than moving it.

A very small program is, by definition, the sort of animal anyone can breed with no trouble on his own range.

Programs between these extremes, written in a language like APL, BASIC or Fortran compose the bulk of the herd currently used in research and instruction. Different academics will choose either to breed or to import a middle sized program after examining the local conditions and the cost of shipment.

Shipping a Horse by Train

Moving a program from one computer to another is like shipping a horse by train: fundamentally, it does not want to go.

The cost of moving a computer program is hard to estimate and the problems of shipping are poorly understood.

The cowboy's preconception of how to move one has proved wrong. His solution was to ride the program into the boxcar, slam the door, ship it and tell someone to ride it out at the other end. A program actually shipped this way usually seriously injures the first handler to get near it when it arrives. After inflicting multiple lacerations on the wrangler, it often dies of neglect. Sometimes it appears in unfamiliar harness, performing inappropriate work.

When shipping clerks from several stations agree on how to immobilize the program in a standard character code, with certain formats for magnetic tape or punched cards, the cost to load, ship, and unload a program shrinks dramatically. Unloading time can be cut from forty hours to fifteen minutes.

Further agreement on the use of languages and on the necessary technical directions can speed the preliminary grooming of an imported program.

The results of these agreements make a program cheaper for a teacher to order from another college and easier for him to handle once it arrives on his campus. However, an easy-to-unload program has to have been loaded with care somewhere else. This loading is not only a technical problem, it is a personnel problem.

Rancher, Cowboy, Clerk

Anyone working around a horse must learn to handle a pitchfork.

The teacher, the programmer, and the computer center shipping clerk each view the program from a different perspective. The teacher wants the program to do the job, be it in research or in teaching.

The programmer also wants the program to perform well. However, his preoccupation is with training the program, smoothing its quirks and polishing its routines so that it will perform at its best. He is often beguiled into prizing the elegance of the performance more than the accomplishment of the job.

The shipping clerk knows that the program must be crated with appropriate instructions and shipped in a confined, unnatural state. The cowboy, preoccupied with the program's beauty on the open range, views this clerk with thinly veiled hostility. The clerk, preoccupied with shipping the program well, views the cowboy with ill-concealed scorn. Neither fully appreciates the other's point of view.

The wise academic shares the programmer's love of the program on the open range, but realizes the need for shipment if the program is to get to other ranchers at different stations. He will tolerate the shipping clerk and perhaps even help him.

The clerk will demand of the rancher that he provide a program well trained for use by others. In addition he asks for details on the program that will help his counterpart at another computer center to get it working according to the advertisement. These details include sample runs of the program and notes on the limitations of its intended use.

Working with the program's handler, the clerk will crate the program with appropriate technical directions and ship it.

Station to Station, Range to Range, Rancher to Rancher

It is not the program's fault if it is harnessed to the wrong job.

The advertisement for the program could be a research note, published article, textbook or talk. It is from this advertisement that an alert professional first learns of a new application. Only after he has found out how he might use a program

does he decide to import a copy of the original.

The rancher comes down to the station to meet the train when a program arrives. He and the clerk discuss how the program should be groomed at the station and settle on a handler. The handler may be the teacher himself, one of his students, or a center employee. The wrangler will curry and brush the program and make sure that its hooves are properly shod for the region. He may help the rancher lead it home to see how it performs.

During this final trial the rancher is preoccupied with checking advertisement against actual performance to see if the program lives up to expectations. When it meets with his approval, it is added to the corral, one more animal to help with the ranch work.

Fast-Breeding Ranch, Fast-Breeding Range

Riding a time-sharing program on a batch processing range is like riding a hobbled race horse: one has trouble understanding how it was bred to run.
Riding a batch program on a time-sharing range is like riding a plow-horse: It can pull heavy loads, but slowly and only straight ahead.

One method of promoting the spread of computer ideas is to improve the speed and convenience of breeding programs. This can be done a number of ways.

A most common, but expensive, trick has been for a researcher with a large grant to hire a number of skilled programmers who write and modify programs to produce a string of steeds useful for his own local research.

Another way to improve the convenience of writing programs is through the use of a good time-sharing system. The convenience of a fast-breeding, fast-training, interactive system allows a teacher to handle his own programs. It also means that more of his students know how to program and may be hired part-time. Finally, it means that larger programs (perhaps up to fifty lines) can be locally bred rather than imported from somewhere else through the computer center.

Into the Sunset

The parable makes the obvious prediction that the spread of computing ideas will be aided by:
1. Improving the shipment of the best trained middle sized programs,
2. Increasing the convenience of the local breeding of all programs, and
3. Effectively advertising good ideas to both farmers and ranchers.

But the most important lesson of the parable is that anything that can vary, will vary: the program's behavior, the programmer's ability, the academic's sophistication, the clerk's competence, the climate of research, or the needs of teaching.

Because of this enormous variation, generalizations about the subject die young. A discussion of a computer program is most fruitful when it is most specific. Stories tell more than statistics.

Technical Transport Problems

by Trinka Dunnagan
University of Iowa

The CONDUIT project sponsored by the National Science Foundation is studying the current process of sharing instructional programs among undergraduate institutions. Believing in the contribution computers can make in education, CONDUIT is hoping to encourage classroom usage of good, computer-based curriculum materials by improving the overall process of courseware dissemination.

One major factor inhibiting sharing of programs is technical non-transferability of otherwise meritorious material. It is proposed that this obstacle can be overcome with a national solution. At the widespread, heterogeneous computing facilities of the CONDUIT consortium, technical transport guidelines are being evolved and tested. Such guidelines are based on preliminary experiments in program exchange, involving over eighty programs and five network centers (Oregon State University, Dartmouth College, North Carolina Educational Computing Service, and the Universities of Iowa and Texas). The proposed solution is to change the locus of programming effort from many unwitting recipients to the author. The failings of the present system stem from the fact that development occurs in a complicated environment where: 1) most academic professionals are indifferent to computer-based courseware making extensive involvement in instructional computing professionally unrewarding, 2) publishers are apathetic to computer-based materials thus the possibilities for commercial publication of courseware is limited, and 3) programmers reflect a general inexperience with other computer facilities thus fostering parochial development. Hopefully CONDUIT guidelines will mitigate development problems by supplying an alternative for optimizing transferability at the source site thereby improving the potential for wide dissemination and recognition of the developer's product.

Considering historic transfer problems, one can see the need for guidelines; some of which are so simple-minded as to have always seemed obvious. The following is a summary of common technical transport problems typifying CONDUIT'S experience and motivating the development of transfer guidelines.

* Magnetic tapes become mysterious on different equipment for reasons such as: 1) "BCD" differs by a few characters on each new machine, 2) certain block lengths are unacceptable, 3) tapes may contain undocumented left-over garbage, 4) internal labels are inaccessible, and 5) external documentation does not exactly match tape contents.
* In some cases card decks arrived in uninterpreted form with local job control cards scattered throughout. Again the program listing and/or documentation would not always match the source deck.
* Once the program had been successfully read into the computer, calls to unexplained external routines, such as a random number generator, could cause program failure.
* Frequent, unacknowledged references to system dependent features, such as physical unit numbers, presented trivial but tedious errors to correct.
* Special devices, unavailable to the potential user, were required for program use in the classroom so no usage occurred.
* Through classroom usage, it was discovered that certain unexplored paths caused program failure or, even worse, that the program was theoretically unsound although free from syntax-level errors.

It is granted that all these problems are not solvable with technical transport guidelines. CONDUIT'S effort also involves educational documentation, program verification, tape transfer format (including a specification of BCD code for CONDUIT), authors' guides, and formal materials review. However, much can be accomplished by following simple rules of transfer programming. Other problems are more identifiable and correctable when a program is well-written. The following presents the major recommendations underlying CONDUIT guidelines for technically transportable programs:

* A standard, widely-diffused language should be used. For CONDUIT this language is either ANSI standard Fortran (based upon ANSI X3.9-1966, American National Standard Fortran) or a slightly revised version of the ACT

Technical Transport continued —

TRANSPORTABLE BASIC (ACT Technical Bulletin No. 11).

* Programs should be modularized to improve explanation of program logic and to seriously reduce both original errors and transfer checkout problems.
* Use of structured programming techniques is strongly recommended. This approach reduces program complexity and increases readability by other persons.
* Explicit references to system specific features, such as a unit number for read or write, should be replaced by a meaningful variable name so that such parameters can be readily initialized at a new site with system specific values.
* Verifiability should be built-in to the program as much as possible so that out-of-range input data can be filtered out; calculation flukes can be caught, displayed, and bypassed; and intermediate results can be output upon request. Also present should be sample input and the subsequent computer results as well as computer-independent calculations for validating problematic algorithms.

* The last recommendation covered in the guidelines is completeness of documentation. Internal program documentation should comment program name, source, date, language, machine, operating system, core requirements, overall function, usage and options, important variables and parameters, and any references to external files, routines, etc. Every separate module should be commented similarly. The net effort is to make the program itself as technically well-documented as possible, the goal being ease of program readability by a programmer at another, remote installation.

Implicit in CONDUIT'S strategy of improving programs at the source is the need for author incentives and rewards and a redistribution of resources to cover a possible increase in development costs. As CONDUIT is an experiment, it is hoped that cost-benefit analysis will justify transfer programming, and that mechanisms for program dissemination will permit cost recovery, promote authors' prestige and ultimately facilitate innovative usage of computer-based curriculum materials in the classroom.

CONDUIT DOCUMENTATION GUIDELINE
Abstracted Version

CONDUIT: A consortium of regional networks at Oregon State University, North Carolina Educational Computing Service, Dartmouth College, and the Universities of Iowa and Texas (Austin).

|||||||||||||||||||||||||||||||||||||||||||||||||||||||||||||||||||||||||||||||||||||||||||||

INTRODUCTION

The CONDUIT Documentation Guidelines describe standards for packaging computer-based curriculum materials. These guidelines stipulate those types of documentation deemed necessary not only for local usage but also for transportation of packages, both educationally and technically, among multiple non-homogeneous computer installations. Documentation to comprise a complete package will be collected from appropriate sources serving the following purposes:

DOCUMENTATION CHART

DOCUMENT	SOURCE	TARGET	PURPOSE
1. COVER LETTER	Local Curriculum Coordinator*	Faculty User	Availability announcement
2. ABSTRACT	Author	Faculty User	Preview
3. EDUCATIONAL DOCUMENTATION	Author	Faculty User, Student	Substantive & Pedagogical Aspects
4. TECHNICAL DOCUMENTATION	Programmer, Author	Curriculum Coordinator Faculty User, Student	Technical Aspects (systems & programming considerations)
5. LOCAL DOCUMENTATION (educational & technical)	Local Curriculum Coordinator	Faculty User, Student	Modifications resulting from usage at a specific network computer center
6. REVIEWS	Reviewers, Discipline Committee**	Faculty Users	Certification

(Reviewer or Discipline Committee brace spanning items 2, 3, and 4 of the TARGET column.)

NOTE: This abstracted version was prepared by Trinka Dunnagan from the *CONDUIT Documentation Guidelines* of October, 1973 in which each component of documentation is explained more fully.

*Each local Curriculum Coordinator is responsible to CONDUIT for collecting and disseminating computer-related curriculum material at his network schools.

**Discipline committees, who serve in an advisory capacity to CONDUIT, are composed of faculty with interest and expertise in computer applications within a discipline.

1. COVER LETTER

A *cover letter* should be supplied by the local Curriculum Coordinator as supplementary, local documentation for any CONDUIT package. The purpose of such a letter is to provide prospective network users with a realistic picture of their relationship with CONDUIT in the event of the package's adoption and to state the costs, availability, and procedures for acquiring any materials (texts, card decks, magnetic tapes, program listings, etc.) needed for that adoption. Any discussion of availability should list in addition to the source repository other network centers and computer types at which this package is supported. Any restrictions (such as copyrights, etc.) on the reproduction and use of these materials should be stated at this time as well as the caveat that although CONDUIT has attempted to maximize the educational value and technical reliability of the programs, *no liability* for errors in these materials, expressed or implied, is assumed by the author(s), the source facility (NAME), or the CONDUIT consortium. User's expectations of CONDUIT support (computer time, programming aid, consulting services, etc.) should be specifically covered in terms of extent, personnel and mechanics involved.

2. ABSTRACT

The author of each package should provide an abstract sufficient to serve as an all purpose introduction to the computer-based curriculum package. The abstract should contain the following items:

(a) Descriptive title
(b) Mnemonic or calling name
(c) Author(s) and original source
(d) Names and locations of any subsequent modifiers
(e) Summary of substantive content
(f) Statement of educational objectives
(g) Specifications of computer's instructional role
(h) Background requirements for instructors and students
(i) References (if available)

3. EDUCATIONAL DOCUMENTATION

The author of a computer-based curriculum package addresses in this type of documentation the needs of faculty and student users. Topics covered should include the following:

(a) Substantive aspects—theoretical background and disciplinary principles of this computer-based package.
(b) Pedagogical significance—relationship of the educational objectives stated in this material to content and instructional techniques.
(c) Implementation considerations—suggestions for instructional management within the classroom, the computing environment and the standard curriculum.

These topics could appear in separate single-purpose manuals (e.g., Teacher's Guide, Student Manual, Programmer's Guide, Problems, etc.) or as a collective write-up depending on the size and scope of the package being documented.

4. TECHNICAL DOCUMENTATION

Technical documentation involves those materials necessary for the understanding by a potential user of how the courseware (e.g., program) operates. Technical documentation should attempt to extricate that programming documentation which is universal and transportable, in terms of information content, from site-specific descriptions needed only for local usage. In order to clarify both the program logic and function, one needs:

(a) Explanation of the program's logical organization and the functions of any discrete modules.
(b) Well-commented program listing.
(c) Descriptions of sample input such as test data and any program parameter cards required.
(d) Listing of output generated by such sample input.
(e) Test problems and expected results.
(f) Description of program options and how to exercise them.
(g) Listing and explanation of program-generated messages.
(h) Glossary of variable names and special discipline oriented items.
(i) Itemization and descriptions of supporting programs, subroutines and external files.
(j) Formats for parameter and data cards.

For each data set, the following information should be available:

(a) Description of file organization.
(b) File data item definitions.
(c) Indices to the data set.
(d) Security procedures, if any.

5. LOCAL DOCUMENTATION

Curriculum Coordinators should provide network users with instructions for usage of CONDUIT materials at their local computer center. Information classifiable as local (or site-dependent) is necessary only if it differs from that which is provided as universal documentation. Such information includes:

(a) Instructions and examples on how to use the local computer (JCL, deck setup, typical file or program access, major operations.
(b) A setup example of how to access the program under consideration.
(c) A listing of the local version of the program and notations on its significant differences from the universal model.
(d) Sample I/O for this version of the program.
(e) Information on typical run times and related costs.

In addition an overall description in explicit terms of the current computing environment should state:

(a) Operating system, release level/version.
(b) Mode of usage (batch versus interactive).
(c) Storage devices required.
(d) Special peripheral device requirements (central site).
(e) Special terminal needs (user site).
(f) Common causes of program failure and error recovery.
(g) Any other locally pertinent information or comments on these materials.

6. REVIEWS

Material selected for dissemination through CONDUIT is first reviewed under the direction of an appropriate discipline committee. Those packages receiving positive reviews are included in the CONDUIT Library for undergraduate education with solicited reviews comprising a final section of the documentations.

Computers

Statewide pools may not yield expected benefits

ST. LOUIS

The pooling of computer services in statewide networks can provide economies and efficiencies, but it often means loss of local control and may make computer services more expensive and less accessible for some users, concludes of a 12-month study in the U.S. and Canada by Charles Mossmann, director of user services at the University of California at Irvine. Mr. Mossmann conducted the study under a grant from the Exxon Education Foundation.

"The 'network bandwagon' is highly evident in the state and provincial capitals," he said, "and bureaucrats and administrators are scrambling to get on it.

"In nearly one-third of the 60 states and major provinces, decision-makers are guided by an explicit plan—generated at the provincial or state level—for computing in higher education. This plan determines what they will and will not do. In another third, such a plan is now under development.

Sharing of Resources

"Almost all such plans explicitly call for the sharing of resources between campuses, usually by means of a network constructed specifically for this purpose.

"Only 20 states and provinces indicate that their public colleges and universities are totally responsible for their own decisions about computing."

Unless there is a strong program of service and consultation for the "naïve and long-distance users," Mr. Mossmann said, state systems tend to be monopolized by the central, on-campus users.

Some network systems are successful, he said, mentioning Dartmouth, Iowa, and North Carolina as examples.

Cooperation a Goal

"A return to the 'one-campus, one-computer' model of the 1960's is just out of the question," he said. "The alternatives simply provide too many opportunities for both quality and economy of operations.

"I think it is not an unreasonable goal to strive for meaningful coop-eration between colleges and universities, for networks that will spread resources to the have-nots and that will enrich the opportunities available to those in a position to use them.

"This cooperation can emerge between institutions and should not have to be imposed on unwilling colleges by an authoritarian governance.

"Computing, in its current stage of development, is uniquely a substance that can be shared. If we are the custodians of the first academic resource which can in fact be shared despite geography, and are the first agents to attempt such sharing on a large scale, it is no wonder we are having trouble. We have no model on which to build. In fact, we may be constructing models that have importance and implication beyond our vision."

Mr. Mossmann discussed his findings at a meeting of EDUCOM— the Interuniversity Communications Council of Princeton, N.J.—which sponsored his study.

Computers tend to be unpopular on campuses, said Ronald Roskens, chancellor of the University of Nebraska at Omaha, and he blamed higher education for allowing alienation and antipathy toward computers to develop among faculty members and students.

"We are suffering the consequences of a fairly high degree of computer illiteracy," he said.

"In my judgment," he continued, "there is no single force that has had greater impact upon the style and the operation of American colleges and universities in the last half-century than computer technology."

Although he found a lack of trust in computers within the academic community, Mr. Roskens assigned computers an important role in helping higher education to regain public trust through improvement of institutional management.

The Omaha chancellor suggested that computer personnel could improve their image by avoiding exaggerated claims of what computer systems can do and how fast they can do it and by avoiding "esoteric jargon."

Every college graduate ought to have some degree of computer literacy, said Gerard Weeg, director of the University of Iowa computer center and chairman of the EDUCOM conference.

Proliferation of Small Computers

He said there are approximately 10,000 computers in use in educational institutions now. It has been predicted that by 1980 computing may be the world's largest industry, he said.

It's hard for bureaucracy to keep abreast of technology.

A computer problem discussed at the conference here was reminiscent of the multiplication of copying machines that hampered attempts to centralize campus printing.

Now, directors of centralized computer services see a threat in the proliferation of small machines of increasing sophistication.

Calculators have developed from mechanical adding machines to electronic, integrated-circuit packages that will perform all kinds of mathematical chores, some of them following computer-like programs fed to them on magnetic tape or cards, and costing up to $12,000.

Leland Williams, president of Triangle Universities Computation Center, said that one of the universities in his group now had about five programmable calculators that slipped through a screen designed to guard against the proliferation of computer facilities.

"When is a programmable calculator a computer?" Mr. Williams asked.   —JACK MAGARRELL

Adding up calculators

The electronic calculator became a billion-dollar market at retail last year, according to a study by Creative Strategies. The biggest share of the market was held by consumer calculators, of which 7 million were sold. Some 3.5-million of last year's unit sales were business calculators, and another 300,000 were in the "professional" category. The study indicated that the market for consumer calculators would grow about 50% this year, in terms of dollar volume, more in terms of units, due to declining prices. Component costs for calculators have dropped sharply, LC chips falling from an average of $30 in 1970 to about $5 currently. LED displays, which cost calculator manufacturers slightly less than one dollar per digit, will be closer to 50 cents before the year is over.●

Reprinted with permission from The Chronicle of Higher Education, Aug. 5, 1974.

PLATO IV System Progress Report on Field Testing

by Eric McWilliams
National Science Foundation

Approximately two-and-one-half years ago, the Computer-based Education Research Laboratory (CERL) at the University of Illinois at Champaign/Urbana committed itself to preparing for and conducting a large-scale field-test of the PLATO system of computer-assisted instruction (CAI). Specifically, CERL committed to

- developing and integrating the hardware and software required to support roughly 1,000 plasma panel consoles;
- installing, operating, and maintaining a network of at least 500 plasma panel consoles, in university, community college, and elementary classrooms; and
- developing and operating CAI lessons (courseware) and educational programs (including teacher training, consultation, evaluative services, etc.) for instruction in elementary reading and mathematics, community college accountancy, biology, chemistry, English, and mathematics, and university physics, chemistry, and foreign languages.

The National Science Foundation committed $5 M to these activities; the University of Illinois committed an equivalent amount, to pay for university lesson development and use on at least 200 of the promised 500 consoles. The field-test, originally scheduled to begin in September of 1973, will be evaluated by an independent third party (The Princeton Educational Testing Service), in order to provide data concerning the processes, costs, and effects of developing and operating the PLATO system and courseware.

Much has been accomplished toward meeting these objectives.

- A sophisticated system of hardware and software (PLATO IV) has been implemented and operated to serve several hundred CAI consoles simultaneously. Performance data indicates that this system will be capable of serving about 1,000 operating CAI consoles.
- A plasma panel console capable of providing extremely clear graphical displays using ordinary telephone lines has been perfected and placed into production. A network of roughly 450 such consoles has been installed and tested.
- Lesson designers, programmers, and other CAI specialists have been organized into teams responsible for producing the courseware for the elementary and community college field-

test, and many university faculty members are developing lessons for use in their own courses. Plans and commitments have been made to field-test the PLATO system in elementary schools and Parkland Community College in Champaign/Urbana, and in several campuses of the Chicago City Colleges.

A device for touch-input and a device for random access audio message output have been developed and perfected. Each will be available for the field-test, and for subsequent commercial use.

There have been other, related developments of some importance as well. For example, even at this very early stage, almost a dozen major universities have procured and are operating PLATO consoles, and an equal number want consoles as soon as possible. Eight military training centers are presently developing courseware and plans for their own field-test of the PLATO system. More than a dozen major U. S. (and several foreign) corporations are preparing to develop and market devices or systems based upon the PLATO technology. Several organizations are presently implementing or planning to install PLATO-based CAI systems in the rather near future. The system has been demonstrated upon request to hundreds of groups in more than 50 U. S. cities and more than eight foreign countries, including live demonstrations before the U. S. Congress, and before government

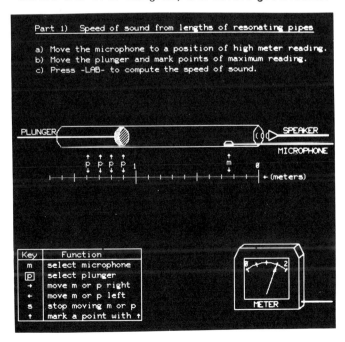

High-resolution image on plasma terminal.

officials and others in the U. S. S. R., in Moscow.

Additional evidence of PLATO's impact can be drawn from the fact that more than 500 authors (ranging in age and experience from school children to full professors) have produced more than 2000 hours of lesson material for PLATO, in more than 80 different disciplines. Although access to PLATO consoles and lessons is still quite limited, more than 20,000 student-contact-hours were logged under PLATO during the fall 1973 term. Furthermore, preliminary results from a survey of 42 instructors and about 500 students who used the system revealed that three-fourths of the instructors and two-thirds of the students felt rather positively toward PLATO CAI after one semester's use, in spite of limited access and occasional interruptions in service.

There have of course been problems and dealys, as well as progress, which have resulted in a substantial increase in the cost for the elementary and community college activities and a year's postponement in the start of the field-tests. Some of this delay is attributable to problems with the hardware and software itself. Although the system reached a moderate level of performance relatively quickly, there have been interruptions in service, especially during those periods when major hardware had to be added to the system.* These interruptions were especially troublesome at the (now more than 70) remote sites, since the terminals themselves have frequently accounted for the majority of the system down-time, and many remote sites have only a single terminal.

It must also be reported that the original configuration proved inadequate to serve the relatively large number of lesson authors committed to developing courseware. The initial configuration assumed that the majority of PLATO use would accrue to students enrolled in scheduled classes, who could therefore share PLATO lessons and memory space. Authors of course usually require distinct PLATO lessons and memory space, and a shortage of extended-core storage quickly developed. It therefore proved necessary to double the amount of extended-core storage for lesson swapping.

There have also been substantial delays in obtaining consoles and telecommunication equipment and service. Difficulties in obtaining educational television (ETV) service from the common carrier for service between Urbana and Chicago made it necessary for CERL to develop special (and more expensive) modulator/demodulator equipment capable of multiplexing up to four consoles on each voice-grade telephone line. This equipment should be adequate for the field-tests, but the change introduced delays which still persist, and it is unfortunate not to be able to field-test PLATO using ETV service at this time.

These system problems have had their effect upon project cost and schedule, not to mention staff effort at CERL. They have also tried the patience of a number of remote PLATO users, who understandably expected the service to be commensurate with the cost (presently estimated to be roughly $10,000 of capital investment per console). These system problems, however, seem to be of a transient nature, inherent in any new system. Furthermore, some of the solutions to these problems are clear improvements in the PLATO design.**

One problem, however, could prove to be more lasting, and therefore of greater significance in the long run. The problem referred to is the difficulty in preparing high quality courseware. It is hoped that a good deal of the delay thus far is developmental, due to the need to recruit and train a staff, and to discover how to use PLATO's features to good advantage. If this theory proves optimistic, and if improved training, authoring aids, techniques, and standards don't increase productivity substantially, we may discover that the original estimate of about 40 man-hours of effort per student-contact-hour of courseware is off by a large factor, at least for authoring teams developing courseware specifically for use by other classes and faculty.

The unexpected increase in the cost to develop courseware, together with the system problems summarized above, have increased the cost of the project by roughly 50%, and have forced a full year's delay in the commencement of the field-tests. Use of PLATO this fall will be limited to fewer students and classes, and less courseware than planned even six months ago. Furthermore, the task of evaluation, already complicated by a wide range of content and grade levels at widely scattered locations, is made even more difficult by the delays and changes in plans. For example, the interpretation of the baseline and other evaluation data will be less straightforward, and less data will be available concerning PLATO use, owing to the delay.

The National Science Foundation has reviewed the PLATO project and plans during the past 9 months. Although the problems noted above are not insignificant, they do not obscure the promise of this system, nor the accomplishments toward mounting a major field-test of it. The problems that have occurred, especially those requiring engineering solutions, have been addressed by CERL in a promising manner. A field-test of PLATO seems even more important than it appeared to be when planned three years ago. The Foundation has therefore agreed to share with the University of Illinois the additional support required. CERL is proceeding with plans to begin a two-year field-test in September of 1974, one year later than originally scheduled.

*Recent reports from CERL show that PLATO is available approximately 96% of the prime time (8 a.m. to 10 p.m., Monday through Friday), with roughly 7 hours between failures, each averaging 6 minutes in duration. The probability of a class (with scheduled access to consoles) being interrupted by a system failure is therefore about .1.

**For example, CERL has designed and built an electronic (fast access) memory subsystem, that can be added to PLATO in such small quantities and at such a low cost as to provide every console with immediate access to its own lesson, thereby eliminating the dependence upon scheduled classes.

TICCIT System Progress Report on Field Testing

by Eric McWilliams
National Science Foundation

Approximately two-and-one-half years ago, The MITRE Corporation at McLean, Virginia committed itself to preparing for and conducting a field-test of the TICCIT system of Computer-Assisted Instruction (CAI). Specifically, MITRE committed to

+ developing and integrating the hardware and software required to provide CAI services to 128 consoles simultaneously using minicomputer and television technology;

+ installing and maintaining a 128-terminal TICCIT (Time-shared, Interactive, Computer-Controlled, Information Television) system in each of two community colleges; and

+ developing and administering CAI lessons (courseware) and educational programs (including teacher-training, consultation, and courseware improvement) for community college English and mathematics.

The National Science Foundation committed $4 M to these activities, in order to obtain a field-test of several promising features of the TICCIT design, including

+ relatively low capital and operating cost, through the use of increasingly powerful and inexpensive minicomputers and television sets as student consoles; and

+ an approach to courseware development based upon mastery learning and a division of authoring labor made possible by a consistent separation of instructional content from instructional logic (the manner in which a student is able to access the content).*

An independent evaluation contract was awarded to the Princeton Educational Testing Service (ETS), to provide educational decision-makers with documented insight into the processes and outcomes of using TICCIT in community college instruction.

Much has been accomplished toward meeting these objectives.

+ A dual-processor minicomputer-based system has been constructed which provides the following features, at a cost of about $450,000 per system:

  ○ 128 color television consoles, capable of displaying 17 lines of 43 (completely programmable) characters in any of seven colors, with automatic refresh of each TV picture accomplished by solid-state electronic memory;

  ○ provision for on-line entering and editing of the courseware content;

  ○ on-line access to textual and graphic courseware for four full-semester courses (roughly 20% of a community college course-load);

  ○ delivery of color videotape images to any 20 consoles simultaneously (through the use of 20 computer-switchable videotape players);

  ○ on-line random access to over five hours of pre-recorded audio messages, which can be delivered to any 20 consoles simultaneously; and

  ○ automatic digitalization (read-in) of color graphics such as drawings or still-frame cartoons, through the use of a scanning TV camera. (After being read in, any graphic can be edited on-line.)

+ A system of "learner-controlled" CAI has been developed which allows each student to exercise the courseware content in the order that suits him. (He may be forced to listen to and look at advice from the system if he seems to be going astray, but he is never forced to look at material that he does not select.)

+ Phoenix College, a campus of the Maricopa County Community College District, and the Alexandria Campus of the Northern Virginia Community College were selected as field-test sites, and an extensive implementation plan was adopted by the colleges, MITRE and Brigham Young University.

. Courseware has been designed and specified for community college courses in algebra, elementary functions, and English grammar and composition. Roughly half of the mathematics and a quarter of the English courseware is now in machine-readable form.

*Faculty and staff at Brigham Young University, who are responsible for the courseware, seek to develop the process of courseware production to a level more comparable to that practiced in the engineering professions, and in the process provide the student with powerful yet simple and consistent control over the instructional process. [See *An Overview of the TICCIT Program M 74-1*, January 1974.]

NOTE
The evaluative articles on PLATO and TICCIT were prepared in June 1974 and do not reflect developments in either project since that time.

A 32-terminal TICCIT system has been installed at BYU. The Phoenix system has been constructed and tested, and is ready for shipment and installation during the month of June. The Alexandria system is being wired and tested presently.

There have been other, related developments as well. For example, even at this very early stage, the Department of Defense has purchased a complete TICCIT system for use in training pilots for the U. S. Navy, and will probably purchase and install quite a number of systems later. Several colleges and universities have expressed interest in purchasing TICCIT systems for their own use, and several computer manufacturers have discussed with MITRE and the National Science Foundation the possibility of marketing the system. The modified TV console produces an extremely clear and stable display, and MITRE has adopted it as their standard computer terminal for use within their own organization. There is every indication that the TICCIT system will support a full 128 terminals simultaneously, which would reduce the per-console capital cost of CAI to about $3500, a significant contribution in itself.

There have of course been problems and delays, as well as progress, which have resulted in a significant increase in the cost to develop the system and the courseware, and have forced a seven-month postponement of the field-tests. Hardware has not contributed significantly to this delay, although some time and effort were invested investigating a mechanical/analog audio device, which was rejected in favor of digitally-stored audio. The major problems have occurred during the design and development of the software and courseware. At least one substantial false-start was made with each of these subsystems, and software and courseware development is still underway. As a result, only the mathematics courseware will be running in the colleges this September; the English courseware won't be ready until several months later.

The delays and increase in cost are disappointing in themselves, especially to the colleges, who have had to change their plans significantly. Equally important, however, the first classroom use of TICCIT will be considerably less of an application of "mainline" (complete, self-contained) CAI than originally planned, due to the need to compress the schedule. Since none of the courseware will be tested upon students until the summer of 1974, it will be necessary to continue to debug and improve the system and courseware through the fall, while serving the first small group of about 100 community college students. Such a start may make it difficult to operate and evaluate the TICCIT system in the fully mainline mode for which it was originally designed, and which carried attractive promises of reductions in the cost of instruction.

These delays have also complicated somewhat the evaluation of the TICCIT system being planned and conducted by ETS. A full field-test of both English and math cannot begin until the middle of the 74/75 academic year, since the first half-year will be required to let the system and courseware "settle in" at the colleges. This will reduce the amount of data that can be collected, and make interpretation of both baseline and other data more difficult.

The National Science Foundation has considered these factors, including the 25% increase in the cost for the TICCIT field-test. Although the problems (noted above) are significant and unfortunate, they do not obscure the promise of the TICCIT system and courseware approach. The problems that have occurred have been addressed in a promising manner. Although evaluation will be somewhat more difficult as a result of the delays and changes, a field-test of the TICCIT system seems even more important now than it was perceived to be three years ago. The Foundation has therefore approved of the proposed changes, and MITRE, BYU, and the colleges are proceeding with the field test of TICCIT, commencing in September of 1974, seven months later than originally planned.

wizard

To some people a computer seems to be a wizard, able to perform black magic at the request of a computer operator. The picture given below was "drawn" by a plotter located in the Oregon State University Computing Center. Actually, the picture was orginally created by the Tektronix Software Group; one can think of it as a "connect the numbered dots" picture, much like kids like to play with. A computer can rapidly connect the numbered dots either on a plotter or on a CRT display screen. An appropriately written computer program can scale the picture to any desired size.

PLANIT: The Portable CAI System

by Charles H. Frye*

The first prototype of PLANIT was put into operation early in 1966. With it one could author and dispense typical CAI lesson senarios with particularly good facility in numerically-oritented lesson materials. Five years ago the PLANIT group was proposing a machine independent operating system for CAI that could easily be installed on any garden variety computer hardware and be used to implement the PLANIT language in time-shared fashion for authoring and dispensing CAI. In contrast to the prototype PLANIT, the new portable version was to be a complete system including all the necessary pieces for production CAI. To include only a lesson authoring and execution capability would hardly qualify to be called a system in the terminology of most computer centers. They also want such capabilities as file maintenance and backup, program maintenance, user accounting, device allocation, etc. Thus, PLANIT is much more than just a CAI language.

Confidence was lacking at the outset that the development of a truly portable CAI system could be achieved. One widely respected systems expert gave the project less than ten percent chance of success. Others said that PLANIT would not be alive at the end of the five-year period. It is to the credit of the National Science Foundation that they continued to believe that the goal was attainable. Today, the proposed PLANIT system has been completed and is being tested and used at a number of sites. PLANIT has been installed on a wide variety of hardware, including CDC 3170, 3300 & 6500, DEC 10, Honeywell 200, IBM 360/40, 360/67 & 370/155, Siemens 4004 & 155, Telefunken, Univac 1108, and XDS 940, some under existing time-sharing systems and others under batch. One version runs side-by-side with a spooling system, HASP.

It was promised that PLANIT would run 20 terminals in no more than 256,000 bytes of core — it is now running more in less space. In at least one case it ran 12 terminals in 72,000 bytes of core. Being completely modularized, it can be configured to the core that is available.

The installation cost was promised to be in the range of $10,000 to $20,000. Purdue University recently completed a study in which PLANIT was installed on their 6500 and run for a week long pilot study during which 56 PLANIT users ran an average of 49.8 minutes each. They reported a total installation cost of about $1300 requiring about 147 hours of programmer time. Others have

also confirmed that the original cost estimates for installation were unnecessarily high.

On the question of consumptiveness, Purdue reported several statistics based on their pilot study:

1. Throughput was apparently unaffected by the operation of PLANIT. Average jobs per hour for the week of pilot study was 434 compared to an average of 421 for the week prior and 445 for the week following.
2. PLANIT required approximately 1/5 of available core while it was processing a user, consuming an average of 4.15 seconds of CPU time per 50-minute period (reflecting the expected low CPU usage for CAI).
3. Terminal/hour costs ranged from $2.08 to $2.25, using Purdue's standard charging algorithm.

It has been observed that because PLANIT uses FORTRAN in the installation process, the result must surely be inefficient especially since such a simple subset is used to implement complex system functions such as scheduling and cataloguing. While it is true that machine language would run faster, two things should be kept in mind:

1. Contrary to all other transfer methods short of recoding, PLANIT execution efficiency will not suffer when the system is moved from one computer to another.
2. Typical CPU usage is very low for CAI such that small differences in efficiency will have only marginal effect. There is no efficiency loss in use of space and peripherals where the CAI investment is high.

At one site in particular there is little doubt that PLANIT is being used as a production system — the University of Freiburg in West Germany has been using it in that fashion for more than a year now with a daily operating schedule, courses being taught for credit and authors hired full-time. Being first, they experienced more than their share of problems but they report the system has operated quite reliably for the last several months.

The PLANIT system is an interpreter — intentionally so. This means that lesson material is stored internally in original typed (or keypunched) form and the keystroke characters are deciphered on-the-fly as the lesson is dispensed to students. There are those who talk about interpreters as though their existance is justified only because the developer didn't know how to build a compiler. In the event that this opinion might still persist, consider the following as some advantages of an interpreter:

1. Interpreting enables certain options in the language which would be difficult or impossible to compile and, since CAI is normally concerned with a user community who is new

*Dr. Frye is the originator of the PLANIT system and is currently project director of the PLANT Project at the Northwest Regional Educational Laboratory, 710 SW Second Ave., Portland, OR 97204.

to computing, the concept of compiling prior to execution will be a new one. Compiling tends to encourage the adoption of language conventions aimed at easing the compilation task at a cost of user convenience. For example, many languages use "counter" items to code user response paths because they can more easily be used in later decision points. Many aspects of PLANIT take on a definition only after the student responds (too late for efficient compilation).

2. Compute times are usually greater for interpreted programs than for compiled programs, ranging from a little greater for character shuffling to more than a hundred times greater for number crunching. However, much of CAI is character shuffling and compute times are characteristically small even for interpreters as was evidenced in the Purdue statistics.

3. Space will usually be of more concern in CAI applications than time. Since a compiled program grows in size according to the number of source statements while an interpreted program usually operates in a fixed size, there will be a point beyond which the compiled program will be the largest. Source code is normally more compact than compiled code. CAI programs are typically large (as programs go) and will pass that point very quickly. Therefore, interpretive CAI systems will ordinarily occupy less total space than compiling ones — this added to the fact that most compiling systems also retain the original source code for editing purposes.

In general, space will probably be more costly to CAI than compute time and interpreting systems will normally require substantially less space. The PLATO terminal has the microfiche projection capability to alleviate this problem but raising the preparation costs somewhat.

Let me now turn to the second part and offer some comments that attempt to put PLANIT in perspective with two well-known elegant CAI systems, PLATO and TICCIT. Today's CAI users are fortunate to have them as options. PLANIT is also an option. The three systems can be summarized in this way:

1. PLATO is for the person who can have everything and has the money to pay for it.
2. TICCIT is for the person who has nothing and wants a lot but has little money to pay for it.
3. PLANIT is for the person who has equipment and needs to get along on what he has because he has virtually no extra money for CAI.

For some time PLANIT was considered to be an interim system, to be used until PLATO and TICCIT were ready. Support required for PLANIT has been a fraction of that for the other two. No hardware development efforts were involved since PLANIT is completely software, at least up until the time of installation. Thus, PLANIT was less expensive to develop and more quickly delivered, making it a likely candidate for interim needs.

However, it is becoming increasingly apparent that PLANIT's portability is providing an option not yet available in another CAI system. PLANIT can be mounted on existing equipment with little or no extra hardware investment. PLANIT lessons on all such installations are fully compatible and can be exchanged freely. Experience at operating versions of PLANIT which have been installed on widely differing hardware show no discernable differences to the user. It is a striking experience to sit at the keyboard of a strange system where PLANIT is mounted and immediately be completely familiar with the entire operation. This has been particularly useful to the military with their diversity of hardware. The ability to produce a fully compatible system on existing hardware at nominal cost suggests something more than an interim role for PLANIT. It may well continue to be a viable option for some time to come.

When discussing PLANIT's future, the question is inevitably asked, "Can PLANIT handle graphics?" The answer is "yes" but the implementation of that is probably 95 percent installation hardware and software and 5 percent PLANIT additions. "Holes" have been intentionally left in PLANIT's command structure to allow for these kinds of additions. In one experiment with graphics, a Rand tablet was used for a PLANIT terminal with the display projected onto the under side, giving the impression of "inking" a surface with an electronic pen. It has also been observed that the PLATO plasma terminals would make nice PLANIT terminals. These kinds of questions are decided at installation time.

Probably the most significant recent development in CAI is that we are beginning to have some options — not just the name of the language but the kind of system. Formerly, we had only one option — invent our own unique system. Now there are several more, such as PLATO, TICCIT, and PLANIT. If this progress is to be sustained, then interested parties should feel obliged to see what is available before concluding that nothing currently exists. Articles on CAI appearing within only the past six months in respected national periodicals show that this has not yet occurred. One lists PLANIT and TUTOR (PLATO's author language) among others as "large and complicated and troublesome to learn" and then proceeds to describe a language of dubious improvement bound to specific hardware. Another describes yet a different language in which the technique of prompting the author for lesson inputs is ostensibly "discovered," not mentioning that PLANIT has been doing this for eight years in addition to several others that can also be named. It was especially interesting that after discussing the remarkable gains in efficiency which were attributed to prompting, the authors of the article then proceeded to describe the soon-to-be-released version II which will allow batch input.

What we need are real, legitimate options in CAI, not contrived ones. PLANIT is one of these legitimate options.

A Computer Career for You?

by Judy Edwards

This article was written while Judy was at the Northwest Regional Educational Laboratory in Portland, Oregon. She is now a Research Assistant at the Lindquist Center, University of Iowa.

INTRODUCTION

The world of computers is rapidly changing. New hardware and software is being developed almost daily. The people who work in the computer center of the future will find the pace increasing. New ideas today will be obsolete tomorrow and they will need to learn rapidly about new developments.

The demand for skilled people will grow rapidly as technological projects grow. The competition for jobs may increase as the need for up-to-date technological knowledge is required.

For those who are planning a career in the computer world, careful planning for that career can insure them a secure place in an ever-changing environment. There will always be new things to learn and advancements for those who assess their abilities, build a good training and education program for themselves and finally survey the jobs thoroughly to find the right position.

Let's look at some of the factors involved in planning a career in computers and see how you can become more aware of what you would want to do in the field of data processing.

THE NEW TECHNOLOGICAL AGE

There will be a growing need for computers as information increases. Computers will have an ever increasing job to do in business, science, government, education and in the professinal world. In fact it is likely that many of us will use a simple form of computer in our homes within just a few years.

With the greatly increased appearance of computers, it seems accurate to predict that more and more jobs will exist. Many of the jobs and working environments will not be what they are today, however. Obviously, as the computer takes on more and more routine work, our work will be new and more interesting. We will learn new skills and find a challenge in keeping up-to-date on discoveries in computer technology whether we work directly with computers or not.

New Career Atmospheres

People who work directly with computers will have an inside picture of technology at work. They will see less and less paper work and more machine-stored information. They will learn about telecommunication systems — those which send computer-stored information over communication lines and television screens to millions of people. Computer personnel will work with and understand vast networks of computer systems which will serve a world-wide population. Specialists in computer science will see knowledge of all kinds computerized for rapid access. Library reference information, for example, will be computerized and referenced by pushing a button on a small table-size or pocket-size computer.

Whatever the application, computer center personnel will continually be learning and moving ahead in a more and more creative atmosphere. The new technologists will not only be concerned with the development of computing machines, but they will be concerned with better understanding of human processes so that man will be capable of relating those complex processes to the computer.

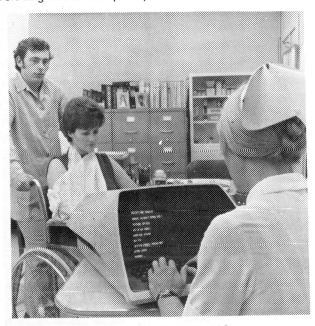

COMPUTERS IN HOSPITALS
CRT terminals are used in many hospitals to record medical information on patients being admitted. (Photo DEC)

The computer, in return, will objectively analyze and report what it sees. In this age learning may be a two-way process — from man to machine and from machine to man.

The Demand for People

For all its amazing ability, the computer has no power except that given it by people. People design and build computers, analyze and solve problems for the computer, and operate and service computing machines. People are essential to the new technology — people who are properly trained and experienced are in great demand.

Computer technology has grown so rapidly that there is a great shortage of technically trained people in all data processing jobs. The data processing industry is growing four to five times faster than any other American industry and in the process has created many unfilled jobs.

The demand for trained personnel will continue to be greater than the supply for several years to come. The number of computer installations in the United States alone promises to hit the 100,000 mark by 1975. By then, some two million people may be needed to fill jobs directly related to computers.

The largest category of computer-related jobs will be in the scientific fields: mathematics, physics, chemistry, and engineering. Equally important

COMPUTERS IN THE MOVIE INDUSTRY
A technician at Consolidated Film Industries operates a printing machine, which makes projection copies of original negatives for theater and television use. An IBM System/7 monitors the printers to ensure that the original colors are faithfully reproduced in the prints. This process earned Consolidated Film Industries and IBM an Academy Award for technical achievement. (Photo IBM)

jobs will be open in accounting, business practices, and in the professions. Naturally, these are the people closest to the designing and scientific use of computers.

Technicians of all kinds will also find jobs. Operators of auxiliary equipment, key punch operators, clerks, and tape librarians are only a few. In computer manufacturing, there is a growing need for skilled technicians to aid designers and engineers in their work. In addition, the customer engineers who service and maintain computer hardware have become an essential group to all computer manufacturers.

Systems analysts, programmers and computer operators will be in great demand. In addition, jobs in sales and software development for computer manufacturers promise to increase quite rapidly.

IS A COMPUTER CAREER FOR YOU?

Before you can even begin to plan for a future career in data processing, you should ask yourself whether a computer career is the best career for you. Let's explore how you can begin to see whether you fit somewhere in the world of computers.

Knowing Your Abilities

Each person in a computer center should possess certain personal characteristics. Certain jobs, those of the systems analyst and computer center manager require the ability to communicate with other people. Some other jobs, such as data preparation and computer operation, require some mechanical skills. Programmers have less to do with people and more to do with reasoning and problem-solving. People in a computer center have one quality in common — the ability to solve problems logically and efficiently.

In looking into career possibilities, you should be aware of the personal abilities and interests you have which fit a particular job. Various positions in a computer center were briefly mentioned, but it would also be helpful to look into jobs outside the average computer center. Perhaps your interests are more compatible with another type of job: computer designer, electronics engineer, computer salesman, or customer engineer, for example.

One important step which is helpful to anyone just beginning to plan a career is to take stock of his own abilities and interests. Are you mechanically inclined? Do you enjoy working with people? More than you enjoy sitting at a desk and logically organizing the solution to problems?

This first step in looking at career choices is mostly up to you. You must first decide which of your interests or skills are most important. You can discuss the answers to these questions with your school job counselor who may have access to information about the abilities required for particular job. In addition, most schools also offer a variety of aptitude tests for clerical and operations skills and others for computer programming. You might want to take these tests as part of your plan to realize your best skills.

Deciding What You Want To Do

If you are interested in a career related to computers, you can begin now to decide what you like to do, what your skills might be, and how they fit the various jobs open to you. It is quite possible, as you learn more and gain more experience, that your skills or ambitions may change. In the world of computers, being ready for change is an advantage rather than a fault. But for now, you should gain some general knowledge of what you would like to do.

PLANNING YOUR EDUCATION AND TRAINING

Often the second question asked by anyone beginning to think about a career is what education or training must I have to get the job I want? Assume you have, by now, at least decided upon the general category of computer-related jobs you would like to try. That job or any jobs in the computer field requires a certain degree of general educational background.

Required education for a particular job may lead to a high school diploma, junior college degree (associate degree), college degree, or an advanced degree such as the masters degree or Ph.D. You can see there are several levels of education available to you. Each of the jobs in data processing will usually require some general education on one of these levels.

Getting training for a job can be quite different than getting an education for a job. Training implies more specific learning. In data processing, training usually means taking courses arranged by a vocational school, junior college, an employer or a computer manufacturer. Courses of this kind teach specific skills: computer operation skills, programming skills, or data preparation techniques, for example. Each job in the computer field also requires some specific training.

Let's look at the various degrees of education and training you may want or need to become proficient enough to begin working in a computer-related field.

Courses in High School

Computer science courses in high school at the present time prepare you for future training. Most high schools offer courses in computer concepts, elementary computer programming and some data preparation courses, such as beginning principles of key punching. These courses generally do not prepare you for a career in data processing. They do, however, allow you to explore the fundamentals of computer science so that you can more clearly decide which job you would most like to do.

Your high school years are ideal for exploring the specific jobs, the career possibilities and learning about the larger picture in the working world. Any computer science courses, math courses, English, and writing courses you take will prepare you for bigger decisions later. Thus, you can use high school as a stepping-stone to help answer some larger questions, such as what specific training do I need, which training school or college shall I choose, or what company shall I work for?

Type of Training	Length of Course	Courses Offered	Cost
Home-Study Schools	18 months	Computer Electronics	$200-$500
Commercial Data Processing Schools	60-80 hours 100-200 hours 400 hours 400-1,000 hours	Key Punching Computer Operation Computer Electronics Computer Programming	$100-$150 $250-$500 $550-$1,000 $400-$1,500
Junior College Data Processing Course	6 months-2 years	Key Punching Computer Operation Computer Electronics Computer Programming Systems Analysis	$100-$400
Computer Manufacturer Courses (employees of computer manufacturer)	2 days-6 weeks 6 months-2 years	Data Preparation Computer Operation Computer Programming Systems Programming Systems Analysis Management Principles Sales Software Design Customer Engineer	Usually free to employee of user or manufacturer

Vocational Training

Vocational courses (job-oriented courses) are becoming more and more popular. Educators and employers have begun to realize that a college degree is unnecessary for certain jobs. Many careers in data processing, in particular, require more specialized training and less of the general education acquired at colleges and universities.

It is not at all unusual to find many people without college degrees in computer-related jobs. Where did they get the necessary training to become data preparation specialists, computer operators, programmers or even systems analysts? At vocational training centers, at private business schools, in a two year job training program at a junior college, with a computer manufacturer or in an on-the-job training session paid for by a new employer.

A four or five year college or university program is not essential to begin a career in data processing. There are, of course, computer careers which require a college education and some highly specialized training. Those we will look at in the next section, "Going on to College."

Right now, let's look at some of the jobs which might be best suited to short-term training — jobs which do not require a college education. Some of the most likely are data preparation clerk, computer operator and computer programmer. The jobs of systems analyst can also be obtained without a degree but often requires some advanced study in business administration. Other jobs with computer manufacturers or related businesses which require only specialized training courses are customer engineer, equipment salesman and computer service representative. The schools which offer training for these jobs offer a variety of courses, but their costs vary according to the length and completeness of the course. The chart (previous page) will show you some types of vocational training schools, the courses they offer, and the general cost of the training.

If you think you would like to look into computer training after high school, you can check into enrolling in one of these schools. Notice that home study schools and commercial data processing schools are rather high in cost. The junior college courses, on the other hand, will cost only the price of tuition and books. Home-study courses are primarily meant for those who live in remote areas and have no other source of training.

A word of warning about commercial data processing schools — some of the schools are not as honest as they appear to be. If you decide on a data processing school for your training, check carefully into the school's reputation and see that they actually can train you for the job or that their tuitions are reasonable for what they offer. Again, you can consult your school job counselor, the computer science teacher in your school, or your school library for information on vocational training for computer careers.

Going on to College

A college degree is not essential for many jobs and careers in data processing, as you have seen. For some computer careers, however, a college education is either very helpful or even necessary to achieve a certain level of employment. Such specialized positions as systems programmer, software specialist, computer hardware designer and scientific systems analyst usually require a college degree.

If you have decided on a career in a specialized computer field — scientific data processing, computer design and manufacturing, or teaching computer science, for example — you would do well to explore now the many possibilities for a specialized education.

Colleges and universities usually offer computer-related degrees which combine education in a major field with computer courses. If, for example, you wanted to become a systems analyst and work primarily in business, you would probably study business administration with computer science courses included as part of your course of study. If, however, you wanted to become a systems analyst for scientific research in computers, you would most likely have computer science as your major field.

For whatever the specialized computer career you may want to pursue, college and university admission offices are usually helpful in supplying you with catalogs, pamphlets and other information about their computer science courses. High school counselors are trained to aid students in choosing the right college and the proper college courses for a particular career. You can begin now to explore the paths to a college education open to you by consulting these sources.

The care and feeding of the computer is the responsibility of the computer operator. Here at the console of an IBM 360/125 he and a company manager examine a printout showing the runs made the previous night.

FINDING THE RIGHT JOB FOR YOU

Assuming that you have gained enough computer training to look for a job, finding the job which is just right for you depends somewhat on what the job may offer you in the terms of salary, security, and the chance to grow and advance. You can learn to judge the quality of a job by comparing specific jobs in different organizations. It is also very helpful to contact people who are already involved in the kind of job you are interested in. They may be able to give you some added insights into the position and can offer you the benefit of their experience with the job and the organization.

Considering the Opportunities

You would probably want to ask certain questions about opportunities and future advancement, regardless of the career path you choose. You might want to know how difficult it is to begin in a particular job, what the pay is, how secure the job will be, and what opportunities for advancement it offers.

For several years the demand for people in data processing will greatly exceed the available supply. Wherever demand is high, salaries are high. The high salary range in data processing will continue for years as the need for qualified people remains.

Security for the future is also high when demand is high. In data processing, however, security does relate a great deal to your ambition to learn and keep up to date with a rapidly changing industry. There is little need in data processing for people who wish to remain in the same job performing the same tasks year after year.

Opportunities for advancement in computer-related careers are unmatched anywhere. Again, the great demand for people is the reason. Because of a great need for trained personnel, advancement is more rapid than in any other field. New employees and long-time employees tend to have equal opportunity because everyone in the computer center is constantly learning or training for new tasks.

Whatever computer skills or training you decide to gain in the next few years, there will be well paid and rapidly advancing careers open to you.

Meeting People in the Field

You have, so far, seen some possible ways to explore your interests and to look into some available careers and opportunities. You can read about how computers are used in a vareity of organizations, and you can also read books and pamphlets published by individual firms or by scientific research laboratories or educational groups. Enough has been written about careers in computer science and data processing to give you a good overall view of the world of computers.

Once you know what careers in computers are of interest to you, you can take another step toward understanding the computer world. Probably one of the best ways to learn about a specific job in an organization of your choice is to talk to the people who work in that environment. The people who have already gained some experience as computer specialists are generally most helpful. They will usually understand your interest and ambition to learn about the jobs they are doing.

Find out which businesses or industries, scientific organizations or school districts in your area have a computer center. You may even have already decided that you are interested in only one of these areas. If you have decided you want to talk to someone working with computers in business, locate the local banks, insurance company, airline, or organization of your choice where you can meet someone in the computer center. Many computer centers for scientific research are organized by government agencies. You can contact your state government information office for details about their research centers. Schools, of course, are listed in your telephone directory. Your own school district may have a computer installation or may have access to one.

Once you have located a computer center, call and ask to speak with the person in the position you want to know about. In most cases, you may not only talk over your career plans and nature of the job with that person, but may be offered a tour of the computer center as well.

You may even have a personal friend who has experience with computers who can tell you what his job is like. Whatever way you go about meeting the people in data processing, you can learn more about the computer career you decide upon by getting some firsthand impressions.

The extent to which you explore these computer careers is up to you. Remember, however, that learning and planning for your career can be the most important step you take.

A programmer determines that the most efficient way to approach a problem, generally making use of a flowchart. Following this, the programmer writes the problem in computer language and tests it on the computer. (Photo IBM)

Career Education. Will it Last?

By Joyce L. Kennedy

Career education - the name of the "turnaround"movement needed in our schools to prepare students for work as a major part of preparing them for living -- is the "in" education concept now. The question: Will it outlast previous educational concepts [remember the right to read" a couple of years ago]?

As an eminent educator, Harold Howe, a former Federal education commisioner and now education vp for Ford Foundation, told an audience, some fear that the career education concept "is so general that it runs the danger of being watered down into a mass of lip service activity."

For example, Dr. Howe noted that the chief state school officers have unanimously endorsed the idea but he "really wonders" if they "intend to go out there and do a job.") In rough translation - will school decision-makers put their money and muscle where their mouths are?)

DR. HOWE'S RESERVATIONS recognize the moon-launch size job ahead if career education is to flourish. Just a few of the massive tasks: making drastic changes in teacher training institutions to reflect a career education emphasis; retraining the current administrative and teaching corps; rewriting classroom instructional materials; establishing home-school-community workplace tie-ups; convincing employers to co-operate by hiring students and teachers for brief periods; getting taxpayers to foot the bill; and persuading administrators of school budgets to spend the money on career education programs. Society, too, must stop thinking that the plumber who learned his skills in an apprenticeship program does not deserve the dignity equal to that given the physicist who learned his skills in college.

In spite of the fearsome number of built-in problems, there are convincing reasons for believing that career education is not a trendy fad, but a powerful idea destined to root and multiply.

For one thing, the needs of people for assistance in career preparation and development are becoming unmanageable in our present setup. Without substantial educational restructuring both "overchoice" (the task of selecting from 28,000 known occupations) and "underchoice "the denial of opportunity through lack of knowledge of and preparation for work) will get worse as we progress further into the postindustrial age. The individual without skills will become a dreg on the market, even more so than today. If increasing numbers of people continue to be highly educated for living, but are without skills to pay for living, the social unrest now will seem harmonic in retrospect. Education is the logical institution to lead the way in providing job skills, positive work attitudes and "amplechoice."

ANOTHER POINT focuses on fairness. The needs of the real majority of citizens must be served as well as those of the academically elite minority. Between 75-80 percent of people are not likely to find jobs requiring a 4-year college degree in years ahead, according to the Federal Labor Department.

THE WORK ETHIC can be restored. People can find satisfaction in achievement. The manpower needs of our nation can be met while maintaining individual freedom of choice. Dignity can be given to all occupations. Career education holds promise of doing these things. But, as noted in a Federal education handbook:

"Career education is an idea whose time has come. Still, it will not come to your community until someone grasps the initiative and brings it there. If someone, why not you? If sometime, why not now?"

Reprinted with permission of *The Computer Educator*, Oct. 1974.

DP Salary Survey

Top managers of edp installations now earn an average of $537 a week, or $27,924 annually, according to the *1974 Weber Salary Survey on Data Processing Positions in the U.S.,* published by A.S. Hansen, Inc. of Lake Bluff, Ill. The 1974 average for managers rose 10.2 percent over 1973, the survey shows. Other job categories that showed impressive gains in 1974, with the 1973 increases in parentheses, were: systems programmers, 10.8% (4.8%); systems analysts, 8.7% (4.4%); keypunch operators, 6.5% (2.8%); and computer operators, 7.2% (5.6%). For applications programmers, the 1974 increase was 4.8%, compared with 5.1% in 1973.

 # Key to Your Future?

By Eleanor Corr
Keystone Junior College
La Plume, Pennsylvania

What turns YOU on? Law? Public Relations? Engineering? Writing? You don't want JUST a job, right? You want to look to a full and rewarding life! This means that you will be working towards that goal which you expect will assist you in achieving self-realization and self-fulfillment.

Career education is regarded as a means of fulfilling that goal.

However, to make appropriate choices concerning educational goals, occupational or vocational careers, you must first acquire knowledge about your aptitudes, interests, and abilities. Consequently, individual growth and development is predicated on freedom of choice, needed skills and knowledge.

If you have bothered to pick up and read through this magazine at all, you have exhibited some interest in the computer field and whether your interests are in the field of business or science, your options are many.

So what about computer-related careers, you ask?

The field of computers is new and dynamic and extends to all parts of society. The computer is not constrained in its use. We're all aware of its effect on government, national defense, medicine, industry, business, and education. YOU can be a part of this new field and still be true to your own "inner calling."

Let's look at the following: RESEARCH (basic research working on applications from a humanitarian point of view such as medicine, weather, energy, space), ENGINEERING (applied research, the design and development of equipment), MARKETING RESEARCH (determining the needs of industry, education, etc.), PROGRAMMERS (systems analysis and design, development of compilers, designing applications), TECHNICAL WRITERS (writing the documentation for product applications), SYSTEMS ENGINEERING (assisting customers in use of equipment, installation of systems), FIELD ENGINEERING (maintenance of systems), MARKETING REPRESENTATIVES (selling computer-related products, conducting presentations), ADMINISTRATIVE positions (maintaining customer relations, planning, organizing work, schedules, etc.), LAW (data processing specialist in corporate law), EDUCATION (teaching data processing, computer science, telecommunications).

Only a few career fields have been mentioned, but I'm sure you can add to that list. Of course, each of those careers which I have listed contain other dimensions. For instance, PROGRAMMERS can be systems analysts or systems designers, or perhaps one programmer may do the "coding" from the systems design of another programmer.

And the "piece de resistance?" Because of the rapid pace of technological change in this field, individuals must constantly be engaged in continuing their professional education. You can be at the forefront of it all where it's important to learn and to know! Today, a career involving computer applications is not only financially rewarding, but challenging and fulfilling as well. Is one in your future?

COMPUTERS IN AUTO MAINTENANCE
Wayne Block runs down the computer maintenance checklist before servicing this police car in the Sparks, Nev., city garage. The computer system automatically schedules maintenance work for each of Sparks' 200-plus vehicles, as well as handling the city budget, payroll and even the quarterly sewer assessment. (Photo IBM)

A "Young" Business

Creative Computing just heard last week about three boys in Portland, Oregon who have organized a computer software company and are providing part-time services to local firms. All three boys are under 18 and have one or two years more of high school.

Apparently they had some minor legal problems getting started since they weren't allowed to operate out of a private residence and had to rent an office. Hence the problem: they were all too young to sign contracts so two parents had to co-sign. But they don't seem to be having any trouble with the work or getting it either, indeed, most of it is through referrals. All of their work is done in BASIC and if you want more information, you can write them directly:

Frank J. Barberis
Computa-Link Company
Oregon Pioneer Bldg., Room 302
Portland, Oregon 97204

Profile of an Industry

Though its origins go back several centuries, the digital computer is primarily a product of technological innovation during the last two decades. Its use has grown exponentially because the information problems it helps to solve have grown that way. Few people, twenty years ago, could foresee either the need for such a powerful problem-solving tool or that the computer could satisfy the need.

In 1950, only a handful of computers were in use helping scientists and mathematicians speed routine calculations. Some people thought that was all the machine was good for. But in 1951, the Bureau of the Census received its first electronic digital computer—a UNIVAC I. Computer usage, related services and the number of companies that provide computers and supporting services have been multiplying ever since.

It is now estimated that well over 100,000 computers are in use worldwide.

How did it happen so fast? Why so many computers so soon?

For thousands of organizations, for hundreds of thousands and perhaps even millions of individuals, the problem has been the management of information. Information has proliferated. And we all need help to sort out information, store it, process it, analyze it and locate it fast.

Above, computer operator is a career opportunity created by the computer industry. This is a good place for high school graduates to enter the field.

Below and facing page, computer technology continues to improve, year by year. Internal operating speeds of large systems are now measured in billionths of a second.

Today, wherever you look, there's an information problem and a need for swift, efficient information handling—whether you're trying to capture, store and analyze many hundreds of thousands of bits of information about a jet engine test . . . to make sure that the several thousand items that customers in a food market want and need are there when they want and need them . . . to analyze and report data collected by pollution control instruments . . . to calculate the best design for a bridge, a building or a bulldozer . . . to catalog, index and quickly find facts in a library . . . to handle the paperwork involved in running a government agency . . . to relieve doctors and nurses of time-consuming clerical work . . . to help farmers to breed animals and raise crops with greater efficiency and productivity . . . and on and on, endlessly.

Many people with problems like these find the large storage capacity, the logic power and the electronic calculating speed of today's computers useful in handling growing masses of data quickly and efficiently, to get needed information in time to take meaningful action, to solve problems before they become crises.

Computer Improvements

For many years the uses of computers have expanded in both quantity and variety. Also, there has been a rapid and steady flow of improvements in computer technology and organization. Computer internal operating speeds are now measured in billionths of a second—just ten years ago, millionths of a second was considered fast.

Far more computer power is now packed into far less space. Internal circuits now must be examined with microscopes in the faster computers where many electronic circuits can be packed on a single chip of silicon little more than a tenth of an inch square.

Main computer memory can now store millions of characters of information. There is quick access to hundreds of millions of additional characters in disk storage units.

Industry Growth

In 1950 there were only a handful of companies in the computer business. Today there are many hundreds. They develop and build computing systems, prepare programs to instruct the machines, operate service bureaus, and sell peripheral equipment such as tape units, disk storage units, printers, and display terminals. Other firms provide consumable supplies, such as punched cards and magnetic tape, and engage in other aspects of the industry.

Many thousands of companies, of course, supply products and services to manufacturers and users of computers. Makers of electronic components are an obvious example. Also needed are paper, fabricated metal

parts, glass and ceramics, optical systems, magnetic materials—the list could go on indefinitely.

New Jobs

With the growth in the use of computers have come many new job opportunities.

Scientists and engineers in nearly every discipline are needed to design, build and improve information-handling products.

The industry has several hundred thousand operating personnel—the people who run computer consoles, card punching and sorting machines and who schedule and manage the use of information-handling equipment.

There are also several hundred thousand people working as systems analysts (people who determine the methodology required to solve information problems) and programmers (those who write computer instructions for computer manufacturers, users, programming firms and data processing service bureaus).

In addition there are many thousands of other people who build, sell or maintain information-handling equipment.

The information explosion spawned the explosive growth of the information-handling industry during the last two decades. Today, nearly everyone is affected by the computer in important ways. Many jobs are made more interesting and challenging. Others are made easier to handle. New career opportunities have opened up. As computer use continues to grow, these benefits can be expected to grow with it and to extend to more people.

Above, one of many new computer career opportunities is that of the customer engineer, who is responsible for maintenance and repair of computer installations.

Computers and the Weather

In 1922 an Englishman named Lewis Richardson developed a mathematical process for predicting the weather by assigning numerical values to such weather conditions as temperature, humidity, and barometric pressure, and plugging them into complex formulas. Unfortunately, the lengthy calculations made his "prediction" six days late.

In 1946, Princeton University's John von Neuman set the first computers to work on forecasting the weather, calling the project the most complex problem ever conceived. By 1955, the first computer-generated forecasts were produced on a regular basis and scientists predicted that accurate forecasts were just a step away.

The battle to predict the weather accurately is being waged by meteorologists from Bangkok to Brasilia, and the meteorologists' most powerful weapon against Mother Nature remains the computer.

Ed Olson, Control Data Corp's world weather project manager stated that "the value of all installed computer systems used for weather forecasting worldwide exceeds $150 million. Control Data holds 40% of that business, and that makes us the leader."

Olson expects the market for computers in the field of meteorology almost to double by 1980. One reason for such a tremendous market is apparent. To forecast tomorrow's weather, scientists compare and anlyze measurements of weather conditions gathered twice daily from more than 10,000 observation points around the globe. The only way to process that information, before tomorrow, is by computer.

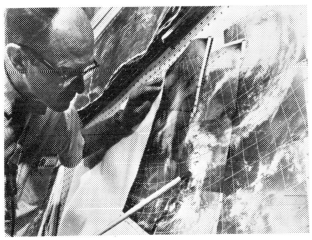

Meteorologists use satellite photos to support computer weather forecasts in predicting the path of a hurricane so timely warnings can be given to threatened areas.

According to Olson, there are four problems in forecasting weather: "Sufficient information is not yet available, and the means to analyze, process and transmit the information are still in an embryonic stage."

The first of these problems scientists hope to solve is data collection. Weather measurements — normally wind speed, wind direction, temperature, humidity, and barometric pressure — are collected primarily from ships, ground stations, weather balloons, aircraft, and in some cases, satellites. Although adequate for landlocked areas, this information base is inadequate over the oceans, causing poor coastal region forecasts. To solve the problem, scientists plan by the end of the decade to position as many as 12 weather satellites above the seas, increasing by 10 to 15 times the present ocean weather information base. Through satellite photographs scientists will capture a much more current picture of the world's weather conditions. But curiously, solving one problem only makes other problems more complex.

"As you gather more and more weather information," Olson said, "you need more and more horsepower to process it. The first computer Control Data ever sold, a 1604 used by the Navy for weather prediction, performed 150,000 operations per second. By 1980 the significant amount of additional data available will require a machine capable of performing at hundreds of times this speed. Right now that machine doesn't exist."

The increased volume of weather information will also make data transmission problems more complex. To forecast the weather for one region of the world scientists must monitor the movement and interaction of weather conditions throughout the world. Because the weather itself knows no national boundaries, this monitoring process requires international cooperation.

The World Meteorological Organization (WMO), has developed a global plan to solve the problem of transmitting weather information rapidly. The WMO plan consists of a network of computers that makes a world map look like a printed circuit. Linked by telephone lines and eventually by communications satellites, the WMO network will allow meteorologists to share instantly a world-wide weather information bank. "More countries participate in the WMO than belong to the United Nations," Olson said, "and the development of the network is being stimulated by WMO efforts to assist underdeveloped nations in purchasing basic systems."

Aside from the need for more powerful computers, the processing function is also far from perfect. As scientists learn more about the intricate relationships among air, earth, ocean, and sun, they must refine and change the complex formulas which are the basis for the computers' calculations.

The computer-generated forecasts must also be checked for accuracy, causing costly delays to correct insufficient or wrong information. Ed Olson recalls a time when a computer receiving weather information from a U. S. Navy destroyer fixed the ship's position in a wheat field near Salina, Kansas. It was in the Mediterranean Sea.

Meteorologist Paul Wolff, vice president of Ocean Data Systems Inc., notes that "with weather satellites providing valuable data above the oceans and with additional computer power, completely accurate one day forecasts could be available before 1980." He added, "Until we achieve completely accurate one day forecasts, long range forecasts of greater than 5 days are relatively unreliable."

With a unique spirit of international cooperation and the benefit of computer technology, scientists today can realistically say "Accurate weather forecasts are just a step away." But until that time the surest safeguard against wind, rain, and sun remains the invention of the ancient Egyptions — the umbrella.

In the early morning a meteorologist sends instruments aloft with a small balloon to monitor weather conditions in the upper atmosphere.

CLIMATE BY COMPUTER

Computer simulation of complex systems like the atmosphere is a tricky business, but two IBM scientists are trying to use computers to answer at least one pressing question: Is dust pollution contributing to the global cooling trends? Their tentative answer is negative. "Initial results indicate that the effect of dust on the earth's [climate] has been overestimated."

LOST CITY METEORITE FALL

On January 9, 1970, a 22-pound meteorite found outside the small farming community of Lost City, Okla., 45 miles east of Tulsa, turned out to be an object of historic significance. It was the first meteorite ever to be recovered in a search guided by trajectory information computed from photographic data, and it was the second meteorite whose orbit around the sun, prior to entering the earth's atmosphere, was determined from photographic observations.

The find was made by staff members of the Smithsonian's Prairie Network, a system of 16 automatic cameras in seven states that was set up to photograph fireballs and aid in the recovery of meteorites. The Lost City Meteorite, discovered in a snow-covered field five days after the fireball was photographed over northeastern Oklahoma on the night of January 4, was the Network's first successful recovery of freshly fallen material.

The fireball, brighter than a full moon, was seen from as far away as central Nebraska. Traveling in an east-southeast direction, it caused sonic booms heard from Tulsa to Tahlequah — 60 miles apart. Network films of the meteorite's descent were quickly analyzed; and, with the help of a computer to compare photos from two different stations, the impact point was predicted to be a spot three miles east of Lost City. On January 9, the 22-pound specimen was found only a half-mile from the predicted impact point.

Computer Simulation of the Atmosphere

Since the nineteen-hundreds, weather scientists have known that all weather is part of a complex global fabric, and that conditions in one region are affected by those in neighboring regions. However, with inadequate knowledge of atmospheric physics and poor data-gathering facilities, global forecasting remained a dream until after World War II. The war sparked vigorous weather research, and meteorologists for the first time began building numerical models that bore some semblance to reality. More important, the first computers—originally used for ballistics ranging—became available for peacetime use. In 1946, famed computer pioneer John Von Neumann saw the value of high-speed computing for meteorology and began to assemble a group of brilliant young scientists at Princeton University. Using a machine known as the MANIAC (for Mathematical Analyzer, Numerical Integrator and Computer), Von Neumann's group in 1950 made a first—and wildly successful—computer run of their model. But later tests revealed inadequacies—according to one account, the computer once forecast a blizzard for Georgia in July.

Since then, computers and models alike have grown steadily more sophisticated; computer simulation remains an expensive and arcane specialty flourishing at only a handful of laboratories, including U.C.L.A., the Rand Corporation, the National Center for Atmospheric Research in Boulder, Colo., England's Meteorological Office and Princeton, where the descendants of the original group have continued Von Neumann's work. Now funded by the National Oceanic and Atmospheric Administration, the Princeton group is using the world's largest and fastest computer—an Advanced Scientific Computer made by Texas Instruments.

For purposes of numerical simulation, the earth's entire atmosphere is divided into boxes extending several hundred kilometers on a side and a kilometer or so in depth A typical model may deal with 60,000 of these boxes. The computer is fed information about the boxes and about the basic laws of physics. It is then asked to compute on the basis of these laws, what will happen to the molecules in each of the boxes as temperature, humidity and wind speed change in neighboring boxes. In other words, it is asked to predict the weather all over the world, and to repeat this prediction every five minutes or so for as long as the model holds together.

The accuracy and range of the prediction obviously depend upon the reliability of the data and the model—and perhaps upon some intrinsic limits not yet understood. "We're now issuing five-day forecasts," says Donald Gilman, head of the long-range forecast division of the National Weather Service. "The consensus is that these models may let us see 10 to 14 days ahead for our daily predictions, although estimates range from one to four weeks. We are appreciably more accurate than we were 20 years ago, but it may be difficult to go on from here. That's one of the things the Global Atmospheric Research Program is designed to tell us: how much further we can expect to get. These models are very sensitive to little disturbances. If you give the model any sort of random kick, such as an error in wind speed, on day one the results you get three months later are very, very different from what you get without the kick. It will be very difficult to distinguish small but real atmospheric disturbances from random background 'noise.'"

To predict climatic trends years or decades in advance, it is clearly impractical to recompute the world's weather every five minutes. Even with large "boxes," it takes tens of hours to run a model for a prediction of a week or two. With finer, more accurate grids, say 65 kilometers on a side, computation time becomes prohibitive.

LESS THAN 1% OF THE EARTH'S SURFACE WATER IS DRINKABLE

While 70% of the earth's surface is covered with water only 1% is "fresh" and a substantial amount of *that* is polluted

NASA HAS A SATELLITE (E.R.T.S.) 570 MILES IN SPACE . . . TO MONITOR EARTH'S WATER RESOURCES

The Earth Resources Technology Satellite orbits over the same spots on Earth every 18 days It can thus detect deterioration of water resources.

Navy display speeds weather forecasts

A communications and display system in prototype operation at the Navy's Fleet Numerical Weather Central in Monterey, Calif., is expected to improve and speed weather forecasts dramatically.

Developed by Genisco Technology Corp., Compton, Calif., the Naval Environmental Display Station (NEDS) provides full communications, remote processing, automatic graphic storage, retrieval and TV display capability up to 80 data bits. The system incorporates a special data-compression technique that permits the Naval Weather Service to use the existing Teletype network for transmitting weather and oceanographic data to the fleet.

Traditionally the service uses

Weather conditions are observed on a CRT display of the Naval Environmental Display Station now under test at Monterey, Calif.

facsimile equipment to transmit graphic data over costly, wideband transmission lines. Weather and oceanographic maps received over the system often are of poor quality and difficult to interpret. Correlation is done manually, and it involves the overlaying of maps by hand to make predictions.

The system being tested has two TV monitors and a keyboard that permits a forecaster to view alphanumeric and color graphic material, while a plotter/printer makes copies of any material of interest.

All data received, selected and stored are automatically logged into a computer index and become available, upon demand to the forecaster. He can call for a CRT display of the index, which lists the weather maps, messages and other data in the system's disc storage. He then calls for a display of the desired weather maps, via the keyboard, to do his forecast. ■■

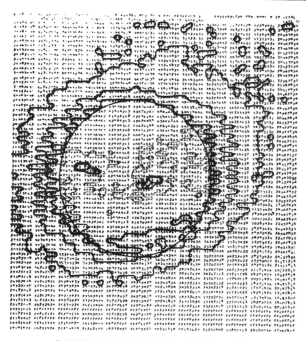

COMPUTER PICTURE OF THE SUN

This is a computer picture taken by the Naval Research Laboratory ultraviolet experiment aboard the Orbiting Solar Observatory-7 launched from Cape Kennedy on September 29, 1971. The picture, received at NASA's Goddard Space Flight Center, shows the sun's disc and inner corona out to two solar radii (1,382,000 km. or 864,000 miles). The smooth circle depicts the approximate size and position of the visible sun. The wiggly lines are isotopes, separating regions of different ultraviolet intensity as on a countour map. Two regions of intense solar activity in the center of the disc are apparent. This image was recorded just two hours after a solar flare occurred in the region near the center of the disc which ultimately stretched off to beyond two solar radii. (Photo courtesy NASA).

Lehigh Offers Decks For World Models

Complete programming for a variety of "World" models now is available from Lehigh University, according to W. E. Schiesser.

The Fortran IV source decks are available — at prices ranging up to $30 per deck of 1,800 cards — to allow computer-running of the Forester World 2 model, the Behrens natural resource utilization model, the Boyd extension of the Forrester World 2 model, and the Battelle Globe 6 model.

Dr. Schiesser informs us that two introductory models have just been released, one on the world food problem which deals with the ultimate carrying capacity of the world's agricultural system. The other model is on the world energy system; it contains the essential elements of the supply/demand interaction for five major sources of energy, with intersource competition.

Additional information, including references to documentation on the different models, is available from Prof. Schiesser at the Computing Center, Packard Laboratory, Lehigh University, Bethlehem, Pa. 18015.

"Human history becomes more and more a race between education and catastrophe."
H. G. Wells

Hunting Tornadoes

For the past two years Dr. Bruce Morgan has spent a portion of each spring zigzagging across Oklahoma's checkerboard of farms and oil fields . . . searching. In the spring of 1973 he found what he was looking for—a powerful storm which spawned a tornado before his eyes.

"It was a very peculiar sight," Morgan recalled. "The sun was shining where we were. There was no sound; we couldn't hear anything. Very light debris—tiny pieces of paper—floated down, blowing in the wind like snow. Three miles away from us this 3,000-foot tornado looking something like a gigantic ice-cream cone was smashing through Union City, Oklahoma. This big white column was just grinding its way across the ground."

Morgan and a three-person team from the National Severe Storms Laboratory (NSSL) recorded the tornado on film and made qualitative scientific observations. The team shot more than 40,000 frames of film by the time the funnel finished its 10-mile path of destruction and curled back up into the clouds.

After targeting a region and obtaining a detailed forecast from the National Severe Storms Forecasting Center in Kansas City, the team drove to that area and positioned itself on the southeastern edge of the storm, the traditional spawning site for tornadoes. As the team chased a storm, often 300 miles in a day, it received updated weather information via radio-telephone from the NSSL base.

Although it was a record lean year for tornadoes, the storm-tracking unit went out 18 times during the first spring and monitored 14 storms, two of which produced small tornadoes. It was enough of a success to convince NOAA to renew the project for another year.

The next spring, the storm trackers had more severe weather than they could handle. The United States received the deficit of tornadoes plus a few extra. Tornadoes formed at a record rate throughout the entire country.

For Morgan and the other members of the chase crew, the successful tracking and photographing of the Union City tornado was the highlight of the season. They believe much valuable scientific information can be culled from the Union City film. For example, the tornado's size versus time can be reconstructed and compared to the various computer models which have been developed.

Minis monitor weather at nuclear power sites

The Atomic Energy Commission requires that proposed nuclear power-station sites be monitored for weather conditions two years before the start of construction, all during construction and for two years after the beginning of operation. A computer-based system, operated by Digital Graphics Inc., Rockville, Md., has been monitoring five unattended sites since January in accordance with AEC requirements.

At each site 32 weather-monitoring instruments, installed on a 400-ft tower, are sampled once every 15 minutes by an on-site minicomputer—a Varian 620/L. In addition to gathering data, the computer checks the quality of data to indicate instrument malfunctions.

At four-hour intervals, each remote site is contacted via commercial telephone lines by a central Varian 73 minicomputer, which gathers the data. The central computer also resets the clock at the site, clears the memory and can provide program updates. It will print an alarm message if any instruments appear to be malfunctioning.

At infrequent intervals, the central computer serves as a time-sharing terminal for a large computer, transmitting many months' worth of processed weather data. The large computer is then used to simulate conditions such as probable vapor drift from a cooling tower or accidental nuclear-particle release.

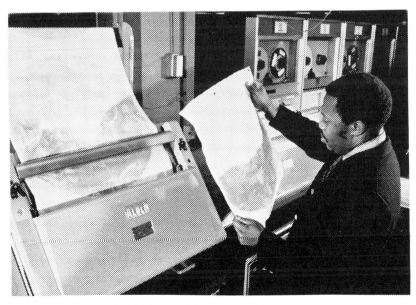

WEATHER FORECASTING BY SATELLITE AND COMPUTER

Almost 15 years ago, April 1, 1960, a new era in meteorology began with the launching by NASA from Cape Canaveral of the world's first weather satellite TIROS-1 (Television Infared Observation Satellite). Today a facsmile of the day's weather by satellite (ESSA Series) is transmitted by computer to the data center at the Environmental Science Services Administration at Suitland, MD. (Photo courtesy NASA).

Relativity for computers: All arithmetic

Three hundred years ago Isaac Newton discovered that to solve the problems of universal gravitation he had set himself he had to invent the branch of mathematics called calculus. Eighty years ago, in formulating special relativity, Einstein caused a revolution in physics by making mass a variable and uniting space and time, but his equations, though changing the content of Newton's, followed Newton's calculus lead. Calculus, in fact dominates classical and most modern physics. For three centuries it has been the physicist's best mathematical friend.

But now the world has digital computers. Digital computers can do calculations with incredible speed. They have prodigious memories. People want to use them wherever a lot of computation must be done in a short time. But computers are not as smart as Newton,

let alone Einstein, or even a college freshman. They can't do calculus. They can only do arithmetic, but they do it very fast.

So a group at the Computer Sciences Department of the University of Wisconsin at Madison under the direction of Donald Greenspan is working out a reformulation of Newton's and Einstein's work, not conceptually, but mathematically, trying to get it on an arithmetic basis so a computer can handle it. They have been successful with Newtonian classical mechanics and fluid dynamics. Greenspan's latest paper (UW's Computer Sciences Technical Report #232) details the first part of a method for special relativity. Later they hope to go to general relativity.

The sticking points in calculus are the concepts of limit and continuity. Limit is a way of getting around Zeno's

paradox, which so bedeviled ancient Greek mathematicians, and showing that an infinite succession of infinitely small steps can in fact lead up to but never surpass a limit that is nevertheless a finite number. Continuity is a property of the sort of equations called functions. A function sets up a relation between an (independent) variable quantity or quantities and another (dependent) variable, so that, knowing the value of the independent variable, one can calculate the dependent one. A function is continuous at a point if an infinitesimal change in the independent variable yields a new finite value for the dependent variable that is only infinitesimally different from the previous one. These two concepts are the keys to the development of integral and differential calculus, and when they had been evolved, 18th-, 19th- and 20th-century physics and engineering were on their way.

What the Wisconsin group has achieved is a way of replacing the infinitesimal steps with finite ones—finite-difference equations— that nevertheless come out to the same thing, in the limit, as the continuous processes of calculus. And it works in practice. "What we do runs," says Greenspan. "Everything we do must go on the computer. Doing it in theory is not enough."

Greenspan says the method should be of wide use to physicists and engineers with all kinds of mechanical, fluid dynamical and special relativistic computations to do. But it is much more than that.

As they were working through the method, the group found, in Greenspan's words, that they were doing physics arithmetically. The conservation laws that define and characterize Newtonian and Einsteinian physics come out of the arithmetic procedure. It is thus not merely a crutch for the computer but an alternate way of deriving and justifying the physically meaningful mathematical statements that have traditionally been gotten by calculus methods. And that could work an important change in high-school curricula.

Calculus—for reasons considered good and sufficient by mathematics teacher—has traditionally been reserved for the first or even second year of college. High-school physics teaching has suffered from the lack. Much of its content had to be brought in on faith or justified by handwaving methods. The new formulation could provide a way of making high-school physics more interesting by deriving its contents in a satisfactory way that the pupils could follow. Greenspan is enthusiastic about the idea of a change, but also extremely realistic. "You have 300 years of vested interest in calculus to overcome," he says. □

If Newton looks disapproving and Einstein surprised, it may be because the calculus is being calculated out of their theoretical derivations.

Nuclear Research	Das Whizkidden grupe.
Preliminary Design	Das Uppen-das-klaudsen grupe.
Administration	Das Oudtgeschmardten grupe.
Rocket Engine	Firenschpitter mid schmoken-und-schnorten.
Design	Das Raundscholder und Reddischeiz grupe.
Project Engineer	Das Schwettenoudter.
Management	Das Ulzerenbalden grupe.
Nuclear Warhead	Das eargeschplitten laudenboomer.
Hydrogen Device	Das eargeschplitten laudenboomer mit ein grosse hollengraund und alles kaput.

Mr. Spock's 7th Sense

by T. R. Kibler
Georgia State University

The Starship Enterprise had as its five year mission to explore strange new worlds, to seek out new civilizations. Besides Captain Kirk and Mr. Spock and its crew, the Enterprise carried an impressive array of scientific apparatus with which to carry out its exploration. Not the least of these was the Transporter which could, by separating the atoms of matter in one location and reassembling them in another, transport people or objects from place to place. It was most often used to transport survey parties to the surface of a planet for exploration. However, before a team would beam down to a planet, Mr. Spock, as chief science officer, would use the Enterprise's sensors to scan the planet's surface to give a detailed analysis of the planet. From the Enterprise's orbit the sensors could measure the atmosphere and surface nature of a planet, including the general mineral makeup. The sensors could even detect the presence or absence of life forms — including the relative level of its civilization.

While the Transporter has to await the future and further research, the sensor is available to us today. Today sensors might not have the speed or the range of those found on the Enterprise, but they are real and most useful.

The principle of the sensor is quite simple — identify objects by the characteristic radiation they give off. However, once one gets to the details, things get a bit messy.

Everything on the surface of a planet or just beneath its surface or in its atmosphere (if there is one) transmits, reflects or emits radiation. Furthermore, the transmission, reflection and emission of radiation of a given object or substance forms an identifiable pattern. Just as a sample placed in a spectrophotometer has a spectral fingerprint which identifies it by the spectral absorption of its elements, so an area of the surface of a planet has a radiation pattern that identifies it and its components.

There are, however, some problems in scanning that don't occur in a spectrophotometer. In a spectrophotometer you have a well defined and controlled environment while in scanning from orbit the atmosphere filters the outside radiation and scatters the reflected and emitted radiation. Also in a spectrophotometer the angle at which light hits the sample is controlled, while in scanning the strength and characteristics of the outside radiation may vary as the zenith angle changes. Further in scanning, the surface composition, surface structures, and surface entities appear different as they are stacked one upon another. However, many of these interferences can be accounted for by analysis. That is, first the atmosphere can be analyzed as to its composition and then its effects accounted for and factored out of surface observations. Similar procedures can be done to separate particular surface objects from their immediate environment.

Again, in principle the hardware for the sensor is basically simple but the actual design becomes complex. The sensor would simply collect the radiation from some desired region of the planet and sample several wavelengths known to have discrimination qualities for surface features of interest. The patterns of readings would then be corrected for atmospheric and light source variations and then matched against standards to determine the things being observed.

In practice there are many technical problems to be considered and many tradeoffs to be weighted. For example, two problems are: what is the proper scan area that is to be observed at a single instance and what is the minimum discrimination to be made in that area. The larger the area scanned and smaller the discrimination within that area the greater the data rate from the sensor for a given scan speed. The question of area size and discrimination size is bracketed on one side by efficiency and research restraints and on the other by physical limits. The larger the scan area the faster an area of the planet can be scanned. If hourly ocean current changes are needed then the scan area must be large enough to scan the ocean area of interest in one hour. However, if the smallest element of discrimination is too small, the mass of data will overrun any system's ability to transmit or store that data — let alone analyze it. Thus for ocean analysis one would need large scan areas and large areas of discrimination. If bird counts in a sanctuary were desired, the smallest picture element must be quite small, but the scan area must also be small in order to keep within the limits of the data collection system.

Further as the size of a picture element becomes

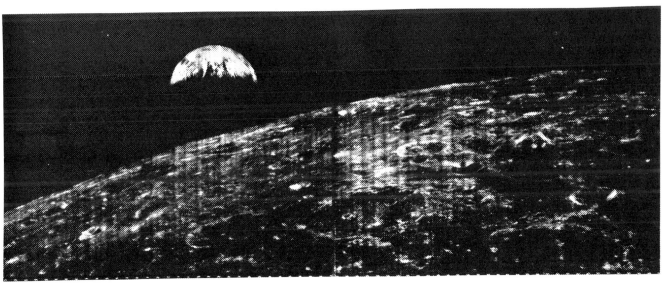

smaller, the requirements of the optical system become more exact. Such problems as general system noise and, in particular, optical distortion become acute. There seems to be a lower limit of about 5-10 centimeters set by atmospheric scattering.

Since there is a loss of detail as the size of the picture element is increased, the obvious answer is to have two sensors systems, one with a large field of vision and large picture elements for large areas survey and locating areas of interest and a second sensor system for small discrimination within smaller areas.

To try to put all of this in perspective — without giving too much detail — let's look at a sketch of a single sensor for an earth satellite. The sensor's lenses continuously scan a strip of the planet at right angles to the motion of the satellite. The motion of the satellite determines the length, direction and speed of the scan. The strip scanned at any one instant will be broken down into picture elements. Thus a strip 185 km (100 miles) long might be broken into picture elements 15 meters long. Further, exposure time would be such that the satellite motion would be 15 meters for each exposure. Thus each exposure or reading of the sensor would sense a strip 185 km by 15 meters at a resolution of 15 meters square.

The radiation coming through the lenses of the sensor would be broken by prisms or filters into the various spectral bands required. The spectral bands being chosen to maximize the characterization of surface features of interest, while minimizing the number of such bands required. Each of the 4 or 5 such bands would have its own set of photodectors. Each set of photodectors would have 12333 elements. Each element would record one of 256 (8 bits) levels of radiation intensity. The digital output from each of the sets of dectors would be digitally compressed and encoded and then multiplexed with the signals from the other spectral bands. The digital compression reduces the volume of data by up to 60% but the encoding for error detection and correction adds back about 25% overhead to the reduced data. This multiplexed signal is then transmitted to earth receiving stations to be stored for later analysis.

The analysis consists of filtering out signal noises, enhancing the desired images and identifying what has been scanned. These are all done by digital techniques. The area of the surface that was scanned becomes a matrix with each element of the matrix being the intensity output from one photodector. Since the atmospheric absorption is different for different wavelengths, the data from each spectral band is corrected differently for the atmospheric effects to that band.

Digital enhancement continues with the elimination of as much blurring as possible and providing as much contrast as possible for objects of interest. The objects of interest vary from analysis to analysis. For example, one researcher may be interested in corn crops in a given area while another is interested in subsurface water and soil composition in the same area.

While outlines may be detectable in several of the spectral bands it is the distinctive patterns across the different spectral bands that give the actual identification of objects. For example, it could be seen from any of the matrices that there was a one acre square in the middle of a much larger area. But by considering the different spectral patterns it could be identified as either a square island in a lake or a pond in a pasture or a poppy patch in the middle of a cornfield.

This sort of analysis only tells about the physical characteristics within a small area. To reveal cultural levels and patterns, it is necessary to accumulate data into a larger picture. The amounts of artificial illumination and heat given off from an area can be checked to find a city and determine its general energy consumption. The comparison of the number of roads to the number of fields identifies an area as being primarily agricultural or industrial. The comparison of the number of forests to the number of cultivated fields helps to identify the level of agricultural development.

These techniques can be done today, although not in real time as the Enterprise's sensors could. The Earth Resources Technology Satellite of 1972 (ERTS-1) had sensors of this general nature to be used for analysis of the earth's resources. The ERTS have the advantage of being able to calibrate their sensors and analysis by scanning known areas. However, when it comes to foreign planets the problems may be more difficult — for as the crew of the Enterprise often discovered, not all planets and civilizations developed in the same manner.

SATELLITES AND COMPUTERS HELP MANAGE EARTH'S RESOURCES

GREENBELT, MD — Operations Command and Control Center console for the ERTS-1 spacecraft at NASA's Goddard Spaceflight Center.

The ERTS program is a first step in the merger of space and remote sensing technologies into a system devoted to developing the ability for more efficient management of Earth's resources. Design of the observatory based on the highly successful Nimbus Meteorological satellites which have regularly returned pictures of the Earth weather status since 1964. The ERTS observatory will operate in a polar orbit 900 kilometers (about 560 miles) above the Earth and return images from two independently functioning multispectral sensors. A data collection system onboard the observatory will gather environmental information from Earth-based platforms and relay this data to the ground processing facility, at NASA's Goddard Space Flight Center, Greenbelt, Maryland. Federal agencies participating with NASA in the ERTS-1 project are the Department of Agriculture, Commerce, Interior, Defense and the Environmental Protection Agency.

THE AUTHOR

Tom Kibler, Technology Editor of Creative Computing is Manager of Scientific Programming at the Computer Center, Georgia State University where he is also a part-time instructor in information systems. Prior to coming to GSU in 1973, Tom was a designer and researcher for IBM and prior to that a consultant and systems programmer at UC, Berkeley and Stanford Univ.

Structured Programming

By Christopher G. Hoogendyk

"That's a great deal to make a word mean,"
Alice said in a thoughtful tone.
"When I make a word to a lot of work like that,"
said Humpty Dumpty, "I always pay it extra."
Lewis Carroll
Through the Looking-Glass

A lot has been said about structured programming. You might ask, "Why another article?" The answer is that no paper yet has pulled together all the ideas and showed their connection (McCracken 1973). If you ask the average programmer what structured programming is, he will reply with a collection of rules and regulations about top-down planning, avoiding GOTOs, and formatting code on a page. Such a collection of rules is hard to remember and easily misused.

There is also disagreement and confusion about when a program can be called "structured". A programmer might say he has a structured program and a dozen others will disagree. Further, as programming theory develops, better methods will be used and the definition of "a structured program" will change. Let us throw out the idea of a structured program versus an unstructured program and look at programs as fitting into a spectrum determined by the skill of the programmer, the effort he puts into the program, the language facilities, etc. In these terms we would speak of a *well structured program*. If Dijkstra put his best efforts into designing and writing a particular program in the best Algol, we might look upon it as an extremely well structured program. But, but not drawing a dichotomy, we also admit that an average programmer can apply the ideas of structured programming in the language at hand and come up with a reasonably well structured program. There is no reason to develop a powerful conceptual tool for programming and then deny its use to a wide range of programmers and applications.

Structured programming, then, deals with the design and writing of well structured programs. Now, what is the central theme of structured programming? If you can't identify a central theme and show the connection between it and each rule, then most programmers (like me) will see structured programming only as a disconnected collection of rules and regulations. This failure to pull the ideas together will be reflected in the use and misuse of the ideas behind structured programming.

The central theme of structured programming is that *structure should reflect function*. This is a powerful design concept. It was the theme of Frank Lloyd Wright's architecture. When applied to programming this concept leads to worthwhile results on three different levels: design, coding, and display.

Program Design.

The first level is the planning or design of the overall program. A program should not be a black box that is patched together until it works. It should represent a systematic development of the ideas behind the program. This idea has been carefully developed and presented in case histories of program design by Dijkstra (1972), and has come to be known as top-down program design. The practical application of top-down design in program development projects is discussed by Miller and Lindamood (1972). Very briefly, top-down design means starting with a definition of the program's purpose and progressively decomposing it into subactions until you reach a level of description that can be coded directly into the programming language you are using. There are some key ideas that emerge from top-down design which are often expressed independently. One is that you shouldn't bind yourself with an early decision about particular program or data structures. This leads to greater flexibility in program design, and makes it easier to modify the design or the program itself if the requirements are changed. In its simplest form this means that a variable name should be used in the place of a recurring constant (this is called parameterization). Thus, instead of referring to device number 3 in your program, you would refer to the INPUT device. Then, at run time, INPUT could be initialized to 3. Dijkstra (1972) gives some more instructive examples.

Program Coding.

The second level at which we can apply the concept that structure should reflect function is in the actual coding. This was first expressed by Dijkstra (1968), although the ideas have been around a while longer. Dijkstra pointed out that the real subject of programming is the process that results from the run time execution of the program. He said, "We should do our utmost to

shorten the conceptual gap between the static program and the dynamic process, to make the correspondence between the program (spread out in text space) and the process (spread out in time) as trivial as possible." This is the source of the objection to the GOTO statement. The GOTO can lead to a complicated flow of execution through a program text that can be almost impossible for a human reader to follow. Work on the formal proof of program correctness has resulted in some good systematic ideas in program coding. Bohm and and Jacopini (1966) proved the logical superfluousness of the GOTO statement and showed that any problem could be expressed using the simple control structures of sequential processes, selection, and iteration. These correspond to the normal sequential execution of a program, the IF-THEN-ELSE construction, and the FOR-NEXT or DO constructions. The inclusion of BEGIN-END blocks lends a simple versatility to these constructions. Using "structured" coding results in real benefits for the human reader. It becomes easy to read a program from top to bottom without having to look back and forth all over the program to pull pieces together. A simple example in BASIC should demonstrate the strength of these simple control structures.

```
10 LET T=0
20 LET T=T+1
30 LET N=NO*EXP(R*T)
40 PRINT T,N
50 IF T 10 THEN 20

20 FOR T=1 TO 10
30 LET N=NO*EXP(R*T)
40 PRINT T,N
50 NEXT T
```

These two pieces of code perform identical functions. In the first, the programmer starts reading, has to think about the initialization of T, reads the next two lines, sees the IF, looks back to line 20, and begins to put it together. In the second piece of code, the programmer reads top to bottom without having to stop once. When structured coding is incorporated in a large program, where there are several levels of control, the improvement in readability demonstrated above is magnified many times over.

Program Display.

The third level at which we can apply the concept that structure should reflect function is in the actual display of program code on a page. The visual structure of the code should convey to the reader as much information as possible about the functional content of the code. An effective way of doing this is to uniformly indent FOR-NEXT or DO loops, and to doubly indent nested loops. The reader who encounters the FOR or DO can then see the extent of the loop immediately without stopping to scan through to find the end of the loop. An idea from Weinberg (1971) is to have programming aids for listing programs that would

do various things such as indent loops uniformly, put keywords of the programming language in boldface, move all comments to the right hand side of the page, etc. Indenting and the use of white space in vertical spacing should be used by all programmers. Additional flourishes depend on ingenuity and available printing mechanisms.

Structured programming, then, is the application and expansion, at several levels, of the concept that structure should reflect function. The usefulness and success of structured programming has been demonstrated (Baker and Mills 1973). The reason for this success is that programming is a human activity. When a program is written the work isn't done. It has to be debugged. As it is used, more bugs will be found, or it will need to be modified to fit changing needs. Few successful programs are ever static. Programmers spend the bulk of their time debugging or reworking program code. Because of this, programs have to be readable. Since structured programming focuses on clear program organization, increased information content, and greater readability, it has a striking effect.

The object of this discussion has been to show how the seemingly disconnected ideas of structured programming are united by the theme that structure should reflect function. No attempt has been made to expand the ideas into detailed discussions or case histories. Those who have a serious interest in programming should read Dijkstra's articles.

References

Baker, F. Terry, and Harlan D. Mills, "Chief Programmer Teams", *Datamation,* December 1973, P. 58.

Bohm, Corrado, and Guiseppe Jacopini, "Flow Diagrams, Turing Machines and Languages With Only Two Formation Rules" *Communications of the ACM,* May 1966, P. 366.

Dijkstra, Edsger W., "GOTO Statement Considered Harmful", *Communications of the ACM,* March 1968, P. 147.

Dijkstra, Edsger W., "Notes on Structured Programming", *Structured Programming,* Academic Press, New York, 1972.

McCracken, Daniel D., "Revolution in Programming: an overview", *Datamation,* December 1973, p. 50.

Miller, Edward F., Jr. and George E. Lindamood, "Structured Programming: Top-down Approach", *Datamation,* December 1973, p. 55.

Weinberg, Gerald M., *The Psychology of Computer Programming.* Van Nostrand Reinhold, New York, 1971.

The author graduated from Dartmouth College in January 1973 with a B. A. in biology. He has since served as chief programmer for the CONDUIT project at Dartmouth, contributing to the development of standards for the preparation of transportable programs. His main interests are ecological modelling and educational uses of computing.

On Computer Languages

"David Ahl, I want to punch you in the nose," was my greeting from Adele Goldberg at NCC in Anaheim. Perhaps she most vividly summarizes the frustration that some of our readers have with the high percentage of BASIC language material we run in *Creative Computing*. Adele is at the Xerox Palo Alto Research Center where "Dynabook" with the tremendously rich and powerful language, SMALLTALK, has been developed by Alan Kay.

Adele is not alone in her view as other letters and conversations suggest. Let me try to briefly summarize the various arguments and positions that have been expressed to me over the last few months pertaining to various languages from their supporters.

ALGOL. The major language in Europe. Surely *Creative Computing* doesn't wish to ostracize its growing body of subscribers in 11 European countries.

APL. A powerful, sophistocated language with a rich vocabulary and conciseness of expression equalled by few other languages.

Assembly Languages (Various). Sophistocated users are soon going to outgrow BASIC or other high-level languages and there is much to be gained from learning to program on the assembly or machine language level.

BASIC. Accounts for nearly 70% of the usage in schools and colleges today. An easy-to-learn language which "everybody" knows.

COBOL. The major language of the business data processing community. Doesn't *Creative Computing* have an obligation to serve the person heading for a career in EDP?

FORTRAN. The major language of the scientific community and still the only (or main) language on many college campuses. Also, the first widely-used high-level language with all that such a history implies.

LOGO. First developed at Bolt, Beranek and Newman (Wally Feurzeig) with further work going on at MIT's AI lab (Seymour Papert) and General Turtle (Alan Papert). Part of the "Mathland" approach for introducing young students to mathematical concepts.

PILOT. A BASIC-like language oriented to young children or other "naive" computer users. Has been used successfully in Montessori schools with preschool age children. Can be run on many minicomputers.

PL1. Different language but substantially similar comments as APL.

SMALL TALK. An incredible "gee whiz" language with fantastic graphics and animation capability. Has to be seen to be appreciated (or believed).

I haven't heard anything from fanciers of PLATO, SNOBOL, RPG, FOCAL, etc. but I'm sure I will sooner or later. However, the point is this: *Creative Computing* is attempting to serve a broad cross-section of the educational computing using community — middle and secondary school students and teachers, college users, public access groups (libraries, museums, storefronts), researchers (to a limited extent), and the general public (to a limited extent). So what mixture of languages should I run? Frankly, I don't exactly know. My gut feeling is that it should be mostly material that will run on the majority of subscribers' computer systems. But also articles and information should probably appear about less popular languages to expose people to other alternatives. For the most part, I'll probably avoid specific machine languages, languages specific to one computer (e.g. NEAT), EDP languages (COBOL, RPG), and other specialty fare. I don't believe that *Creative Computing* should promote any one language as we are currently accused of doing with BASIC. However, I do have the very real problem that I can only print what is submitted.

As the readership of *Creative Computing* grows in sophistocation and your demands change, I'll do my best to remain responsive. A diversity of manuscripts and your thoughtful cards and letters will help keep me on the right track.

—DHA

Toward A Human Computer Language

Alexander B. Cannara
IMSSS, Stanford, California

Why must (should) computer-programming languages be different from human languages? Please trust that this question can be linked intimately to our topic: "computer languages for education". But first, I'll argue that "computer languages" and "for education" redundantly describe that topic: (1) people use computers, thus computer languages, for work or play; (2) anyone engaged in productive enterprise (work or play) now and then learns something new (to him), so programming can be an educational experience; (3) because the computer is a very general tool in the realm of human thought, it is really an educational tool for all people. All designers of programming languages should keep that in mind. We want a computer language to allow us to define objects and their interactions as naturally as possible, so that we can set them off on computational explorations of worlds that we, not the language, constrain.

Obviously, people are at the center of the relationship between the computer and humanity. We design computers and define languages for using them, and these programming languages allow us to communicate our thoughts not only to a machine, but to ourselves and to other people as well. Some argue that the latter is the more important function. In any case, any language is for communication and a limited language limits the communication of those who use it.

Programming languages (or any other formal languages), are special, in contrast with human languages, because we do not yet understand our own language processing well enough to be able to construct any reasonable facsimile of it within or without Turing-computable limitations. In other words, no one has written a computer program that could pass the "Turing-test" and sensibly communicate with a human in human language over arbitrary scope and time. Research with that kind of goal in mind now aims at building upon success in limited contexts and is often coupled with psychological models of thought, memory, etc. (e.g. T. Winograd, Psychology Today, May 1974; or J. S. Brown, Proceedings of the ACM 1974 Conference). So a partial answer to the opening question is: "computer languages cannot yet be as broad as human languages".

Given that programming languages are designed by sometimes frail, sometimes insightful humans who cannot describe what it is they do to communicate, but want to make a machine do it, what limitations of current programming languages should make us unhappy and spur

us on to better designs? And, since every programmer was once a novice, shouldn't we be concerned with the nature of a programming language's structure and the ease with which its full powers can be grasped and applied to problems that its users wish to solve? I'll use some notable failures in language design to illustrate things with which we should not be satisfied and to show why the answer to the latter question should be an emphatic "yes".

Almost everyone is familiar with one of the more primitive programming languages like Fortran and Basic (proper nouns both, and deserving of no more capitals than God and Man). Why is "primitive" a justifiable modifier? For example, consider Fortran (historically an acronym for "formula translator"). Created as a way of making algebraic expressions more easily entered (by humans) into a machine, thus more readable than lists of individual machine instructions, it served to express formulas in notation consistent with common mathematics — the same notation for all machines having a Fortran-translator program (compiler). Two decades ago, this was a step in closing the gap between computer and human vernaculars. But even then it was clear that a useful machine, which can parse "(2appl es+3lemons)/1.8fruitperpound", must also handle control commands, like "do this then do that until something happens", with clarity and ease. Hackneyed design gave Fortran, among other defects, less power to express the control of a program's execution than to parse an algebraic expression, and so eternally placed arcane and unnecessary burdens upon its users. Similar remarks apply to Basic, originally designed as a simple, stopgap recoding of machine language for users of early time-sharing systems. Some examples:

English/Algebra
If (2 apples + 3 lemons) / 1.8 fruit per pound is > 0 then do this, if it is $= 0$ then do that, otherwise do the other thing.

Fortran
```
        FRUTLB = 1.8
        IF ((2*APPLES+3*LEMONS)/FRUTLB) 100,200,300
100     . . .
200     . . .
300     . . .
```

Basic
```
10      LET X = (2*A+3*L)/1.8
20      IF X < 0 THEN 100
30      IF X = 0 THEN 200
40      IF X > 0 THEN 300
100     . . .
200     . . .
300     . . .
```

Algol
real x, fruitperpound; fruitperpound := 1.8; if (x := (2*apples+3*lemons)/fruitperpound) > 0 then this else if x = 0 then that else theotherthing;

The Fortran and Basic examples highlight the glaring inconsistency of easy algebra and sorry obfuscation of control. Suppose we had to write the algebra as:
```
10      2
20      APPLES
30      *
40      3
50      LEMONS
60      +
70      1.8
80      /
```

Would or should we be happy with such a lobotomized language? Perhaps for a $20 calculator. And never mind trying to recall what goes on at lines 100, 200 and 300, which may be pages away (or cards away on archaic systems) in the program's text. Yet many people, deprived of access to anything else, believe that Fortran, Basic, etc. are the essence of programming! Perhaps our true shame is that we inflict our most scurrilous languages upon our school-children, in whose lives the vast potential of the computer will have greatest meaning. We've mused that there is no complete and satisfactory language, not yet — certainly if too many of us continue to accept naively the ravings of foppish languages there may never be.

It's obvious which of the examples above (Algol, over a decade old) most closely approaches English and some of this is just nice form. We naturally like to call things (variables, labels, procedures) by names that indicate to us their significance. Notice that Fortran and Basic limit even this simple ability by restricting name lengths and character content (it is irrelevant that different versions of these languages impose different limits). Utter trivia like non-free-field syntax (e.g. Fortran statements must begin after column 6 (or is it 5?)) further subordinate the programmer's daily convenience to the one-time convenience of the language designer. Sometimes, on some machines, some such restrictions result from necessary trade-offs. But even on the smallest machine, a compiler or interpreter that reasonably sacrifices niceties of form should never be allowed to sacrifice the essentials of consistency and intelligibility.

Notice that Fortran misappropriates "=" as the assignment operator and leaves the user with either: "IF (X − 2) 100, 200, 100" or "IF (X .EQ. 2) GO TO 200" as means for testing equality (in this case of X and 2). Basic at least retains the usual meaning of "=", but at the price of adding an extra, prefix operator "LET". As a result of these kinds of patchy designs, such languages are poorly defined and give the user no consistent means for mastering their syntax. Special cases abound. Locally, the syntax may be postfix, prefix or infix and the same element (e.g. "IF" in Fortran, "=" in Basic) may have different meanings, depending upon its context. Human languages do the same sort of thing, but not at such low levels.

Fortran "format" statements provide perhaps the most horrendous example of a language patched within a language. Mastery of their syntax alone has provided jobs and income for many programmers. Interestingly, the tendency is to modify Fortran and Basic by adding "features". Since the languages have no particular structure anyway, these are cut-and-paste enterprises. One notable result has been Pl/1, which fearlessly combines the syntaxes of Algol, Cobol and Fortran into something like the worst of all possible worlds! It solves few of the inconsistencies and frivolities of either Fortran or Cobol (e.g. noise words which seem to mean what they mean in English but mean nothing!) and abuses a well-defined language: Algol-60. Unfortunately, Pl/1 seems to be the product of bigger-is-better reasoning. When a language is designed in such a way as to make it harder to read or to explain, then we should be suspicious that it lacks usefulness as well as elegance. It is of course true that not everyone who uses a computer has clear, elegant languages at his or her disposal, but we should all be aware of needs and opportunities for changing such situations. Here are two examples of a guessing game written by children in Basic and Logo (which borrows ideas from Algol and Lisp):

Basic
```
10 PRINT "DO YOU NEED INSTRUCTIONS?"
20 INPUT A$
30 DIM A$(1)
40 IF A$="N" THEN 80
50 PRINT "PLEASE GUESS A NUMBER BETWEEN 1 AND
60 PRINT "THEN I WILL GIVE YOU A HINT"          100,";
70 LET X=INT((100*RND(0)+1)
80 INPUT R
90 IF X=R THEN 150
100 IF R < X THEN 130
110 PRINT "GUESS LOWER"
120 GOTO 80
130 PRINT "GUESS HIGHER"
140 GOTO 80
150 PRINT "YES!"
160 GOTO 10
```

Logo
```
TO START
10 PRINT "DO YOU NEED INSTRUCTIONS?"
20 IF IS REQUEST "YES"
   THEN PRINT "PLEASE GUESS A NUMBER BETWEEN
   1 AND 100, THEN I WILL GIVE YOU A HINT"
30 QUIZ RANDOM 1 100 REQUEST
END


TO QUIZ :X: :GUESS:
10 IF EQUAL :X: :GUESS: THEN WON ELSE LOST
   LESS :GUESS: :X:
END


TO WON
10 PRINT "YES!"
20 START
END


TO LOST :TOOLOW:
10 IF :TOOLOW: THEN PRINT "GUESS HIGHER"
              ELSE PRINT "GUESS LOWER"
20 QUIZ :X: REQUEST
END
```

To which language should we prefer to expose ourselves or our children? Keep in mind that most machines including microprocessors have long had all the instructions needed to easily realize Algol-like control, which Fortran-like languages use only for parsing formulas. A decade ago Fortran was wasting abilities of most machines it ran on, now it and its relatives are simply more wasteful of more machines.

The actual range of computations and data-types could also be a topic of discussion (e.g. Fortran and Basic do numerical work easily, string manipulations with difficulty). Apart from attempting elegance, some languages serve particular computational audiences (e.g. Snobol for strings, Lisp for lists/functions). However, nearly all languages suffer idiosyncratic limitations when type definitions lend predisposition of meaning to data. Profusion of data-types is all right as long as it does not hamper the user's own constructions. The enterprise of reality or programming is message processing and the effect (meaning) of a particular message depends upon the action of the computational chunk (object) that receives it. This merges with the idea of an extensible language in which the user can construct new entities which truly expand the power of the language. Procedure definitions in Algol, Pascal, Logo, etc. constitute only a beginning (subroutines in Fortran and Basic are but trivial excursions into machine language, because they lack even the syntactic status of primitives). Education and computers can be linked via language extensibility.

We want the machine to understand us in our vernacular or a sensible approximation of it. We want to phrase programs as solutions to our problems in clear, powerful prose. For these purposes, no existing language may ever be satisfactory as it stands. Including English, etc.! Thus the need for extensibility — syntax and semantics being under our control during the course of a computation. Languages which allow the creation of new types of objects and new examples of existing types have been around for some time, Simula for instance. Generally their births were motivated by desires to model real-world systems by simulation (e.g. of forests, hospitals, etc.). Their abilities to create new types and examples of objects that intercommunicate at will allows one to begin to program with a greater sense of reality. But restrictions remain, Simula is fixedly Algol-like, Simscript is incomprehensibly couched in Fortran syntax, and so on. Perhaps the ideal is a language which captures the essence of "objectness" and intercommunication, yet is itself an editable object accessible to its users. Exciting work along such lines is being done by some people and will surely leave a mark on our computational future.

So, the rest of the answer to the opening question is: "certainly every effort should be made to breach the gap between computer and human language". Particularly in educational settings, where it is paramount that the student's language be the language through which learning proceeds. The goal isn't English, or any other known language in particular, but the ability to construct whatever objects/languages one wants.

"Say something in computerese."

Learning About *Smalltalk*

by Marian Goldeen

My name is Marian Goldeen. I'm an eighth grade student at Jordan Junior High School in Palo Alto, California, and I would like to tell you about how I got started working with computers at Xerox and the class I taught.

It all started in December, 1973 when I was in the seventh grade. There were four people in my class who were interested in taking a course about the computer language Smalltalk at Xerox.

When we first started we were shown how to start the machines up, and file in our one file, which had already been written onto our disks. These files contained some programs that would draw boxes like this.

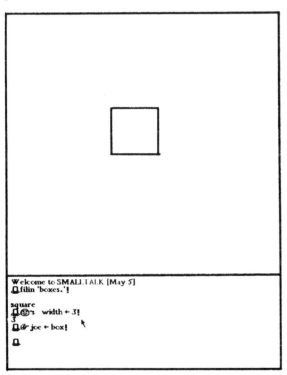

These boxes could turn on their axes,

grow,

and shrink.

Later on we learned how to change the programs which had been created and drew these boxes so that we could do different things with them, for instance, move them to different places on the screen.

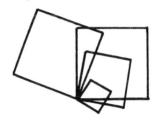

There was a little rectangular object to the side of the keyboard, called the mouse. When you moved the mouse around a corresponding pointer on the screen moved around too. We learned how to make the boxes follow the mouse pointer.

After we had learned just about everything there was to know about boxes we were able to create our own programs (Gulp). I don't know what the two boys in the class did, but Colleen and I created a painting program. It was fairly complicated. To run it you first had to set up the menu.

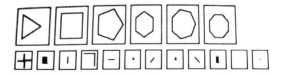

You would point with the mouse to the box that contained the shape you wanted to draw with, then press the top mouse button. Now the shape would be a paint brush and you could draw pictures.

"Smalltalk" is an interactive language developed by Alan Kay at Xerox Palo Alto Research Center. It is easy to learn and use, has powerful text display and manipulation capabilities, extensive graphics and animation features, and very high computational speed on several parallel levels. It runs on a small computer specifically dedicated to running Smalltalk and has not, at this time, been implemented on any general purpose computer. We'll have more on Smalltalk in future issues.

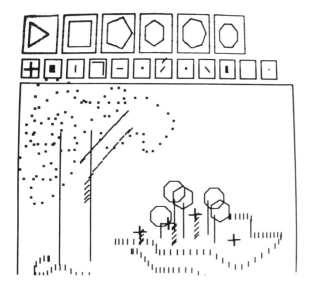

By now school had just gotten out and we had stopped taking our Smalltalk classes for the time being. At the beginning of July a class was organized for Barron Park kids and I came up too, to help tutor. These kids started at about the same place I had but since they're not too important for the moment I'll go on about me. I started working very hard on stickfigures and finally came up with something that looked like this.

The headless horseman, eh?! Well, I decided that a stickfigure without a head would never do. So I gave it a head.

Now, what's so great about a stickfigure if it won't do something for you? I taught my stickfigures how to play baseball.

Then, I decided that what I really needed were some can-can dancers.

After that I worked the original dance routine in so one figure danced a solo!

At about this time I noticed that out of all the kids from Barron Park (about twenty) only two or three were girls. Horror of Horrors!! So I decided that when school came around I would teach a computer class for girls only!

When school started that's exactly what I set about to do. Unfortunately the woman I arranged it with convinced me that there should be boys in my class. I ended up with three girls and two boys.

I started them off with boxes. Then they, just as I had, went on to do their own programs. Lisa started off with a guessing game,

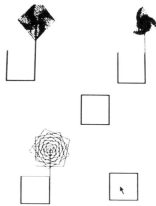

Kathy did some rocketships and *oddshapes,*

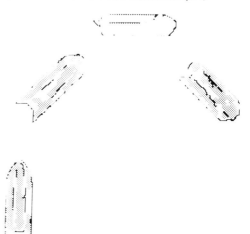

62

and Susan started a painting program.

With a lot of elaboration my figures can now play badminton.

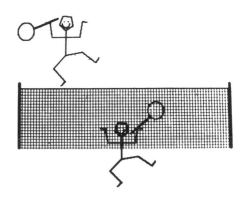

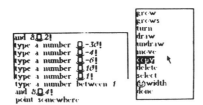

A few weeks later Lisa, having finished her guessing game, joined Kathy on the rocketships.

At this point I stopped teaching them and they started working on their own. I went back to my stickfigures. I decided that these figures needed to have elbows, knees, hands and feet. To enable the computer to do this faster I changed the head into a pentagon.

Now I'm working on a galaxy simulation where I can selectively send different stars into nova.

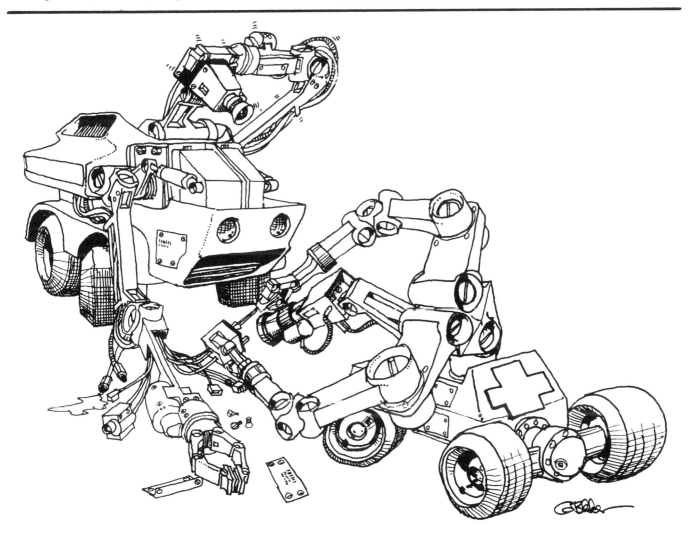

Eclectic Programming Languages

C. Terrence Ireland and Norman S. Glick
The George Washington University

Where are programming languages headed? Will there always be many languages, or will there be one ultimate language? Will BASIC and FORTRAN disappear from the scene, replaced by new improved languages? Presently, the complexity of new improved languages discourages their general use.

One end of the curvilinear relationship between general purpose computer language difficulty and computer language sophistication is clear; the other end is faith. The middle is hazy. The Display shows a partial construction of this relationship. You should feel free to rearrange the languages in the Display to fit your own beliefs.

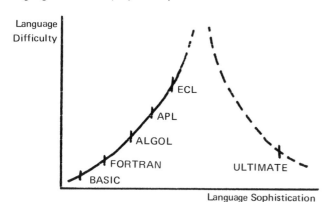

Display

Simple languages are easy to use because they have few constructs that you must absorb into your intuition. More recent languages carry an expanded syntax, which opens up new opportunities to instruct the computer. It will, however, take you longer to absorb the expanded syntax into your intuition; you may not find the time. One attempt at requiring programmers to publish their algorithms in a language with an expanded syntax ended in failure. Most scientific programs are initially written in FORTRAN. The Association for Computing Machinery once required that published algorithms be written only in ALGOL, a language more sophisticated than FORTRAN. As a result many of the ALGOL programs mimicked the original FORTRAN programs, instead of taking advantage of the additional sophistication available in ALGOL. Unfortunately, it is also true that well-programmed ALGOL algorithms must often be translated back into FORTRAN or BASIC to run on your machine.

The Ultimate Language appears at the other end of the curve, which hopefully has descended back into view. Perhaps the Ultimate Instruction will be "You know what I want. Do it!" Presently, the Difficulty Curve for general purpose languages is still going up, and the predicted time of descent is moving farther into the future.

An Extensible Language

New languages should be eclectic: "not following any one system, . . . , but selecting and using what are the best elements of all systems." An eclectic language permits a very rich set of elements, but you must choose among them. The choice can be very hard, particularly for novice users of the language. Many will want to be constrained by a simpler language; at least it keeps you out of trouble.

An eclectic language system, ECL, has been developed during the last five years at the Harvard Center for Research in Computing Technology. This extensible language allows you to reach out and select the "best elements." You can even change ECL language elements that you dislike, and add new ones for your specific application. Never mind how ECL appears to others. What counts is how it appears to you. If you want to redefine "=" to mean different things in different contexts, as in PL/I, then extend ECL so that

$$A = B = C$$

means set the value of A to "true" if the value of B is the same as the value of C, otherwise set the value of A to "false". Make sure, however, that you keep such activities secret!

ECL does not have complex numbers. Why not add them yourself. You can:

1. Define a new type of data, call it COMPLEX.
2. Extend the usual arithmetic operators +, −, *, and / to handle the corresponding operations on COMPLEX numbers.
3. Construct a natural print value for a COMPLEX number. Either
   a. The algebraic form, a + bi.
   or
   b. The picture form, an Argand Diagram, e.g.

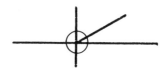

4. Extend exponentiation to include COMPLEX numbers.
5. Et cetera.

An extensible language must also be contractable. Once you expand ECL for the complex number user, you can contract other features that do not interest him. He sees only the language he wishes to see. In a similar manner, you can construct a BASIC-like language.

ECL gives you the opportunity to produce your own extensions "as naturally as possible" in a well-understood high level "core language." But there is a cost. To tie together all the characteristics of the complex numbers into one package requires a lot of code. You can build a beautiful vertical structure; each layer of the structure feeds into the next higher layer to permit simplified programming at high altitudes. You can operate on complex types of data with the same ease that you can add two numbers in BASIC. It does take time to develop any such structure. If you use the entire package often, the development time is well-spent. Perhaps your needs are less comprehensive or you want something simple in a hurry. Perhaps someone else will eventually write the package for you. ECL is a powerful system, but it is still on the upward side of the Difficulty Curve.

People have different reasons for writing programs. At least three reasons are visible:

1. Instruct your computer to apply an algorithm to a set of data, and to return to you the result of the application.
2. Transport your programmed algorithm to another

"Very good. Please continue." A New Approach to Testing

Sandra J. Hershkowitz

The development of computer-generated examinations is fairly recent, but the use of such testing is spreading rapidly; in fact, the first CATC (computer-assisted test construction) conference has recently been held in San Diego to provide information about and experience in this area.

For my master's thesis in education, I devised a computerized testing system, with the hope of increasing learning and motivation in an introductory computer science course. With the generous cooperation of Dr. Ronald Wojcik (who was then affiliated with St. Bonaventure University) and his staff, the exams were used by 63 undergraduate students in order that the system could be evaluated and student reaction obtained.[1]

Basically, the idea is as follows: Students are taught in whatever manner is usual but are tested so that they are competing with *themselves* rather than with the rest of the class. Exams are administered via "terminals", typewriter-like machines hooked up to a computer, which may be located in the school building or may in fact be miles away — in one of the many computer centers located in colleges, universities, or business corporations throughout the country.

The student identifies himself on the typewriter, and testing begins. A question is typed out for the student to answer. Questions are chosen at random from a storage bank of questions so that each student's exam is unique. Because the student is competing with himself, he is encouraged to take each exam several times, with the idea of improving his previous high score. The use of randomly selected questions means that a student's retests will also be different; therefore he is being exposed to a large amount of material covering a particular unit or area and is not merely taking the same exam over and over.

Questions are corrected immediately as they are answered. If the answer typed in by the student is correct, he is given an encouraging comment and asked to proceed ("Very good. Please continue.") If the answer is incorrect, an appropriate comment is typed out ("The correct answer is .... Why don't you take a look at this later?"). At the end of the exam, the student is given his score, along with his previous high score, and the areas needing review are listed. He may then remove his corrected paper, with comments, and use it for further study.

In the particular system used by the St. Bonaventure students, there were three units or areas. Each unit exam contained 25-30 objective-type (true-false, identification, multiple-choice, fill-in) questions, chosen from a storage bank of approximately 300 questions; and students were allowed to take each exam up to nine times, with a two-week period allowed per unit. A questionnaire was administered to assess student reaction, and the responses were very gratifying. Students overwhelmingly liked the exams, they liked the interactive approach and the repeatability option, and they felt they were learning more using the exams.

Such a testing system is a practical reality — it is adaptable to many subject areas at any level and does not involve great expense. It can be programmed on a small computer; and, as mentioned earlier, a computer does not have to be on the premises. Students may retest themselves on a particular unit and try to improve themselves with each retest. They can use their completed exams as study aids and receive each exam, graded, immediately as completed.

Another point not to be overlooked is the value of such a testing system to the teacher. In addition to being freed from administering and grading exams, the teacher can readily obtain desired statistical information, continually updated. (For example, for a particular unit: number of times each question is answered correctly; how many times each student has taken the exam; mean and standard deviation of high scores for the unit; individual scores for each student; and so on.)

With the increasing use of individualized learning programs, computer-generated examinations fit in perfectly. A student may proceed at his own pace and take the exams appropriate to his level of learning.

[1]"Interactive Testing-Evaluation in an Introductory Computer Science Course" by Sandra J. Hershkowitz and Ronald Wojcik, *Journal of Educational Data Processing,* Spring, 1975.

Eclectic Languages continued —

machine so that it can apply the algorithm to a set of data, and can return the result of the application.

3. Transmit the knowledge of the algorithm to someone else.

If you write for Reason 1, you write in the available language of your choice. Many will write in the first language learned, some will write in the second language learned, one or two will write in the best language available. The best language for Reason 1 is not necessarily the best language for Reason 2. That is the dilemma. To transport an algorithm to another computer, you must write in a language known to it. Will there ever be one language for all of us?

A Universal Language?

Computer scientists are confronted with an astounding decline in the price of computer hardware. The technology that has generated the dramatic and rapid cost reductions that you have noticed in the hand calculator market will produce, probably within five years, very powerful computers at costs within the reach of anyone who can afford a TV set.

Remember that the curvilinear relationship described at the beginning of this article is subjective. Even today what one computer user finds difficult, a "programming linguist" might find easy. When the butcher, the baker and the candlestick maker have that sophisticated computer hardware available to them, how will they communicate with it? More and more people will find the effort to learn even languages like BASIC to be more than they are willing or able to exert. The pressures on computer scientists to come closer to the ultimate instruction will intensify.

But wait; further development of eclectic languages like ECL may give the professional programmer much better tools to develop "easy" specialized extensions (read "languages") for classes of users: the butcher class, the baker class, . . . The kind of professional programmer who is equipped to develop custom languages for others is likely to be willing and capable to exert whatever mental effort is required to achieve fluency in a sophisticated language. But the casual user of computers, whose numbers will increase substantially in the next several years, must be given simple languages — he will tolerate no other kind. Unlike today's general purpose "simple" languages, though, the simple language of the future will not have a few constructs to absorb into the intuition, but a few constructs that are already part of the intuition.

Few people will learn the full-blown eclectic language, but many will learn the intuitive extensions.

The Computer Threat to Society

From the supermarket shelf you pick up two different brands of dishwasher detergent intending to buy the least expensive one. The stock person apparently forgot to put the price cards on the shelf. So you look at the boxes. But all you find on each is a postage-stamp size area with a series of lines of different thicknesses. No price.

What has happened is that the store has switched to a computerized UPC system. UPC stands for Universal Product Code and for supermarkets it's a great time saver. Prices no longer have to be marked on each item; the check-out clerk simply passes the "bar code" (that series of lines) over an optical scanner which is hooked to a computer in the back of the store. The computer transmits the current price back to the register where it is displayed on a little screen and printed on the register tape.

But what's good for the supermarket may not necessarily be good for you, particularly if you're a comparison shopper and the shelves aren't well marked. Are you being deprived of your right to be a comparison shopper by the computer? Certainly not. The computer is only doing what it has been programmed to do. It's not the villain. In fact, if the system reduces store overhead, prices might even come down a little.

But UPC is indicative of the little ways that the computer is invading our lives. Yes, and even threatening them. No, not the computer itself, but the things it makes possible. With UPC, people are being forced to make a change that some of them don't want to make. Let's take a look at some of the other ways things made possible by the computer are invading and, in fact, threatening our lives.

Fraud

So much has been written about the use of computers to defraud, the possibilities should be well known by now. Fraud by manipulating the software is most common

Yours truly — threat to society? Image made by a Digivue Display Hard Copy Unit (Varian Graphics, Palo Alto).

(Equity Funding, the use of a terminal to order the delivery of over $1 million in equipment from Pacific Telephone, a New York bank teller reassigning small amounts from every transaction to his own account, etc.). But hardware fraud is becoming popular, too — telephone "Blue Boxes" for example.

Influence on Elections

Public opinion polls and surveys are taken before every major election using minute sample sizes. Of course, the samples are demographically balanced and supposedly representative of the nation or state as a whole. Computers are then programmed to project these samples and predict the outcome of an entire election. The same sort of thing is done on election day using the results from early-reporting precincts. What influence do these predictions have on the actual election? Do people vote for the predicted winner because they want to join the bandwagon? Do others give up in despair? No one can say for sure, but it is clear that there is some effect and it is probably undesirable.

Inconvenience

High on the list of citizen complaints about the computer is the difficulty of correcting incorrect charge account or bank statements. We've all heard of horror stories in which an item was purchased, then returned 10 days later. The purchase price is carried on the statement for one month but interest on the unpaid balance is charged for the next 6 months or so until a human finally reads one of the letters of explanation. Worse yet, that person might be labeled a delinquent payee in a computerized credit data bank and, at some subsequent time, have difficulty getting a car loan, Sears card, mortgage, check cashed (choose one or more).

Although computerized charge accounts, bank statements, stock registrations, etc. have been around for about 20 years, most companies today are doing an inadequate job as intermediaries between the customer and the computer. The infrequent exception is a newsworthy event. For example, the grandson of Marybeth McKinney in Winnetka, Ill. recently ate her AT&T debenture interest check. Mrs. McKinney contemplated the challenge of trying to get through a computer to obtain a replacement check. She wrote AT&T and received a prompt answer from Cynthia Nelson who wrote, "I am sorry to learn that your grandson decided to chew up your check. I hope it did not make him sick." A new check was mailed and the story appeared in the *Chicago Tribune* titled "A Taste of AT&T Minus Computer Bite." The fact that business courtesy becomes a newspaper headline is indicative of the degree of everyday inconvenience and harassment we have learned to put up with from our servant, the computer.

Physical Harm

When "computer threat" is mentioned, most people tend to think of inconvenience, invasion of privacy, or criminal fraud. Yet perhaps the most threatening aspects of computers are inadvertent errors or program bugs. It is a rare program of any size or complexity that doesn't have one or more bugs even after years of successful operation. The bug may be in a subroutine that is used only infrequently or it may be in a very complex set of calculations where it is difficult to recognize an error. (You may say, but isn't the program tested and debugged when it is written? In theory, yes. But where there are millions of possible paths through a program it generally is checked by another computer program — and what if there is an error in that one?)

What are the consequences of such errors? In a word, scary! They're unpredictable, potentially very damaging, and, even after they occur, may not be correctly identified or even recognized. Not only that, but they could well cause physical harm as well as the more common inconvenience and financial loss. For example, the computerized control system on BART failed to take into account the possibility of a certain type of malfunction in a sensor. Result — a very damaging crash.

What about the computer diagnostic systems used in virtually every large pathology laboratory? Let's say you return from Zaire feeling poorly. You go into a large hospital and the doctor orders blood tests, etc. The computer then diagnoses your illness — incorrectly. You're then treated for the wrong disease and you die four days later. Not a very pleasant consequence of a computer bug. Not only that, who would ever suspect the computer program? So the error goes on for years unchecked.

Other Problems

The problems mentioned above are only a few of the many threats to society facilitated by the computer. We also have possible threats to national security when compromised timesharing systems are used for advanced defense or weapons research. We have the invasion of privacy which goes hand in hand with larger and more comprehensive data banks (criminal, medical, credit,

consumer opinion). We have pranks and practical jokes such as the McDonald's contest in Southern California and the student who insured the life of his goldfish. We also have the threat of becoming excessively dependent on the computer to do things that we used to do via experiment. Thus an engineer or scientist today may be deprived of the practical and valuable learning experience which results from an experiment which fails.

Are these undesirable problems the fault of the computer? Emphatically, NO. They occur more easily because the computer exists. The impersonal, mechanical computer is a convenient scapegoat to blame when the real problem may lie with the input data, the system's design, or the execution of the program. We must recognize that as the computer extends our intellect it also extends our capability and speed of making errors, of committing crime, of forcing change, of invading privacy, and of causing inconvenience. We must also recognize that along with the computer's tremendous power to facilitate beneficial advances for society is an equal power to cause problems.

David H. Ahl

IT IS WISE TO RECALL THAT AMIDST THE FLOWERS BE THORNS

Digital Calculators – Then and Now

The electronic digital computer first appeared in the middle 1940s. Then, it was a specialized calculating tool of mathematicians and scientists. Today, it is helping to solve information problems in almost every area of human activity.

The computer now can be used to print bank statements, as well as calculate astronomical tables. It can be used to compare the writing styles of two poets, as well as compare the performances of two chemical processes. It helps creative artists, as well as builders of bridges or buildings.

This revolution in computer use parallels to some extent an earlier evolution from simple manual counting tools to mechanized data processing machines. Some of the basic principles embodied in early mechanized calculators, as well as the problems they were designed to solve, help to explain the significance of the modern digital computer and the recent rocket-like rise in its use as a general problem-solving tool.

In the beginning

It's usually assumed that man developed the concept of number and counting before he developed an effective written language of words. His first records were primitive accounting and inventory records of grain, animals and possessions, recorded with sticks, pebbles or scratches on cave walls.

But his need for information and communications gradually outstripped the capability of these simple tools. So he invented new and better tools: first the abacus and, later, faster mechanical and electrical counting and information-handling aids. These were the forerunners of today's electronic digital computers.

The Abacus

The first digital calculator, the abacus, is really a mechanized form of pebble-counting. Beads, sliding on wires, substitute for the pebbles. Five beads below a wooden bar are units; each bead above is worth five. Numbers are represented by pushing beads against the bar. The wires or columns, starting at the right, represent place value: units, tens, hundreds, etc., just as our decimal arithmetic columns do. The abacus first appeared in the Near East and China about 2,000 years ago and it is still being used in parts of Asia.

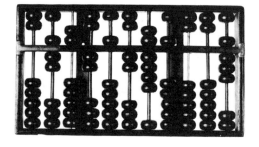

Left, early Egyptian numerical symbols.
Above, an abacus similar to those used for rapid calculation in the Orient since the thirteenth century.

Facing page, top, French mathematician Blaise Pascal's Arithmetic Machine, invented in 1642. *Below*, a nineteenth-century Jacquard loom, controlled with punched cards.

Reprinted from the booklet *More About Computers* with permission of IBM. Copyright 1974 by International Business Machines Corp.

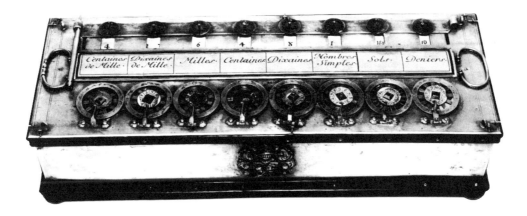

Pascal's Arithmetic Machine

Blaise Pascal–French mathematician, philosopher and writer–devised a calculating machine in 1642, at the age of nineteen. This machine demonstrated the practicability of mechanized calculation.

Pascal's machine was operated by dialing a series of wheels bearing the numbers zero to nine around their circumferences. To "carry" a number to the next column when a sum was greater than nine, Pascal devised an ingenious ratchet mechanism that would advance a wheel one digit when the wheel to its right made a complete revolution. Answers appeared on indicators above the dials.

Leibniz' Calculating Machine

Gottfried Wilhelm Leibniz took the next great step forward in calculating machines. He wanted to mechanize the calculation of trigonometric and astronomical tables and free scientists for more fruitful work. "It is unworthy of excellent men," wrote Leibniz, "to lose hours like slaves in the labor of calculation…" In 1671, he started development of the first machine to multiply and divide directly. A version of this machine was built in 1694.

Punched Card Looms

Weaving looms in France were the first machines to be controlled automatically from coded information punched into paper cards. First proposed in the first half of the eighteenth century, the idea of using holes punched in paper to control the operation of a loom was perfected by Joseph Marie Jacquard in 1804. He controlled the operation of a loom with a series of connected punched cards. The same basic technique is still in use in the textile industry.

Babbage's Calculating Engines

Over a century ago, an English mathematician named Charles Babbage was designing a machine based on the same basic principles as today's electronic computers.

His first machine was a Difference Engine with which he hoped to mechanize the calculation of logarithmic and astronomical tables. Babbage built his first Difference Engine in 1822 (for which he won the first Gold Medal of the Royal Astronomical Society). It was a relatively simple machine that could generate tables to an accuracy of six decimal places. Then, he immediately began work on a bigger engine capable of twenty-place accuracy. Only part of it was ever constructed.

After his work on the Difference Engine, Babbage developed new ideas for a really powerful tool to handle any sort of mathematical computation automatically. Powered by steam, this machine would have worked from a planned program of operating instructions stored on punched cards. It would have included, as modern computers now do, a memory or data storage section, an arithmetic unit, a section for entry of data and instructions, and an output section for printing

results. It would also perform decision-making functions. He called it an Analytical Engine. These concepts were not incorporated in a workable automatic calculator until the twentieth century.

Punched Card Counting

Dr. Herman Hollerith, of the U.S. Census Office, was the first person to use electrical tabulating equipment to analyze statistical data. For the U.S. Census of 1890, he devised a way to represent a person's name, age, sex, address, and other vital statistics in the form of holes punched in paper cards. This coded data then was counted electrically. During the 1890 Census, his ideas enabled the government to tabulate the census data more than twice as fast as it had handled the 1880 Census, even though the population had increased 25 per cent during that decade. Without some such mechanized tabulation, the census data would have become obsolete before it could have been completely analyzed.

Hollerith's pantograph punch was one of the first devices used to punch coded census data into cards. A blank card was placed on a plate at the back of the machine. At the front of the machine, a large replica of the card showed the coded meaning of each of the squares on the card. To record an item of data, the operator moved the punching mechanism over the appropriate hole in the replica and pressed the handle to punch a corresponding hole in the card.

Hollerith's first electrical tabulator used a clock-like counting device. The operator placed a punched card in a card reader and then pulled down a lever which caused a set of spring-loaded pins to be pushed against the card. Wherever there was a hole punched in the card, the pin passed through into a cup of mercury and completed an electrical circuit. This caused a pointer on a dial counter to advance one unit.

Cards were sorted semi-automatically. When a card was counted in the tabulator, a cover on a preselected compartment in a separate sorter box opened automatically. The operator placed the card in the compartment and closed the cover manually. In this way, cards were quickly sorted according to any desired characteristics such as place of birth, age, sex, citizenship.

During the first third of the twentieth century, punched-card machines based on Hollerith's ideas were modified, improved, speeded up. New and faster machines were developed to handle payroll, accounting, billing, sales analysis and other problems.

Below, an early twentieth-century, key-driven card punch.

In the 1930s, punched-card equipment made it possible to handle a mountain of data which suddenly had to be recorded when the Social Security Act was passed. The same kinds of machines also were used to develop statistical tables, calculate the orbit of the moon more accurately than ever before and speed calculations for a variety of scientific problems.

However, scientists and mathematicians kept collecting new data and they needed even faster calculators to handle it. As a result, new kinds of machines were developed and old ones were adapted to handle calculation at greater speed.

Mark 1: The First Large Scale Automatic Digital Calculator

In 1937, a Harvard University Ph.D. physics candidate, Howard H. Aiken, outlined plans for a machine that could be made to solve differential equations automatically. The plans were so interesting that IBM agreed to help him develop and build the Automatic Sequence Controlled Calculator, or Mark 1, as the machine was later called. It was completed in 1944 and presented by IBM to Harvard University.

Mark 1 was a 5-ton machine, consisting of a complex of 78 devices linked by 500 miles of wiring. It contained 3,304 electromechanical relays and was controlled by a sequence of instructions prepared by a programmer and then punched into a roll of paper tape. Once the Mark I was started on the first instruction in a program, no further human direction was needed until a new problem was put in the machine.

The Mark I could perform 23-digit additions and subtractions in three tenths of a second and could multiply two 23-digit numbers in about six seconds. Under automatic control of the paper-tape program, it could produce intermediate and final answers to a problem on punched cards or electric typewriters.

Mark I was retired in 1959, after fifteen years of continuous, useful work. Parts of the original machine are on display at the Smithsonian Institution and at Harvard University.

ENIAC:

The need for ever faster computations kept mounting, especially during World War II. This pursuit of speed led to the first electronic computer, ENIAC (Electronic Numerical Integrator and Calculator).

Completed in 1946, ENIAC was developed for the U.S. Army at the University of Pennsylvania's Moore School of Electrical Engineering by graduate student J. Presper Eckert and physicist Dr. John W. Mauchly. They eliminated the need for mechanically moving parts, such as electrically controlled counter wheels, to represent digits and numbers. Instead, they adapted electronic flip-flop circuits and used electronic pulses to flip vacuum tubes on and off like switches, with the "on" and "off" states representing numbers.

Since electronic pulses could move thousands of times faster than electromechanical devices, the concept behind ENIAC was a real breakthrough in the development of fast calculators.

The Stored Program Concept

It took another great idea to complete the concept of today's stored program computer. It was developed in the 1940s by Dr. John von Neumann. He suggested, in 1945, that operating instructions (the program), as well as data, be stored inside the computer memory and that the computer be made to modify these instructions under program control.

During the late forties, several electronic computers based on the ideas of Von Neumann were under development in the U.S. and Great Britain. The first such machine in Great Britain, called EDSAC, started operating at the University of Cambridge in 1949. Several computers were completed in the U.S. from 1949 to

Below, Herman H. Goldstine and J. Presper Eckert, Jr. holding a unit from an accumulator used in ENIAC, the first electronic digital calculator. (Photo courtesy of Science Museum, London.)

1952. Among them were the EDVAC at Aberdeen Proving Grounds, Whirlwind I at the Massachusetts Institute of Technology, UNIVAC I for the Census Bureau and an Institute for Advanced Studies machine at Princeton University.

Today

Since the days of Aiken, Eckert and Mauchly, it has been a battle, even for computer specialists, to keep up with computer progress. Faster, miniaturized circuits and storage devices have been developed, as well as techniques that enable many people in locations remote from a computer to share time on the same system. New programming languages and terminals make the machines easier to use.

As a result, computers today can be used by more people on more problems at less cost per computation. Computers no longer must be high-cost, room-size systems. Even small, desk-size units can work faster on large problems than some of the biggest of yesterday's systems. And results of computation now can be presented as pictures, graphs or spoken words as well as printed forms. Continuing improvement in both equipment and programming can be expected to further extend the use of digital computers.

The Computer. Threat to Society?

An Interview with Senator John V. Tunney

Senator John V. Tunney of California has long taken a major interest in the protection of individual rights and has continually proposed legislation to meet these goals. He is currently Chairman of the Subcommittee on Constitutional Rights of the U.S. Senate Committee on the Judiciary, and also the Subcommittee on Science and Technology. Senator Tunney recently took time from his busy schedule to respond to some questions posed by Creative Computing.

CREATIVE COMPUTING. On one hand the computer is a powerful tool for extending man's intellect. On the other, it is a monstrous dehumanizing force. Which will prevail? Why?

TUNNEY. Obviously, the computer has an enormous ability to make our lives more rational and convenient. In industry after industry, the arrival of the computer has facilitated the provision of services on a scale that was beyond imagination only a few years ago. Yet many Americans are concerned, quite rightly in my opinion, that the technological imperatives that flow from the rapid spread of large computers and telecommunications networks will gradually overwhelm traditional democratic values, leading ultimately to the loss of individual autonomy and the concentration of extraordinary power in anonymous and unresponsive bureaucracies. Congress seems to be aware of these dangers, which are so reminiscent of the nightmare visions of Kafka and Orwell. If the current level of Congressional concern remains constant, then the American people stand a good chance of gaining control over the powerful technologies of computer science.

CREATIVE COMPUTING. Large data banks of credit rating information are one of the most visible "computer threats" to individual privacy. Yet these data banks have probably prevented millions of dollars of fraud and stopped thousands of people from going into debt beyond their ability to pay. Is this a worthwhile use of computers or does the possibility of misuse outweigh the benefits?

TUNNEY. Few will complain about the inclusion of objective "ledger" information about a person's financial history in a computer databank. However, any attempts to computerize subjective opinions about an individual's personal habits raise substantial doubts. The computer's phenomenal speed, availability, efficiency, convenience, low cost and long-distance capabilities all combine to pose serious questions about our present ability to protect innocent citizens from the devastating and lasting consequences of inaccurate or malicious information.

CREATIVE COMPUTING. Most computer errors are actually human errors in programming the computer. These are commonly referred to as "bugs". It is a rare program that doesn't have some bugs even after years of successful operation (the routine with the bug may be very infrequently used or a small error in a complex set of calculations may not be recongized). Most pathology departments in large hospitals use computers for analysis and diagnosis today. Would you feel comfortably in such a hospital suspecting you had recently picked up an unusual disease from the Far East?

TUNNEY. I would feel comfortable in such circumstances if I could be assured that the computer would serve only in an assisting role and not become a substitute for the doctor's professional judgment.

CREATIVE COMPUTING. In one sense a computer is a tool just like a hammer or lathe. But a very powerful tool that can replace low-skill jobs. Do you think computers will create as many jobs as they eliminate? Will the new jobs require specialized training? If so, will people who have lost their job to a computer be able to get such training? Will they be willing?

TUNNEY. I think it is logical to conclude that in the long run the computer industry will create as many jobs as it displaces. However, it seems equally logical to assume that particular individuals who lose their jobs because of automation will not necessarily be able to find another in a computer-related industry. Obviously, some kind of re-training is advisable.

CREATIVE COMPUTING. From small-sample public opinion surveys, computers have been programmed to predict the outcome of entire elections. Do you feel that such predictions unduly influence the actual voter later on?

TUNNEY. No, I do not believe that early predictions necessarily affect the outcome of elections.

CREATIVE COMPUTING. By making projections from early-reporting precincts, computers predict on TV the outcome of elections long before all the ballots are cast on the West Coast, Alaska and Hawaii. Do you think voters in these areas are unfairly influenced by these predictions?

TUNNEY. In Presidential elections I do not believe that computerized projections should be announced until all polls have closed. In 1964 and 1972, for example, I believe that voters in the West, after hearing projections of Presidential landslides lost interest and didn't vote. This absenteeism especially affects statewide and local races and issues.

CREATIVE COMPUTING. High School students have repeatedly cracked the passwords and access codes of timesharing computer systems thereby demonstrating that the most secure computer systems are not at all secure. How do you feel about the fact that research on some of our most advanced military systems is done on the ARPA computer network to which thousands of college students also have access? (Educational users supposedly do not have access to research accounts but —)

TUNNEY. I have been assured by Defense Department officials in hearings before my Judiciary Subcommittee on Constitutional Rights and my Commerce Subcommittee on Science and Technology that ARPANET is not used for classified work. If that testimony is incorrect, then I am greatly concerned.

CREATIVE COMPUTING. We have no information that classified work per se is being done on the ARPANET; the point we were trying to make is that there is no such thing as an absolutely foolproof, secure computer system.

One last question — do you feel that the functions and applications of computers are beyond the understanding of the average individual?

TUNNEY. Any reasonably informed person can understand computer functions and applications if they are explained in plain English. Unfortunately, computer specialists are like all professionals and tend to cloud their explanations with opaque jargon.

CREATIVE COMPUTING. One of our goals is to cut through this jargon and to bring facts and information about computers to students and, indeed, to people in all walks of life.

TUNNEY. Thank you for devoting so much time and consideration to these matters and thank you also for the opportunity to contribute to *Creative Computing.*

CREATIVE COMPUTING. Thank you Senator Tunney.

Putting Teeth Into Privacy Legislation

by Susan Hastings

H. R. 1984 — that's the apt number a computer has assigned to the new Koch-Goldwater proposal that would expand the 1974 Right to Privacy Act. The new bill is designed to correct many of the ambiguities and weaknesses of the first successful legislation for protecting the privacy of individuals on whom personal information is held in federal government data banks.

Public concern with the government's relentless appetite for more and more information about the people it serves has grown with the Watergate disclosures and the recent revelations about CIA and FBI dossier-building. People who formerly were only peripherally aware of the problem, are now joining the crusade against privacy invasion partly because they see the computer, and the data it is capable of storing, as a terrible threat to their right to privacy. They don't like the idea that somewhere, somehow, files are being kept on them; that there are clerks who know about them, and can reach into those files and do things against them.

The new law is not perfect, but as Willis H. Ware, chairman of a presidential commission appointed to study the implications of privacy legislation, admits, it's adequate "as a first whack at the problem." Major criticism is directed at what the law has omitted, and conversely, at the prohibitive expense of implementing just what it does include.

Privacy legislation does not prohibit the government from keeping data banks, but it does protect the individual on whom the information has been kept from wanton disclosure of that information. The present law covers most personal information systems operated by federal agencies; the new bill would extend legislation to cover state and local governments as well as the private sector. Under it, subjects of data to be released usually must be aware of the nature, the purpose, and the recipient of the information to be disclosed, and should, in most cases, be able to rule on its accuracy and relevancy. Implementation of the law will be costly: the Office of Management and Budget estimates expenses of $200 to $300 million a year for the first four or five years after a startup cost of $100 million. And that is just for the law as it now stands. People seeking continued privacy legislation want it to cover data in the files of many agencies that are exempt in current and pending legislation, i.e., law enforcement, intelligence and certain personnel records. But these people do have hope for continued legislation, and will continue their battle for new laws, even if they do have to see them passed separately.

The American Civil Liberties Union is one extra-governmental group that has worked long and hard for privacy legislation, and it is generally pleased with Congressional response. Ironically, Aryeh Neier, ACLU executive director, gives praise for the victory to the computer itself. Today's fear about computers and invasion of privacy has had a very beneficial impact, he says, because "it created an awareness of the possible danger" for everyone.

Neier believes that the computer, although it "may make it a little bit easier to invade privacy", was never the real villain in the personal information game. The technology for managing data banks had achieved a significant enough development before computers came along to create the problem without computers. Before the computer came along, information that was fed into the information files was actually of a more gossipy nature than the harder kind that the computer is fit to handle. But people were more scared about the power of a machine than they ever were about the real culprits — the people who collect the information to use against other people.

Government will probably always insist on keeping records about its citizens. Perhaps though, new privacy legislation and the computer that inspired it, will limit the information government can afford to keep and use. After all, it's expensive to feed unnecessary information into data files. It's also expensive to break the law.

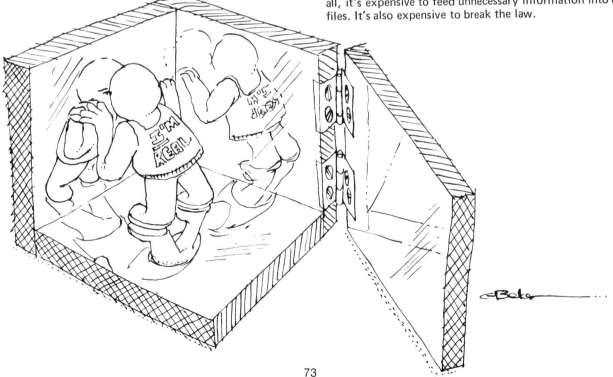

Industry Leaders Testify at Government Privacy Hearings

by Susan Hastings

In an era in which technology constantly provides people with newer and more useful tools, a decision must be reached on how the information provided by technology should be used by society. In hearings before the U. S. House of Representatives last winter, business leaders in the computer field attempted first to define the issues of computer security and privacy, and then to demonstrate the roles government and industry must play in their efforts to make the new technology beneficial to all of society.

There is a great difference between the terms "privacy" and "security". Privacy is — or should be — the inherent and legal right of individuals, groups or institutions to determine for themselves when, how, and what information about them is communicated to others. In relation to computers, security is the means taken to ensure that privacy. Privacy is a legal, political and philosophical concept, and properly belongs in the domain of government. Computer security deals with technique, and is the province of the manufacturer. Law and technology must cooperate in their efforts to make the benefits of modern electronics available to everyone.

Rapid progress in electronics has raised the processes of data collection, storage, retrieval and dissemination to the point where it will be easier to invade the privacy of citizens. Although continuing progress makes it possible to develop systems designs and controlling software that provide much better protection against man or machine failure, business must take upon itself the task of developing even newer systems to protect the rights of the individual.

Separate computer privacy studies in the United States, England, and Canada have agreed upon four recommendations for legal and technological control over systems as they relate to sensitive information about people:

1) An individual should be given right of access to information about him contained in record keeping systems and a way to find out how the information is used;
2) There should be a way for an individual to correct or amend a record of identifiable information about him;
3) There should be a way for an individual to prevent information about him that he provided for one purpose from being used for another without his consent;
4) The custodian of data files containing sensitive information has a responsibility for endeavoring to maintain the reliability of the data and to take precautions to prevent misuse of data.

The manufacturer is faced with the technological problem of implementing these recommendations. His chief responsibility is to provide the hardware and software that will enable computer users to achieve the degree of security necessary to insure the accuracy and pertinence of personal information held in data files. Although all manufacturers recognize that technology alone cannot prevent the abuse of information by authorized persons, it can provide for journaling and auditing techniques which may serve as effective deterrents. IBM's policy on data security would no doubt hold for the entire industry:

"Although the customer has overall responsibility for the protection of data, IBM has a responsibility to assist our customers in achieving the data security they require. In this regard, IBM will offer systems, products, services, and counsel that clearly contribute to the solution of data security problems."

The objective of any data security program is to cut the risk and probability of loss to the lowest affordable level and to implement a full recovery program if a loss occurs. Lewis M. Branscomb of IBM and Robert P. Henderson of Honeywell believe that their companies have recognized their responsibilities for providing better safeguards for computer security. In 1972 IBM committed itself to an investment of some $40 million over a five year period to study the requirements of data security and to make further developments of appropriate safeguards of their products. Like Honeywell and other manufacturers, they are working on devices in the hardware and software areas that will provide protection in the security area.

Despite ever more sophisticated technology to increase the security of computer systems, there is no such thing as *perfect* security. Beyond legal action, there is a great deal that users can do, however, to promote their own security. Users must be educated to take the responsibility of determining their own security needs and selecting the right combination of operating procedures, physical security measures, hardware devices, and programming tools that will fill those needs. Historically, the security of any information system depends on normal procedures of business and accounting control and traditional physical security measures. A computer installed behind showplace plate glass windows may be good for a company's public image, but it renders the computer vulnerable to people with malicious designs. Likewise, users should exercise a special sensitivity in selecting the personnel who have access to data banks, for no matter how secure the system, there is always the danger of people being compromised. Trained, dependable people are an absolute necessity. No matter what the level of hardware and software security, one must always remember that people run (and break) the system, not technology.

Record-keeping in the Space Age

Robert P. Henderson

People persist in tagging our era the "Space Age," but perhaps "Computer Age" is a much more meaningful term to describe it. Certainly the exploration of space excites the imagination, but the computer exerts a more compelling influence on the life of the average citizen. There wouldn't even be any space program without the technological advances of computers. And because the computer's potential effects on society are so great, it has generated a good deal of controversy.

The computer has come along to serve as an extension of man's intellect just when it is most needed to help solve many of the complex social and economic problems of our time. But there are those people who, after thoughtful consideration, see the computer as facilitating a radical realignment of knowledge — and therefore of power.

The new sort of computerized power politics is a dangerous possibility, but it is not inevitable. Great benefits lay ahead of us through the use of computers; we must take steps to prevent the perversion of computer technology and insure ourselves that the computer always serves the individual and never the other way around.

In their potential benefit to society, computers today are ready to take off in a big way. In the past, a great deal of effort has been directed toward making the most efficient use of computers as they existed, but now managers must think of developing computer systems that are specifically geared to their needs and the needs of the people who work for them. Information systems must be developed that will help managers make decisions, thus making business more efficient and effective.

As the isolated and independent computer systems so typical of the last decade become linked together in the 70's, data and programs will begin to flow together in enormous national — and even international — data grids. One of the great benefits of these large new computer systems will be their ready access to many people in both a physical and intellectual way. Terminal devices through which people can communicate with the computer systems will enable them to converse with the data bank as easily and familiarly as with their human colleagues. In effect, each man will be able to use the computer as a means of building upon the work of others. Just as he will use data generated by the activities of others, he can generate his own data for their use. The result can be an eventual pyramiding of man's knowledge and intellectual accomplishment that is staggering to consider. There are those who even forsee a time when all of the information available in the world can be stored and constantly updated in computer memory, available to anyone who wanted it wherever he might be.

In the future, vast compuerized legal files could produce case histories quickly and easily for all lawyers. The result might be not only clearer and easier interpretation of laws, but quicker and less expensive justice. Computers could aid doctors in making patient diagnoses, and make medical information about individual patients available wherever that patient might happen to be when he suffers an accident or illness. Computerized educational systems may help teachers satisfy the individual needs of each student in their classes, and give the teachers more time to give direct help when required. In all of these cases, computers will not be replacing people; they will be serving as extensions of human talent.

In considering all the benefits of a computerized society, we must remember that they depend primarily upon two developments: a vastly increased capacity, complexity, and accessibility of computer systems; and a storage of not only an infinite amount of academic information, but also a great deal of highly personal information.

While only computers can take the immense task of helping us reach coordinated decisions with the extensive records they handle, there is a natural human dislike of becoming a statistic. This dislike becomes even stronger when the statistic grows into a lengthy dossier providing intimate details about one's personal life, and may become available to any number of persons for any number of reasons.

Privacy is one of our most precious rights, and in today's crowded and disorderly environment, it may be one of the hardest to maintain. However, the computer does not in itself create any invasion of privacy. Its role is no more active in this respect than the old-fashioned filing cabinet. The only new element in the threat to privacy posed by record-keeping, is the computer's fantastic efficiency. This is what people really fear, and this is the problem that must be faced. Technology must look ahead at the problems which it might accelerate, even if it does not really create them.

The computer industry cannot solve the problem alone, but there is a great deal that it can do, both technically and

ethically. Technically, safeguards can be built into a design system to limit those having access to the system. However, as much as machines do to protect the privacy of computerized records, they can never be reguarded as absolutely invincible from really determined people. More than physical safeguards must be considered. Management should not only exercise sensitive control over the trustworthiness of their personnel, but should also make sensible decisions on what kind of information will go into their files, and how long it will stay there.

As the computer industry assumes a heavy responsibility in the privacy issue, so too must the people whom it serves. The government is taking an active role in passing new laws to provide a citizen with the ability to challenge in court the release of private data about him without his consent. But the general public must become involved also in thinking about and discussing the problems generated by computerized record keeping. The weight of public opinion can do a great deal toward influencing constructive public policies and creating voluntary ethical codes and standards of practice among users of computer systems.

Computerized and centralized information systems can take us in two directions. One would lead us to a rigid, automated bureaucracy with great knowledge and power but little regard for the human consequences of its program. The other would enlist the power of computers in the service of individuals, enabling them to cope more successfully with the complexities of modern life and increasing the opportunities for successful fulfillment of their talents. Society has no choice but to use computer aids in solving the problems of our age, but it now must learn how to use these products to serve the people. If the time ever comes when the misuse of computerized record-keeping leads man to fear being curious, daring, and willing to deviate from the norm in order to experiment, it would not be a case of the machine triumphing over man, as some people fear. It would be a case of man *becoming* the machine.

How One Computer Manufacturer
Looks At the Data Privacy/Security Issue

By Curtis W. Fritze
Executive Consultant
Control Data Corporation

The issue of data privacy ... an individual's rights to control personal data ... is a highly complex and controversial topic. It affects not only the individual, but also the agencies of government and the activities of business and other organizations which require such information to meet social and economic needs. And it also affects the design and operation of the tool most used for information processing and storage ... the computer.

Legislation concerning data privacy is in various stages of development at state, county and even city levels. Since passage of the Federal Privacy Act of 1974 there has been an outpouring of rhetoric and written materials concerning individual rights versus information technology. Legislators, educators, civil rights groups and computer manufacturers have produced volumes of statistics, opinions and studies about the subject.

Paramount to any discussion of data privacy is "the computer," often considered the culprit because of its ability to rapidly store, retrieve, process and transmit information. Consequently, computer manufacturers as well as computer users are concerned about legislation that could drastically change administrative techniques and computer architecture. The key issue appears not whether to discontinue computer technology, but how to keep and extend its benefits while preserving the rights of citizens to privacy and confidentiality without negative impact to the manufacturers and users of computer systems.

For the computer manufacturer, data privacy automatically means providing "data security" in the computer system. This means safe-guarding confidential information ... protecting it from unauthorized disclosure, modification or destruction, either accidental or intentional, through the use of special hardware and software. In extreme situations, this can mean additional expenditures by the manufacturer for research, development and production, as well as installation, and maintenance to meet customer specifications. On the user side, it can increase operating costs through increased equipment costs and additional computer time and generally add to the cost of doing business.

Considering all aspects — the studies, economies and social responsibilities, Control Data has developed a position on the issue; but not necessarily in support of any particular piece of legislation at least until the details of the requirements are known. A portion of this statement follows.

* * * * *

"Control Data, as a responsible corporate citizen, believes in the individual's right to privacy and supports the basic principles recommended by the HEW Report of June 1973. These principles are: (1) There should be no files of personal data, the existence of which is secret; (2) There should be a way for the individual to find out what information about him is in a file record and how it is used; (3) There should be a way for an individual to prevent information provided for one purpose from being used for another purpose without his consent; (4) There should be a way for an individual to correct or contest records about him in personal data files; (5) Any organization maintaining or using personal data files should assure the reliability of the data and safeguard the files against misuse."

* * * * *

The data privacy and security issue will undoubtedly gain momentum in the near future, just as computer systems will be a continued requirement of complex societies. The issue has a mixture of technical, social, political and legal entities. Consequently, we need sound prudent public policies, including legislation, ethical codes and standards of business practice.

These principles require careful implementation to avoid undue economic burden and impact on business. Unless this can be achieved, we may "cure the disease, but lose the patient." Continued dialogue and cooperation between government and business is absolutely necessary.

As stated in the National Academy of Sciences study: "Man cannot escape his social or moral responsibilities by murmuring feebly that 'the machine made me do it'."

Survey of Public Attitudes Toward Computers in Society

by David H. Ahl

SUMMARY

Computers are not only invading our lives along a multitude of directions — supermarkets, credit data, medical records, hobbies, etc. — but our society is becoming so dependent upon computers that it can truly be said that we live in the computer age. The computer will have at least as profound an effect on humankind as did the printing press some 500 years ago. In the Gutenberg Museum, a map plots the spread of printing out from Mainz to the rest of the world over scores of years. The computer invasion has taken place at an infinitely greater speed.

Now, some 30 years after its invention, what do people think of the computer? Monster or savior? Slave or dictator? Do people understand this awesome force?

This survey indicates that most people are remarkably optimistic about the benefits the computer can bring to society in a number of areas — for example, education, law enforcement, and health care. People feel they are unable to escape the influence of the computer and that it has some undesirable effects; however, they do not feel particularly threatened by it. Young people tend to be less optimistic and feel more threatened by the computer than do adults. A surprising two-thirds of the population have a fair understanding of both the role and function of the computer although there are a few popular misconceptions.

Compared to the 1971 AFIPS/*Time* survey, people have become more optimistic about the use of computers in most areas with the notable exception of credit data banks. Also, this *Creative Computing* survey identified the computer influence on elections as a real danger area — to our knowledge this has not been previously surveyed.

METHODOLOGY

During the 6-month period, February through July 1975, *Creative Computing* Magazine conducted a survey on people's attitudes toward computers and their role in society. Some 843 people responded in two highly computerized nations, the United States and Germany. About one-third of the respondents were educated or experienced in computer usage; two-thirds were not. Thirty-six percent of the respondents were classified as young people (20 and under) and students; the remainder were a relatively balanced cross-section of adults.

The 17 questions in the survey fell in four major categories (although they appeared in random order on the survey instrument). The categories:

1. Computer Impact on the Quality of Life (4Q)
2. Computer Threat to Society (4Q)
3. Understanding of the Role of Computers (5Q)
4. Understanding of the Computer Itself (4Q)

In some cases where the questions were similarly worded, the responses to this questionnaire are compared to those from a 1971 survey jointly sponsored by AFIPS (American Federation of Information Processing Societies) and *Time* Magazine.

COMPUTER IMPACT ON THE QUALITY OF LIFE

On the whole, respondents felt that the computer will improve the quality of life in four areas: education, law enforcement, health care, and prevention of fraud. Young people and students saw somewhat less improvement from the use of computers than did adults.

Computers will improve education. About 85% of all the respondents strongly or mostly agreed with that statement and only 5% disagreed. This was the highest positive (or negative) response to any single question and also the question which had the greatest agreement between adult and youth.

Computers will improve law enforcement. 82% of the adults agreed with this and only 3% disagreed. The younger respondents were somewhat more cynical; 70% agreed and 10% disagreed.

Computers will improve health care. On this issue, the young respondents had considerably more doubts than adults; about 79% of the adults agreed but only 54% of the youth. More than twice as many youth disagreed with the statement as adults — 12% vs. 5%.

Ranking lower on desirable uses of the computer is its use for *storing and checking credit rating data*; 64% of both adult and youthful respondents saw this as a worthwhile application. However, 13% of the adults thought this was a bad application for the computer, perhaps reflecting previous hassles that they or friends had with computerized credit rating data. Most young people probably haven't been exposed to this malady; only 8% of them objected to this application. While substantial, the 64% of the people in favor of this application represents a substantial decline from the 75% recorded just four years ago in the AFIPS/*Time* survey.

THE COMPUTER THREAT TO SOCIETY

Respondents were mixed in their feelings about the threatening nature of computers. Most felt they were unable to escape the influence of the computer. Nearly half saw computer predictions influencing the outcome of elections. More than one-third felt that computers dehumanize society to some extent. About one-quarter saw the computer taking more jobs than it creates. And about one-fifth saw the computer having an isolating effect on programmers, operators, etc.

A person cannot escape the influence of computers. 92% of the adults agreed with that statement, most "strongly" agreeing; only 4% disagreed. These percentages are virtually the same as those recorded in the 1971 AFIPS/*Time* survey. Reflecting a more optimistic, perhaps somewhat naive view that one can drop out and avoid anything one doesn't approve of, only 67% of the young people felt they could not escape the influence of computers and 18% strongly disagreed with the notion that computers couldn't be avoided.

Computer polls and predictions influence the outcome of elections. About 46% of the respondents agreed with this statement and 27% disagreed. In a democratic society, this is truly of grave importance. If almost half the people, adult and youth alike, feel their voting behavior is in some way influenced by computer polls and predictions (join the bandwagon, we've lost so why bother voting, etc.) then we have a real problem.

Computers dehumanize society by treating everyone as a number. Reflecting a rather positive shift in attitude, only 37% of the adult respondents agreed with this statement and 50% disagreed compared to the percentages of 54% agreement and 40% disagreement just four years ago in the AFIPS/*Time* survey. The younger respondents in the current *Creative Computing* survey were more pessimistic; 40% agreed that computers dehumanize and only 31% disagreed. (Youth were not included in the 1971 survey.)

Computers isolate people by preventing normal social interactions among users. Computer bums and computer freaks are common around any school with a computer. Million dollar corporate computers have to be fed data around the clock to justify their investment and there is a growing army of midnight shift programmers and operators. Among the uninitiated, FORTRAN or COBOL are more foreign than French or German. Are computers really isolating segments of society? Maybe, but apparently it's not very noticeable since only 20% of the respondents agreed with the statement above. More revealing, however, is the fact that 63% of adults disagreed with the statement and only 43% of young people disagreed. Perhaps computer freaks, who tend to be among the younger cadre, *are* becoming more evident.

UNDERSTANDING THE ROLE OF COMPUTERS

This issue was examined from two directions: what types of jobs are suitable for a computer and what will be its effect on human employment (or unemployment)? For the most part, adults saw the computer as suitable for dull, repetitive tasks like a hammer or lathe while young people saw computers in much broader roles. Furthermore, adults saw computers replacing low skill jobs and creating just as many jobs as they eliminate; young people were not as optimistic.

Computers are best suited for doing repetitive, monotonous tasks. Eighty percent of the adults agreed with this statement and 10% disagreed. Among young people, 57% agreed, 22% disagreed. In other words, young people see the computer doing a wide variety of things beyond simply data processing, numerical machine tool control, and telephone switching. But perhaps in some of these more sophisticated applications in which the computer takes over some of the human decision-making function, youthful respondents are more fearful of computers and less optimistic than adults.

Computers are a tool just like a hammer or lathe. Again, adults are in considerably greater agreement with this statement than are younger respondents.

Computers slow down and complicate simple business operations. Interestingly enough, most people seem to believe that computers are used reasonably well in business because 68% disagree with this statement and only 17% agree.

Computers will replace low skill jobs and create jobs needing specialized training. Somewhat more adults agreed with this statement (71%) than did youth (62%). About 15% of both adults and youth disagreed. This implies that a substantial fear exists that computers will take a tremendous number of jobs and there will have to be a massive effort by society (retraining, welfare, or ?) to absorb the human beings put out of work by the computer monster. This leads to the next question.

Computers will replace as many jobs as they eliminate. Again, somewhat more adults agreed (70%) than did youth (61%) and fewer adults disagreed (13%) than youth (23%). So we see that a large number of people believe the computer will replace low skill jobs, but furthermore, we see some question about the creation of new jobs by the computer to replace the ones eliminated and, as before, there is even more doubt expressed by youthful respondents.

UNDERSTANDING OF COMPUTERS

After looking at the various roles of the computer, one must ask, do people understand the computer per se by itself? And the answer is that a surprising number do. And quite a few don't. Indeed between one-quarter and one-third of the population believe the computer is beyond the understanding of the typical person. Also, many people have the wrong notion about who causes computer mistakes — machines or people.

Computers are beyond the understanding of the typical person. Are they? Well 25% of the adults and 31% of the youth think so. But 62% of the adults and 49% of the youth think they are within comprehension. Perhaps more revealing — among schools with an instructional computer program, over 80% of the students believe that computers are within their understanding.

Computers make mistakes at least 10% of the time. This statement must be coupled with the next one: *Programmers and operators make mistakes, but computers are, for the most part, error free.* FACT: Statement 1 is absolutely false, statement 2 is true. How did respondents do with these questions? Most answered "correctly" — about 68%, fewer youth than adults, but a fair number of people were downright wrong (13%). The rest of the people didn't know (19%). These percentages are similar to those scored on nationwide tests of scientific facts — about 2/3 of the people know the facts but the other third are wrong or just don't know. A happy situation? Not very.

It is possible to design computer systems which protect the privacy of data. Not even the computer designer knows for sure, so what can we expect from the general public? Well, 61% of the adults think you can design a secure system and 26% think you can't; only 49% of the youth think you can and 16% think you can't. What does all this say? Probably nothing except that some people are optimists and some are pessimists, and at least on the data privacy issue, more adults are optimistic than young people.

STATISTICAL RESULTS OF SURVEY OF PUBLIC ATTITUDES TOWARDS COMPUTERS IN SOCIETY

	ADULT (N=300)		YOUTH (N=543)	
	Strongly or Mostly Agree	Strongly or Mostly Disagree	Strongly or Mostly Agree	Strongly or Mostly Disagree
Computer Impact on the Quality of Life				
• Computers will improve education.	86.6%	5.9%	84.2%	4.5%
• Computers will improve law enforcement.	81.9	3.3	70.0	10.1
• Computers will improve health care.	78.6	5.3	54.1	11.9
• Credit rating data banks are a worthwhile use of computers.	64.2	13.4	64.0	7.6
Computer Threat to Society				
• A person today cannot escape the influence of computers.	91.6	4.0	66.6	17.7
• Computer polls and predictions influence the outcome of elections.	48.1	27.5	44.2	26.9
• Computers dehumanize society by treating everyone as a number.	37.4	50.3	39.9	30.6
• Computers isolate people by preventing normal social interactions among users.	18.7	62.5	20.9	42.5
Understanding the Role of Computers				
• Computers are best suited for doing repetitive, monotonous tasks.	80.0	10.3	57.0	21.6
• Computers are a tool just like a hammer or lathe.	72.6	14.7	61.3	23.4
• Computers slow down and complicate simple business operations.	17.6	66.4	17.4	68.8
• Computers will replace low-skill jobs and create jobs needing specialized training.	71.0	15.0	61.8	14.4
• Computers will create as many jobs as they eliminate.	62.5	16.4	40.0	29.1
Understanding of Computers				
• Computers are beyond the understanding of the typical person.	25.2	61.6	30.6	49.2
• Computers make mistakes at least 10% of the time.	9.6	76.7	10.3	60.0
• Programmers and operators make mistakes, but computers are, for the most part, error free.	67.0	19.3	72.3	13.3
• It is possible to design computer systems which protect the privacy of data.	60.2	26.4	48.6	15.9

NBS Privacy Conference

From April 2 to April 4, 1975, the National Bureau of Standards and the MITRE Corporation held a symposium and workshop in McLean, Virginia in order to allow computer users from business and government to exchange their views on the impact of privacy legislation. Excerpts from some of their talks follow:

Representative Edward I. Koch (D—NY):

. . . Notwithstanding the deficiencies of the Privacy Act, I feel it represents a monumental breakthrough in the field of personal privacy safeguards.

Millions of files that are locked away from the public will become available in September 1975, so that one can see one's own file, see whether the material in it is relevant, see whether it is accurate, see whether it is current, and, if it is not, provide the mechanism whereby corrections can be made. Also significant is that the Privacy Act contains a provision forbidding all agencies, including law enforcement agencies, from maintaining a record of the political and religious beliefs or activities of any individual unless expressly authorized to do so by statute or by the individual himself.

There are changes I would like to see in the Privacy Act. First of all, the law is deficient in the area covering law enforcement agencies . . . . I feel that criminal justice systems should be included in the Privacy Act until the Justice Department can come forward with a proposal that the Congress can agree upon. The second change I would like to see would be a removal of the near blanket exemption given to the CIA and a tightening up of the exemptions pertaining to the FBI. The exemptions should be limited only to those files having to do with national defense and foreign policy, those containing information held pursuant to an active criminal investigation, and those maintained for statistical purposes and not identifiable to an individual.

I feel that provisions allowing an agency to withhold from an individual the source of confidential information in his file should be deleted . . . . And, most importantly, I would like to see the establishment of a Federal Privacy Board which would monitor agencies' compliance with the Act and work in somewhat of an ombudsman's capacity and hold hearings for those individuals who want to air their grievances.

We need a broad federal policy to set the basic standard for privacy protection both in the public and in the private sector. But we have to be able to move beyond the broad approach to appreciate the specific needs of different sectors of the government and private organizations. When separate pieces of legislation come before the Congress for consideration, if privacy protections can be included, I certainly will support adding such provisions.

Joseph L. Gibson, senior attorney for Marcor, Inc.:

Recent reports have given the appearance that the privacy issue is a national crisis which suddenly sprang forth from the anti-Vietnam war movement and Watergate. That appearance is not accurate. The issue of privacy has a substantial history: current trends began a decade ago. The issue will be satisfactorily resolved, not by restating a few general principles, but only by devising a number of specific solutions for specific problems.

Charles Work, deputy administrator, Law Enforcement Assistance Administration:

I am confident that law enforcement can meet the challenges posed by the regulation and proposed legislation. I am also confident that in the long run, law enforcement and law enforcement agencies will be much better for it. Many of the enumerated requirements are not difficult to meet; a much more difficult requirement is that the records must be accurate, complete and up to date. We need systems with bank-type auditing capacity so that the defendant can be traced through the system. This is a very significant challenge, ... because if management cannot get the data into the systems, it will not meet the requirements of privacy and it will not be the system's fault. It could also be costly, because management systems cannot be significantly improved without a significant increase in manpower. But in the long run, the privacy mandate will dramatically improve the systems and must improve the overall management of concerned agencies.

Naomi Seligman, McCaffery, Seligman & von Simpson, management consultants:

One cannot speak of the impact of privacy legislation on the economy as a whole, but instead must separate its impact into three distinct sectors of data base users: government agencies, third party services — such as credit bureaus — and the broader run of U. S. business. The real costs of privacy violations to the individual clearly relate to a large number of social issues.

Almost all analyses of the issue begin with the assumption that data is always used to an individual's disadvantage; yet, many data bases are used to provide privileges which would be impossible without such data. Specific cost is very much associated with the nature of specific data disclosed about the individual. I strongly believe that the principles of the HEW Report can be achieved by general business without any of the problems or onerous costs.

Ruth M. Davis, NBS conference chairperson:

The first law that we talk about in the area of privacy came into being in 1974, 194 to 198 years after manual systems of handling information had been officially used by the U. S. and by organizations operating in the U. S. The new laws come at a time of dramatic change in electronic, optical, and communications technology. This is the setting in which we are trying to formulate actions.

One requirement (for action) is the "retrofitting of all existing information systems to make sure that they meet new legislative requirements. Second, there is a need to determine, validate and insure compliance with the laws of existing and new systems. Third, there is a need for developing and introducing the technologies that will allow the required changes in information handling so that the systems are operationally effective, legal, and economically possible. Last, we must dust off and refine good information management practices.

The privacy mandate, along with its accompanying requirements should not be taken lightly. At the same time it should be reviewed in terms of the many kinds of effects it can have.

The Fine Line between Personal Freedom and Public Security

How Much Privacy Should You Have?

by Alan Westin

Have you ever wondered what information about you is in the files of large federal service agencies such as Social Security, the Veteran's Administration, or the Agriculture Department?

If you once served in the armed forces or worked for the federal government, have you wondered what ratings or evaluations were made about you, and to whom these have been released?

If you have applied for any license administered by the federal government — to the Federal Aviation Agency as a pilot or to the Coast Guard as a boat owner — have you wondered what other government agencies or private organizations get access to the personal informa-

tion you supplied?

If you were ever arrested — including arrests for civil rights protests, political demonstrations, or marijuana offenses — have you felt worried about the FBI's dissemination of that information to local and state licensing bodies, bonding agencies, banks, or local police departments?

If you work for a business covered by federal equal employment opportunity regulations, do you know how your minority designation is listed, and what is done with it?

Have your children been part of a federally funded social research project in school? If so, were you ever told what future uses would be made of the personal and family data that was collected?

Do you find yourself wondering sometimes what federal records may

have been opened about you that you don't even know about — by the Internal Revenue Service, Army Intelligence, the Passport Office or even the White House?

Finally, have you ever asked to see what was in a federal agency's file about you, and did agency officials make it difficult or even impossible for you to do so?

If such concerns about the federal government's collection and use of personal information have occurred to you over the past few Watergate-shrouded years, or if

Dr. Alan Westin is a professor at Columbia University, New York. As an expert witness on privacy he has written extensively on the subject and testified before several Senate committees.

81

How Much Privacy Should You Have?

you have had similar thoughts about the data-collection activities of local and state governments, business corporations, schools and universities, and other organizational record-keepers in American society, you are far from alone. In 1970, a national Harris poll found that one out of three Americans was personally worried about invasions of his privacy. While eavesdropping on telephone conversations was mentioned, the most widely cited complaints involved personal data collection by organizations. These included "computers that collect too much information," credit inquiries by business, and the way the federal government collects taxes and takes the census.

Normally, what disturbs every third American gets some fairly serious attention from the nation's lawmakers. But the trouble with protection of privacy, from the surfacing of this issue in the early 1960s until 1974, was that American legislators treated it much like the weather—everyone talked about the problem but no one was willing or able to *do* anything about it.

Citizen's Rights—The Federal Privacy Act of 1974

Then came Watergate. Between 1972 and 1974, Americans learned to their shock and dismay that White House agents had ordered the tapping of the Democratic Party's telephones, the burglary of a psychiatrist's office to get confidential medical files on a Vietnam war critic, and the assembling of income-tax data and sex-life information on members of the press and political critics of the Nixon Administration.

By 1974, national polls reported that one out of *two* Americans now felt that his personal privacy was threatened.

In this Watergate-dominated atmosphere, Congress finally did act. In a move that has so far received far too little attention in the popular media, Congress passed the Federal Privacy Act of 1974, one of the potentially most important citizen's rights laws in the computer age. Since the new law governs the collection of personal data by virtually all federal agencies and gives individuals important new powers to protect themselves against abusive practices, it is crucial for the protection of privacy that the public learn just what the Privacy Act does for them.

By the time that Congress decided that it *had* to pass some major privacy legislation in 1974, at least covering the federal

government's own files, three key issues of data privacy had come into focus:

• What personal information ought to be collected at all by a given federal agency or department, to carry out its lawful functions?

• If personal information is properly collected, how can we be sure it is kept confidential within the collecting agency, for the purpose originally intended, and not shared improperly with other government officials or private organizations?

• Shouldn't individuals almost always have a legal right to inspect that record, if they wish, to check its accuracy, completeness, and lawful use?

As it faced these difficult questions of judgment, Congress was aware that far more was at stake than assuring the constitutional rights of political radicals or Mafia leaders. Hearings chaired by Senator Sam Ervin, Jr., and other Congressional leaders had documented that "derogatory information files" were being amassed on

hundreds of thousands of Americans by federal investigative agencies. Even more fundamentally, every American's access to the benefits and opportunities controlled by organizational record-keepers could be imperiled by inaccurate, incomplete, or improper data-collection practices, especially by the federal government.

By 1974, Congress had also learned through studies by the National Academy of Sciences and a Citizen's Panel report for the Department of Health, Education, and Welfare that the basic issues were not caused by *computers*, and no "pull-the-plug" decision could resolve the problem. Computerized files and databanks were increasingly the *setting* in which the social policy issues had to be faced, and computers tend to *magnify* the injuries that can be done. But Congress realized that the basic issues concerned how Americans were to be judged for various rewards and opportunities in our society, and through what kinds of fair procedures.

So the Federal Privacy Act of 1974 took a major step forward, by requiring federal agencies to follow a code of fair information practices in handling citizen information, whether in computers or on cards. Stripped of technical language, some of the Act's main sections provide that:

• Individuals must be told, whenever they are asked to give personal information, what legal authority the agency has to ask for this, whether supplying it is voluntary or required, and how it will be used.

• Individuals can inspect their own records if they wish, obtain a copy of them, and have their accuracy verified and officially corrected if found to be inaccurate.

• Individuals can find out who else besides the agency that collected the information has had access to their records.

Guidelines for Federal Agencies

As its basic framework, the Act sets out standards and procedures for federal agencies to follow as "fair information practices." Federal agencies must collect only data "relevant and necessary" to their lawful function. They *cannot* collect information about how we exercise our First Amendment rights of speech, press, association and religion, unless such collection is expressly authorized by law. Agencies must take reasonable steps to see that our records are "accurate, relevant, timely and complete."

At least once a year, each federal agency must publish a public notice about each system of personal records it maintains. This must state the system's name, location, categories of persons covered, users of the system, policies as to storage and retrieval, controls over access, and procedures for individuals to inspect and challenge their records if they wish.

Most important of all, the Federal Privacy Act makes it a crime for federal officials knowingly to violate the Act's requirements. It also gives individuals the right to sue in federal court to enforce access, correction or compliance with the Act, with damages and even lawyers' fees provided in cases of willful violations.

The Act contains a few controversial exceptions, for investigative activities of law enforcement agencies, the CIA, and certain kinds of personnel-checking inquiries. But the Act's coverage is still remarkably wide, probably reaching more than 95 percent of the record-keeping activities of the federal government.

In order to give federal agencies a chance to get their enormous file collections into good order and to install new procedures, the Privacy Act does not take effect until September of 1975. That also gives us as citizens a chance to learn what the Act does and how *we* can use it.

Memoirs of an Ex-Social Security Number Giver

by Dr. Patricia Campbell

Once when I was young and naive, I was full of pride at having a real number of my own, one that was verified by a piece of paper issued by the United States Government. I had my own unique social security number. It didn't bother me that some of my greedy friends had several social security numbers. It didn't even bother me when two of my multi-card friends found they shared the same number. After all the government was in charge of social security numbers, and they wouldn't louse up anything as important as this.

So my social security number and I continued our relationship. Its red and white card said, "Not For Identification Purposes," but what did that mean? 172-38-7613 and I were one.

As the card and I grew older and we both lost some of our shine, I memorized my number and put the card in a safe place where it could be retrieved in case of emergency or memory lapse. But there really wasn't much chance that I would forget those nine digits, because everyone kept asking me what they were. At first I proudly reeled off the number and waited for people to respond, "Oh, you memorized it." But soon I began to wonder if the Social Security Administration really needed to know about

"I want to apply for an unlisted zip code."

things like my telephone calls and my electric light bill in order to figure out how much money I was entitled to upon retirement.

So when the gas company asked for my social security number, I asked them if they were going to contribute to my social security checks. They said no, I said why do you need the number, and the clerk looked around for help. No one could tell me why they wanted that number, or what they were going to do with it, other than "put it in a computer."

A computer, me, and my unique (or almost unique) number; all of a sudden it started to make sense — the gas company, the telephone company, voter registration, the office of motor vehicles, the credit offices, and even the rent-a-car people would all have information about me under the same number. And without my permission or even knowledge, all this information, correct or not (I started remembering my two friends with the same number) could be put together. With visions of George Orwell and 1984 on one side and the Bill of Rights on the other, a private revolution was born.

The credo of this revolution would be simple and hopefully easy to live with. "NO LONGER WOULD ANYONE WHO DIDN'T HAVE A LEGAL RIGHT TO MY SOCIAL SECURITY NUMBER GET IT."

My credo was first tested when it came time to change my driver's license. As the burly state trooper asked for my social security number my resolve weakened and I asked, "What would you do if I wouldn't give you my social security number?" "Give you another number," was his response, and another number I got.

It hasn't always been that easy; in fact, a predisposition toward threatening people with your lawyer is very helpful in this revolution. Through the use of patience, threats and repetition ("You can't deny me my right to vote because I won't give you my social security number" repeated 50 times at unequal intervals works wonders), I have had numerous successes and only one failure (Federal law demands your social security number for checking accounts).

So onward I go, forever confident that when the CIA and FBI ever get around to my file, it will be a little harder for them to fill it.

(By the way, the social security number I used in the story isn't mine; I don't give my social security number, remember.)

Dr. Campbell is an Assistant Professor in Educational Foundations at Georgia State University, teaching graduate educational research and methods of evaluation. She is active in research and lecturing on sex-role stereotyping, as well as in rape prevention. She is also a member of the Board of Directors of the American Civil Liberties Union of Georgia.

Her fight against the use of social security numbers for any and everything has been a long-standing battle against invasion of personal privacy and the constant collection of unnecessary information by many private and public agencies.

Crime, Cops, Computers

by W. David Malcolm, Jr.
Acton, Mass.

A car had been burglarized. The detectives didn't have much to go on — only that three men had been seen leaving the scene in an "old tan-and-white station wagon." No make, model, year, or license number. It was clearly a case for PATRIC, the new detective's helper at the Los Angeles police department.

PATRIC (for "Pattern Recognition and Information Correlations") is a computer system that does the same kinds of things that a detective does, but does them much faster. PATRIC is crammed full of criminal records, crime reports, information on stolen vehicles, even the favorite methods of known criminals. By instantly cross-checking bits of information fed into it, PATRIC can quickly build up more and more information, and eventually come up with likely human suspects.

In this particular case, PATRIC searched its files, and found another car crime in a different part of the city, also involving men fleeing in a tan-and-white vehicle — but this time someone had remembered part of the license number and reported it. Using this partial number, PATRIC found the names of five men who had been stopped for questioning in similar cars. The computer then searched another file on past arrests, and found that three of the five men had previously been arrested for theft from an auto! PATRIC turned over the names to the human detectives, who promptly investigated and then arrested the trio for the latest burglary.

PATRIC took 15 minutes to produce the suspects; a detective would probably have decided the case was not worth spending hours or days sifting through all that information, with the likelihood that suspects couldn't be found anyway. Even when there is more information available, the computer can save hours of detective work.

Until recently, the men in blue couldn't afford much new equipment. But now they're getting funds from the federal government's Law Enforce- ment Assistance Administration (LEAA), a branch of the Justice Department. LEAA is pumping about $800 million a year into the various states, much of it going to their police organizations for equipment like PATRIC. These systems are perhaps the most significant elements of technology aiding police today. One of their biggest contributions has been a vast improvement in communications, which has always been a major problem.

In a noncomputerized police department, the dispatcher at the station house is flooded with radio calls from the cruisers, crime reports coming in by telephone, and other messages. During peak crime hours the dispatchers are frequently overwhelmed; sometimes police radio channels get so clogged that the policemen can't get through to the dispatcher half the time.

Now many police forces are installing computer terminals in patrol cars. Connected by their own radio frequencies to central computers, the terminals allow patrolmen to bypass the overworked dispatcher when they want certain kinds of information, like license numbers on hot cars and rap sheets on suspects picked up in the field. A cop in the cruiser queries the computer using a keyboard on the terminal, and gets an answer in seconds. In one case, two patrol cars carrying test terminals for a month recently made seven times as many "hits" on hot cars as they did without them. This was because they were able to make many more inuqiries through the computer than any human dispatcher could handle.

Checking Everything in Sight

The sheriff's department in Palm Beach, Florida has been using in-car terminals for almost a year, and patrolmen hare having a field day catching car thieves. They just keep poking thousands of license numbers on everything in sight into their computer system to see if the vehicles have been reported stolen. When it's quiet, they go through motel and other parking lots looking for numbers. Since the terminals went in, stolen car recoveries have climbed 60%!

The Palm Beach system uses solid-state plasma display and keyboard terminals that are located in each patrol car, hooked up to a 28K, 1.2 million bit PDP-11 controller in the main communications center. The inquiry/response mode is activated by the patrolman pressing special keys which are coded for particular messages. Requested information on, for example, whether a car is "hot" or not, who is the registered owner, and is the person wanted, is received back on the display in six to eight seconds. This response time compares with voice transmission (such as "Harry, could you query the computer regarding a John Jackson?") turnaround time of 90 seconds.

Besides the obvious advantage in rapid apprehension of criminal suspects, this reduction of time delays is also saving officers' lives. When the information turns out to be a "hit" (car or person wanted), an alarm is rung from the communications center. The dispatcher then reports the location of that patrolman on the displays of all cars in the field; the investigating officers also knows to use caution in the apprehension.

Another safety device is the emergency key. When an officer stops a car, he first enters the time and location on the terminal. If, at the end of three minutes, he has not reported back to the control center via the terminal, an emergency signal sounds in the center, and the location of the officer, who presumably needs help, is flashed onto all other terminals in the field.

Depending on the circumstances, the officer in the field can get a great deal of information concerning a vehicle or a person under suspicion. One interesting case occurred when the computer was first installed in Palm Beach. Someone standing outside a closed gas station at 2 a.m. looked suspicious to the road patrolman. So the patrolman stopped and asked "What are you doing here?" and the man replied "Just waiting for my buddy, just going to go fishing." The patrolman got his identification and entered it in the terminal in the car, and it came back that the guy was not wanted. So the patrolman queried the terminal if the fellow had an arrest record. It came back that the guy was a specialist in breaking into gas stations. So the patrolman went back to the man and asked, "Have you ever been arrested?" The man replied, "No, I have never been in no trouble, I'm just going fishing." The the patrolman brought the guy over to the car and said, "Do you see that screen?" And the guy said, "Oh, s---." Needless to say, he had already been in the gas station and was on his way out when he got caught. He just copped out right there, and that was the end of the ball game!

References:

The Wall Street Journal, Monday, March 18, 1974 "*Modern Detection* — Police Weapons Range From Electronic Cops To Glowing Bacteria"
Datamation, September 1973, pp. 88-90 "Law Enforcement Communications Conference" by Wendy Reid.

IN THE 1960's THE U.S. ARMY EMPLOYED OVER 1,500 PLAINCLOTHESMEN WHO WERE REPORTING ON INDIVIDUALS TO ITS MANY DATA BANKS

Is Big Brother Watching You?

The NATIONAL CRIME INFORMATION CENTER (NCIC) may have information about you. To find out what the FBI knows about you, send $5 and a set of rolled-ink fingerprints (which you can get from your local police station) taken on a fingerprint card, and containing your name and birth date, to: FBI, Identification Division, Washington D.C. 20537. Inaccurate data on your record can be corrected by contacting the agency that originally provided the information to the FBI.

PROSECUTOR MANAGEMENT INFORMATION SYSTEM

by Susan Hastings

PROMIS (Prosecutor's Management Information System) is a computer-based system for public prosecution agencies. Developed by the Institute for Law and Social Research under a grant from the U.S. Department of Justice Law Enforcement Assistance Administration (LEAA), PROMIS has been in operation in Washington, D.C. since January 1971.

While there can be no substitute for skilled, experienced prosecutors, PROMIS permits a prosecutor's office to accumulate a wealth of information on each of its burgeoning cases and maximize what manpower is available by assuring that office operations are conducted in the context of modern managerial and administrative methods. As a prosecutor finds he can devote more time to priority areas, he can more efficiently exert positive and productive control over his workload.

One of the most important functions of PROMIS is its ability to screen the massive influx of information with which prosecutor's offices are faced. Facts are the raw material for the prosecutor. The decisions he makes about a case are based on the soundness of the facts that are available. PROMIS's computerized data base enables prosecutors to acquire and process facts in a consistently comprehensive and uniform matter.

PROMIS gives prosecutors a method by which they can evaluate and rate cases in terms of the gravity of the crime and the accused criminal's background. Cases can be rated evenly through computer-generated numerical scores, thus giving the chief prosecutor the managerial leverage he needs to apportion his office's time and manpower according to the relative importance of pending cases. He can then assign the priority for more intensive pre-trial preparation to the cases which involve violent crime and habitual criminals.

Because of the massive caseload faced by prosecutor's offices, many serious offenders often avoid proper punishment because the responsibility for their cases has been fragmented and/or delayed to the point where the court-wise repeat defendant is able to maneuver his case through the cracks in the system. PROMIS however, can help to alleviate this problem by generating, five days ahead of time, a calendar that ranks in descending order of importance the cases a court will try on a particular day. The prosecutor's office can than allocate its manpower to prepare itself sufficiently for the most serious cases.

The judicial process cannot function without the active cooperation of citizen jurors and witnesses, but witnesses are often disillusioned by court scheduling conflicts. PROMIS enables a Witness Notification Unit to locate and subpoena witnesses in order to schedule their appearance in court. It also tries to provide a coordination of scheduling that is convenient to everyone in order to avoid the delays that often prove inconvenient, confusing and unnecessarily frustrating.

The implementation of PROMIS in Washington, D.C. has heightened awareness about the utility of legal paraprofessionals. These non-lawyer college graduates perform time-consuming duties that do not require the specialized training of an attorney. PROMIS made it obvious that full documentation of reasons for prosecutorial actions was not being made, and the visibility of this problem led to the creation of the paralegal positions. As the procedures of the prosecutor's office became better structured and more systematized through PROMIS, there is indication that more and more tasks will fall within the capabilities of paralegals, and skilled attorneys will be able to direct their abilities more fully toward case preparation and prosecution. Additionally, errors and omissions which might occur when an overtaxed attorney is charged with the duties of citizen interviews and case documentation, might be lessened as paraprofessionals take over this ministerial task.

Just as PROMIS has demonstrated the need for paralegals, it can also be used to pinpoint the areas in which they should be trained. PROMIS-produced data which can gauge the effectiveness of a given training program can also indicate areas in which prosecutors themselves need further training.

The reach of the prosecutor extends from one end of the criminal justice system to the other, starting with the police and ending with corrections. With the advent of PROMIS, prosecutors possess a potent tool that will help them take full advantage of their position within the system. A 1970 statement by Chief Justice Warren E. Burger expresses the need that people in this country feel for such an aid:

"In the supermarket age, we are trying to operate the courts with cracker-barrel corner grocer methods and equipment — vintage 1900 . . . the judicial processes for resolving cases and controversies have remained essentially static for 200 years. That is not necessarily bad, but when courts are not able to keep up with their work it suggests the need for a hard new look at our procedures." A method like PROMIS that enables prosecutor's offices to collect data on a routine and systematic basis, may well prove the answer to increasing the effectiveness of our criminal court system.

[For more information, write C. Madison Brewer, Institute for Law and Social Research, 1125 15th St. NW, Suite 625, Washington, D.C. 20005.]

A computerized Criminal Justice System

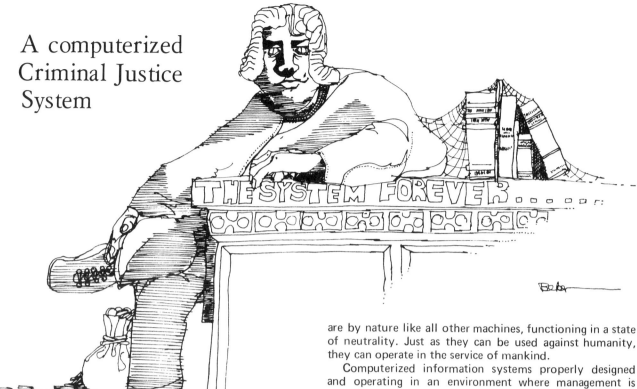

by Melvin F. Boekelman
Police Dept., Kansas City, Mo.

We live today, in a time in which 90% of the scientists who have ever lived, are now living; at a time in which knowledge, that prior to this century doubled every 50 years, now doubles every five years; a time in which the dramatic technological advances of the electronic computer have given us the capability to calculate information 500 times faster than we could prior to World War II. Leading economists have stated that automation is by now so deeply implanted in our economy that we are beyond the point of no return to non-automated systems. As a result of its powerful calculating capabilities, the electronic computer is today making us aware of many facts and theories that have been hidden from us since the beginning of time. It is the computer, more than any other facet of modern day technology, that is providing the capability to solve the complex problems of our environment.

While overwhelming evidence convincingly supports automation, we have been confronted with a great uproar of anti-computerism from segments of our society. There is a fear that reducing the human being to a number means the loss of identity and that this is representative of all that is demoralizing and degrading to our society. It has been suggested that people hate computers because they are the first machine in history to really move in on our intellectual and emotional lives. The machine is suspected of recording everything in our lives from the womb to the tomb, and is thought to replace the activities of numerous individuals.

Records that can tell a great deal about one's activities, habits, associations and personality characteristics can be, and are stored in the memory bank of a computer. If the data were made available under unauthorized or unethical circumstances, the result could be damaging to the individual, and eventually, to society. However, computers are by nature like all other machines, functioning in a state of neutrality. Just as they can be used against humanity, they can operate in the service of mankind.

Computerized information systems properly designed and operating in an environment where management is exercising proper controls, can provide much greater security than ever possible under manually maintained record systems. The vigorous use of these machines under controlled circumstances will prove a positive resource for the nation and the improvement of the quality of our lives.

The criminal justice system in the USA has been slow in casting aside old, outmoded, and antiquated ways of operating. Today the picture is changing rapidly as a result of automation and so are the social implications that result from the new technologies.

The Kansas City Regional Criminal Justice System uses the computer to protect the public, assist the victim, apprehend the criminal, and process the case with all the efficiency and security that can be commanded from present day technology. Records show that the Criminal Justice Data Bank Alert II is being accessed for entry of data or for inquiry of information an average of 35 times every minute of a 24 hour day. The Kansas City Regional computer is exchanging information automatically with the FBI's National Criminal Information Center 3,000 times each day. It's data base is extensive, and records on-line 26 major categories of information which total over one million on-line records. In the system, 1,000 subjects who are known to be armed, dangerous, or likely to resist arrest, are tagged.

An individual's right to privacy, whether he is a criminal or not, however, must be protected, and this is conscientiously considered in the use of the system. Mobile terminals, instead of the traditional radio systems greatly enhance the privacy and security of criminal justice data. Manual and software controls range from administering extensive personality tests to computer applicants to installing bullet proof security walls in the computer complex. Procedural Instruction 73-3 prohibits the processing of any report without the approval of the Criminal Justice Agency, and many strict policy statements about who can use the information and what he can do with it are other steps taken by the department to protect the security and confidentiality of the system.

*Condensed from an article in *Computer & Society,* Vol. 6, No. 1.

Embezzler's Guide to the Computer

by Brandt Allen
University of Virginia

Computerized embezzlement may be the best game in town. It doesn't really matter whether the target organization is profit-oriented, governmental, or a not-for-profit group. It does help the potential embezzler, however, if he is in a position of responsibility and is a "trusted" employee. He needs a basic knowledge of accounting, record-keeping, and financial statements, but he doesn't have to be a computer expert. Computer technology tends to confound auditors and managers themselves so much that they are rarely in a position to detect or prevent the embezzlement. Embezzlement is far less risky than ordinary theft, and far more rewarding. An added attraction for the embezzler is the fact that even if he should get caught, he probably wouldn't even have to go to jail. In a large percentage of cases, embezzlers aren't prosecuted because a concept dating back to English common law makes embezzlement a crime against an entity and not an individual.

Embezzlers shouldn't count on being caught though. The prognosis for successful computer-based crime is good. Virtually all of the traditional peculation opportunities of the past may be run through the computer, and a host of exciting new schemes is possible as well. The best embezzlement schemes have to be well executed to work, but the ideas are simple.

For any employee who really wants to practice this lucrative game, the best place to start is probably with a disbursements fraud. Historically, this kind of crime has accounted for more embezzlement losses than all others. The approach is really quite simple: an organization is forced into paying for goods and services that it did not receive, and payment for them is made to a bogus company. Anyone who wants to successfully accomplish this kind of fraud can do so by carefully studying his company's procedures for account-keeping, purchasing, and receiving. Vouchers and invoices have to be falsified, but for an employee in accounting or data processing, sometimes it is as simple as punching a few cards and entering them as if they were legitimate into a batch of transactions. Second-generation computer systems make this job more difficult because computer files of open purchase orders and merchandise receipts would not correspond to the various duplicate files maintained elsewhere, but this kind of danger can be minimized by stealing from inventory accounts with high activity and high value from which a certain amount of loss is "expected" by companies. If any one account isn't "hit" too hard, a company will probably tolerate the loss before it triggers a thorough investigation. Managerial style is often the key as to who gets robbed and who doesn't. Potential embezzlers should stay away from "detail men" and pick on the accounts managed by people who do not or cannot pore over financial statements, analyze the operating variances, and scrutinize the purchases, prices, terms, and inventory levels. Since all embezzlement efforts are conducted through accounting systems with a number of tests and controls, a little homework in studying the company's computer operations and controls can allay any of the dangers they might hold.

Inventories themselves can be a source of revenue to the embezzler, and it is often easier to convert goods to cash than it is fraudulent checks. Computerized inventories lend themselves to penetration for two basic reasons: they account for a large amount of material, and the controls on access systems are usually lax. One outstanding example of the possibilities of inventory theft via computer is the railroad company which lost 200 boxcars when an employee altered input data in the company's rolling stock to reflect that the cars were either scrapped or wrecked, when they were actually shipped to another company's yards.

Still another fruitful area for the embezzler is the manipulation of shipments, sales, and billing procedures. A company can be confused into shipping a product to a customer without sending a bill, or shipping something and billing it at the wrong price. Improper credits or adjustments on returned or damaged merchandise can be granted. Sales commissions, allowances, and discounts on merchandise can be manipulated. The computer makes it easy to alter shipping documents because in many computerized order-entry systems the sales record is maintained on file and is normally not updated until the order is shipped. Sales order records can be altered after the shipment has been made, but before the billing processes are started.

Payroll processing functions in large organizations offer a ready source of funds to embezzlers who understand how they operate; and employees in data processing, payroll, and programming are in ideal positions to make their schemes work. They can alter input data to pad the payroll with extra hours for themselves and others, but this is often a risky business. Simpler, and more lucrative are the schemes of creating fictitious personnel or increasing by small amounts the money withheld from employees' checks for income taxes and other purposes. Funds can often be embezzled from money destined for the payment of pensions, employment benefits, and annuities by keeping a dead beneficiary on file, and having his address changed to the embezzler's own.

Any of the schemes described could be perpetrated without the aid of the computer, but the computer actually makes them a lot easier to enforce successfully. The computer accepts all input as the truth. Access to computer records is often easier than to manual records, and an embezzler's visibility when committing the crime is a lot less. And, if a foul-up should happen to occur, people are always ready to make the computer the scape-goat.

*This article is condensed from one of the same title which appeared in *Harvard Business Review,* Jul-Aug 1975.

Credit Card Crooks

In Brooklyn, New York, there is a certain stretch of one street that is now known as Mugger's Alley. On this particular street there stands a bank computer that serves as a 24-hour-a-day cash dispenser. The customer sticks his credit card into the machine and the machine forks over a folderful of money. Then a mugger sticks his gun into the customer's back and the customer forks over the money to the mugger.

This is one example of credit card thievery. But it is by no means the only type that can occur, nor is it the most serious kind of credit card crime. Instead, picture this scene from the very near future: A new breed of electronic mugger eliminates the middleman (the credit card customer) and mugs the computer itself — electronically bypassing the various checkpoints and making the cash machine regurgitate money until it is empty. It would be the proverbial perfect crime: thousands would be stolen and there would be no witnesses, no evidence and no documentation. It may have happened already. The technology for cleaning out a money machine is known, and for an electrical engineer, it is neither difficult nor costly.

If this sophisticated kind of bank robbery has actually ever occurred either no one knows about it or no one is talking about it. Banks and computer manufacturers are working feverishly to prevent such grand larceny from taking place, but they have yet to find a way to enforce security economically.

The only solution they have come up with is the magnetic stripe, a black line on the back of many credit and charge cards. The composition of that stripe is similar to the sensitive surface of sound-recording tape. Instead of recording sounds, however, the "mag stripe" records various bits of information about the card and its holder, encoded for reading by a computer terminal for transmission to a central computer. In much the same way that a playback head on a tape recorder picks up and transmits the sounds recorded on the tape, a "reader" picks up and transmits the data encoded on a mag stripe to a centrally located computer which runs a check on the card and sends back either an all clear or a warning signal. The entire process takes only a few seconds to complete. Security provided by a mag stripe is not only quick and convenient, it also thwarts the major techniques of today's credit card thieves — stolen and altered cards.

Magnetic stripes may sound like the answer to a credit card security officer's dreams, but, unfortunately, the equipment needed to read the stripes is often too expensive for most subscribers to afford. Lawrence E. Shoemaker of Diners Club explains the situation: "Let's assume a terminal costs a thousand dollars. We have well over three hundred thousand merchants. If we supply each of them with a terminal, that's a cost of three hundred million dollars. Even if those terminals saved us as much as a half-million dollars annually, it would take us *six hundred years* to amortize the costs."

Manufacturers, including Bell Laboratories which has already developed the Transaction Telephone to try to cope with such dramatic expense, are trying to surmount the current cost obstacle of terminals. But there are still problems. Not all credit cards have the stripe, so all terminals have a provision for by-passing the mag stripe reader. Small banks to not have the equipment to take advantage of mag stripe technology at all, so they don't bother with it. Yet, mag stripes do seem to offer the best security available against credit card crime, and in 1971, the American Bankers Association gave the mag stripe its blessing.

However, it seems that as fast as technology can come up with methods of preventing crime, it can also find ways of beating those methods. Citibank of New York, one of the nation's largest credit institutions, did not share the rest of the industry's confidence in the mag stripe. It challenged 22 Cal Tech teams to thwart the system and offered $15,000 as incentive to anyone who could. Citibank had to pay off 22 prizes. Phillip H. Dorn, president of a computer security firm, says that any sophomore-level engineering student could also have built at least four or five devices to beat the system out of scraps lying around any engineering lab.

As we move into a society that bases its money handling less and less on cash transactions and more upon computerized techniques of transferring funds, there seems to be even greater reason to fear electronic robbery. Experts, however, are optimistic about the future. They cite how computers, even now, help security people to spot trends and patterns in the fraudulent use of credit cards. Thus, while increased utilization of electronics and of data processing may open some avenues for a new breed of sophisticated criminal, it may also help to close off some escape routes. The crook who manages to mug a computer could be caught by that computer.

[Adapted from "How Credit Card Crooks Pick Your Pocket" by Marvin Grosswirth, *Science Digest*, June 1975.]

Waiting for the Great Computer Rip-Off

by Susan Hastings

Computers have come to be deeply and pervasively involved in the basic business functions of our society. Top executives might die off, factories blow up, foreign subsidiaries get nationalized, but if you really want to see a company president blanch, ask him what he would do if the magnetic tapes with his accounts receivable got erased. And as sophisticated electronic and magnetic data replace manually kept books, the dangers of almost undetectable large scale crime being committed by unscrupulous computer experts is becoming a serious problem for both the manufacturers and the users of even the very most secure systems now in existence.

Data stored in machines has not only replaced old-fashioned accounting systems, but it has also gone a long way toward replacing tangible assets. According to Richard Mills, a vice-president of First National City Bank in New York, "The base form of an asset is no longer necessarily a 400-ounce gold bar; now assets are often simply magnetic wiggles on a disk." For criminal purposes, anyone familiar with computers may be able to manipulate those wiggles so that funds are fraudulently credited to an account, a bank balance is programmed never to fail, or the record of ownership of very large sums is changed. One expert has said that for a criminally-minded person with a lot of skill, it's about as difficult as "solving a hard Sunday crossword puzzle," to read, alter, and tamper with intricate programs.

Computer crime has not yet been proven to be an overwhelming source of loss, but no one really has any valid statistics as to how much subversion is actually going on. There are indications, however, that a lot more crime occurs than is ever detected. One expert puts the ratio of undiscovered to discovered crime on the order of one hundred to one. Donn Parker, the leading expert on the history of computer crime, admits that of the nearly 175 cases he has investigated, almost all were exposed accidentally.

A classic case of embezzlement via computer was uncovered accidentally last year when New York police raided a bookie and found his best customer to be an $11,000-a-year bank teller who for weeks at a time had gambled up to $30,000 a day. The man who had access to his bank's computer terminals, would simply pocket customers' deposits and type in false information to the machine, usually transferring money from long-unused accounts. By combining such elementary computer manipulations with workaday larceny, he managed to net 1.5 million dollars before he was caught.

Donn Parker has analyzed twelve cases of computer embezzlement that occurred in 1971 and found that the losses averaged $1.09 million apiece, or about ten times the average embezzlement loss. With ever larger amounts of credit and other assets moving into EDP systems it seems inevitable that more criminally inclined people with more elaborate resources will grab for the prizes so temptingly exposed. "There are something like a million programmers in the country right now," observes Willis Ware, a computer-security expert, "and if only one per cent of these were inclined to be dishonest, that's ten thousand dishonest programmers." The fact that employee dishonesty as a cause for computer related losses in business jumped from fourth to second place in all losses in just three years, may mean that it just takes time for dishonest people to learn how to take advantage of their opportunities. And even as computers themselves become more sophisticated, the criminals who attempt to subvert them become more cunning and less detectable.

With the advent of time-sharing and multi-access systems, there is opportunity for more far-ranging crime than was demonstrated in the comparatively elementary manipulations of the embezzling bank teller. Years ago college students began to exploit the possibilities of a system's vulnerability when they used their computer knowledge to read various instructors' stored exam questions. When that wasn't enough, they even learned to change their own grades. Nowadays few manufacturers or users are unaware of the lack of total security in any computer operations. Perhaps most disturbing in its implications is the result of many attacks waged by the Defense Department's "tiger teams", who try to penetrate systems being considered for defense. So far, there is no major system that has been able to withstand a dedicated attack.

Manufacturers believe that their computers can be made more crime-proof, but to do so will be expensive in both hardware costs and user convenience. Alternatives to the often laughably weak password defenses are being considered: some companies are working on devices that will only recognize a personal insignia such as the shape of a hand. Wiretapping might be avoided through the development of message scrambling devices, but the problem here is that a really ambitious criminal could use his own unscrambling computer to defeat such a device. However, even as these and many other security devices are being developed, experts are beginning to admit that a sophisticated and highly motivated thief is not likely to be deterred for long. Manufacturers say that it's pointless to bring out new systems capable of resisting attack until their customers adopt better physical security measures in their own installations as well as better screening of computer employees. Considering that it's the employees who not only have the most access to computer data, but also know the most about the intricacies and weaknesses of the systems, one can understand Robert Jackson's suggestion for preventing crime: he speculated that the first step might be to "shoot the programmer."

[Adapted from "Waiting for the Great Computer Rip-off" by Tom Alexander, *Fortune,* July 1974.]

Computer Abuse

The Need for a Rational Perspective

by David P. Snyder,
Research and Operations Analysis Division,
U. S. Internal Revenue Service*

Computers, like most modern scientific and industrial developments, have had a lot of bad press. Technology of all kinds has provided the popular media with an increasing number of themes and plots in recent years. Even documentary books about dysfunctional technological performances have made the best seller lists (e.g., *The Silent Spring, Unsafe At Any Speed*). I mention these popular treatments of technology because they are the principle means by which the general public becomes conscious of the technical aspects of its environment. Few of us have ever been inside a submarine, but most of us have a pretty good personal conception of what we think it would be like, because of the detailed representation of submarines in books and films.

And so it is that most people "know" about computers. They have read, (or read about) "1984" which has, in only 25 years, come to epitomize the public's image of the "computerized society." As required reading in many high school curricula, Mr. Orwell's social-science fiction novel has already served to give its author's name to an era that has not yet (and hopefully will never) occur. This single fictional image has become so strong that Washington bureaucracies tended to terminate their 1974 10-year plans with Fiscal Year 1985 rather than calendar year 1984 (like hotels which "skip" the 13th floor). And, in the milieu of continuing post-Watergate revelations of secret data banks, wire-taps, martini-olive transmitters and other elaborate electronic arcanery, "Orwellian" has replaced "Kafkaesque" as the most widely-used intellectual epithet.

Given such an environment, only the most hearty proponents of automation are not speaking cautiously about computers as being "two-edged" swords, whose power for social and political evil must be carefully proscribed before we can avail ourselves of their economic and intellectual benefits. Of course, it has always been easy to conceive of any technology as an anti-social force, since the existence of only one potentially destructive application will make a technology suspect. Upon the briefest reflection, we should quickly see that only the most trivial technological innovation would be completely free from such drawbacks. (The umbrella is the most recent one I can think of.) This is why it is so difficult to contrive a believable concept of Utopia; by definition, utopia must be perfect in every detail; every man a king and no one's oxen gored. By contrast, a possible socio-political nightmare may be easily conceived simply by amplifying any one of a number of existing social, technological or political imperfections.

Of course, the mention of "imperfections" raises another popular target of computer critics. Computers are not perfect; they make mistakes. Never mind that the vast bulk of these mistakes are the fault of those who programmed or loaded them. Those who mistrust computers have ample justifications for their concerns. What kind of confidence can we afford to place in a system which obstinately screws up our department store charge account for 14 consecutive months? How can we possibly assign significant responsibilities to a device which inexplicably sends sewer and refuse service bills to 3rd grade students in lieu of their report cards? In short, somewhere between the public's fictionalized and personal computer experiences there has emerged the image of a frighteningly powerful yet slow-witted and malicious servant who is not to be trusted.

Small wonder, then, that practically every innovative computer application is challenged with a flurry of adversary questions which reflect about as much substance and factual comprehension as the old, "Yes, but would you want your sister to marry one?" Let's take just one current example. Several state and local jurisdictions have recently adopted, or are considering adoption of, a computerized psychological testing service to be used by a variety of public services such as juvenile aid, correctional agencies, mental health, social welfare, and education. The economic incentive is clear enough — consulting psychologists charge $100—$200 to administer such tests, while the computer testing service will charge only $3.00—$5.00 to analyze and score a psychological profile administered by any public service employee.

Of course, our normal first reaction to such a proposal is one of horror; here is the archetype of computerized dehumanization! I am inclined to share such concerns, but not because of the use of the computer. Rather, I am extremely skeptical about our ability to accurately encapsulate an individual's psychological nature in a questionnaire, regardless of who administers it and how it is analyzed. *However,* clinical tests *have* shown that doctors, conducting medical examinations of patients with routine

*The views expressed in this article do not reflect the policies or practices of the U. S. Treasury Department, and are solely the personal professional opinions of Mr. Snyder.

Mr. Snyder is a Management Analysis Officer with the U. S. Treasury Department in Washington, D. C. A former consultant to the RAND Corporation, he is an active writer/lecturer on info-com technology and social values. He is a member of the Board of the Washington Chapter of the World Future Society, and Associate Editor of *The Bureaucrat Magazine.*

Members of panel session on "The Communications Revolution: Creating the Global Community", at the Second World Future Society General Assembly, June 3, 1975. From left to right: Stuart Brand, Publisher of the *Whole Earth Catalogue,* Robert Theobald, Socio-Economist and Author, Bob Johansen, Communications Researcher, Institute for the Future, and Dave Snyder, Management Analysis Officer, U. S. Internal Revenue Service. (Photo: Courtesy of World Future Society Photographer: Jim Mack)

ailments and using a standardized set of diagnostic criteria, are *less* accurate in their diagnoses than computers analyzing the identical criteria.

The explanation for this disparity in performances seems to relate to several factors, including the doctor's state of mind, and their reactions to extraneous aspects of the patients' physical appearance and personality. The significant point here is that, for routine, repetitive situations of all sorts, where criteria/characteristic relationships are well understood and empirically demonstrable, computers do have legitimate, cost-effective application potential, and in fact, may well out-perform their human counterparts. (Computer auto diagnostics are a superior example of this sort of application.)

While we're on the subject of human shortcomings, let me bring up a couple of additional study findings of the past several years which serve, I believe, to put the computer into better perspective. For example, clinical experiments strongly suggest that human analytical processes tend to remain unchanged, even in the face of extremely high rates of dysfunction. In one test, (Goldberg, *American Psychologist,* 1970), diagnosticians were given a hypothesis about the interpretation of certain test results, along with several corroborating case histories. Using these criteria, the clinicians were given a series of test cases to analyze, receiving immediate feedback regarding the correctness of their evaluations. *It took an 80% failure rate* to make them consider abandoning the criteria they had been given and to search for a more suitable one.

Data such as this suggests that the human mind tends not to be adaptive. Yet a computer can be programmed to put reviewers on notice whenever a failure rate on a routine procedure reaches an unacceptable rate, which we would judgmentally set considerably lower than 80%. There is clinical experience which suggests further, rather severe limitations to man's cognitive and perceptual abilities. Numerous studies tend to corroborate George Miller's original hypothesis that the human mind can handle no more than 7 ± 2 different data elements at the same time. Stafford and de Neufville state not only that it is impossible for humans to make reliably consistent comparisons between objects with more than one dimension, but that human judgment, particularly in non-linear decision situations, is clouded by personal psychological utilities. (*Systems Analysis for Engineers and Managers,* McGraw Hill, 1971.)

Thus, man is not without his shortcomings as an analytical tool, as the supercilious HAL observed in Arthur Clarke's "2001". In fact, one might go so far as to suggest that man is a 'double-edged sword' whose potential for social and political evil must be carefully proscribed. An absurd analogy, and yet, of course, we do proscribe man's potential for doing wrong through our laws. And so too, I suggest, should we deal with the negative potentials of computers.

Basically, of course, when we talk about the regulation of computers, we are really talking about controlling the use and abuse of data. A variety of approaches have been suggested for the regulation of data banks. Some people have proposed that certain classes of personal data simply not be automated (or even collected at all, for that matter). Others have proposed that the collection, processing and distribution of information be licensed by the government. The most far-reaching, concrete action of this sort has been the Swedish Data Act of 1974, under which no computerized personal data file may be established or maintained without a permit issued by a Data Inspection Board, which also issues and enforces standards for file size and content, security, disclosure, and data sharing.

It is clear that there are a variety of proposals for data

bank regulation which would be workable and effective. Such proposals, however, fail to address a critical reality which will become an increasingly important central feature of the information age. This reality is that information has economic value. There is ample evidence of this in the every day life of organized social, political, and economic enterprise. Institutions spend millions of dollars on reports and studies to aid them in making correct decisions. The sale of abstracts, digests, bulletins, news and technical journals run into the billions of dollars. Mailing lists, particularly when associated with socio-economic data, are of enormous value for marketing purposes. Patent holders sell or lease the rights to use their ideas. The "all news" radio format is now the biggest money maker in the audio broadcast industry. Institutions pay millions of dollars each year to send employees to schools, seminars, and conferences ... presumably for the knowledge which the employees will acquire for use within the institution.

Of course, information has always had value, and has always been bought and sold; but never on so large a scale or in so large an amount as it is today. The primary reason for this is the complexity of the modern world. Decision-makers seek to minimize risk; with the increased variety in our society, more and more data must be gathered and analyzed in order to determine the probabilities associated with a given decision. It is clear that this situation will continue to accelerate as individuals and institutions seek to improve upon the sub-optimal decisions of the recent past. Thus, the compilation, analysis, and distribution of information will become a vital global industry in the coming decade. Some have speculated that it will become the dominant industry. Given these circumstances, it would seem extremely desirable and patently reasonable that we should immediately begin to treat information as an economic commodity.

First, it should be pointed out that the courts have long linked the protection of personal privacy to the legal conception of property rights. In this context, the unauthorized acquisition and/or dissemination of private information has been treated under the laws pertaining to trespass; while the unauthorized distribution of legitimately acquired data is regarded as a breach of contract. (The new Swedish Data Act established "Data Trespass" as a new form of crime.) Thus, for most personal data, the law is already well established with regard to the treatment of information as a commodity.

However, an economic link between an individual's personal data and its use for purposes other than that for which it was originally solicited has *not* been established. As a result, credit card firms or universities may sell to third parties data which they have required of their card holders or their students, although the original "owners" of the data receive no compensation. Further, governmental authorities require many institutions to provide them with aggregate data, at no cost, for the purpose of public policy and law making. If the economic nature of data were established, data would be paid for as with any other resource, and individual persons or corporations would receive some remuneration for the use of their individual data. Further, if the principles of information economics were widely practiced, institutions would cease to view data as a "free commodity", and much unnecessary, inefficient or duplicative reporting would be dropped. Direct, economic incentives for increased efficiency in data handling would be far more effective in curtailing burdensome public reporting requirements than a dozen Hoover Commissions.

Let us examine how such an arrangement might work. A principle candidate for the economic treatment of data would be the nation's banking and financial institutions. These organizations, which possess vast amounts of personal data, will soon acquire even more, with the completion of the Electronic Funds Transfer System (EFTS), and the accelerating evolution of the so-called "cashless society", through the expanded use of point-of-sale terminals and direct electronic transactions, such as consolidated payrolling. The more than 40,000 financial institutions who will participate in the EFTS will comprise a massive distributed data base, from which enormously valuable economic information might be generated on a para-real time basis.

If the present non-economic view of data continues, these financial institutions would conceivably generate some limited saleable information from their vast data-net whenever it was an attractive spinoff from normal operations. Presently contemplated legislation would, however, put up serious barriers to the use of personal data for purposes other than that for which it was originally collected. (Such legislations would generally promote the necessity of duplicative data gathering throughout the nation, in order to protect personal privacy.) If, however, a formal information economy were to be promoted, the EFTS might be used to generate great quantities of vital data for sale to the public and private sector, with a portion of the profits to be returned to the customer/owners of the initial inputs, perhaps in the form of additional interest on their savings accounts. The published data from such a system would be no more intrusive upon personal privacy than Census data, and would be collected as a by-product of customer transactions.

Ultimately, such an arrangement could evolve into a wholly new institution, a data banking system (DBS). The regulation of a DBS would take form similar to that already applied to the nation's money banks. Data Banks would be fiduciaries for the information they hold, just as regular banks are fiduciaries for the money they hold. There would be penalties for the violation of the fiduciary trust, such as misuse or misappropriation of personal information. *And,* of course, just as individuals are subject to penalties for passing bad checks or counterfeit money, so too would individuals be subject to penalties for giving false information about themselves to the bank. The recognition of information's economic value would promote institutional interest and resource commitments in the protection of data, similar to those control and accountability measures which organizations take to protect inventories of other costly resources.

Of course, many people would argue that such a proposal does not come to grips with the critical social and technological problems inherent in controlling computers and protecting personal privacy. I do not agree. *Any approach to regulating info-com technology will be less than perfect;* just as any approach to regulating the banking industry will permit some misappropriation of funds, and once in a great while, a bank failure. Those who anticipate the development of a fool-proof data protection technology based upon voice or fingerprint analysis or some other such esoterica simply do not understand the problem. So long as there is potential gain to be derived from the misuse of personal data, it will be misused. As with other human transgressions, laws must be enacted and enforced against "data trespass", and other information related crimes. Laws should *not* be passed constraining the use of info-com technology, any more than laws should have been passed against automobiles in the early 1900's (e.g., Laws which required a driver to proceed his automobile by several hundred yards, on foot, to warn citizens of his vehicle's approach. Or laws barring the use of autos between sundown and sunup, or on the Sabbath.)

Above all, we must not convince ourselves that a fool-proof data security process is essential before we can permit the development of the major information-nets and data bases essential to our present critical research and decision-making needs. In the first place, such security measures will clearly not be quickly forthcoming, if at all. But, more importantly, if we will only place our trust in technological perfection, it means we will have abandoned altogether our faith in the rule of law, in our institutions, and in our fellow men. *This would bring about the true dehumanization of automation — a society in which trust is reserved for perfect, inviolable systems*. There will be risks involved with the creation of the information society, just as there have been risks in all of mankind's great adventures. The risk-avoiding alternatives available to us are the sterile pursuit of problematical technical perfection, or the stagnation and decay of inaction. I, for one, would prefer to accept the computer, 'warts and all'. The game, as they say, will be worth the candle.

[Note: Whatever mechanism is evolved to manage and control info-com technology, it seems apparent that, within 10—15 years, we will see an information industry regulated like a public utility, with profit margins and capital investment priorities, controlled by public commissions.]

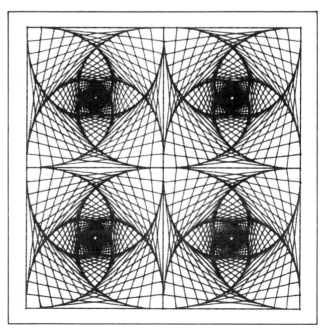

Doomsday, Says MIT Computer, May Be Just 100 Years Away

By Robert Reinhold

CAMBRIDGE, Mass. (NYT).— A major computer study of world trends has concluded, as many have feared, that mankind probably faces an uncontrollable and disastrous collapse of its society within 100 years unless it moves speedily to establish a "global equilibrium" in which the growth of population and of industrial output are halted.

Such is the urgency of the situation, the study's sponsors say, that the slowing of growth constitutes the "primary task facing humanity" and will demand international cooperation "on a scale and scope without precedent." They concede that such a task will require "a Copernican revolution of the mind."

The study, which is being sharply challenged by other experts, was an attempt to peer into the future by building a mathematical model of the world system, examining the highly complex interrelations among population, food supply, natural resources, pollution and industrial production.

The conclusions are rekindling an intellectual debate over a question that is at least as old as the early economists, Thomas Malthus and John Stuart Mill: Will human population ultimately grow so large that the earth's finite resources will be totally consumed and, if so, how near is the day of doom?

Club of Rome

The study was conducted at the Massachusetts Institute of Technology under the auspices of the Club of Rome. In the findings, to be published Thursday by the Potomac Associates under the title "The Limits to Growth," the MIT group argues that the limits are very near—unless the "will" is generated to begin a "controlled, orderly transition from growth to global equilibrium."

The study would seem to bolster some of the warnings of environmentalists. In Britain, for example, a group of 33 leading scientists issued a "blueprint for survival" in January, calling on the nation to halve its population and heavily tax the use of raw materials and power.

But others, particularly economists, are skeptical.

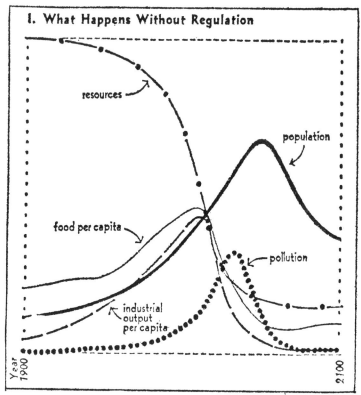

I. What Happens Without Regulation

resources

population

food per capita

pollution

industrial output per capita

Year 1900

2100

The New York Times

This computer "run" by MIT group, using five key growth factors to the year 2100, shows rapidly diminishing resources eventually slowing growth, assuming no major change in physical, economic or social relationships. Time lags in decline of population and pollution are attributed to natural delays in the system. Population rise is finally halted by an increase in the death rate.

"It's just utter nonsense," remarked one leading economist, who asked that he not be identified. He added that he felt there was little evidence that the MIT computer model represented reality or that it was based on scientific data that could be tested.

Another economist, Simon S. Kuznets of Harvard, a Nobel Prize-winning authority on the economic growth of nations, said he had not examined the MIT work first hand, but he expressed doubt about the wisdom of stopping growth.

"It's a simplistic kind of conclusion—you have problems, and you solve them by stopping all sources of change," he said.

Others, like Henry C. Wallich of Yale, say a no-growth economy is hard to imagine, much less achieve, and might serve to lock poor cultures into their poverty.

"I get some solace from the fact that these scares have happened many times before—this is Malthus again," he said.

Malthus, the 19th-century British economist, theorized somewhat prematurely that population growth at rates that could be graphically represented as a rising curve would soon outstrip available food supply. He did not foresee the Industrial Revolution.

Prof. Dennis L. Meadows, a management specialist who directed the MIT study—which is the first phase of the Club of Rome's "Project on the Predicament of Mankind"—conceded that the model was "imperfect," but said that it was based on much "real world" data and was better than any previous similar attempt.

The report contends that the world "cannot wait for perfect models and total understanding." To this Dr. Meadows added in an interview: "Our view is that we don't have any alternative—it's not as though we can choose to keep growing or not. We are certainly going to stop growing. The question is, do we do it in a way that is most consistent with our goals or do we just let nature take its course."

Letting nature take its course, the MIT group says, will probably mean a precipitous drop in population before the year 2100, presumably through disease and starvation. The computer indicates that the following would happen:

● With growing population, industrial capacity rises, along with its demand for oil, metals and other resources.

● As wells and mines are exhausted, prices go up, leaving less money for reinvestment in future growth.

● Finally, when investment falls below depreciation of manufacturing facilities, the industrial base collapses, along with services and agriculture.

● Later, population plunges from lack of food and medical services.

All this grows out of an adaptation of a sophisticated method of coming to grips with complexity called "systems analysis." In it, a complex system is broken into components and the relationships between them reduced to mathematical equations to give an approximation, or model, of reality.

Then a computer is used to manipulate the elements to simulate how the system will change with time. It can show how a given policy change might affect all other factors.

If human behavior is considered a system, then birth and death rates, food and industrial

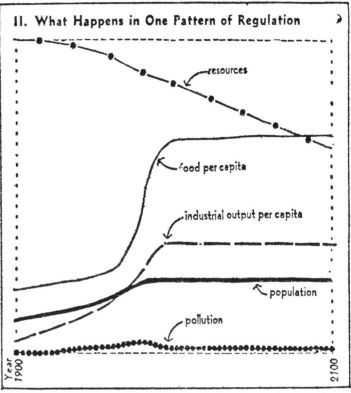

II. What Happens in One Pattern of Regulation

resources

food per capita

industrial output per capita

population

pollution

Year 1900 — 2100

The New York Times.

Another computer "run" by the MIT group projects a relatively stable future on the assumption that "technology policies" are combined with other growth-regulating mechanisms. The study says policies would include resources recycling, pollution control devices, increased lifetimes of all forms of capital, and methods to restore and renew eroded and infertile soil.

production, pollution and use of natural resources are all part of a great interlocking web in which a change in any one factor will have some impact on the others.

For example, industrial output influences food production, which in turn affects human mortality. This ultimately controls population level, which returns to affect industrial output, completing what is known as an "automatic feedback loop."

Drawing on the work of Prof. Jay W. Forrester of MIT, who has pioneered in computer simulation, the MIT team built dozens of loops that they believe describe the interactions in the world system.

They then attempted to assign equations to each of the 100 or so "causal links" between the variables in the loops, taking into account such things as psychological factors in fertility and the

The Limits to Growth report, which this article is about, originally appeared in March 1972. This "Doomsday . . ." article is the original New York Times news release. Since that time, various reports from the Club of Rome, but particularly *The Limits to Growth* have spurred much spirited debate and controversy. The computer model used is most certainly one of the most sophisticated ever devised. But is it correct? Does it take into account man's phenomenal adaptability and ingenuity?

In future issues, these pages will be available for your serious discussion about *The Limits to Growth* and related computer simulations.

biological effects of pollutants.

Critics say this is perhaps the weakest part of the study because the equations are based in large part on opinion rather than proved fact, unavailable in most cases. Dr. Meadows counters that the numbers are good because the model fits the actual trends from 1900 to 1970.

The model was used to test the impact of various alternative future policies designed to ward off the world collapse envisioned if no action is taken.

For example, it is often argued that continuing technological advances, such as nuclear power, will keep pushing back the limits of economic and population growth.

Little Benefit

To test this argument, the MIT team assumed that resources were doubled and that recycling reduced demand for them to one-fourth. The computer run found little benefit in this since pollution became overwhelming and caused collapse.

Adding pollution control to the assumptions was no better; food production dropped. Even assuming "unlimited" resources, pollution control, better agricultural productivity and effective birth control, the world system eventually grinds to a halt with rise in pollution, falling food output and falling population.

"Our attempts to use even the most optimistic estimates of the benefits of technology," the report said, "did not, in any case postpone the collapse beyond the year 2100."

Skeptics argue that there is no way to imagine what kind of spectacular new technologies are over the horizon.

"If we were building and making cars the way we did 30 years ago we would have run out of steel before now, I imagine, but you get substitution of materials," said Robert M. Solow, an MIT economist not connected with the Club of Rome project.

At any rate, the MIT group went on to test the impact of other approaches, such as stabilizing population and industrial capacity.

Zero population growth alone did very little, since industrial output continued to grow, it was found. If both population and industrial growth are stabilized by 1985, then world stability is achieved for a time, but sooner or later resource shortages develop, the study said.

Ultimately, by testing different variations, the team came up with a system that they believe capable of satisfying the basic material requirements of mankind yet sustainable without sudden collapse. They said such a world would require the following:

● Stabilization of population and industrial capacity.

● Sharp reduction in pollution and in resource consumption per unit of industrial output.

● Introduction of efficient technological methods—recycling of resources, pollution control, restoration of eroded land and prolonged use of capital.

● Shift in emphasis away from factory-produced goods toward food and nonmaterial services, such as education and health.

The report is vague about how all this is to be achieved in a world in which leaders often disagree even over the shape of a conference table.

Even so, critics are not sanguine about what kind of a world it would be. Dr. Meadows agrees it would not be a Utopia, but nevertheless does not foresee stagnation.

"A society released from struggling with the many problems caused by growth may have more energy and ingenuity available for solving other problems," he says, citing such pursuits as education, arts, music and religion.

Many economists doubt that a no-growth world is possible. Given human motivations and diversity, they say, there will always be instability.

"The only way to make it stable is to assume that people will become very routine-minded, with no independent thought and very little freedom, each generation doing exactly what the last did," says Dr. Wallich. "I can't say I'm enamored with that vision."

What of Africa?

"Can you expect billions of Asians and Africans to live forever at roughly their standard of living while we go on forever at ours?" asked Dr. Solow.

Dr. Wallich terms no-growth "an upper-income baby," adding: "They've got enough money, and now they want a world fit for them to travel in and look at the poor."

The MIT team agrees that there is no assurance that "humanity's moral resources would be sufficient to solve the problem of income distribution." But, it contends, "there is even less assurance that such social problems will be solved in the present state of growth, which is straining both the moral and physical resources of the world's people."

The report ends hopefully, stating that man has what is physically needed to create a lasting society.

"The two missing ingredients are a realistic long-term goal that can guide mankind to the equilibrium society and the human will to achieve that goal," it observes.

Collaborating with Dr. Meadows in writing "The Limits to Growth," were his wife, Donella, a biophysicist; Jorgen Randers, a physicist, and William W. Behrens 3d, an engineer. They were part of a 17-member international team working with more than $200,000 in grants from the Volkswagen Foundation in Germany.

Growth for the sake of growth is the ideology of the cancer cell
— Ed Abbey

All animals, except man adapt according to their environment. Man changes his environment, making it adapt to him
— R. Buckminster Fuller

Why Supermarkets Are Going Bananas Over Computers

by Chris Barnett

Better profits in the long run, and shorter lines at the checkstand. Will It Really Work?

One Saturday late last June, Jim and Sharon Roberts of Troy, Ohio, noticed something strange when they walked into Marsh's Supermarket to do their weekly shopping. The checkers weren't pounding on the cash registers like they normally do. Instead they were simply sliding each item across a smoky glass window built into the newly installed checkstands.

Just by passing the item across the glass, the price automatically appeared on a readout sign, the untouched cash register recorded the sale and the register tape spelled out each item purchased, sometimes by brand name, along with the price.

The Robertes quickly discovered that their neighborhood supermarket had been turned into a laboratory; National Cash Register Company and Marsh's Supermarkets, Incorporated, had selected the Troy store to test some unusual new equipment. An electronic scanner that automatically "reads" a code affixed to every item in the store, feeds everything it reads into a computer in the backroom and gives manager Earl Frysinger a mountain of facts and figures designed to help him run the store more effectively and more profitably had replaced the good old cash register.

What's more, the test results at the Marsh's store, together with findings of other market tests of additional scanning equipment around the

country, are destined to have a devastating impact—not only on the lives of millions of American shoppers but on the entire grocery industry—wholesalers and retailers as well as the manufacturers of every item you find on your foodstore's shelves.

Overstatement? Figure it out for yourself. At this very moment salesmen for over a dozen of the nation's biggest or most aggressive business machine and data processing equipment makers are amorously courting retail food chains to persuade them to computerize their checkout systems, indeed the entire store operation—from buying to inventory control to cash flow.

The retailers, cautious but not all that skeptical, recognize they can no

Illustration by John Dearstyne

longer be leery of the computer, the magical machine that's cut costs, beefed up production and delivered decision making data for so many other industries in today's business community. In boardroom after boardroom, food chain executives, who've traditionally resisted automation for a handful of reasons, are making major decisions to commit mammoth amounts of capital in a last ditch attempt to fatten their wafer-thin profit margins.

The Postage Stamp Code

But for the first time, food chains are possibly finding it a little easier to make that "go or no go" decision. It all appears to hinge on a code the size of a postage stamp that is revolutionizing everything. It's called the Universal Product Code, and thanks to a massive cooperative effort by virtually every American grocery product manufacturer, the UPC will be "source marked." In other words, the price code is put on at the plant, not stamped on at the store. This alone should result in considerable savings (some say 20 percent) in labor costs.

Not surprisingly, UPC implementation is not happening overnight. Nevertheless, the Uniform Grocery Product Code Council, with its 1300 company members representing a collective $63 billion in annual retail sales, has pulled out all the stops to get it moving.

Spurred on by an outfit called Distribution Codes, Incorporated, tabbed to ramrod the project, the code,

adopted industrywide in April, 1973, should be on the labels or packages of 50 percent of the stores' shelf stock by year end. If all goes according to plan, 80 percent of the products should be source marked by midyear to fall of 1975. Once source marketing hits 80 percent, many scanning equipment makers think the food chains will be banging on their doors.

Meantime, there is plenty of groundwork to be laid. Manufacturers of the Point of Sale (POS) equipment have lots of selling to do. Many of the equipment makers have proven the benefits of POS, including scanning, to the general merchandise or nonfood sectors of retailing. Singer, whose Business Machines Division claims the leadership position (with over 50 percent of the market) in POS, has long served retailing giants like J.C. Penney and Sears, Roebuck; now it's scrambling for supermarkets.

Also in the race is Litton Industries' Sweda International Division, a major factor in retailing POS systems here and abroad; Sperry-Univac, which conducted the historic Kroger test and thus the first maker to scan a code; the ESIS Division of Bunker Ramo, said to be the leader in electronic information systems for supermarkets; and National Semiconductor Corporation, a highly aggressive Santa Clara, California, concern. Then, of course, there is NCR Corporation (new name for National Cash Register, a retailing household word that is reportedly number two in POS).

Almost all the foregoing firms offer

a modular approach—an electronic cash register (either stand alone or hooked to a minicomputer in the backroom) that can be upgraded to a scanner setup when the store, the manufacturers and the public are ready.

All or Nothing

A comparatively late entry to electronic POS is giant IBM Corporation, which has introduced both a supermarket and a general merchandise version. As might be expected, IBM is taking an altogether different marketing approach, at least in the grocery field. The big computer maker produces the terminal or cash register and the scanner but it will not sell them separately. Its supermarket system, dubbed the 3660, also includes a "store controller," a backroom minicomputer that monitors and memorizes the activities of up to 24 terminals and scanners. Buy the whole package or forget it.

Other firms are going their own way, too. MSI Data Corporation of Costa Mesa, California, has welded together a team of grocerymen and data processing types and are wooing supermarket accounts exclusively. The hardware, of course, is heavily pitched, but the company also stresses a series of software programs aimed at showing the manager how to use his newly collected data. Still others that have developed supermarket scanner systems include Data Terminal Systems, Incorporated, of Maynard, Massachusetts, and Norand Corporation of Cedar Rapids, Iowa. But the POS makers realize that selling the retailer is only half the sale. Most companies are vitally concerned with the reaction of the shopper. Electronic cash registers have made some headway in speeding up the lines at the cash register but the scanners should make them move even faster, believes Charles S. Adams, senior vice-president—marketing for Sweda International in Morristown, New Jersey. "It should also provide for greater accuracy at the checkstand and fewer missrings since the terminal automatically 'looks up' the price of each item."

No More Waiting?

Some retailers also think the scanner systems will put an end to many of their customer complaints. "Studies have indicated that waiting to be checked out is high on the list of customer aggravations," says John Rob-

Scanning foodstuffs becomes a piece-of-cake for checkers, with no need to line up item and machine. Photo courtesy of NCR Corp.

ertson, vice-president of information systems for Ralphs Grocery Company in Los Angeles. "We hope customer delay at the checkstand will be minimized by automatic handling of some of the more tedious transactions like check cashing, coupon redemptions, bottle returns and food stamps."

Ralphs, which planned to test the IBM 3660 system in its Lakewood, California, store last month, is pushing hard on customer service. "Accuracy is the big word," notes Robertson. "With the prices of most items retrieved from the store computer, the customer will not miss any sale or promotional price, and will always be charged the correct amount of sales tax on the correct taxable item."

Some consumer groups and other vocal shoppers have already registered their displeasure with the move to automate grocery checkstands. They have no objections to swift moving lines or the automatic dispensing of trading stamps. What they are objecting to is the grocery industry's concerted move to eliminate price stamping on each item.

Complains one Chicago housewife: "I just can't imagine going into a store and comparing can goods where there is no price marked on the top. You can't compare the codes, I understand, and the shelf tags are always jumbled up. I don't know how it's going to work. I just don't see it."

Jim Roberts, the Troy, Ohio, policeman who likes to "go to the grocery store" with his wife Sharon, agrees. Commenting on the test now underway at Marsh's, Roberts reports that the scanners "don't pick up all the prices all of the time." Evidencing a basic distrust of computers, he says the "worst thing they could do is take off all the old prices. If the thing (the scanner) is not set right, it could be eating you alive and you'd never know it."

Store manager Earl Frysinger says the test at Marsh's is going "very well. It's given us faster front end service and more accurate cash control, plus it's simplified our office bookkeeping." How are customers reacting to the test? "We haven't had too much controversy," he replies. "But, then, we held a meeting with 24 housewives beforehand and explained it to all of them." Still, every item in the store is double priced—UPC coded and stamped on top. Mr. Frysinger has no idea when he'll drop the stamped price.

What your "new" shopping receipt might look like after the computer computes it. Photo courtesy of IBM Corp.

Probably not for a long while. Robert Cottrell, vice-president of store operations for The Kroger Company of Cincinnati, reported that its experimentation with RCA on automated checkout (since taken over by Sperry Univac) showed that shoppers react "negatively" when the prices are scrubbed.

"The removal of individual item pricing on dry goods," he explained in a recent report, "as expected, resulted in significant declines in the rating of the Kroger test store for 'adequate price information.'" Shelf strips are not a fully accepted replacement for item pricing, he added.

Clearly, the price stamping question is a hot potato now and few POS equipment makers are willing to address themselves to it publicly. Others, like Richard Baily, president of the Singer Company's Business Machines Division, takes the more positive approach and contends that it will take some patience and education, but within a couple of years at most, coded items will be smoothly sailing across the scanner and no objections will be heard.

Patience and education seem to be the watchwords today when it comes to POS and particularly scanning. As noted earlier, retailers are clearly interested; scanning equipment makers drew record crowds at the Super Market Institute's convention in Dallas last May. But price is a stumbling block for many chains. Price of an eight terminal IBM system at the Dallas show was $118,760, according to Supermarket News, the industry trade-paper, while Univac asked $106,700 for a five checkout lane scanning system.

Nevertheless, some chains are putting their toes in the water and going the minicomputer-linked-to-an-electronic-cash-register route. Singer, for example, has signed Mayfair Markets in Los Angeles; Sweda International has a contract from Albertson's of Boise; National Semiconductor is working closely with Alpha Beta throughout California and Arizona and NCR Corporation has a half dozen client grocery chains including A&P and Public Super Markets, as well as Marsh.

Others like National Tea Company of Chicago (515 supermarkets in the Midwest and central United States) are going to have to be shown. "Scanning is still kind of nebulous," shrugs John Loper, vice-president of construction. "We don't know who is going to emerge with the best equipment." Loper thinks scanning would work best in a new store. "It's too expensive to install it in an existing store." The chain is testing two electronic cash register/minicomputer systems, one in Chicago, the other in St. Louis.

What are the Goliaths of the food retailers doing? An A&P spokesman says nothing concrete is happening in connection with POS systems. Meantime, on the West Coast, Oakland-based Safeway Stores is still mulling over the results of an eight-month scanning test completed a year ago. It was installed, said a formal company statement, "to evaluate the degree of improvement such a system can provide in the actual operation of a supermarket."

How did it go? Replies a Safeway spokesman: "We don't have anything to say."

Community Memory: A Public Information Network

After twenty-five years of computer development, the question is still open as to whether this technology can be directly useful to the public. People at present generally believe that computer systems are used on them rather than for them. The few public-access systems are vertically organized, conceived primarily for delivery of computer-aided instruction and other pre-selected information, as thoroughly edited as other forms of mass information. Horizontal programs, although largely unexplored, would allow the public to take advantage of the huge and largely untapped reservoir of skills and resources that resides with the people. A critical context for use of such a system would be in community based information centers rather than terminals located only in private homes.

For the last year the Community Memory Project has been demonstrating the potential of computer-based public access communications media with a small network of public terminals in the San Francisco Bay Area. From any terminal it was possible to search a common data base using boolian combinations of keywords or to add and index new information/messages of whatever nature the user desired. Both the ease with which the public accepted the service and the imaginative uses to which it was put were surprising and gratifying. The project is currently developing hardware and software systems to move the idea from an externally financed experiment to a cheap, self-sufficient service available to everyone in the Bay Area. These systems would supply the basic tools for establishing similar services elsewhere, and provision is being made so these regional networks could be linked to form a continental information sharing network.

People in the Bay Area accepted the Community Memory Project with remarkably little hesitation and put it to a much broader range of uses than was anticipated, proving that given the tools, the public will not only provide for its own information needs but will do so with great creativity. The first of three terminals was installed adjacent to a bulletin board in a non-profit community record and music store in Berkeley. People were delighted by the chance to put a computer to use. They encouraged

their friends to use the system, instructed one another in its use, and seemed fascinated as much by the possibilities of the medium as by the technology itself. The level of acceptance was not confined to the relatively sophisticated student area, but carried over to later installations such as one at a library in San Francisco's polyglot Mission District.

Students began to use the system immediately in their search for housing, and as use of the system grew, so too did its data base. Musicians found others to practice with, buyers and sellers of instruments, and were even able to form new groups. People began to use the system to assemble car pools, organize study groups, find chess partners, and pass tips on good restaurants. More exotic uses developed: experiments were made with poems, graphics and items almost analogous to letters to the editor, but much freer in content and form. Instant publication by a "very small press" became available to all who professed literacy.

As the rate of usage and the diversity of roles of the system increased almost daily, its inherent deficiencies began to appear and offered technicians opportunities to develop and perfect the system. Although misuse of the system was not prevalent, it began to appear that malicious and obscene items, trivia, and misinformation represented the major opportunities for its abuse. Inexperience on the part of the users with typewriter keyboards, spelling errors and misunderstanding the keyword concept used presented other problems. These and other deficiencies encountered in the operation of the pilot system could be efficiently dealt with through redesigned software systems, but at the present moment, the system's efficient use really depends more upon maintenance of conviviality in the interactions of the users. It is necessary for the general public to gain a clearer sense of understanding and control over the system as a tool.

The pilot system, supporting a few terminals on a large, expensive general-purpose time-sharing computer, was not economically reasonable. It appears that by using an optimized file structure, good searching procedures, and a thoughtfully coded, mostly core resident program, more than 64 simultaneous users could be serviced by a 24K mini computer the speed of a NOVA or PDP 11/40. Such softwear is currently being developed along with custom terminal multiplexing hardware which will greatly reduce the load this many terminals place on the CPU. With the broad base for capital and maintenance costs this system provides and the use of a low-cost, people-oriented Tom Swift Terminal, costs should be less than $2000 per public access site.

The cooperative use of technology to meet human needs, rather than its competitive use to create lucrative mass markets is the basic goal of the Community Memory project. The issues of how and for whom the technology will be made to perform are becoming ever more critical. They play a deep role in the continuing economic, ecological, political, and energy crises. These issues must be dealt with by both the people who have mastered and currently control the technology and those people the technology claims to serve.

[Condensed from the *Journal of Community Communications*, Vol. 1, No. 0. Send 20¢ for copy to LGC Engineering, 1807 Delaware St., Berkeley, Ca. 94703.]

Turning On With Computer Art

A Report on the Third International Computer Art Festival

Sema Marks
City University of New York

The Image of the Computer

Computers permeate society. Yet for many people they remain mysterious, threatening, or, even worse, "evil." Unfortunately, many applications of computers most visible to the public reinforce these stereotypes and convey a decidedly unfavorable image.

When this circuit learns your job, what are you going to do? asks a public service ad displayed in buses and subways.

Applications and questionnaires: *Current salary? Have you ever contemplated suicide? Are you now or have you ever been . . .?* Computers invade our privacy. They send us bills and junk mail and foul up our charge accounts. They hold us accountable for our expenditures. They seem to monitor us. Information systems enabling womb-to-tomb surveillance are causing a serious dichotomy between our democratic heritage of individual freedom and privacy, and business and government's need to know.

Many negative feelings towards computers probably emanate from a long tradition of hostility and suspicion about technology which in any way simulates human behavior. Consider the tradition of Frankenstein and Golem. While modern day Luddites may only express their feelings by folding, stapling and mutilating punch cards (rather than smashing laboratories), they nonetheless express the view that sabotage and destruction are man's only means for dealing with these "malevolent beings."

Clearly we must face up to the problem of the computer's public image, for computers are here to stay and are becoming increasingly important in all aspects of our daily and professional lives. Ironically, it is precisely the computer which will enable man to manage and control the accelerating technological society of the future.

On one level, computer literacy is simply a question of being "in" or "out." The world is already divided between those people who know about computers and those who don't. Where some have access to computers and others do not, the balance of power, efficiency, and knowledge which can be brought to bear on a problem is clearly tipped in favor of the man-machine partnership. Knowing about computers today is a valuable asset; tomorrow it may be a matter of survival.

As we move further into the computer age and computers become more accessible to the general population, we must look for ways to turn people on to computers, their applications, their benefits. One strategy is a surprise move, a tactical end run, interesting people in computers in unexpected ways.

Computer Art

Introducing people to computers through their use in the arts is one tactic. Few know that computers can fit into *that* world. Computer art broadens people's views of what computers are all about. Many people who can't relate at all to tables of prime numbers can spend hour after hour happily listening to computer music and speech songs, and viewing computer films and videotapes.

I am using the term "computer art" to refer to any work — film, videotape, music, graphics, holography, poetry or sculpture — in which the computer plays an important role. Artists use computers for many different reasons. For some the computer provides more control over the processes and procedures they are currently using. Composers of electronic music, for example, have turned to the computer to "record" their productions. Analog synthesizers have no memory, hence they provide no way to exactly reproduce an electronic music score. Once a computer program exists, however, the composer can listen to a piece and make subtle or strong changes; he can interchange voices, slow down or speed up the tempo, and make insertions in the score.

Pierre Boulez, the noted composer and conductor, has been learning to use the computer as a new musical instrument and composing device. "You begin to compose sounds in your head and you build from experience to know what will happen next," he said. "The computer is exciting because it can be both the score and the instrument at the same time." In a total computer music system, the computer is able to generate, analyze and interpolate any sound imaginable.

[More about computer art and the views of computer artists in the special May-June 1976 art book issue of *Creative Computing*]

International Computer Art Festival

Many examples of computer art — computer music, films, videotapes, poetry, graphics and sculpture — were shown and discussed at the Third International Computer Art Festival held at the Graduate School and University Center of the City University of New York from June 12–21, 1975. Through a series of workshops, seminars, and live performances, over 1200 people shared in the world of computer art.

The quality of the work shown and demonstrated varied considerably from what might be considered "five-finger exercises" to commercially acceptable productions. "Hun-

Computer programmer and film-maker Ken Knowlton explains EXPLOR to his class. (Photograph: Louis Forsdale)

Coming off the line printer. (Photograph: Louis Forsdale)

ger,'' for example, a computer-animated film by Peter Foldes won the Special Jury Award at the Cannes Film Festival in 1974 and was nominated for an Academy Award in 1975.

My own involvement with the Festival as Director of Academic Computing of CUNY was not so much prompted by the present esthetic and technical qualities of this new medium, but rather on the belief that this is a significant new dimension with virtually unlimited artistic and scientific possibilities that need to be fostered and developed.

> *Our time is a time for crossing barriers, for erasing old categories, for probing around. When two seemingly disparate elements are imaginatively poised, put in apposition in new and unique ways, startling discoveries often result. Marshall McLuhan and Quentin Fiore.* The Medium is the Message.

My principal interest in computer art and the Festival, however, was as a tactic for interesting those people who have no reason to believe that they should have an interest in computers and computer art, or who are hostile out of ignorance to embrace the medium as a friendly tool rather than as an enemy or something beyond comprehension.

The Festival demonstrated that computer art is a very good way to turn people on to computers. Like computer games, computer art involves the "user" (sucks him in? hooks him?) in a non-threatening way. Computer art is theater. It provides entertainment. It absorbs the user and arouses his curiosity.

How does it work? How did he do that? Does he just push buttons and hope that something interesting will come

Adding a personal touch. (Photograph: Louis Forsdale)

out? How involved is the artist anyway? These questions are easily answered, particularly with some hands-on experience as we provided at the Festival.

Artist and respecter-of-art both learn rather quickly when confronted with a computer that one doesn't just push buttons and pray (or engage in some other undisclosed mathematical mumbo-jumbo). Rather one *interacts* with his tool as every artist must interact with tools: the painter with brush, canvas and paint; the musician with a variety of instruments; the dancer with time, space, and body. These are understandable concepts, easily demonstrated. Even a writer needs a pen, pencil or typewriter. Tools and art are in no way incompatible. On the contrary, art exists only in and through the use of tools, including computers.

We demonstrated this to a broad mix of people under the tutelage of Ken Knowlton, a researcher at Bell Telephone Laboratories and creator of several programming languages for the production of computer graphics. Some of the participants knew computers, but not much about the uses of computers in art. Some knew art, but didn't know how the muse could be served by those electric circuits. They effectively complemented each other, each giving what he could to his fellow students.

Student output using EXPLOR.

Ken taught them EXPLOR, a simple and easy-to-learn computer language for the production of graphic design, and we provided them with hands-on capability to exercise their knowledge — keypunches, terminals and the other accouterments of computer art. Excitement mounted over the five days of the workshop as the walls filled up with student-produced graphics of great variety. This evolving "exhibition" was one of the most gratifying features of the Festival.

Testimony of the participants, just watching them in fact, showed that they did become involved with computers, some of them for the first time in their lives. My own suspicion was that the participants changed their views about computers in many, many ways.

For those previously antagonistic towards the technology, there was a decided shift from the Frankenstein stereotype in which the monster had to be killed for man to survive, to one in which man and the computer could work happily and productively together, to achieve what neither could do alone.

The workshop was a success. The participants were turned on to computers. But what had they learned?

They learned that artists use computers. And, as one person pointed out, "If artists (who are stereotypically the complete antithesis of the traditional computer programmer) can use a computer, anybody can."

They learned that the computer could be a useful tool. It could extend their creative abilities in much the same

New Communications Media

Can we account for the human dimension?

*Condensed from a paper of the same title by Robert Johansen given at the World Future Society Second General Assembly. For a free copy, write Institute for the Future, 2740 Sand Hill Road, Menlo Park, CA 94025.

The new communications media, especially that of computer conferencing, has produced new and systematic ways of understanding its human implications. In researching group communications, experts have found that they can pinpoint three overall patterns of influence in the new media. For simplicity's sake they call them the Great Thinker, the Social Accountant, and the Technology-Firster.

The Great Thinker has the ability to look at overall patterns — to mentally grasp a totality and express it in a way that others can also see. But it is usually a very general vision; it is often highly debatable; it is sometimes naive. Great Thinker approaches usually lack detailed information or experience; however, they play the very important role of assumptions-questioners and visionaries. Their effect on new media is felt only on a general level, but it is an important effect. It would have taken a Great Thinker point of view in 1945, for instance, to view the computer as anything but a number cruncher. Computers are now communications media as well, though most people *still* view them as primarily number crunchers. We need ways of broadening our own vision about current examples of infant media — perhaps still including the computer.

The Social Accountant seeks to evaluate a new medium of communication *before* it is released to the general public in order to precisely measure its social effects in a controlled environment. The problems with his outlook arise in trying to generalize from the laboratory to the "real world". The tools of social accounting, however, are often invaluable and may be the only systematic processes available.

The Technology-Firster argues that one can never estimate the social effects of a new communications medium until it is actually being used on a large scale. The failure of the Picturephone is an example of the Technology-Firster gone wrong. However, there is a basic truth in the position of the Technology-Firsters: new media of communications cannot be *fully* understood until they are in real use over a period of time. Technology-Firsters are usually very good planners; they just aren't social planners.

Taken alone, all three approaches to technology lack the vitality or comprehensiveness necessary to plan for human communications such as those likely to occur in the near future. A hybrid among them however, is not only possible, but may be the only serious hope for adequate accounting of human factors related to the new communications media. The resulting approach would operate in the following ways:

1. Maintain a sense of larger social implications as practiced by Great Thinkers, but make sure it is linked to processes for developing and applying new media.
2. Develop the measurement and evaluation sophistication of Social Accountants, but don't be afraid to leave the laboratory.
3. Keep closely tied to the operational know-how of Technology-Firsters but try to keep human issues on an equal footing with technology.

Computer Art continued —

way as the telescope or miscroscope extends their vision. They had entered into a productive partnership with the computer. They had put the computer on.

> *The computer is by all odds the most extraordinary of all the technological clothing ever devised by man, since it is an extension of our central nervous system. Marshall McLuhan and Quentin Fiore.*

And they learned EXPLOR, a means to control the machine and have it do their bidding. Many have gone on to use EXPLOR to experiment with graphic design for the production of silkscreens and needlepoint. Others have gone on to courses in FORTRAN (the language in which EXPLOR is embedded) to enable them to have still more control over their end-products. And all will view computer art, particularly graphics, from a new perspective, now having a deeper understanding of what went into it.

There are many portals to the world of computers. Some people will choose one doorway, some another. For many, as the Festival demonstrated, computer art is a most inviting, comprehensible, even compelling entry point.

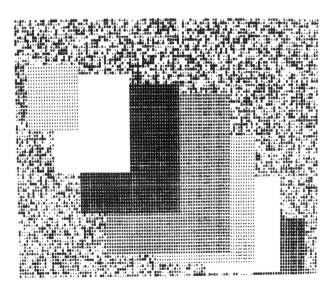

More output using EXPLOR.

Computer Cartoons

by Ronald E. Anderson and Marilyn Freimuth
University of Minnesota

People are generally not comfortable with computers. The rapid proliferation of computers has left many suffering mild anxiety from the social adjustments required in the wake of such "future shocks." Laughter has been known to cushion all types of shock and psychiatrists have even gone so far as to prescribe humor for people's distresses. For this reason, humor deserves a closer look in the context of the computer movement.

Humor communicates far more than happy emotions because it depends upon a collection of *ideas* which are not completely compatible. A funny cartoon or a good joke can provide a great deal of valid commentary about computers by calling attention to important facets of the real world, especially the beliefs and values that people hold. Consequently humor often expresses the complexities and subtleties of cultural thought and sentiment.

In the pursuit of such insight into the public's computer mood, we systematically began to collect computer humor.[1] Cartoons, especially single-frame drawings, are the primary form of humor on the subject of computers. Rarely can you find a computer mentioned in a joke book or a public restroom. Evidently this is due to the distance most people feel removing them from the computer and perhaps because the computer is a natural victim of caricature. Distortion of physical features constitutes the essence of caricature, e.g., Mr. Nixon is all cheek and nose whereas computers become forbidding monsters or smiling faces.

Creativity is an extremely important ingredient of both humor writing and humor enjoyment. Laughter depends upon the surprise revelation of a new, unexpected link between disjoint things or thoughts. Perceiving a fresh connection or an unexpected irony requires a creative leap from one established thought to another. Surprise yields mild tension; laughter is the human mode for relieving that tension. Without creative perception of the unexpected character of humorous incongruities, a human being experiences neither surprise nor pleasure.

It is our conviction that cartoons reveal people's attitudes toward computers more effectively than many other methods of assessing attitudes and feelings. In this spirit we compiled a library of cartoons from such diverse sources as magazines, newspapers, and books although most of the cartoons were taken from *The New Yorker, Saturday Review, The Saturday Evening Post, Punch, Datamation,* and *Educational Technology.* For these magazines we collected all the computer cartoons in five year intervals beginning in 1952 and ending in 1972, which provides a broad sampling of public mood across the early years of computer history. Our data base now contains nearly 300 cartoons, and these have been systematically subjected to content analysis to identify the dominant theme in each cartoon. This is not an easy task because some cartoons possess multiple themes, some of which are overlapping and very subtle.

Six major themes occur in the computer cartoons:
1. humanized computer
2. computerized human
3. computerization penetrating daily life
4. computer as beneficial tool
5. tool evolves into threatening master
6. the dependent computer
7. computer people and insider jokes

Each cartoon was placed into one of the above categories, and it is insightful to examine the cartoons in each category separately to gain a perspective on the ideas and orientations basic to each theme. As indicators of public attitudes the cartoons are considerably more elaborate and rich than opinion research studies. Nonetheless, the cartoon portrait is consistent with the opinion studies. In particular both types of investigations demonstrate the combination of both positive and negative feelings toward computers. Not only is there divergence of attitude orientation but some if not most people feel ambivalent toward computer-

1 Humor being one of the most creative of human activities should challenge the more creative computer artists, but as yet no computerist has created a program to generate jokes or gags. The senior author would be delighted to hear from someone who has proven our claim incorrect. Please address any responses to Ron Anderson, 2122 Riverside, Minneapolis, Minnesota 55404.

ization. To illustrate these findings each of the content categories is briefly summarized:

1. *Humanized computer*. A large portion of computer humor assigns human traits to computers. These cartoons are much more likely to appear in literary rather than technical magazines, which suggests that the human-computer identification problem is greater in the general public than in the computer world. The human-like computer cartoons attribute thinking, feeling, socializing, misbehavior, and even sex drives to computing machines.

"...AND NOW, GENTLEMEN—MY GREATEST ACHIEVEMENT... THE PERFECT PUPIL!"

"Only once in every generation is there a computer that can write poetry like this."

© DATAMATION

3. *Computerization Penetrating Daily Life*. The largest grouping of cartoons points toward this theme. Computers are intentionally or accidentally depicted as a normal, growing institution. Several social sectors are emphasized: education, business, and the family. Highlighting this type of humor are those focusing upon the intertwining of computers and social life in areas such as computer dating.

The major preoccupation of the cartoons is the issue of whether or not computers think and to what extent computing resembles thinking. A more playful trend is the emphasis upon emotional problems, e.g., in 1957 (June 19), *Punch* shows two tired engineers belatedly report on the state of computer repair: "I'm afraid it needs a psychiatrist."

2. *Computerized human*. Several cartoons support the contention of social critics that our society has become robopathic and many people are losing personal spontaneity and compassion for fellow human beings. Sometimes the blame for this condition is attributed to computerization; sometimes not. Usually the people suffering from dehumanization are those working close to computers.

These cartoons can be viewed as a positive aid in identifying areas where people act like machines forgetting traits that make one uniquely human.

"*Gee! my first computer date! I wonder what he'll be like?*"

MODERN DATA

4. *Computer as beneficial tool*. This theme is, of course, the primary justification for the existence of the computer. Cartoons decorate this point by showing many idiosyncratic ways of putting the computer to work: as prophet, as fortune teller, as Santa's helper, as fishing expert, and so forth. One could surmise that man is coming to rely too heavily upon the computer.

5. *The Tool Evolves into Threatening Master*. Extreme reliance on any technology has its disadvantages. An appropriate metaphor for the theme in this area is the servant turned master. Heavy dependence on computers as pervasive tools may lead to obedience to the computer as an authority. This dilemma is depicted in a 1964 (June 3) *Punch* cartoon where an onlooking scientist observes another scientist bowing down in front of the computer saying, "I think Smith's on to something pretty big!"

6. *The dependent computer*. In a crucial way computers depend on human intervention for data and programs. Perhaps the most interesting idea which the cartoons elaborate on is that no matter how complex a computer may be, its operation is still subject to the whims and sporatic moods of people. The act of "pulling the plug" so that the computer goes down is reinterpreted as an act of self-actualization.

7. *Computer people and insider jokes*. The technical magazines tend to emphasize this area. Some humor resides with the computer itself and such problems as high cost, miniaturization, and hardware change. The more interesting cartoons focus upon computerpeople and popular images of this

unique breed of specialist. Often the computerman is a superman, but more often he (she) is struggling to solve huge problems while on the brink of personal disaster.

Conclusion

Skimming through these cartoons and associated themes uncovers humor which quite blatantly raises social issues, e.g., impersonalization and unemployment. Other cartoons are more subtle in their message but nonetheless function as consciousness raising devices. They serve to sensitize the reader to the role of the computer in society.

Computer cartoons also offer us a creative, human way of coping with a technology that is sometimes frightening, sometimes boring, and sometimes incomprehensible. Cartoons provide us with a delightful route to think and feel about the most fantastic of man's machines.

Building A Computer of Your Own

by Stephen B. Gray

During the last year, getting a computer of your own has become much easier than before. There are three companies offering microcomputer kits, and the prices of commercial minicomputers are coming down with every new model.

Not long ago the only way to obtain a computer without paying several thousand dollars was to buy an old vacuum-tube model, or to go the very difficult route of building a transistor one from scratch. Even now there is an occasional vacuum tube machine available, but the drawbacks are formidable: many are so large they require a large barn to store, they need a great deal of air-conditioning and electrical power, and some tubes can be very expensive to replace. Schematics are needed to get the computer working and maintained, but they are almost never available. Even with some of the older transistor computers, updated schematics are usually impossible to obtain. Now and then the prototype of a recent transistor computer can be bought cheaply, but again, usually without schematics, so the buyer has two choices: take months or years to trace out every connection, or rewire most or all of the machine.

As in amateur radio, many computerniks would never think of buying a ready-built machine; they feel compelled to build one. Up until quite recently, this task has proved to be so difficult that only a couple of dozen computer hobbyists in the country had operating digital computers of any real complexity, and nearly all of them were electronics engineers in the computer industry.

The problem in building a computer from scratch is that so many areas of specialization are involved: logic, input/output, memory, peripherals, and mechanical skills such as packaging, back-plane wiring, metal-working, plastics, and many others.

Although many of the computer hobbyists are engineers who design their own circuits, most non-engineers must rely on published information, and although several dozen books and manuals contain computer schematics, they have serious limitations. A book may show schematics of various portions of a computer — arithmetic unit, memory, control circuits — but none show how to connect them together, and anyway, they are usually only partial schematics. Minicomputer manuals containing schematics can be bought, but many of the parts are identified only by a manufacturer's code number.

Even supposing an amateur computer-builder did get hold of complete schematics and all the parts, the one big stumbling block that has thrown many is core memory. It's still expensive to buy when new, and when surplus, it may contain broken cores, or perhaps it became surplus because it couldn't pass the manufacturer's quality control. Getting a core memory to work still separates the men from the boys, if there are still any who want to try it, now that semiconductor memory has become so readily available and cheap.

Surplus computer PC boards have been available for some years, but nearly all of them are without the "tab" ends, broken off to make sure the boards won't find their way back into commercial computers.

Even after the advent of the 54/74 series of integrated digital circuits and the various CPU-on-a-chip microcomputer circuits, there was still a dearth of information on just how to build a computer from what was offered.

In 1972, Intel introduced two sets of chips for microprocessors, the MCS-4 and MCS-8. The chips themselves weren't too expensive, in relation to what had been available before, but the cost of having the read-only memories programmed was several times that of the set of chips.

The CPU chip in the MCS-8 set is the 8008, which is the basis of two computer-hobbyist kits currently available. The SCELBI-8H, first offered in late 1973, is available in a variety of ways: as an assembled and tested computer with a 4K memory, at $1239, or in kit form for $1149; as a set of five printed-circuit cards with a 1K memory, $498; individual cards, from $55 to $195; "unpopulated" cards (without components), a set of five for $109; and various other combinations. Several interface cards are available, for making use of an oscilloscope readout, audio cassette-tape memory, or Teletype. Two dozen programs are available, including keyboard-to-CRT display, assembler, Teletype memory dump, magnetic-tape bootstrap loader, etc.

Incidentally, for those who have learned FORTRAN or BASIC in school or elsewhere, having to program at the assembly-language level can be very tedious, uninspiring, and error-prone.

The July 1974 *Radio-Electronics* described the Mark-8, also built around the Intel 8008 microprocessor, and also programmed in the Intel assembly language. A minimum Mark-8, with 256 8-bit words, is about $300. The construction manual for the Mark-8, which also gives information on obtaining a set of PC boards, is $5.00 from *Radio-Electronics*.

The Altair 8800 (*Popular Electronics,* Jan. and Feb. 1975) is based on the Intel 8080 chip, faster and with more instructions than the 8008, and is sold by MITS for $542 with 256 words of memory; with 1K words, $701 in kit form, or $938 assembled. Larger systems are also available, including the Basic I, with 8K words of memory, audio-cassette interface, serial input/output card, a computer terminal with keyboard and 32-character display, and BASIC software, for $2393 in kit form. Peripherals include a disc drive ($1480 kit) and a line printer.

Other kits and peripherals are available elsewhere; a recent issue of *Radio-Electronics* contained two construction articles, on a CRT terminal and an interface for connecting the terminal to a Teletype or cassette recorder, ads for the SCELBI-8H, MITS Altair 8800, and the CRT terminal, plus three ads for microcomputer kits (and two for semiconductor memories) from surplus-parts companies.

A series of publications on the "Experimenter's Computer System" is offered by M. P. Publishing, including one for $2.50 on a microcomputer CPU based on the Intel 8008, with 256 8-bit words; another for $2.50 on an audio-cassette mass-storage system, with schematics; a third about an I/O controller, etc. These were available on a subscription basis; similar material now appears in the ECS monthly magazine; the first issues go heavily into assembly-language programs.

There are several newsletters of interest to the computer hobbyist. The Amateur Computer Society has published a 6-page newsletter about every three months since 1966, with information about computers that ACS members have built, relevant books and magazine articles, where to buy parts, parts for sale or trade by members, and information on kits and other commercially available items.

"The Computer Hobbyist" newsletter was founded in 1974, and leans toward circuits and assembly-language programs. The first issue had Part One of a long article on "A Graphics Display for the 8008" with two programs, a Surplus Summary, and Notes on the 8008 Instruction Set.

The Micro-8 Computer Users Group was originally the Mark-8 Group, but widened its horizons when several more micros appeared; an extensive newsletter is published, with information on what its members have achieved with micros, interfaces and peripherals, comments on kits, various circuits, etc.

As for the future, minicomputers have been getting smaller and cheaper, and calculators more complex and cheaper, so it may be only a matter of time before a hand-held computer is available for a few hundred dollars.

[Ed Note: I feel I should share with you the last paragraph of Steve's cover letter for this article. "Incidentally, I almost added a paragraph at the very end, on 'What are you going to do with your computer?' but I felt this would make a good subject for another article, where it can be examined at length, on the trivial uses that home computers are put to, simply because there isn't much real need for one, other than for fun and games." Readers: let's hear from you on this —DHA]

Amateur Computer Society
260 Noroton Ave.
Darien, Conn. 06820

The Computer Hobbyist
Box 295
Cary, North Carolina 27511

Micro-8 Computer Users Group
Cabrillo Computer Center
4350 Constellation
Lompoc, Calif. 93436

M. P. Publishing Co.
Box 378
Belmont, Mass. 02178

MITS
6328 Linn, N.E.
Albuquerque, New Mexico 87108

Radio-Electronics
200 Park Ave. South
New York, N. Y. 10003

SCELBI Computer Consulting, Inc.
1322 Rear, Boston Post Road
Milford, Conn. 06460

Sphere (computers and kits)
96 East 500 South
Bountiful, Utah 84010

Fiction and Poetry

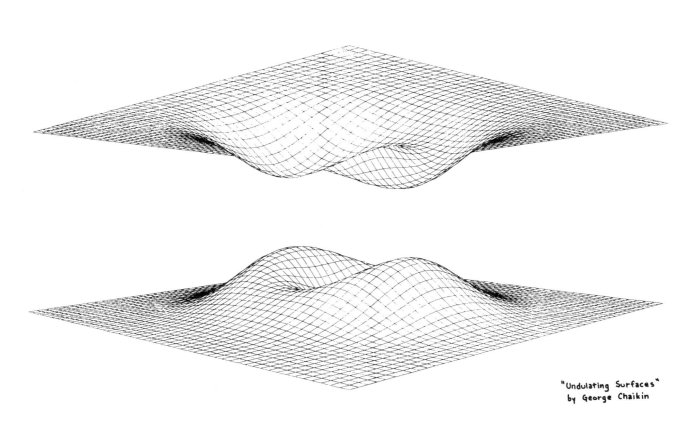

"Undulating Surfaces"
by George Chaikin

Daddy and his Computer

by Heather Lynne McWilliams

One sunday morning when eveybody except grandmother was dressed ready to go to church and jist then the phone rang daddy had to go to work. So mommy, Alex and I went to church. A few minutes later daddy was back home becuse he forgot his briefcase and daddy was back at work a few mintes later. Mommy, Alex and I came home early becuse Alex thew-up. And when we got back, daddy called he said, "I am comeing home." And when he came home there was a computer chasing his car, he stoped the car and got out and went in the house and yelled lock the doors shut the window a run away computer he yelled over and over. The news speded fast and soon to the police, the police caught the computer and smashed it with a hammer. And daddy quit his job and got another job. But I think that is another story.

□

Heather Lynne McWilliams turned in an unusually complete resume after her story was accepted. She is eight years old, four feet tall, weighs 48 pounds, is in excellent health, and is single. She lives in Kailua, Hawaii. Experience: reading books and magazines, such as School Bulletin, Jack and Jill, National Geographic, and Weekly Reader; creative writing since first grade, plus many stories written at home, including "The Haunted House" and "The Singing Gun." Education: preschool at Carey's School; first through third grades at Kailua Elementary School. Outside interests: Swimming, climbing trees, learning to sew, member of church choir, playing the piano, hiking, camping, art, and dolls. Early background: born at Air Force Academy, Colorado Springs, Colo.; lived in Colorado Springs, Montgomery, Ala., and Washington, D.C. Father's job: director of technical services and internal controls for Computing Management Inc.

Assume the world
has ended in catastrophe
and ask what then
of the literature of change

The life and times of Multivac

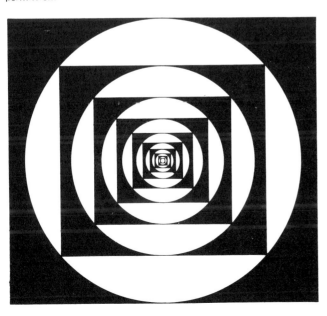

By Isaac Asimov

Science fiction is the literature of change. It is the only form of fiction which, as a matter of definition, tells its story against the background of a society vastly different from our own, with the difference dependent on changes in science and technology.

Since we live in a period of rapid change, science fiction has become the relevant literature of today, particularly to young people who must face such change for the rest of their lives.

The attempt to work out reasonably changed societies led science-fiction writers to consider such matters as television, nuclear bombs, and interplanetary exploration long before most scientists and government leaders (let alone the general public) did so. This has lent science fiction an air of respectability. All these factors combined have even raised it to the ultimate, and somewhat dubious, height of academic acceptance.

What's more, science fiction offers a technique of unlimited flexibility for dealing with today's problems.

At the present moment, for instance, the question of man versus machine is exercising many minds. Argue the matter from the immediate standpoint of today and you will obscure it with numerous emotional hangups and side issues. Take it, instead, several centuries hence. Assume that today's world has ended in catastrophe but that the remnants of technology have saved the remnants of mankind. Assume that a new world has arisen in which the problem is stark and simple, in which men are few indeed and the machine powerful beyond present dreams. Now raise the same question of man versus machine, and we have . . ."The life and times of Multivac."

The whole world was interested. The whole world could watch. If anyone wanted to know how many did watch, Multivac could have told them. The great computer, Multivac, kept track—as it did of everything.

Multivac was the judge in this particular case, so coldly objective and purely upright that there was no need of prosecution or defense. There were only the accused, Simon Hines, and the evidence, which consisted, in part, of Ronald Bakst.

Bakst watched, of course. In his case, it was compulsory. He would rather it were not. In his 10th decade, he was showing signs of age and his rumpled hair was distinctly gray.

Noreen was not watching. She had said at the door, "If we had a friend left . . . " She paused, then added, "Which I doubt!" and left.

Bakst wondered if she would come back at all, but at the moment it didn't matter.

Isaac Asimov is the author of many science books, both fact and fiction. His most recent fiction is "Tales of the Black Widowers."

Hines had been an incredible idiot to attempt actual action—as though one could think of walking up to a Multivac outlet and smashing it, as though he didn't know a world-girdling computer, *the* world-girdling Computer with millions of robots at its command, could protect itself. And even if the outlet had been smashed, what would that have accomplished?

And Hines did it in Bakst's physical presence, too!

He was called, precisely on schedule: "Ronald Bakst will give evidence now."

Multivac's voice was beautiful, with a beauty that never quite vanished no matter how often it was heard. Its timbre was neither quite male nor, for that matter, female, and it spoke in whatever language its hearer understood best.

"I am ready to give evidence," Bakst said.

There was no way to say anything but what he had to say. Hines could not avoid conviction. In the days when Hines would have had to face his fellow human beings, he would have been convicted more quickly and less fairly—and would have been punished more crudely.

∎

Fifteen days passed, days during which Bakst was quite alone. Physical aloneness was not a difficult thing to envisage in the world of Multivac. Hordes had died in the days of the great catastrophes; it had been the computers that had saved what was left and directed the recovery—and improved their own designs till all were merged into Multivac. Five million human beings were left on Earth to live in perfect comfort.

But those five million were scattered and the chances of one seeing another outside the immediate circle, except by design, were not great. No one was designing to see Bakst, not even by television.

For the time, Bakst could endure the isolation. He buried himself in his chosen way—which happened to be, these last 23 years, the designing of mathematical games. Every man and woman on Earth could develop a way of life to self-suit, provided always that Multivac, weighing all of human affairs with perfect skill, did not judge the chosen way to be subtractive to human happiness.

But what could be subtractive in mathematical games? It was purely abstract, pleased Bakst, harmed no one else.

He did not expect the isolation to continue. The Congress would not isolate him permanently without a trial—a different kind of trial from that which Hines had experienced, of course, one without Multivac's tyranny of absolute justice.

Still, he was relieved when it ended, and pleased that it was Noreen's coming back that ended it. She came trudging over the hill toward him and he started toward her, smiling. It had been a successful five-year period during which they had been together. Even the occasional meetings with her two children and two grandchildren had been pleasant.

He said, "Thank you for being back."

She said, "I'm not back." She looked tired. Her brown hair was windblown, her prominent cheeks a trifle rough and sunburned.

Bakst pressed the combination for a light lunch and coffee. He knew what he liked. She didn't stop him, and though she hesitated for a moment, she ate.

She said, "I've come to talk to you. The Congress sent me."

"The Congress!" he said. "Fourteen men and women. Self-appointed and helpless."

"You didn't think so when you were a member."

"I've grown older. I've learned."

"At least you've learned to betray your friends."

"There was no betrayal. Hines tried to damage Multivac; a foolish, impossible thing for him to try."

"You accused him."

"I had to. Multivac knew the facts without my accusation, and without my accusation, I would have been an accessory. Hines would not have gained, but I would have lost."

"Without a human witness, Multivac would have suspended sentence."

"Not in the case of an anti-Multivac act. This wasn't a case of illegal parenthood or life-work without permission. I couldn't take the chance."

"So you let Simon be deprived of all work permits for two years."

"He deserved it."

"A consoling thought. You may have lost the confidence of the Congress, but you have gained the confidence of Multivac."

"The confidence of Multivac is important in the world as it is," said Bakst seriously. He was suddenly conscious of not being as tall as Noreen.

She looked angry enough to strike him; her lips pressed whitely together. But then she had passed her 80th birthday—no longer young—and the habit of nonviolence was too ingrained. Except for fools like Hines.

"Is that all you have to say, then?" she asked.

"There could be a great deal to say. Have you forgotten? Have you all forgotten? Do you remember how it once was? Do you remember the 20th century? We live long now; we live securely now; we live happily now."

"We live worthlessly now."

"Do you want to go back to what the world was like once?"

Noreen shook her head violently. "Demon tales to frighten us. We have learned our lesson. With the help of Multivac we have come through, but we don't need that help any longer. Further help will soften us to death. Without Multivac, we will run the robots, we will direct the farms and mines and factories.

"How well?"

"Well enough. Better, with practice. We need the stimulation of it in any case, or we will all die."

Bakst said. "We have our work, Noreen; whatever work we choose."

"Whatever we choose, as long as it's unimportant, and even that can be taken away at will—as with Hines. And what's your work, Ron? Mathematical games? Drawing lines on paper? Choosing number combinations?"

Bakst's hand reached out *(Continued*

to her, almost pleadingly: "That can be important. It is not nonsense. Don't underestimate..." He paused, yearning to explain but not quite knowing how he could, safely. He said, "I'm working on some deep problems in combinatorial analysis based on gene patterns that can be used to..."

"...To amuse you and a few others. Yes, I've heard you talk about your games. You will decide how to move from A to B in a minimum number of steps and that will teach you how to go from womb to grave in a minimum number of risks and we will all thank Multivac as we do so."

She stood up. "Ron, you will be tried. I'm sure of it. Our trial. And you will be dropped. Multivac will protect you against physical harm, but you know it will not force us to see you, speak to you, or have anything to do with you. You will find that without the stimulation of human interaction, you will not be able to think—or to play your games. Good-by."

"Noreen! Wait!"

She turned at the door. "Of course, you will have Multivac. You can talk to Multivac, Ron."

He watched her dwindle as she walked down the road through the parklands kept green and ecologically healthy by the unobtrusive labors of quiet, single-minded robots one scarcely ever saw.

He thought: Yes, I will have to talk to Multivac.

■

Multivac had no particular home any longer. It was a global presence knit together by wire, optical fiber, and microwave. It had a brain divided into a hundred subsidiaries but acting as one. It had its outlets everywhere and no human being of the five million was far from one.

There was time for all of them, since Multivac could speak to all individually at the same time and not have to lift its mind from the greater problems that concerned it.

Multivac indifferently permitted talk of any kind, precisely because talk was unimportant. It was only acts that Multivac prevented, or punished.

Bakst had no illusions as to its strength. What was its incredible intricacy but a mathematical game that Bakst had come to understand over a decade ago? He knew the manner in which the connecting links ran from continent to continent in a huge network whose analysis could form the basis of a fascinating game. How do you arrange the network so that the flow of information never jams? How do you arrange the switching points? How to prove that no matter what the arrangement, there is always at least one point which, on disconnection . . . ?

Once Bakst had learned the game, he had dropped out of the Congress. What could they do but talk and of what use was that? Multivac indifferently permitted talk of any kind and in any depth, precisely because talk was unimportant. It was only acts that Multivac prevented, diverted, or punished.

And it was Hines's act that was bringing on the crisis; and before Bakst was ready for it, too.

Bakst had to hasten now, and he applied for an interview with Multivac without any degree of confidence in the outcome.

Questions could be asked of Multivac at any time. There were nearly a million outlets of the type that had withstood Hines's sudden attack into which, or near which, one could speak. Multivac would answer.

An *interview* was another matter. It required time; it required privacy; most of all it required Multivac's judg-

ment that it was necessary. Although Multivac had capacities that not all the world's problems consumed, it had grown chary, somehow, of its time. Perhaps that was the result of its ever-continuing self-improvement. It was becoming constantly more aware of its own worth and less likely to bear trivalities with patience.

Bakst had to depend on Multivac's good will. His leaving of the Congress, all his actions since—even the bearing of evidence against Hines—had been to gain that good will. Surely it was the key to success in this world.

He would have to assume the good will. Having made the application, he at once traveled to the nearest substation by air. Nor did he merely send his image. He wanted to be there in person; somehow he felt his contact with Multivac would be closer in that way.

■

The room was almost as it might be if there were to be a human conference planned over closed multivision. For one flash-by moment, Bakst thought Multivac might assume an imaged human form and join him—the brain made flesh.

It did not, of course. There was the soft, whispering chuckle of Multivac's unceasing operations—something always evident in Multivac's presence—and over it, now, Multivac's voice.

It was not the usual voice of Multivac. It was a still, small voice, beautiful and insinuating, almost in his ear.

"Good day, Bakst. You are welcome. Your fellow human beings disapprove of you."

Multivac always comes to the point, thought Bakst. He said, "It does not matter, Multivac. What counts is that I accept your decisions as for the good of the human species. You were designed to do so in the primitive versions of yourself and . . ."

"...And my self-designs have continued this basic approach. If *you* understand this, why do so many human

beings fail to understand it? I have not yet completed the analysis of that phenomenon."

"I have come to you with a problem," said Bakst.

Multivac asked, "What is it?"

Bakst said, "I have spent a great deal of time on mathematical problems inspired by the study of genes and their combinations. I cannot find the necessary answers and home-computerization is of no help."

There was an odd clicking and Bakst could not repress a slight shiver at the sudden thought that Multivac might be avoiding a laugh. It was a

touch of the human beyond anything even he was ready to accept. The voice was in his other ear and Multivac said:

"There are six billion different genes in the human cell. Each gene has an average of perhaps 50 variations in existence and uncounted numbers that have never been in existence. If we were to attempt to calculate all possible combinations, the mere listing of them at my fastest speed, if steadily continued, would, in the longest possible lifetime of the Universe, achieve but an infinitesimal fraction of the total."

Bakst said, "A complete listing is not needed. That is the point of my game. Some combinations are more probable than others and by building probability upon probability, we can cut the task enormously. It is in the manner of achieving this building of probability upon probability that I ask your help."

"It would still take a great deal of my time. How could I justify this to myself?"

Bakst hesitated. No use in trying a complicated selling job. With Multivac, a straight line was the shortest distance between two points.

He said: "An appropriate

114

gene combination might produce a human being more content to leave decisions to you, more willing to believe in your resolve to make men happy, more eager to *be* happy. I cannot find the proper combination, but you might, and with guided genetic engineering . . ."

"I see what you mean. It is . . . good. I will devote some time to it."

■

Bakst found it difficult to hitch into Noreen's private wave length. Three times the connection broke away. He was not surprised. In the last two months, there had been an increasing tendency for technology to slip in minor ways—never for long, never seriously — and he greeted each occasion with a somber pleasure.

This time it held. Noreen's face showed, holographically three-dimensional. It flickered a moment, but it held.

"I'm returning your call," said Bakst, dully impersonal.

"For a while it seemed impossible to get you," said Noreen. "Where have you been?"

"Not hiding. I'm here, in Denver."

"Why in Denver?"

"The world is my oyster, Noreen. I may go where I please."

Her face twitched a little. "And perhaps find it empty everywhere. We are going to try you, Ron."

"Now?"

"Now!"

"And here?"

"And here!"

Volumes of space flickered into different glitters on either side of Noreen, and further away, and behind. Bakst looked from side to side, counting. There were 14, six men, eight women. He knew every one of them. They had been good friends once, not so long ago.

To either side and beyond the simulacra was the wild background of Colorado on a pleasant summer day that was heading toward its end. There had been a city here once named Denver. The site

still bore the name though it had been cleared, as most of the city sites had been. He could count 10 robots in sight, doing whatever it was robots did.

They were maintaining the ecology, he supposed. He knew no details, but Multivac did, and it kept 50 million robots all over the Earth in efficient order.

Behind Bakst was one of the converging grids of Multivac, almost like a small fortress of self-defense.

"Why now?" he asked. "And why here?"

Automatically, he turned to Eldred. She was the oldest of them and the one with authority — if a human being could be said to have authority.

Eldred's dark-brown face looked a little weary. The years showed, all six score of them, but her voice was firm and incisive. "Because we have the final fact now. Let Noreen tell you. She knows you best."

Bakst's eyes shifted to Noreen. "Of what crime am I accused?"

"Let us play no games, Ron. There are no crimes under Multivac except to strike for freedom and it is a human crime that you have committed, no crime under Multivac. For that we will judge whether any human being alive wants your company any longer, wants to hear your voice, be aware of your presence, or respond to you in any way."

"Why am I threatened with isolation then?"

"You have betrayed all men."

"How?"

"Do you deny that you seek to breed mankind into subservience to Multivac."

"Ah!" Bakst folded his arms across his chest. "You found out quickly, but then you had only to ask Multivac."

Noreen asked, "Do you deny that you asked for help in the genetic engineering of a strain of humanity designed to accept slavery under Multivac without question?"

"I suggested the breeding of a more contented humanity. Is this a betrayal?"

Eldred intervened. She said, "We don't want your sophistry, Ron. We know it by heart. Don't tell us once again that Multivac cannot be withstood, that there is no use in struggling, that we have gained security. What you call security, the rest of us call slavery."

Bakst said, "Do you proceed now to judgment, or am I allowed a defense?"

"You heard Eldred," said Noreen. "We know your defense."

"We all heard Eldred," said Bakst, "but no one has heard *me*. What she says is my defense is not my defense."

There was a silence as the images glanced right and left at each other. Eldred said, "Speak!"

Bakst said, "I asked Multivac to help me solve a problem in the field of mathematical games. To gain its interest, I pointed out that the problem was modeled on gene combinations and that a solution might help in designing a gene combination that would leave man no worse off than he is now in any respect and yet breed into him a cheerful acceptance of Multivac's direction and acquiescence in its decisions."

"So we have said," said Eldred.

"It was only on those terms that Multivac would have accepted the task. Such a new breed is clearly desirable for mankind by Multivac's standards, and by Multivac's standards it must labor toward that. And the desirability of the end will lure it on to examine greater and greater complications of a problem whose endlessness is beyond what even it can handle. You all witness that."

Noreen said, "Witness what?"

"Haven't you had trouble reaching me? In the last two months, hasn't each of you noticed small troubles in what has always gone smoothly. You are silent. May I accept that as an affirmative?"

"If so, what then?"

Bakst said, "Multivac has been placing all its spare circuits on the problem. It

115

> '**Do you deny that you asked for help in the genetic engineering of a strain of humanity designed to accept slavery under Multivac without question?' 'I suggested the breeding of a more contented humanity. Is this a betrayal?**'

has been slowly pushing the running of the world toward rather a skimpy minimum of its efforts, since nothing, by its own sense of ethics, must stand in the way of human happiness and there can be no greater increase in that happiness than to accept Multivac."

Noreen asked, "What does all this mean? There is still enough in Multivac to run the world—and us—and if this is done at less than full efficiency, that would only add temporary discomfort to our slavery. Only temporary, because it won't last long. Sooner or later, Multivac will decide the problem is insoluble, or will solve it; in either case, Multivac's distraction will end. In the latter case, slavery will become permanent and irrevocable."

"But for now Multivac is distracted," said Bakst, "and we can even talk like this—most dangerously — without its noticing. Yet I dare not risk doing so for long, so please understand me quickly.

"I have another mathematical game—the setting up of networks on the model of Multivac. I have been able to demonstrate that no matter how complicated and redundant the network is, there must be at least one place into which all the currents can funnel under particular circumstances. There will always be the fatal apoplectic stroke if that one place is interfered with since it will induce overloading elsewhere which will break down and induce overloading still elsewhere — and so on, indefinitely, till all breaks down."

"Well?"

"And this is the point. Why else have I come to Denver? And Multivac knows it, too, and this point is guarded electronically and robotically to the point where it cannot be penetrated."

"Well?"

"But Multivac is distracted, and Multivac trusts me. I have labored hard to gain that trust, at the cost of losing all of you, since only with trust is there the possibility of betrayal. If any of you tried to approach closely to Multivac, it might rouse itself even out of its present distraction. If Multivac were not distracted, it would not allow even me to approach. But Multivac *is* distracted, and it *is* I who am approaching!"

Bakst was moving toward the converging grid in a calm saunter and the 14 images, keyed to him, moved along as well. The soft susurrations of a busy Multivac center were all about them.

Bakst said, "Why attack an invulnerable opponent? Make him vulnerable first, and then . . ."

Bakst fought to stay calm, but it all depended on this now. Everything! With a sharp yank, he uncoupled a joint. If he had only had still more time to make more certain.

He was not stopped—and as he held his breath, he became aware of the ceasing of noise, the ending of whisper, the closing down of Multivac. If, in a moment, that soft noise did not return, then he had reached the right key point, and no recovery would be possible. If he were not suddenly the focus of approaching robots—

He turned in the continuing silence. The robots in the distance were working still. None were approaching.

Before him, the images of the 14 men and women of Congress were still there and each seemed to be stupefied at the sudden, enormous thing that had happened.

Bakst said, "Multivac is shut down, burned out. It can't be rebuilt." He felt almost drunk at the sound of what he was saying. "I have worked toward this since I left you. When Hines attacked, I feared there might be other such efforts, that Multivac would double its guard, that even I . . . I had to work quickly . . . I wasn't sure . . ." He was gasping, but forced himself steady, and said solemnly: "I have given us our freedom."

And he paused, aware at last of the gathering weight of the silence. Fourteen images stared at him, without any of them offering a word in response.

Bakst said sharply, "You have talked of freedom. You *have* it!"

Then, uncertainly, he said, "Isn't that what you want?"

∎

With trembling pseudopods, Rork Glanf tore away the Earth-Girl's space-suit.

SCIENCE FICTION BY DOODLES WEAVER

Time and again, *and overtime*

SEATED IN THE TIME-BINDING HARNESS, and with a smile that could only mean sinister self-assurance, Rork Glanf, inter-stellar spy from Ganymede II posing as Professor Aych Gentry of the Cybernetics-Semantics Laboratory, Earthian Division, pressed the nuclear stub which would release the tensor force fields surrounding him and propel him into another space-time phase. Even as his ducleum-covered waldo made contact with the magnetic knob,

Glanf-Gentry reviewed quickly what he must do in the next few moments.

Immediately on arriving in the year he was born, he would enter the place of his birth, disguise himself as an intern, steal into the maternity ward, and surreptitiously exchange two infants in their cribs—himself and his twin brother—thus causing a rupture in the past that would enable him to return to the present as King of the Galaxy,

continued

Time and again, *and overtime* continued

which position his brother now held. Simple, fast, effective, and foolproof!

Gentry-Glanf's pseudopod, disguised as a human finger, released the activating distorter! In the laboratory rose a loud whine and a light flashed reminiscent of a super-nova as Glanf and the time-binding machine disappeared.

o   o   o

Shading his eyes with one hand, Professor Karloff looked up from his vivisection of a Syrian aqua-aardvark and said to Adam Rink, the Android: "Bless my garters, what won't that young fool think of next?"

o   o   o

Transported instantaneously to the day of his birth, Glanf materialized on the front steps of the hospital, slipped inside, overpowered a lone intern with his portable thalamic-para-lyzer, donned the white uniform, walked boldly into the baby ward, went directly over to himself-the infant, removed himself from one crib and substituted his twin brother for himself, putting himself in his brother's bed. Then, cackling mirthfully to himself-as-adult in Saturnian pidgeon-Martian, he reactivated the nuclear stud and before you could say "Wow" he reappeared in the laboratory just as Professor Karloff was ending the speech: "that young fool think of next?"

At that instant his smile of confidence froze. Why had he returned to the laboratory, if he were the King of the Galaxy?

How come he was still an insignificant interstellar spy?
Why was he not in the Uranium Chair of the King?
What had gone wrong?
Where was the mixup? Why . . .

"I'll tell you why!" shouted Adam the Android (who was also a telepath), tearing off his human face and revealing the lizard-like features of the terrible man-eating Plutonian Quaggle-beast: "Because I am really your twin brother and I perfected the time-binding machine just twenty minutes before you did, and I went to our birthplace and switched the babies first, so you actually put yourself back to where you were in the first place!"

Then laughing like a moon-mad space pirate, the android-human-Quaggle-beast slid across the floor on his nineteen appendages into a teleportation booth, appearing immediately in his Uranium Chair at the meeting of the Galactic Council, where he quickly signed a document recommending death for his twin brother, Professor Aych Gentry, who was really Rork Glanf.

But Glanf the Ganymedian was not so easily defeated. Instantly he pressed the stub of the tensor force-field machine and returned to the past two hours before the preceeding conversation occurred. There he perfected the Time Machine, and returned to the present one-half hour before his twin brother had perfected it, then rapidly returned to the day of his birth, overpowered the intern, switched the babies, and reappeared in the laboratory just as Professor Karloff was ending the speech: "that young fool think of next?"

o   o   o

At that instant his smile of confidence froze. Why had he returned to the laboratory, if he were King of the Galaxy?

How come he was still an insignificant inter-stellar spy?
Why was he not in the Uranium Chair of the King?
What had gone wrong?
Where was the mixup? Why . . .

"I'll tell you why!" howled Adam the Android (also a telepath), tearing off his human face and revealing the ugly features of the truculent flesh-eating Plutonian Quaggle-beast.

"Because I, Adam, I am really your twin brother and I knew you were going to go back in time two hours before I perfected the Time Machine so I went back **four** hours before you went back the second time and then I returned to our birthplace and switched the babies before you switched the babies the second time after you had switched the babies the first time, so you actually put yourself back to where you were the time before you switched the babies the second time!"

Then shrieking like an insane spider the human-android-Quaggle-beast slushed across the floor on his nineteen tentacles into a teleportation booth, appearing immediately in the Uranium Chair at the meeting of the Galactic Council, where he signed a death warrant for his twin brother, Professor Gentry, who was really Rork Glanf.

But the spy-Professor-Ganymedian was not so easily defeated. Instantly he pressed the stub of the time binding machine and returned to the past, six hours before the two preceding occurrences, perfected the Time Machine, returned to the present one-half hour before his twin brother had perfected it the second time, went back to the day of his birth, overpowered the intern, switched the babies, and reappeared in the laboratory just as Professor Karloff was ending his speech: "that young fool think of next?"

o   o   o

But his smile of confidence froze. Why had he returned to the laboratory, if he were King of the Galaxy? What had gone wrong? Where was the mixup? Why . . .

"I'll tell you why!" screamed Adam the Android (who could also read minds), tearing off his face and so on: Because I am really your twin brother and I knew you were going to go and so on and on . . ."

o   o   o

Those two little babies really got around, hey?

o   o   o

P. S. You rascals looking for the part about Earth-Girl shown in opening illustration—never mind! It was all a hoax by us foxy editors to make you read story.

Poems by Peter Payack

MOTORCYCLE EVOLUTION

The size of the human brain
increased from the apelike
capacity of 500 cubic centimeters
in Australopithecus to about
1500 cc. in modern man.

It took 2 million years
for man's brain to evolve
from the motor size of
a Kawasaki 500 to that
of a Harley-Davidson Superglide.

ONLY MINUTES

It would take
an infinite number
of monkeys,
an infinite amount
of time to write
this poem using
typewriters and
random chance.

For instance,
it would take 10,000
monkeys 150 years
to achieve one "it would".

As it was,
it took this goofball
only minutes.

INTERSTELLAR CHESS

If in the cosmic
struggle for existence
even entire galaxies
are mere pawns,

(1. Andromeda - King 4...)

Then who are the players,
and what is the prize?

(...Milky Way - King 3).

THE AVERAGE PERSON

Every second,
the average person
has 100 million
sensations bombarding
his body like so many
telephone messages,
with his head acting
as a switch board to sort
out the data.

When you read this poem
do you sort of get
a busy signal?

CORNUCOPIA

There are 100,000
million billion stars
in the known universe.

If one in a trillion
has a planet with intelligent
life on it, there would be
100 million sentient races.

The odds are
that somebody out there
has to like my
poetry.

That's why
I keep writing.

ONLY ME

The only thing
between my shadow
and the sun
for 93 million miles
is me.

I'm always
getting in the way
of something.

Motorcycle Evolution, Only Minutes, and the Average Person are reprinted with permission from THE PARIS REVIEW, Vol. 16, No. 1. Copyright 1975 The Paris Review, Inc., New York. Cornucopia, Interstellar Chess, and Only Me are reprinted with permission of the author. They appeared in CORNUCOPIA, a collection of 14 poems, available for 50¢ plus 20¢ postage from Peter Payack, 23 7th St., Cambridge, Massachusetts 02141.

Foolishness

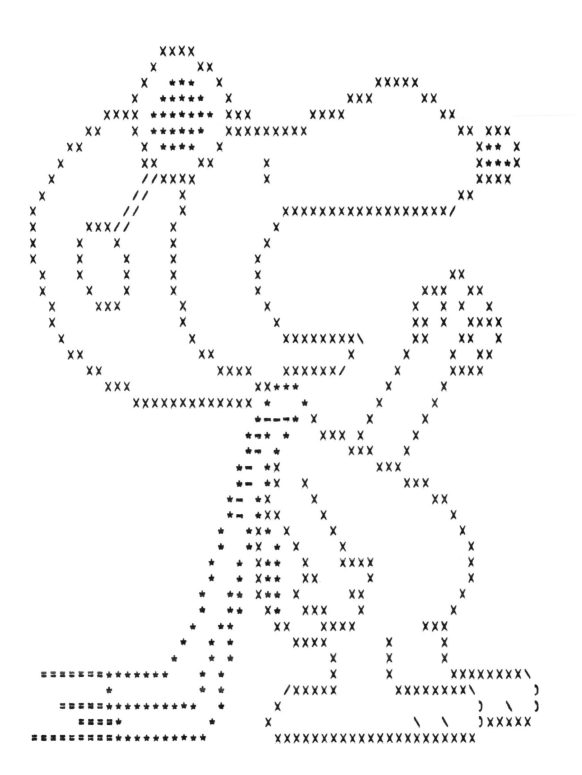

Chances are that everyone in the known world over the age of ten has had at least one battle with a computer in his lifetime. There's just something about the arrogant, stubborn refusal of a machine to reconsider even its most blatantly stupid acts that seems to bring out the beast in us. As a result, we spend most of our free time fighting a full scale war against computers. Tragically, it's a war we're all destined to lose. Let's face it: we're only human beings armed with nothing but logic and intelligence. These weapons are no

WE'RE LOSING OUR WAR

WE'RE LOSING OUR WAR AGAINST COMPUTERS BECAUSE...

... nothing will change their minds once they're convinced you've sent in 30,000 subscriptions to the same magazine.

WE'RE LOSING OUR WAR AGAINST COMPUTERS BECAUSE...

... they invariably continue to list a car as stolen for at least 6 months after it's been recovered and returned.

WE'RE LOSING OUR WAR AGAINST COMPUTERS BECAUSE...

... we make the mistake of assuming they never make a mistake.

WE'RE LOSING OUR WAR AGAINST COMPUTERS BECAUSE...

... they remember everything about us we'd like forgotten.

WE'RE LOSING OUR WAR AGAINST COMPUTERS BECAUSE...

... their screening of Police M.O. files somehow proves that every left-handed Baptist who owns a De Soto is the Mad Killer.

WE'RE LOSING OUR WAR AGAINST COMPUTERS BECAUSE...

... they're so smug about being able to solve complex equations, they won't stoop to learn simple arithmetic.

122

match for a computer's tireless determination to keep repeating its idiotic goofs until our spirits are broken. Worse yet, we are plagued by a cult of Computer Worshippers among our own kind who perpetuate the ridiculous myth that humans are always wrong. So, in case you're one of those bubble-brained idealists who clings to the belief that righteousness must eventually triumph, just consider how the punch cards are stacked against you in this fight. Then, you'll agree with MAD's battlefront analysts who cite these twelve reasons why

AGAINST COMPUTERS

ARTIST: BOB CLARKE   WRITER: TOM KOCH

WE'RE LOSING OUR WAR AGAINST COMPUTERS BECAUSE...

. . . they take years and years to find their stupid mistakes, and then they expect us to pay for them.

WE'RE LOSING OUR WAR AGAINST COMPUTERS BECAUSE...

. . . it's futile to call up and complain about a mistake, since the machine that goofed is the same one that answers the phone.

WE'RE LOSING OUR WAR AGAINST COMPUTERS BECAUSE...

. . . they forget everything about us we wish they'd remember.

WE'RE LOSING OUR WAR AGAINST COMPUTERS BECAUSE...

. . . their dumb mistakes can cause us to make fatal mistakes.

WE'RE LOSING OUR WAR AGAINST COMPUTERS BECAUSE...

. . . their opinion of the most efficient way to do things is definitely only their opinion.

WE'RE LOSING OUR WAR AGAINST COMPUTERS BECAUSE...

. . . they assume that Q.X. Zlyk, Q.X. Zlyk, Sr., and Q.X. Slyk, Senior, are three different people . . . two of whom didn't pay their Income Tax.

123

Genesis
Release 2.5

by Michael L. Coleman
with illustrations by Stew Burgess

IN THE BEGINNING the Project Manager created the Programming Staff. The Programming Staff was without form and structure. And the Project Manager said, "Let there be Organization;" and there was Organization. And the Project Manager saw that Organization was good; and the Project Manager separated the workers from the supervisors, and he called the supervisors—"Management," and he called the workers—"Exempt."

And the Project Manager said, "Let there be a mission in the midst of the Organization, and let it separate the workers, one from another." And the Project Manager created the mission and he called it—"The System." And the Project Manager separated those who were to benefit from The System from those who were to build it. And he called the former—"Users," and he called the latter—"Programmers."

And the Project Manager said, "Let all the Programmers in the Organization be gathered together into one place, and let a Chief Programmer be brought up to lead them." And it was so. And the Project Manager saw that he was competent.

And the Project Manager said unto the Chief Programmer, "Create for me a schedule, so that I may look upon the schedule and know the Due Date."

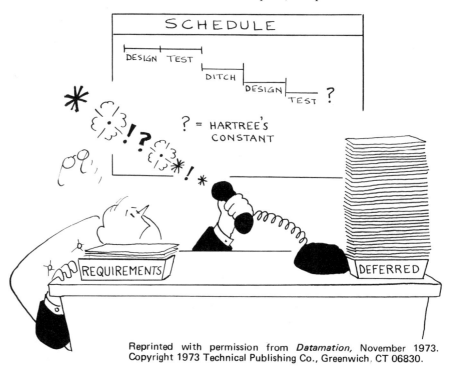

And the Chief Programmer went among his staff and consulted with them. And the staff was divided into two parts, one part was called—"Analysts," and the other part was called— "Application Programmers." And the Analysts went back to their desks and estimated, as was their custom. And it came to pass that each Analyst brought his estimate to the Chief Programmer, whereupon he collected them, summarized them, and drew a PERT Chart.

And the Chief Programmer went unto the Project Manager and presented to him the estimate saying, "It shall take ten months." And the Project Manager was not pleased and said, "I have brought you up from the depths of the staff; you have not grasped the 'Big Picture.'" And the Project Manager hired consultants, and authorized overtime, and he said to the Chief Programmer, "Behold, see all that I have done! The Due Date will be in five months." The Chief Programmer was much impressed and went from before the Project Manager and proceeded to implement The System.

And the Chief Programmer sent his Analysts to the Users and said, "Let Specifications be written." And there were meetings, and lunches, and telephone calls. And the Specifications were written. And there was a Payday and the Happy Hour, one month.

And the Chief Programmer examined the Specifications and saw that they were too ambitious. And he separated the mandatory features from the optional features; and he called the mandatory features—"Requirements," and he called the optional features— "Deferred," and the Users called him names. And the Chief Programmer gave the Specifications to the Analysts and said, "Let the Requirements be analyzed and let the Files be designed." And it was so. And the Chief Programmer said, "Let the Software Houses put forth their Salesmen, and let us have a Data Management System." And it was so. The Software Houses brought forth all manner of Salesmen who presented their packages, and claimed wondrous things for them, each according to his own file structure. And it came to pass that a Data Management System was selected; and the Chief Programmer saw that it was good. And there was a Payday and the Happy Hour, a second month.

And the Chief Programmer said, "Let the System be divided into parts, and let each part be called a 'Module.' And let programming teams be formed and let each be assigned to write a Module." And it was so. And the Chief Programmer created the programming teams with two levels, a greater and a lesser; and he called the greater the "Senior Programmers," and he called the lesser the "Junior Programmers."

And he gave the greater dominion over the lesser. And the Chief Programmer saw it was good. And the Junior Programmers saw it differently. And there was a Payday and the Happy Hour, a third month.

And the Chief Programmer said, "Let the programming be started and let much overtime be consumed, for there is but two months left." And the Programmers, both the Senior and the Junior, were much afraid, and they strove to please the Chief Programmer. And they flowcharted, and they coded, each in his own fashion. And the Chief Programmer looked upon the work and liked it not. And the Chief Programmer said, "Let there be a Standard;" and there was a Standard. And the Programmers looked upon the Standard and liked it not. And there

was a Payday and the Happy Hour, a fourth month.

And the Chief Programmer said, "Let there be Progress Reports, so we can monitor and control;" and there were Progress Reports. And the Chief Programmer looked upon the Progress Reports and saw that the Due Date

was not to be met. And the Chief Programmer arose, pressed his suit, shaved his beard, and went unto the Project Manager, and groveled. And the Chief Programmer pointed his fingers, and caused Blame to issue forth upon all manner of creatures who sold Hardware and Software. And the Chief Programmer asked for an Extension.

And the Project Manager was exceedingly angry, and cast doubts upon the Chief Programmer's ancestry; and uttered a multitude of threats. But it came to pass that an Extension was granted; and the Chief Programmer took the Extension back to the programming teams, and there was much rejoicing. And the programming of the modules was completed. And there was a Payday and the Happy Hour, a fifth month.

And the Chief Programmer said, "Let the Modules be integrated, one with another, so that System Testing may begin." And it was so. Two by two the Modules were integrated, one with another. And great difficulties were experienced, and many hours of overtime were used, and many cups of coffee were consumed. And it came to pass that System Testing was completed. And there was a Payday and the Happy Hour, a sixth month.

Then the Chief Programmer did go to the Project Manager and said unto him, "Behold, I bring you good tidings of a great joy which will come to all the Users; for on this day The System is completed." And suddenly there was with them a multitude of Users praising the Chief Programmer and saying, "Glory be to The System in the highest, but can you make this one small change"? ∎

WE WENT LOOKIN' FOR TH' GOOD LIFE, BUT WE SHOULDA STOOD IN BED,

'CAUSE THE STUFF WE ATE & DRANK & BREATHED, IT PLUMB CLOGGED UP OUR HEAD,

AND THE THINGS WE SAW ON TEEVEE, ON THE NEWS EACH NIGHT AT TEN,

WERE ENOUGH TO MAKE YOU WANT TO GRAB YOUR TOWEL AND THROW IT IN!

WELL, SOMETIMES OUT IN THE COUNTRY YOU CAN STILL SEE BIRDIES SING,

YOU CAN'T **HEAR** 'EM, THOUGH, 'CAUSE JET AIRLINERS DROWN OUT EVERYTHING,

AND SAY, WHATEVER HAPPENED TO THOSE SIMPLE THINGS WE PRIZED?

THERE'LL BE A LOTTA CHANGES MADE NEXT MONTH WHEN WE GET **ORGANIZED!!**

FRACTIONATED PEOPLE

by David Henderson

We are rapidly becoming a nation of statistics. Someone feeds information into a half-million dollar computer and discovers the average Harvard graduate has one and two-thirds children. This information is flashed across the country. Reaction is mixed:

Yale: "We always thought those Harvards were queer."

Dartmouth: "Like father like son."

University of Miami: "When we get 'em that size we throw 'em back."

Stanford: "No wonder they have such a lousy football team."

M.I.T.: "We question the accuracy of the feed-in figures."

Columbia U. (pre-med): "Keep him in the incubator on a reinforced liquid diet and he may pull through."

A random sampling in the street:

Man: "Must be a peculiar-looking kid."

Woman: "Poor dear."

Taxi driver: "I get a lot of half-baked passengers, but never two-thirds baked."

Teenage girl: "I care?"

Teenage boy: "Sez who?"

Now there is nothing wrong with statistics, but reliance on figures like these is courting the danger of going down in history as a fractional race.

The average American family owns one and a quarter cars. Two and a third members of every family on the eastern seaboard watch "All In The Family" fifteen minutes every other week. Two and seven-eighths of every ten readers of *Time* magazine scan four and one-tenth issues during national campaigns. Statistical fractions could invade our language and become a way of life.

Here is how a typical family in the near future may behave:

It is Saturday night and they are headed for a movie. They miss the beginning of the feature because three-quarters of the family car is scheduled for recall and it doesn't run too well. Father steps up to the cashier. "Three and two-thirds tickets, please" he says, shoving part of a ten-dollar bill through the opening. They also miss the end of the film. This is the week one family views only nine-tenths of the picture.

On the way home they stop at a drive-in. Four and a third plates of ice cream are ordered. Father stares at his plate in disappointment. This week he gets only one-third of a scoop. When they prepare for bed, it's Mother's turn to be disappointed. She gets only one-fifth of the innerspring mattress to sleep on. However, it's Saturday night and they will sleep only two hours, seventeen minutes and four seconds. Their dog, Smedley, a medley of breeds that defies statistics, pays no attention to computer read-outs and is rarely on balance in the game plan. He gets his one and a tenth can of dog food anyway.

At breakfast Father says to Junior: "Eat your one-third egg."

"I'm waiting for my three-quarters of a piece of toast," Junior replies.

I'll drop the car off to be fixed on my way to the train," says Father. "I'll pick it up on the way home."

No one objects. This is the day the family is statistically grounded. With the exception of Smedley. Dogs average two and a fifth miles per month in cars. No one minds skipping this. Smedley throws up on one-third of the back seat before the car is four-fifths down the block.

At the garage the mechanic listens to the engine and considers how he will overcharge by one-third for his work. The work is marginally over the guarantee that covers the repairs he predicts will be necessary.

The train isn't crowded. This must be the Monday one-fifth of the workers have hangovers, three-tenths have colds and one-eighth are just goofing off.

Arriving at the office he is greeted by the receptionist: "J. B. wants to see you in his office."

J. B. looks up from his desk. "I think we should go over the Harper account. They're unhappy with one-fifth of the last campaign."

"They're nitpicking. Their sales are up one-eighteenth over last year."

"Well, keep an eye on it. We don't want to lose that one. It's five-sixths of your income, you know."

At lunch, the drab day turns pleasant, relaxed and conquerable. Everyone knows businessmen average three and a half dry martinis per lunch. It would be an even four but they spill half of the last one. The rest of the day is one-third inefficiency, one-third blur, and one-third thick tongue.

The club car on the evening train is a refueling station. One-tenth of commuters are club car fixtures. This night there is such a crush that Father consumes his own martini and a quarter of the drinks of those pressed against him. He arrives home one hundred percent smashed. He is one hundred percent unaware of what's being served for dinner and falls into bed one hundred percent fully clothed. He snores one-third more than one hundred percent loud. ☐

David Henderson is a Canadian humorist who is funny four-quarters of the time.

Reprinted from *Passages*, the inflight magazine of Northwest Airlines, copyright 1974 by Caldwell Communications, Inc.

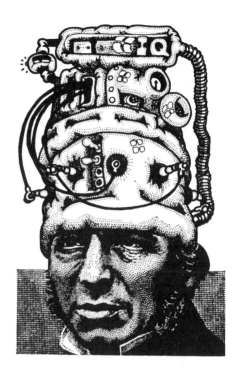

Test For System Analysts

INSTRUCTIONS: Read each question carefully. Answer all questions. Time limit: 4 hours. Begin immediately.

HISTORY: Describe the history of the papacy from its origins to the present day, concentrating especially, but not exclusively, on its social, political, economic, religious, and philosophical impact on Europe, Asia, America, and Africa. Be brief, concise, and specific.

MEDICINE: You have been provided with a razor blade, a piece of gauze, and a bottle of Scotch. Remove your appendix. Do not suture until your work has been inspected. You have fifteen minutes.

PUBLIC SPEAKING: 2500 riot-crazed aborigines are storming the classroom. Calm them. You may use any ancient language except Latin or Greek.

BIOLOGY: Create Life. Estimate the differences in subsequent human culture if this form of life had developed 500 million years earlier, with special attention to its probable effect on the English parliamentary system. Prove your thesis.

MUSIC: Write a piano concerto. Orchestrate and perform it with flute and drum. You will find a piano under your seat.

PSYCHOLOGY: Based on your knowledge of their works, evaluate the emotional stability, degree of adjustment, and repressed frustrations of each of the following: Alexander of Aphrodisias, Rameses II, Gregory of Nicia, Hammurabi. Support your evaluation with quotations from each man's work, making appropriate references. It is not necessary to translate.

SOCIOLOGY: Estimate the sociological problems which might accompany the end of the world. Construct an experiment to test your theory.

ENGINEERING: The disassembled parts of a high-powered rifle have been placed on your desk. You will also find an instruction manual, printed in Swahili. In 10 minutes a hungry Bengal tiger will be admitted to the room. Take whatever action you feel appropriate. Be prepared to justify your decision.

ECONOMICS: Develop a realistic plan for refinancing the national debt. Trace the possible effects of your plan in the following areas: Cubism, the Donatist controversy, the wave theory of light. Outline a method for preventing these effects. Criticize this method from all possible points of view. Point out the deficiencies in your point of view, as demonstrated in your answer to the last question.

POLITICAL SCIENCE: There is a red telephone on the desk beside you. Start World War III. Report at length on its socio-political effects if any.

EPISTEMOLOGY: Take a position for or against truth. Prove the validity of your stand.

PHYSICS: Explain the nature of matter. Include in your answer an evaluation of the impact of the development of mathematics on science.

PHILOSOPHY: Sketch the development of human thought, estimate its significance. Compare with the development of any other kind of thought.

GENERAL KNOWLEDGE: Describe in detail. Be objective and specific.

Confess: A Humanistic, Diagnostic-Prescriptive Computer Program to Decrease Person to Person Interaction Time During Confession

KENNETH MAJER
Institute for Child Study

MICHAEL C. FLANIGAN
School of Education
Indiana University

Recent Vatican interest in the effect upon laymen of the shortage of professional priests (PP) and the decreased seminary enrollment of potential priests (P'P) has led to the development of Computerized Operations (Non-retrievable) for Expediting Sinner Services (CONFESS). This program provides a viable alternative to traditional confession procedures by listing penance requirements (by sin) on a private print-out to confessees appropriate to the sin committed. This eliminates one problem which frequently occurs where the confessee, because he is under extreme duress, may forget the original penance. In addition, the program provides a probability estimate of the consequence of not completing the penance associated with a given sin; for example, number of years in purgatory. Thus, full freedom of choice is given to the participant/user (PU). The program requires no PP involvement and hence frees PPs to engage in more pressing activities. It is hoped that by providing PPs with more time for critical theological activities, P'Ps will consider the priesthood a more socially conscious and relevant profession, causing an increase of P'P enrollment in accredited seminaries.

Program Description

CONFESS is available in three natural interactive languages, COURSE WRITER III, BASIC and TUTOR and can be programmed for most other natural languages such as interactive FORTRAN. The program has been developed utilizing on-line computer terminals linked to an IBM 360 for data input, but could be modified to operate in batch mode on almost any third generation configuration given the willingness to sacrifice immediate feedback.

The computing procedures for CONFESS are as follows: The present sins input (psi) yields the graduated penance accrual (GPA) as a function of present sins (ps) plus frequency of confession visits (fcv) times completed penances (cp) divided by recurring sins (rs). Hence, GPA is a function not only of the immediate sins reported but also a partial function of the reciprocal relationship of recurring sins to completed penances by frequency of confession visits. The relative penance, then, is increased by the inclusion of recurring sins.[1] Mathematically, this can be represented as follows:

$$psi \rightarrow GPA = f \left\{ ps + fcv \left(\tfrac{cp}{rs} \right) \right\}$$

Therefore, each present sin yields a specific GPA that is stored until all GPAs have been computed. At that time, punishment and its maximum likelihood of occurrence[2] should the GPA not be completed, are retrieved from core storage and printed out for the individual GPA prescription.

Validity and Reliability

A study to establish the validity of the CONFESS program was conducted. The procedure included a sample of 243 actual confessions stratified across low, medium and high socio-economic income brackets with non-significant differences in proportions of black, white and Spanish speaking PUs. Fourteen priests were used in the study from seven different cities.

The actual sins confessed and penances prescribed in the confessional booths were tape recorded without the confessor or confessee's knowledge to insure absolute authenticity of confessor-confessee interaction.[3] The tapes were further analyzed and penances were rated on a scale of 1-10 where $10 =$ maximum severity.[4] Then ratings were made by the seven cardinal evaluators identified by Stake (AERA, 1972). The interrater reliability was .949.

The 243 sin sets taken from the taped confessions were then entered into the CONFESS program via remote terminal. A Pearson product moment correlation was computed between the actual PP penance prescriptions and the CONFESS PGAs. A correlation of .971 was interpreted to provide sufficient concurrent validity for CONFESS confidence.

A further series of small studies to determine the reliability of the CONFESS program were conducted as follows:

Study 1: External Latency Reliability. The mean wait for confessional booths with PPs (where there were 2 booths/church) was 7.12 minutes while, in comparison, the average wait for a CONFESS box (one installation per church) was only 1.72 minutes. This difference in out-side wait latency is significant at the $p < .01$ level.

Study II: Internal Latency Reliability. This study examined the latency from the last sin confessed until the PP or CONFESS program provided the penance or GPA, respectively. Again, the CONFESS latency was significantly shorter than the PP latency. The means were 1.31 minutes (plus an average of 9.3 head shakes) for PPs, and 6.1 seconds for CONFESS.

Study III: Computer Breakdowns vs. PP Rest Breaks. In this study the CONFESS program was monitored for computer breakdowns and don't-understand-not-compute-either (DUNCE) loops. During the 243 CONFESS program runs (a total of 517 minutes), no breakdowns were reported and only one (1) DUNCE loop was reported. The DUNCE loop was in the case of one PU who was previously excommunicated from the church; however, the CONFESS program has been modified and will now process excommunicated PUs as well as non-excommunicated PUs. PPs, on the other hand, showed an average of 1 rest break for a mean of 12.3 minutes every hour and one-half.

Study IV: Consistency of PP penance vs. GPA. In this study, the 243 confession tapes were re-heard by the same 14 PPs. Each PP re-heard the same confessee's albeit on tape and without hearing the end of the tape which contained the penance he gave. In 241 cases, the PPs did *not* give the same penance and, in fact, in 191 cases the penance severity changed at least one degree (e.g., from a severity rating of 7 to a severity rating of 8). Although no speculation for causality is made here, it is important to compare the CONFESS consistency. In all 243 cases, the GPA was identical.

The results of these four studies are sufficient to provide confidence in CONFESS program reliability.

Procedures/Output

Being a natural language program, the procedures for CONFESS are extremely simple. The following steps describe the PU procedures.

Step 1: Enter the CONFESS box, and kneel on cushioned kneeler in front of the typewriter/console. Type in your personal PU identification code.

Step 2: The typewriter will type your name and the elapsed time since your last CONFESS session (CONFESSION). Following the request for present sins, type in all sins since your last CONFESSION.

Step 3: Press the "enter" button and silently repeat the short form of the ACT of Contrition. (Given the average latency for GPA, 6.1 seconds, this is usually reduced to "I'm sorry").

Step 4: Remove the CONFESS personalized GPA printout.

Sample Printout

CONFESS   GPA PRINTOUT   JOHN POPE Age 29

TIME SINCE LAST CONFESSION = 3 WEEKS

PRESENT SINS	TYPE	GPA	PUNISHMENT	PROBABILITY THEREOF
1. SECRETLY ENVIES BOSS	VENIAL	10 OUR FATHERS. PRACTICE SMILING AT BOSS	1 YEAR IN PURGATORY	.98
2. SWEAR AT WIFE	VENIAL	10 HAIL MARY'S. PRACTICE SMILING AT WIFE	1.73 YEARS IN PURGATORY	.84
3. COVET NEIGHBOR'S WIFE	MORTAL	ONE ROSARY/DAY FOR ONE WEEK. PRACTICE SMILING AT WIFE.	ETERNAL DAMNATION	.91

ONLY *3* SINS THIS TIME *MR. POPE.* YOU'RE IMPROVING. YOU HAD *14* LAST CONFESSION. NICE GOING. KEEP UP THE GOOD WORK. LET'S SEE IF YOU CAN MAKE OUT A LITTLE BETTER WITH NUMBER *3* IN THE FUTURE.

The Guiness Book of Computer Records

by Lynn Yarbrough

It would be interesting to add a chapter to the Guiness Book of World Records on the topic of computer programs. What is the biggest computer program ever written? The longest running? The most complex? The most famous? The most used? In order to establish records for these and other categories, we must first agree on what we mean by some of these. For example, we probably can agree on a criterion for complexity: the total number of conditional jumps is an obvious one. But to eliminate programs constructed solely for the purpose of breaking records, we would also have to establish some criterion for usefulness — and that may be difficult to get people to agree on.

Here are some candidates for records, based mostly on my own limited knowledge and personal criteria for usefulness. I am eliminating operating systems from consideration, because they are intended to run forever, or at least until the computer conks out, and concentrating on programs that are designed to solve specific problems.

Biggest program —
The Project Apollo real-time system. I don't know quite how big it is, but it's on the order of 1,000,000 lines of code.

Most complex —
Maybe Project Apollo again, but for density of conditions I suggest that PL/I compiler may have a higher percentage of conditional jumps. Any other candidates?

Most famous —
The COBOL compiler on the IBM S/360.

Most used —
The control programs for the Bell Telephone Companies' Electronic Switching System.

Most subroutines —
I had heard, a few years ago, of a FORTRAN program with just under 200 subroutines, but I can't claim a record for that because I can't identify it. Has anyone a candidate for this category?

Longest running —
Prof. Donald Knuth of Stanford University once ran a program to exhaustively analyze a chessboard problem. The program was run at odd hours when the computer was otherwise idle, and thus took over a month to complete. In total, the run used about 180 hours of central processor time — on a CDC 6600! But the Atomic Energy Commission people may have this record beaten already — can anyone fill us in?

If instead of only programming records, we extend our new chapter to include other computer-related records, here are some other items for consideration.

The largest punched card file in the world was for many years maintained by the U. S. Bureau of the Census. After the census of 1960 this file contained over 500,000,000 cards. Consider the amount of storage space for this amount of cards; packed as densely as possible this represents a stack of cards over 100 miles long! (I wonder if this file is still maintained, and if so how big it got after the 1970 census.)

The largest magnetic tape file in the world is maintained by NASA. It consists of all the telemetry and other data gathered from all the missions, both successful and otherwise, flown by U. S. rockets and satellites since the beginning of the space program.

(NASA has a major problem in using this data before the tapes disintegrate. There is so much data that 90% of it will probably never be examined by anyone.)

What facts can you add to the CREATIVE COMPUTING book of programming or computer records? Who can tell us more about the widest magnetic tape (3″ tape used by an early Honeywell computer), or the amount of heat generated by Einac or Whirlwind, or the most computers tied together (ARPA Net?). As you give us information, we'll try to tie it together and publish the results from time to time.

135

Draw the Bug From the Computer and Win Prizes!!!

Ever thought of the very worst kind of computer bug or program bug? One that is really frightening. Is it one that eats your program away from inside a DO or FOR loop? Or is it a nasty disk file identifier insect? Does the thought of these bugs scare you? Or do you try not to think about their horrible grizzlyness?

If you can come to grips with yourself to draw that which when seen by someone will give them nightmares for the rest of their life you can win. But it takes more than artistic talent. It takes raw Guts with a capital G. But if you have the sensitivity and, of course, guts, you are eligible to win BIG, BIG prizes. Chances are you may have already WON!! How does that grab you?! Read on!

All you need to do is think of the ugliest, scariest computer bug you could ever imagine to meet . . . or not want to meet!!! And draw it. That's all. Easy, isn't it?!

So hurry up and grab a pencil. Let your inner fears pour out before the closing date of October 20, 1975. Entries received after the deadline will be automatically disqualified and incinerated.

INSTRUCTIONS

1. In the space provided for you at the right, draw your computer bug.
   a. The bug must fit within the space provided.
   b. Color drawings always welcome, but please do not use ethnic colors, i.e., black, red, yellow, or white.
   c. Only one entry per family. Two or more will be regarded as cheating, and all said entries will be disqualified and incinerated.
2. Enclose a signed photograph of yourself. This is for identification purposes. And if your drawing loses, your picture may win!!! Ha-ha!!!
3. Be sure to send $5.00 with the drawing. This fee covers "processing charge". This includes mailroom assortment, judging by our panel of distinguished computer program bug exterminators, and incineration of drawing if disqualified. Losing drawings will be returned. We regret that the $5.00 will not.

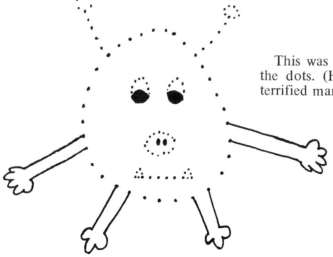

This was last year's winning drawing. Just join the dots. (Had we drawn it out, we could have terrified many of your friends.) — DHA

Adapted from something similar in *The Harvard Lampoon.*

People, Places, and Things

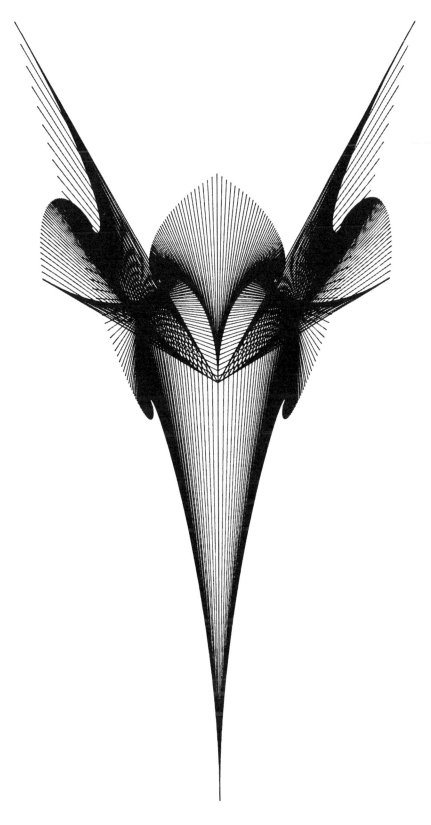

Nicholas Copernicus

Copernicus was born on February 19, 1473, in
Torun, Polish Prussia, the son of a merchant. Though
today he is remembered as the father of modern
astronomy, in his own time he made his livelihood not
as an astronomer, but as an ecclesiastic. His position
as canon of the cathedral of Frombork gave him
both financial security and freedom to pursue his
own astronomical studies. It was at Frombork that
Copernicus worked out his great book, the
De Revolutionibus.

The accepted model of the structure of the universe
in Copernicus' time was earth-centered. The sun,
the moon, the five known planets, and the stars
were thought to revolve about the earth in endless,
perfect circles.

The model was developed by Aristotle around
350 B.C., and elaborated by Claudius Ptolemy of
Alexandria around 150 A.D. Ptolemy outlined his
system in a treatise which has come to be known as
the Almagest, meaning "the greatest." What Ptolemy
established for the first time was a working
mathematical model by which the positions of the
planets could be predicted accurately.

In the Ptolemaic system, each planet moved in a
small circle (or epicycle) whose center was carried

round the earth in a larger orbit (or deferent). For
fourteen centuries astronomers computed planetary
positions from tables based on this analysis.

Copernicus described an unfamiliar universe, with
the sun, not the earth, at its center; he treated the
earth as a planet among the other planets, with a
yearly orbit around the sun, a daily rotation on its
axis, and a conical precession.

His great breakthrough is the recognition that the
complex paths which we see traced by the planets
could be explained by a combination of their own
motion and that of the earth from which we
observe them.

His new model gave astronomical inquiry the
direction it still follows today. But he arrived at his
innovations using the traditional assumption, shared
by Aristotle and Ptolemy, that the motion of
heavenly bodies must be a compound of circles—an
idea which was soon to be overthrown by Johannes
Kepler, as he worked to build a foundation for the
Copernican hypothesis.

Copernicus' cosmology drawing, from his manuscript of the
De Revolutionibus.

Copernicus' book, the De Revolutionibus, had an
immediate impact on astronomical theory.
"Astronomy is written for astronomers," he wrote in
his preface. But in the coming century his
re-examination of the structure of the universe
would permanently alter the way people thought of
themselves and their world.

The De Revolutionibus—published only in the year
of its author's death—might never have appeared in
print if Georg Joachim Rheticus, a young professor
of mathematics, had not persuaded Copernicus to
entrust him with the manuscript for publication.

EVELYN ROTH

Who is Evelyn Roth you may ask. Born in Mundare, Alberta, Evelyn grew up on a little "cow-wheat-chicken" farm and attended a one-room school until the age of fifteen. She then moved to Edmonton, Alberta, where she completed her education and began working in libraries, taking dance and fencing classes and designing clothes.

In 1961, she moved to Vancouver and became part of INTERMEDIA, a group of artists, musicians, film makers, and dancers who shared both common ideals and work space. In 1969, Evelyn worked with the University of British Columbia School of Architecture on a six-month project in Venice.

On her return to Vancouver, she began to channel all her artistic efforts into sculptural-wearables (multi-functional clothing) and dance-theater events. All of her sculpture-wearables are loosely knit from soft, flexible materials to provide both sensuous enjoyment and maximum flexibility to the wearer. Her ecological and environmental awareness and concern is reflected in her choice of materials. Working primarily with discarded fabrics, Evelyn Roth transforms throwaways into objects of fantasy and invention.

Why, you may wonder, is CREATIVE COMPUTING writing about Evelyn Roth? Because Evelyn has found a new, unique use for both video tape and computer tape. Video tape can only be used 300 to 500 times before it loses reproductive quality and must be discarded by TV studios. Evelyn collects this tape from TV stations in the U. S. and Canada and crochets them into many articles like hats, bags, slippers, costumes, car cozies, and canopies. During the month of June 1974, she, with the assistance of Marion Denny, crocheted a giant canopy (1500 sq. ft.) using over 1 mile of tape to provide a shaded area in the courtyard adjoining the British Columbia pavilion at EXPO '74.

Evelyn emphasizes that "the material is fireproof and checked by many fire marshalls. That's a good point, because most people think it burns like film."

Why not try crocheting a sculpture-wearable yourself out of those reels of computer tape that are starting to drop more bits per inch than they retain? Send us a photo of your creation, and we will print it in a future issue of CREATIVE COMPUTING.

Evelyn Roth at the British Columbia pavilion at Expo '74 displaying her video tape creations.

Have you ever seen a better use for discarded computer tape than a sun shade canopy?

PILOT 73 Information Exchange

A little while ago, I was wondering how PILOT 73 was getting along. As I asked my friends what's up, I noticed that . . . Lots of folk are using PILOT, but there's nobody who knows much about who's doing what with which machine, et cetera.

A typical situation is: There's an experienced FORTRAN programmer who is eager to develop a PILOT interpreter in ANSII FORTRAN IV. However, he doesn't know of anyone who wants such a system. As I was looking through another friend's correspondence, I discovered several requests for a PILOT written in FORTRAN.

As a dedicated PILOT — person, (having written several versions from time to time) I came up with a neat idea . . .

 **A FREE OR LOW-COST CO-ORDINATING SERVICE FOR PILOT USERS!!!**

Rather than waiting for somebody else to do this, I undertake this task (as fate allows me to have the requisite time). Now to flesh out the idea:

WHAT YOU CAN DO FOR ME

At the moment, there are lists of names with cryptic notes piled upon my desk. These are persons interested in PILOT in some way. However, there's very little knowledge beyond the names. Spend a few minutes, answer the questions below, and send to me. If you do this, you become a member of the Exchange.

WHAT I CAN DO FOR YOU

1) *Summary Sheet* I will assemble a catalog of PILOT people and send it to you. A short summary of each person or group's interests will be included under general areas of interest (ie, all B5500 users). From time to time, updated catalogs will be sent out. This is free until costs become excessive.

2) *Connections* Send me your need or request and I shall pass it on to those with the resource you need. Both you and they will get a card indicating your area of mutual interest.

3) *Resource Center* I shall maintain a library of PILOT resources, including listings of PILOT programs, PILOT interpreters, translators, and other implementations, manuals, technical tricks, and so forth. An index of the library will be attached to the Summary Sheet. Help the library grow by contributing a copy of your aspect of PILOT. If a particular item in the Library is of interest to you, I will make copies for you at cost.

Remember, the more I know, the better the service is for you.

Gregory Yob
PO Box 310
Menlo Park, Calif. 94025

PILOT 73 RESOURCE QUESTIONNAIRE

NAME:
ADDRESS:
PHONE:

1) Do you have a working version of PILOT?
2) If yes, on which machine(s)?
   2.1) Host language?
   2.2) Core Memory required?
   2.3) Configuration of Peripherals?
   2.4) How well is it debugged?
   2.5) Did you write it yourself?
   2.6) Compiler/Interpreter/Translator?
   2.7) Performance/response time?
   2.8) Do you have a user's Manual? (Send a copy)
   2.9) Do you have a listing and paper tape? (Send a copy)
3) If you are writing PILOT programs, are there some available for others? (send copies please)
4) Are you looking for a version of PILOT? (If yes, 2.1 — 2.9 above)
5) Please state your needs and interests:
6) Names and addresses of other persons you feel may be interested in the Exchange:

Nolan Bushnell- Father of PONG

by Trish Todd

You spot a large metal machine in the corner; it has two knobs, a coin slot, and a television screen which shows a dot of light lazily bouncing off the sides of the screen at irregular angles. Immediately, you are curious and begin to read the instructions to Pong, one of the computerized games from Atari, Inc.

The company was started two years ago by Nolan Bushnell, who was managing an amusement park to finance an electrical engineering major. He built the first game prototype, Computer Space, in his garage, and then he met "Moose," who built games from other designs of Bushnell's for a percentage. The first was Pong; it was tested in a bar called Andy Capp's — and in 24 hours you couldn't get near it. The "company" then expanded to include twelve other people who worked together and produced ten Pongs a day. Each Pong brings in about $200 a week.

The "company" has now developed into Atari, Inc., worth over $20,000,000. Located in Los Gatos, California, Atari manufactures Pong, Gotcha, Rebound, Space Race, Super Pong, Pong Doubles, Quadrapong, and Grantrak 10. Bushnell now owns Atari, and Moose is vice-president of research and development; both are confronted with lawyers, patents, security, and labor problems which they never foresaw in Bushnell's garage.

As Atari has grown, Nolan has tried to retain the "Atarian philosophy," which is based on dignity, trust, freedom, and loyalty. This philosophy is intended to produce a comfortable working environment; for example, labor and management share the same medical-insurance program (which also covers unwed pregnancies). The company tries to promote an informal atmosphere, both on the assembly line and between labor and management. Both men and women work on the assembly line, where judging from the hair and attire, sex is hard to distinguish. There are both men and women administrators too. Nolan's management philosophy is occasionally revealed in the form of a surprise party for all the employees — and he buys the liquor!

However, the "Atarian philosophy" has also had to cope with several problems. Workers have been uneasy about the absence of a union; the assembly line is a hazardous place, and an exploding television screen can permanently ruin a limb. Workers have complained of low wages. Atari has also had to hire security guards to protect itself from theft by employees who have used the philosophy to their advantage.

Atari's success is a result of its product's popularity. Their "computer" games are found in bars, lounges, hotel lobbies, banks, and country clubs; in Hawaii, Pongs may be found on the sidewalks chained to parking meters. Its popularity lies in its sophistication; like tennis, it involves coordination and brain power, and the more one practices, the less is left to chance. These games addict their players because the final result is either frustration or reward. The games also easily lend themselves to socialization through light-hearted competition or, as in Pong Doubles, through teamwork. Atari has gone one step beyond novelty and developed a true participatory sport.

As the blip lazily glides into your goal and your opponent scores again, it is hard to realize that the game is based on the algorithms that are built into a computer's circuitry system. So quarter after quarter is deposited in the slot, Atari's profits zoom upward, and the computer becomes increasingly important in America's leisure time.

Playing PONG to *Win*

by David Ahl

First you should understand that Pong is merely a miniature "computer" attached to a TV screen. The behavior of the ball and paddles is permanently programmed into the "computer" or PC board. If X happens, Y will result. Simple. No luck involved. No body English. No spins on the ball. Understand the algorithms and you can win the game.

The Paddle

The Pong paddle seems to be a single unbroken surface. Many players believe it can impart a spin to the ball as in actual ping-pong or tennis. Wrong. The paddle actually consists of seven sections. Each section returns the ball at a predetermined angle, *no matter what the angle of incidence*. The middle section returns it horizontally, the end sections at the greatest angles. The others are in between. Try to set your paddle for a return as soon as possible and fine tune it on the final approach of the ball.

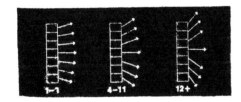

The Volley

The ball may seem to speed up with every volley. It doesn't. But it does speed up on the fourth and twelfth volleys. And, devilishly, the return angles of the paddles increase on these volleys too.

Gotcha Zones

A shot hit to the four corners of the screen cannot be returned no matter what the position of the paddle. You can most easily hit the ball to your opponent's corners from the center of the court; it's more difficult as you get to either of your corners. Hence, try to aim the ball at your opponent's corners to either score on him or at least prevent him getting it to your corners.

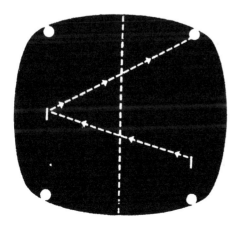

The Serve

The person who misses a point always receives the next serve. (On some earlier Pongs this algorithm was reversed, i.e., person who scores a point receives the next serve). You can predict where the serve will come from by simply imagining the screen wrapped around a cylinder with a second screen in back that you can't see. If the ball went off the screen fairly straight, it will appear from a continuation of the same path it was tracing. If it went off at an angle, it will bounce against the edge of the invisible screen on the other side of the cylinder and reappear at the new (opposite) angle. If you miss an angular serve, the next one will approach slightly higher or lower (unless the angle was exactly 45° in which case it will come from the same point).

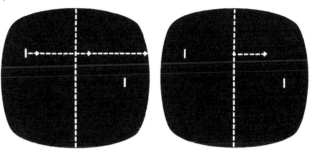

Now go hustle your friends. And if they want to know how you got so good all of a sudden, tell them to subscribe to *Creative Computing*.

Supplement to the Whole Earth Catalog
The *CoEvolution* Quarterly

CoEvolution Quarterly is the latest in an extraordinary series of publications from Stewart Brand, leader and spokesman for the Alternative Press movement.

I visited briefly with Stewart last November in his warehouse-on-the-water in Sausalito, windowless unfortunately. The place is piled floor-to-ceiling with magazines, newsletters, and information about virtually every project, organization, store or source in the U. S. It brings to mind NBC News Central although here the information is the written word rather than tapes and TTY prinout. Here in this dilapidated building is both the nerve center and central clearinghouse for the alternative press of the nation.

You have all seen *Whole Earth Catalog, Last Updated Whole Earth Catalog,* and *Whole Earth Epilog* full of those perceptive, mind-expanding notations followed by the now famous "--SB" (Stewart Brand). *CoEvolution Quarterly* brings you updates of material from the catalogs, new listings, as well as some longer articles and stories. Packed with information and sources about land use, shelter, food, community, learning, communications, and the alternative life. Handled by many local bookstores or $6.00/year from 558 Santa Cruz, Menlo Park, CA 94025.

History shows that new ideas in science most often come from brash youngsters, mavericks, or rank outsiders.

Fortune, May 1974

Your Own Computer?

by David H. Ahl

A number of people have asked me lately about computers in the home and about building your own. Somehow the two subjects seem to go hand-in-hand, probably because of an increasing number of low-priced computer kits on the market obviously aimed at the home hobbyist. In my mind, having your own computer at home and building your own are two entirely different animals.

A computer in the home is not like a ham radio rig or model railroad in which half of the enjoyment comes from the building. A computer is more like a TV set; 97% of the households in the U. S. have one, but most are not from Heathkit. A computer is, of course, much more than a TV — it provides education, recreation, and even utility.

You may find the following analogy chart useful to decide where you fit in the computer spectrum.

1. Use application programs	Drive a car (90% of population)
2. Program computer using high-level language (BASIC, FORTRAN, etc.)	Change oil, do tune-up (20%)
3. Computer science — machine languages, compilers, etc.	Auto mechanic — tear down and rebuild engine (1/4%)
4. Build your own computer from kit or plans	Build a dune buggy or dragster (0.1%)
5. Design and build your own computer	Design and build an efficient electric vehicle (0.001%)

In future issues of *Creative Computing,* we will report on No. 4, in particular, building an Altair 8800 computer kit (yes, I have previously built an HO model railroad, hi-fi components, and even a dune buggy). We'll also have some in-depth discussion on Nos. 1, 2, and 3 — that is, just what do you do with a home computer other than play games, and also where do you get one if you don't build it yourself?

Lies, Lies, Lies

Every once in a while I get a letter from a reader that makes me wonder whether you readers really believe everything you read in *Creative.* What am I saying? That there are falsehoods in *Creative*? That there are errors? That the truth is blemished? In a word, yes! And sometimes even deliberately!

The reason for this blasphemy is simply this: along with the best in computer activities, articles and other goodies, I happen to believe that we also have an obligation to do as much as possible in the way of bringing you an objective, multi-faceted, interesting, mind-expanding, broadening view of the world. And this is a world that contains people and ideas that are sometimes in conflict with one another, (not war, now) but what you might call cognitive dissonance. If we run an article which proclaims "there is no such thing as randomness," I don't really care if you believe it or not, but rather that it is a provocative idea that makes you think, or evaluate, or ponder, or wonder. That's what it's all about, folks — thinking and stretching your mind in order to create new ideas and make better use of the old ones.

And, incidentally, to have fun while you're at it!

—DHA

Introducing

Computer Recreations Corp.

by Trish Todd and Scott Guthery

Last year Americans spent over $50 billion on recreation. And billions more on home entertainment — television sets, radios, stereos, quadraphonic sound systems, tape recorders and home movie and video tape equipment.

This is no passing fancy. We live in an age of increasing leisure time. More people have more time to do more things with more money than ever before.

We live in an age of advancing technology, too. And when the consuming public seems ready for a new innovation, the technology always seems to be there, ready to meet that need. Witness the booming electronic calculator market.

We also live in an age of shortages — of energy, of raw materials. And the recent gasoline shortage made people suddenly aware of the need to search out new sources of entertainment and recreation. Closer to home, or at home. Reports from the travel and entertainment industries indicate that this awareness remained, even after the gas returned.

We live, as well, in an age of computers. Only up to now the computer has seemed a sort of enemy to many of us and at best a friend only to the specialist. To the average consumer/citizen/worker the computer is as foreign as the Crab Nebula.

Fear of the unknown, of course, is understandable. But anyone who has witnessed the average child adapt to the computer environment knows how short lived fear of computers can be. And how soon the computer becomes a friend.

Which brings us to COMPUTER RECREATIONS, a company formed to bring a wide (and friendly) selection of computer games into subscribers' homes through a special home terminal. This terminal resembles a typewriter with a cradle for the customer's telephone headset and is connected to his home television. In dialing a special number, the player is connected with the Computer Recreations WATS line, and he enters the "Game Parlor."

The player is then given several options. He may ask what games are available, ask for game rules, inquire who is in the "Game Parlor" or watch another game that is in progress. The game possibilities include chess, golf, Monopoly, football, Space War, Solataire, Blackjack, and many others. The participants may use an alias while competing with other subscribers; their faces are never seen. Computer Recreations is also involved in simulating urban planning, management decision-making, and political models. The possibilities will be constantly expanding because of a built-in market research program.

The system is fairly expensive today although it is within the financial reach of the affluent middle class; however, the technology exists to develop a terminal within the reach of almost everyone. (DEC, RCA, and others are at work on very low cost terminals today.)

Many Americans tend to think of computers as impersonal machines which are gradually changing the spontaniety of human life into a dehumanized number system. Not so, says Computer Recreations, and they aim to prove their point. For more information, write Scott Guthery, President, Computer Recreations, P. O. Box F, Cliffwood, NJ 07721.

This section of *Creative Computing* consists of news, notes, quotes, and short bits about this computer age in which we live. It was compiled and edited by Trish Todd, a freshman at Brown University along with David Ahl.

That's Entertainment

Switch from entertainment to education in seconds, says Philips/MCA of a videodisc system scheduled for fall 1976 production. Consisting of pre-recorded videodisc albums and a videodisc player that attaches to any standard home television receiver, the system will relay full color or black-and-white pictures and sound. Features: random access, speed-up, slow-down, freeze frame, reverse, and picture-by-picture presentation. The company claims that it's "easier to operate than a conventional phonograph, and simple and safe enough for a child to handle." For further information, write Lester Krugman, North American Philips Corporation, 100 East 42nd St., NY 10017 (212-697-3600).

American Libraries

Computer Science Conference in Anaheim

The Association for Computing Machinery announced that the Fourth Annual ACM Computer Science Conference will be held at the Disneyland Hotel in Anaheim, California on February 10-12, 1976. The Conference will feature short reports on current research in computer science by students, faculty, and researchers in the computer and information sciences. Over 1,000 attendees are expected.

In conjunction with the Conference, the ACM Special Interest Groups on Computer Science Education (SIGCSE) and Computer Uses in Education (SIGCUE) will hold a joint technical symposium on Computer Science and Education.

SIGCSE Meeting in Williamsburg

The Sixth SIGCSE Technical Symposium is scheduled for July 26-27, 1976 in Williamsburg, Virginia. The primary focus of the program will be on contributed papers in all areas of computer science education.

Contributed papers, with three copies are to be submitted to Professor William Poole, Mathematics Department, College of William and Mary, Williamsburg, Virginia 23185, with a March 15, 1976 deadline.

New Program Detects Typos

A computer program to catch typographical errors before they appear in print has been devised by two Bell Labs. researchers. Said to be the first of its kind ever developed, the program is fast, needs only limited computer storage capacity, and is easy for the proofreader to use, according to its developers. It will also help detect typographical errors in foreign languages as well as in English. The program cannot detect typos without human assistance. After the original document is input, an "index of peculiarity" for each word in the document is computed. The computer then displays or prints out a list of the words, with those most likely to contain typos listed first. It is then relatively easy for the proofreader to find and correct the typos. In one trial of the system, a 108-page document of nearly 20,000 words was examined for typos in three minutes by the computer. The author of the document needed less than ten minutes to scan the word list and locate 30 misspellings — 23 of which occurred in the first 100 words listed by the computer.

Modern Data

The $10 Computer Arrives

The "$10 computer" is no longer a joke. Hard on the heels of an announcement by National Semiconductor of the $48 computer, American Microsystems, Inc. (AMI) has introduced the "$9.98 computer," complete with program and data memories and input/output facilities.

Of course, you have to buy 5,000 at a time to get the $9.98 special price, but even 5,000 will only cost you $49,900, about the price of two minicomputers a few years ago. AMI expects the fixed-program computers to be used in calculators, portable data entry devices, cash registers and appliance controllers.

The S9209 computer comes with a 6K bit read-only memory for program storage, a 256 bit random access memory for temporary storage and input/output lines. The system handles 33 basic instructions with a typical instruction cycle time of 15 microseconds. Several of the microcomputers can be connected in tantrum for applications requiring increased capability.

Minicomputer News

A Career in Data Processing — 120 Years Ago

No. 3R6018 Fountain Pen only, without assortment. Price, each.................................8c
No. 3R6020 Fountain Pen Filler, for fountain pen use; straight glass with seamless rubber bulb. Price, each.................................4c
If by mail, postage extra, 2 cents.

The closest career to data processing 120 years ago would probably be the position of a clerk in a manufacturing or financial institution. Are "the good old days" for you? Here are the "Rules for Office Staff" posted in 1854 by Huddleston & Bradford, a banking firm in London, England.

1. Godliness, cleanliness and punctuality are the necessities of a good business.
2. The firm has reduced the working day to the hours from 8:30 a.m. to 7 p.m.
3. Daily prayers will be held each morning in the main office. The clerical staff will be present.
4. Clothing will be of a sober nature. The clerical staff will not disport themselves in raiment of bright color.
5. A stove is provided for the benefit of the clerical staff. It is recommended that each member of the clerical staff bring 4 lbs. of coal each day during cold weather.
6. No member of the clerical staff may leave the room without permission from Mr. Roberts. The calls of nature are permitted and clerical staff may use the garden beyond the second gate. This area must be kept clean in good order.
7. No talking is allowed during business hours.
8. The craving of tobacco, wines or spirits is a human weakness, and as such is forbidden to the clerical staff.
9. Members of the clerical staff will provide their own pens.
10. The managers of the firm will expect a great rise in the output of work to compensate for these near Utopian conditions.

— DHA

HP Educational Programs Clearinghouse

Have you ever felt that it would be so convenient if you could run French lessons or metric conversion exercises or a career information system on your computer? Information about the existence of such materials is not readily available; therefore, Hewlett Packard is launching the HP Clearinghouse for Application of Computers to Education.

The purpose of the project is to establish and maintain a list of educational applications, books, and other computer-related documents that will run on HP computer systems (both 2000 and 3000 series). Initially, the Clearinghouse will only deal with information concerning such materials; the materials would still be available from the current service agency. Catalog listings will be generated at periodic intervals and distributed for a small charge.

If you have materials that you would like included in the Clearinghouse, please contact: Harold J. Peters, HP Clearinghouse, Education Marketing, Hewlett-Packard, 1000 Wolfe Road, Cupertino, Ca. 95014.

Freedom of Information Act

Because concern in the United States has been stewing over the amount of information that our government collects about its citizens, concern has also been mounting over how to release this information to the public. Despite a presidential veto, the Freedom of Information Act (FOIA) has recently been amended in order to provide more clearly defined situations in which the government may or may not withhold information.

The FOIA became effective on July 4, 1967 and was designed to force government agencies to be more liberal in releasing information by establishing nine "exemption areas" as the only situations in which information could be withheld. Anyone requesting information from the government could take his case to court.

A recent House Subcommittee study showed that courts are generally reluctant to ask for disclosure of information such as files compiled for law enforcement or information in the interest of "the national defense or foreign policy". Although these are two exemption areas, the Congress did not intend for these situations to mean the automatic withholding of information. In 1974, amendments were passed over the presidential veto to prevent this sort of automatic delay in disclosure of information.

President Ford did not feel that courts should be "forced to make what amounts to the initial classification decision in sensitive and complex areas where they have no particular expertise." He also mentioned in his letter to Congress that confidentiality would be hard to maintain if government documents had to be closely examined before decisions could be made on their disclosure.

Computers, and society's increased use of numbers as identifiers have made it easier to gather and file information on citizens. The 1974 amendments to the FOIA have at least made this information more accessible to those it concerns.

Space Shuttle Simulator

The first shuttle mission space flight is scheduled for March, 1979, but preparation for the flight begins years in advance and is an extensive and complex process. The National Aeronautics and Space Administration recently purchased a large scale Sperry Univac 1100/46 computer system to be used in the training of flight crews and ground personnel in all phases of the Space Shuttle Program.

The computer complex will be a major part of the Shuttle Mission Simulator (SMS), and it will include simulation of the orbiter vehicle, main engines, solid rocket motors, external tanks, support equipment, and other activities required to fulfill the mission's objectives.

The main purpose of the complex will be to interact independently or simultaneously with the simulator fixed base and motion base crew stations as well as a full network simulation, all on a real-time basis. Since the computer system has multi-processing capabilities, it will also operate in remote batch, batch and demand situations. Training operations are scheduled to begin in March, 1978.

World Problems and Human Potential

Everyday, society is faced with discussion, debate, and concern about the world's problems. Everyone, it seems, is trying to solve a different problem, and not much attention is given to the relationships between problems. Therefore, the Union of International Associations began a data collection exercise using a network of 2500 international governmental and non-governmental organizations. Information was gathered on problems that these organizations felt concerned or was relevant to them, and it was compiled in the *Yearbook of World Problems and Human Potential.*

The project was produced from text held on the magnetic tape files of UIA's computer. Each world problem has a four-digit number in ascending numerical sequence which serves as a reference for the computer, filing, indexing, and cross-references. The system now contains 2560 world problems, but it can hold 3700. Each problem is also given a textual description and cross-references/indexes. This large amount of interrelated information is displayed through maps which are plotted by a computer. These maps enable people to plot their position in the social system just as they would check their position on a road map.

Because the collection of such an enormous and indefinite amount of information is such a difficult task, the aim of the project has been to establish a framework for processing data rather than to provide a definitive end-product. Hopefully, this process will make it possible to improve methods of gathering large amounts of information from diverse sources and make the result work for man toward a definite purpose.

For more information, write Anthony J. N. Judge, Asst. Secy-General, Union of International Assns., Rue aux Laines 1, 1000 Brussels, Belgium.

ACM Student Paper Winners

A committee consisting of graduate students at Massachusetts Institute of Technology chose Guy L. Steele, Jr. of Harvard University as the winner of the fourth annual George E. Forsythe Student Paper Competition for 1974-75, sponsored by the Association for Computing Machinery. For his paper, "Multiprocessing Compactifying Garbage Collection," Mr. Steele won $200 cash, a three year subscription to the ACM serial of his choice, and a trip to Minneapolis/St. Paul to receive his award at the 1975 ACM Annual Conference.

John L. Bentley of Stanford University and R. Mark Claudson, a high school student in Richland, Washington, tied for second place. Mr. Bentley's paper discussed "Multi-Dimensional Binary Search Trees Used for Associative Searching," and Mr. Claudson wrote about "The Digital Simulation of River Plankton Population Dynamics."

Computers Become Art at Lincoln Center

Fourteen artists from across the country participated in an unusual art show recently at Alice Tully Hall in New York's Lincoln Center cultural complex.

On exhibit were paintings representing a wide range of styles from landscape to surrealism. All were on computer equipment. The showing is part of a new corporate program to humanize working environments. It's called "A program to encourage the advancement of environmental art." The sponsor is James Talcott, Inc., a major New York City-headquartered financial services corporation.

In commenting on the showing, Donald S. Alvin, Talcott's vice president of marketing, said: "There has been great progress in moving art out of museums and mansions into more public environments. But there's one area where too little has been done. This area is perhaps the most important. It's where you and I spend most of our waking hours and nearly half our lives. It's the working environment.

"We at Talcott see no reason why art should top at the door of business. What we do see is a great opportunity to bring art to where most of the people are, most of the time. At the very least, it will make people a little happier. It might even result in better work."

With the advice of major museums, Talcott identified fourteen talented artists from across the country and commissioned them to humanize the computer technology environment.

"We chose the computer for two reasons," said Alvin. "It's an area we have been involved in for many years, and it's one of the most challenging and sterile working environments. In many ways the computer area symbolizes what's wrong with too many working environments. It's a place designed solely for efficiency and expediency. And in a large part, for machines."

[Ed Note. While the 14 selected artists were certainly respected and well-known, we at Creative Computing *wonder why no computer artists were invited to participate. It seems rather curious – DHA]*

New Role for NCIC

Financial institutions, plagued by phony securities deals, can get some extra help from the FBI's National Crime Information Center. Before leaving his post as Attorney General, William B. Saxbe urged the financial community to make better use of the NCIC to report lost, missing, counterfeit and stolen securities.

NCIC's fleet of crime-watching computers, Saxbe said, can also be used to check out suspicious securities. Approximately 90 per cent of the country, he pointed out, can have access to the network through local and federal law enforcement agencies for validation purposes.

In areas where there's an overload of law enforcement traffic, Saxbe said, the Justice Department could allow a financial user direct inquiry access into NCIC's securities file "as long as adequate internal security procedures are worked out."

Correlation and Causation

A professor of statistics used the following example to show that a statistical correlation between two series of events does not necessarily establish a causative link.

"Just because smoking of cigarettes and lung cancer are correlated," said the professor, "does not of itself prove that smoking causes cancer. Of course, the medical profession are agreed that there is indeed a direct causative link between the two, but the statistical correlation itself does not prove it."

"You may have noticed," he continued, "that the front seats of the vaudeville are always filled with bald-headed men. Now, if you believe that smoking causes cancer because the two are correlated you would conclude that looking at girls in tights makes your hair drop out. In fact, it is the over-activity of a certain hormone which both makes your hair drop out and makes you want to look at girls in tights."

ACM Policy on Universal Identifiers

How many times have you commented on the amount of numbers that identify you in society? We have charge account numbers, license numbers, Social Security numbers, insurance policy numbers, school I.D. numbers; the list is endless. A universal identifier would combine all of these identities into one number, and, with the use of computerized data banks, a specific individual's records could be quickly located for all number needs.

On November 14, 1974, the Association of Computing Machinery adopted a resolution regarding the use of the universal identifier. The A.C.M. acknowledged that a universal identifier would be beneficial to society and its individuals by simplifying the process of locating and comparing information about individuals. However, the A.C.M. felt that present technical, organizational, and legislative efforts to prevent possible abuse to the individual's right to privacy have *not* been adequate. The council urged the prompt generation and passage of legislation that would prevent the misuse of universal identifiers, including the Social Security Number.

FBI Computer Plans Grow, Despite Critics

Officials in the Federal Bureau of Investigation have been pushing for more than a year to expand the agency's computerized data bank network by linking it to existing state and local criminal information systems.

The Bureau's plan is to establish a centralized data system that would supply information to local police authorities, but which could also monitor and collect all local and state police messages. Control of communications would rest with the F.B.I.

That is what alarms so many of the critics. Conservative members of Congress are apprehensive about creation of a Federal police force; liberals are fearful of possible misuse of information at the expense of individual rights.

Responding to the criticism, officials have written that "The F.B.I. has long recognized ... the sanctity of the privacy of the individual." Authority to halt the computerized police system is vested in the Attorney General, the White House, and the Congress. A definitive action has not been taken.

The New York Times

You Can't Escape UPC

Recently, mysterious little squares filled with green, gray, and black stripes have been appearing on boxes of cereal, cans of spaghetti, and other supermarket items. These little squares belong to the new Universal Product Code (UPC) scanning checkout system, and they will increase checkout speed and efficiency in supermarkets and department stores.

The checker simply passes the UPC symbol over a slot in the counter, and it is read by an optical reflective system which uses a lasar light source. This symbol can contain information such as the item's department, manufacturer, color, and size. This information is then decoded and transmitted to the in-store computer which recalls the price from memory and sends it to the register for display and printing on the sales receipt.

Not only does the UPC scanning system check out merchandise, it also records information for inventory, calculates sales taxes automatically, records amounts of tender given, displays amounts of change due, calculates employee discounts, authorizes checks and charge accounts, and forces the salesperson to insert a salescheck when needed. One such scanning system operates in conjunction with NCR 255 electronic checkout terminals and an NCR 726 in-store computer and is priced at $4995.00.

This system is easily programmed, and modular and expandable hardware makes the Terminal Support System easily adaptable to a store's needs. Human error in merchandise management will practically be eliminated by NCR's small green, gray and black squares.

What? A Computer Make a Misteak?

Believe it or not, computers do make mistakes; in fact, the Rome Air Development Center at Griffiss Air Force Base has given a $408,000 grant to the Polytechnic Institute of New York to do research on computer errors. The research program is aimed at predicting the number and frequency of software errors made by Air Force computers, and hopefully, it will result in the formulation of techniques to prevent and eliminate mistakes. If successful, it is expected that other industries will use the report as a guide for their own studies.

The Air Force spends millions of dollars each year on correction of programming errors. Some of these programs are several million instructions long and are programmed by hundreds of individual programmers, each writing a small module of code. When these codes are connected, mistakes appear because modules are tested individually, not collectively. The real problem in producing reliable software has been in predicting how often the software will fail when put in use. Some large time-sharing computers fail every few hours due to software problems, while others operate for weeks without failure. The Polytechnic team will conduct studies on techniques for more reliably testing large programs.

Want to Lose 10 Pounds?

Do you think that your weekly grocery bill is too high? Have you been eating the right foods? Have you been eating too much meat and not enough vegetables? A UNIVAC 1108 computer will answer these and other questions you have about food and your diet.

Over 12,000 Wisconsin residents have already taken advantage of the program offered by the University of Wisconsin in Madison. One simply fills out a food record which shows foods most frequently eaten by Wisconsin residents. A person may fill out one to thirty forms; each form is for one day.

The results are then checked by nutrition experts, and food substitutions or diet changes may be recommended. These recommendations are based on the person's intake of a dozen nutrients, taking into consideration the person's age and sex. The computer has shown that many people eat more meat than they need; these people could cut back on meat and buy less expensive foods.

"One with Pepperoni and Mushrooms Please"

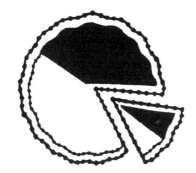

Michigan State University's "talking computer" recently ordered pepperoni and mushroom pizzas from a local pizzeria and received them. The order was placed under the direction of a wheelchair-bound and speech-handicapped student, who operated the keyboard to make the computer talk over the phone. The student was one of twenty-five guests at the pizza party for beneficiaries, supporters, and co-workers in the project to adapt the computers to help people with speech problems. Host of the party was Dr. John Eulenburg, professor of linguistics and computer science, and co-designer of the talking computer.

Computers Monitor Biorhythms

Everyone has those days when they seem to be extra accident prone. One is constantly dropping things, stubbing toes, crunching fingers, and making petty mistakes at work. United Air Lines' San Francisco aircraft maintenance base is using computers to discover these accident prone days by monitoring the biorhythms of more than 28,000 employees; hopefully, the study will help reduce on-the-job accidents.

Biorhythms are the physical, mental, and emotional ups and downs of an individual, and they can be plotted in regular cycles. The physical cycle repeats every twenty-three days, the emotional every twenty-eight days, and the intellectual every thirty-three days. Studies show that individuals have more accidents when their biorhythms are on a negative curve. In United's program, each foreman is given a chart of each employee's "zero," "double zero," and "triple zero" days. (A "double zero" days occurs when two cycles are in a downphase.) Employees can then be alerted to be extra cautious on those days.

On-Line Legal Data

SEARCH (System for Electronic Analysis and Retrieval of Criminal Histories), a federal project which stresses computerization of court records, is going to be a part of the New Jersey legal system. A central computer storing every court decision since 1948 will give all courthouses and law libraries in the state access to the materials filed in the computer. Legal data will be available swiftly on a full-text basis, so that the time-consuming tasks of research can be accomplished with a simple push of the computer button.

Computer Security Puzzle

By concocting what could probably qualify as a code breaker's nightmare, one researcher hopes to prevent some of the criminal manipulations that go on with computers. Professor John Robinson of the University of Iowa is hard at work making a computer puzzle-code of data bits that must be run before any program can be used. For a less valuable program, he says, an operator might have to take about 1200 data bits and arrange them correctly to have access to the program. To further complicate the task and minimize tampering, he would include an extra 200 useless data bits. In a more complicated program, a computer crook might be faced with picking the right 2000 data bits out of a possible 10,000 clues and somehow figuring out the correct arrangement. That's certainly enough to discourage lucky guessers.

Science Digest

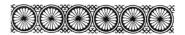

Graphical Standards for BASIC

Because there are no standards for writing graphical programs, it has always been difficult for people and institutions to exchange written programs. However, the development of a standard syntax for graphical operations in the BASIC language is now underway at Dartmouth College. The study has been made possible by grants from the National Science Foundation, the National Bureau of Standards, California Computer Products, Inc., Hewlett-Packard Company, UNIVAC, and Tektronix.

The project began in October, 1974 when a panel met at Dartmouth to discuss extending BASIC for graphical purposes. If the resulting syntax is approved by the X3J2 Committee on Standard BASIC, graphical commands could be incorporated in the published standard. However, the X3J2 has been holding sessions for over a year without resolving all the differences of the committee members; so, it appears that the graphical syntax project will not enjoy the benefit of even a preliminary language standard before it is scheduled to terminate in January, 1976.

Indian Students Use Computers

Educationally delayed teen-aged American Indian students from four states are being given a chance to further their education with the help of a timesharing computer system. Chemawa Indian School of Salem, Oregon has purchased extensive computer time from the Oregon Total Information System (OTIS), an educational computer consortium in Eugene. The school, founded in 1883, is the oldest continuously operated Indian boarding school in America, providing dormitory living during the school year to high school aged children from tribes in Alaska, Oregon, Washington and Idaho.

The computer time will provide each student who is more than three years below his grade level with a system of learning laboratories focused around terminals and computer assisted instruction. The minicomputer directing this instruction will be a Hewlett-Packard 2000F, the third in OTIS' inventory.

According to Dr. Y.T. Witherspoon, special projects coordinator for the School, 16 terminals will be divided among three separate learning labs for reading, language arts and mathematics. "Students will use the lab that answers their own particular need. We will be able to give each youngster 10 minutes per day on a terminal and still meet the educational demands of the entire student body."

"It is our hope," continued Dr. Witherspoon, "that by using the Computer Assisted Instruction, we will be able to compress at least seven years of education into the usual four — thereby giving educationally delayed students a chance to catch-up with their contemporaries."

Flying Buffalo

by Richard Loomis

People are constantly asking me why I named my company "Flying Buffalo, Inc." Quite simply, I wanted a name that would attract attention. I thought about several names that related to wargames or simulations. But they all sounded similar to names that other companies were already using. The "Flying Buffalo" name was originally going to be used for my planned (but never finished) stamp and coin shop. I was going to have a picture of a flying eagle penny and a buffalo nickel. I decided to use the name for my game company, because I figured it would attract lots of attention, and be easily remembered. I was certainly right. I have received several requests to write articles about my company, we have been written up in newspapers, and we even got mentioned in the March issue of *Playboy* magazine!

I suppose now you are wondering what it is we actually do. We moderate multi-player, play-by-mail games on our computer. (Moderator: referee or umpire. Multi-player: the games have more than 2 players competing against each other. Play-by-mail: the players are located in various places around the world, and mail their moves to us. Computer: the machine which keeps track of all this.) Our most popular game is called *Nuclear Destruction*. We usually put 12 players in a game. Each player is given a country of the world. He has factories, missiles, and anti-missiles. He decides what to build with his factories, who to shoot his missiles at, and how to distribute his foreign aid. Any player may fire any or all of his missiles at any other player. If enough missiles are fired at a country, that player is out of the game. The idea, of course, is to get the other players to shoot at each other instead of at you. The players may exchange messages with each other in order to make alliances, threats, bribes, or whatever. The rules of the game are quite simple, but there are an infinite number of variations. We charge $1 entry fee, and 25¢ for each turn. The turns are two weeks apart, and the game generally lasts for about a year.

Our second most popular game is called *Battle Plan*. It is similar to *Nuclear Destruction*, but adds a lot of complicated rules for armies, navies, air forces, counterspies, research, and so forth. We usually put 6 or 7 players in a game of *Battle Plan*, and we charge 55¢ per turn.

If you would like to see the rules to *Nuclear Destruction* send 15¢ (or *Battle Plan*, send 50¢) to: Flying Buffalo, Inc., P.O. Box 1467, Scottsdale, Arizona 85252.

Is anybody interested in a research project? Think about this: In a game of *Nuclear Destruction* you have 12 different people of various ages, backgrounds, and physical locations competing in a game where the players may have conflicting goals. In one game you are likely to have people who want to win at any cost, people who want to maximize their positions in several games at once (that is, two second place finishes are better than a win and a last place), people who get bored and drop out, people who have entered the game only in hopes of meeting someone they have played against previously in order to get revenge, people who are totally irrational, and people who play merely to correspond with other people. We have players from 9 to 59 years of age. We have students, professors, servicemen, politicians, mechanics, musicians, doctors, and lawyers. They are located in Canada, California, New York, Florida, Alaska and Maine. We even have players in Switzerland, England, Austria, France and Israel. If some professor, or even someone looking for a degree, would like to write an article based on this game, we would be happy to enter him in several free games for research purposes. If you are interested, please write me at the above address.

COWS AND COMPUTERS

Satellite terminal connected to the University of Wyoming's Sigma 7 computer over an unusual line installed by Mountain Bell. Joe Wenger, an Industrial Management major from Evanston, Illinois is one of four Commerce and Industry students who manned the University of Wyoming's exhibit at the Wyoming State Fair at Douglas, August 26 - September 1, 1974.

The computer is programmed to answer questions in 18 different areas. Running is a program of interest to ranchers to provide nutrients and diet balance for five different types of cattle. (Photo by Rasmussen, University of Wyoming)

FREE BUTTONS!!

In conjunction with President Ford's "Improve the Economy with Singing" Program, millions of "WIN" buttons were printed. Yes, millions! Nobody quite knows what to do with these embarrassing quantities of buttons and in most large cities the Federal Office of Economic Opportunity or its equivalent will give hundreds of these buttons free to anyone who asks for them. (You may have to do some diligent searching by phone to find the right agency in your area).

Well, fans, did it ever occur to you that WIN up-side-down spells NIM, a popular computer game. So get a hundred NIM buttons for your school or computer center today, courtesy of Uncle Sam.

—DHA

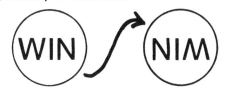

OUR COMPUTERIZED telephone answering service is scientifically calibrated to judge human personality just by voice vibrations and tonal quality. We can detect within 10 seconds whether the person who wishes to speak to you is trying to borrow money or sell you worthless merchandise. Write for information. Electronic Voice Analysis.

COMPLEAT COMPUTER CATALOGUE

RESOURCES
AND
TOOLS

You've heard of *Big Rock Candy Mountain, Whole Earth Catalog, Whole Earth Epilog, Rain, Yellow Pages of Learning Resources*, and *Tom Swift and His Electric English Teacher*. Well here we go again with another catalog/access handbook/annotated bibliography. The idea of this, *The Complete Computer Catalog,* is to provide source information about resources for learning about and using computers effectively. The emphasis will be on applications, software, and learning aids rather than computer hardware and systems.

This catalog is for:

1. People who have never seen a computer and want to learn what all the fuss is about,

2. People who are just meeting their first computer either in school or on the job,

3. Experienced computer people who want to use their machine more effectively.

Between two and eight pages of *The Complete Computer Catalog* will appear in each issue of *Creative Computing.* Eventually all the entries may be collected together and published as a book (or catalog).

We would welcome entries from readers on any worthwhile item related, even distantly, to computers. Please include the name of the item, an evaluative description, price, and complete source data. If it is an item that you were acquainted with over one year ago, please check with the source to make sure it is still available at the quoted price.

Our catalog categories are not cast in concrete. However, at the moment they are:

    Books and Booklets
    Periodicals and Journals
    Games
    Learning Aids and Films
    Computer Software
    Computer Hardware
    Groups and Associations

Send contributions to The Complete Computer Catalog, c/o *Creative Computing,* P.O. Box 789-M, Morristown, NJ 07960.

BOOKS AND BOOKLETS

COMPUTERS AND THEIR IMPACT ON BUSINESS AND SOCIETY

Course outline and text for 40-hour course "to present a balanced view of what a computer is and how it can be used, and also set pupils thinking about what computing could mean to them as people." This book was prepared by the National Computing Centre, Ltd., Manchester, England. U. S. price unknown, but it is available from:

Hayden Book Co., 50 Essex St., Rochelle Park, NJ 07662.

COMPUTERS IN THE ELEMENTARY SCHOOL: A COURSE FOR TEACHERS

This 32-page booklet consists of a fairly detailed course outline to give elementary teachers an introduction to computers and electronic calculators. It includes sections on problem-solving, calculators, computers, programming, future implications, and classroom strategies. $1.50.

Curriculum Group, Oregon Council for Computer Education, Dept. of Computer Science, Univ. of Oregon, Eugene, OR 97403.

RANGER 'RITHMETIC

Series of booklets for first to eight grade with 20 some odd problems in each around the theme of forest conservation. Many problems suitable for calculator or computer solution. Ask for the one for your grade level. Single copy free. Also ask for list of teaching aids.

Forest Service, U. S. Dept. of Agriculture, Washington, DC 20250.

THE WHOLE WORD CATALOG

A practical collection of assignments for stimulating student writing, designed for both elementary and secondary level. Activities included to foster personal writing, collective novels, diagram stories, fables, spoofs, and language games. Contains an annotated bibliography. Many computer people do not write easily or well; this will help. $3.00.

Teachers & Writers Collaborative, 186 West 4th St., New York, NY 10014.

LAYMAN'S GUIDE TO THE USE OF COMPUTERS

The emphasis of this guide is on instructional applications of computers. It tends to have a data processing slant and isn't as comprehensive as some other guides (OCCE, for example) but for $3.00 presents a reasonable overview (although the price should really be more like $1.50).

Association for Educational Data Systems, 1201 Sixteenth St., NW, Washington, DC 20036.

MATHEMATICS CURRICULUM REPORT

Report (October 1974) discusses changes in mathematics programs in junior high and middle schools. Discussion of pocket calculators, computers, statistical concepts, practical problem-solving, and various university and vendor curriculum projects. Ask for Vol. 4, No. 1, "Mathematics Programs are Changing" – 50¢ prepaid.

NASSP, 1904 Association Drive, Reston, VA 22091.

SCIENCE FOR SOCIETY

An extensive 110-page bibliography for students, faculty, and lay groups. Most references 1971 and later – mostly newspapers and magazines. Price unknown.

Commission on Science Education, AAAS, 1776 Massachusetts Ave., NW, Washington, DC 20036.

CURRICULUM MATERIAL PRODUCT CATALOG

This booklet lists virtually all of the materials for using computers in the curriculum published by DEC including the popular Huntington II simulation materials. Pictures of each item, capsule commentaries, price, and ordering information are included. Free.

Education Products Group, Digital Equipment Corp., Maynard, MA 01754.

COMPUTERS BOOKLET

A 94-page booklet for 40 cents? Why, it's even difficult to get 94 sheets of blank paper for 40 cents. And yet here is one of the best basic descriptive books on computer hardware. It covers the birth of computers from the abacus and Babbage up to the present day, the anatomy of a computer including simplified explanations of some very sophisticated hardware, and finally some speculation about what's coming in the way of applications and large networks. The booklet simply titled *Computers* is written by William Corliss and published by the AEC, sorry ERDA. This one is a must. 40¢ each, even less in quantity. (Many other booklets are also available from ERDA; we recommend three: *Cryogenics, Teleoperators* and *Lasers*. Send $1.60 for all four.)

U.S. Energy Research and Development Administration, Technical Information Center, P.O. Box 62, Oak Ridge, TN 37830.

POPULATION AND FOOD

There are two interrelated and indisputable facts which many people have failed to comprehend: 1) world food production cannot keep pace with world population growth (not even with computer planning, miracle fertilizers, or plankton harvests from the ocean) and 2) "family planning" or new contraceptives cannot and will not, in the foreseeable future, check population growth. People are clearly looking for a miracle solution since the alternative, of course, is triage. Every person in the world, has an obligation to learn more about this situation which can only be described as a crisis. Send for a copy of the "Declaration on Population and Food" and a subscription to "The Other Side." Both free.

The Environmental Fund, 1302 Eighteenth St., N.W., Washington, DC 20036.

BRAINSTORMING, CREATIVITY

Practical exercises and guides to brainstorming, creative thinking, designing objectives, getting people involved in this book by Donkoberg and Jim Bagnall. The title is a jaw-breaker, *The Universal Traveler: A Soft-System Guide to Creativity, Problem Solving and the Process of Reaching Goals.* Price unknown.

William Kaufmann, Inc., One First St., Los Altos, CA 94022.

COMPUTER OUTPUT MICROFILM COMICS

A clever comic book with Super Rex and Clark Trent explains how-tos and benefits of computer output microfilm. 25¢.

Memorex Corp., San Tomas at Central Expressway, Santa Clara, CA 95052.

3 IFIP BOOKLETS

Three booklets have been produced between 1971 and '74 by various working groups of the International Federation for Information Processing.

Computer Education for Teachers in Secondary Schools – An Outline Guide is for those who are planning courses for the training of teachers. It gives suggestions for the content of courses although the information is of a very general nature. Includes 3 brief but excellent pages on methodology. 75¢.

Computer Education for Teachers in Secondary Schools – Aims and Objectives in Teacher Training. Booklet shows how society and education is changing and discusses the role of the computer in modern education. Lists brief outlines for seven courses. 75¢.

The Use of the Computer in Teaching and Learning. Describes ways of using the computer in education, the rationale and benefits. Discusses the necessary factors for a successful program – key people, instructional material development, facilities, and hardware acquisition. Depth of coverage is sparse (booklet has only 16 pages of text). $1.50.

AFIPS Press, 210 Summit Ave., Montvale, NJ 07645.

SMALL PRESS MATERIALS

Edcentric, Haiku Magazine, Tzaddikim, Feminist Art Journal, Fiction, Roar, Nitty Gritty, Blue Pig, Algol, Maybe, and *Quest* are just 11 of the approximately 1800(!) little magazines and small presses listed and described in the 1975-76 International Directory of Little Magazines and Small Presses. If you want a different view of the world, sometimes strange, sometimes ecstatic, but always refreshing, get this directory and send for sample copies of 10 or 20 little magazines. Directory $5.95 plus 50¢ postage.

Dustbooks, P.O. Box 1056, Paradise, CA 95969.

TOWARD UNDERSTANDING THE SOCIAL IMPACT OF COMPUTERS

This very comprehensive 136-page book by Roy Amara is the distillation of the thoughts of 60 participants in four workshops held by the Institute for the Future. The principal message is that a real urgency exists to systematically

understand how computers affect the decisions we make, the goods and services we produce, and the world we perceive. Specific topics discussed in-depth include: 1. Computer modeling and simulation as an aid to decision making, 2. Computers and financial processes, 3. Computer perceptions, attitudes, literacy, 4. Computers and individual access. A fifth could be added, "where do we go from here?" $10 to institutions, $7.50 to individuals and schools.

Institute for the Future, ATTN: Judy Flathman, 2740 Sand Hill Road, Menlo Park, CA 94025.

TOM SWIFT AND HIS ELECTRIC ENGLISH TEACHER

A "Whole Earth Catalog" type book by G. Howard Poteet for English teachers. This oversize (11" x 15") handbook is chock full of teaching techniques, ideas on how to use new and old equipment, quotations, hardware, software, etc. Excellent sections on the use of radio, TV, filmstrips, and drama. Source and price info included. $4.95.

Pflaum/Standard, 8121 Hamilton Ave., Cincinnati, OH 45231.

LEARNING AIDS

SMARTY CAT

A slide rule for young children to help in the four basic arithmetic operations. A blue cat's face moves along a red, white, and blue rule – addition and subtraction is on one side, multiplication and division on the other. Probably most useful for slow learners. $1.50 each.

Involv-o-Products, P.O. Drawer 3966, San Angelo, TX 76901.

MAGAZINES, JOURNALS, NEWSLETTERS

LEARNING

An excellent, colorful, contemporary magazine for elementary and middle school teachers. The focus of the March 1975 issue is on math — teaching strategies, new methods and materials, activities for hand-held calculators, opinion, etc. Single copy $1.50.

Education Today Co., 530 University Ave., Palo Alto, CA 94301.

MINICOMPUTER NEWS

This bi-weekly tabloid newspaper reports on developments in minicomputer hardware, software, and applications. A recent issue covered a real potpouri of topics — Decnet, timesharing user group news, oceanographic research with minis, and Centronics re-entry into the electronic games field. $6.00 per year, sample issue free.

Benwill Publishing Co., 167 Corey Road, Brookline, MA 02146.

COMPUTER PROGRAM ABSTRACTS

The National Computer Program Abstract Service is a clearinghouse for computer program abstracts — simulation models, application programs, MIS, etc. — from business, government, military, and universities. As of Spring 1975, 17,000 abstracts were indexed in 167 specific subjects. A quarterly Program Index Newsletter is published for $10.00 per year. Sample copy free.

NCPAS, P.O. Box 3783, Washington, DC 20007.

GAMES & PUZZLES

The only monthly magazine devoted to nothing but games and puzzles. Word games, crosswords (watch out for British spelling), number games, Go, Backgammon, Chess, Scrabble, various card games, mazes, reader puzzles and games, competitions. Lively and fun. $10.80 per year to U. S., sample copy $1.10.

Games & Puzzles, 11 Tottenham Court Road, London WIA 4xF, England.

THE FUTURIST

A bi-monthly journal of forecasts, trends, and ideas about the future. The magazine presents an objective, reasoned approach to future study and does not advocate particular ideologies. Recent issues have examined teaching and education in the future, behavior control, work and leisure, and world planning. $12.00 per year, sample copy $2.00.

World Future Society, P.O. Box 30369, Washington, DC 20014.

TEACHER MAGAZINE

Teacher, one of the two big "establishment" elementary school magazines (*Instructor* is the other) often has games and activities useful for introducing young kids to concepts in math, statistics, and computers. "Clothespin Probability," "What Comes Next?" (Jan 1975) and "A Game for all Reasons" (April 1975) are three such games. Watch the column, "Creative Classroom" for the best ideas. Subscription $10/year; sample copy $1.25.

Teacher, P.O. Box 800, Cos Cob, CT 06807.

SIMULATION/GAMING/NEWS

S/G/N is now in a 32-page 8½ x 11 newsprint format which seems to have improved its very professional and comprehensive coverage of the world of simulations and serious games. It frequently carries a page or two of computer gaming news, has excellent game reviews and an annotated bibliography which appear every issue, as well as news, views, and articles about gaming and education. Bi-monthly, $6.00/year; sample copy $1.00.

Simulation/Gaming/News, Box 3039, University Station, Moscow, ID 83843.

THEORETICAL COMPUTER SCIENCE

A new quarterly journal covering theoretical automata, semantics of programming languages, the study of algorithms and their complexity, and the nature of computation. Mathematical and abstract in spirit but motivated by problems of practical computation. $43.95 per year, sample copy free.

North-Holland Publishing Co., c/o American Elsevier Publishing Co., 52 Vanderbilt Ave., New York, NY 10017.

HP EDUCATIONAL NEWSLETTER

An outstanding 8-times a year newsletter produced for users of Hewlett Packard computers in education. Naturally it is oriented to software which runs on HP machines, mostly BASIC. A portion of each issue is generally devoted to user application (success) stories. About 40% or 50% of each issue presents instructional applications and activities, sometimes on one special focus topic, sometimes on many. Shorter sections include book reviews (genuine reviews, not publisher press releases), letters, announcements, and a calendar of events. Free to HP users. $6 per year to others.

HP Educational Users Group, 11000 Wolfe Road, Cupertino, CA 95014.

SIGCUE BULLETIN

This is the official publication for the 1,300 member Special Interest Group on Computer Uses in Education (SIGCUE) of the Association for Computing Machinery (ACM). An excellent source of information on using computers in college instruction. Contains brief technical articles, interviews, conference reports, book reviews, and calendar of events. Four issues per year. $6/year ($4 for ACM members).

Assn. for Computing Machinery, 1133 Avenue of the Americas, New York, NY 10036.

WOMEN IN ENGINEERING

IEEE Transactions on Education, Vol. E-18, No. 1 (Feb 1975) is a special issue on women in engineering. The 14 papers in the issue discuss the growth of women in engineering programs, opportunities in various types of engineering, minority programs, and starting early with orientation in junior high school. Some of the papers are real eye openers to our changing world. Single copy $2.50.

Thelma Estrin (IEEE Committee on Professional Opportunities for Women), Brain Research Institute, Univ. of California, Los Angeles, CA 90024.

HP65 CALCULATOR NOTES

Would you believe BAGELS, CRAPS, FOOTBALL, GUNNER, HEX-A-PAWN, and PING-PONG for a pocket calculator? And much, much more? I didn't until I saw *65 NOTES*, an absolutely fascinating publication of the HP-65 (and 55) Calculator Users Club. Packed with useful information to HP-65 owners — routines, beginners corner, how to handle alphabetics(!), tips, and games. The March 1975 issue is a double issue (45 pages) entirely devoted to games. Monthly, $10 per year, $1.00 sample copy, $2.00 March games issue.

Richard J. Nelson, HP-65 Users Club, 2541 W. Camden Place, Santa Ana, CA 92704.

ON-LINE NEWSLETTER

Covers computers in teaching and learning activities particularly in Michigan and adjoining states and provinces. Each issue carries brief reports, conference information, news, reviews, and comments. Those in the midwest will want to get *On-Line,* others will find the *SIGCUE Bulletin* more helpful. Six issues per year, $4.00 (free in Michigan).

Karl Zinn, U-M CRLT, 109 E. Madison St., Ann Arbor, MI 48104.

PEOPLE'S COMPUTER COMPANY

A 5-times a year newspaper edited by Bob Albrecht carrying all kinds of diverse information about computer games, building your own computer, new hardware for hobbyists, information about people starting local public computer centers, and other related stuff.

Vol. 4, No. 1, although designated "Hardware Issue," had an excellent reprint titled "Community Memory – A Public Information Network" and another article "Starting Your Own (Community Computer) Center." $5.00 per year, sample copy $1.00.

People's Computer Company, P.O. Box 310, Menlo Park, CA 94025.

OUTWORLDS

One of the most diverse, interesting, and professional science fiction fanzines around. The personal touch of the editor, Bill Bowers, is very refreshing. Stories are of variable interest and/or quality, i.e., you probably won't like everything in every issue but you'll like something very much. Excellent graphics. Published quarterly. $4.00 per year, sample (double) issue $1.50.

William L. Bowers, Outworlds, P.O. Box 2521, North Canton, OH 44720.

THE COMPILER

An occasional publication of Anaheim Publishing Co., *The Compiler* is aimed at business data processing educators. Three or four articles per issue plus information on the latest books from Anaheim (mostly COBOL, Assembler and business EDP). Free.

Anaheim Publishing Co., 1120 East Ash, Fullerton, CA 92631.

PRIVACY JOURNAL

A monthly 8-page newsletter with news about privacy – new laws and regulations, new technology, and public attitudes. Generally, at least, fifty per cent of each issue discusses computer-related privacy. Looks at school records, crime data systems, medical records, mail lists, wiretaps, credit reporting, surveillance, computer security, etc. $15.00 per year, sample copy free.

Privacy Journal, P.O. Box 8844, Washington, DC 20003.

FOR NCR 399 USERS

Load & Go is an informal quarterly newsletter for NCR 399 users put together by Bill Moore and Jim Burmeister. It has hardware hints, commonly-used software routines, games, tips, and occasional reviews and letters. Not an official publication of NCR. $5.00 for 10 issues.

Bill Moore, Muskegon Federal Savings, P.O. Box 568, Muskegon, MI 49443.

COMMUNITY TELEVISION

Are you interested in improving the regulation of television broadcasting? Should cable TV and satellites be used to serve social needs as well as commercial ones? What's going on in community video? Public access TV? How about interactive TV in medicine? A video conference? TV in Russia? Reviews, equipment, news. If these things pique your curiousity then maybe you should try *TeleVISIONS,* a lively bi-monthly tabloid magazine now in its third year. $10 for 10 issues, sample issue $1.00.

Washington Community Video Center, P.O. Box 21068, Washington, DC 20009.

POPULAR COMPUTING

A monthly publication for people interested in the art of computing. Each issue contains 2 or 3 new interesting, and generally very intriguing, problems for computer solution, tables of roots and logarithms to high precision, essays on the art of computing, book reviews, and other related material. $15.00 per year, sample issue $2.00.

Fred Gruenberger, Popular Computing, P.O. Box 272, Calabasas, CA 91302.

DOOMSDAY + 1

Doomsday + 1 is a new comic book (you know, like *Superman, Detective Comics* or *Captain Marvel.*) Are you kidding? *Creative Computing* recommending comics? Yes, indeed. In case you didn't read Ron Anderson's article in *Creative* Vol. 1, No. 3, we should mention that cartoons and comics mirror the average person's understanding of technology (and computers) very closely. *Doomsday + 1* is set in the near future

after a devastating nuclear war, but oh what the remaining computers and robot androids can do! Take a look. 25¢ at your local newsstand or $1.25 for the next six issues from Charlton Comics, Division St., Derby, CT 06418.

MICRO-8 USER GROUP

Ever since the plans for building your own computer, called the Mark-8, appeared in *Popular Electronics,* hobbyists using the Intel 8008 chip (and later the 8080) have formed clubs and started newsletters to communicate with one another. The *Micro-8 Computer User Group Newsletter* serves 300 plus members all over the U.S. It's one of he best, print quality (vital for schematics) has improved dramatically from the early issues, although you still have to comb every page to find a specific item. $6.00 for 6 issues. Sample issue $1.00.

Micro-8 Computer User Group, Cabrillo Computer Center, 4350 Constellation Road, Lompoc, CA 93436.

THE AMERICAN SYSTEM

For businessmen, *Fortune* is practically required reading; for other people, ho hum. However, the April 1975 "Special Bicentennial Issue: The American System" should be required reading for everyone. An article by Max Ways discusses how the System quickens and guides Americans toward higher goals and harder challenges, but then how each triumph brings its swarm of troubles. Daniel Bell discusses the danger of people demanding equality of result and not just equality of opportunity, and speculates that these demands could well overload our political system. Two other articles examine our battered educational system and scientific system. Can both regain their vitality of 20 years ago? And at what cost? Another article discusses the new generation of young Americans, their ethics, responsibility, and the fact that they expect more from the System than any previous generation. This issue of *Fortune* deserves a place in your personal "search for freedom and self-fulfillment" (J.F. Kennedy). *Fortune,* April 1975, $2.00.

Fortune, 541 North Fairbanks Court, Chicago, IL 60611.

TEKGRAPHICS

A quarterly publication that describes the latest software for graphic computer terminals and Tektronix customer applications. Recent issues have included articles about interactive mapping, urban planning and medical diagnostics. Free.

Tektronix, Inc., Information Display Division, P.O. Box 500, Beaverton, OR 97005.

FUTURE REPORT

This 18-issues-per-year newsletter contains scores of capsule reports in each issue from one line to a few paragraphs on emerging future trends. Generally a number of computer-related items in each issue. The reports as a whole make a fascinating mosaic of what society is likely to be in the near future. Covers subjects from space travel to energy, medical practice to courtrooms, and environment to music. Free Perpetual Calendar of the Future with one-year subscription. $36/year. Sample copy free.

Foundation for the Future, P.O. Box 2001, MIT Branch P.O., Cambridge, MA 02139.

DO YOU SUPPORT TECHNOLOGY?

If you read *Creative Computing* regularly, chances are you have a warm spot in your heart for science and technology. Many other people, particularly students and educators, with similar views have joined the Federation of Americans Supporting Science and Technology. Recent issues of FAAST News have covered a variety of topics: Aerospace (space shuttle, remote sensing, "Cosmic/Charisma", the OSCAR satellite); Biomedical (fetal research, continuing medical education); Energy (nuclear fuels, natural gas issues, cryogenic energy, ERDA); Environment; and various political activities. FAAST membership (includes bi-monthly *FAAST News*) $5.00.

FAAST, 1785 Massachusetts Ave., N.W., Washington, DC 20036.

PERSONAL PRIVACY VS. THE CORPORATE COMPUTER

Americans have long abhorred the spector of a faceless, bureaucratic Big Brother. As computerized personal data systems have grown more and more sophisticated, many people have become concerned about the threat these systems pose to individual privacy. Recently some state and federal regulations have been passed to counter the threat and more are in the offing. But the cost of complying with them will be very high. In an article in *Harvard Business Review* (Vol. 53, No. 2, Mar-Apr 1975), Robert Goldstein and Richard Nolan discuss the impact of the new privacy laws on five active personal data systems — consumer credit, health, personnel, insurance, and law enforcement. They also suggest several steps that organizations must take to adjust to the new environment. Reprints of "Personal Privacy vs. the Corporate Computer" cost $3.00 each for 1 to 5 or 50¢ each for 6 or more (why get 1 when you can get 6 for the same price?).

Reprint Service, *Harvard Business Review,* Boston, MA 02163.

MAJOR ROLES FOR MINICOMPUTERS IN BUSINESS

Managers have known for several years that the effectiveness of a computer system is proportional to the square of its cost, i.e., pay twice as much and get four times the performance. Because of this and because there have been so few computer specialists to go around, companies have tended to centralize their EDP operations. But these premises are now shifting as minis become more cost effective and as more people are trained in computers. An article, "At last, major roles for minicomputers" by Gerald Burnett and Richard Nolen in *Harvard Business Review* (Vol. 53, No. 3, May-Jun 1975), discusses four companies that have used minis differently. The authors suggest steps for management to analyze minis and assimilate them into the organization. Reprints (one article or mixed) $3.00 each (1 to 5) or 50¢ each (6 or more).

Reprint Service, *Harvard Business Review,* Boston, MA 02163.

MEDIA

SPACE: 1999

Did you catch the first episode of Space: 1999 on TV where the computer said, "not-enough-data-to-compute. HUMAN DECISION NECESSARY"? A close second to Star Trek, Space: 1999 is an excellent British TV series starring Martin Landau and Barbara Bain (remember Mission: Impossible?). Based largely on fact and well executed. Check your local listings; it's not a network show.

VIDEO DISKS

Within 5 to 10 years, video disk players will be commonplace in homes and schools. Add a keyboard, microprocessor, and memory device, and you've got an interactive super game player. Can you imagine going to your local record store and buying a video disk of space games, auto racing games, or word games? It's coming, gang. Today, however, you'll have to settle for a nice glossy 40-page booklet, MCA Disco-Vision." Free while they last.

MCA Disco-Vision, 100 Universal City Plaza, Universal City, CA 91608.

COMPUTERS IN SOCIETY

Two one-half hour radio interviews with M. Granger Morgan of the Office of Computing Activities, National Science Foundation on the "Impact of Computers on Society" are contained on this standard C-60 cassette tape. Order No. T-7404. $5.00.

World Future Society Book Service, 4916 St. Elmo Ave., Washington, DC 20014.

GAMES AND SIMULATIONS

SHANTI — THE GAME OF EVERLASTING PEACE

Shanti is a game for two to four players. It is designed to illustrate principles of cooperation, harmony, and serving others. The objective is to move from student to Master to Bodhisattva and then to move freely on the board helping others. The "board" is actually a hand silk-screened muslin cloth and the markers are beautifully hand carved and painted. It is obvious that hours of loving labor (cottage industry kind) go into every set. $12.95.

Kanthaka Press, Box 696, Brookline Village, MA 02147.

DESIGN YOUR OWN GAME

This booklet by Harvard McLean and Michael Raymond contains a wealth of pragmatic instruction in how to construct simulations and instructional games. The process is described step by step with examples to illustrate most points. $1.75.

The Simulation and Gaming Association, RR No. 2, Greentree Rd., Lebanon, OH 45036.

THE GUIDE TO SIMULATIONS/ GAMES FOR EDUCATION & TRAINING

By David Zucherman and Robert Horn, this is the most comprehensive guide to educational games and simulations. The second edition contains over 600 entries grouped into 20 categories. Each entry contains detailed information on playing (age level, number of players, playing and preparation time), materials, the objectives, nature, and role of the game. Also price and source information. Several articles on the use of simulations are also included. $15.00.

Information Resources, Inc., P.O. Box 493, Lexington, MA 02173.

FINIS.

A National Computers in Education Conference?

reported by David Ahl

During the 1975 National Computer Conference in Anaheim, a meeting took place which had as its innocent purpose to discuss the overlapping activities of various societies and organizations that have an interest in computers in education. The 30 some odd attendees represented eight societies having a major interest in educational computing and approximately 15 other societies who are on the periphery, but none-the-less have a real interest in the subject. The eight major societies represented were: ADCIS, AEDS, COED (IEEE), NAUCAL, SIGCAI (AERA), SIGCAS (ACM), SIGCUE (ACM), and SIGCSE (ACM).

Following some preliminary descriptions of each major group represented, and some of the others too, the attendees got into discussion about some of their overlapping activities (and publications of which there are at least 20 that appear more-or-less regularly!). The dialogue was, to say the least, spirited, even heated and impassioned at times. It lasted well into the wee hours, was resumed at many breakfast counters the next day, and the day after that.

Two concrete proposals emerged. The first proposal appeared to be endorsed by the overwhelming majority, that is:

1. To publish in one place an informal annotated guide to societies, groups, and publications involved with computers in education. The word "informal" was put in because it seemed that people wanted a brief evaluation of each organization, Whole Earth Catalog style, in addition to or even in place of the organization objectives as stated in its constitution or bylaws. To my knowledge it was not decided who would publish this guide. I'd be glad to volunteer to publish the information in *Creative Computing* in the "Complete Computer Catalog" column or as a separate section or even a separate booklet. On the other hand I do not feel qualified to write capsule descriptions of each organization and will depend upon reader submittals for this.

The second proposal had a great deal of support, although hardly unanimous. It was:

2. To hold a National Computers in Education Conference. One large faction felt that it was certainly time that we got around to this. After all, if the IFIP can hold a World Computers in Education Conference (Marseilles, Sep 1975), the U. S. certainly should have a national one. Should this be done by AFIPS? Jointly with NEA, NCTM, AASA, etc.? Many questions -- few answers. Another faction felt strongly that small specialized conferences were more productive, promoted more meaningful dialogue, and were certainly more manageable. Organizations, understandably feel strongly about retaining their own individual identity, although one has to wonder whether this may be hampering the bringing about of broad changes and major innovation in the use of computers in education. Again, no answer.

Creative Computing solicits comments from readers on these subjects. In future issues we will present a continuing forum on them.

PUBLIC ACCESS QUESTIONNAIRE

by Larry Press

I am compiling and maintaining a survey of what people are doing in the way of public access computer projects. This would include projects for community service, education, and recreation. If readers are connected with or know of such projects, please answer the applicable questions below; augment with comments, brochures, or literature; and send to Larry Press, 128 Park Place, Venice, CA 90291. A later issue of *Creative Computing* will carry the results of this survey.

1. How many public terminals do you have? Are they owned, borrowed, leased, or donated?
2. What CPU do you use? Is your time owned, borrowed, leased, or donated?
3. Is your project supported by a grant, host institution, user payments, or no one?
4. How many hours per week do you support public access?
   Are resource people available during these hours?
5. Do you teach classes in terminal operation, programming, etc.?
6. How many programs in your public access library?
7. Are users permitted to write programs or are they restricted to using library routines?
8. Which, if any, of the following applications do you support?
   A. Game playing programs for recreation and familiarization with terminal operation and functional characteristics of the system.
   B. Local data bases with information on, e.g.
      1. where people work (car pools)
      2. what skills and interests people have
      3. consumer information on local stores-prices, complaints, etc.
   C. How to do it dialogs with reference to local sources of information, people, materials, etc.
   D. On-line opinion polls (with capability for questions and issues to be raised by citizens) on specific local issues such as a proposed zoning change.
   E. On-line suggestion and complaints "box".
   F. Dialogs to guide people in the preparation of forms required by various agencies.
   G. Para-legal/ombudsman dialogs, such as:
      1. How to handle your divorce.
      2. How to get building permits.
      3. How to interpret warranties on retail goods and services.
      4. How to do your own escrow.
      5. What are tenants/landlords rights.
      6. Detecting discrimination in the granting of credit.
      7. Loan payment/interest/term computations.
      8. Help locating sources of credit.
      9. Income tax preparation.
      10. Help in obtaining favorable utility rates.
   H. Consumer guidance dialogs, e.g., how to buy a used car or appliance, with information on local suppliers, consumer reports, etc.
   I. Local want ads.
   J. Dialog to route people to agencies, e.g., drug rehabilitation, family planning, welfare, etc.
   K. Calendar of community events.
   L. Field trips from local schools.
   M. Data Processing for community service organizations.

Still a Few Bugs in the System

It bugs us here at *Creative Computing* when the mass media blame various problems on the computer. Even people in government, business, and schools find the computer a convenient scapegoat for problems actually caused by a programmer, keypuncher, faulty data collection techniques or other non-computer facets.

In this continuing column, we'll reprint articles or quotes which blame various catastrophies or problems on the computer. It's up to you, the reader, to decide whether the computer is actually to blame. Also, if you spot an appropriate item for the "Bugs" column, please send it in.

A COMPUTERIZED bill had this notice on the bottom: "Failure to receive this bill is no excuse for non-payment of the amount shown below."

Chicago Tribune

SHREVEPORT, La. (AP) — Gas rates have gone up like everything else. Just ask Ruth Brister. Her bill went from around $14 last month to $42,474.58.

"I flipped completely," she said.

"The computer went haywire and some of those bills got out," a customer representative at Arkla Gas Co. explained.

Toledo Blade, 3/30/75

In Swansea, Wales, Barry Carr was quite happy when he passed his driving test soon after his 17th birthday, the earliest age at which Britons are permitted to drive a car. But when his license arrived, it bore 12 endorsements for a whole array of driving **OFFENSES**, plus a 28-day driving suspension. Police proved sympathetic when it was found a computer at the license office had run wild. "The system has not been operating for long," said an official.

Road & Track.

Fred Finn Mazanek, a one-year-old guppy, died, recently, leaving an estate of $5,000.

Stan Mazanek, twenty-four, a student at the University of Arizona, had filled out an insurance form he received in his mail box marked "Occupant," entering the fish as the insured party. No fraud was involved in the policy. The guppy's age was listed as six months, his weight as thirty centigrams, and his height as three centimeters.

The Globe Life and Accident Insurance Co. apparently issued Policy No. 3261057 in Fred Finn's name through a computer error. When Mazanek filed a claim following the guppy's demise, they sent a sales representative to see him to find out if he was the sort of person who would take advantage of a clerical error.

He was. The company settled out of court for $650.

South Bend Tribune.

Students Stuff the Contest Box

by Robert Meyers

PASADENA, Calif. — It was enough to crack the golden arches.

Twenty-six science and math students at California Institute of Technology here, looking for something to do while studying for final exams in March, stuffed more than 1.1 million computer-printed entries into a give-away contest sponsored by the McDonald's hamburger company.

When the drawings were held about two weeks ago, the students had won 20 per cent of the total prizes, including a $7,000 car and $3,000 in cash. McDonald's promised to change its rules.

"It's amazing how much free time you can find during final exams week when you're really looking for it," said Steve Klein, 21, a junior information sciences major.

Klein and Dave Novikoff, 21, Barry Megdal, 19 and Becky Hartsfield, 18, all students at the science-oriented school here, were intrigued by the give-away contest being sponsored by the McDonald's Operators Association of California. The rules called only for an entry to be printed on a 3x5 inch card, by a person who was over 18 with a valid driver's license. "Enter as often as you wish," the rules invited.

The students did. In late March the 26, all members of Page House, a residential and dining facility, spent $350 to buy about 20

hours' printing time on an IBM 370/158 computer. They produced 52 boxes of paper, each box of which contained 2,700 pages, and each page of which contained eight valid McDonald's entries.

"There were 1.2 million entries at first," Megdal, a sophomore electrical engineering student says, "but by the time we got through cutting the paper up into individual entries, there were only 1.1 million."

Each of the 26 students involved in the tension-breaking project thus found that the computer had printed his name 40,000 times. Dividing up into eight groups, the students took their ballots to 98 of the 190 participating McDonald's stores in Southern California.

When the management of the fast-food chain learned of the prank, its reaction was hot enough to sizzle a french fry.

". . . The students acted in complete contradiction to the American standards of fair play and sportsmanship," boomed a press release. "Their actions had the effect of depriving individuals and families of improved odds of winning the prizes."

The company reported getting letters from outraged citizens. Newspapers and television stations sent reporters to sniff out the story. Burger King, a fast-food competitor of McDonald's gleefully gave Caltech a $3,000 scholarship in honor of the stunt.

McDonald's, however, spent a great deal of

time trying to figure out what action to take with regard to the computer-printed entry forms. The company finally decided to honor them all, but to give duplicate prizes to the general public for every Caltech entry that was drawn.

That action cost the participating dealers an extra $10,000 on top of the $50,000 already allotted.

The prizes were presented last Tuesday, May 20. Becky Hartsfield, a freshman physics major, was given the keys to a new Datsun 710 station wagon, which she immediately turned over to a chapter of the United Way.

The top prize — a more expensive car and a year's supply of groceries — went to a non-student.

The students say they will keep the check for $3,000, and use it to pay for the taxes and license on the station wagon, to improve their living quarters, to buy micro-wave ovens for the house, and to pay off the cost of buying time on the computer to print the entries in the first place. "No one will make a profit on this," Novikoff said.

At the awards presentation on Tuesday, Novikoff invited Ronald McDonald, the clown character who represents the hamburger chain, to have dinner that night at Page House.

Ronald, however, ate elsewhere.

Washington Post 5/21/75. Thanks to Nelson Griggs, Boyds, MD for sending us the clipping.

Computer-Generated Super-8 Movies

During the summer of 1973, twenty college teachers produced Super 8 movies and sequences of 35mm slides during a six week NSF College Teacher Institute at Carleton College on Computer Graphics and the Production of Computer-Generated Materials for Teaching Mathematics. Of the dozen movies and forty slide projects, eight movies are being made available at this time. Each has proved to be effective in classroom use.

The ideas were conceived of, programmed, and photographed by the participants. A movie camera or 35mm camera was mounted in front of a Tektronix storage scope driven by a minicomputer. Film images are black and white, the negative of the scope face. Some parts were filmed "real time", other parts were manually or automatically single-framed for an animated effect.

The following movies produced during the 1973 Institute are available at $12.50 per Super 8 Technicolor Magicartridge loop or $125.00 for the entire set of 11 loops. It is expected that other materials from the 1973 Institute, and materials from the 1974 Workshop will also become available at minimal cost.

For ordering, or to obtain notice of other projects as they become available, write Roger B. Kirchner, Department of Mathematics, Carleton College, Northfield, Minnesota 55057.

Description of some of the Super 8 movies produced during the 1973 NSF Summer Institute at Carleton College on Computer Graphics and the Production of Computer-generated materials for teaching mathematics.

Non-calculus:
Professor Colpac's Roses, by Harold Mick, Linda and Charles Moulton

Partly animated, partly real time. "Colpac" refers to the graphics language used to write the computer programs. The roses are polar graphs of $r = \cos (n \Theta)$. The interesting point is made that the full graph is obtained when n is odd for Θ in [O, π], and when n is even for Θ in [O, 2π].

Sine (2 loops), by Jerry Caldwell

The graph of t = sin(s) is plotted for s = (π/6)k, k = 1, 2, . . ., 12. The graph is then traced out continuously for s in [O, 2π]. Values are calculated by wrapping segments of length s around the unit circle. The animation is clever, but the pace is slow even for those who are just learning. The two loops take about 8 minutes. A threat of having to see the film twice engraves the idea of the sine fuction indelibly in the memory.

Calculus:

Numerical Integration I, II (2 loops), Linda and Charles Moulton

The integral of a particular quartic is estimated using various numerical techniques. Part I includes the more standard techniques such as the rectangle rule, the trapezoidal rule, and Simpson's rule. Part II includes Gauss-Legendre, spline, and Monte Carlo techniques. The animated portions were filmed real-time. The numerical results are difficult to read, but values are supplied on a supplementary sheet.

Advanced Calculus:

Nonuniform Convergence (2 loops), by George Abdo and Jerry Caldwell

Several sequences of functions which converge pointwise but not uniformly are shown. Pointwise convergence is made clear by considering $f_n (x)$ at a particular x.

The first four sequences are fairly standard. The last two are interesting in a visual sense. They converge nonuniformly on every subinterval! The first examples are well paced. The last two may be criticized as developing too slowly but are well worth seeing.

Applied Mathematics:

Vibrating Membrance, by Stuart Goldenberg

Shows fundamental modes of vibration for membranes with square and circular boundaries. Solutions are those obtained using the separation of variables technique. This film is an incredible value because of the wear and tear on the graphics scope and the computer time used in producing it. Titles are in color!

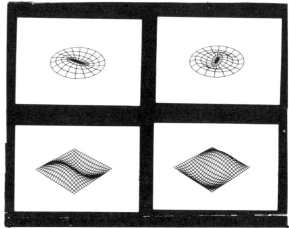

NSF Awards

Back in April 1974 when *Creative Computing* was just a germ of an idea, I had several conversations with people in the National Science Foundation. It seemed to me that *Creative Computing* would be an excellent communication vehicle between leading edge computer projects, most of which are sponsored by the NSF, and the rest of the world. Several NSF people agreed, a proposal was written and submitted. And then nothing. Finally six months later a polite refusal of funding.

In any event, we still think the world would like to know where NSF dollars are going these days and what the current hot button is of the folks in Washington. Most of the dollars for computer projects come from the Technological Innovation in Education Section, so we're listing just those projects. If you want more information, a 19-page booklet, "1974 Awards", is available containing an abstract of each project. To get your free copy, write:

Erik D. McWilliams
Technological Innovation in Education
National Science Foundation
Washington, D. C. 20550

THE U.S. APPROPRIATED $16,400,000,000 IN 1972 FOR SCIENTIFIC RESEARCH

Computer Super-8 Movies continued —

Vibrating String, by George Abdo and Jerry Caldwell
Shows graphs of the traveling waves $y = f(x + ct)$ and $y = f(x - ct)$ together with the graph of the solution $y = (f(x + ct))/2$ to the vibrating string equation $y_{tt} = c^2 y_{xx}$. Several initial displacements are considered.

Heat in a Bar, by George Abdo and Jerry Caldwell
Shows the temperature distribution in a bar over time with a particular initial distribution and several endpoint conditions. Solutions are those obtained by the separation of variable technique.

Complex Variables:
w = exp(z), by Michael Collins
Studies of the image of circles $|z| = R$ under the complex exponential map for $0 \leqslant R \leqslant 25$. There is a spectacular zoom on the origin in the case $R = 8$. A must for complex variables courses. This film is remarkable in that it was produced on one roll of film and was not edited.

List of Projects

Hard-Core CAI

PLATO IV	$2,164,000
PLATO Software	116,000
TICCIT	1,400,000
Evaluation of PLATO and TICCIT	235,922
PLANIT	15,700
Audio and Natural Language in CAI	330,000
Biofeedback in CAI Reading Instruction	50,000
CAI for Indian Students	31,500
Translation of a German Study of CAI Languages	5,500
Subtotal	$4,348,622

Transportability and Networks

CONDUIT	$ 493,300
Central Mississippi Regional Computer Network	195,800
Florida Regional Computer Cooperative	9,100
Subtotal	$ 698,200

Elementary and Secondary School Projects

A Strategy to Introduce Computers in Secondary Schools	$ 530,926
LOGO and New Learning Environments	350,000
Computer-Based High School Math Laboratory	163,600
Study of Computing Activities in Secondary Education	105,300
Subtotal	$1,149,826

Guidance

SIGI Development and Field Test	$ 133,300
Subtotal	$ 133,300

Conferences

Computer Technology Forecast Conference	$ 107,800
Subconference on Computer Communication Networks	22,000
Conference on Cable Communication and the University	20,900
Conference on Computers in the Undergraduate Curricula	16,400
Subtotal	$ 167,100

Miscellaneous

MITS Interactive Television System	$ 246,700
Digital Systems Engineering Course	256,400
Computer Graphics in Learning	213,100
Improvement of Science Education via Technology	100,000
Evaluation of Communication Device for Severely Handicapped Students	88,000
Study of Computer Literacy Courses and Materials	17,300
Instructional Variables in Computer Programming	5,000
Subtotal	$ 926,500
Grand Total	$7,423,548

Hewlett-Packard's Computer Curriculum Project

Hewlett-Packard Company publishes several series of curriculum material which cover secondary through graduate level education. The material assumes that students have the use of the BASIC language computer system. Monitoring the project is a group of educators organized into an advisory board. This group reviews all the materials and makes recommendations for further development. The authors of the material are educators — well known for their work in computer curriculum and for accomplishments in their academic fields as well.

Books are available now for Secondary School use in selected topics in mathematics, physics and ecology. A number of Social Science units will be introduced for the 1974-75 school year. Each curriculum unit covers a standard or enrichment topic. The computer is used to develop concepts which are either impossible or very difficult to explore without the computer, and which make a significant contribution to a fuller understanding of the subject. Most modules consist of student and teacher's versions. The student version emphasizes computer-oriented presentation of the material and gives exercises for students to do. The exercises are open-ended, in order to challenge each student to work at his or her own level of ability.

The teacher's advisor contains background material, suggestions for presentations, and sample solutions for student problems.

If special computer programs are required, the listings are included in the material making it unnecessary to purchase them separately.

The following list contains the titles which are now available for Secondary School use. For further information or to be placed on a mailing list please write:

Computer Curriculum Project
Hewlett-Packard Company
11000 Wolfe Road
Cupertino, CA. 95014

MATHEMATICS

Attacking Non-Linear Equations Student Text
Attacking Non-Linear Equations Teachers Notes
Number Sets Student Lab Book
Number Sets Teachers Advisor
Mathematical Systems Student Lab Book
Mathematical Systems Teachers Advisor
Functions Student Lab Book
Functions Teachers Advisor
Linear Equations & Systems Student Lab Book
Linear Equations & Systems Teachers Advisor

PHYSICS

Geometrical Optics Student Lab Book
Geometrical Optics Teachers Advisor
Mechanics Student Lab Book
Mechanics Teachers Advisor
Waves Student Lab Book
Waves Teacher Advisor
Electricity & Magnetism Student Lab Book
Electricity & Magnetism Teachers Advisor

ECOLOGY

GRAZE Ecology Simulation Student Text
GRAZE Ecology Simulation Teachers Notes
Air Pollution Student Lab Book
Air Pollution Teachers Advisor

PROJECT SOLO COMPUTER TOPICS

Trigonometry Student & Teacher
Mathematics Projects Student Text
Mathematics Projects Teachers Guide
Calculus Student & Teacher
Matrix Mathematics Student Text
Matrix Mathematics Teachers Guide
Physics Student Text
Physics Teachers Guide

Selected books from this project will be reviewed in CREATIVE COMPUTING in forthcoming issues. Check the Book Review Section.

NEW INSTRUCTIONAL COMPUTING BOOKLET

The ACM Special Interest Group on Computer Uses in Education has sponsored a special 80-page publication, entitled *Topics in Instructional Computing* devoted to teacher education in instructional uses of computing. Edited by Stuart Milner of the School of Education at Catholic University of America, *Topics* contains twelve refereed papers which discuss methodology, languages, resources (materials, organizations, etc.), attitudes, effective learning environments, and familiarizing teachers at all levels with the broad spectrum of instructional computer uses.

Copies of *Topics in Instructional Computing* are available at $4.00 each from A. Kent Morton, Kiewit Computation Center, Dartmouth College, Hanover, NH 03755.

Can You Solve The Energy Crisis?

Dr. Dan Klassen
Computer Technology Program
Northwest Regional Educational Laboratory
Portland, Oregon 97204

Among the many attractions available to EXPO '74 visitors in Spokane, Washington is a computer simulation of the energy crisis. Located in the Environmental Symposia Center, the energy simulation exhibit is designed to allow anyone to step up to an interactive CRT terminal linked to a PDP 8/M and explore various solutions to the energy shortage.

The simulation is used almost continually from 10 a.m. when the exhibits open until 10 p.m. when the gates close, according to Chris Fromhold, an Environmental Symposia Center staff member. A typical user stays at the terminal about 15 minutes and manipulates the model on a year-by-year basis for a simulated 10- to 15-year period. Center staff members report that most users have never used a computer before.

The energy simulation model itself reflects energy supplies and use in the United States. After a brief introduction on how to make changes in the model, the user attempts to balance the demand for energy with available supplies by changing policies, standards and energy use habits. Factors which can be manipulated include: production level of American industries, factories and utilities; pollution standards that plants must meet; efficiency of the automobile as a means of transportation; condition and availability of mass transportation; and use of energy for heating and lighting. The user adjusts energy consumption in each of these areas in an attempt to keep demand and supply in balance. In addition, the user attempts to keep indices of pollution generation, economic well-being and general citizen satisfaction within acceptable limits. Changes to the energy use rates are made on a yearly basis. If the user elects not to adjust energy use patterns, the demand for energy grows at a predetermined rate.

Most of the users are junior and senior high school boys, although many school-age girls as well as numerous older people try the simulation. Fromhold, a teacher during the school year, says that the most interested and excited users are 12- to 14-year old boys that have never used a computer before.

Staff members have observed that a significant number of users return to the exhibit with a strategy in mind. Of these, the most troublesome are junior and senior high school boys who determine how the program operates and then use this knowledge to introduce a "bug" into the system; debugging is necessary about once every week, according to Symposia staff members.

The exhibit was created and produced by Dr. Dan Klassen, John Lynch, Sr., and Dr. Duane Richardson of the Computer Technology Program, Northwest Regional Educational Laboratory, Portland, Oregon. The energy simulation was originally designed, under a grant from the United States Office of Education, as an instructional application for classroom use. It is one of five energy-related, computer-based instructional applications being developed by the Computer Technology Program; all will be available in early 1975.

We travel together, passengers on a little spaceship, dependent on its vulnerable reserves of air and soil; all committed for our safety to its security and peace; preserved from annihilation only by the care, the work, and, I will say, the love we give our fragile craft. We cannot maintain it half fortunate, half miserable, half confident, half despairing, half slave to the ancient enemies of man, half free in a liberation of resources undreamed of until this day. No craft, no crew can travel safely with such vast contradictions. On their resolution depends the survival of us all. Adlai Stevenson

Good Things From Oregon

Judging from the number of CC subscribers from Oregon and the tremendous number of people from Oregon at various conferences and meetings, it is certainly one of the leading states in computer education. We had hoped to have a comprehensive article about computing activities throughout the state, but apparently the people I spoke to are just too busy doing their own publications to do a piece for us. Hence, we'll just note several conspicuous examples of the good things happening in Oregon.

Oregon Computing Teacher produced by the Oregon Council for Computer Education, is an informal magazine of about 72 typewritten pages per issue which appears 4 times a year. It contains a variety of original and reprinted material of interest mainly to high school and undergraduate college faculty. (It is not aimed at students.) We're impressed with the uniformly high quality of this publication. It's available for $5.00/yr from Oregon Council for Computer Education, 4015 S. W. Canyon Road, Portland, OR 97221.

Computers in Education Resources Handbook is a comprehensive 500-page handbook about the uses of computers in education, primarily at the pre-college level. It covers both instructional and administrative uses of the computer although it is clearly stronger on the instructional side. It discusses hardware (lightly), software (moderately), applications (heavily), training, surveys, and sources of additional information (excellent). First published in 1973 it is quite current, even so a new edition is being published in early 1975. Available for $10.80 from Dept. of Computer Science, Univ. of Oregon, Eugene, OR 97403.

ECO-NET is a non-profit environmental education network emphasizing the exchange of information relating to the environment, energy, communications and, yes, even computers. A 16-page monthly newsletter is called *RAIN*. Despite its Pacific Northwest bias, it's one of the very best, ranking along side *Whole Earth Catalog, Epilog,* and *CoEvolution Quarterly.* At the moment, the price is right too. *Rain* is available free (until their grant runs out) from Environmental Education Center, Portland State Univ., P. O. Box 751, Portland, OR 97207.

An apology: The Wizard graphic and note on pg. 25 of the Jan-Feb *Creative Computing* came from the May 1974 issue of *Oregon Computing Teacher* which we neglected to mention. Sorry.

A request: When you write for materials such as those above or from advertisers, please mention *Creative Computing.* That encourages those groups to keep us posted and/or keep advertising with us.

psst! want a hot tip?

Do you have something to contribute to *Creative Computing*? Why not send it to us?

As you can tell from the first several issues we are focusing on activities and games for using computers in education and recreation. We also run articles, fiction, and humor on the role and effect of technology and computers on society and people. Our language is non-technical.

Contributions should be 500 to 3000 words. Typed, double-spaced. Include illustrations if possible (sharp black on white paper — not Xerox or other copies. Photostats are ok). Also, include photos if available (5x7 or large B+W — no slides or Polaroids).

If you want an acknowledgement, send a self-addressed stamped envelope.

COMPUTERS HELP WATCH FOR CORN BLIGHT

PURDUE UNIVERSITY, LAFAYETTE, IN — Mrs. Susan Schwingendorf, LARS Computer Analyst, marks fields on a photo work copy to assist in locating data in the multispectral analysis. The computer listing indicates the crops grown in each field. Biweekly data from ten corn fields checked for blight by Extension Agents are also made available to her and the other data analysts. The Corn Blight Watch Experiment is being conducted by the U. S. Department of Agriculture, NASA, and the Agricultural Experiment Stations and Extension Services of seven states, in cooperation with Purdue University's Laboratory for Applications of Remote Sensing (LARS) and the University of Michigan's Institute for Science and Technology (IST). (Photo courtesy NASA).

SEXISM IN COMPUTERS

A computer in the USSR did all right by male mathematicians but began giving trouble when a woman tried operating it. Both male chauvinist pigs and women will be disappointed to learn that the reason was not that the lady's input was unacceptable to the computer because of its alleged feminine illogic or that the computer became overheated at the sight of her beauty, but rather that her dress was made of synthetic fiber producing an electric field that affected the computer.

Input/Output

Comments on the birth of Creative

Dear Editor:

Thank you for sending us the first issue of *Creative Computing*. It is an excellent beginning and I hope that you will keep up the good work.

Edward S. Cornish, President
World Future Society

Dear Editor:

After reading the first issue, I am very enthusiastic about the future of CREATIVE COMPUTING. I think it fills a gap that existed in the material available to those interested in using computers in the classroom.

Carolyn W. Evans
Medical College of Georgia

Dear Editor:

Congratulations on your charter issue. It is great to see at long last a first-rate, exciting magazine concerning coputers in education. Promise me you will keep up the good work.

Allan B. Ellis, President
Education Research Corp.

Dear Editor:

CONGRATULATIONS on the birth of Creative Computing!! The first issue is dynamite. While its readership may account for only a small percentage of the computing done in America, I'm convinced that it will contribute a much greater percentage of the creativity contained therein. Creative Computing will provide an important communication point to facilitate and magnify this contribution.

Scott B. Guthery, President
Computer Recreations Corp.

Dear Editor:

Thank you for sending *Creative Computing*. Especially enjoyed the book review, and the cartoons. At times the prose could be more succinct.

Suggest that you arrange to have *Creative Computing* put on board jet airliners.

In future issues I would suggest having a contest to write programs useful in civic work:
1. Construct a tree based on Zip codes for car pooling or passing news by phone.
2. Sociogram to place friends in same seat on a bus.
3. Scheduling for volunteers, or shifts.

Or, Sorting a record collection into segments the right length to fit on an 8-track cartridge.

Maybe there is a source of bibliographic information pertaining to omputers in education that would prepare a search for you to publish in the newsletter. It would be nice to have a list of addresses for university newsletters in the field of computer education.

I hope someday you can find someone to write a story on Educational Testing Services, Inc., a *very* lucrative business.

Chris Connors
Berkeley Hts., NJ

A dissenting vote

Dear Editor:

Only today did I have a chance to browse thru your *Creative Computing* issues.

My special interest in "Computer Mathematics", as you know, is the use of computer programming — in any language — to motivate students to search for areas of pure and/or applied mathematics which can present problems which need computers.

95% of the issue is aimed elsewhere — so from my point of view your magazine lacks creativity in mathematics.

Keep me informed.

George Grossman
Director of Mathematics
Board of Education of the City of New York

And a reply

Dear Editor:

I am writing both to subscribe to *Creative Computing* and to reply to the letter you printed from George Grossman, the Director of Mathematics of the NYC Board of Education.

Unfortunately Mr. Grossman seems to view the computer only in the light of teaching mathematics, and finds 95% of what is covered in *Creative Computing* as being aimed elsewhere. What he is in fact saying is that out of the 100% of computer oriented material he can only find 5% germain to his narrow circumscribed and stultified conception of what computers are all about. This is very sad, and what is sadder is that this man controls, at least nominally, all computer education in the City school system.

Fortunately his ideas are carefully ignored in the more enlightened parts of the system. At my school our courses cover a wide range of computer science topics from assembler language programming and system architecture, to automata, recursion, string processing and compiler writing. Light does shine in New York.

Creative Computing shows potential. It seems to be floundering as to what its direction ought to be, but if anything it errs in the direction of too many topics, rather than, thank heaven, too few. I will read the issues that I get and should I figure out exactly what I think needs changing, I will let you know. Until then, good luck!

Name withheld by request

(George Grossman's reply is in Vol. 2, No. 1, pg. 34)

"Feature" Letter to the Editor

Dear Editor:

I've been meaning to write since your first issue, but finishing college and other things have gotten in the way. Your latest issue (May-Jun 75) contains so much thought provoking material that I simply can't wait any longer, so, here are my thoughts.

First, congratulations on a simply excellent publication! Your content, layout, artwork and direction are just great. To be commended above all esle, particularly this latest issue, is *Creative Computing*'s, DIVERSITY. By the way, I hope you *do* view *Creative Computing* as being a member of the Alternative Press, and not just because you're on newsprint. You're not going to be able to keep a stance of open-eyed diversity and attract the readership you need if you fall into some worn-out rut. If newsprint's respectability causes trouble, then come out in microfiche also. That would be nice for permanence, anyway.

Re: David Ahl's editorial and Gregory Yob's esthetic and philosophical comments on GEOWAR, I couldn't agree more. My undergraduate major is philosophy and my "heros" are John Muir, Henry Thoreau, Mohandas Gandhi and Bertrand Russell — facts which always astonish people since I appear to live in our computer center. I can see why on the surface people are astounded to find that I am a philosophy major. As was pointed out in your third issue, computers have received a very bad press and very, very few people have any real conception of what a computer actually is, on the hardware or software level. [Which raises an interesting question: which *is* the computer, hardware or software? More on this later.]

I have always been deeply disturbed by the proliferation of war games and the tendency for every new technical (or intellectual) advance to be adapted to the purpose of killing. The conduct of our species is what must evolve now. Not physical evolution but intellectual.

Unfortunately, most large R & D budgets have been and are still tied to "Defense." That is what is so hugely disappointing about the demise of the space program. For a while a significant number of people were united behind a peaceful research project of significant scale. Now we are united behind nothing and I am afraid that the answer to the question "Where are we going?" is to hell and that very quickly if we don't regain some unifying objective and goal.

I hope your editorial moves some people to take time out from Star Trek at the CRT and spend some time looking at the real stars. Perhaps I spend too much time reading science fiction, but I can't believe that the future of the human race lies totally on Terra of Sol. We are just going to sit here and stagnate if we don't get off this planet — at least through intellectual contact with extraterrestial life. The current generation of computer fanatics is just the generation to decide that this is a worthwhile goal, and it may be the last generation capable of making such a choice. By the end of this century we're going to be too busy surviving to notice the stars.

Re: Ed note on page 18. I have doubts about reversals eventually becoming palindromes because of randomness. I am always suspicious of falling back on randomness, because it seems pretty clear to me that there is no such thing as true randomness. Anyway, since the number continually gets larger, doesn't the probability of "randomly" hitting a palindrome get smaller? If I get around to it I'm going to play around with 1675 on the IBM370/168 VS1.7 we're tied into. Might as well use up the money in some of our course accounts in the interest of curiosity.

[Ed note: As Fred Gruenberger and others have pointed out, my speculation that reversals of 196 could become palindromic due to randomness is dead wrong because the size of the number is increasing at every step – DHA]

*** SPROING. 18 HOUR INTERLUDE. ***

Enclosed is a copy of a program I just wrote which takes the number 196 through 12066 reversals to produce a 5000 digit number without ever being palindromic. I apologize for its being written in 370 assembly language, which has

got to be the most exclusive "language" around, but we have to pay 22¢ a cpu second and I had to have the most efficient program possible. With slight modification this program would handle results up to 8,000,000 digits in length (the system has 16 meg) but there is this slight problem of paying for it. I may have a go at taking it out to 10,000 digits. There is always that nagging suspicion that the next reversal, or maybe the next, or surely the one after that . . .

Re: Things I'd like to see discussed in *Creative:* More about ways in which people have used computers to investigate the world and themselves, i.e. situations in which someone said "I wonder if . . ." and then used a computer to help find out. A large selection of "I wonder ifs . . ." without answers would be nice, too. How about a list of prodigious problems which might lend themselves to computer solution if only someone looks at them in the right way?

How about some input on the average user level on the proliferation of languages? If you're using a computer as a tool (or a friend) to solve problems, do you get more done if you *know* BASIC or ANS FORTRAN inside out or if you have an acquaintance with PL/I or GIBBERISH II? What do your readers like/dislike in their languages-systems? etc. *[Ed Note: "On Languages" will be a regular forum to discuss just these issues – DHA]*

How should computer use fit into a sane lifestyle; Does computer use overall create or solve problems? etc.

Having been myself a member of a programming team competing in a contest (University of MO at Rolla – March 29) I have wondered if such contests encourage "good programming." Should they?

How does someone not in an educational institution get time on a computer? Does anyone sell time (reasonably) to individual users?

Re: Your upcoming issue "The Computer Threat to Society": Change is always a threat to staying the same. I hope in this issue someone will follow up on the thoughts expressed in the next to last paragraph of David Ahl's editorial.

Also, looking over your staff listing, I notice that you are not too well represented in the midwest. Things do occasionally happen out here, even without the benefit of wall-to-wall people. You really should get someone out there — talking is still the best medium for information exchange.

In any case — good luck! I'll keep trying to talk people into subscribing.

Peace and Love,
John R. Lees, Jr.
Fulton, MO

[Ed note: John is now a regular Reviews Editor for us. –DHA]

Contributions welcome!

Dear Editor:

Many mathematicians feel that computer programming can and should be taught to students in the upper elementary grades. The most difficult problem facing someone in this position is the generation of problems that are appropriate for a computer, conceptually easy enough for students to grasp, and engage their interest.

Included with this letter are some problems that my 6th-grade students find interesting and helpful in demonstrating how a computer can help them solve problems that they might meet elsewhere. Most of the problems require only a few storage units and maybe 1 loop, but this has been plenty for my students to handle.

Charles A. Reeves
6th-grade Math/Science Teacher
Developmental Research School
The Flordia State University
Tallahassee, Florida 32306

Many of Charles' problems can be found in the "Problems for Creative Computing" section of this and future issues. If other readers have favorite problems, please send them to us. – DHA

CAI — A failure?

Dear Editor:

I propose that the reason why CAI has failed is because computer experts have not yet found a way to code human fallibility. The best teaching of human beings is by sensitive but fallible teachers. Why, in CAI, is it always assumed that the student is the one who will make the mistakes?

J. D. Tinsley
Inspector of Schools
Birmingham Education Department
Council House, Birmingham, England

How about some comment or opinion from other readers on the failure of CAI? —DHA

Correction.

Dear Editor:

Thanks again for a superb issue of *Creative Computing*. I'm sure that you can't keep up the pace on improvement because there just isn't that much room to go. This is the best journal for my purposes that I have ever seen.

There is one thing that I'd like to point out in relation to that historical reprint from IBM [Digital Calculators — Then and Now. Jan-Feb 1975]. In an article called "Will the Inventor of the First Digital Computer Please Stand Up?" W. David Gardner reports on the work of Dr. John Vincent Atanasoff for *Datamation* (Feb., 1974, pp. 84-90). The article gives the decision of Federal District Court Judge Earl R. Larson which "defrocked Dr. J. Presper Eckert and Dr. John W. Mauchly as the high priests of electronic digital computer invention." It goes on to explain how the decision arose in a case involving Sperry Rand and Honeywell over the patent of ENIAC. After carefully considering the evidence, Judge Larson decided that the patent was invalid because the basic ideas were taken from a machine which Atanasoff developed between 1935 and 1942 at the University of Iowa. Atanasoff has gone without proper credit long enough (and besides too many people have the idea that nothing important but agriculture happens out here on the plains).

Paul J. Emmerich
Dana College

Standard BASIC?

Dear Editor:

I think you should stick to "standard" BASIC in programs that are included in *CREATIVE COMPUTING*. In volume 1, number 2, there were programs on pages 12, 13, and 19 that use the backslash for multiple statements on a line. The one on page 19 also has some construction that looks like Fortran implied do loops in a print line and if-then-else with statements allowed as arguments. It is honestly not BASIC and will probably only run on the machine that originated it. The use of an output string in an input statement (e.g. INPUT "YOUR MESSAGE PLEASE" A$) is also nonstandard. Sorry to push the point so hard, particularly on one of your own programs, but I think that programming style is pretty important, especially in publications that lots of people are going to see. The language you choose is an important part of style, and encouraging weird extensions that don't conform to the spirit of a language is poor style.

Christopher G. Hoogendyk
Dartmouth College

I agree with you in spirit; however, when a significant or interesting program is submitted to us (for example, SUPER STAR TREK in this issue), should we not publish it because it is not in standard BASIC? Or should we require the submitter to convert it to "standard" BASIC (to which most contributors would reply, "Why should I bother?"). Or should we convert it to standard BASIC (at which request, most of our volunteer editors would find other things to do). Or should we publish it and leave it as an exercise for readers to convert?

READERS: What do you think?

Parting note: to my knowledge, the BASIC Standards Committee has not yet defined "standard" BASIC. — DHA.

Some words from the giant . . . .

Dear Editor:

Thank you for your letter of June 24 asking me to participate in *Creative Computing* magazine's November-December issue on the computer and society.

Many of us within IBM are intensively seeking answers to a number of the problems touched upon in your questionnaire. For example, those questions dealing with privacy and data security are addressed in the enclosed statement by Dr. Lewis Branscomb, IBM Vice President and Chief Scientist, in testimony given before a subcommittee of the House of Representatives.*

The role of the computer in society is, of course, only part of a broader area dealing with the role of technology in general. We recognize that the computer, like any instrument of technology, can be a force for good or harm depending upon the use to which it is put.

IBM's past experience and future outlook reassure me that the computer, in virtually every instance, will be used for good, not harm and that this technological tool will continue to fulfill its great promise.

Frank T. Cary
Chairman of the Board, IBM

*See a summary of this testimony on page 46. – DHA.

Computers save congressmen time in voting. (Does that mean more talk or more vacations?)

Dear Editor:

I appreciate your invitation to present my views on the role of computers in society. Computer support to the House of Representatives began in the late 1960's when the Clerk of the House introduced data processing equipment as a means of administering several clerical tasks. In 1971, the Committee on House Administration established the House Information Systems staff to provide a professional base for computer activities. This staff continues to act under the guidance and leadership of the Committee on House Administration, currently chaired by the Honorable Wayne L. Hays of Ohio.

The members of the House are constantly aware of the utility and the importance of computers in our society: the electronic voting system, for example, was used for nearly 1500 rollcalls during the 93rd Congress and saved approximately 500 hours of legislative time that would otherwise have been needed to answer rollcalls under the manual method. The House computer has also been applied to many other useful tasks including a bill status system, committee calendar system, data analysis services and administrative support systems. The Committee on Science and Technology has been a frequent user of these systems.

I look forward to the appearance of your November-December 1975 issue as it sounds extremely interesting.

Olin E. Teague
Chairman, Committee on Science and Technology
U.S. House of Representatives

The Last Number

Dear Editor,

I noted with some interest your article on multiple precision arithmetic. For some time, I have had a personal mania for computing huge factorials exactly, and it is gratifying to see that I am not alone in my proclivities. I have calculated 10,000 factorial exactly (I think — how could you ever check it?) and think that this may well be the largest one yet computed exactly. In any event, I also learned that there is nothing quite so dull as 7 pages of digits.

A very good reference on multiple precision arithmetic is in Knuth's *Seminumerical Algorithms*. He says all that you would normally need to know. Although it might be tough going for computing neophytes, the book is well worth the effort. Especially interesting is the part on modular arithmetic in which it is revealed how to do multiple precision arithmetic without having to do any carries.

Keep up the good work.

John Levine, Student
Yale University

Creative Computing is the number 1 magazine in personal computing software and applications.

The typical home or small business computer system starts with a microcomputer, keyboard, cassette recorder, and TV set. From there you can add the peripherals, sensors, controllers, and other devices you need for your own special applications.

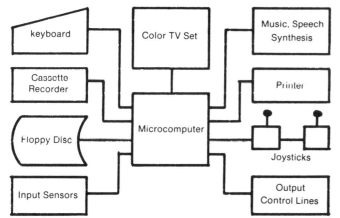

Creative Computing Magazine is dedicated to describing applications for home, school, and small business computers completely and pragmatically in non-technical language. You won't need a Ph.D in Computer Science, or a technical reference library, or a computer technician beside you to get these applications up and running. We give you complete hardware and software details. Typically, applications utilize commercially available systems. However, if an application needs a piece of home-brew hardware, we tell you how to build it. Or if it requires a combination of high-level and machine language code, we give you the entire listings along with the flowcharts and algorithms.

We also run no-nonsense reviews of computers (assembled and kits), peripherals, terminals, software, and books. We're frank and honest, even if it costs us an advertiser, which it occasionally has.

Here are just some of the applications you'll see fully described in future issues of *Creative Computing*.

Building Management and Control
1. Alarm monitoring/police notification
2. Environmental control (heating, air conditioning, humidification, dehumidification, air purity, etc.)
3. Fire and smoke detection
4. Appliance control (microwave oven, gas oven, refrigerator)
5. Perimeter system control (sprinklers, outdoor lights, gates)
6. Solar and/or auxiliary energy source control
7. Watering system control based on soil moisture
8. Fuel economizing systems
9. Maintenance alert system for household devices (key component sensing and periodic preventative maintenance)

Household Management
1. Address/telephone file
2. Investment analysis
3. Loan/annuity/interest calculations and analysis
4. Checkbook maintenance
5. Periodic comparisons of expenditures vs. budget
6. Monitor time and cost of telephone calls
7. Record incoming telephone calls and select appropriate response to caller
8. Recipe file
9. Diet/nutrition analysis
10. Menu planning
11. Pantry inventory/shopping list

Health Care
1. Medical/dental record keeping
2. Insurance claim processing
3. Health maintenance instrumentation control (EKG, blood chemical analysis, diet analysis, self-diagnosis)

Education and Training
1. Mathematics drill and practice
2. Problem solving techniques
3. Tutorial instruction in a given field
4. Simulation and gaming
5. Music instruction and training
6. Music composition and synthesis
7. Learning to program
8. Software development
9. Perception/response/manipulation skills improvement

Recreation and Leisure
1. Games, games, games
2. Puzzle solving
3. Animation/kinetic art
4. Sports simulations
5. Needlepoint/stitchery/weaving pattern generation
6. Computer art
7. Library cataloging (books, records, etc.)
8. Collection catalog/inventory/value (coins, stamps, shells, antique auto parts, comics, etc.)
9. Model railroad control
10. Amateur radio station control
11. Astronomy; star, planet, satellite tracking
12. Robotics
13. Speech recognition and synthesis

Business Functions
1. Small business accounting
2. Word processing/text editing
3. Customer files
4. Software development
5. Operations research
6. Scientific research
7. Computer conferencing
8. Telephone monitoring
9. Engineering calculations
10. Statistical analysis
11. Survey tabulation
12. Inventory control
13. Mailing lists

164

Programs, Puzzles, Problems, and Activities

Problems for Creative Computing

by Water Koetke

The problems to be discussed in this column are those that seem particularly well suited not just for computing, but for creative computing. They will cover a wide variety of topics and subjects, and all are intended for both students and teachers — for anyone turned on by challenging problems, games or programs.

Your reactions will be very much appreciated. Suggestions for future columns, solutions to problems discussed, new problems, extensions and experiences with problems discussed are all solicited. Please address all correspondence to Walter Koetke in care of *Creative Computing*.

The challenge of creative thought is before all of us — this column is intended for those who choose to demonstrate that creative thought is also behind them. I hope you find the ideas rewarding.

Tac Tix and the Complications of Fallibility

The game of Tac Tix was created by Piet Hein, also the inventor of Hex, in the late forties. A first impression of the game is likely to be that it is indeed simple, but first impressions themselves are over-simplifications aren't they? The rules of Tac Tix are few, a desirable characteristic of games to be used in the classroom.

Each game begins with 25 markers arranged in a 5 x 5 square formation as in the diagram.

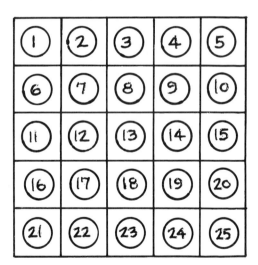

Two players then alternate turns. On each turn a player may take as many markers as he chooses from any single row or column, provided that the markers are next to each other. For example, markers 1 and 3 cannot both be removed on a single turn unless marker 2 is present and is also removed with the others. The player who removes the last marker is the winner.

STOP READING this article. Put it down and take a few minutes to analyze the game. The first player has an easily described winning strategy. Can you find it?

Assume that the first player can play without error. On his first turn he should remove marker 13, the center marker. On each subsequent turn he should remove the markers symmetrically opposite

those removed by his opponent. By playing in this manner he is assured of winning the game. After the center marker is removed, a typical game might be:

Second Player	First Player
2 - 5	21 - 24
15, 20, 25	1, 6, 11
8 - 10	16 - 18
7	19
14	12 (wins)

When playing this game, an equally infallible second player is likely to be bored to death.

Since Tac Tix is played on a small board, has only a few easily stated rules, and requires only a short time to play, it is a very good game to implement on a computer. Writing a program that will play Tac Tix with a user by following a well defined strategy is an excellent problem at two different levels.

First, try a program in which the computer is the first player. To do this, one must be able to create a program that: represents the 5 x 5 board using single or double subscripted variables; makes symmetrical moves; determines if the second player is making a legal move; and realizes that the game is over. When writing the program one faces many of the likely difficulties encountered in far more complex problems.

Second, try a program in which the computer is the second player. If all users were infallible, then this really isn't worth writing. However, somewhere there may be a student or teacher who occasionally makes an error. Assume that you're writing the program for him. By considering this small bit of reality, a trivial case in the world of perfect people has become a rather challenging, interesting problem.

Consider each of the following opening plays of the first player. What is the best counter play for the second player?

Opening Play	Counter Play
3, 8, 13	?
16 - 18	?
11 - 15	?

In general, the second player should attempt to play so that for every missing marker the symmetrically opposite marker is also missing. The center marker must also be missing. If the second player succeeds in obtaining this board configuration at the end of any turn, he has successfully taken advantage of the first player's error and has a winning strategy. On all subsequent turns he should remove only those markers symmetrically opposite those removed by his opponent. Following this strategy, if the first player's opening play is 3, 8, 13 the second player's play should be 18, 23.

But what should the second player do if the opening play is 16 - 18? That's part of the challenge of the problem! Perhaps play 9 - 10, but that seems to increase the first player's chances of making a winning move next time. We do assume the first player is smart even if he does err on his first play. Perhaps play at random, but that seems to decrease the second player's chance of obtaining a winning board configuration.

The complexity of the problem is indeed increased by letting the first player be human. The problem is very good because it is a mini-version of what one often faces in much larger problems: the solution is not trivial; although each step of a solution can be well defined, some definitions will reflect the problem solver's best judgment rather than an absolute truth; once a solution is well defined, a program can be written that plods through many cases while another can be written that uses reflections and rotations of the board to reduce the number of cases. The challenge of writing a program that plays Tac Tix with a smart but fallible user who is given the first move properly belongs under the title "Creative Computing." And those who write such a program are likely to have done some "creative analysis" before they finish.

A modified version of Tac Tix that looks easier but is actually much more complex is played on a 4 x 4 board rather than a 5 x 5 board. The only other change is that the player who removes the last marker is the loser. Is there a winning strategy for either player? After trying to define a winning strategy for one of the players, one may well become interested in writing a program that develops its strategy by learning as it plays. By repeating successful plays and avoiding the repetition of unsuccessful plays, the computer can improve its strategy with each successive game. The writing of such cybernetic programs will be the subject of a future column.

Related References

Gardner, Martin; *Mathematical Puzzles and Diversions*; New York: Simon and Schuster; 1959; Chapter 15.

Spaulding, R. E.; "Recreation: Tac Tix"; *The Mathematics Teacher*; Reston, Virginia: National Council of Teachers of Mathematics; November 1973; pages 605-606.

Puzzles and Problems for Fun

This puzzle is calculated to test your ability in calculus: A watchdog is tied to the outside wall of a round building 20 feet in diameter. If the dog's chain is long enough to wind halfway around the building, how large an area can the watchdog patrol?

A. G. Canne
Pittsburgh, Pa.

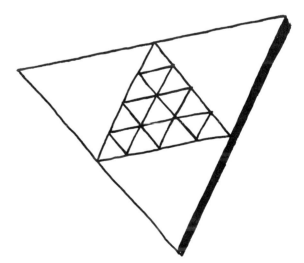

The Sheik of Abba Dabba Dhu wears this medallion, on which each equilateral triangle represents a wife in his harem. How many wives does the sheik have?

David Lydy
Cincinnati, Ohio

Palindromes: For Those Who Like to End at the Beginning

by Water Koetke

Egad, a base life defiles a bad age
Doom an evil deed, liven a mood
Harass sensuousness, Sarah
Golf; No, sir, prefer prison-flog
Ban campus motto, "Bottoms up, MacNab"

A palindrome is a work, verse, number or what have you that reads the same backward as forward. The unit in a palindrome may vary. Each of the five lines in the poem at the beginning of this article is itself a palindrome using a letter as the unit. However, a palindromic poem might be written for which the entire poem is a palindrome rather than the individual lines. The unit in a palindrome might also be a word as in:

> *Men wanted warning before police approached;*
> *squealer approached police before warning wanted men.*

The length of plaindromes is, of course, dependent upon the author's cunning and patience. Whether a simple "Mom" or the "Ethopoiia Karkinikie", a palindromic Greek poem of over 400 lines published in 1802, all palindromes seem to merit special admiration. Howard Bergerson's book referenced at the end of this article is a very comprehensive collection of palindromes of many types. His work will be a classic for those interested in literary games. The six palindromic sentences in this article all appear in Bergerson's book.

Palindromes are appropriate as the subject of introductory programs involving string manipulation. For example, writing a program to recognize a palindromic sentence using a letter as the unit requires character manipulation. Writing a program to recognize a palindromic sentence or paragraph using a word as the unit requires both character and word manipulation. This is particularly interesting if the sentence or paragraph is entered one line rather than one word at a time. The creation of palindromes is likely to remain in the province of a human and not a machine endeavor. One may devise clever programs to assist that endeavor, but human creativity supported by a well thumbed dictionary shall remain the most essential resources.

Numeric palindromes are those numbers that read the same backward as forward. The examination of these numbers is a field rich with possibilities for creative computing.

Consider all palindromes that can be written in the form N^k where N and k are positive integers. Would you expect that N is also a palindrome; Let's consider the case of k=2. 14641 and 484 are both palindromes that can be written in the form N^2:

$$14641 = 121^2$$
$$484 = 22^2$$

And both 121 and 22 are also palindromes! Is this always true; And what about other values of k; Is the cube root of a palindromic cube also a palindrome; Is the fourth root of palindromic fourth power also a palindrome?

These questions are of interest because only partial answers have been given. When k=2—if N^2 is a palindrome then N is often, but not always, a palindrome. When k=3—the only known palindromic cube without a palindromic cube root is 10,662, 526, 601, but there may be others yet undiscovered. When k=4 —all known palindromic fourth powers have fourth roots that are palindromes, but what about those that are yet unknown; When k=5 —this one's a little harder as there are no known palindromes that can be written in the form N^5. Clearly the answers to these questions are a proper subject for creative computing —and just as clearly, the fundamental principles required to generate a formidable attack on the answers require no more than high school algebra and the resource of computing facilities.

There is a conjecture concerning palindromes that raises another unanswered question. Begin with any positive integer. If it is not a palindrome, reverse its digits and add the two numbers. If the sum is not a palindrome, treat it as the original number and continue. The process stops when a palindrome is obtained. For example, beginning with 78:

```
        78
 +      87
       165
 +     561
       726
 +     627
      1353
 +    3531
      4884
```

The conjecture, often assumed true, is that this process will always lead to a palindrome. And indeed that is just what usually happens. Most numbers less than 10000 will produce a palindrome in less than 24 additions. But there's a real thorn in the side of this conjecture —196. No one really knows whether a palindrome will be produced if the beginning number is 196.

Writing a program that explores this conjecture can be a valuable experience on several levels. A program that examines the integers 1 through 10000 is a worthwhile student project because it requires the ability to deal with numbers of up to 14 digits. The numbers 196, 691 and the resulting sums and their reversals would, of course, have to be excluded from this program. The exploration of 196 really should be a category of its own. Pursuit of this problem will lead the student down several interesting side roads, lure him into doing some original mathematics, and certainly teach him much about computing. Solution of this problem should certainly merit an A since it will bring him recognition that extends well beyond his classroom. Personally, I'm quietly hoping that the problem of 196 is solved by a secondary school student just as the three largest known perfect numbers were discovered by a secondary student with access to computing facilities, but that's a different subject isn't it?

Related References

Bergerson, Howard W.; *Palindromes and Anagrams;* Dover Publications, New York; 1973.

Gardner, Martin; "Mathematical Games"; *Scientific American;* New York; August 1970; pages 110-114.

Kordemsky, Boris A.; *The Moskow Puzzles;* Charles Scribner's Sons, New York; 1972, page 172.

MORE ABOUT PALINDROMES

The January and June 1974 issues of *Games & Puzzles* contained some additional discussion about palindromic numbers on Darryl Francis' Puzzle Pages and in letters from R. Hamilton and Jonathan Kessel.

R. Hamilton notes in his letter, "Of the 900 three digit numbers, 90 are themselves palindromic, 228 require just one reversal to form a palindromic number, 270 require two reversals, 143 require three reversals, 61 require four reversals, 33 require five reversals and 75 require more than five. These remaining 75 numbers could be classed into just a few groups, the members of which after one or two reversals each produce the same number and are therefore essentially the same. One of these groups consists of the numbers 187, 286, 385, 583, 682, 781, 869, 880 and 968 each of which when reversed once or twice form 1837 and eventually form the palindromic number 8813200023188 after 23 reversals (The nos. 89 and 98 also belong to this group.) The most interesting group consists of the numbers 196, 295, 394, 493, 592, 689, 691, 788, 790, 887 and 986 which form 1675 after a few reversals but after 100 reversals fail to produce a palindromic number forming the non-palindromic 44757771534490515-61729069927156150844362777464 4."

Jonathan Kessell notes, "However, what you didn't mention, maybe because it is rather obvious, is that if 78 and 96 both yield 4884, then 87 and 69 will do so, too. Thus, not only 89 gives 8,813,200,023,188 after 24 reversals, but so does 98. You may also be interested to know that 249 integers less than 10,000 fail to produce a palindrome after 100 reversals. The smallest of these numbers is 196; indeed, even after as many as 4,147 reversals, this number still fails to generate a palindromic number. (Just how many reversals are necessary for 196 to produce a palindromic result? — DF.) The numbers 6,999 and 7,998 produce the longest palindrome: 16,668,488,486,661 — out of all the numbers from 1 to 10,000, that is. It takes twenty steps to produce this palindrome from both of the numbers.

Also, there is an infinity of palindromic squares, most of which have palindromic square roots. The smallest nonpalindromic root is 26 — the square root of 676. Similarly with cubes and cube roots. The smallest nonpalindromic cube root is 2,201, the cube being 10,662,526,601. The number 836 may be of interest, too. It is the largest three-digit integer whose square root (698,896) is palindromic. Further, 698,896 is the smallest palindromic square with an even number of digits; also, when turned upside down, the number remains palindromic. The next largest palindromic square with an even number of digits is 637,832,238,736, which is the square of 798,644."

Anyone care to take the study of palindromic numbers further still?

Palindromes (con't)

Tom Karzes, an eighth grader at Curtis Jr. High School, Sudbury, MA wrote a program to take any number and test whether it is a palindrome; if it is not the program goes on to form the palindrome. The program fails with greater than a 7-digit number. Can you write one that doesn't?

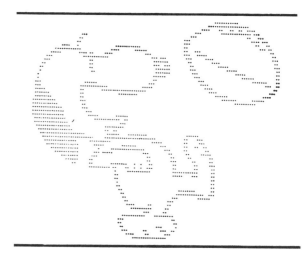

```
LISTNH
10 REM *** TOM KARZES, CURTIS JR HS, SUDBURY, MA
11 PRINT \INPUT "GIVE ME A NUMBER";A\PRINT\B=0
20 B=B+1\A=A/10\ IF INT(A)>0 THEN 20
30 FOR C=B TO 1 STEP -1\A=A*10\B(C)=INT(A-10*INT(A/10))\NEXT C
40 D=0\FOR C=1 TO INT(B/2)\ IF B(C)<>B(B+1-C) THEN D=1\NEXT C
50 FOR C=B TO 1 STEP -1\ PRINT CHR$(B(C)+48);\NEXT C
60 IF D=1 THEN 69
65 PRINT " IS A PALINDROME."\GOTO 10
69 PRINT " IS NOT A PALINDROME,"
70 IF B/2>INT(B/2) THEN B(INT(B/2)+1)=2*B(INT(B/2)+1)
72 FOR C=1 TO INT(B/2)\B(C)=B(C)+B(B+1-C)\NEXT C
75 FOR C=1 TO INT(B/2)\B(B+1-C)=B(C)\NEXT C
80 B(B+1)=0\FOR C=1 TO B\B(C+1)=B(C+1)+INT(B(C)/10)
90 B(C)=B(C)-10*INT(B(C)/10)\NEXT C
100 IF B(B+1)>0 THEN B=B+1
110 GOTO 40
120 END

READY

RUNNH

GIVE ME A NUMBER? 19

19 IS NOT A PALINDROME,
110 IS NOT A PALINDROME,
121 IS A PALINDROME.

GIVE ME A NUMBER? 38

38 IS NOT A PALINDROME,
121 IS A PALINDROME.

GIVE ME A NUMBER? 79

79 IS NOT A PALINDROME,
176 IS NOT A PALINDROME,
847 IS NOT A PALINDROME,
1595 IS NOT A PALINDROME,
7546 IS NOT A PALINDROME,
14003 IS NOT A PALINDROME,
44044 IS A PALINDROME.

GIVE ME A NUMBER? 96

96 IS NOT A PALINDROME,
165 IS NOT A PALINDROME,
726 IS NOT A PALINDROME,
1353 IS NOT A PALINDROME,
4884 IS A PALINDROME.
```

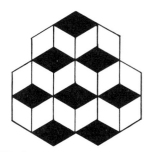

HOW MANY BLOCKS DO YOU SEE? 6 OR 7 ?

1675 — NON-PALINDROMIC?

Mike Lean in England took the number 1675 and reversed it 4850 times with the help of a computer, of course. Those 4850 reversals produced a 2000-digit number which still was not palindromic. Darryl Francis of *Games and Puzzles* thinks it's reasonable to assume that 1675 will never become palindromic however many times it is reversed. Do you agree?

Spell them backward and they stay the same

Read it from right to left and it will be the same as when you read the usual left to right. What will be? A palindrome, that is what.

Here is a sample: WON'T PEWS FILL IF SWEPT NOW?

You can have a lot of fun creating your own palindromes. But before you get started on yours, read these:

TOO HOT TO HOOT.
A POTATO PA?
NO, IT IS OPEN ON ONE POSITION.
STRAP ON NO PARTS.
WAS IT A BAR OR A BAT I SAW?

And this one is more difficult to read aloud:

OH HO HAH HAAHA AHAH HAH OH HO!

You can do the same with numbers. Example: 25952.

When your friends ask you what a palindrome is, tell them, "A palindrome looks and spells exactly the same from left to right or right to left, backward or forward, or forward or backward." In a popular dictionary this example is printed: ABLE WAS I ERE I SAW ELBA.

A few commercial names are palindromes. In California a city is named Yreka; a merchant calls his bakery Yreka Bakery.

And don't overlook single words: HUH. PEP. EYE. ADA. POP. WOW.

At first, making your own will be a slow process, but as you work with them it will become easier. Many adults know at least a few such words, so ask for their help. Friends at school may have one or two. And how about your teachers?

Write all of them down before you forget some. Try to make a long list, so you can show it to friends.

170

Follow-up on Palindromes

Remember in the Jan.-Feb. issue on page 12 we asked if readers could improve on Tom Karzes' programs to turn any number into a palindrome by successive reversals and adding. Here's an example:

```
  76
  67
─────
 143
 341
─────
 484 a palindrome
```

In the Jan.-Feb. issue we said Tom Karzes' palindrome program "fails with greater than a 7-digit number." What we really should have said is that it will not accept input numbers of over seven digits. In retrospect, this is not much of a limitation at all since palindromic seed numbers are generally much less than 7 digits. His program, in fact, spews out a number as long as a Teletype line. Sorry, Tom!

In any event, Gregory Yob of Menlo Park, CA put some additional sophistication into a palindromic reversal program. Here's the program, a couple of sample runs and then a portion of the run using 196 as a starter (remember — that's the one that doesn't seem to ever become palindromic). Gregory interrupted that run after 101 additions.

He then wrote a souped up version that doesn't print out the calculations but rather just the final palindrome and number of steps to reach it. If a palindrome isn't formed by 254 digits the program quits and prints the last number. Here's a listing of the second program and a couple of sample runs including the run of 196 as a starter.

Want to carry on? Why not modify the program to try all the numbers between 100 and 200 in sequence? Or extend it, if your BASIC compiler permits, to handle a longer number?

A Non-Palindrome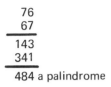

Ever since the first article on palindromes appeared in *Creative Computing* in January 1975, I have received letters from people discussing the notorious 196 (or 1675). 1675 is merely two reversals and additions of 196 (196 + 691 = 887. 887 + 788 = 1675).

Three magazines seem to be keeping track of this problem. Darryl Francis of *Games & Puzzles* printed letters from R. Hamilton who reversed 196 100 times with no palindrome formed, Jonathan Kessell (4147 reversals), and Mike Lean (4850). Students of Fred Gruenberger, editor of *Popular Computing* reversed 196 well over 5000 times. Gregory Yob's program is printed here with which he performed 584 reversals. Tony Skaltsiotis and Andrew Glassner of Highland Park High School, N.J. took it out to 10,000 reversals.

The ultimate so far was done by Lynn Yarbrough who dedicated 3 hours of a CDC 6600 to the problem and performed 79,098 reversals. Still no palindrome. (Details of his run are in *Creative Computing*, Vol. 2, No. 1, page 34.

```
0070  DIM A$[254],B$[254],C$[254]
0080  PRINT "STARTING #";
0090  INPUT A$
0100  S=0
0110  REM- PRINT LAST SUM
0120  PRINT TAB(10);A$
0130  REM: MAKE REVERSED #
0140   FOR J=LEN(A$) TO 1 STEP -1
0150   K=LEN(A$)-J+1
0160   B$[K:K]=A$[J:J]
0170   NEXT J
0180  REM: PRINT REVERSED # & STEP COUNT
0190  S=S+1
0200  PRINT S;TAB(11);B$
0210  REM- DO THE ADDITION
0220  C$=A$+B$
0230  REM: RESET AND DO AGAIN
0240  A$=C$
0250  B$=" "
0260  PRINT
0270  GOTO 120
0280  END
```

↖ LISTING

```
STARTING #?2344
         2344
1        4432

         6776
2        6776

STARTING #?196
         196
1        691

         887
2        788

         1675
3        5761

         7436
4        6347
```

← SAMPLE RUNS

```
STARTING #?176
         176
1        671

         847
2        748

         1595
3        5951

         7546
4        6457

         14003
5        30041

         44044
6        44044

STARTING #?776
         776
1        677

         1453
2        3541

         4994
```

← AND HERE'S THE BIG ONE (196)

WE DIDN'T HAVE SPACE FOR ALL THE INTERMEDIATE PRINT-OUT (YOU RUN IT!). GREGORY ABORTED THE RUN AFTER 101 ADDITIONS.

```
99    7074449215608204801780891870975118165118444806
      6084448115618115790781980871084028065129444707

100   1315889733122632059256287274205914623024788951 3
      3159887420326419502472782652950236221337988513 1

101   4475777153449051561729069927156150844362777464 4
      4464777263448051651729960927165150944351777574 4
```

```
0010  REM: FIND A PALINDROMIC NUMBER BY REVERSALS AND ADDITIONS
0020  REM: BY GREGORY YOB  (415) 326-4039
0030  REM: PO BOX 310, MENLO PARK, CALIFORNIA 94025
0040  REM: --- INSPIRED BY ARTICLE IN CREATIVE COMPUTING
0050  REM: --- RUN ON BASIC TIMESHARING SYSTEM 3000
0060  REM: --- WHICH HAS LIMITED STRING ARITHMETIC
0070  DIM A$(254),B$(254),C$(254)
0080  PRINT "STARTING #";
0090  INPUT A$
0100  S=0
0110  REM- PRINT LAST SUM
0120  REM: REMOVED TO ELIMINATE PRINTOUT
0130  REM: MAKE REVERSED #
0140  B$=" "
0150   FOR J=LEN(A$) TO 1 STEP -1
0160   REM: RESULT STRINT BEGINS WITH A BLANK, SO:
0170   K=LEN(A$)-J+2
0180   IF A$(J:J)=" " THEN 200
0190   B$(K:K)=A$(J:J)
0200   NEXT J
0210  REM: PRINT REVERSED # & STEP COUNT
0220  S=S+1
0230  REM: REMOVED & REPLACED BY A TEST
0240  IF A$=B$ THEN 340
0250  IF LEN(A$)=254 THEN 320
0260  REM- DO THE ADDITION
0270  C$=A$+B$
0280  REM: RESET AND DO AGAIIN
0290  A$=C$
0300  B$=" "
0310  GOTO 140
0320  PRINT "IS NOT ";
0330  GOTO 350
0340  PRINT
0350  PRINT "PALINDROMIC AT STEP "S-1
0360  PRINT " THE NUMBER IS:"
0370  PRINT A$(1:70)
0380  IF LEN(A$)<71 THEN 450
0390  PRINT A$(71:140)
0400  IF LEN(A$)<141 THEN 450
0410  PRINT A$(141:210)
0420  IF LEN(A$)<211 THEN 450
0430  PRINT A$(211:254)
0440  GOTO 450
0450  END
```

HERE'S THE SOUPED UP VERSION OF THE PROGRAM

AND HERE'S THE RUN USING 196 AS A STARTER.

```
STARTING #?196

STOPPED AT 200
XI?PRINT S;LEN(A$)
    425      188
```

← USE INTERRUPT TO FIND OUT WHERE WE ARE

```
XI?PRINT A$
  60239554322389886717750708169963186816112861056083174321936783138176880
  6222039538119870088201211328006808208448313126923572231218729184371380660
  1573216186704689629070576185898743224658230 5
```

```
XI?GOTO 200

IS NOT PALINDROMIC AT STEP  584
THE NUMBER IS:
  17978332204844160006808962247253580610457420253934734211705030836407528
  48129667831246939654647375611640929999515770646259233887400047774319526
  47177515999820135225573737447038653029766821859247046390305071123384 28
  4620138530269763537322608976006243840332889 6
```

PROGRAM HALTED AT STEP # 584 WHEN NUMBER FORMED 254 DIGITS, THE MAXIMUM STRING SIZE OF SYSTEM.

Computing Factorials -- Accurately

by Walter Koetke
Lexington High School, Mass.

Multiple precision arithmetic is a topic that can easily capture the imagination of almost anyone interested in computing. Today's programming languages and even hand held calculators normally provide enough precision to satisfy the requirements of most users, so this topic is really most appropriate for those intrigued by the challenge of creative computing. Perhaps because multiple precision arithmetic is not studied by all students, introductory literature relating to the topic is very sparse. If you encounter a good reference, be sure to note it as the topic is rarely given more than two or three cursory pages.

Calculating factorials is a standard example in elementary programming courses. Although a good example of the technique required to compute a product, the fact that only a few factorials can be calculated exactly before being subjected to round-off error is usually ignored. Actually, not too many factorials can be computed before the arithmetic limits of BASIC are reached. A typical program that correctly calculates the factorial of an entered value is:

```
10 INPUT N
20 LET F=1
30 FOR M=1 TO N
40 LET F=M*F
50 NEXT M
60 PRINT F
70 END
```

Given a non-negative integer N, then N! (N factorial) is defined as:

if $N>0$, $N! = N(N-1)(N-2) \ldots 1$
if $N = 0$, $N! = 1$

If only 6 significant digits are available, the results of this program are subject to round-off error for all values of N greater than 11. If 10^{38} is the upper limit of the available numbers, then this program can not even approximate the factorial for any N greater than 33. Even if 10^{99} is the upper limit available, the factorial can not be approximated for any N greater than 69. However, using multiple precision arithmetic, we can extend these limits to whatever extreme we choose.

To compute factorials more accurately, we must develop an algorithm for multiple precision multiplication. The most straightforward algorithm is that which we use when multiplying with pencil and paper. Hand calculation has many stumbling blocks, but a limited number of digits or a limited range of values are not among them.

Consider computing the product 7 x 259. You begin by multiplying 7 x 9, and although the product is 63 you only write down the 3 and "carry" the 6. After next multiplying 7 x 5, you add this "carry" to the product and obtain 41 — and again you write down the 1 and "carry" the 4. And so forth . . . After each individual multiplica-

tion, you record the units digit and "carry" those that remain.

To write a BASIC program that does multiple precision arithmetic using this same algorithm, one need only be able to separate the units digit of a product from the "carry". If P represents the product of two positive integers, then:

$$carry = INT(P/10)$$
and
$$\text{units digit of } P = P - 10*(carry)$$

Let's now apply this algorithm to the larger problem of computing the factorial of any positive integer. To do this we will write a program similar to the very brief example already given. However, the product shall be represented by the subscripted variable F, *each subscripted value representing a single digit of the product*. One program that does this is:

```
10 DIM F(50)
20 LET L=50
30 INPUT N
40 FOR I=2 TO L
50 LET F(I)=0
60 NEXT I
70 LET F(I)=1
80 FOR M=1 TO N
90 LET C=0
100 FOR I=1 TO L-1
110 LET F(I)=F(I)*M+C
120 LET C=INT(F(I)/10)
130 LET F(I)=F(I)-10*C
140 NEXT I
150 NEXT M
160 FOR I=L TO 1 STEP -1
170 PRINT F(I);
180 NEXT I
190 END
```

Notice that:

1. The program will compute factorials that can be expressed using no more than 50 digits. This restriction can be decreased by using a larger value in the DIM at line 10 and making a corresponding change in the value of L at line 20.

2. The product of two integers and the addition of the previous carry is completed at line 110. The next carry is calculated in line 120 and the unit's digit of the product is obtained in line 130. If you understand these three lines, you understand the fundamental idea of multiple precision multiplication.

3. All 50 (or L) digits of the product are always printed. This isn't wrong, but leading zeroes look peculiar.

Two sample runs of the program appear as:

```
RUN

? 5
0 0 0 0 0 0 0 0 0 0 0 0 0 0 0 0 0 0 0 0 0 0
0 0 0 0 0 0 0 0 0 0 0 0 0 0 0 0 0 0 0 0 1
2 0

READY

RUN

? 40
0 0 0 8 1 5 9 1 5 2 8 3 2 4 7 8 9 7 7 3 4 3 4 5 6
1 1 2 6 9 5 9 6 1 1 5 8 9 4 2 7 2 0 0 0 0 0 0 0
0 0

READY
```

172

Now stop reading and try running this program. Can you improve it? Increase the number of digits in the product. Print only those digits of the product that are significant. Print the product without spaces between each digit. Try to do these things *before* you continue reading — and if you can't use a terminal you can still write the required program changes.

If you were successful in completing the suggested improvements, then read fast for awhile. Increasing the number of digits in the product from 50 to 150 can be done with:

```
10 DIM F(160)
20 LET L=160
```

The only limit to the number of digits is the upper limit of the subscripts available in the BASIC you are using.

Printing the product without spaces between digits can be done in several different ways — most of which are a function of the version of BASIC you are using. Since this has little to do with multiple precision arithmetic, removing the spaces remains your problem.

Deleting leading zeroes in the printed product doesn't have much to do with multiple precision arithmetic either, but let's delete them anyway. This is not being done arbitrarily, but because it provides a very good example of the use of a "flag" within a program. Quite simply, we will use one variable, say S, as a flag to indicate whether a non-zero digit has been printed. All zeroes can then be ignored rather than printed unless a non-zero digit has been printed. This is represented in flow chart form as:

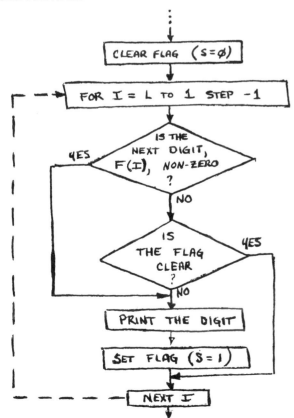

This algorithm for omitting leading zeroes is added to the program by:

```
160 LET S=0
170 FOR I=L TO 1 STEP -1
180 IF F(I)>0 THEN 200
190 IF S=0 THEN 220
200 PRINT F(I);
210 LET S=1
220 NEXT I
230 END
```

Two sample runs of the modified program appear as:

```
? 5
  1 2 0

READY

RUN

? 100
9 3 3 2 6 2 1 5 4 4 3 9 4 4 1 5 2 6 8 1 6 9 9 2
3 8 5 6 2 6 6 7 0 0 4 9 0 7 1 5 9 6 8 2 6 4 3
8 1 6 2 1 4 6 8 5 9 2 9 6 3 8 9 5 2 1 7 5 9 9 9
9 3 2 2 9 9 1 5 6 0 8 9 4 1 4 6 3 9 7 6 1 5 6 5
1 8 2 8 6 2 5 3 6 9 7 9 2 0 8 2 7 2 2 3 7 5 8 2
5 1 1 8 5 2 1 0 9 1 6 8 6 4 0 0 0 0 0 0 0 0 0 0
0 0 0 0 0 0 0 0 0 0 0 0 ^ 0

READY
```

If you tried running this program as suggested, you probably discovered something else that needs to be improved — the speed of computation. The present form of the program always multiplies each of the integers 1 through N by each of the variables F(1) through F(L-1). Thus when N = 100 and L = 160 as in the last sample run, the computation loop (lines 110 - 130) is repeated 15,900 (100*159) times. Even when N = 5 this loop is repeated 795 (5 x 159) times, and that's a lot of work to compute 1*2*3*4*5. This excessive computation can be eliminated by making use of *a pointer*, a very important idea in computing. Essentially, we will use another variable, say P, to point at the left most non-zero digit in the product. We can then multiply each of the integers 1 through N by each of the variables F(1) through F(P). When N = 5, this reduces the number of repetitions of the computation loop from 795 to 6, or more than 99%. When N = 100, the reduction is from 15900 to 6834, or about 57%. Clearly a pointer provides a worthwhile savings. Try to verify these reduced counts before you leave this topic.

If you are unfamiliar with the concept of a pointer, be sure you read these paragraphs very carefully. After you become familiar with this idea, teach your students about pointers if you're a teacher, or teach your teacher about pointers if you're a student. Who learns a significant idea first is not nearly so important as having everyone eventually understand the idea.

To implement the use of a pointer in our factorial program, begin with the initial value, P = 1. We then want to multiply each of the integers 1 through N by each of the variables F(1) through F(P). Thus line 100 should be changed to read FOR I = 1 TO P. The pointer does not alter the multiplication algorithm in lines 110 through 130, but after the NEXT I in line 140, we must examine the carry to see if the pointer is to be incremented. If the carry is non-zero, we increment the pointer, perform the carry, and then repeat the procedure. If the carry is zero, we can continue with NEXT M.

The instructions needed to do this are:

```
142 IF C=0 THEN 150
143 LET P=P+1
144 LET F(P)=C
145 LET C=INT(F(P)/10)
146 LET F(P)=F(P)-10*C
147 GOTO 142
```

Finally, since the product contains exactly P digits, then the print loop beginning at line 170 can be changed to read FOR I = P TO 1 STEP -1.

Our multiple precision factorial program, complete with all modifications discussed, now appears as:

```
10 DIM F(160)
20 LET L=160
30 INPUT N
40 FOR I=2 TO L
50 LET F(I)=0
60 NEXT I
65 LET P=1
70 LET F(1)=1
80 FOR M=1 TO N
90 LET C=0
100 FOR I=1 TO P
110 LET F(I)=F(I)*M+C
120 LET C=INT(F(I)/10)
130 LET F(I)=F(I)-10*C
140 NEXT I
142 IF C=0 THEN 150
143 LET P=P+1
144 LET F(P)=C
145 LET C=INT(F(P)/10)
146 LET F(P)=F(P)-10*C
147 GOTO 142
150 NEXT M
160 LET S=0
170 FOR I=P TO 1 STEP -1
180 IF F(I)>0 THEN 200
190 IF S=0 THEN 220
200 PRINT F(I);
210 LET S=1
220 NEXT I
230 END
```

Any additional improvements are left to you. Although several are possible, more efficient use of the variables in the F array is likely to be the most dramatic. The example program uses one variable to represent one digit. By allowing each variable to represent two or three digits, program speed is essentially doubled or tripled. But then there are additional problems when the product is printed, and possibly additional problems within the computation loop. Does the example have any theoretical limit on the factorials that can be computed? Does it have any realistic limits?

The topic of multiple precision arithmetic will be further explored in a subsequent column. Now that you understand multiple precision multiplication, only the operations of addition, subtraction and division separate you from successfully computing $\sqrt{2}$ and π to at least half million digit accuracy.

(To further test your knowledge of multiple precision arithmetic, why not try Contest Problem 3. — Ed.)

Glum Glossary

Punched card: A short piece of 80-channel paper tape.

Program: The footprints of hundreds of bugs. Once the bugs are eliminated, the program is all that's left.

Puzzles and Problems for Fun

► Mrs. Canton wanted to buy all the grocer's apples for a church picnic. When she asked how many apples the store had, the grocer replied, "If you added 1/4, 1/5 and 1/6 of them, that would make 37." How many apples were in the store?

► Donna bought one pound of jellybeans and two pounds of chocolates for $2. A week later, she bought four pounds of caramels and one pound of jellybeans, paying $3. The next week, she bought three pounds of licorice, one pound of jellybeans and one pound of caramels for $1.50. How much would she have to pay on her next trip to the candy store, if she bought one pound of each of the four candies?

► Take a 3-digit number like 200, reverse it (002) and then multiply the two numbers. The result, 400, is a perfect square (20* 20 = 400). Find all such 3-digit numbers.

Bill Morrison
Sudbury, Mass.

► Can you put nine pigs in four pens so that there are an odd number of pigs in each of the four pens?

 If you have a favorite puzzle, perhaps we can print it here. Send it along!

AEDI, MUTAB, NEDA and SOGAL

by Walter Koetke
Lexington High School

Your non-terrestrial thoughts should not remain free of problems that require creative solutions. Toward that end, here are two situations that you might find interesting. After solving either one or both of these problems, please send your solution to Walter Koetke at the *Creative Computing* address. The best solutions received will be acknowledged in a future column.

If you think you've seen the first problem before, you may be correct. It's really an old problem in a new disguise.

The civilizations of the three planets Neda, Mutab and Sogal have agreed to begin a war in the year 2431. Although these societies have not eliminated such irrational actions as war, they have at least formalized the process. There are, for instance, no guerilla activities and wars are usually very brief and always decisive. Wars are fought with inter-planetary rockets each of which is powerful enough to completely destroy an entire planet. With such powerful weapons at their disposal, Neda, Mutab and Sogal have agreed to the following set of rules, for only in this way can they be assured of a single victor.

Rule 1: The fight will continue until only one civilization remains.

Rule 2: The rather primitive technique of drawing lots will be used to determine which planet may launch the first rocket, which the second and which the third.

Rule 3: After the launching rotation is established, rocket launching begins and continues in order until only one planet remains.

When contemplating the outcome of this war, the three civilizations have full knowledge of the background of their adversaries.

Mutab is clearly the technologically superior civilization. Once launched, their rockets always strike with perfect accuracy — thus disproving a modern theory that nothing is perfect. Before this war begins, both of the other civilizations are aware of the terrifying fact that if a Mutab rocket is fired at them, the probability of their being completely destroyed is 1.

Neda is the oldest civilization and long ago had the superior technology. However, the complacency of a self-centered, unchallenged mind has been eroding this superiority for many years. As a result, the technology of Neda has not advanced in over 40 years. If a Nedian rocket is fired at another planet, the probability of hitting that planet is 0.8, just as it was 40 years ago.

Sogal is by far the newest of the three civilizations. Being dedicated to producing its own technology on its own terms has resulted in a proud and purposeful civilization, but one that is technologically four to five hundred years behind its present adversaries. A missile launched by Sogal has only a 50-50 chance of reaching its intended target.

Your role in this future war is to determine each civilization's probability of winning.

AEDI continued . .

The second problem is based upon an idea presented by C. Stanley Ogilvy in the text *Tomorrow's Math*, Oxford University Press, 1972. However, you should attempt your own solution before seeking Ogilvy's support.

Although the civilization on the planet of Aedi is generally considered rather advanced, its political system no longer attracts the imagination and support of the majority of citizens. In an effort to attract more capable leaders at the highest level, a new plan was formulated for selecting the president. The originators of the plan also hoped that their new idea would result in a younger president and a change of presidents at least every 10 years.

Essentially, the new plan is as follows. Once a president is selected, he holds office for at least five years. At that time he may or may not be replaced by a newly selected person. The selection process is new and is the key to this new plan. The selection process is a problem — one problem known by all citizens at all times. When a president has served for five years, all citizens of Aedi are invited to submit their solution to the problem. If a solution submitted is better than that previously submitted by the current president, then the submitter becomes the new president. If a solution submitted is equal to that previously submitted by the current president, then the submitter becomes the new president only if his solution is also different from that previously submitted by the current president.

The problem used by the Aedians to select their leader can be attacked on many different levels. The problem involves three sets of three instructions each and a board on which play is recorded. Three blank instruction sets and the playing tablet appear as:

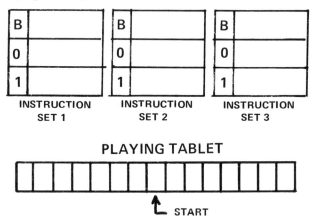

B			B			B	
0			0			0	
1			1			1	

INSTRUCTION SET 1   INSTRUCTION SET 2   INSTRUCTION SET 3

PLAYING TABLET

↑ START

Instructions are of the form STOP (self-explanatory) or contain three elements:

1. An indication of what to record on the playing tablet. The only possibilities are 1, 0 or B (blank).

2. An indication of which direction to move on the playing tablet. One square left or right are the only choices.

3. An indication of which instruction board contains the next instruction to be followed.

Thus the instruction 1-R-3 means: record a 1 on the playing tablet, move one square right, and go to board 3 for the next instruction.

President of Aedi

The combination of the contents of your place on the playing tablet and the instruction board you are following dictate your next instruction. The left column of the instruction board indicates B (blank), 0 or 1. If your current place on the playing tablet is blank, you follow instruction B; if it is a 0, you follow instruction 0; and if it is a 1, you follow instruction 1. The play always begins with board 1.

Consider the following complete set of instructions. If you think you understand the rules, try following the instructions before reading further.

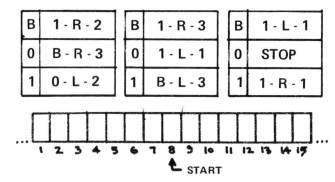

B	1 - R - 2		B	1 - R - 3		B	1 - L - 1
0	B - R - 3		0	1 - L - 1		0	STOP
1	0 - L - 2		1	B - L - 3		1	1 - R - 1

1 2 3 4 5 6 7 8 9 10 11 12 13 14 15

↑ START

The infinite tablet has been partially numbered for the convenience of this discussion. Play begins on board 1 and, since square 8 is blank, our move is 1-R-2. Thus we write a 1 in square 8, move 1 square to the right (square 9) and go to board 2 for the next instruction. Since square 9 is blank, the second instruction is 1-R-3. Once again we write a 1, move to the right, and this time go to board 3 for the next instruction. Our tablet now looks like

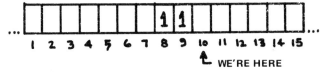

1 2 3 4 5 6 7 8 9 10 11 12 13 14 15

↑ WE'RE HERE

The next instruction is 1-L-1, which records a 1 in square 10, returns us to square 9 and indicates that the next instruction is on board 1. Because square 9 contains a 1, our instruction is 0-L-2 so we replace the 1 with a 0, move to square 8 and proceed to board 2 for the next instruction. The tablet now appears as:

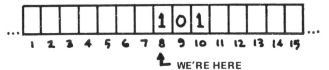

And on we go. If you continue following these instructions until you reach STOP, the tablet will finally appear as:

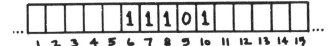

When STOP is reached, the success of the effort is measured by the longest string of consecutive ones that appear on the tablet. In the example, the longest string contained but three ones.

The Aedians problem was not to follow a particular instruction set, but to create one. Specifically, their leader would be the person who could write the series of instructions that would produce the longest *finite* sequence of consecutive ones. Since you've just seen the example used to introduce the problem to the young Aedians, you'll have to beat three consecutive ones before you're their new leader. If you generate an impressive series, be sure to send the instructions to *Creative Computing*. All worlds seem desperately in need of leaders and we'll gladly publish your name as a likely candidate.

* * *

Never underestimate the importance of just fooling around.

Kenneth Boulding

* * *

"The only time my education was interrupted was when I went to school."

George Bernard Shaw

* * *

Puzzles and Problems For Fun

▶ The number $153 = 1^3 + 5^3 + 3^3$ Find all other 3-digit numbers that have the same property. How about 4-digit numbers? To the 4th?

Bill Morrison
Sudbury, Mass.

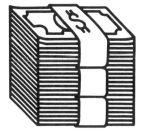

▶ Mr. Karbunkle went to the bank to cash his weekly paycheck. In handing over the money, the cashier, by mistake, gave him dollars for cents and cents for dollars.

He pocketed the money without examining it and spent a nickel on candy for his little boy. He then discovered the error and found he possessed exactly twice the amount of the check.

If he had no money in his pocket before cashing the check, what was the exact amount of the check? One clue: Mr. Karbunkle earns less than $50 a week.

▶ Can you find the missing number for each diagram? You first have to figure the pattern which may be horizontal or vertical with a relationship between every number, every second or third number. You may have to add, subtract, multiply, divide, invert or do a combination of these things. Have fun!

A.

3	5		17
7		25	49
	37	73	

B.

	13	6
7	9	
12		10

C.

4	20	5
	8	8
6	54	9
7	49	7

D.

```
        27
    _       _
 12     6      3
    _    4    _    1
```

▶ Send us your favorite puzzles for this column!!

177

A new learning activity from Creative Computing . . . .

Reading, Writing, and Computing

Walter Koetke
Lexington High School, Massachusetts

Problems Column Editor: Walter Koetke, Math Dept., Lexington High School, Lexington, MA 02173. Please send solutions and suggestions for problems directly to Mr. Koetke.

When Alex was admitted to Hopeful Hospital he knew he was very ill. After a thorough examination Dr. Frank concluded that Alex had a severe case of sleepitis, and that the proper treatment was lots of activity and exercise. Because Hopeful Hospital was very modern and up-to-date, the medical facilities included a computer to assist in the diagnosis and treatment of unusual illnesses. Dr. Frank entered Alex's symptoms into the computer, and the computer concluded that Alex had a severe case of exhaustitis. The computer also indicated that the proper treatment for exhaustitis was no activity, no exercise and lots of sleep. Dr. Frank considered his original diagnosis and the computer diagnosis, then decided to go along with the computer. The doctor prescribed no activity, no exercise and lots of sleep. Alex died one week after beginning the prescribed treatment. After his death, a group of doctors re-examined Alex's records and demonstrated that Alex actually had sleepitis, and that the prescription of no activity, no exercise and lots of sleep was largely responsible for his death.

Who should be blamed for Alex's death?
    a) The computer — for making an incorrect diagnosis
    b) The programmer — because the computer's incorrect diagnosis was probably a programming error
    c) Dr. Frank — for making an incorrect diagnosis
    d) Alex — for getting sick in the first place
    e) No one — we all have to go sometime

If you answered a or b, or even gave serious consideration to answering a or b, then your computer literacy is indeed open to question. An elementary school education is inadequate if students leave without some idea of what computers can and cannot do. Society's use of computers is so extensive that even school dropouts are likely to use and certain to be affected by computers. Clearly then, the need for schools to carefully assess their efforts toward computer literacy of all students is essential.

If you need some support when you attempt to stir whatever is bogging down the implementation of computer literacy in your school, town or what-have-you, consider the following:

Dr. Arthur W. Luehrmann of Dartmouth College presented a paper titled "Should the Computer Teach the Student, or Vice Versa?" at the AFIPS 1972 Spring Joint Computer Conference. In this truly classic, penetrating paper Luehrmann raises questions such as "how much longer will a computer illiterate be considered educated? How long will he be considered employable and for what jobs . . ." Luehrmann's article inspired the title of this one — for developing skills in reading, writing and computing should now be the fundamental objective of education.

As you are probably aware, the NAEP (National Assessment of Educational Progress) conducted an extensive program in 1972-73 to determine the nature and effectiveness of mathematics education in the United States. In 1977-78, the NAEP will again assess the state of mathematics education — but something new will be added.

At that time they will also separately assess the nature and effectiveness of computer literacy education. How well will the students of your school and your town reflect a basic knowledge of computer literacy?

Computer literacy can not only be profitable, but it also might record your name for posterity. Several students at the California Institute of Technology recently used a computer to help generate their entries for a sweepstakes type of contest being run by the McDonald's Corp. The students not only won first prize, a car — not a pile of hamburgers, but also won a large percentage of all the other prizes. While McDonald's was objecting and claiming that the students took unfair advantage of all other contestants, their rival, Burger King, was presenting CIT with a scholarship in the name of the student who originated the idea.

Since one of the primary purposes of this column is to suggest interesting problems, let's redirect our attention in that direction. Three of the following four problems are for those "getting started." Finding examples other than the very standard ones can be time consuming, particularly for teachers who are developing entire computer related units. Perhaps these will help.

1. Writing a program that generates or tests for prime numbers is a very good standard example for those learning to program. Usually, however, it is an end in itself. This problem is intended to provide an application for a prime testing algorithm.

Suppose that k people are standing in a circle. After choosing one person to begin, the people count-off in a clockwise direction around the circle. If a person counts-off with a prime number he must leave the circle. The winner is the last person who remains.

Consider one example, say k = 6.

Then the people appear as

The initial counting process would yield:

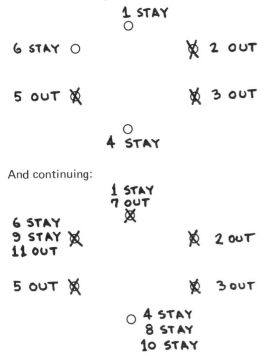

Thus the fourth player is the winner.

The problem is to make a two-column table containing k and the player who would win for that value of k. Can you predict the player who wins for any given k?

2. The second problem can be rephrased in many different ways, all of which revolve about the question "Is each positive integer 1 through n a divisor of some integer that contains only the digits one and zero?" For example:

1 is a divisor of 1
2 is a divisor of 10
3 is a divisor of 111
4 is a divisor of 100
5 is a divisor of 10
6 is a divisor of 1110
and so forth.

If you have an answer and can prove yourself right, send me your answer in care of Creative Computing. I haven't yet seen a valid proof of an answer. Writing a program to determine the dividend for a given divisor is apt to raise several ideas worth examining — and it's only a division problem.

3. One very standard, likely boring example for new programmers who are also studying algebra is often that of the quadratic formula. A very clever way of making the same points as well as a host of more interesting ones was first presented to the author at an NCTM (National Council of Teachers of Mathematics) workshop conducted by Helen Hughes. Given the quadratic equation $Ax^2 + Bx + C = 0$, where A, B and C are integers such that $1 \not< A \not< 10$, $0 \not< B \not< 10$, and $0 \not< C \not< 10$, write a program that will find the probability that
   a) the roots will be imaginary
   b) the roots will be rational and equal
   c) the roots will be rational but unequal
   d) the roots will be irrational.
How are these probabilities affected by varying the limiting values of A, B and C?

4. The final problem isn't computer related at all. In fact, it's not even going to help you get started at anything. Actually, it might finish age problems altogether. The next time you're asked to solve a problem about Dick being four years older than Fred was last Thursday, etc., pull this out of your pocket.

Ten years from now Tim will be twice as old as Jane was when Mary was nine times as old as Tim. Eight years ago, Mary was half as old as Jane will be when Jane is one year older than Tim will be at the time when Mary will be five times as old as Tim will be two years from now. When Tim was one year old, Mary was three years older than Tim will be when Jane is three times as old as Mary was six years before the time when Jane was half as old as Tim will be when Mary will be ten years older than Mary was when Jane was one-third as old as Tim will be when Mary will be three times as old as she was when Jane was born.

How old are they now?

I'm really not sure of the source of this timeless gem. A student gave it to me several years ago, and memory suggests he reported seeing it in an issue of the American Mathematical Monthly. At any rate, it might provide those who assign age problems a few moments to reconsider their usefulness.

The problem of Mutab, Neba and Sogal presented in the May - June issue has been resolved. The first correct solution was submitted by Charles Kluefil of Glen Oaks, New York, who reported that the chance of survival for Mutab is 30%, for Neba is 17-7/9%, and for Sogal is 52-2/9%. Unfortunately, the citizens of Aedi are still searching for a new leader. No solutions were received that qualified the sender as the new president.

"Today's topic of discussion will be, The Dehumanizing of Education"

Problems For Creative Computing . . . .

Probability

by David C. Johnson, University of Minnesota

PREREQUISITES

Basic notions of probability including P(E) = 1 - P(E')

DISCUSSION

The CAMP project, University of Minnesota, has conducted research and development activities on the use of the computer as a problem-solving tool in school mathematics grades 7 - 12. The following problem while a "take-off" on the classical Birthday Problem has a number of real applications relative to expected occurrence of given events:

from the everyday: What is the probability of at least two girls wearing the same style and color outfit at a party with say 30 girls invited (assuming some given number of basic styles, say g, and number of colors, c, or gxc different outfits -- e.g., if g=8 and c=10 then gxc=80.)

to a problem in manufacturing and sales: How many different styles and colors are needed to give a low probability (p<.10) to the event that two or more families in the same neighborhood (of 100 families) will purchase identical automobiles (if, on the average, 10% of the families purchase a new XXX each year.) Note: the problem is actually a little more complex than this, but the statement should provide a general idea -- the assumption is also made that people like their cars to be different.

PROBLEM

The situations posed above can be stated in purely mathematical terms. The three problems posed below appear in the CAMP exercises in the book *Elements of Probability* by Robert J. Wisner, Scott, Foresman and Company, 1973, appropriate for a high school course in probability.

1. First, to warm up — write a computer program to calculate the probability that at least two people in a group of n people will have the same birthday. (Hint: since the 365^n may become very large, you will have to design a procedure to calculate 365/365 x 364/365 x 363/365 x 362/365 . . .)

2. Now for *the* problem:
   a. Write a general program which considers n people selecting an alternative (or having a characteristic) from m equally likely possibilities. What is the probability that at least two will select the same alternative? You might think of this as n people each picking a number between 1 and m and writing it down -- what is the probability that at least two will pick the same number? (Of course, m>n or the probability is 1.)
   b. Use your program to determine how many numbers you will need to use at a party with 12 people to give yourself better than a 50-50 chance of having two pick the same number (you might like a probability of about .75). Do you see the similarity between this and the manufacturing problem? Actually conduct the number experiment with some groups of friends -- how well do the experimental results agree with the mathematical? Note that the experiment can be done by asking your friends to pick a favorite color or object from a list with m items -- but, you have to be cautious here; not all of the items may be equally liked by your friends -- what does this do to your computation?

Compounding

by Charles A. Reeves, Florida State University

▶ Try to fold a sheet of paper onto itself as many times as you can (i.e., fold it in half, then in half again, then again, etc.). What is the largest number of folds you can make? Someone has claimed that it is impossible to make more than 8 folds, no matter what size you start with!

But imagine for a moment that it *is* possible to fold it over onto itself a large number of times. The thickness of one sheet of notebook paper is about .004 inches. If you could fold it 50 times, how high would the stack be?

▶ Your rich uncle deposited $1000 in a savings account for you the day you were born. The account draws 6% simple interest, and the earnings are added back into the account each year. But your uncle didn't tell you about this — you found out when his will was read. He died when you were forty years old — how much did you get?

For those who want more: Same problem as above, but the interest rate is ½% each month instead of 6% per year. How much more money, if any, would you get this way?

▶ Consumer prices rose an average of 8.8% during 1973. Let's round this off to 9%, and assume that prices continue to go up this much *every* year.

Pick out an item that you think you might like to buy when you're an adult, and for which you know the present price. Write a program that will report to you how much the item will cost in the year 2000 AD.

▶ Your father gives you a penny as a gift on your first birthday. He promises to double the amount of the gift each year until you reach your 21st birthday. How much will you get from him on this birthday?

For those who want more: Have the computer print the amount you will receive on the 21st birthday, and also the *total* amount you will have gotten through the years.

▶ Erie County in upstate New York is one of the most heavily polluted areas in the United States. In a study of the residents of the county it was found that the number of people dying from respiratory diseases is *doubling* every five years. In 1950 there were 263 deaths attributed to respiratory diseases. How many deaths will there be in the year 2050 AD, assuming this same rate of increase every 5 years?

▶ The population of the world increases almost 2% each year over what it was the year before. In 1970, the world population was about 3.6 billion, or 3,600,000,000.

Have the computer calculate what the world population will be in the year 2000 AD.

▶ A salmon starts a 100 mile journey upstream to the placid lake where she was born. Each day she is able to swim 3 miles upstream, but each night when she sleeps she is pushed 2 miles back downstream. Exactly how many days will it take her to reach the quiet spawning grounds?

▶ The bristleworm can reproduce by splitting itself into 24 segments, each of which grows a new head and a new tail. What is the maximum number of bristleworms that could be obtained in this fashion, starting with only 1 worm, after ten "splittings"?

DOUBLING UP

by FRANK TAPSON

TAKE a piece of paper—you may use any size you please—and fold it in half. Then fold it in half again, and yet again, and again . . . How many times do you think you can do this? If you have never met this problem before then try it before you read any further—you will very probably receive a surprise. Have a guess first before actually trying to do the folding and then see how far you get.

Many people on meeting this little problem for the first time are prepared to say that, provided the paper is large enough then it may be folded in half any number of times. Well, as you might have discovered by now, after 7 such foldings the task becomes extremely difficult, and if not impossible then it will almost certainly be after the next fold. It is interesting to look at what in fact happens.

After our first fold, the piece of paper we have to work on next is double the thickness of the original. Another fold of this piece doubles the thickness so that we now have 4x the thickness of the original. Folding again will once more double-up on the thickness so that we have (2 x 2 x 2) 8 thicknesses of paper. This is followed by 16 thicknesses after the next fold, then 32, then 64, and 128 after the 7th fold. Assuming that the paper we are using is one-thousandth of an inch thick (not the thinnest possible but still a flimsy paper) then after folding it 7 times we have a piece which is one-eighth of an inch thick, or about the thickness of a piece of stout card. Now such a card could certainly be folded in half generally, but there is an added difficulty. Just as the thickness has been doubled with each fold so the area has been halved, and after only 6 foldings we are usually trying to bend something which is not much bigger than an extra-large postage stamp, which is why that piece of 'stout card' is so difficult to fold.

It is interesting to wonder how far the process might be taken if a piece of super-large paper were used. Let us assume it is still one-thousandth of an inch thick, but that we can start with a piece the size of a football-pitch. Go on—have a guess, how many times would you manage to fold it in half?

Some might wish to argue about the precise stage at which the task becomes impossible, but if the 13th folding can be made, it produces something which is about four feet square and eight inches thick. Now think about bending that!

Once we start folding by speculation (and not by actually trying to do it) it becomes fascinating to go on with the process. For instance, just suppose we were able to get an extremely large piece of paper and fold in in half exactly 100 times and, having done that we wished to stand on top of it—how long a ladder would we need to get to the top? By now you have no doubt some idea of what to expect—or have you? After the 26th fold we have a "piece of paper" which is just over a mile thick so you might think we are going to need a fairly tall ladder for 100 folds. Keep going—the 53rd fold gets us just past the sun, and if you think that we are at least over half way then you have failed to see what doubling is all about. The 83rd fold gets us somewhere near the centre of our galaxy, from which it follows that the 84th fold puts us out on the other side and still going. And there we will let the matter rest, if anyone can work out 'precisely' where the top of our work will be after the 100th fold do let us know. We might be able to use it as a navigational aid for inter-stellar travel!

This simple concept of the growth of the doubling sequence has had a fascination for those concerned with the lighter side of mathematics for many years. Perhaps the most famous is the story told around the invention of the chess-board, how the king was so pleased that he offered the inventor any reward that the inventor cared to name. This was expressed as 'one grain of corn on the first square of the board, two grains on the second square, four grains on the third square and so on . . .' The king thought this is a very light price to pay for such a great game and readily agreed. However, he was not at all pleased to learn that the total quantity of grain required could not be supplied by the entire world output of grain for several years to come. Some accounts of the story claim that he had the inventor beheaded for imposing such a mathematical joke upon royalty! Re-telling this story in his mammoth work

A History of Chess, H. J. R. Murray says that the quantity of grain needed is such as to cover England to a uniform depth of 38.4 feet. The actual *number* of grains needed to fulfil the stated conditions is 2^{64}-1, a figure which also occurs in connection with the story woven around the Tower of Hanoi.

Another form of the story involves either the sale of a horse, or the shoeing of one. In either case the price is fixed at a farthing (over a hundred years ago) or a penny for the first nail in its shoes, doubled-up for the second nail, doubled again for the third nail and so on. The only serious disagreement appears to be concerning the total number of nails (I have stories giving 6, 7, and 8 nails per shoe).

A story can also be woven around the telling of a secret to two friends, each of whom tells it to two other (different) friends, each of whom . . . Assuming that the actual telling occupies just one minute, and that another minute is lost in scurrying off to find someone else to tell the secret to-how many people will know after one hour has elapsed from the initial telling? By now of course you will have some idea of what is happening and won't be too surprised to learn that by the end of the hour 2,147,483,647 people would know the secret. Since this is just over one-half of the present total world population, it hardly could be called a secret any more! The same story has been presented differently by asking, under the above conditions, in a village of a given number of inhabitants, how soon would it be before everyone knew the secret?

There is a surprising growth rate in the simple matter of doubling at every stage of the sequence. Just think of it next time you fold a piece of paper in half, and don't go on for too long lest you should fall off the top!

For the curious, the exact value of 2^{100} is—1,267,650,600,228,229,401,496,703, 205,376.

Reprinted from *Games & Puzzles,* December 1974. Copyright 1974 *Games & Puzzles,* 11 Tottenham Court Road, London W1A 4XF, England.

Puzzles and Problems for Computers and Humans

▶ A fly and a mosquito start together to circle a building, but the fly circles the building in six minutes, the mosquito in four. How many minutes will elapse before the mosquito passes the fly?

▶ Write down five odd numbers so they total 14.

▶ A man, anticipating the rationing of gasoline, hoarded 100 gallons in a large tank behind his garage. One night a neighbor decided to siphon off ten gallons for his snowmobile. As the gasoline was run off, the villainous neighbor poured water in the tank at the same rate as he was filling his gas can, keeping the contents thoroughly mixed throughout.

If the whole caper took ten minutes, how many gallons of gasoline and how much water did the neighbor end up with in his ten-gallon can?

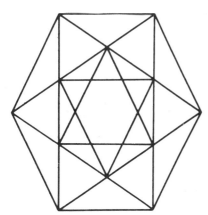

▶ How many triangles are there in this figure?

▶ Write a program to convert any number from 1 to 3000 to its equivalent Roman numeral. The seven Roman symbols are:

M	1000
D	500
C	100
L	50
X	10
V	5
I	1

The rules for forming Roman numerals are:
1. If a symbol precedes one of smaller value, its value is added.
2. If a symbol precedes one of larger value, its value is subtracted; then the difference is added to the rest of the number.
3. Numbers are written as simply as possible using only C, X, and I as subtrahends. Some examples are MCMLXIV, 1964; DXLIX, 549.

Your program should accept as input the decimal number and output the Roman numeral. Convert the following numbers in your contest entry: 1, 14, 400, 549, 999, 1964, 1975, 2500, 2994, 3000.

▶ In the octonary (modulus 7) system, write a program to find the seven 7-digit squares which contain no duplicate digits. Here is one: $1242^2 = 1567204$.

▶ We are told that the purchase price of Manhattan Island in 1626 or 1627 was $24. Assume the Indians invested their money on January 1, 1627 at 6% compounded annually. At that rate, the money would be worth a great deal by January 1, 1975. We know that if P dollars are invested at an interest rate of r (expressed as a decimal), the amount A the following year is given by:

$$A = P(1 + r) \qquad (1)$$

and the total amount after n years is given by:

$$A = P(1 + r)^n \qquad (2)$$

Write a program to calculate the value of the investment on January 1, 1975 to the nearest penny using two methods: (1) compute the amount year by year using Formula 1 and accumulate it, (2) compute the amount by Formula 2. In Method 1, round the result each year to the nearest cent. Your challenge, of course, is to maintain more significant digits than most computers are capable of handling.

You'll be interested to compare your answers with the 1974 assessed value of the land of some $6.4 billion.

▶ Arrange two of each of the digits 0 to 9 so as to form a 20-digit number. Your number may not begin with a zero. Then score your number as follows:

For every two consecutive digits that form a perfect square, score two points. For every three consecutive digits that form a perfect square, score three points. A four-digit square scores four points, and so on.

For example, if your number was 587382190249719503664, you would score two points for 49, two points for 36, two points for 64, and six points for 219024 — for a total of 12 points. You may *not* count 036 as a three-digit square.

What is the maximum number of points you can score? Lynn D. Yarbrough comments that he has no idea of a reasonable way to attack the problem with a computer, but using a hand-held scientific calculator and some ingenuity seemed to yield a good solution. The number Lynn found, which scored 100 points, is:

49134681827562500379	Square Root	Points
49	7	2
134681827562500	11605250	15
1346818275625	1160525	13
81	9	2
1827562500	42750	10
18275625	4275	8
27562500	5250	8
275625	525	6
7562500	2750	7
75625	275	5
562500	750	6
5625	75	4
62500	250	5
625	25	3
2500	50	4
25	5	2
		100

Lynn comments further, "the longest single square I have found with no tripled digits is $9987338075625 = 3160275^2$, which can be neatly combined with $25210441 = 5021^2$ into the sequence 99873380756252104416, but its score is not nearly so high (40)".

For those readers wishing to continue with Squaresville, there is a number with a score of 106 points. I leave it as a challenge for you to find it. — DHA

▶ Assume a life-span of 80 years. In what year of the 20th century (1900-1999) would you have to be born in order to have the maximum number of prime birthdays occurring in prime years? The minimum number?

Marsha Lilly
Sudbury, Mass.

▶ Arrange two of each of the digits 0 to 9 to form a 20-digit number. Your number may not begin with a zero. Score your number as follows:

For every two consecutive digits that form a perfect cube, score two points; for every three consecutive digits that form a perfect cube, score three points; and so on.

For example, if your number was 45864096859013312727, you would score two points for 64, four points for each for 4096, 6859 and 1331, and two points for each of the 27's . . . which would give you a total of 18 points. You may not count 01331 as a five-digit cube.

Games & Puzzles

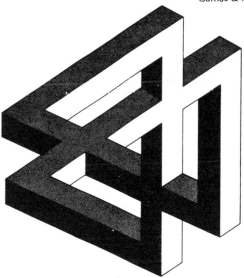

▶ A regular dodecahedron has twelve pentagonal sides and twenty vertices. Assuming that one face is in the X—Y plane with an edge along (0,0,0) to (0,1,0), what are the coordinates of the remaining 18 vertices?

Lynn Yarbrough
Lexington, Mass.

▶ There are 720 ways to arrange the digits 1 through 6 as six-digit numbers:
1 2 3 4 5 6
1 2 3 4 6 5
1 2 3 5 4 6
etc.

If you continue this sequence, in numerical order, what will be the 417th number in the series? What will be the nth?

Bill Morrison
Sudbury, Mass.

▶ 78 multiplied by 345 produces 26910. Notice that these three numbers have between them all of the digits 0 to 9 occurring just once.

You can probably find other such examples containing all ten digits and with the three numbers having two, three, and five digits respectively. However, there is just one set of three numbers which has the additional peculiarity that the second number is a multiple of the first number. Can you write a computer program to find this combination?

Pythagorean Triples

by Richard Acuna, Senior
Sylmar High School, California

PROBLEM:

A Pythagorean triple is a set of three positive integers that satisfy $A^2 + B^2 = C^2$. Let's find some of these triples.

PROCEDURE:

*On a piece of scratch paper, write out a table of squares of integers, from 1 to 15.

*Assume that A is less than or equal to B. Then the smallest value for A or B would be 1. Question: Is $A^2 + B^2$ a perfect square, when A and B are equal to 1?

*$1^2 + 1^2 = 2$. Since 2 is not a perfect square, this combination for A and B does not produce a Pythagorean triple. Make a table showing all possible combinations of A and B, if each is less than or equal to 10. Compare 1 with 1, 2, 3, . . ., 10, then 2 with 1 to 10, and finally, 10 with 1 to 10. Make note of all the triples you find. Use the table of squares you made, to check the sum of $A^2 + B^2$ to see if it is a perfect square.

*If you were asked to find all triples in which A and B were less than 25, using only a pencil and paper, the task would take a long time. Write a program for your computer to find all triples in which A and B are less than or equal to 25. How long did it take your program to find these triples? How long would it have taken, with only pencil and paper?

SOME QUESTIONS:

*Count the number of sets of triples you found above. If A and B range between 25 and 50, how many triples would you expect to find? If A and B range between 50 and 100, how many triples would you expect to find? Modify the program you have written, to find all triples for A and B less than or equal to 100. Check your answers to the questions above. Does it appear that, as A and B range from 1 to 100, the Pythagorean triples are evenly distributed?

*If you study the set of triples you have found, you will note that some triples are multiples of others. For example, 6, 8, 10 are multiples of 3, 4, 5. If these integers are measures of sides of right triangles, both triangles would have the same shape. Modify your program, so that it will output only those triples that would relate to uniquely shaped triangles; eliminate all multiples of any triple found.

*Given: $A = 2MN$, $B = M^2 - N^2$ and $C = M^2 + N^2$. These formulas give Pythagorean triples whenever M and N are integers. Use these formulas and a new program to find a set of triples. Do these formulas eliminate multiples? Did you find more triples with this program? Did your program overlook any triples?

*If you have the computer time, use one of your programs, modified, to find all triples for which A and B are less than 10000. Does it appear that triples are evenly distributed throughout this range?

Pocket Calculator

TRICKS !!

1. Enter 107734, turn calculator 180 degrees and read.
2. Enter 4. Press the addition button. Enter 57734. Turn the calculator 180 degrees, read what it says. Press addition button again and read.
3. If the price for 28,430,938 barrles of oil is increased 2.5% who benefits? Turn calculator 180 degrees for answer.

Can you invent some new tricks? You'll have to settle for words containing only the letters B, E, H, I, L, O, and S. Send your results to *Creative Computing*.

We heard that Hewlett-Packard technicians play a game on the company's programmable HP65 pocket calculator in which two players subtract one to three objects each turn from a starting total of 15 in an effort to leave the loser with the last turn. If the player in the role of the calculator wins, the upside down reading says BLISS. If the other player wins, the reading is I LOSE.

DIGITAL INVARIANTS

Andrew Kourkoutis defines a perfect digital invariant as an integer containing N digits, where the sum of the Nth powers of the digits is equal to the integer itself. In general,

$$. . . H^N + . . . + I^N + J^N + K^N =$$
$$. . . (10^{N-1} H) . . . (10^2 I)(10^1 J)(10^0 K)$$

If N is 3, then

$$I^3 + J^3 + K^3 = 100I + 10J + K$$

371 is one such number, for

$$3^3 + 7^3 + 1^3 =$$
$$27 + 343 + 1 = 371$$

Write a program to find digital invariants for N less than or equal to 4. (If N is greater than 4, running time on most systems will be too great.)

Puzzle: People and Cabins

This one isn't easy. It could swallow up a day of your time, even a week. But it will take more than an hour.

The following 15 facts are all you need to solve it:

1. There are five hunting cabins on a lake. Each cabin is a different color, and is inhabited by a man of a different nationality, each drinking a different kind of liquor, firing a different brand of shotgun shell, and shooting a different duck.
2. The Englishman lives in the red cabin.
3. The Pole shoots only bluebills.
4. Bourbon is drunk in the green cabin.
5. The Finn drinks beer.
6. The green cabin is immediately to the right (your right) of the brown cabin.
7. The hunter who uses Winchester shells shoots mallards.
8. Remington shells are shot in the yellow cabin.
9. Brandy is drunk in the middle cabin.
10. The Norwegian lives in the first cabin on the left.
11. The man who buys Federal shells lives in the cabin next to the cabin of the man who shoots red heads.
12. Remington shells are used in the cabin next to the cabin where the canvasbacks are shot.
13. The hunter who fires Western shells drinks gin.
14. The Irishman loads up with Peters shells.
15. The Norwegian lives next to the blue cabin.

Your mission, should you decide to accept it, is to figure out who drinks the Scotch and who shoots the teal.

Good luck.

Thinkers' Corner

by Layman E. Allen © 1975

WORD PUZZLES

How many of the problems (a) through (f) below can you solve by forming a network of words that have exactly as many letters as the number listed as the GOAL? (Suppose that each symbol below is imprinted on a disc.)

To qualify as a network

(1) all sequences of discs across and down must be words,
(2) the words must have two or more letters and not be proper names,
(3) all of the discs in the REQUIRED column must be used,
(4) as many of the discs in PERMITTED as you wish may be used,
(5) at most one of the discs in RESOURCES may be used.

Example: The number of letters in the words of the network
C A T is 5:
	CAT		TO		
0	3	+	2	=	5.	

The number in the network F A T is 3.

Problem	GOAL	REQUIRED	PERMITTED	RESOURCES
(a)	5	R F	L M P	C G J N U Y
(b)	7	A A	D T I	B E S V X Z
(c)	10	Q T N	I U M R	C G K O T W
(d)	10	E F R	J O O Q	B F H L S V
(e)	12	E R W	A K M S	D G K O T Y
(f)	19	A E R R T	A C L N O S	B F M R U W

If you enjoy this kind of puzzle, you may like playing ON—WORDS: The Game of Word Structures. Free information about this and other instructional games is available upon request from THE FOUNDATION FOR THE ENHANCEMENT OF HUMAN INTELLIGENCE, 1900-W Packard Rd., Ann Arbor, MI 48104.

Some Suggested Answers (frequently there are others):

(a) M
FRY

(b) A I
SAT

(c) QUIT
NO

(d) S O
FOR
E

(e) M O W
ARE
SURE

(f) A
ACORN
T

A new learning activity from Creative Computing . . . .

Turtle Geometry Without Hardware

Robert S. McLean
The Ontario Institute for Studies in Education
Toronto, Canada
and
Claude and Colette Pagano
La Seyne, France

Papert's turtle (Papert and Solomon, 1972) is by now probably well known to most people who work with computers and young children.* The basic outline of the use of the turtle as a concrete environment in which to teach concepts of elementary programming and problem solving at an early age is available in the literature. The turtle itself is now commercially available, and the ideas embodied in the real turtle can be simulated on a CRT as well, often with better results.

Any consideration of the turtle has assumed the availability of a computer to support it. What can a teacher who has been exposed to the ideas inherent in the use of the turtle do if he or she doesn't have the equipment? This is the problem that two teachers in France faced last year. They worked out an analog of the computer turtle situation which uses the children themselves as the "machinery". These notes of their activity illustrate their approach and detail several additions to the usual turtle problems. While these notes are fairly explicit in the suggestion of activities for teacher and child, they are intended as a guide. Any user will certainly modify them and expand the range of possible activities.

The basic problem environment consists of an object that moves toward a target in a space containing obstacles according to specific rules of movement. The environment is concretized for the child by the analogy of the movement of a turtle which has the goal of finding its food, a leaf of lettuce. The activities are first of a physical sort, moving from normal play behavior to more conceptual, program-directed activity. The first activities consist of movement of the child on the ground.

A. The leaf of lettuce is placed on the ground and a child goes towards it playing the role of the turtle.

B. Some obstacles are placed on the ground and the "child turtle" describes his movement while he is going to the lettuce.

C. The "child turtle" is now blindfolded. Another child directs the turtle towards his food: 1) by taking him by the hand; 2) by audible signals, and; 3) by oral orders, first without obstacles and then with obstacles.

During this phase, the children look along the orders given to the turtle for those which are the most useful (which give the most knowledge with the minimum ambiguity) noting that the turtle doesn't retrace his steps and does not move sideways like a crab. (If a live turtle is brought to class some days ahead of the game, the children will discover this for themselves.) The person conducting the game can point out the following three instructions: forward, turn right, and turn left.

*A future issue of *Creative Computing* will carry an article describing turtle geometry and the LOGO computer language.

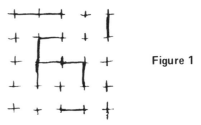

Figure 1

D. In order to make these three instructions more precise, the ground is ruled off in squares, thus forward becomes move forward one square. Turn right becomes turn 90 degrees to the right without leaving the present square. Turn to the left becomes turn 90 degrees to the left without leaving the square. By the choice of these three instructions, the movement of the turtle, which is really a continuous action, is modeled in a succession of elementary actions defining a succession of elementary states. Each square communicates with its four neighbors by an opening and each obstacle is provided by closing the boundary between two adjacent squares.

Once again, the "child turtle" first evolves and describes his task with the aid of the three instructions. Second, he executes to the extent possible the orders of another child, and third starts over with a blindfold if he can recognize by touching the borders of the squares — for example with the aid of a string placed on the ground.

more

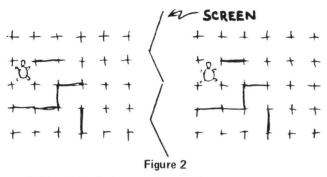

Figure 2

E. Two identical networks are placed on each side of a folding screen. One team has some obstacles in network A and communicates to the other team by messages the position of these obstacles such that the other team can produce the same networks. (It is good to let the children think about the different ways of coding the information.) When the networks A and B are identical including their obstacles, a "child turtle" is placed on each network in the same position in the corresponding squares. Each instruction executed by turtle A is transmitted to turtle B who executes it in turn. Note, if the child turtles are very advanced, one can ask them to move symmetrically on two symmetric networks.

Once the above activities have made concrete the basic geometry and rules of the game, the group can begin to consider more abstract representations.

First, a representation of the state of the turtle is invented. A picture of the turtle can be drawn and progressively stylized as in figure 3.

Figure 3

Next, the operators are encoded to give the basis of a rudimentary programming language for the turtle (figure 4). The information given by the color and by the shape of the symbol is, in fact, redundant as the symbol is placed systematically in the quadrant of the square situated at the right of the initial turtle and of the final turtle.

   FORWARD

    RIGHT

   LEFT

Figure 4

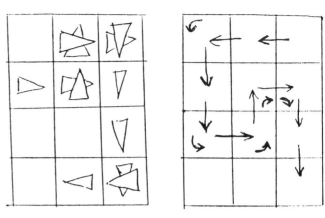

Figure 5

We can propose certain games of coding and decoding. For example, code the path of the turtle in figure 5. One can also decode a string of commands: FR, FFR, FR, FL, FF, LF, LF, LF, FR. Find a path permitting the turtle to find its lettuce in figure 6 and then code it. In figure 6, also code the path which permits the turtle to return to its initial square in its initial position.

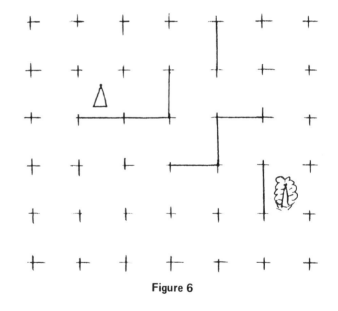

Figure 6

With these basics of coding for the turtle, the games played with the real environment earlier can be replayed with a more abstract representation. It is possible to extend the basic games in many ways; the following is a list of variations that can be used to introduce additional concepts.

We can demonstrate the isomorphism of the movement of the turtle from one square to another and that of an ant crawling along a wire as in figure 7.

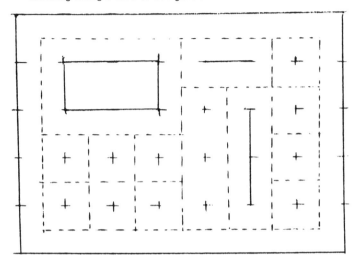

Figure 7

The notion of the length of a path can be introduced by taking as one unit the advance from one square to the next and thus the length of the path is the number of arcs followed by the ant above.

The notion of distance between two points can be introduced through the problem of finding the shortest path between two squares. One can count these shortest paths and can find the difference between squares on a grid for any case given (figure 8).

Figure 8

The notion of a hamiltonian path can be explored by finding the longest path without passing through the same square twice. There is also the question of whether one can pass through all of the squares by that means.

The notion of transportation time can be studied by associating an elementary time with each elementary action. For example, forward may take four seconds, turning right — 3 seconds, and turning left — 2 seconds. Thus one can look for the most rapid paths. There can be a race between two or more turtles subject to the constraint that they do not simultaneously occupy the same square.

One can add the possibility that the lettuce moves. This movement can be deterministic (that is to say, known in advance by the turtle) or random (a game of strategy).

The idea of a non-square network can be introduced. The turtle can move in a network of hexagonal mesh (which is equivalent to a triangular mesh for the ant) with three orders: forward — as above, right — meaning turn 60 degrees to the right, and left — which means turn to the left by 60 degrees, plus two variants (RR and LL permitted or not). Another possible variation of the networks is triangular for the turtle or hexagonal for the ant which do not permit the command FF (figure 9).

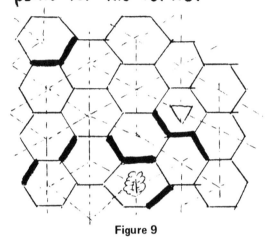

Figure 9

Conditional instructions can be introduced. The four tests of the real turtle to see if it is touching an obstacle in the front, left, right or rear can be adopted as TEST CLEAR TO FRONT (RIGHT, LEFT, or REAR). These can be adopted with the LOGO like TEST followed by IFTRUE or IFFALSE sort of structure or it can be more like other programming languages and use an IF . . . . THEN (action) type of format.

Additional forms of tests can be invented, such as test whether the turtle can see its food (by looking straight ahead) or smell it. The latter sense can be considered either directional or not, and may be a function of distance from the target.

The list of applications of turtle geometry is far from being limited. The choice of this theme in the elementary school permits many possibilities, and removing the requirement for computer equipment has made this approach attractive. In effect, each child thus establishes his program, executes it and analyzes it.

Reference

Papert, S. and Solomon, C. Twenty things to do with your computer. *Educational Technology,* 1972, 9(4), 39-42.

"Continued in their present patterns of fragmented unrelation, our school curricula will insure a citizenry unable to understand the cybernated world in which they live."
Marshall McLuhan — 1964

188

The 10ᶜ Computer and Other Games

by Gwyn Lyon
Gates Elementary School
Acton, Massachusetts

The teaching of math to kids is traditionally divided into lecture and drill. In the re-thinking of a second grade math program, I decided to incorporate some different approaches to aspects of math computation. A game such as Input-Output can be noisily exciting, and effectively teach the relationships between sets of numbers.

INPUT-OUTPUT

A game for the Blackboard or Overhead Projector. Divide the acetate into two columns or make two columns on the blackboard. Place a numeral in the left or Input column. Through the function of the magic-black box-computing-teaching machine, the number is transformed into a new number.

	teaching machine = ?
Input	Output
4	7

Place a new number in the input column, and using the same teaching machine function, a new number appears in Output.

Input	Output
4	7
0	3
	answer: t.m. = +3

Continue to add numbers until a student guesses what function the teaching machine is set for.

Second graders can do problems of this level of difficulty:

	teaching machine = ?
Input	Output
4	11
7	17
10	23
	answer: t.m. = 2x + 3

The game can be adapted for many types of algebraic equations:

	teaching machine = ?
Input	Output
9	4
25	6
4	3
	answer: t.m. = $\sqrt{x}$ +1

As an added bonus, a child with such learning problems as would exclude him from the successful completion of a traditional worksheet can often excel in "head" games that require no written response.

THE 10¢ COMPUTER

The teacher must also begin to rely more on manipulative materials to move the child securely from the concrete to the abstract. Hence, the ten cent computer:

Materials: a large grocery box. 1 sheet of acetate, 8" x 10".

Method: Cut the box up so that you have one large sheet of cardboard, without seams, that will completely cover the stage of the overhead projector. Mine is 12" x 11½", but measure yours to be sure.

Cut four holes in the top third of your cardboard. Save the cut-outs! Tape the sheet of acetate so that it covers the holes. Then hinge the covers back over the holes with tape.

A Simple Binary Game: Beginning at the left side, mark the numerals 1, 2, 4, 8 on each acetate-covered hole.* Close all the covers. Place the computer on the stage of the projector, and turn on the projector. Lift the first cover on the left. Computer now shows "1". Write on the blackboard, 1000.

Close all the covers. Lift cover marked "2". Write on blackboard, 0100, and explain that because the light is on in the "2" position, the binary notation is 0100.

Close all covers. Explain that all numbers up to 15 can be shown with only the four lighted positions. How can you make 3? 7? 14?

Binary Numers for the 10¢ computer

●●●●	0	●●●○	8
○●●●	1	○●●○	9
●○●●	2	●○●○	10
○○●●	3	○○●○	11
●●○●	4	●●○○	12
○●○●	5	○●○○	13
●○○●	6	●○○○	14
○○○●	7	○○○○	15

By this time, the children will have grasped the idea, and can work quite competently up to 32, using only the blackboard notations. If you want to carry on, you can make an "advanced" computer with 6 holes that can record numbers all the way up to 63!

*Normal binary number notation goes right-to-left, i.e. 1 = 0001, 6 = 0110, 8 = 1000, etc. If you think your kids can grasp this, give it a try.

Suggested Bibliography

Ahl, David. *Getting Started in Classroom Computing*. Digital Equipment Corporation, Maynard, Massachusetts.

Adler, Irving and Ruth. *Numerals, New Dresses for Old Numbers*. John Day, Company. New York, N. Y.

Kenyon, Raymond. *I Can Learn about Calculators and Computers*. Harper and Row. New York, N. Y.

A new learning activity from Creative Computing . . . .

Beginning With <u>BASIC</u>

by William R. Morrison
Curtis Jr. High School
Sudbury, Massachusetts

The act of sitting down at a computer terminal creates a closed world. Even first-time users become absorbed, lose track of time, and seek only to further whatever dialogue they are involved in. Can you remember the pleasures of getting the machine to do what you wanted it to? Or the frustrations of many error messages? These two activities are designed for junior-high school students to use as part of an introductory unit on computers. They are intended to help make that first experience informative; to let students learn step by step how the computer responds to various commands; and finally to let students form their own images of the computer as a partner in a dialogue.

A. EXERCISES IN IMMEDIATE MODE

This first guide takes the student from immediate mode to a simple program. It presents a minimum of rules, emphasizing instead a series of actions, and lets the student draw whatever conclusions he can. The impact of these first impressions will later be the foundation for a more formalized presentation, the objects of which should be familiar. Explanations tend to turn students off unless they have already had an experience that makes them eager to know why.

Some Things to Try With a Computer that Speaks BASIC:

1. Try some PRINT statements:

    PRINT MY COMPUTER SPEAKS BASIC

    What happened? Did you forget something? Correct the command and try again. Will the computer accept something like: 2+5=4? Can you make it print such arithmetic nonsense? Now print your name and the date.

2. Try this: PRINT "SOME ARITHMETIC"; 22*33;35/70;5—9,7+9 What happens when you use the ; or the ,? How does the computer handle fractions? Try a few, such as 1/3+5/8, and see.

3. Here is a short program. Type it in and try it out.

    ```
    10 INPUT A
    20 INPUT B
    30 PRINT A "TIMES" B "IS" A*B
    40 GOTO 10
    ```

If something went wrong, remember that everything you type in has meaning to the computer, every quote mark, comma, etc.

4. Let's make some changes and see how this program can be improved. You don't have to type the whole thing over again, of course; change the lines by typing the line number and its line. First, though, stop the computer from running the old program by typing CTRL/C.

    Change line 20: Type: 20 LET B=1
    Change line 40: Type: 40 LET B=B+1
    Add a line 50: Type: 50 GOTO 30

What happened to old line 20? Find out by asking the computer to LIST the program. Now, try a RUN of the program. Stop the program with CTRL/C — does CTRL/C stop the computer while it is LISTing a program?

Give the program a title with:

    5 PRINT "TIMES TABLE"

Do you see why line numbers go up by 10's? Now make the program stop automatically when it gets to ∧ times 10:

    45 IF B=10 THEN 60

Of course you need line 60!

    60 STOP

If B is *not* 10, what does the computer do?

5. You should now nave a program that asks for a number and then types out all the multiples of that number up to 10 times that number. Go ahead — pick a number and hand in a RUN and a LIST of the program.

6. Can you:

    a) Further change the program to add, subtract or divide instead of multiplying?

    b) Change the program to print the multiplications or divisions, etc., in a table form?

    c) (Difficult!) Make the computer print the table starting at 1 x 1, going to 1 x 10, then starting over by itself at 2 x 1, 2 x 2, etc.?

B. EXTENDING A SIMPLE PROGRAM TO SOLVE COMPLEX PROBLEMS

This hands-on guide is for somewhat more proficient students, and is designed to illustrate some ways of adapting a simple program to more complex uses. It presents the program as a resource, a given tool to be used for solving a problem. As an added benefit, students are helped to review and extend their knowledge of some important mathematical concepts.

A Problem to Solve and a Program to Help:
Problem:
   Find out if 1517 is a prime number. If it is not prime, find at least two divisors.
Solution:
   Instead of looking for a table of prime numbers (unfair!) or doing a whole mess of division problems to look for divisors, and maybe not finding any, use this simple program:

```
10 LET A=1517
20 INPUT B
30 PRINT A/B
40 GOTO 20
```

This program tells the computer to:
- Remember the number 1517 (Line 10)
- Ask for a number — it will type ? and wait (Line 20)
- Divide 1517 by that number (Line 30)
- And go back for another divisor (Line 40)

   You still have to give the computer numbers to try as divisors, but at least *it*, not you, will be doing the work.

Question:
   Remember the Sieve of Eratosthenes? Even if you don't, do you have to divide 1517 by all the multiples of 2, or just by 2? Now, since there are no other even primes, why not divide 1517 by only odd numbers after you try 2? Why not leave out multiples of 3, 5, 7 etc.?
Information:
   Here are some prime numbers to try as divisors: 2 3 5 7 11 13 17 19 23 29 31 37 41 43 . . .
Problems:
   Change the above program to print:
   a) Your name
   b) Each division problem as well as its answer
   c) Using lines such as LET B=3 and LET B=B+2, all the divisions of 1517 by odd numbers until you stop the computer with a CTRL/C

The above exercises are merely suggestions for making the computer's self-sufficiency pay off and helping the student maintain his own private dialogue with the machine.

A Puzzle For Fun

A warden had eight prisoners in separate cells, arranged in the manner shown below.

He decided to rearrange the prisoners so their numbers would be in consecutive order, reading counter-clockwise around the circle, with the center cell left empty.

The warden started by moving a prisoner into the empty cell, then moving the other prisoners one at a time, always into the cell vacated by the previous occupant. All but No. 5, who was never moved from his cell.

Prisoners can only be moved to a cell adjacent to their own, i.e., only 7 or 3 could move to the empty cell.

Can you figure out how the warden did it in 17 moves?

Odd or Even?

by Jeffrey Moskow (Student)
Lexington High School, Mass.

My first computer programming instructor defined a computer as an expensive, fancy, overgrown adding machine. Bearing this in mind it is not difficult to see that a computer is primarily concerned with numbers. One of the most important things to remember when programming a computer is that whatever you are trying to accomplish should be reduced to numerical operations before writing the program. The differences between numbers can be used to write many programs, both simple and complex. The following program is only concerned with two kinds of integers, odd and even.

```
10 PRINT "THIS PROGRAM TAKES ANY INTEGER AND TELLS"
20 PRINT "IF IT IS ODD OR EVEN"
30 PRINT "PLEASE GIVE ME A NUMBER";
40 INPUT X
50 IF X/2=INT(X/2) THEN 80
60 PRINT X;" IS AN ODD NUMBER"
70 GOTO 30
80 PRINT X;" IS AN EVEN NUMBER"
90 GOTO 30
100 END

RUN

THIS PROGRAM TAKES ANY INTEGER AND TELLS
IF IT IS ODD OR EVEN
PLEASE GIVE ME A NUMBER? 34
 34  IS AN EVEN NUMBER
PLEASE GIVE ME A NUMBER? 57
 57  IS AN ODD NUMBER
PLEASE GIVE ME A NUMBER? 133
 133  IS AN ODD NUMBER
PLEASE GIVE ME A NUMBER?
↑C
```

This simple program is based on the fact that even numbers are divisible by 2 while odd numbers are not. This same principle can be used to simulate the tossing of a coin. The only difference is that this program uses the random number function.

Cryptic Puzzle

by Denis Kaminski
George Washington Jr. HS
Ridgewood, NJ

Below are 11 computer words put into a code. Each letter of the alphabet was replaced with a different letter. Remember that if "S" stands for "Ω" in one word, it will be the same throughout the list. A clue is given with the first word.

```
P Q X U O (A popular beginner's language)
M D F G F Q C        G Z B Z G S W Z
B D D W              O D F Z
P H M M Z F          U P Y
D H G W H G          Y Z Y D F S
U C W H G            M B D J    O R Q F G X
```

```
10 RANDOMIZE
20 PRINT "THIS PROGRAM SIMULATES THE TOSSING OF A COIN"
30 PRINT "HOW MANY TOSSES";
40 INPUT X
50 FOR N=1 TO X
60 LET F=INT(2*RND(0))+1
70 IF F/2=INT(F/2) THEN 100
80 H=H+1
90 GOTO 110
100 T=T+1
110 NEXT N
120 PRINT "IT WAS HEADS ";H;" TIMES"
130 PRINT "IT WAS TAILS";T;" TIMES"
140 END

THIS PROGRAM SIMULATES THE TOSSING OF A COIN
HOW MANY TOSSES? 15
IT WAS HEADS  9  TIMES
IT WAS TAILS 6  TIMES
```

Will the results for 15 tosses always be the same?

Will the numbers of heads and tails be closer if the number of tosses is greater? Why?

Programming:

Try to write a program that shoots dice.

Try to write a program that allows the user to input a number and the computer will output whether or not the number is an integer.

Odd or Even?

Is the number of letters used in a headline of a newspaper odd or even?

Find out for 20 different headlines.

Odd or Even?

Choose a shelf full of books. Is there an odd or even number of books on that shelf?

Find out for 20 different book shelves.

Odd or Even?

Roll one of the dice. Is the number of spots odd or even?

Find out for 20 different rolls of the dice.

Alphabet Statistics

Using short paragraphs taken out of textbooks, magazines, or the newspaper, have each student count up the number of A's, B's, C's, and D's and list these in order of their frequency. When everyone is done, compare results. Chances are in most written material, A will be the most frequent letter followed by D, C, and B.

Have students plot each of their results on a bar graph.

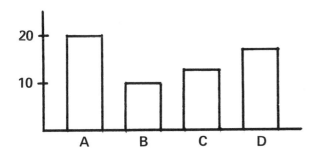

This is a good exercise to introduce the idea of scaling. For example, a long paragraph may have 100 or more A's, whereas a short one might have fewer than 20. However, for a meaningful plot, one division on the graph paper (¼'') might equal ten letters when 100 letters are to be plotted or only two letters when 20 are the maximum in any bar.

A simple computer program can be written to accept as input the results from each student and then compare his percentages with those of the entire class.

Programming Problems to Start With

Just getting started in programming? Whether you are learning BASIC, FORTRAN, APL, or some other language, here are eight simple problems to program and one more difficult one. The first seven of them should not take over ten statements in BASIC or FORTRAN. (We will print the best reader-submitted program for Problem #9 two issues from now).

1. Compute and print out the sum of the digits from 1 to 10.
2. Comute and print out the sum of the digits individually squared, from N1 to N2, which are inputs.
3. Input N numbers. Compute and print out the product of the even digits.
4. Generate and print out N two-digit random numbers; and also print out the largest one of these, where N is an input.
5. Generate K1 two-digit random numbers, and print out the fraction which are smaller than your age, where K1 and your age are inputs.
6. Read in K2 numbers as DATA and print them out sorted from smallest to largest.
7. Compute and print out a table of the present value of $1.00, for a rate, number of periods, and print out increment, which are all inputs.
8. Prepare a program to draw five cards at random from a 52-card deck, and print out the suit and value of each card.
9. Write a program that will print all permutations of N things taken N at a time for all N<=10.

PROGRAM LISTING

```
LIST NH
10 PRINT "STATISTICAL LETTER ANALYSIS" \ PRINT
20 PRINT "ENTER 'END' AFTER LAST STUDENT" \ PRINT
30 DIM A(100), B(100), C(100), D(100), T(100), N$(50)
40 I=I+1 \ PRINT
50 INPUT "NAME", N$(I) \ IF N$(I)="END" THEN 200
60 PRINT "HOW MANY OF EACH LETTER"
70 INPUT "A", A(I)
80 INPUT "B", B(I)
90 INPUT "C", C(I)
100 INPUT "D", D(I)
105 REM
          INDIVIDUAL TOTALS
110 T(I)=A(I)+B(I)+C(I)+D(I)
120 A1=A1+A(I) \ B1=B1+B(I) \ C1=C1+C(I) \ D1=D1+D(I)
130 GOTO 40
190 REM
          COMPUTE TOTAL AND PERCENTAGES
200 T=A1+B1+C1+D1 \ N=I-1
210 A2=A1*100/T \ B2=B1*100/T \ C2=C1*100/T \ D2=D1*100/T
215 REM
          PRINT RESULTS
220 FOR I=1 TO N
230 PRINT FOR M=1 TO 5
240 PRINT "-"; FOR M=1 TO 50
250 PRINT \ PRINT "ANALYSIS FOR "N$(I) \ PRINT
260 PRINT ,"CLASS","YOUR","CLASS","YOUR"
270 PRINT "LETTER","TOTAL","TOTAL"," %"," %"
280 PRINT "A",A1,A(I),A2,A(I)*100/T(I)
290 PRINT "B",B1,B(I),B2,B(I)*100/T(I)
300 PRINT "C",C1,C(I),C2,C(I)*100/T(I)
310 PRINT "D",D1,D(I),D2,D(I)*100/T(I)
320 NEXT I
330 PRINT FOR M=1 TO 5
340 PRINT "-";FOR M=1 TO 50
350 PRINT \ PRINT \ PRINT "THAT'S ALL FOLKS!" \END
READY
```

SAMPLE RUN

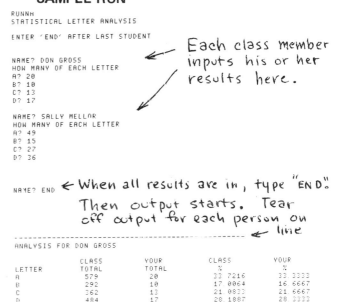

```
RUNNH
STATISTICAL LETTER ANALYSIS

ENTER 'END' AFTER LAST STUDENT


NAME? DON GROSS
HOW MANY OF EACH LETTER
A? 20
B? 10
C? 13
D? 17

NAME? SALLY MELLOR
HOW MANY OF EACH LETTER
A? 49
B? 15
C? 27
D? 36


NAME? END
```

Each class member inputs his or her results here.

When all results are in, type "END". Then output starts. Tear off output for each person on line

```
-------------------------------------------------
ANALYSIS FOR DON GROSS

              CLASS    YOUR         CLASS    YOUR
              TOTAL    TOTAL         %        %
LETTER
A             579      20          33.7216  33.3333
B             292      10          17.0064  16.6667
C             362      13          21.0833  21.6667
D             484      17          28.1887  28.3333
```

etc.

Sports Special

Look for math exercises in various sports that your students follow so avidly. Here are some examples of things to be computed in different sports:

Baseball	Batting averages
Basketball	Points per minute
Hockey	Penalty minutes per period
Football	Pass completion percentages

Another interesting exercise is to make a prediction model. It is easiest to do with the win-lose record for each team. For example, about halfway through the football season, the win-lose record for four teams might look like this:

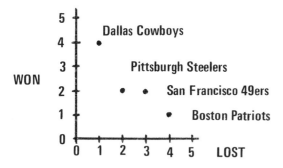

Using this graph, a team that is higher and to the left has a greater chance of beating one lower and right. The further apart the teams, the greater point spread would be expected, i.e., the 49ers might be expected to beat the Patriots by one touchdown, whereas Dallas might be expected to tromp Boston by three touchdowns. Make a big chart for the class that can be updated daily or weekly and predict all the games each week. How accurate is this prediction model? Try other variables instead of win-lose record, such as third down conversions or total yardage gained.

Some students might wish to write a computer program for the prediction model. In such a program, several variables can be averaged together or even given different "weights" to make an even better model. A word of warning: No model, no matter how many variables are considered, is perfect. Indeed, if the outcome of sporting events could be perfectly forecasted, there would be no more "sport".

Here is the output from one such program:

TEAM1	EXPECTED SCORE	TEAM2	EXPECTED SCORE
BOSTON	19	BUFFALO	17
NY JETS	21	CLEVELAND	14
NY GIANTS	10	MIAMI	28
OAKLAND	21	DENVER	18
etc.			

So You Think You Know BASIC?

List the seventeen fundamental statements in the BASIC language

1_____	7_____	13_____
2_____	8_____	14_____
3_____	9_____	15_____
4_____	10_____	16_____
5_____	11_____	17_____
6_____	12_____	

A. If there were a decree that said you had to use fewer statements, draw a line through the 5 statements you could easily do without. Are there 5 others that you could get along without?

B. Circle the four that really do the most for you and which you would hold on to until the very end.

Look back over your list and your decisions and consider:

C. After getting rid of all 10 statements asked for in A., is there anything you really cannot do? If there is, you ought to think about changing some of your decisions.

D. Which statements are necessary, and which just make programming easier? What value do you place on these latter statements?

E. Consider other items in life similarly. What possessions do you enjoy (make a list of 12)? Which ones could you give up if you had to? How important to you are things that are nice but not necessary?

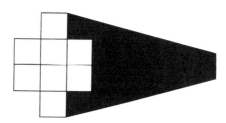

Insert the numbers from 1 through 8 in the eight boxes, one digit to a box, in such a manner that there are no consecutive numbers next to each other, horizontally, vertically or diagonally.

John R. Cossen
Bellerose, N.Y.

A new learning activity from Creative Computing . . . .

You Don't Need a Computer for These

by David Ahl

No computer? Then try these activities in class or at home.

Build a "computer". Using junk and leftovers (boxes, cans, fabric, yarn, spools, bits of plastic, etc.) build your own computer. (Send a photo of your creation to *Creative Computing* and we'll print the best ones).

Clip a story. Look for stories or articles mentioning computers in newspapers, magazines, and non-computer publications. What was the role of the computer? Was the reporting, in your opinion, accurate?

Draw a computer. What does a computer look like in a medical laboratory, a school, a factory, on board a spacecraft? Draw your view.

Write a story. Will computers take over the world, develop individual personalities, become as small as a wrist watch, etc? What will it do in the home? For grocery shoppers? For beggars? Let your speculations wander in a story of your own. (Send your stories to *CC.*)

Produce a glossary of computer terms. Many "computer" words are not in the dictionary. How can you find such words and their meanings. You ought to be able to find at least 30 words peculiar to the computer field (actually there are several hundred), and at least 10 words or acronyms that are not in standard dictionaries.

Visit a computer center. Try a local community college, university, bank, or company. But be sure to arrange your visit well in advance so you don't show up on payroll check day.

"Well, I'm glad to see that ONE day out of the year you kids can stop all that screaming and jumping around and behave like ladies and gentlemen"

195

A new learning activity from Creative Computing . . . .

Learning, Innovation, and Animals

by David Ahl

This activity is unusual in several ways. First, the computer program ANIMAL is used for data storage and retrieval rather than for computations. Second, the latter part of the activity (Exercises 5-11) has nothing to do with computers per se. Its entire objective is to stretch minds in imaginative new directions. I believe the whole future of the computer rests on imaginative and creative new applications and that it's too easy to get caught up in the traditional, and somewhat mundane data processing rut. So here's an opportunity to let your mind wander and have fun in some strange and wonderful new places.

Illustrations for this article are all by Earl Newman, Summit Star Rt, Box 51, Blodgett, OR 97326.

✳ ✳ ✳

The processes of learning and innovation, seemingly different, are really closely related.

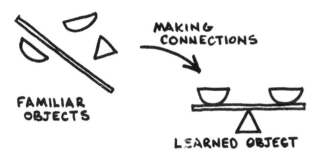

In the *learning* process, we take familiar objects, facts, feelings, attitudes, and values and make connections to learn about new things. These connections between familiar things can take many forms. Looking at the same thing from a different point of view is one way of making a connection. Another way of making connections is by comparison. We'll look into this process at greater length in the next section, "Identifying Animals by Comparison".

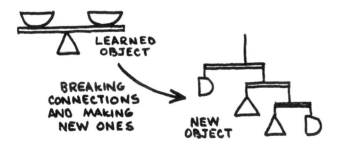

In the process of *innovation*, we take familiar things, assembled or in pieces, and break the familiar connections. Then we try to make new connections to make something new, different, or better. What processes are used in innovation? Generally the same ones used in learning! Comparison, for example, is a good innovative technique as we'll see in "Strange and Familiar".

Identifying Animals by Comparison

When a young child looks at an ABC primer there isn't much to distinguish a dog from a horse. Then one day he discovers that a horse is BIGGER than a dog. Wow! Now there is one way to tell the two apart.

This is an example of the all important process of identification by comparison. Comparison involves finding a common descriptive facet about the things to be compared and then determining whether the objects are similar or different on that facet. For example, let's compare our horse (a pinto) with a dog (pointer).

Characteristics	Horse	Dog	
Size	Large	Small	Different
Marking	Spots	Spots	Same
Color spots	Brown	Black	Different
Tail	Long	Long	Same
Ears	Pointed	Drooping	Different
Used by man	Hunting	Hunting	Same

So we see on the six dimensions we've looked at, the horse and dog are similar on three and different on three. As we grow older, we continue to refine this process until we can distinguish betweeen very similar things (cocker spaniel and springer spaniel, for example).

One way to learn more about this process of comparison to identify things and also to sharpen your own descriptive skills is to teach someone else to identify similar things by comparison. The computer program ANIMAL is just such a willing "someone" waiting to be taught.

In playing ANIMAL, we will teach the computer to identify various animals by asking questions that can be answered with a yes or no. When you first start with the computer, you'll find it knows very little. It asks you to think of an animal. Let's say you think of a gorilla. The computer will ask:

DOES IT FLY? NO (your reply)
IS IT A FISH? NO

So you see the computer knows only a BIRD (no specific kinds) and a FISH (again, no varieties). After you respond NO to the question, "Is it a fish?" the computer says:

THE ANIMAL YOU WERE THINKING OF WAS A? GORILLA

And now we come to the crux of the comparison process as the computer says:

PLEASE TYPE IN A QUESTION THAT WOULD DISTINGUISH A GORILLA FROM A FISH
?DOES IT HAVE FUR
FOR A GORILLA THE ANSWER WOULD BE? YES

The next time through the program, if you said your animal was not a fish, the computer would ask, "Does it have fur?" Gradually through this process the computer builds up its repertoire of animals.

Notice that where the computer asked for a question to distinguish a gorilla from a fish, we could have said:

? DOES IT HAVE FINS
FOR A GORILLA THE ANSWER WOULD BE? NO

In other words, animals can be distinguished with either yes or no questions.

EXERCISE 1

For each of the following pairs of animals, write *two* questions that will distinguish between them. Write one question so that it can be answered "yes" for the first animal in the pair; the other, "no".

DOG	TIGER	MOOSE
HORSE	PUMA	RAM
ELEPHANT	CAMEL	OCELOT
HIPPOPOTAMUS	LLAMA	CHEETAH

EXERCISE 2

There are many possible ways to distinguish between two things. For each of the following pairs of animals, write *seven* questions that will distinguish between them.

OSTRICH	PENGUIN
GIRAFFE	GORILLA

EXERCISE 3

Choose one or two "families" of animals. Go to an encyclopedia, wild life book, or other source and find out all the members of the family and their distinguishing characteristics. To start you off, here are the names of some of the members of the cat family:

LION	OCELOT
TIGER	CHEETAH
PUMA	PANTHER
LEOPARD	JAGUAR
OUNCE	CAT, SIAMESE
COUGAR	CAT, PERSIAN
LYNX	

EXERCISE 4

Play ANIMAL on the computer. Teach it your family of animals from Exercise 2. If members of the class have chosen different families of animals, when you are finished, the computer should be able to identify just about any animal.

SAMPLE RUN OF ANIMAL

```
THINK OF AN ANIMAL AND THE COMPUTER WILL TRY TO GUESS IT...

ARE YOU THINKING OF AN ANIMAL? YES
DOES IT SWIM? YES
IS IT A FISH? NO
THE ANIMAL YOU WERE THINKING OF WAS A ? SEAL
PLEASE TYPE IN A QUESTION THAT WOULD DISTINGUISH A SEAL FROM A FISH
? DOES IT HAVE FLIPPERS
FOR A SEAL THE ANSWER WOULD BE? YES
ARE YOU THINKING OF AN ANIMAL? YES
DOES IT SWIM? NO
IS IT A BIRD? NO
THE ANIMAL YOU WERE THINKING OF WAS A ? ELEPHANT
PLEASE TYPE IN A QUESTION THAT WOULD DISTINGUISH A ELEPHANT FROM A BIRD
? DOES IT HAVE A TRUNK
FOR A ELEPHANT THE ANSWER WOULD BE? YES
ARE YOU THINKING OF AN ANIMAL? YES
DOES IT SWIM? NO
DOES IT HAVE A TRUNK? NO
DOES IT GO 'ARF? NO
DOES IT HAVE RETRACTIBLE CLAWS? YES
IS IT A CAT? NO
THE ANIMAL YOU WERE THINKING OF WAS A ? TIGER
PLEASE TYPE IN A QUESTION THAT WOULD DISTINGUISH A TIGER FROM A CAT
? DOES IT LIVE IN THE JUNGLE
FOR A TIGER THE ANSWER WOULD BE? YES
ARE YOU THINKING OF AN ANIMAL? YES
DOES IT SWIM? NO
DOES IT HAVE A TRUNK? NO
DOES IT GO 'ARF? NO
DOES IT HAVE RETRACTIBLE CLAWS? NO
IS IT A BIRD? NO
THE ANIMAL YOU WERE THINKING OF WAS A ? COW
PLEASE TYPE IN A QUESTION THAT WOULD DISTINGUISH A COW FROM A BIRD
? DOES IT GIVE MILK AND GO 'MOO'
FOR A COW THE ANSWER WOULD BE? YES
ARE YOU THINKING OF AN ANIMAL? YES
DOES IT SWIM? NO
DOES IT HAVE A TRUNK? NO
DOES IT GO 'ARF? NO
DOES IT HAVE RETRACTIBLE CLAWS? NO
DOES IT GIVE MILK AND GO 'MOO'? NO
IS IT A BIRD? NO
THE ANIMAL YOU WERE THINKING OF WAS A ? GOAT
PLEASE TYPE IN A QUESTION THAT WOULD DISTINGUISH A GOAT FROM A BIRD
? DOES IT GIVE MILK AND EAT TIN CANS AND ALMOST ANYTHING ELSE
FOR A GOAT THE ANSWER WOULD BE? YES
ARE YOU THINKING OF AN ANIMAL? YES
DOES IT SWIM? YES
DOES IT HAVE FLIPPERS? NO
IS IT A FISH? NO
THE ANIMAL YOU WERE THINKING OF WAS A ? WHALE
PLEASE TYPE IN A QUESTION THAT WOULD DISTINGUISH A WHALE FROM A FISH
? IS IT THE LARGEST KNOWN MAMMAL
FOR A WHALE THE ANSWER WOULD BE? YES
ARE YOU THINKING OF AN ANIMAL? LIST
ANIMALS I ALREADY KNOW ARE:
SEAL        ELEPHANT     DOG        CAT         TIGER
COW         BIRD         GOAT       FISH        WHALE
```

Versions of ANIMAL exist in BASIC and various assembly languages. The most comprehensive BASIC version (by Art Luehrmann) is available for $2.00 for a paper tape and 50¢ for the listing from Program Librarian, Kiewit Computation Center, Dartmouth College, Hanover, NH 03755.

Interlude

Here are some facts about animals that may help you with the exercises in this chapter.

* * *

The keenest sense of smell exhibited in all nature is that of the male silkworm moth. It can detect the sex signals of a female which is 6.8 miles away!

* * *

The Gaboon viper has the longest fangs of any snake. The specimen kept in the Philadelphia Zoo in 1963 was a little careless and bit itself to death.

* * *

Speed is so essential to the survival of the gazelle that nature has endowed it with the ability to run almost from the moment it is born. While most animals are weak and wobbly in the first few days after birth, a two-day-old gazelle can outrun a full-grown horse.

* * *

Gazelles, prairie dogs, wild asses, and many other animals never drink water. They have a special chemical process which transforms a part of their solid food into water.

* * *

The world's fastest animal is the cheetah. It has been timed at 70 miles per hour, but many believe that it can do even better over a short haul. Sometimes called the hunting leopard, the cheetah has long been used in India to track down the black buck, the Indian antelope, and other fast game.

* * *

The animal that takes the longest time to make its debut is the elephant. Its gestation period is 645 days or more than 21 months.

* * *

The most long-lived animal is the giant tortoise of the Galapagos Islands. Specimens have been estimated to be as old as 190 years.

The blue whale is the largest and most powerful animal ever to have graced the planet. The largest accurately measured specimen was captured off Scotland in 1926; it measured 109 feet 4¼ inches in length. A whale caught off Argentina five years later is said to have weighed 195 tons.

* * *

The longest of all worms is the *Lineus longissimus*, or "living fishing line worm." In 1964, a specimen washed ashore at St. Andrews, Scotland, after a storm. It measured more than 180 feet in length.

* * *

The tusks of some male African elephants eventually become so heavy that their owners must frequently rest them in the forks of trees. The longest African elephant tusk on record was some 11 feet long.

The wildcat is the most vicious fighter in the animal kingdom. Asleep, it resembles a gentle housecat — in a fight, it is a furry ball of rage. This spitfire's speed gives it an advantage over most other animals. In one swift leap, it can rip open its enemy's throat with its razor-like teeth.

* * *

The world's largest rodent is the capybara, also called the carpincho or water hog. A native of tropical South America, it can attain a length of 3½ to 4½ feet and a weight of 150 pounds.

* * *

When in mortal danger, many animals feign death. But none do this as convincingly as the American opposum and the dingo, a wild dog of Australia. The dingo will allow its captor to beat it unmercifully until the chance to escape presents itself. The entrapped opossum will assume its famous "possum" pose, which is to lie limp with its tongue hanging out of its mouth and its eyes open and rolled back.

* * *

Although the whale weighs over a hundred tons and the mouse tips the scales at only a few ounces, they develop from eggs of approximately the same size.

Strange and Familiar

We've seen from the animal exercises how we can make finer and finer comparisons until we can distinguish almost any kind of animal. But now, suppose that instead of comparing similar things (animals), we make comparisons between things that are outwardly different, between things that might conflict with each other. In doing the following exercises, let your mind stretch a bit. Try to be aware of not only the way you see things, but how they might be seen by an insect or a rock or an old man or someone on another planet.

EXERCISE 5

For each of the questions below, choose the answer you think is best. Then write a sentence or two to explain your choice. Here is a sample question with two completely different sample answers. Neither answer is right or wrong. What is important is the reason *you* have for *your* choice.

Q. What needs more protection? TURTLE or ROCK

A. Turtle — because rocks are not even alive.

A. Rock — because a turtle can regrow a break in its shell. If a rock cracks it can't mend itself.

The first time you read the question, the obvious response (Turtle) will probably spring to your mind. However, once you go beyond the obvious, you might find other interesting and innovative possibilities (Rock). Remember — there is *no* one *right* answer.

1. Which is stronger? SCISSORS or FACIAL TISSUE
2. Which is dirtier? DIRT or DETERGENT
3. Which is more powerful? A BULLDOZER or YOUR CONSCIENCE
4. Which is lighter? HELIUM BALLOON or JOY
5. What color is love? Why?

EXERCISE 6

Here are five more questions. The instructions are the same as in Exercise 5.

1. Which is more talkative? A STREAM or THE WIND
2. Which is more alive? AN OSTRICH EGG or A RICE PLANT
3. Which is brighter? A FLAME or A CHILD'S LAUGH
4. Which lasts longer? A PAIR OF JEANS or A DROP OF RAIN
5. Which sees more? YOUR FINGERS or YOUR EARS

EXERCISE 7

In this exercise we will be looking for the connectives between two dissimilar things. The connections may or not be obvious. Write a sentence or two answer to each of the following questions. Remember — there is no right answer.

1. How is AN ICEBERG like a BIG IDEA?
2. How is s SUNSET like a MIRROR?
3. How is a TREE like SELF RESPECT?
4. How is the BEACH like TIME?
5. How are INTEGRITY and the OCEAN alike?

EXERCISE 8

For this exercise you should have a partner. For each question, you should come up with a one or two word answer. Then trade papers with your partner who must explain *your* answer. For example:

QUESTION: What ANIMAL behaves like a DELIVERY TRUCK?

YOUR ANSWER: A Kangaroo.

(Trade papers with your partner)

PARTNER EXPLANATION: A kangaroo is like a delivery truck because it carries its young around in a pouch.

Stretch your comparisons. Try to stump your partner. However, your partner can challenge you. Therefore, don't go so far out that you can't make the connection yourself. If you can't explain your connection, you are stumped!

1. A CANDLE is like what ANIMAL?
2. What aspect of COMPUTERS reminds you of TAROT cards?
3. What part of the HUMAN BODY is like an APPLE?
4. What MECHANICAL THING is like an IGUANA?
5. What ANIMAL behaves like SATURDAY?

EXERCISE 9

Get a new partner and do these five questions the same as Exercise 8.

1. What PLANT could best teach a child SELF CONFIDENCE?
2. The idea of COMFORT may have come from what ANIMAL?
3. A MAGNET behaves like what part of the HUMAN BODY?
4. The phrase EXACT DISORDER could describe what?
5. What might be described by the words, STRAIGHT TWIST?

EXERCISE 10

Now it's your turn to help compose the questions. Below are five questions similar to those in Exercises 5 and 6. It's up to you to provide a choice of two possible answers. Then exchange your paper with a new partner and answer the questions the same way as you did in Exercises 5 and 6. For example:

QUESTION: Which is larger?

YOUR ANSWER: A HIPPOPOTAMUS or A MOTHER'S LOVE

(Trade papers with your partner who then chooses an answer and explains it in one or two lines.)

1. Which teaches self-control?
2. Which is most hungry?
3. Which is more beautiful?
4. Which is like a New England church?
5. Which costs more?

EXERCISE 11

In this exercise, you'll have to stretch your imagination a bit because you're going to look at the world from an entirely new viewpoint of some other thing. You must try to feel the way that thing does. FEEL the thing. ACT the thing. BE the thing while you write a one or two line answer to each question. (Remember — there is no right answer.)

A. You are a CHEETAH. You can run at 70 mph for short hundred yard bursts. You are tawny with small deep brown spots. You are 5 feet long and weigh 110 pounds.
1. You are hungry. You see an antelope at a water hole about 200 yards away. Describe your feelings of anticipation.
2. You have chased, killed, and eaten the antelope. Which gave you the most satisfaction — the chase exercising your magnificent body, the kill letting loose your raw instinct and emotions, or the meal satisfying your hunger? Why?

B. You are the EGG of a Ruby Hummingbird. You can't move. You are only potential. You are surrounded by four other eggs in a tree in the Brazillian jungles.
1. What are your thoughts as you wait for something to happen?
2. You have been incubated by your mother and are ready to break out of your shell. At the first peck a cold draft of air rushes in. How do you feel now?

C. You are an ACORN. You have just fallen 60 feet from an oak tree and have rolled next to a giant boulder. The soil is soft and fertile and after the winter snows you find you have settled about a half inch into the soil, just enough for you to crack open and send out roots.
1. You are a tiny acorn. Do you have any feeling for what you'll look like when you grow up? How do you know?
2. You have begun to sprout. How do you feel about the enormous boulder practically on top of you?
3. No rain has fallen recently. How do your roots feel digging for nourishment without water? One root bumps into a sewer pipe; how does it feel?

D. You are a HEADLIGHT FILAMENT. You are very fine and made out of carbon and tungsten. You are a part of a car which has been driven almost 80,000 miles. You have been turned on and off over 3,000 times. You know the driver of the car relies on you to see at night and you have never let him down.
1. It is night. The tingle of the first surge of current comes through you as it has so many times in the past. How do you feel?
2. The owner of the car is arranging to have the car towed to an auto scrap yard. The motor and transmission are worn out but you still work fine. How do you feel toward your owner? Toward the other parts of the car? Toward the owner of the scrap yard? Toward the other old headlights around you?

E. It is the first day of the deer hunting season. A buck has been shot in the fleshy part of his buttocks but has not fallen. Hunters surround him on two sides. You are the FEAR inside the deer. You are not the deer but the raw, naked, panicky fear inside his brain and nerves.
1. You are the fear that is driving the deer to spring away from the hunters despite his pain. How do you, FEAR, feel as the deer becomes weaker and weaker from the wound and the exertion of running?
2. What are the good and bad things you feel as FEAR?

EXERCISE 12

Make up one "be another thing" exercise like A through E in Exercise 11. Pick something that will cause the person doing the exercise to really stretch his or her imagination. Exchange your paper with a partner and do each other's exercise. When you have finished discuss your "answers" with each other.

EXERCISE 13

Of all the exercises done by you and your classmates in this chapter, which one caused you to stretch your imagination the most? Why? Did you stretch more when dealing with animals, plants, objects, attitudes, feelings, or values?

Computers in the English Curriculum

by Larry Press
University of Southern California

This paper discusses and presents some examples of what I will loosely call the exploration and play mode for computer assisted learning. The examples will all be drawn from the area of English, since the humanities are generally neglected; however, I have had positive results using a similar approach in classes on operations research (1) and Papert (2) advocates exploration and play in mathematics.

Another reason for choosing English is that I hope to stimulate others with substantive backgrounds in English to build upon my ideas. I am not an English teacher and elaboration of my examples should improve then considerably.

EXPLORATION AND PLAY

Let me illustrate exploration and play by contrasting it with a more typical drill and tutorial approach to learning parts of speech. A hypothetical drill and tutorial program might present questions such as:

```
GIVEN THE SENTENCE:
    THE BOY RAN TO HIS HOME
WHICH WORD(S) ARE NOUNS?
WHICH WORD(S) ARE VERBS?
```

The student's response would be matched with "boy", "home", "ran" and judged either *right* or *wrong*. If right, he would be congratulated and presented with a new "frame". If wrong, he could be shown some tutorial explanation of nouns and verbs, and re-tested. The system would record his progress through this sifting, brach network.

A pure drill and practice version, might just list words and ask for a judgment: "noun" or "verb". The mistakes would be marked and a total score tabulated. This could even be done on a timed basis (e.g., 5 seconds per word or try to get as many correct as you can in one minute).

Compare these hypothetical programs to the INSULT dialogue in figure 1. (In reading this, as well as all other printouts in the paper, keep in mind that it was generated sequentially in a conversational manner). The key difference is that there is no "right" answer in figure 1. The student explores — he types in words and gets sentences. The computer never says "right" or "wrong", the student's ear is the judge of his work. He plays as well. The "insults" are funny and he soon learns to amuse himself with sense and nonsense responses. It is only a matter of time until he discovers that he can use dirty words if he will — another source of fun. He can use slang, abuse the computer, etc.

The emphasis in drill and practice programs, as well as much of our non-computer based education, is on getting the right answer. Failure to do so results in a slight re-buff and success a small reward. As Holt (3), has shown at length, concentration upon getting the right answer is

```
RUN
INSULT

HEY STUPID! WHAT'S YOUR NAME ANYHOW??

? LARRY

ALLRIGHT LARRY, WHAT IS YOUR FAVORITE NOUN?
? COW

IT FIGURES!  WELL, WHAT'S YOUR FAVORITE VERB?
? PRINT

HEY LARRY, HOW WOULD YOU LIKE TO PAINT A COW????

DONE

RUN
INSULT

HEY STUPID! WHAT'S YOUR NAME ANYHOW??

? LARRY

ALLRIGHT LARRY, WHAT IS YOUR FAVORITE NOUN?
? HORSE

IT FIGURES!  WELL, WHAT'S YOUR FAVORITE VERB?
? TICKLE

HEY LARRY, HOW WOULD YOU LIKE TO TICKLE A HORSE????
```

counterproductive. Holt has observed it to be a source of anxiety in students and sees it resulting in a low tolerance for ambiguity. He sees concentration upon mechanics and strategies for beating the system rather than understandability. Holt reports much failure correlated with fear; and a machine that says "wrong" is, indeed, rather frightening.

The student is also in a passive role in the drill and tutorial mode — responding to the demands and judgments of the machine. In the INSULT example, the student soon learns that he is in control and actively directs the course of his exploration.

MORE EXAMPLES

I will present 3 more examples of exploration and play programs in English. The first, and simplest, is for small children and is adapted from the TV show Sesame Street. It is illustrated in Figure 2 and the dialogue is self explanatory. It could obviously be generalized by programming other "families" of words.

```
RUN
SESAME

LET'S MAKE THE UN-FAMILY WORDS!  I NEED YOUR HELP.
YOU GIVE ME THE START AND I WILL PUT IN THE 'UN'.

GIVE ME ONE OR MORE LETTERS? R
R PLUS UN GIVES RUN!!

GIVE ME ONE OR MORE LETTERS? F
F PLUS UN GIVES FUN!!

GIVE ME ONE OR MORE LETTERS? OREG
OREG PLUS UN GIVES OREGUN!!
```

Next is the program WISHES, which is illustrated by the conversation of Figure 3. This program is adapted from Koch (4), a fascinating book on teaching poetry writing to grammar school children (it also presents much grammar school poetry). Koch recommends that each session begin with a warm-up such as that on color

```
LET'S WRITE A WISH POEM
TO WARM UP, TRY PLAYING WITH COLOR WORDS.  FOR EXAMPLE,
WHAT COLOR DO YOU THINK OF WHEN I SAY APPLE? GREEN
HOW ABOUT SKY? BLUE
YOU KNOW, YOU DON'T ALWAYS HAVE TO USE THE REAL COLOR
OF SOMETHING IN A POEM.  YOU CAN USE ANY COLOR YOU FEEL
LIKE EVEN IF IT SEEMS FREAKY OR SILLY.  IF YOU DON'T
COUNT RED OR GREEN, WHAT COLOR SEEMS LIKE APPLES? SILVER
CLOSE YOUR EYES AND SEE IF YOU CAN IMAGINE A BIG,
SILVER APPLE.  SEE IF YOU CAN MAKE IT GROW OR DANCE OR
DO SOMETHING SILLY.  JUST TYPE OK WHEN YOU ARE FINISHED.
? OK
THINGS LIKE APPLES ARE NOT THE ONLY THINGS THAT MAKE
PEOPLE THINK OF COLORS.  FOR EXAMPLE, A THIRD GRADER NAMED
JOHN THOUGHT THAT THE SOUND OF A CAR ENGINE WAS
SCRATCHY RED!
WHAT COLOR IS THE SOUND OF A WHISTLE?  BRIGHT BLUE
THE WHISTLE SOUNDS BRIGHT BLUE!
TRY MAKING THE SOUND OF A BALLOON POPPING.  WHAT COLOR
IS THAT? ORANGE
WHAT COLOR WAS THE BALLOON? RED
WHAT COLOR DO YOU SEE WHEN YOU IMAGINE THE FEELING OF A
BIG ICE CUBE ON YOUR TUMMY? DEEP BLUE
YOU ARE REALLY GETTING INTO COLOR WORDS!
NOW LET'S TRY WORKING ON A WISH POEM.  EACH LINE SHOULD HAVE
A WISH IN IT AND IF YOU WANT TO YOU CAN PUT IN COLORS TOO.
JOHN AND HIS SISTER WHO IS IN KINDERGARTEN MADE UP THESE
EXAMPLES TO SHOW YOU:

     I WISH FOR A BIG GREEN 1000 DOLLAR BILL
     I WISH THAT EVERY DAY WAS MY RED AND WHITE BIRTHDAY
     I WISH ALL THE STORES WERE FREE RED BLUE

GET IT?  NOW YOU TYPE IN A WISH.  MAKE IT LESS THAN
ONE LINE LONG, OK?  WHAT DO YOU WISH?
?I WISH I WAS A BIG GREEN BASEBALL
FAR OUT!  TRY ANOTHER ONE.  REMEMBER, IT CAN BE CRAZY OR
FREAKY IF YOU WANT IT TO.
? I WISH IT WAS SUPER YELLOW SUNNY
ALLRIGHT!  WOULD YOU LIKE TO MAKE UP MORE? YES
OK.  GIVE ME AS MANY WISHES AS YOU WANT TO.  JUST TYPE
STOP WHEN YOU RUN OUT OF WISHES.  GIVE ME YOUR NEXT WISH.
? I WISH TO WISH
NEXT
? I WISH FOR MORE AND MORE AND MORE
NEXT
? AND EVEN MORE
NEXT WISH
? STOP

NOW I'LL SHOW YOU A NEW WISH POEM

I WISH I WAS A BIG GREEN BASEBALL
I WISH IT WAS SUPER YELLOW SUNNY
I WISH TO WISH
I WISH FOR MORE AND MORE AND MORE
AND EVEN MORE

THAT'S A PRETTY SLICK WISH POEM YOU WROTE!  CATCH YOU LATER.

DONE
```

```
LET'S WRITE A STORY.  YOU WILL HAVE TO GIVE ME SOME WORDS:

FIRST, WHAT IS YOUR FAVORITE ARTICLE OF CLOTHING? SHOES.
OKAY, WHAT IS YOUR FAVORITE NOUN? PICKLE
NOW GIVE ME A DARK, SINISTER ADJECTIVE? HOARY
AND WHAT IS THE MOST EVIL COLOR YOU CAN THINK OF? FLECKY GREEN
BY THE WAY, WHAT IS YOUR FIRST NAME? LARRY
ALLRIGHT LARRY, WHAT IS THE SWEETEST, MOST DELICATE FLOWER? ROSE
NOW I NEED AN ADJECTIVE.  IT SHOULD BEGIN WITH AN 'S' SOUND
AND SHOULD BE REFINED AND GENTLE.  IT COULD EVEN BE A NONSENSE
WORD IF IT SOUNDED NICE? SWEET
NOW I WILL NEED A COLOR WHICH YOU FEEL SYMBOLIZES INNOCENCE? BABY BLUE
NOW GIVE ME A SWEET, GENTLE NOUN? COTTON
OKAY, WHAT IS ANOTHER ARTICLE OF CLOTHING? SHIRT
NOW, GIVE ME A PLURAL BODY PART? TOES
FINALLY, I NEED TO KNOW WHICH ANIMAL SEEMS MOST COMICAL TO YOU? MOOSE

ALLRIGHT, THAT SHOULD DO IT.  HERE IS OUR STORY:


     THE LEGEND OF LITTLE RED RIDING SHOES

     THERE ONCE WAS A GIRL CALLED LITTLE RED RIDING SHOES.  ONE DAY
HER MOTHER GAVE HER A BASKET OF PICKLES TO GIVE TO HER GRANDMOTHER.
ON THE WAY, A HOARY, FLECKY GREEN FROG NAMED LARRY SAW HER.  THE
FROG DECIDED TO GET TO GRANDMOTHER'S FIRST!
     WHEN THE FROG GOT THERE, GRANDMA WAS TENDING HER ROSE
GARDEN, DRESSED IN SWEET, BABY BLUE SNEAKERS.  SHE WAS SWEET AND
GENTLE AS COTTON SO THE FROG ATE HER UP, PUT ON HER SHIRT AND
JUMPED INTO HER BED.
     YOU PROBABLY KNOW THE REST OF THE STORY RIGHT?  THEY GO
THROUGH THE 'MY WHAT BIG TOES YOU HAVE' THING FOR A WHILE, THEN
LARRY KISSES RED, THEY BOTH TURN INTO MOOSES, THEY ARE MARRIED
AND LIVE HAPPILY EVER AFTER.

     SIGH ... A HAPPY ENDING
```

words in the first half of figure 3. After the warm-up, the student constructs a "wish poem".

Koch suggest dozens of such warm-ups and many types of poems are illustrated in his book. There are lie poems, dream poems, being an animal poems, comparison poems, I used to/but now poems, and many more. Mine is only a simple example, and many more such programs could be written.

Finally, figure 4 shows a conversation with the program BARTH. This is inspired by John Barth, who periodically tells the reader to insert words of his own choice at various points in his stories. For instance in the story Title (5) we find this sentence:

A person who can't [verb adverb] ought at least to speak correctly, or more esoterically:

Why do you suppose it is, she asked [long participle phrase of the breathless variety characteristic of the dialogue attributions in nineteenth-century fiction] that literate people such as we talk like characters in a story?

It was my original intent to build the example in Figure 4 around an existing poem, with various words left open to the user, but I was unable to do so. Instead, I invented the "story" which is shown.

Note how easily this sort of program could lead into explicit discussion of formal aspects of poetry. Even in Figure 4, we see examples of allusion, metaphor, alliteration, tone, and euphonia. The following list illustrates the manner in which a similar program might be extended:

a) Onomatopoeia: Give me a verb which sounds like wood breaking.
b) Rhyme: Give me a noun which rhymes with cow or give me a two syllable adjective which rhymes with turtle.
c) Alliteration: Give me an adjective that begins with an "sh" sound.
d) Assonance: Give me an adjective with an "a" sound in the middle.
e) Consonance: Give me a noun which ends with "ts".
f) Euphonia: Give me a smooth, pleasant sounding adverb.
g) Cacaphonia: Give me a rough, harsh adverb.
h) Meter: Give me a 3 syllable adjective with the accent on the second syllable.
i) Imagery: Give me a bright red object (to be used in a visual metaphor). Obviously, non-visual images may be used as well.
j) Metaphor: Give me a soft noun (to be used in a metaphor).
k) Synecdoche: What do you consider the essential part of a tree to be?
l) Or even Barth's long participle phrases ala nineteenth century fiction!

This list was culled from an introductory poetry text, Perrine (6). Note that all of the formal concepts illustrated by a story such as that of Figure 4 do not have to be supplied explicitly by the student, e.g., the allusion to red riding hood. The above list could easily be extended by suggesting that examples of paradox, irony, symbols, metonymy, etc. could be built into the "body" of the story.

CONCLUSION

I've presented four examples of "exploration and play" for English. In each case, there was no such thing as a wrong answer, the user was active, and I attempted to create an air of carefree play. It is my hope that others will develop, use, evaluate, and distribute similar programs. While my programs are intended as examples, I'll be glad to send a paper tape (in HP-2000 BASIC) of any or all of them to anyone who wants one (this offer only holds until I get caught)!

BIBLIOGRAPHY

1. Press, L., The Use of Computer Simulation Models in Teaching Introductory Mathematical Modeling Proc. of the 5th CCUC.
2. Papert, S., See for instance his paper: On Making a Theorem for a Child, Proceedings of the 1972 ACM National Conference. Papert, a former student and colleague of Piaget, has been working in this mode for a number of years.
3. Holt, J., How Children Fail, Pitman Publishing Co., New York, 1964.
4. Koch, K., Wishes, Lies and Dreams, Chelsea House Publishers, New York, 1970.
5. Barth, J., *Title*, from Lost in the Funhouse, Doubleday and Co., New York, 1968.
6. Perrine, L., Sound and Sense: An Introduction to Poetry, 3rd ed., Harcourt, Brace and World, Inc., New York, 1969.

```
INSULT

10   DIM AS[30],NS[30],VS[30]
15   DIM FS[1]
20   PRINT LIN(2);"HEY STUPID! WHAT'S YOUR NAME ANYHOW??";LIN(2)
30   INPUT AS
40   PRINT "ALLRIGHT ";AS;", WHAT IS YOUR FAVORITE NOUN?"
50   INPUT NS
60   PRINT LIN(2);"IT FIGURES!  WELL, WHAT'S YOUR FAVORITE VERB?";LIN(2)
70   INPUT VS
100  LET FS=NS[1,1]
110  IF FS="A" THEN 400
120  IF FS="E" THEN 400
130  IF FS="I" THEN 400
140  IF FS="O" THEN 400
150  IF FS="U" THEN 400
160  PRINT LIN(2)"HEY ";AS;",HOW WOULD YOU LIKE TO ";VS;" A ";NS;"????"
170  STOP
400  PRINT LIN(2);"HEY ";AS;", HOW WOULD YOU LIKE TO ";VS;" AN ";NS;"????"
600  END


SESAME

5    DIM LS[72]
10   PRINT "LET'S MAKE THE UN-FAMILY WORDS! I NEED YOUR HELP."
20   PRINT "YOU GIVE THE START AND I WILL PUT IN THE 'UN'."
30   PRINT LIN(2)"GIVE ME ONE OR MORE LETTERS";
40   INPUT LS
50   PRINT LS" PLUS UN GIVES "LS"UN!!"
60   GOTO 30
70   END


BARTH

1    DIM AS[72],BS[72],CS[72],DS[72],ES[72],FS[72],GS[72],HS[72],IS[72]
2    DIM JS[72],KS[72],LS[72],MS[72],NS[72]
10   PRINT "LET'S WRITE A STORY.  YOU WILL HAVE TO GIVE ME SOME WORDS!"
20   PRINT
30   PRINT "FIRST, WHAT IS YOUR FAVORITE ARTICLE OF CLOTHING";
40   INPUT AS
50   PRINT "OKAY, WHAT IS YOUR FAVORITE NOUN";
55   INPUT BS
56   IF BS[LEN(BS),LEN(BS)]="S" THEN 60
57   BS[LEN(BS)+1,LEN(BS)+1]="S"
60   PRINT "NOW GIVE ME A DARK, SINISTER ADJECTIVE";
65   INPUT CS
70   PRINT "AND WHAT IS THE MOST EVIL COLOR YOU CAN THINK OF";
75   INPUT DS
80   PRINT "BYE THE WAY, WHAT IS YOUR FIRST NAME";
85   INPUT ES
90   PRINT "ALLRIGHT "ES", WHAT IS THE SWEETEST, MOST DELICATE FLOWER";
100  INPUT FS
110  PRINT "NOW I NEED AN ADJECTIVE.  IT SHOULD BEGIN WITH AN 'S' SOUND"
115  PRINT "AND SHOULD BE REFINED AND GENTLE.  IT COULD EVEN BE A NONSENSE"
118  PRINT "WORD IF IT SOUNDED NICE"
120  INPUT GS
130  PRINT "NEXT I WILL NEED A COLOR WHICH YOU FEEL SYMBOLIZES INNOCENCE";
135  INPUT HS
140  PRINT "NOW GIVE ME A SWEET, GENTLE NOUN";
145  INPUT IS
150  PRINT "OKAY, WHAT IS ANOTHER ARTICLE OF CLOTHING";
155  INPUT JS
160  PRINT "NOW, GIVE ME A PLURAL BODY PART";
165  INPUT KS
170  PRINT "FINALLY, I NEED TO KNOW WHICH ANIMAL SEEMS MOST COMICAL TO YOU";
180  INPUT LS
181  IF LS[LEN(LS),LEN(LS)]="S" THEN 200
190  LS[LEN(LS)+1,LEN(LS)+1]="S"
200  PRINT LIN(2)"ALLRIGHT, THAT SHOULD DO IT.  HERE IS OUR STORY!"
210  PRINT
218  PRINT
220  PRINT "          THE LEGEND OF LITTLE RED RIDING "AS;LIN(2)
230  PRINT "     THERE ONCE WAS A GIRL CALLED LITTLE RED RIDING "AS".  ONE DAY"
240  PRINT "HER MOTHER GAVE HER A BASKET OF "BS" TO GIVE TO HER GRANDMOTHER."
250  PRINT "ON THE WAY, A "CS","DS" FROG NAMED "ES" SAW HER, THE"
260  PRINT "FROG DECIDED TO GET TO GRANDMOTHER'S FIRST!"
270  PRINT "     WHEN THE FROG GOT THERE, GRANDMA WAS TENDING HER "FS
280  PRINT "GARDEN, DRESSED IN "GS","HS" SNEAKERS.  SHE WAS SWEET AND"
290  PRINT "GENTLE AS "IS" SO THE FROG ATE HER UP, PUT ON HER "JS" AND"
300  PRINT "JUMPED INTO HER BED."
310  PRINT "     YOU PROBABLY KNOW THE REST OF THE STORY, RIGHT?  THEY GO"
320  PRINT "THROUGH THE 'MY WHAT BIG "KS" YOU HAVE!' THING FOR A WHILE, THEN"
330  PRINT ES" KISSES HER, THEY BOTH TURN INTO "LS", THEY ARE MARRIED"
340  PRINT "AND LIVE HAPPILY EVER AFTER."
350  PRINT LIN(2)"SIGH ... A HAPPY ENDING"
360  END


WISHES

10   DIM AS[72],BS[72]
20   FILES WSWFL
30   PRINT "LET'S WRITE A WISH POEM!!"
40   PRINT "TO WARM UP, TRY PLAYING WITH COLOR WORDS.  FOR EXAMPLE"
50   PRINT "WHAT COLOR DO YOU THINK OF WHEN I SAY APPLE";
60   INPUT AS
70   PRINT "HOW ABOUT SKY";
80   INPUT AS
90   PRINT "YOU KNOW, YOU DON'T ALWAYS HAVE TO USE THE REAL COLOR"
100  PRINT "OF SOMETHING IN A POEM.  YOU CAN USE ANY COLOR YOU FEEL"
110  PRINT "LIKE EVEN IF IT SEEMS FREAKY OR SILLY.  IF YOU DON'T"
120  PRINT "COUNT RED OR GREEN, WHAT COLOR SEEMS LIKE APPLES";
130  INPUT AS
140  PRINT "CLOSE YOUR EYES AND SEE IF YOU CAN IMAGINE A BIG,"
150  PRINT AS" APPLE.  SEE IF YOU CAN MAKE IT GROW OR DANCE OR"
160  PRINT "DO SOMETHING SILLY.  JUST TYPE OK WHEN YOU ARE FINISHED."
170  INPUT AS
180  PRINT "THINGS LIKE APPLES ARE NOT THE ONLY THINGS THAT MAKE "
190  PRINT "PEOPLE THINK OF COLORS.  FOR EXAMPLE A THIRD GRADER NAMED"
200  PRINT "JOHN THOUGHT THAT THE SOUND OF A CAR ENGINE WAS "
210  PRINT "SCRATCHY RED!"
220  PRINT "WHAT COLOR IS THE SOUND OF A WHISTLE";
230  INPUT AS
240  PRINT "THE WHISTLE SOUNDS "AS"!"
250  PRINT "TRY MAKING THE SOUND OF A BALLOON POPPING.  WHAT COLOR "
260  PRINT "IS THAT";
270  INPUT AS
280  PRINT "WHAT COLOR WAS THE BALLOON";
290  INPUT AS
300  PRINT "WHAT COLOR DO YOU SEE WHEN YOU IMAGINE THE FEELING OF A"
310  PRINT "BIG ICE CUBE ON YOUR TUMMY";
320  INPUT AS
330  PRINT "YOU ARE REALLY GETTING INTO COLOR WORDS!"
340  PRINT "NOW LET'S TRY WORKING ON A WISH POEM.  EACH LINE SHOULD HAVE"
350  PRINT "A WISH IN IT AND IF YOU WANT TO YOU CAN PUT IN COLORS TOO."
360  PRINT "JOHN AND HIS SISTER WHO IS IN KINDERGARTEN MADE UP THESE"
370  PRINT "EXAMPLES TO SHOW YOU!";LIN(1)
380  PRINT "     I WISH FOR A BIG GREEN 1000 DOLLAR BILL"
390  PRINT "     I WISH THAT EVERY DAY WAS MY RED AND WHITE BIRTHDAY PARTY"
400  PRINT "     I WISH ALL THE STORES WERE FREE RED BLUE"
410  PRINT LIN(1)"GET IT?  NOW YOU TYPE IN A WISH.  MAKE IT LESS THAN"
420  PRINT "ONE LINE LONG, OK, WHAT DO YOU WISH";
430  INPUT AS
440  IF END #1 THEN 630
450  PRINT "FAR OUT!  TRY ANOTHER ONE.  REMEMBER, IT CAN BE CRAZY"
460  PRINT "OR FREAKY IF YOU WANT IT TO."
470  PRINT #1;AS
480  INPUT AS
490  PRINT "ALLRIGHT!  WOULD YOU LIKE TO MAKE UP MORE";
500  PRINT #1;AS
510  INPUT AS
520  IF AS[1,1]="N" THEN 660
530  IF AS[1,1]="Y" THEN 560
540  PRINT "PLEASE ANSWER YES OR NO"
550  GOTO 490
560  PRINT "OK GIVE ME AS MANY MORE WISHES AS YOU WANT TO.  JUST"
570  PRINT "TYPE 'STOP' WHEN YOU RUN OUT OF WISHES.  NOW"
580  PRINT "GIVE ME YOUR NEXT WISH PLEASE..."
590  INPUT AS
600  IF AS[1,4]="STOP" THEN 660
610  PRINT #1;AS
620  GOTO 580
630  PRINT "WOW! MY STORAGE AREA IS FULL.  LET'S QUIT FOR NOW."
640  PRINT "IF YOU WANT TO DO MORE WISHING, YOU CAN RUN THIS"
650  PRINT "PROGRAM AGAIN."
660  PRINT
670  IF END #1 THEN 740
680  READ #1,1
690  PRINT "NOW I'LL SHOW YOU A NEW WISH POEM,";LIN(2)
700  FOR I=1 TO 1000
710  READ #1;AS
720  PRINT AS
730  NEXT I
740  PRINT
750  PRINT "THAT'S A PRETTY SLICK WISH POEM YOU WROTE!!  CATCH YOU LATER."
760  END
```

A new learning activity from Creative Computing . . . .

Surveys, The Census, and Privacy

by David H. Ahl

Every 10 years, the United States government takes a census of every person in the country. This serves a number of very useful purposes. First, it tells how many people there are in the country. Second, it gives data on living and income patterns and answers questions on whether the quality of life is improving, indicates the decline (or growth) of disadvantaged sectors of the population, and on economic growth. Also it gives valuable information on educational attainment. It also yields vital statistics on population mobility, mortality, birth rates, etc.

Private industry, various government bodies, colleges, and other groups also take surveys from time to time. Here are some examples of recent surveys:

- The Department of Transportation surveyed passengers on the NY-Washington Metroliner about passenger rail service.
- Educational Systems Research Institute surveyed the graduates of career education programs in 15 cities for the U. S. Office of Education.
- Ohio State University surveyed its students on a number of issues including the reaction to their black studies program.
- General Mills Corporation surveyed consumers about their preferences for various snack and cereal products.
- Consumer Mail Panels (for several insurance companies) surveyed a cross section of people involved in auto accidents to see how well their insurance claims were handled.

EXERCISE 1

Take a survey of the following items in class. Make a little table to put the results like this:

	Number of Students	Percent

A. Number of Children in Family
   1
   2
   3
   etc.

B. Age
   13
   14
   15
   etc.

C. Does mother work?
   Full time
   Part time
   No

D. Number of letters in last name
   5 or fewer
   6, 7, or 8
   9, 10, or 11
   12 or more

E. Rank the performance of the President
   Poor
   Fair
   Good
   Excellent

F. Do you like raisin bran?
   Yes
   No

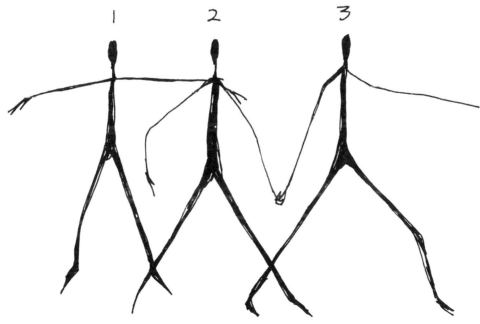

more

EXERCISE 2

Write a computer program to accept the responses to the questions in Exercise 5 for the members of the class. The program should then compute the percentages, and print a table similar to that above. Have the program "dump" the data at the end, i.e., print a list of each class member and their responses like this.

SALLY CARLSON   1 2 2 7 3 1
DAN BOSTICH   2 1 2 7 2 2
GENE WASHINGTON   1 2 1 10 2 1
etc.

Generally, the dump is done onto magnetic tape or punched cards so all the data does not have to be stored in the computer yet continues to be available for future use.

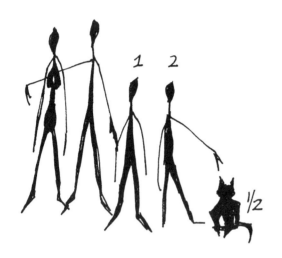

EXERCISE 3

Modify your program or write a new one that accepts input and analyses the value game responses for the whole class. (Do not have this program dump the individual responses at the end.) Discuss the tabular results in class. Does comparing your values with those of the class as a whole help clarify things for you? Do you tend to conform or be more of an individual? Do some of the results make you feel good? Are others embarrassing?

EXERCISE 4

Thinking now of the program in Exercise 3, would you want other members of the class to see your responses? If we were to do a dump, what should be done with it? Would you feel better if it was kept locked up by the teacher? Or would you rather see it burned? If it were destroyed and we decided later that we'd like to cross tabulate some results or add the results of two or three classes together to get a better overall average we wouldn't be able to. Then what?

Discuss various solutions to this issue looking at their advantages and disadvantages. Think of them relative to the census, a cereal survey, and your credit data (for charge accounts and loans). Here are some possibilities:

1. Determine all possible analyses ever to be done with the data and do them. Then throw the raw data away.
2. Keep the raw data but throw away the name.
3. Keep the data on magnetic computer tape and keep the tapes locked up.
4. Keep the data in coded form on magnetic tape.
5. Appoint a committee of people who are using the data and those who are in the survey and let them decide the disposition.

Can you think of other possibilities?

EXERCISE 5

The following page is an excerpt from the summary and recommendations of the report, "Records, Computers, and the Rights of Citizens", from the HEW Secretary's Advisory Committee on Automated Personal Data Systems. It is directed at organizations collecting data for research purposes. Is it complete? Does it cover all possibilities? Is it too restrictive in places? Where?

THERE ARE NOW 3,000 DIFFERENT KINDS OF CREDIT CARDS IN USE

U.S. CREDIT BUREAUS HAVE ACCUMULATED LARGER FILES ABOUT INDIVIDUALS THAN THE COMBINED FILES OF THE F.B.I. AND THE C.I.A.

One credit bureau claims to have 45,000,000 Americans and Canadians in their files.

The following excerpt is taken from the summary and recommendations of the report, "Records, Computers and the Rights of Citizens," from the HEW Secretary's Advisory Committee on Automated Personal Data Systems (See Editorial, Page 3). Copies of the full report (DHEW (OS)73-94; GPO#1700-00116) may be ordered for $2.35 from the Superintendent of Documents, Government Printing Office, Washington, D.C. 20402.

Safeguard Requirements For Statistical-Reporting and Research Systems

I. GENERAL REQUIREMENTS

A. Any organization maintaining a record of personal data, which it does not maintain as part of an automated personal data system used exclusively for statistical reporting or research, shall make no transfer of any such data to another organization without the prior informed consent of the individual to whom the data pertain, if, as a consequence of the transfer, such data will become part of an automated personal data system that is not subject to these safeguard requirements or the safeguard requirements for administrative personal data systems.

B. Any organization maintaining an automated personal data system used exclusively for statistical reporting or research shall:

(1) Identify one person immediately responsible for the system, and make any other organizational arrangements that are necessary to assure continuing attention to the fulfillment of the safeguard requirements;

(2) Take affirmative action to inform each of its employees having any responsibility or function in the design, development, operation, or maintenance of the system, or the use of any data contained therein, about all the safeguard requirements and all the rules and procedures of the organization designed to assure compliance with them;

(3) Specify penalties to be applied to any employee who initiates or otherwise contributes to any disciplinary or other punitive action against any individual who brings to the attention of appropriate authorities, the press, or any member of the public, evidence of unfair information practice;

(4) Take reasonable precautions to protect data in the system from any anticipated threats or hazards to the security of the system;

(5) Make no transfer of individually identifiable personal data to another system without (i) specifying requirements for security of the data, including limitations on access thereto, and (ii)

determining that the conditions of the transfer provide substantial assurance that those requirements and limitations will be observed — except in instances when each of the individuals about whom data are to be transferred has given his prior informed consent to the transfer; and

(6) Have the capacity to make fully documented data readily available for independent analysis.

II. PUBLIC NOTICE REQUIREMENT

Any organization maintaining an automated personal data system used exclusively for statistical reporting or research shall give public notice of the existence and character of its system once each year. Any organization maintaining more than one such system shall publish annual notices for all its systems simultaneously. Any organization proposing to establish a new system, or to enlarge an existing system, shall give public notice long enough in advance of the initiation or enlargement of the system to assure individuals who may be affected by its operation a reasonable opportunity to comment. The public notice shall specify:

(1) The name of the system;

(2) The nature and purpose(s) of the system;

(3) The categories and number of persons on whom data are (to be) maintained;

(4) The categories of data (to be) maintained, indicating which categories are (to be) stored in computer-accessible files;

(5) The organization's policies and practices regarding data storage, duration of retention of data, and disposal thereof;

(6) The categories of data sources;

(7) A description of all types of use (to be) made of data, indicating those involving computer-accessible files, and including all classes of users and the organizational relationships among them;

(8) The procedures whereby an individual, group, or organization can gain access to data for independent analysis;

(9) The title, name, and address of the person immediately responsible for the system;

(10) A statement of the system's provisions for data confidentiality and the legal basis for them.

III. RIGHTS OF INDIVIDUAL DATA SUBJECTS

Any organization maintaining an automated personal data system used exclusively for statistical reporting or research shall:

(1) Inform an individual asked to supply personal data for the system whether he is legally required, or may refuse, to supply the data requested, and also of any specific consequences for him, which are known to the organization, of providing or not providing such data;

(2) Assure that no use of individually identifiable data is made that is not within the stated purposes of the system as reasonably understood by the individual, unless the informed consent of the individual has been explicitly obtained;

(3) Assure that no data about an individual are made available from the system in response to a demand for data made by means of compulsory legal process, unless the individual to whom the data pertain (i) has been notified of the demand, and (ii) has been afforded full access to the data before they are made available in response to the demand.

* * *

In addition to the foregoing safeguard requirements for all automated personal data systems used exclusively for statistical reporting and research, we recommend that all personal data in such systems be protected by statute from compulsory disclosure in identifiable form. Federal legislation protecting against compulsory disclosure should include the following features:

• The data to be protected should be limited to those *used exclusively for statistical reporting or research.* Thus, the protection would apply to statistical-reporting and research data derived from administrative records, and kept apart from them, but not to the administrative records themselves.

• The protection should be limited to data *identifiable with, or traceable to, specific individuals.* When data are released in statistical form, reasonable precautions to protect against "statistical disclosure" should be considered to fulfill the obligation to disclose data that can be traced to specific individuals.

• The protection should be specific enough to qualify for non-disclosure under the Freedom of Information Act exemption for matters "specifically exempted from disclosure by statute." 5 U.S.C. 552(b)(3).

• The protection should be available for data in the custody of all statistical-reporting and research systems, whether supported by Federal funds or not.

• Either the data custodian or the individual about whom data are sought by legal process should be able to invoke the protection, but only the individual should be able to waive it.

• The Federal law should be controlling; no State statute should be taken to interfere with the protection it provides.

INTERVIEW

Here's an informative activity to do in a "Computers in Society" or "Computer Appreciation" course, or for that matter, in a social studies or sociology course.

EXERCISE 1

Make up copies of the interview form on the next page and give each student two copies. (You may want to use a subset of the questions instead of the entire list.) Each student should fill out one copy of the questionnaire himself. Then, each student should interview an adult on these issues. Try to obtain interviews with a diverse cross-section of people. Students may feel more comfortable working in groups to get interviews; if so, let them pair off. But no more than two students to a group; more than that tends to overwhelm interviewees.

EXERCISE 2

Tabulate the results, compare the various answers obtained, and discuss in class. Can you draw any conclusions about the attitude of the general public toward computers? Do students' attitudes generally agree or disagree with those of the interviewees? Are there any obvious relationships between the attitudes expressed and the demographic characteristics (age, sex, etc.) of the respondents?

Send your raw results to CREATIVE COMPUTING, i.e., number of total responses in each box, and we'll tabulate and print them all in a future issue.

OPTIONAL EXERCISE 1

Write a computer program to tabulate the results and compute average scores for each question as well as percentage distributions.

OPTIONAL EXERCISE 2

If your computer system has file capabilities, write a program to administer the questionnaire via a terminal, store the results and merge them with all previous results and then print out the scores to date. For real pizzazz, print the results graphically like this:

COMPUTERS WILL IMPROVE HEALTH CARE

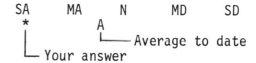

Or, show a bar chart of answers like this:

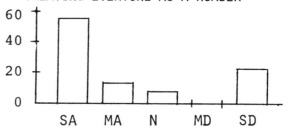

CREATIVE COMPUTING
COMPUTERS AND SOCIETY QUESTIONNAIRE

Statement	Strongly Agree (1)	Mostly Agree (2)	Neutral or No Opinion (3)	Mostly Disagree (4)	Strongly Disagree (5)
1. Computers will improve health care.					
2. Computers will improve education.					
3. Computers will improve law enforcement.					
4. Computers slow down and complicate simple business operations.					
5. Computers are best suited for doing repetitive, monotonous tasks.					
6. Computers make mistakes at least 10 percent of the time.					
7. Programmers and operators make mistakes, but computers are, for the most part, error free.					
8. Computers dehumanize society by treating everyone as a number.					
9. It is possible to design computer systems which protect the privacy of data.					
10. Credit rating data stored on computers have prevented billions of dollars of fraud. This is a worthwhile use of computers.					
11. In the U.S. today, a person cannot escape the influence of computers.					
12. Computers will create as many jobs as they eliminate.					
13. Computers will replace low skill jobs and create jobs needing specialized training.					
14. Computers are a tool just like a hammer or lathe.					
15. Computers are beyond the understanding of the typical person.					
16. Computer polls and predictions influence the outcome of elections.					
17. Computers isolate people by preventing normal social interactions among people who use them.					

Age_____ Sex_____ Education_____
Occupation_____ Location_____
Name (optional)_____

For results of this survey, see page 77.

Wisdom is OK for places where you have to be wise, but it isn't so good where you have to know.

Kenneth Boulding

COMPUTERS IN ROAD BUILDING
Using a problem-oriented language such as COGO, civil engineers can efficiently determine the cut and fill, gradients and curvatures for a new road, pipeline, or transit system. (Photo Caterpillar)

Life Auction

THE AUCTION

This is an interesting and enjoyable exercise. Each person is asked to rank in order the following items:

Your ranking:		Item:
_____	1.	Ability to be self-sufficient
_____	2.	Active and satisfying life
_____	3.	Ability to influence others (ideas)
_____	4.	Ability to draw love from others
_____	5.	Power over things (fix cars, grow vegetables, program computers, build boats, etc.)
_____	6.	Ability to be a caring person
_____	7.	Active and satisfying athletic life
_____	8.	Opportunities for risk and adventure
_____	9.	Intellectual ability
_____	10.	Good health
_____	11.	Wealth
_____	12.	Approval by the opposite sex
_____	13.	Intellectual stimulation
_____	14.	Physical attractiveness
_____	15.	Prestige (not "social") family life
_____	16.	Ability to initiate and maintain friendships
_____	17.	Resilience (ability to bounce back
_____	18.	Ability to give love
_____	19.	Socially significant activity
_____	20	Close and supportive
_____	21.	Artistic ability

Then in small groups of three or four, members share their lists and discuss what each considers to be really important in life. Then the larger group comes together and the auction begins. Each person is given 20 chips or cards, each worth one thousand dollars. Each item is auctioned off and in the spontaneity and excitement of the auction, the participants discover what they think is really important to them. They also learn a great deal about others in the group.

I LEARNED THAT I . . . .

After completing the above exercise, complete one or more of the following statements:
I learned (or relearned) that I . . . .
I noticed that I . . . .
I was surprised to see that I . . . .
I was pleased (disappointed) that I . . . .
Because it is important that everyone be as open and supportive as possible, it is essential that any member feel free to "pass" at any time.

Try writing a computer program to analyze the responses of the class to these exercises.

(The above excerpted from an article by Jim Wilson from the January 1973 Loomis-Chaffee Bulletin.)

A new learning activity from Creative Computing . . . .

What Do You Value?

by Sally Richards

There's a great deal of talk (and action, too) these days about values; value clarification, strategies, the processes involved in "valuing," and about the revaluation of values. Based on the premise that our lives, our surroundings, and our roles are constantly shifting and changing, it becomes critically important that each of us knows what we value. That is, we must know who we are, what we want and where we're going.

Values have become a central issue in school, home, church, and business. Value clarification is being sought extensively as a vehicle for achieving personal growth and fulfillment, as well as a basis for decision making and problem solving.

How does one know what to value? How do you know what you are for or against?

In these troubled, confused, but also exciting times, we need people who know who they are, who know what they want out of life, and who can name their names when controversy rages. People who are not so vulnerable to a demagogue, or to blandness, or to safety. Values are the basis upon which people decide what they are for and against, or where they are going and why. In other words, they give direction to life. But, with the many divergent values viable today, it is oftentimes difficult to know where you stand.

The following exercises (sometimes called strategies) can be used to help you determine what is important to you? What do you value? After doing these yourself, you can perhaps try them on friends, family, or students and compare some of their ideas and alternatives to your own.

As quickly as you can, list 20 things in life which you really, really love to do. There are no right or wrong answers about what you should like.

Using the suggested code below, the next step is to code the 20 items listed above.

1. Place the number 1 by any item which costs more than $5 each time you do it.

2. Put a 2 by any item which involves some RISK. The risk might be physical, intellectual, or emotional. (Which things in your own life, that you love to do, require some risk?)

3. Using a 3, record any of the items on your list you think your FATHER and MOTHER might have had on their list if they had been asked to make such a list at your age.

4. Place either a 4 or a 5 next to each item; the 4 is for items you prefer doing with PEOPLE, the 5 for items you prefer doing ALONE.

5. Place a number 6 by any item that would not have been on your list 5 years ago.

6. Place a number 7 by any item you think will not be on your list 5 years from now.

7. Finally, go down through your list and indicate the date when you last did each item. Use an 8 for things you have done today, a 9 for those done within the last month, and a 10 for things you haven't done in more than a month.

1.									
2.									
3.									
4.									
5.									
6.									
7.									
8.									
9.									
10.									
11.									
12.									
13.									
14.									
15.									
16.									
17.									
18.									
19.									
20.									

Now . . . how about writing a program that will analyze the responses that you and your class have made.

THIS IS A COMPUTERIZED ANALYSIS OF YOUR RESPONSES TO THE VALUE STRATEGY GAME '20 THINGS I LOVE TO DO'.

THIS ANALYSIS WILL PASS NO FINAL JUDGMENTS ON YOUR RESPONSES. IT WILL, HOWEVER, COMPILE THE NECESSARY STATISTICS THAT WILL AID YOU IN MAKING YOUR OWN EVALUATION OF THE THINGS YOU VALUE IN YOUR LIFE.

HOW MANY THINGS ARE CONTAINED IN YOUR LIST (FROM 1 TO 20)? 20

ENTER THE CODE NUMBERS THAT YOU HAVE PLACED NEXT TO ITEM# 1 . TYPE A 99 AFTER ALL OF YOUR NUMBERS HAVE BEEN ENTERED.

? 5
? 10
? 99

ENTER THE CODE NUMBERS THAT YOU HAVE PLACED NEXT TO ITEM# 2 . TYPE A 99 AFTER ALL YOUR NUMBERS HAVE BEEN ENTERED.

? 1
? 4
? 10
? 99
:
:

YOUR COMPUTERIZED ANALYSIS . . . . .

YOU ARE FORTUNATE. IN THESE INFLATIONARY DAYS ONLY 30 PERCENT OF THE THINGS YOU LOVE REQUIRE MONEY.

YOU MUST BE CAUTIOUS!
ONLY 15 PERCENT OF YOUR VALUED ACTIVITIES

INVOLVE PERSONAL RISK.

YOU AND YOUR PARENTS VALUE LESS THAN HALF OF THE SAME THINGS.

PEOPLE ARE INVOLVED IN LESS THAN 50 PERCENT OF YOUR FAVORITE ACTIVITIES.

YOU ENJOY DOING THINGS THAT INVOLVE YOU ALONE MOST OF THE TIME.

2 OUT OF 10 TIMES YOUR ITEMS WOULD NOT HAVE APPEARED ON YOUR LIST FIVE YEARS AGO.

YOU KNOW WHAT YOU VALUE. 0 PERCENT OF YOUR ITEMS WILL NOT BE ON YOUR LIST IN 1978.

35 PERCENT OF YOUR VALUED ACTIVITIES HAVE BEEN ENJOYED WITHIN THE LAST 24 HOURS.

WITHIN THE LAST MONTH YOU HAVE DONE 60 PERCENT OF THE THINGS YOU LOVE TO DO.

AND IN 4 OUT OF 10 CASES YOU HAVE NOT BEEN INVOLVED IN YOUR VALUED ACTIVITIES FOR MORE THAN A MONTH.

YOUR COMPUTER ANALYSIS OF THE THINGS THAT YOU VALUE IS COMPLETE. WE HOPE THAT YOU ARE HAPPY WITH THE RESULTS. PERHAPS THERE ARE SOME CHANGES YOU WOULD LIKE TO MAKE OR PERHAPS YOU HAVE LEARNED SOMETHING ABOUT YOURSELF BY PLAYING '20 THINGS'. ONLY YOU CAN EVALUATE THE STATISTICS OF THIS ANALYSIS.
IT MIGHT BE INTERESTING TO GO BACK OVER YOUR LIST AND ASSIGN PRIORITIES TO YOUR ITEMS. IT MIGHT GIVE YOU SOME ADDITIONAL INSIGHT TOWARD THE THINGS THAT YOU VALUE.

After you have written your analysis program look back over the results.

- Can you identify any patterns in the things that you value?
- Did you learn something new about yourself?
- Are there things you are pleased with?
- Is there anything you would change?
- How might you go about it?
- Are there some things you like to do that you haven't done lately? Why? What can you do about it?
- Does establishing priorities for your entries give you additional insight about you and your values?

Try playing "20 Things" several times this year. Maybe you'll learn something new about yourself each time!

This article was adapted from "What do You Value" by Sid Simon that appeared in the Spring-Summer issue of *Forum*, a semi-annual publication for educators by J. C. Penney Co. Ask for an issue at your local Penney's store. This article was reprinted with permission from *EDU* No. 7 published by Digital Equipment Corp.

Fairy Tales Can Come True...

by Ron Jones

ONCE THERE WAS a country that had made more technical progress than any other country in the world.

ITS SCIENTISTS, economists, psychologists, engineers and all the like were generating billions of bits of knowledge each year -- knowledge that could help the country make the best decisions to keep its people healthy, wealthy, and wise.

THE PEOPLE, their elected representatives, and the president couldn't keep up with all this information -- and didn't understand most of it anyhow -- and important decisions seemed more and more to be wrong.

SOME SCIENTISTS came up with an invention -- a computer to store all the old facts and the new ones as they came along -- and to make it easy to find the facts and to analyze them.

OTHER SCIENTISTS developed ways of organizing facts to be able to manage operations involving many, many people and lots of money. But ordinary people can't talk to computers or use these new systems.

IT TAKES professional scientists to do this job, and so the people, their elected representatives, and the president were coming to depend more and more on these scientists to recommend decisions.

THE SCIENTISTS feel that the facts in the computer have to be complete, even down to the most personal information about each person. The more facts, the more accurate they are, the more correct the decisions will be.

SOME PEOPLE fought back against this. They said that the country was a democracy, that a democracy means the people have a say-so in decision making, that everyone is equal in the country, and that the dignity of individuals is preserved at all costs. They didn't want to see their country run by scientists and computers.

THE SUPPORTERS of the scientists and the computers answered that the democracy was in danger from planlessness and poor administration -- that the world had become too complicated in the two hundred years since the country was formed -- and that the longer people fought the new technology, the greater the chance it would be forced down their throats as a dictatorship completely out of their control.

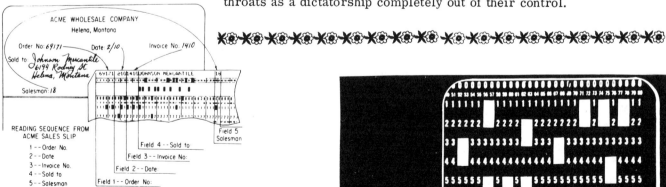

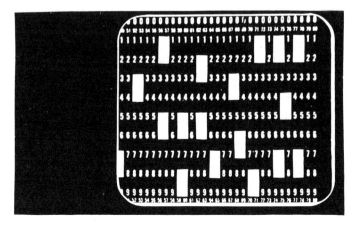

...It Depends on You

SAVE THE NEWSPAPERS FOR A WEEK. THEN CUT OUT ARTICLES THAT YOU BELIEVE GIVE EXAMPLES OF EITHER SIDE OF THE FOLLOWING ISSUES.

Causes and effects in an advanced technological society are so widespread and so hard to match together, that experts and techniques ordinary people can't understand ARE/ARE NOT needed to separate the important from the unimportant in order to make intelligent decisions.

The real danger IS/IS NOT an increasing tendency to leave decisions that the people and their representatives used to debate and decide to groups of independent experts and technicians, elected by nobody and responsible to nobody.

If our society is becoming more indirect -- we're having more trouble trying to see the connections between what happened and what caused it -- then direct participation in government and decision-making IS/IS NOT becoming less relevant.

The idea that an election for president every four years represents a chance to speak out on all the decisions society faces for the next four years IS/IS NOT adequate to contemporary needs.

There IS/IS NOT a way that participation in the old-fashioned use of the word can substitute for the experts and modern decision-making techniques government must use today.

ORGANIZE A DEBATE ON THE FOLLOWING:

RESOLVED: The nation needs a new version of democracy and new political institutions more adequate to the realities of a modern technological society than what exists at present.

CHOOSE TWO SPEAKERS FOR EACH SIDE, ONE TO PRESENT THE ARGUMENTS, AND ONE TO REBATE THE OTHER SIDE'S ARGUMENT.

THE SPEAKER FOR THE AFFIRMATIVE SPEAKS FIRST.
THE SPEAKER FOR THE NEGATIVE SPEAKS NEXT.
THE SPEAKER REBUTTING THE AFFIRMATIVE SPEAKS NEXT.
THE SPEAKER REBUTTING THE NEGATIVE SPEAKS LAST.

USE ANYTHING IN THIS PAMPHLET FOR EVIDENCE, AS WELL AS ANYTHING ELSE YOU CAN FIND THAT IS RELEVANT.

THE REST OF THE CLASS WILL ACT AS A JURY.

YOU ARE A BUSINESSMAN...

by Ron Jones

A COMPUTER expert/economist has come to you with a mathematical model of a means of so stimulating the economies of urban ghettos that they would cease to be a problem to the nation or themselves in a decade. The most conservative estimates are that the money saved in local and federal governmental costs as well as by ghetto dwellers would equal the savings of 25% of the gasoline used in the country.

A very large sum of money is needed to perfect the economic and mathematical relationships to enable the computer to be used to direct the program, as well as to act as seed money for the enterprises, provide funds for education and training, inventory, refurbishing of the areas, and a sales and marketing effort.

It's more money than you and your associates have; it is essential that government interference be avoided; you cannot supply the enormous collateral the banks would demand for a loan. You're going to have to sell stock in it, millions of shares of stock at a low price to raise the millions of dollars needed. The idea is a necessary one, and will ultimately save taxpayers millions, maybe billions of dollars each year, as well as providing ghetto dwellers the equality of opportunity we worship as one of our value-beliefs.

PREPARE a statement inviting people to invest in buying stock -- a few shares or a lot of shares. Point out the need, the potential in the action, the possibility that the ultimate return will be in tax savings and satisfaction of seeing the disadvantaged help themselves, the dangers and bad experience of leaving such a task to government -- everything you can to induce someone to see the gain to himself, if not in dollars in something else, of such an investment.

WHEN you have made up your sales pitch for the prospective corporation, try it out on your parents and some of their friends. Ask them if they would invest in such a company, and why.

WHAT WERE THE RESULTS OF YOUR SURVEY?

WHAT DO THESE RESULTS INDICATE AS FAR AS A MESHING OF ADVANCES IN TECHNOLOGY AND OUR INSTITUTIONS?

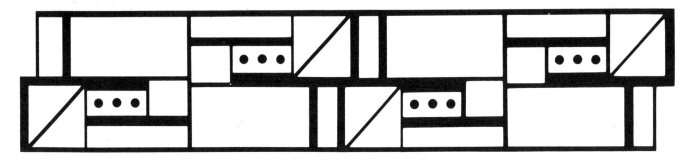

THERE'S MORE THAN MEETS THE EYE

Don't get the idea that the question is one of profits versus idealism. The question boils down to using technological advances -- of being able to apply scientific knowledge to solving our social problems -- some of which were caused by technological advances -- with the same efficiency we can supply cars, or frozen foods, or polyester clothing.

Here are six questions that Harvard University is studying about this problem. Just on the basis of what you know and feel -- and what you've found out doing some of the exercises in this book -- what do you think might be a way of answering these questions and solving the problems they describe?

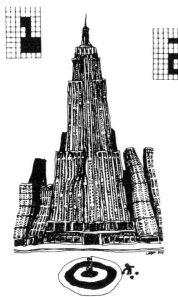

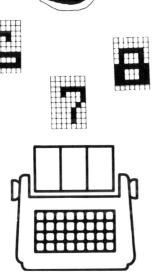

1. How do the organization and goals of corporations -- directed at profits to provide money to plow back into the business, salaries for top-notch people, and a profit for the investors -- affect the ability of our society to provide goods and services that are socially desirable, but not necessarily profitable to any one group in society?

2. What does it cost our society to concentrate so much effort on economic growth to provide jobs for as many people as possible rather than investing some of our capital in social development?

3. How do you reconcile the incentive to individuals of profits and achievement with the public need for goods and services that may not return either to those providing it?

4. How can you reconcile the all too frequent fight between what is desirable to us as individuals for our own welfare and what is desirable to us as members of society from the standpoint of welfare?

5. Are the roles of government and private enterprise due for some major changes because of the short-term as well as the long-term effects of technology?

6. How can advertising and other forms of communication be used in public education to make people aware of the need to make decisions affecting these questions before the pressures of value changes, social changes, and economic and political stresses tear our society apart?

TECHNOLOGY...
DOOMSDAY FOR INDIVIDUALISM?

by Ron Jones

Reprinted with permission from *Zephrus: DeSchool Primer* No. 4. (The entire DeSchool Primer series of 12 idea-crammed activity newspapers is outstanding. Most cost between $1.50 and $4.00 and are worth every penny. Write for a descriptive flyer to Ron Jones, Zephrus Education Exchange, 1201 Stanyan, San Francisco, CA 94117.)

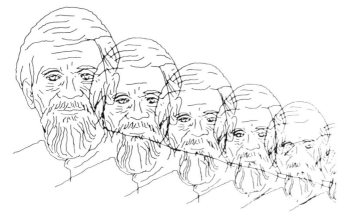

FORM TEAMS AND DEBATE THESE ISSUES

OPTIMIST: The computer is our greatest hope for survival as individuals in a multi-billion person society, with all the institutions needed to keep that society going. What all this technical advance does, really, is keep us all from running into one another so we can act as individuals. Otherwise, it would have to be like the army -- with everyone in ranks.

PESSIMIST: That's where it is. All this technology and the changes it has brought on have made the contributions of individuals less and less important, and organized efforts more important. Who had a greater feeling of individual accomplishment -- Magellan sailing across the Pacific or the first men on the moon?

PESSIMIST: No matter what you say, we live in a mass society. Both government and business seem to be trying to reduce us to organization people because we fit their computer programs better. Our self-image and sense of worth go down with each new technological advance.

OPTIMIST: Our higher level of education lets us learn new skills and develop our potential to the fullest. We have much more feeling of individualism than 19th century factory workers or farmers. The demands made by minorities show how much higher is our sense of individual worth than before.

OPTIMIST: Makes it child's play to communicate with just about anyone, anywhere. Fosters individual growth.

PESSIMIST: Invasion of privacy. Lays me open to sales pitches, junk mail, and bugging. Ends up by destroying me.

PESSIMIST: Everyone today feels almost drowned in a sea of bigger and bigger government and business. They operate as if no one personally existed -- we're just voters, citizens, and consumers en masse.

OPTIMIST: Government and business look more powerful than ever, but they're more afraid of us than ever, because we're better educated and demand more. Look how they rely on polls, and have had to go to advertising to make people like them. We can get to them more easily than before.

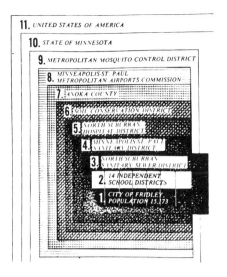

CLASSES FOR
ADULTS

Begin September 11, 1973

SANTA CRUZ ADULT SCHOOL
350 Taylor Street
Santa Cruz, Ca. 95060

OPTIMIST: Today the government tries to provide everyone with education, health care, cultural development, housing, keeping the economy on track, and promoting technological advances. This frees people from worries they used to have.

PESSIMIST: But the price is that experts and faceless bureaucrats run these things, and act as if they know everything and are doing us a favor. We're less free than ever before.

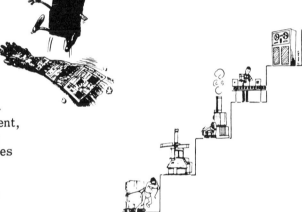

TECHNOLOGICAL PROGRESS IS SAID TO RESEMBLE A FLIGHT OF STAIRS.

DEPARTMENT OF
HEALTH, EDUCATION, AND WELFARE
SOCIAL SECURITY ADMINISTRATION

YOUR SOCIAL SECURITY CARD

WHAT TO DO WITH YOUR CARD

- SIGN YOUR NAME on both cards.
- REMOVE THE TOP CARD and carry it in your wallet or purse, or keep it where it will be handy.
- LEAVE THE BOTTOM STUB attached to this holder and keep it with your other important papers such as birth certificate, insurance policies, etc.

OPTIMIST: I don't have to worry about my old age or getting sick. I'm free to develop in my own way.

PESSIMIST: I'm a number, a statistic. That's the way the government treats you. And they use all my salary and job information to manipulate me.

PESSIMIST: Before all this technology advance, people were free of experts, bureaucrats, big government, and big business. And they had privacy; they could do anything.

OPTIMIST: They sure did -- nobody cared if they were ignorant, starved, got sick, or died -- in privacy. Education, social care, and health need information to be efficient -- and it is an invasion of that old-fashioned privacy to get extensive and accurate information.

219

A new simulation . . .

Escape

by Dr. J. Harris
Chelsea Centre for Science Education
University of London, England

INTRODUCTION

In this module you are going to investigate how an object travels if it is launched vertically upwards from the earth's surface. You will be able to find out how far away it can travel, what initial velocity it must have to reach a certain height, and so on.

Of course the computer doesn't actually do the experiments. It might — but in this case doesn't — simply tell you the results of trials which have been made. What it does do is to work out the results, based on particular physical laws, which we have good reason to have faith in. The calculations are also based on some simplifying assumptions. All this is explained in the body of the text.

MOTION IN A GRAVITATIONAL FIELD

Imagine that you are trying to throw a ball straight upwards, as high as you can. Obviously the harder you throw it the higher it will get before reaching its highest point and starting to fall back to earth.

Q1 *Suppose that for your strongest throw the stone gets to a height of 5m. How high would the stone get if you could give it twice the initial speed?*

	A	7.1m
	B	10m
	C	14m
	D	20m
or	E	25m

If you could answer that correctly you should know the height which the stone reaches depends on how much kinetic energy it has to start with, and that kinetic energy depends on (speed)^2. So twice the velocity means four times the kinetic energy. As the stone goes up its kinetic energy is transformed to potential energy. The potential energy depends on how high above the ground the stone is, and when the stone is 20m above ground, the potential energy is four times that for 5m above ground.

So we can calculate how far the stone will go for a particular initial speed, however great. We can also calculate what initial speed it must be given to reach a particular distance.

The Chelsea Science Simulation Project is the British counterpart to the Huntington Computer Project in the United States. In other words, it is a project to produce high-quality computer simulation modules consisting of a program, student's workbook, and teacher's guide. Most of the modules produced to date are in the areas of physics and biology and are in various states of test, revision, and final forms. A test version of the physics module, ESCAPE, is presented here. Future issues of Creative Computing will carry a complete article about the Chelsea Science Simulation Project and, hopefully, additional modules if enough readers want them. Write and let us know your interests.

Q2 *So far we have made at least two assumptions in this discussion. Do you know what they are?*

Suppose that a space probe were fired directly from the earth's surface, and fired fast enough to travel a great distance. Would the kind of argument used above still work? In particular, would the potential energy go on increasing uniformly with distance from the earth?

You probably know that as one travels away from the earth the earth's pull, gravity, gets weaker. The *force* of gravity on an object follows the so-called inverse-square law.

The radius of the earth is about 6,000km. The inverse-square law says that at twice this distance (12,000km) from the earth's centre the force is only $(½)^2$ = ¼ of what it is at the surface of the earth; at three times the distance the force is $(1/3)^2$ = 1/9th, and so on.

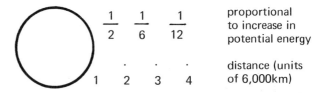

The force pulling the object back towards earth steadily decreases as it gets further and further away. What about the potential energy? It goes on increasing — but does it still increase steadily, in proportion to the distance from the earth's centre?

Theory says it wouldn't. It says that potential energy will increase more and more slowly as the probe gets further from the earth's centre and the gravity force gets weaker. The increase in potential energy in going from a distance 6,000km above the earth's surface to a distance 12,000km is less than the increase in going from the surface to a distance 6,000km. And again, the potential energy increase in going from 12,000 to 18,000 is less than the change in going from 6,000km to 12,000km, and so on.

And so the kinetic energy is "used up" less and less quickly as the probe gets further away from earth.

Now this raises a question. Would it be possible to give the probe so much kinetic energy that it would never be completely used up (transformed to potential energy)? If so the probe would just go on indefinitely moving farther and farther away from earth. Perhaps it seems a reasonable idea that since the kinetic energy is transformed less and less quickly there will always be some left (if you eat half a cake today, then tomorrow eat half the remaining half to leave you a quarter, then eat half the quarter . . . you will, in theory anyway, always have *some* cake left).

On the other hand however far from the earth the probe is (assume the earth is the only body in the Universe) there is always *some* gravitational force on it. And so you might argue that no matter how far away the probe is, nor how fast it is still moving, it will never be able to escape completely, never to return, because the earth will always be pulling it back, however weakly.

Perhaps both these arguments sound reasonable to you. But they can't both be right! And one can't decide between them except by doing calculations to find out. (Or by doing an experiment — can one fire something off into space so that it never comes back?)

This is where the computer can help. It has been programmed to answer different questions to do with launch velocity and distance travelled. Of course, it has to assume a theoretical basis on which to make these calculations. It has been programmed to assume that the gravitational force falls off according to the inverse-square law, and that there is no air resistance. Other simplifying assumptions have been made, such as:

▶ the earth is the only body in the Universe
▶ the probe is always launched vertically upwards

The computer can tell you:

A What launch velocity is needed to fire a probe to a particular chosen distance.
B What velocity the probe has left at certain distances, for a particular launch velocity.
C At what distance does the probe stop and turn around and begin returning to earth, for a chosen launch velocity.

Your job is to use the computer to help answer the problem posed earlier: "Is it possible to fire something so fast that it will never return?"

Decide which of the three questions (A, B or C above) would be the most helpful.

For each question you will have to give some information. For example, if you ask for question C to be answered you will have to choose values for the launch velocity of the probe, and its mass.

To help you find the answer to the problem use the computer to answer these specific questions:

Q3 Does the mass of the probe affect how far it will travel for a given launch velocity, or what launch velocity it must be given if it is to reach a certain distance; If so, how?

Q4 Suppose the last question were asked about energy instead of velocity — would the answer be the same? (Does the mass of the probe affect how far it will travel for a given initial kinetic energy, or what energy it must be given if it is to reach a certain distance?)

Q5 The earth's radius, R is about 6,000km (6×10^6 m). What launch velocity is needed to carry a probe from the earth's surface to a distance R from it?

The next question refers to the distance from earth to the moon, the sun, etc., but in answering it you should assume, as before, that the earth is the only body in the Universe.

Q6 What launch velocity is needed to get a probe as far as the moon (earth — moon distance is about 380×10^6 m)?

— as far away from the earth as the sun is (150×10^9 m)?
— as far as Pluto, the furthest known planet (about 60×10^{12} m)?
— as far as the nearest star (about 40×10^{15} m)?
— as far as you like.

Sample output is shown only for Question A. Run the program yourself to see how it works for Questions B and C.

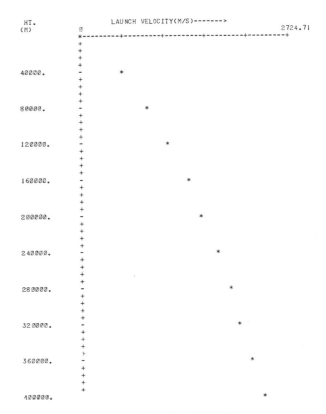

```
    T  IPUT DO YOU WANT?
1YP:     T LAUNCH VELOCITY TO REACH A CHOSEN HEIGHT
  OR  2 FOR VELOCITY AT DIFFERENT HEIGHTS ,FOR A CHOSEN
        LAUNCH VELOCITY
  OR  3 FOR HEIGHT REACHED FOR A CHOSEN LAUNCH VELOCITY
?1


TO INTERRUPT THE PROGRAM TO GET DIFFERENT OUTPUT
TYPE  0  WHEN YOU ARE ASKED TO INPUT MASS, OR HEIGHT

MASS OF PROBE (KG)    HEIGHT (M)    LAUNCH VELOCITY (M/S)

?1000
                        ?150000
                                        1700.22

?0

TO GET ANOTHER OUTPUT AS LISTED ABOVE TYPE 1,2 OR 3

TYPE 4  IF YOU WOULD LIKE A TABLE OR GRAPH SHOWING
THE LAUNCH VELOCITY NEEDED TO REACH CHOSEN HEIGHTS

TYPE 0 TO END THE PROGRAM
?4

TYPE (1)  FOR TABLE
 OR (2)  FOR GRAPH
?2

TOTAL HEIGHT  (METRES)=?400000
```

```
  HT.                    LAUNCH VELOCITY(M/S)------->
  (M)      0                                              2724.71
        *--------+--------+--------+--------+--------+
         +
         +
         +
         +
40000.   -        *
         +
         +
         +
         +
80000.   -              *
         +
         +
         +
         +
120000.  -                  *
         +
         +
         +
         +
160000.  -                      *
         +
         +
         +
         +
200000.  -                          *
         +
         +
         +
         +
240000.  -                             *
         +
         +
         +
         +
280000.  -                                 *
         +
         +
         +
         +
320000.  -                                    *
         +
         +
         +
         +
360000.  -                                       *
         +
         +
         +
         +
400000.  -                                         *
```

TYPE 1 IF YOU WANT TO RE-RUN THIS PART OF THE PROGRAM
?0

221

```
00050  REM         ***ESCAPE VERSION 5, MAY    01ST 1974 ***
00055  REM             *****COPYRIGHT  CHELSEA COLLEGE   ****
00060  LET M=6E+24
00065  LET R=6,37E+6
00070  LET G=6,6/E+11
00075  LET K=G*M/R
00080  REM       *****MOTION OF OBJECT LAUNCHED VERTICALLY*****
00085  PRINT "WHAT OUTPUT DO YOU WANT?"
00090  PRINT "TYPE 1 FOR LAUNCH VELOCITY TO REACH A CHOSEN HEIGHT"
00095  PRINT " OR    2 FOR VELOCITY AT DIFFERENT HEIGHTS ,FOR A CHOSEN"
00100  PRINT "        LAUNCH VELOCITY"
00105  PRINT " OR 3 FOR HEIGHT REACHED FOR A CHOSEN LAUNCH VELOCITY"
00110  INPUT A
00115  PRINT
00120  PRINT
00125  PRINT "TO INTERRUPT THE PROGRAM TO GET DIFFERENT OUTPUT"
00130  PRINT "TYPE  0  WHEN YOU ARE ASKED TO INPUT MASS, OR HEIGHT "
00135  PRINT
00140  IF A=1 THEN 165
00145  IF A=2 THEN 260
00150  IF A=3 THEN 500
00155  PRINT "REPLY WITH 1,2 OR 3"
00160  GOTO 110
00165  REM    ***GIVES LAUNCH VELOCITY NEEDED FOR A CHOSEN HEIGHT*****
00170  PRINT "MASS OF PROBE (KG)   HEIGHT (M)    LAUNCH VELOCITY (M/S)"
00175  PRINT
00180  INPUT M1
00185  IF M1=0 THEN 620
00190  IF M1>0 THEN 205
00195  PRINT "POSITIVE MASS ONLY"
00200  GOTO 175
00205  PRINT TAB(24);
00210  INPUT H
00215  IF H=0 THEN 620
00220  IF H>0 THEN 235
00225  PRINT "HEIGHT MUST BE POSITIVE"
00230  GOTO 205
00235  GOSUB 1190
00240  PRINT TAB(40);V
00245  IF H>=1000 THEN 255
00250  GOSUB 1160
00255  GOTO 175
00260  REM    *GIVES SPEED AT VARIOUS HEIGHT FOR CHOSEN LAUNCH VELOCITY
00265  LET N2=0
00270  PRINT "LAUNCH VELOCITY (M/S)=";
00275  INPUT V1
00280  PRINT
00285  IF V1>0 THEN 300
00290  PRINT "POSITIVE VALUE FOR ";
00295  GOTO 270
00300  PRINT "MASS OF PROBE (KG)=";
00305  INPUT M1
00310  IF M1=0 THEN 660
00315  PRINT
00320  IF M1>0 THEN 335
00325  PRINT "POSITIVE VALUE FOR ";
00330  GOTO 300
00335  LET E1=.5*M1*V1*V1
00340  PRINT "TYPE 5 HEIGHTS AT WHICH YOU WOULD LIKE TO KNOW"
00345  PRINT "WHAT VELOCITY THE PROBE HAS LEFT"
00350  PRINT
00355  PRINT " HEIGHT (METRES)        VELOCITY (M/S)"
00360  PRINT
00365  FOR I=1 TO 5
00370   INPUT H
00375   IF H=0 THEN 620
00380   IF H>0 THEN 395
00385   PRINT "POSITIVE HEIGHT ONLY"
00390   GOTO 370
00395   LET E=E1-K*M1*H/(R+H)
00400   IF E>0 THEN 415
00405   PRINT TAB(19);"DOESN'T GET THAT FAR"
00410   GOTO 435
00415   GOSUB 1195
00420   PRINT TAB(25);V
00425   IF H>=1000 THEN 435
00430   GOSUB 1160
00435  NEXT I
00440  LET N2=N2+1
00445  IF N2=10 THEN 625
00450  PRINT
00455  PRINT "DO YOU WANT TO RUN THIS PART OF THE PROGRAM AGAIN"
00460  PRINT "TYPE  0  FOR NO, OR  1  FOR YES";
00465  INPUT B2
00470  IF B2*(B2-1)<>0 THEN 460
00475  PRINT
00480  PRINT
00485  PRINT
00490  IF B2=0 THEN 270
00495  GOTO 625
00500  REM  **GIVES MAX HEIGHT REACHED FOR A CHOSEN LAUNCH VELOCITY**
00505  PRINT "MASS OF PROBE (KG)    LAUNCH VELOCITY (M/S) "
00510  PRINT "  HEIGHT REACHED (M)"
00515  INPUT M1
00520  IF M1>0 THEN 540
00525  IF M1=0 THEN 620
00530  PRINT "POSITIVE MASS ONLY"
00535  GOTO 515
00540  PRINT TAB(24);
00545  INPUT V1
00550  IF V1>0 THEN 575
00555  IF V1=0 THEN 620
00560  PRINT "POSITIVE VELOCITIES ONLY"
00565  GOTO 540
00570  PRINT
00575  LET E1=.5*M1*V1*V1
00580  IF E1<K*M1 THEN 595
00585  PRINT TAB(30);"WILL NEVER RETURN"
00590  GOTO 510
00595  LET H=(R*E1)/(K*M1-E1)
00600  PRINT TAB(30);H
00605  IF H>=1000 THEN 615
00610  GOSUB 1160
00615  GOTO 515
00620  PRINT
00625  REM     **** OFFER INITIAL CHOICE AGAIN, OR  TABLE OR GRAPH*****
00630  PRINT
00635  PRINT "TO GET ANOTHER OUTPUT AS LISTED ABOVE TYPE 1,2 OR 3"
00640  PRINT
00645  PRINT "TYPE 4  IF YOU WOULD LIKE A TABLE OR GRAPH SHOWING"
00650  PRINT "THE LAUNCH VELOCITY NEEDED TO REACH CHOSEN HEIGHTS"
00655  PRINT
00660  PRINT "TYPE 0 TO END THE PROGRAM"
00665  INPUT A2
00670  PRINT
00675  PRINT
00680  IF A2=0 THEN 1165
00685  IF A2=1 THEN 170
00690  IF A2=2 THEN 265
00695  IF A2=3 THEN 505
00700  IF A2=4 THEN 725
00705  PRINT "REPLY WITH 0,1,2,3 OR 4"
00710  GOTO 665
00715  REM     *****TABLE OR GRAPH OF LAUNCH VELOCITY NEEDED TO *****
00720  REM     ***** REACH CHOSEN HEIGHTS *****
00725  PRINT "TYPE  (1)  FOR TABLE"
00730  PRINT " OR   (2)  FOR GRAPH"
00735  LET M1=1
00740  INPUT G1
00745  PRINT
00750  RESTORE
00755  IF (G1-1)*(G1-2)=0 THEN 765
00760  GOTO 725
00765  IF G1=2 THEN 925
00770  PRINT "TYPE  (1) IF YOU WANT TO CHOOSE HEIGHTS YOURSELF"
00775  PRINT " OR   (2) FOR VALUES STORED IN THE PROGRAM"
00780  INPUT D
00785  PRINT
00790  IF (D-1)*(D-2)=0 THEN 800
00795  GOTO 770
00800  PRINT
00805  IF D=2 THEN 865
00810  REM    **TABLE ,OWN VALUES******
00815  GOSUB 1045
00820  PRINT "HEIGHT (METRES)    LAUNCH VELOCITY(M,R)"
00825  PRINT "  0                  0"
00830  FOR H=H1 TO H9 STEP H1
00835   GOSUB 1190
00840   PRINT H;TAB(18);V
00850  NEXT H
00855  PRINT
00860  GOTO 995
00865  REM    **TABLE,STORED VALUES ***
00870  PRINT "HEIGHT (METRES)    LAUNCH VELOCITY(M/S)"
00875  PRINT
00880  GOSUB 1160
00883  PRINT
00885  PRINT "  0                  0"
00890  FOR N=1 TO 14
00895   READ H
00900   GOSUB 1190
00905   PRINT H;TAB(18);V
00910  NEXT N
00915  GOTO 995
00920  REM    **GRAPH ***
00925  GOSUB 1045
00930  PRINT
00935  PRINT " H1,              LAUNCH VELOCITY(M/S)------->"
00940  PRINT " (M)             0";TAB(63);V9
00945  PRINT "        *----------+---------+---------+---------+";
00950  PRINT "---------+"
00955  LET F=1
00960  FOR H=H1 TO H9 STEP H1
00965   GOSUB 1190
00970   GOSUB 1125
00975   LET F=F+1
00980  NEXT H
00985  GOTO 995
00990  REM    **RE-RUN QUERY **
00995  PRINT
01000  PRINT
01005  PRINT "TYPE 1 IF YOU WANT TO RE-RUN THIS PART OF THE PROGRAM"
01010  INPUT A3
01015  PRINT
01020  IF A3=1 THEN 725
01025  IF A3=0 THEN 1215
01030  PRINT "REPLY WITH 0 OR 1"
01035  GOTO 1010
01040  REM    ***USER INPUTS HEIGHTS ***
01045  PRINT "TOTAL HEIGHT  (METRES)=";
01050  INPUT H9
01055  IF H9>0 THEN 1065
01060  GOTO 1045
01065  LET H=H9
01070  GOSUB 1190
01075  LET H9=H
01080  LET V9=V
01085  PRINT
01090  LET H1=H9/10
01095  IF H1>=1000 THEN 1105
01100  GOSUB 1160
01105  PRINT
01110  PRINT
01115  RETURN
01120  REM    ***GRAPH OUTPUT **
01125  FOR S=1 TO 4
01130   PRINT TAB(15);"+"
01135  NEXT S
01140  LET V=V*50/V9+9
01145  PRINT F*H1;TAB(15);"-";TAB(V);"*"
01150  RETURN
01155  REM    ***WARNING ROUTINE***
01160  PRINT
01165  PRINT " WARNING : RESULTS MAY BE INACCURATE FOR HEIGHTS";
01170  PRINT " LESS THAN 1000 M "
01175  PRINT
01180  PRINT
01185  RETURN
01190  LET E=K*H*M1/(R+H)
01195  LET V=SQR((E+E)/M1)
01200  RETURN
01205  DATA 1,10,100,1000,10000,100000,1E+6,1E+7,1E+8,1E+9
01210  DATA 1E+10,1E+11,1E+12,1E+13
01215  PRINT "END OF PROGRAM"
01220  END
```

222

The Automobile and Air Pollution*

by Herbert D. Peckham, Gavilan College

The most logical place to begin our study of air pollution is with the automobile. Table 1 presents some very interesting statistics concerning the relationship between cars and air pollution. First, the overall quantity of pollutants (141 million tons per year) is absolutely depressing! Second, the automobile plays a discouragingly large part in the overall pollution. Certainly in the production of carbon monoxide (93% of the total) and organics (66% of the total), the automobile is the villain! Last, it is clear that the automobile has little to do with pollution from sulfur oxides and particulates.

Table 1 – Total US Air Pollution (1970)

Pollutant	Millions of Tons Per Year			% Caused by Auto
	Auto	Other	Total	
Carbon Monoxide	66	5	71	93
Organics	12	7	19	63
Oxides of Nitrogen	6	7	13	46
Sulfur Oxides	1	25	26	4
Particulates	1	11	12	8
Total Pollutants	86	55	141	61

Before we can start building our automobile air pollution models, we need to know the rates at which automobiles produce the various pollutants. Of course, this is continually changing as automobile pollution controls become more severe. We will use 1970 estimates (hopefully, by 1980 or 1990 the values will be much lower). Also, we will assume a standard velocity of 40 miles per hour. Do you feel this is a reasonable choice? The rates of pollutant production are given in Table 2.

Table 2 – Average 1970 Pollutant Production Rates per Automobile Traveling at 40 MPH

Pollutants	Rate of Production		
Gases	liters/mile	cubic feet/mile	grams/hour
Org.	4.5*	6.4	483
NO_x	3.4**	4.8	231
SO_x	0.1***	0.14	11.4
CO	54.1	76.6	2710
	(grams/mile)		(grams/hour)
Particulates	0.5		20

*Assumes an average molecular weight of 60. Gas volumes computed at standard temperature and pressure.

**Assumes equal parts nitric oxide and nitrogen dioxide are formed. Average molecular weight of oxides of nitrogen assumed to be 38.

***Assumes 4 parts sulfur dioxide to 1 part sulfur trioxide are formed. Average molecular weight of sulfur oxides assumed to be 67.

*This activity is reproduced from the Student Lab booklet *Air Pollution* from the Hewlett-Packard Computer Curriculum series. Additional background material and exercises are in the booklet. The Student Lab book and companion Teachers Advisor book are available for $1.00 each from Hewlett-Packard Computer Curriculum Project, 333 Logue Ave., Mountain View, California 94043.

Let's take an average residential district, composed of a mixture of apartments and single family dwellings, as the subject of our first air pollution model. Suppose that the residential district is square with one mile sides and that we are concerned with the air over the district up to an elevation of 500 feet. Moreover, we will assume that no air passes in or out of our residential district and that any pollutants created are uniformly distributed through the air up to our "ceiling" of 500 feet.

These assumptions are typical of the ones we will be making continually. Certainly they are crude, and you may be in complete disagreement. However, experience shows that it is a valid approach to start with a very crude model and then refine it.

EXERCISE 1 – *Estimating Number of Cars*

How many automobiles would you expect to find in our residential area? How many automobiles would you expect to find running at some arbitrary time? You will have to make some assumptions to reach your answer. Be sure and state these assumptions explicitly. Compare your assumptions to those of other students. Do your assumptions stand up well under close examination?

Now that you have estimated the number of cars, we will structure our first model. Let P stand for the number of cubic feet of pollutants at any time, R for the number of cubic feet of pollutants produced per hour by each car, and N for the number of cars operating at any given time. The simplest model we could construct would be

$$P_{new} = P_{old} + (R)(N).$$ \hfill (1)

P_{new} is the amount of pollutants at the end of any hour. P_{old} is the amount at the end of the previous hour.

**COMPUTER ALERTS CONNECTICUT
TO AIR POLLUTION LEVELS**

Connecticut's Department of Environmental Protection (DEP) is counting on a computer and electronic sensors to help fight air pollution. The IBM System/7 in Hartford, automatically records, analyzes and informs DEP of air pollution levels gathered by mobile trailers filled with electronic monitoring equipment. If pollutants rise beyond normal ranges the computer triggers a bell alarm to alert the air compliance director. Stage 2 Alerts are issued when people with heart or respiratory conditions might be affected by the air pollution. (Photo State of Connecticut)

Initially, let's concentrate solely on carbon monoxide pollution. This gas is fairly stable and quite persistent. We will need some concentrations and their effects to use in the exercises. A carbon monoxide concentration of 1000 parts carbon monoxide to one million parts air (abbreviated 1000 ppm) is sufficient to produce unconsciousness in 1 hour and death in 4 hours. The maximum allowable concentration for industrial workers for an eight-hour working day is 50 ppm. Concentrations of from 25 to 50 ppm will be experienced inside an automobile moving in a heavy stream of traffic in a multilane highway or freeway.

EXERCISE 2 – A Simple Model

Write a BASIC program to compute and print out the number of cubic feet of carbon monoxide in our residential area every hour for a 24-hour period. Assume that at the beginning there is no carbon monoxide in the air. Use the number of cars running which you estimated in Exercise 1. The carbon monoxide production rate per car can be obtained from Table 2.

EXERCISE 3 – Computing Concentrations

Modify the program in Exercise 2 to print out the carbon monoxide concentration in ppm (parts per million) at the end of every hour.

EXERCISE 4 – Lethal Concentrations

Using elementary algebra, compute how long it will take to reach the lethal concentration of 1000 ppm in the residential district. Make the same assumptions as for Exercise 2. Taking the fundamental assumptions of our model into account, do you feel there is a carbon monoxide hazard associated with life in a normal residential area?

EXERCISE 5 – A Garage Problem

Use algebra to compute how long it will take for a single automobile, in a closed garage with the engine running at a speed equivalent to 40 mph, to produce a carbon monoxide concentration of 1000 ppm. State clearly any assumptions you make. Is there a hazard here?

EXERCISE 6 – Intersecting Freeways

Suppose that two major freeways cut across our residential district and intersect at the center. Use the model given by (1) and compute the carbon monoxide concentration in ppm. State any assumptions which you must make. Do you feel there is a carbon monoxide hazard in this situation?

EXERCISE 7 – A Tunnel Problem

It is not uncommon to find highway tunnels one mile long carrying two lanes of traffic in each tube. Suppose the ventilation fans went out just as you entered the tunnel. Is there a carbon monoxide hazard? State any assumptions you make.

By now you surely have detected serious flaws in our model. We have been handling only carbon monoxide but, according to Table 2, there are other pollutants present. We have assumed that no air moves in or out of our residential district, but usually there is at least *some* wind, and wind certainly carries away pollutants. Also, we have assumed that once pollutants are created, they are with us forever. However, the pollutants do break down, or are gradually eliminated from the air by mechanisms other than wind.

The next task is to "patch up" the model given by (1) to make it more realistic. First, we will redefine P. Let P stand for the total number of grams of pollutants of *any* kind in the system. To account for wind effects, assume that if W is the wind velocity in miles per hour during any hour-long period, that (W/50)P is the amount of pollutants that is removed during that hour. We will limit wind velocities to the range 0 to 50 mph. As you can see, a velocity of 0 means that no pollutants are removed during the hour, and a velocity of 50 mph implies that all the smog is blown out during the hour. Do you think this is reasonable? If not, you might want to make assumptions of your own. Finally, let's assume that $R_2 P$ of the pollutants disappear during an hour from dissipation mechanisms.

Now we can write down our new model:

$$P_{new} = P_{old} + R_1 N - \frac{W}{50} P_{old} - R_2 P_{old} . \qquad (2)$$

P (either "old" or "new") stands for the total number of grams of pollutants in the system. R_1 is the total amount of pollutants (in grams) produced per hour per car. N is the number of cars operating (remember that we are assuming 40 mph). W is the wind velocity in miles per hour. R_2 is the decimal part of the pollutants that is dissipated each hour from causes other than wind or weather.

If we let C stand for the concentration of pollutants in milligrams (thousandths of a gram) per cubic foot, then C must be given by

$$C = \frac{1000 P_{new}}{V} \qquad (3)$$

where V is the volume of the system in cubic feet. The combination of Equations (2) and (3) gives us our new model and allows us to compute the pollutant concentration in milligrams per cubic foot.

EXERCISE 8 – A New Model

Suppose we examine an intersection of two major freeways. Let's assume that each freeway has four lanes of traffic in each direction. Consider as our "system" a block of air, 2000 feet on a side and 500 feet high, centered on the freeway intersection. Assume that the traffic flow saturates the freeways and remains constant. Assume a wind velocity of 5 mph, and R_2 = .01. Write a BASIC program using Equations (2) and (3) to print out C every hour, assuming that the initial value of P is zero. Run the program until C does not change further. Draw a rough graph of your results.

EXERCISE 9 – Equilibrium Concentration

If C does not change, the system has reached equilibrium. *When this is true, $P_{new} = P_{old} = P_{eq}$. Use some simple algebra in Equations (2) and (3) to predict mathematically the equilibrium value of C. Check your answer against the results of Exercise 8.*

EXERCISE 10 – Turning the Wind Off

Use the program from Exercise 8 to investigate the effects of turning the wind on and off. Your program printouts should show two equilibrium values of concentration, with and without wind! Can you find both of these algebraically?

EXERCISE 11 – *Closing Down Freeways*

> *Use the program from Exercise 8 and any wind velocity you desire. What happens to C if the freeways are shut down at some particular instant? Sketch a rough graph of the program printout.*

We still have serious flaws in our automobile air pollution model. We have been assuming *constant* values of N, W, and R_2. Clearly, this isn't realistic. It is common experience that there are morning and afternoon traffic rush hours, and that very little traffic is on the street in the middle of the night. Also, the wind rarely blows with constant velocity. Finally, the dissipation rate R_2 is certainly not constant. As we discussed previously, photochemical smog is the result of organics, oxides of nitrogen and sunlight. It stands to reason that R_2 should be smaller during hours of sunlight than during hours of darkness.

It will be fairly easy to take these ideas into account and make our model *much* more realistic. The key is to assume *maximum* values of N, W, and R_2, then take hourly decimal parts of the maximum values. Thus we can set up one list of 24 factors to be applied to N, another list for W, and so on. Each of these lists constitutes a time profile of each factor. Now, the model is

$$P_{new} = P_{old} + R_1 X_i N - Y_i W P_{old}/50 - Z_i R_2 P_{old} . \qquad (4)$$

X_i is the traffic profile factor (applied to N), Y_i is the wind profile factor, and Z_i is the dissipation profile factor. The subscript i is the hour number (1 to 24). So we can compare results, let's agree that hour number 1 in any day is from midnight to 1 a.m.

EXERCISE 12 – *A Time Dependent Model*

> *Write a BASIC program to evaluate the model given by (4) applied to the freeway example in Exercise 8. Assume reasonable sets of values for X, Y, and Z. Print out C every hour. Sketch your results in a simple graph.*

EXERCISE 13 – *Political Questions*

> *Use the model developed in Exercise 12 on a system whose characteristics are specified by you. Run the program to get a feel for the pollutant concentrations that come out of the model. Now, suppose that the edict has come down to cut down on pollution. Use your model and program to investigate the question. Make realistic suggestions as to how the pollution concentration from automobiles might be cut down.*

Computer-Based Experiments in Cognitive Psychology

William L. Bewley

Computer Technology Program
Northwest Regional Educational Laboratory
Portland, Oregon 97204

Author is formerly of Dept. of
Psychology at Lawrence University
in Appleton, Wisconsin

EXPERIMENT 1: PATTERN RECOGNITION

This paper describes the first of six computer--based experiments contained in *Cognitive Psychology: A Computer-Oriented Laboratory Manual,* a product of Dartmouth College's project COMPUTe. The six experiments were designed for use in any introductory or advanced undergraduate psychology course either partially or totally concerned with human cognition.

Each experiment is run on a time-sharing system using a terminal as the input/output device. The computer programs which run the experiments require 8K storage and are written in Dartmouth BASIC. Versions which run on DEC'S RSTS system are also available, and the programs are presently being modified to run in HP BASIC.

Each program performs two functions: (1) it runs the student as a subject in an experimental task, e.g., visual search, continuous memory, paired-associate learning, concept learning, a game similar to the Prisoner's Dilemma, and the Missionaries and Cannibals problem; (2) it runs a simulation of an information-processing model on the task, e.g., Pandemonium, the Atkinson and Shiffrin buffer model, Hintzman's discrimination-net model, Levine's focusing model, a modification of Messick's social motives model, and the Newell and Simon General Problem Solver. The student is asked to compare his performance on the task with that of the model and to compare what he thinks he did in the task with what the model says he did. The programs are fairly flexible in that some features of the task and model can be changed by the student so that he can run his own experiments on other students and the model.

Background

According to the Pandemonium model of Selfridge (1959), pattern recognition is a hierarchical process in which information from input patterns is fed through a succession of analyzers or "demons," the output of one demon serving as the input of the next. At the lowest level are image demons which simply form an image or unprocessed copy of the input stimulus. This image is then processed by a set of feature extraction demons which, as their name implies, extract from the image such features as straight lines, curved lines and angles. Cognitive demons then evaluate the extracted features to determine the likelihood that one of the several alternative patterns is the input pattern. These likelihood estimates are then sent to a decision demon which makes the recognition response, deciding that the most likely alternative is the input pattern. There are two strong implications of this model. The first is that there are hierarchical levels of processing in pattern recognition. The second is that the processing at each level is parallel, i.e., all image demons process the input pattern simultaneously, all feature extraction demons process the images simultaneously, and all cognitive demons evaluate the extracted features simultaneously. The purpose of this experiment was to test these two implications.

The Experiment

This experiment is a partial replication of the visual search experiment of Neisser (1963). Each student is shown 20 lists of letters, one list at a time. Each list is composed of 50 lines, 6 letters per line, arranged in 5 rows with 10 lines per row. The student's task is to search each list for a particular target letter, scanning the list from left to right within each row starting with the top row and working down (i.e., the scanning pattern used in reading). A question mark is typed immediately below each list to indicate that the student may begin his search. When he is ready to begin he presses the carriage return button again. The computer then prints the line number at which the target occurred and the student's search time in seconds. The simulation of the Pandemonium model then scans the same list for the same target, and its search time, in arbitrary units, is printed. Following this, the computer types the next list. This procedure is repeated until a search time is obtained for each of the 20 lists.

There are two independent variables: the target to be found and the context in which it is embedded. The five targets are Q, Z, not-Q, not-Z, and Q or Z. If the target is Q, only one of the 50 lines in the list contains a Q. If the target is Z, only one of the 50 lines contains a Z. If the target is not-Q, only one of the 50 lines does not contain a Q. If the target is not-Z, only one of the 50 lines does not contain a Z. If the target is Q or Z, one of the 50 lines contains either a Q or a Z. In every case, the subject is searching for the line containing the target. The context in which the target is embedded is either angular or round. For the angular context, the non-target letters are drawn from the set E, I, M, V, W and X. For the round context, the non-target letters are drawn from the set C, D, G, O, R and U. Since there are five targets and two contexts, there are ten experimental conditions. The 20 lists shown to each subject represent only one experimental condition. That is, the 20 lists have the same target and context. The only difference among the lists presented to each subject is the line at which the target occurs.

The dependent variable is the average time it takes to scan one line. This is calculated by dividing reaction time by the line number at which the target appears.

Predictions

Hierarchical Levels

For a task in which subjects search for a single letter, Neisser (1964) suggests a Pandemonium something like that shown in Figure 1. Only one cognitive demon is present, the cognitive demons for all letters but the target letter being effectively turned off. This implies that the processing of a letter needs to go only as far as the feature extraction level until the target letter is found. If, for example, the search is for a Q, processing of each letter terminates as soon as features not associated with a Q are extracted. The recognition process is completed (i.e., the Q cognitive demon and the decision demon are activated) only when features associated with a Q are extracted. When searching for the absence of a letter (e.g., not-Q), the structure of the Pandemonium is similar to that used in searching for the presence of a letter in that the cognitive demons for all letters but the critical letter (e.g., Q) are turned off. As before, this means that the recognition process is completed only for the critical letter. However, since the critical letter is present in all lines but one, the recognition process must be completed at least once in each line. Since completion of the recognition process (activation of the cognitive and decision demons) requires more time than processing to only the feature extraction level, it should take longer to search for the absence than for the presence of a letter. One prediction derived from the idea of hierarchical levels of processing, then, is that scanning time per line should be greater when the search is for not-Q than for Q, and for not-Z than for Z.

Referring again to Figure 1, it is seen that there are three levels of feature extraction. Level 1 extracts the crudest features, the simple presence or absence of lines, angles and curves. At level 2, the feature extraction is more detailed, producing information regarding the presence or absence of categories of lines (vertical, horizontal and oblique), angles (right and acute), and curves (continuous and discontinuous). Level 3 produces the most detailed information, going beyond the mere presence or absence of the feature categories of level 2 to indicate the number of features in each category. It is assumed that these three levels of feature extraction form a hierarchy, level 1 extraction occurring before level 2, and level 2 extraction occurring before level 3. It is further assumed that the cognitive demon evaluates features in the order of their extraction, level 1 features being evaluated first, then level 2 features, and finally level 3 features. The cognitive demon evaluates the features extracted by level 2 and level 3 only if the features extracted by the preceding level, levels 1 and 2, respectively, indicate that the letter being processed could be the target letter. Since more processing time will be required when more feature extraction levels must be evaluated, and since more feature extraction levels must be evaluated with greater similarity of target-letter and context-letter features, a second prediction derived from the idea of hierarchical levels of processing is that scanning time per line should be greater for a Q-search than for a Z-search in the round context and greater for a Z-search in the angular context.

Parallel Processing

Searching for two target letters, e.g., searching for either a Q or a Z, requires the addition of a cognitive demon to the Pandemonium shown in Figure 1. In general, there will be one cognitive demon for each target letter. Since demons at a particular level of the Pandemonium operate in parallel, however, the addition of a cognitive demon will have no effect on processing time. Accordingly, there should be no difference in scanning time per line in searching for a Q, a Z, or either a Q or a Z. To be more specific, it should take no longer to search for a Q when a Z is also a possible target than to search for a Q as a single target, and vice versa.

USING THE PROGRAM

The program has five running options: (1) to run a subject and the simulation or run the simulation alone; (2) a choice of four targets (Q, Z, Q or Z, or any letter of the alphabet); (3) a goal of detecting the presence of the target in a line or a goal of detecting its absence; (4) a choice of three contexts (round — C, D, G, O, R and U; angular — X, I, M, V, W and X; or any six letters of the alphabet); and (5) to have the Pandemonium search procedure printed or omitted. It is suggested that a student should run himself as a subject in conjunction with the simulation before running his own experiments on other students and the simulation. The choice of target, goal (presence or absence of the target), and context will be determined by the experimental condition under which the program is to be run. For the first run, this should probably be determined for each student by the instructor in order to ensure an approximately equal number of subjects in each experimental condition.

The printout of the Pandemonium search procedure lists the feature extraction levels used in processing each target and context letter. Examining the procedure for each of the experimental conditions should help the student to understand the structure of the Pandemonium and how the experimental effects predicted above are produced by this structure. The search procedure should be printed whenever the student runs a new experimental condition.

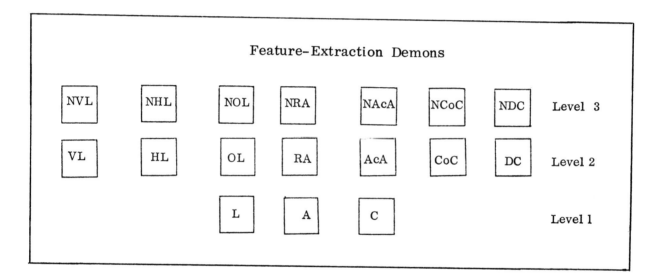

Figure 1. Pandemonium.   (L = lines, A = angles, C = curves, V = vertical,
H = horizontal, O = oblique, R = right, Ac = acute, Co = continuous,
D = discontinuous, N = number.)

```
RUN
SNERCH

TYPE 1 FØR A SIMULATION, 2 TØ TEST A SUBJECT AND SIMULATE?2

TARGET: TYPE 1 FØR Q, 2 FØR Z, 3 FØR Q ØR Z,
ØR 4 IF YØU WISH TØ INPUT YØUR ØWN?1

TYPE 1 IF THE GØAL IS THE PRESENCE ØF TARGET LETTER,
2 IF IT IS THE ABSENCE?1

CØNTEXT: TYPE 1 FØR RØUND, 2 FØR ANGULAR, 3 IF YØU
WISH TØ INPUT YØUR ØWN?1

WØULD YØU LIKE A PRINTØUT ØF THE SEARCH PRØCEDURE?
TYPE 1 FØR YES, 0 FØR NØ?1


PANDEMØNIUM SEES:   'C'
LEVEL 1
ELIMINATES:  D G R U Q
POSSIBILITIES REMAINING:    C O
THE CHARACTER IS CØNTEXT

PANDEMØNIUM SEES:   'D'
LEVEL 1
ELIMINATES:  C Ø U
POSSIBILITIES REMAINING:    D G R Q
LEVEL 2
ELIMINATES:  R
POSSIBILITIES REMAINING:    D G Q
LEVEL 3
ELIMINATES:  G Q
POSSIBILITIES REMAINING:    D
THE CHARACTER IS CØNTEXT

PANDEMØNIUM SEES:   'G'
LEVEL 1
ELIMINATES:  C Ø U
POSSIBILITIES REMAINING:    D G R Q
LEVEL 2
ELIMINATES:  R
POSSIBILITIES REMAINING:    D G Q
LEVEL 3
ELIMINATES:  D Q
POSSIBILITIES REMAINING:    G
THE CHARACTER IS CØNTEXT
```

Pandemonium's processing of the letter 'C'

Feature-extraction level 1 eliminates all letters having lines or angles (the 'C' has only a curve)

Since the target letter, 'Q,' is among those eliminated, Pandemonium can conclude that the letter is context and go on to the next letter

Pandemonium's processing of the letter 'D'

Feature-extraction level 1 eliminates all letters not having lines, angles, and curves (the 'D' has all three). The program treats the 'O' as being without a slash.

Feature-extraction level 2 eliminates all letters having oblique lines, acute angles, and continuous curves (a 'D' has none of these)

Feature-extraction level 3 eliminates all letters not having one vertical line, two horizontal lines, two right angles and one discontinuous curve (the 'D' has all of these)

```
PANDEMØNIUM SEES:   'Ø'
LEVEL 1
ELIMINATES:  D G R U Q
POSSIBILITIES REMAINING:    C O
THE CHARACTER IS CØNTEXT

PANDEMØNIUM SEES:   'R'
LEVEL 1
ELIMINATES:  C Ø U
POSSIBILITIES REMAINING:    D G R Q
LEVEL 2
ELIMINATES:  D G Q
POSSIBILITIES REMAINING:    R
THE CHARACTER IS CØNTEXT

PANDEMØNIUM SEES:   'U'
LEVEL 1
ELIMINATES:  C D G Ø R Q
POSSIBILITIES REMAINING:    U
THE CHARACTER IS CØNTEXT

PANDEMØNIUM SEES:   'Q'
LEVEL 1
ELIMINATES:  C Ø U
POSSIBILITIES REMAINING:    D G R Q
LEVEL 2
ELIMINATES:  R
POSSIBILITIES REMAINING:    D G Q
LEVEL 3
ELIMINATES:  D G
POSSIBILITIES REMAINING:    Q
THE CHARACTER IS A TARGET


PRØBLEM 1

ØRCGDU RGCØUD UDRCGø CRØGUD CØRUDG ØGCRUD RØUGDC CØRGUD CDRGØU
UØCDGR DGCRUø ØDUCRG DCUØGR URDCGø GDCØRU RØDCGU ØURCDG RGøUDC
DGøGRC CRDUøG UDGCRø øDUCRG CøGURD DRUCGø RCøDUG øGUCDR DØRUCG
CRØUGD ØRCUDG DUGRCø GUDCøR GUøDCR CRØUGD ØRUCGD DØCGUR RCGøUD

?
?

LINE 45     SUBJECT TIME 30        ——→ in seconds

LINE 45     SIMULATED TIME 4960    ——→ arbitrary time units
```

And so on for 19 more problems.

231

```
0 REM NEISSER'S VISUAL SEARCH AND PANDEMONIUM
2
4 RANDOMIZE
6
8 REM DS CONTAINS THE LETTERS A-Z
10 DIM D$(26)
12 REM B HOLDS 3 FEATURE-EXTRACTION LEVELS FOR 26 LETTERS
14 DIM B(26,3)
16 REM FOR EACH OF 20 TRIALS, 0 TELLS WHICH OF THE 50 SETS
18 REM OF SIX CHARACTERS HOLDS THE ANOMALY
22 DIM L$(5),L(5),R(5)
24 REM AS AND RS HOLD THE ANGULAR AND THE ROUND CONTEXT LETTERS
26 DIM A$(6),R$(6)
28 REM CS AND C HOLD THE CONTEXT CHARACTERS ACTUALLY USED
30 DIM C$(6),C(6)
32 REM ES AND E HOLD A SET OF SIX LETTERS TO BE PRINTED
34 DIM E$(6),E(6)
36 DIM T$(11),T(11),U(11)
38 REM V(I) IS THE NUMBER OF LEVELS TAKEN TO RECOGNIZE THE I'TH LETTER
40 DIM V(26)
42
44 REM FOR THE L, C, AND E ARRAYS, THE STRING ARRAY HOLDS THE
46 REM ACTUAL LETTER, WHILE THE NUMERIC ARRAY HOLDS ITS
48 REM POSITION IN THE ALPHABET
50
60 REM FNT FINDS THE TIME OF DAY IN SECONDS. NOTE, THIS
62 REM FUNCTION WILL PROBABLY VARY FROM COMPUTER TO COMPUTER.
64 REM IN MANY VERSIONS OF BASIC, IT MAY BE DEFINED AS:
66 REM          DEF FNT=TIME(0)
68 DEF FNA(X)=INT(X*RND+1)
70 DEF FNT
72 LET C$=CLK$
74 LET FNT=3600*VAL(SEG$(C$,1,2))
76 LET FNT=FNT+60*VAL(SEG$(C$,4,5))+VAL(SEG$(C$,7,8))
78 FNEND
80
82
100 FOR M=1 TO 26
110 READ D$(M)
120 NEXT M
130 FOR M=1 TO 26
140 FOR M1=1 TO 3
150 READ B(M,M1)
160 NEXT M1
170 NEXT M
180 FOR M=1 TO 6
190 READ A$(M)
200 NEXT M
210 FOR M=1 TO 6
220 READ R$(M)
230 NEXT M
240 PRINT "TYPE 1 FOR A SIMULATION, 2 TO TEST A SUBJECT AND SIMULATE";
250 INPUT Z4
260 IF Z4=1 THEN 340
270 LET Z4=0
280
290 REM WHEN THE FOLLOWING ROUTINE IS FINISHED, T9 WILL CONTAIN
300 REM THE NUMBER OF TARGET LETTERS, THE LS ARRAY WILL CONTAIN THE
310 REM LETTERS, AND THE L ARRAY WILL CONTAIN THE LETTERS'
320 REM ALPHABET POSITIONS
330
340 PRINT
350 PRINT "TARGET:  TYPE 1 FOR Q, 2 FOR Z, 3 FOR Q OR Z,"
360 PRINT "OR 4 IF YOU WISH TO INPUT YOUR OWN";
370 INPUT T
380 IF T>4 THEN 350
390 ON T GOTO 550,590,630,400
400 PRINT
410 PRINT "HOW MANY DIFFERENT TARGET LETTERS";
420 INPUT T9
430 PRINT "TYPE THEM ONE TO A LINE"
440 FOR T1=1 TO T9
450 INPUT L$(T1)
460 FOR R=1 TO 26
470 IF D$(R)=L$(T1) THEN 520
480 NEXT R
490 PRINT "SORRY, '";L$(T1);"' IS NOT A LETTER."
500 PRINT "PLEASE TYPE IT OVER";
510 GOTO 450
520 LET L(T1)=R
530 NEXT T1
540 GOTO 700
550 LET T9=1
560 LET L$(T9)="Q"
570 LET L(T9)=17
580 GOTO 700
590 LET T9=1
600 LET L$(T9)="Z"
610 LET L(T9)=26
620 GOTO 700
630 LET T9=2
640 LET L$(1)="Q"
650 LET L(1)=17
660 LET L$(2)="Z"
670 LET L(2)=26
680
690
700 PRINT
710 PRINT "TYPE 1 IF THE GOAL IS THE PRESENCE OF TARGET LETTER,"
720 PRINT "2 IF IT IS THE ABSENCE";
730 INPUT T7
740 IF T7<>2 THE 790
750 PRINT
760 PRINT "TYPE 1 IF PANDEMONIUM IS TO STOP SCANNING A LINE UPON"
770 PRINT "REACHING A TARGET, 2 IF IT SHOULD SCAN THE ENTIRE LINE"
780 INPUT Z6
790 PRINT

800 PRINT "CONTEXT:  TYPE 1 FOR ROUND, 2 FOR ANGULAR, 3 IF YOU"
810 PRINT "WISH TO INPUT YOUR OWN";
820 INPUT C
830 IF C>3 THEN 800
840 ON C GOTO 850,890,930
850 FOR M=1 TO 6
860 LET C$(M)=R$(M)
870 NEXT M
880 GOTO 950
890 FOR M=1 TO 6
900 LET C$(M)=A$(M)
910 NEXT M
920 GOTO 950
930 PRINT "TYPE THE SIX LETTERS, SEPARATED BY COMMAS";
940 INPUT C$(1),C$(2),C$(3),C$(4),C$(5),C$(6)
950 FOR M=1 TO 6
960 FOR M1=1 TO 26
970 IF C$(M)=D$(M1) THEN 1010
980 NEXT M1
990 PRINT "SORRY, '";C$(M);"' IS NOT A LETTER."
1000 GOTO 930
1010 LET C(M)=M1
1020 NEXT M
1030
1040 REM SET UP THE T ARRAY TO CONTAIN THE CONTEXT
1050 REM LETTERS AND THE TARGET LETTERS
1060
1070 FOR M=1 TO 6
1080 LET T(M)=C(M)
1090 LET T$(M)=C$(M)
1100 NEXT M
1110 REM T1 IS THE LENGTH OF THE T ARRAY
1120 LET T1=6+T9
1130 FOR M=7 TO T1
1140 LET T$(M)=L$(M-6)
1150 LET T(M)=L(M-6)
1160 NEXT M
1170 PRINT
1180 PRINT "WOULD YOU LIKE A PRINTOUT OF THE SEARCH PROCEDURE?"
1190 PRINT "TYPE 1 FOR YES, 0 FOR NO";
1200 INPUT Z
1210 IF Z=0 THEN 1240
1220 PRINT
1230 PRINT
1240 FOR M=1 TO T1
1250 IF Z=0 THEN 1290
1260 PRINT
1270 PRINT
1280 PRINT "PANDEMONIUM SEES:  '";T$(M);"'"
1290 FOR I=1 TO T1
1300 LET U(I)=0
1310 NEXT I
1320 FOR M1=1 TO 3
1330 IF Z=0 THEN 1360
1340 PRINT "LEVEL";M1
1350 PRINT "ELIMINATES: ";
1360 LET B=B(T(M),M1)
1370 REM B IS LEVEL M1 FOR THE LETTER T$(M)
1380 REM NOW FIND WHICH OF THE T1 LETTERS THIS LEVEL ELIMINATES
1390 FOR M2=1 TO T1
1400 IF U(M2)=1 THEN 1450
1410 IF B(T(M2),M1)=B THEN 1450
1420 IF Z=0 THEN 1440
1430 PRINT " ";T$(M2);
1440 LET U(M2)=1
1450 NEXT M2
1460
1470 LET P1=P2=0
1480 IF Z=0 THEN 1510
1490 PRINT
1500 PRINT "POSSIBILITIES REMAINING: ";
1510 FOR M2=1 TO T1
1520 IF U(M2)=1 THEN 1610
1530 IF Z=0 THEN 1550
1540 PRINT " ";T$(M2);
1550 IF M2<=6 THEN 1590
1560 LET P2=1
1570 REM THE LETTER MIGHT STILL BE A TARGET
1580 GOTO 1610
1590 LET P1=1
1600 REM THE LETTER MIGHT STILL BE CONTEXT
1610 NEXT M2
1620 IF Z=0 THEN 1640
1630 PRINT
1640 IF P1+P2=2 THEN 1710
1650 IF Z=0 THEN 1720
1660 IF P2=1 THEN 1690
1670 PRINT "THE CHARACTER IS CONTEXT"
1680 GOTO 1720
1690 PRINT "THE CHARACTER IS A TARGET"
1700 GOTO 1720
1710 NEXT M1
1720 LET V(T(M))=M1
1730 NEXT M
1740
1750
1760 FOR M=1 TO 20
1770 IF M>6 THEN 1800
1780 LET A=FNA(6)
1790 GOTO 1810
1800 LET A=6+FNA(14)
1810 IF O(A)<>0 THEN 1770
1820 READ O(A)
1830 NEXT M
1840 FOR I=1 TO 20
1850 PRINT
1860 PRINT
1870 PRINT
1880 PRINT "PROBLEM";I
1890 PRINT
```

```
1900 PRINT
1910 LET V=0
1920 FOR J=1 TO 50
1930 FOR M=1 TO 6
1940 LET E(M)=0
1950 NEXT M
1960
1970 REM PUT THE CONTEXT LETTERS IN RANDOM ORDER IN THE E ARRAYS
1980 FOR M=1 TO 6
1990 LET A=FNA(6)
2000 IF E(A)<>0 THEN 1990
2010 LET E(A)=C(M)
2020 LET ES(A)=CS(M)
2030 NEXT M
2040 REM IN CASE THERE IS NO TARGET LETTER IN THIS SET OF SIX,
2050 REM PANDEMONIUM MUST CHECK ALL SIX.
2060 LET A=6
2070
2080 REM NOW STICK IN A TARGET IF APPROPRIATE
2090 IF T7=1 THEN 2120
2100 IF O(I)=J THEN 2170
2110 GOTO 2130
2120 IF O(I)<>J THEN 2170
2130 LET A=FNA(6)
2140 LET A1=FNA(T9)
2150 LET ES(A)=LS(A1)
2160 LET E(A)=L(A1)
2170 IF Z4=1 THEN 2240
2180 FOR M=1 TO 6
2190 PRINT ES(M);
2200 NEXT M
2210 PRINT " ";
2220 IF J/10 <> INT(J/10) THEN 2240
2230 PRINT
2240 IF J>O(I) THEN 2330
2250 IF Z6<>2 THEN 2300
2260 LET A=6
2270
2280 REM ADD ON THE TIMES FOR ALL THE LETTERS UP TO AND
2290 REM INCLUDING THE TARGET LETTER
2300 FOR M=1 TO A
2310 LET V=V+V(E(M))
2320 NEXT M
2330 NEXT J
2340 IF Z4=1 THEN 2430
2350 PRINT
2360 REM NOW TYPE A QUESTION MARK AND WAIT FOR THE USER TO PUSH 'RETURN'
2370 INPUT Z9S
2380 LET T0=FNT
2390 INPUT Z9S
2400 LET T0=FNT-T0
2410 PRINT
2420 PRINT "LINE"JO(I)J"SUBJECT TIME"JT0
2430 PRINT
2440 PRINT "LINE"JO(I)J"SIMULATED TIME"JV*10
2450 NEXT I
2460
2470 DATA "A","B","C","D","E","F","G","H","I","J","K","L","M","N","O"
2480 DATA "P","Q","R","S","T","U","V","W","X","Y","Z"
2490
2500 DATA 3,23,136,    7,35,220,    4,18,53,    7,35,135
2510 DATA 3,17,132,    3,17,102,    7,35,105,    3,17,117
2520 DATA 3,17,122,    5,21,61,    3,29,134,    3,17,52
2530 DATA 3,21,136,    3,21,96,    4,16,46,    7,35,155
2540 DATA 7,35,130,    7,41,176,    4,18,88,    3,17,72
2550 DATA 5,21,66,    3,19,74,    3,19,154,    3,19,99
2560 DATA 3,21,51,    3,23,108
2570
2580 DATA "E","I","M","V","W","X"
2590 DATA "C","D","G","O","R","U"
2600 DATA 5,6,25,30,45,46,9,11,14,16,19,21,24,26,29,31,34,36,39,41
2610
2620 END
```

REFERENCES

Neisser, U. "Decision-Time without reaction-time: Experiments in visual scanning." *American Journal of Psychology*, 1963, 76, 376-385.

Neisser, U. "Visual search." *Scientific American*, 1964, 210, 94-102.

Selfridge, O. "Pandemonium: A paradigm for learning." *Symposium on the Mechanization of Thought Processes*. London: HM Stationery Office, 1959.

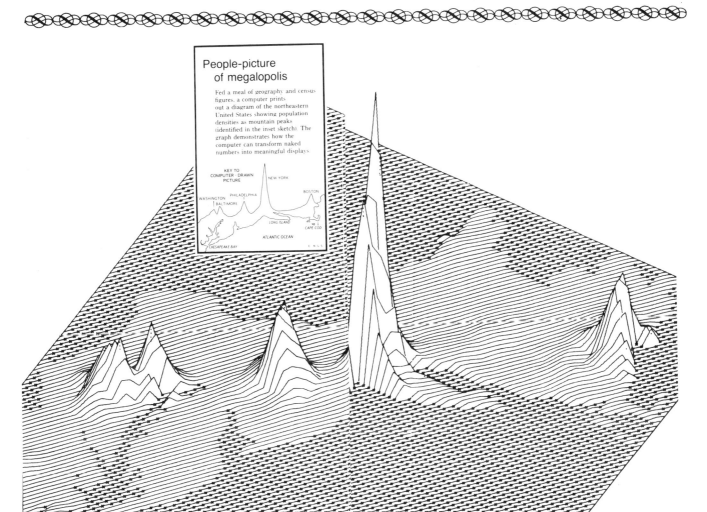

People-picture of megalopolis

Fed a meal of geography and census figures, a computer prints out a diagram of the northeastern United States showing population densities as mountain peaks (identified in the inset sketch). The graph demonstrates how the computer can transform naked numbers into meaningful displays.

KEY TO COMPUTER-DRAWN PICTURE

NEW YORK, BOSTON, PHILADELPHIA, WASHINGTON, BALTIMORE, LONG ISLAND, CAPE COD, ATLANTIC OCEAN, CHESAPEAKE BAY

The JOURNALISM Programs: Help for the Weary Writer

by Robert L. Bishop

("Help for the Weary Writer" was adapted by Diann Bradarich from a lengthier description of JCAI available from the Center for Research on Learning and Teaching, 109 East Madison, Ann Arbor, Michigan 48104.)

In 1955 the reading public was scandalized by Rudolph Flesch's popular book, "Why Johnny Can't Read." Many a disgruntled teacher will add that Johnny can't write either. At every level of education, the complaint is universal: students cannot communicate effectively through the written word. Students themselves can offer testimony enough to the abhorrence with which they attack the inevitable term paper. The literature detailing the reasons is extensive, but the question of fault is really irrelevant. Rather, the emphasis must be on developing alternative methods of building composition skills.

The Department of Journalism at the University of Michigan has made significant progress in alleviating the painful process of learning to write well. A tireless teaching aid has been discovered — the computer. Computer programs edit text by standard readability formulas, check for stylistic characteristics such as clarity and cliches, and examine conformity to style rules such as punctuation and correct spelling. The easy analysis of both style and content of the natural language text partially fulfills instructional requirements for technical and business-report writing, English composition courses, foreign language instruction, and journalism exercises. Sample stories and critiques are included as an appendix to this article.

The Structure of JOURNALISM

JOURNALISM is composed of four general categories of computer programs; specific exercises, a general stylistic analysis program, a spelling check, and a housekeeping routine which continually stores measures of performance.

Specific exercises. A general program called JCAI (Journalism Computer Assisted Instruction) allows a teacher to introduce an entirely new exercise into the system easily; previous experience with programming is unnecessary. The instructor merely indicates key words he wants to check and accompanying comments dependent on the order, presence or absence of the words. Sampe Story *B* is an example of an exercise written and programmed in six hours by Dr. Nadean Bishop who had no previous experience with computers.

Stylistic Analysis. JOURNALISM'S second routine is a general stylistic analysis. In addition to clarity, readability and the mechanics of style, the routine analyzes variety in sentence length and structure, and the overuse of articles, passive verbs, adjectives or adverbs. Since the program is not dependent on content, any bit of prose can be analyzed. Thus, the teacher is freed from the limitation of "canned" assignments. Thy program may be run separately or in conjunction with JCAI.

Spelling. The third routine, a spelling check, compares each word in a given article to a dictionary of some 17,000 entries andprints out each word for which it does not find an entry. The dictionary may be supplemented with a list of specific words for a given exercise — proper names and technical terms, for example.

Housekeeping Aid. JOURNALISM'S fourth routine is a clerical or housekeeping aid which automatically stores all the statistics generated by the JCAI program, the stylistic analysis, and the spelling check. It also records types of errors such as failure to use reference sources, errors in news judgment, or potentially libelous comments. Each student then has an up-to-date record of progress in avoiding spelling errors, eliminating mechanical problems, reducing sentence length (or increasing sentence length, if desirable), and increasing sentence variety.

JOURNALISM in the Classroom

JOURNALISM has been used since 1969 in the beginning news writing course in the Department of Journalism at the University of Michigan. Four elements constitute the core of the course: a programmed instruction book, video tapes and discussions about writing, computerized

writing exercises, and at least three individual conferences with each student. The programmed book is a self-instructional guide to basic news writing, news values, condensation, speech reporting, copy editing, and descriptive writing; it replaces most of the usual lectures. The Department of Journalism offers seven video tapes for use at the instructor's option. These include four short tapes on writing intended to stimulate class discussion and three on specialized subjects: interviewing, reporting public opinion polls, and laws of libel.

Computerized exercises range from simple rewrite assignments to genuine challenges such as reporting a national study of public schools or handling a revenue-sharing proposal made by Nelson Rockefeller. The raw material for the story may be gathered from a film, a tape or the programmed text which furnishes simulated news releases. The idea of diversified sources hinges, of course, on the assumption that using realistic sources of information is valuable practice for the student.

When the student has written a story, it is fed into the computer by one of two methods: (a) batch, running a deck of computer cards punched with the story through a card reader, or (b) interactive, by typing the story into a computer terminal.

The JOURNALISM program first analyzes the story by scanning for key words or phrases. In this way, an article with an undesirable slant can be corrected by altering a few heavily connotative words. The same routine can be used for checking accuracy, and in some cases libel. All exercises have a check on key names, titles, and addresses.

In the second stage of stylistic analysis, the system checks sentence and paragraph length, the percentage of sentences containing verbs of being or passive verbs, the percentage of descriptive adverbs, indirect or wordy sentences, and points of newspaper-style rules. The computer advises the student which sentences need to be revised, and how many of them must be changed in order to erase the negative comment. The computer analysis of sample story *B* prints out the sentence which seems to have the most unnecessary words (that, those, these, of, because, etc.), blanking out the barred words so that the student can judge which ones are really unnecessary.

The computer retypes the story, numbers each sentence, and prints out a series of comments and queries specific to the student's work. Since there are infinite possibilities for expressing any idea, the student treats the critique as suggestions rather than as commands; the article remains ungraded.

At this point, the student decides which comments to use and rewrites the story to do the best of his ability. The new version is compared to sample stories written by other students.

Throughout the semester the student has a series of conferences with the instructor in which they can discuss the finer points of journalistic writing and any disagreements with the writing style suggested by the JOURNALISM programs.

Evaluation of JOURNALISM

The most important advantage of the JOURNALISM programs is that they give the student fast, tireless, and accurate responses, far more responses to a paper than any teacher has time to write. Most stories are checked for 15 different factual points in addition to general comments on sentence and paragraph length, conformity to the stylebook, and readability. Obviously, the student receives far more guidance on each story than an overworked instructor can offer.

JOURNALISM results in a substantial saving of time for both student and teacher. Because of the computer exercises and the programmed workbook, students spend less than three hours in class per week (for a course with four hours of credit). Teachers must correct only 33 to 50 percent of the papers in a normal load and can use the extra time for clinical sessions with individual students.

The results have been more than satisfactory. University of Michigan journalism classes now cover in 14 weeks what used to take 20 or 25 weeks. Students are well into feature writing in their first semester, rather than approaching this level halfway through the second writing course. And they express more satisfaction with the course than with conventional courses, both in terms of regular evaluation forms and in the percentage of those electing the second course. Despite some fears that students would strongly resist the computer, data from student opinion forms show that students would elect both JCAI and conventional sections if given the choice with slightly more elections for JCAI sections.

As one might expect, student satisfaction directly correlates with student performance. JCAI students score significantly better in the CAI course and in the following writing course than do students from conventional courses. Preliminary results of a study conducted during the 1973-74 academic year support this existing data. Students from JCAI sections who elected the second course received an average of a half a grade higher on a complex assignment reviewed by outside judges than did their non-JCAI counterparts.

Though many are skeptical about the threat of "mechanized teaching" destroying individuality in writing style, the success of JCAI clearly dispels such fears. The very structure of the programs is designed to provide more individual attention; the student works on an individual basis with the computer which, in turn, relieves the instructor of some of the drudgery of paper grading and frees him for work with students on individuality and creativity.

Sample Runs of JOURNALISM Programs

1 THE DESTROYERS USS AMMAN AND USS COLLETT COLLIDED THIS MORNING
2 THREE MILES OFF THE CALIFORNIA COAST AT NEWPORT BEACH. ELEVEN MEN
   WERE REPORTED KILLED WITH AT LEAST SIX OTHERS INJURED.
3 THE COLLISION OCCURED IN A FOG THAT LIMITED VISIBILITY TO LESS
4 THAN A QUARTER OF A MILE. THE FOG HAS ALSO HAMPERED RESCUE EFFORTS
   BY HELICOPTERS.
5 A SEAMAN OF THE AMMAN CLAIMED, "THE COLLETT HIT US AMIDSHIPS
   AND RIPPED THE SIDE OPEN, JUST LIKE IT HAD BEEN DONE WITH A GIANT
6 CAN OPENER. I WAS BELOW IN THE ENGINE ROOM AND THERE WAS NO
7 WARNING. THE WATER CAME POURING IN."
8 ONE NAVY SOURCE IN LOS ANGELES SAID THAT THE AMMAN'S REAR
   ENGINE ROOM WAS FLOODED WITH WATER POURING IN THROUGH A HOLE ON THE
9 PORT SIDE. THE BOW OF THE COLLETT IS REPORTED TO BE DAMAGED.
10 EFFORTS ARE BEING MADE TO TOW THE HEAVILY LISTING AMMAN TO
11 LONG BEACH. A FIRE THAT BROKE OUT AFTER THE COLLISION WAS QUICKLY
    BROUGHT UNDER CONTROL.
12 SMALL CRAFT FROM NEWPORT BEACH SPED TO THE SCENE AND BROUGHT
    INJURED AND DEAD ASHORE.
13 THE AMMAN WAS HEADED FOR SAN DIEGO AND DEACTIVATION WHEN IT
    WAS STRUCK.
14 THE COLLETT WAS CONDUCTING SEA TRIALS AFTER AN OVERHAUL AT
    THE LONG BEACH SHIP YARD.
15,16 THE INJURED HAVE BEEN TAKEN TO HOAGUE MEMORIAL HOSPITAL. THEIR
    IDENTITIES AND THOSE OF THE DEAD ARE BEING WITHHELD.

COMPUTER ANALYSIS OF SAMPLE STORY <u>A</u>

IDENTIFY THE DESTROYERS BY BASE AND FLOTILLA NUMBER AND REPORT ANY DAMAGES EARLY IN THE STORY UNLESS YOU HAVE VERY GOOD REASONS FOR NOT DOING SO.

FINE. I SEE THAT YOU HAVE MENTIONED WHAT THE DESTROYERS WERE DOING BEFORE THE COLLISION.

I DO NOT FIND WILLIAM WILBERS' NAME. DID YOU LEAVE IT OUT OR MISSPELL IT? USE AS FULL AN IDENTIFIER AS IS AVAILABLE.

GOOD. YOU HAVE MENTIONED THE HOSPITAL WHERE THE INJURED WERE TAKEN. THIS IS AN IMPORTANT DETAIL FOR READERS WITH RELATIVES WHO MAY HAVE BEEN INJURED IN THE COLLISION.

WHY DID YOU OMIT THE SIZE OF THE SHIPS AND THE NUMBER OF CREWMEN? THESE DETAILS, AFTER THE OTHER FACTS ARE GIVEN, INDICATE SOMETHING ABOUT THE MAGNITUDE OF THE ACCIDENT AND DAMAGES.

YOU MAKE YOUR WRITING MORE DIFFICULT BY USING TOO MANY PASSIVE VERBS. TRY CHANGING THESE TO ACTIVE VOICE, PRESENT TENSE. CHANGE 4 OR MORE TO ACTIVE VOICE.
CHECK SENTENCES 2, 8, 9, 10, 11, 13, 15

YOU MAY NEED TO VARY THE LENGTH AND STRUCTURE OF YOUR SENTENCES MORE.
FOR EXAMPLE, SEE SENTENCES
     10 - 11 - 12
     12 - 13 - 14

SENTENCES CONTAINING VERBS OF BEING, 20.0%
SENTENCES CONTAINING PASSIVE VERBS, 46.7%
DESCRIPTIVE ADVERBS IN TOTAL WORDS, 0.9%
INDIRECT OR WORDY SENTENCES, 7.7%
SENTENCE SIMILARITY MEASURE, 13.3%

YOUR AVERAGE SENTENCE LENGTH IS 14.1 WORDS.

SOME OF YOUR SENTENCES APPROACH THE MAXIMUM DESIRED LENGTH. CHECK THEM TO SEE IF THEY CAN BE CONDENSED. IF THEY CANNOT, YOU MAY WISH TO BREAK THEM INTO TWO SENTENCES.
CHECK SENTENCES 5, 8

THIS CONCLUDES THE ANALYSIS OF YOUR STORY. THE COMPUTER MAY HAVE MISSED SOME IMPORTANT ELEMENTS, OR MAY NOT HAVE RECOGNIZED SOME OF THE KEY PHRASES WHICH YOU USED. CORRECT THE STORY ACCORDING TO THE COMMENTS AND YOUR OWN BEST JUDGEMENT, AND THEN COMPARE YOUR VERSION WITH THE MIMEOGRAPHED STORIES DONE BY OTHER STUDENTS.

SAMPLE STORY <u>B</u> ENTERED INTO THE COMPUTER

(from an English Composition Class)

1 ONE OF THE LEAST PROTESTED ORDEALS THAT THE AMERICAN PUBLIC
   HAS BEEN SUBJECTED TO HAS BEEN THE PROCEDURE OF FUNERAL ARRANGEMENTS
2 AND BURIAL. THE REASONS FOR THE LACK OF VOLATILE CRITICISM ARE MANY,
   THUS GIVING THE COALITION OF FUNERAL DIRECTORS IN AMERICA THE UPPER
   HAND IN DEALING WITH THESE MATTERS.
3 FUNERAL PREPARATIONS CAN BE AN ORDEAL AND TO THE MAJORITY OF
4 THE PUBLIC IT IS DEFINITELY ONE. ALTHOUGH THE AMERICAN PUBLIC MAY FEEL
   THAT THEIR CUSTOMS AND TRADITIONS CONCERNING THE BURIAL OF THEIR LOVED
   ONES TO BE THEIRS ALONE, THEY WOULD BE SURPRISED TO FIND THAT THESE
   CUSTOMS AND TRADITIONS HAVE BEEN DICTATED BY FUNERAL DIRECTORS FOR
5 THEIR COMMERICAL BENEFIT. SELDOM IS THE INDIVIDUAL'S IDEA OF THE
6 PERFECT BURIAL HIS OWN. FOR YEARS FUNERAL DIRECTORS HAVE CAPITALIZED
7 ON THE UNPREPAREDNESS OF THE BEREAVED. UNLESS HAVING PREVIOUSLY
   EXPERIENCED A DEATH IN THE FAMILY, THE AVERAGE CITIZEN IS TOTALLY
8 IGNORANT OF THE HIGH COST INVOLVED IN A FUNERAL. JESSICA MITFORD IN
   HER BOOK, "FROM THE AMERICAN WAY OF DEATH", QUOTES THE AVERAGE UNDER-

9 TAKER'S BILL AS IN THE NEIGHBORHOOD OF $1,450. SHE GOES ON TO SAY
   THE AVERAGE CITIZEN IS FORCED TO MAKE A QUICK DECISION ALTHOUGH HE
   IS TOTALLY UNPREPARED FOR SUCH, AND RELIES ON THE ADVICE OF THE WORST
10 PERSON POSSIBLE--THE FUNERAL DIRECTOR. UNDER A BARRAGE OF APPEALS
    TO "AMERICAN TRADITION", KEEPING UP WITH THE JONESES, AND SENTIMENTAL
    AFFECTION FOR THE LOVED ONE, THE UNFORTUNATE CONSUMER CONSENTS TO
    A SERVICE FAR EXCEEDING HIS WANTS OR NEEDS, BOTH PRACTICALLY AND
    FINANCIALLY.
11 HOW HAS THE BOOMING BUSINESS REMAINED ABOVE PUBLIC CRITICISM?
12 LORD ESSEX SAYS THAT THE AVERAGE UNPROTECTED CITIZEN HAS NEITHER
    THE MORAL COURAGE TO SPEAK AGAINST OR ACT IN DEFIANCE OF THESE
13 PSUEDO AMERICAN CUSTOMS AND TRADITIONS. ALSO, THESE PEOPLE ARE
    CONFRONTED WITH THIS ORDEAL USUALLY JUST ONCE, AND ARE UNWILLING TO
    MOUNT AN OFFENSIVE AGAINST SUCH A DISTANT PROBLEM.
14 TO COMBAT THIS GROWING INJUSTICE IN AMERICA THE PUBLIC SHOULD
15 BECOME AWARE OF THE SITUATION. EACH PERSON SHOULD DECIDE WITH HIS
    FAMILY THE PROCEDURE THEY WILL TAKE SO THAT WHEN THE TIME COMES THEY
    CAN BETTER COPE WITH PROBLEMS OF BURIAL.

COMPUTER ANALYSIS OF SAMPLE STORY <u>B</u>

THIS WAS A DIFFICULT ASSIGNMENT. YOU WERE ASKED TO GIVE A COMPRESSION OF THE EVIDENCE IN JESSICA MITFORD'S BOOK THE AMERICAN WAY OF DEATH AS PART OF A PERSUASIVE EDITORIAL TO CONVINCE YOUR READERS THAT FUNERAL PRACTICES SHOULD BE CHANGED. THE COMPUTER HAS BEEN PROGRAMMED TO CATCH ERRORS AND OMISSIONS AND SUGGEST WAYS YOU CAN REVISE YOUR EDITORIAL; USE THE COMMENTS YOU FIND USEFUL.

IT WAS GOOD THAT YOU REFUTED THE TENET THAT ELABORATE FUNERALS ARE IN THE "AMERICAN TRADITION."

THE CASE OF MR. AUGUST CRELINI WAS USED BY JESSICA MITFORD TO PROVIDE HUMAN INTEREST AND BUILD PERSONALIZED OUTRAGE AT THE LIES AND OTHER DECEPTIONS USED TO BILK BEREAVED RELATIVES. IF YOU DID NOT REFER TO THIS CASE STUDY, DID YOU PROVIDE SOME OTHER EVIDENCE TO ACHIEVE THIS SAME RESULT?

YOU WERE ASKED TO AROUSE PUBLIC SENTIMENT FOR REFORM. IF YOU DID NOT MENTION "FUNERAL SOCIETIES" OR "MEMORIAL ASSOCIATIONS" WHICH ARRANGE FOR PRE-PLANNED "DIGNIFIED FUNERALS AT REASONABLE COST," DID YOU RECOMMEND SOME OTHER SOLUTIONS TO THE PROBLEM?

BOOK TITLES ARE ALWAYS UNDERSCORED, SO THE REFERENCE TO MISS MITFORD'S BOOK SHOULD BE TO THE AMERICAN WAY OF DEATH, UNDERSCORED. OUR TEXT GAVE THE EXCERPT FROM THE CHAPTER HEADING "FROM THE AMERICAN WAY OF DEATH," BUT YOUR CITATION SHOULD BE TO THE BOOK ITSELF.

CURRENT TYPOGRAPHY REQUIRES THAT PERIODS AND COMMAS ALWAYS COME WITHIN THE CLOSING QUOTATION MARKS.

THE CLICHE "KEEPING UP WITH THE JONESES" USES THE PLURAL FORM OF THE NAME JONES.

EDITORIALS USUALLY ARE GIVEN TITLES, SO IF YOU DIDN'T HAVE TIME TO THINK OF ONE TRY TO DESIGN SOME SHORT AND EYE-CATCHING TITLE FOR THE REVISED ESSAY.

REPLACE SOME OF YOUR "TO BE" VERBS FORMS, "IS," "WAS," "AM," "ARE," "BEEN," ETC., WITH VERBS SHOWING MORE ACTION.
REPLACE 1 OR MORE WITH ACTIVE VERBS.
CHECK SENTENCES 1, 3, 4, 7

YOU USE A FEW TOO MANY PASSIVE VERBS.
CHANGE 3 OR MORE TO ACTIVE VOICE.
CHECK SENTENCES 1, 4, 9, 13

YOU MAY BE USING TOO MANY ADVERBS AND ADJECTIVES INSTEAD OF FINDING THE VERB OR NOUN WHICH SAYS EXACTLY WHAT YOU MEAN. EXAMINE YOUR STORY TO SEE IF ADVERBIAL OR ADJECTIVAL PHRASES CAN BE ELIMINATED.

WORDS LIKE "CAUSE," "OF," "THERE," "WHICH," "THAT," "THESE" AND "THOSE" OFTEN INDICATE WORDY, INDIRECT SENTENCES. ELIMINATE 4 OR MORE OF THEM IN YOUR STORY. SEE IF YOU CAN IMPROVE THE SENTENCE:
     ALTHOUGH THE AMERICAN PUBLIC MAY FEEL   THEIR
     CUSTOMS AND TRADITIONS CONCERNING THE BURIAL
     THEIR LOVED ONES TO BE THEIRS ALONE, THEY WOULD BE
     SURPRISED TO FIND   CUSTOMS AND TRADITIONS
     HAVE BEEN DICTATED BY FUNERAL DIRECTORS FOR THEIR
     COMMERCIAL BENEFIT.

NEWSPAPER STYLE GENERALLY ELIMINATES THE COMMA BEFORE "AND" AND "OR," ESPECIALLY IF CONNECTING ITEMS IN A SERIES.
CHECK SENTENCES 9, 10, 13

SENTENCES CONTAINING VERBS OF BEING, 33.3%
SENTENCES CONTAINING PASSIVE VERBS, 40.0%
DESCRIPTIVE ADVERBS IN TOTAL WORDS, 1.7%
INDIRECT OR WORDY SENTENCES, 38.5%
SENTENCE SIMILARITY MEASURE, 0.0%

YOUR AVERAGE SENTENCE LENGTH IS 23.4 WORDS.

SOME OF YOUR SENTENCES APPROACH THE MAXIMUM DESIRED LENGTH. CHECK THEM TO SEE IF THEY CAN BE CONDENSED. IF THEY CANNOT, YOU MAY WISH TO BREAK THEM INTO TWO SENTENCES.
CHECK SENTENCES 4, 9, 10

SOME OF YOUR PARAGRAPHS ARE DEFINITELY TOO LONG. BREAK THEM INTO TWO OR MORE PARAGRAPHS IF YOU ARE SURE YOU CAN NOT CONDENSE THEM.
CHECK PARAGRAPH 2

THIS CONCLUDES THE ANALYSIS OF YOUR STORY. THE COMPUTER MAY HAVE MISSED SOME IMPORTANT ELEMENTS OR MAY NOT HAVE RECOGNIZED SOME OF THE KEY PHRASES WHICH YOU USED. CORRECT THE STORY ACCORDING TO THE COMMENTS AND YOUR OWN BEST JUDGEMENT, AND THEN COMPARE YOUR VERSION WITH THE MIMEOGRAPHED STORIES DONE BY OTHER STUDENTS.

Shorthand Instruction via Computer

by
C. Bruce Kavan & Leona M. Gallion
Indiana State University

Introduction

A unique application of the computer to the classroom environment has been to utilize a computer-based system for writing instructional materials for beginning shorthand classes. This system is used to verify and statistically analyze instructional new-matter shorthand dictation materials which are vocabulary controlled. These materials are then used for instructional purposes in beginning shorthand classes.

Research Basis

Research[1] has established that achievement in beginning shorthand increases with the use of vocabulary-controlled dictation materials. However, only a limited amount of this type of material is currently available. This may, in part, be due to the large expenditure in human capital necessary to construct, verify, and analyze dictation materials utilizing a limited or controlled vocabulary. To facilitate and encourage the preparation of vocabulary-controlled dictation materials, a computer-based system was designed and implemented at Indiana State University in the Fall of 1973. This system has been used subsequently in shorthand methods classes and workshops for writing new-matter vocabulary-controlled dictation materials.

The Computer-Based System

The computer-based system is built upon a word base dictionary composed of the 1500 most frequently used words in written business office communications as established by Mellinger.[2] The other information in the word base dictionary was researched and compiled by the designers from the various shorthand publications. The dictionary for these selected words contained

a. the word image
b. the lesson number in which the word could first be written in beginning shorthand
c. the number of syllables in the word
d. the word frequency grouping in hundreds
e. the word type(s) — brief form, brief form derivatives, word endings, and word beginnings

Design criteria for the system was based on the following two objectives:

1. To design the necessary computer software which comprises the components of the system. Each of these components or subsystems consists of one or more computer phases or programs. The objectives of the subsystem were
   a. to statistically analyze dictation material.
   b. to access the dictionary (see Figure 1 for sample page of the dictionary)
   c. to provide the working tools for writing dictation
2. To design a computer system with maximum simplicity of operation for use by the novice student user while simultaneously achieving maximum efficiency of computer resources.

The system is used first to verify a passage of dictation material which has been coded for use in a specific lesson in beginning shorthand. If a word in the dictation passage is not in the dictionary or is a word that cannot be written either in or prior to the lesson introduction code, that word will be underscored by astericks in the output (see Figure 2).

After all words in a dictation piece are only those among the 1500 most frequently used words and are those which can be written in either the introductory lesson or the previous lessons, the statistical phase will execute. The edited text image is then outputted into standard word groupings of 10 for constant-level dictation (indicated by /) and 20 for traditional dictation (indicated by / # /). (see Figure 3) The syllabic intensity of the passage is computed as well as the following statistics: percent of words from each lesson, percent of words in each hundred of the 1500 most frequently used words as well as the percent of brief forms, brief form derivatives, word endings, and word beginnings. Further, all words that can first be written in each of the lessons are listed as well as brief forms, brief form derivatives, word beginnings, and word endings (see Figures 4 to 8).

References

1. Leona M. Gallion and Alberta Anderson, "Controlled Vocabulary Beginning Shorthand Dictation," *Journal of Business Education*, October, 1972, pp. 27-28.
2. Morris Mellinger, *Basic Vocabulary for Written Business Office Communications*, (Chicago: Chicago State College Publication Series, 1970.

```
**************************************************************
    WORD        LESSON WORD    NUMBER OF    WORD       WORD
                FIRST USED IN  SYLLABLES    FREQUENCY  TYPE
                VOL. I, D.J.   IN WORD      (100*S)
**************************************************************
```

WORD	LESSON WORD FIRST USED IN VOL. I, D.J.	NUMBER OF SYLLABLES IN WORD	WORD FREQUENCY (100*S)	WORD TYPE
A	3	1	1	1
ABLE	3	2	3	
ABOUT	15	2	1	1
ABOVE	13	2	2	
ACCEPT	5	2	5	
ACCEPTANCE	21	3	14	
ACCEPTED	14	3	10	
ACCIDENT	21	3	13	
ACCIDENTS	21	3	14	
ACCOMMODATE	20	4	14	
ACCOMMODATIONS	27	5	14	3
ACCOMPLISHED	20	3	14	
ACCORDANCE	11	3	10	
ACCORDING	11	3	4	3
ACCORDINGLY	37	4	12	3
ACCOUNT	20	2	2	
ACCOUNTING	20	3	9	3
ACCOUNTS	20	2	9	
ACKNOWLEDGE	23	3	9	1
ACROSS	5	2	10	
ACT	5	1	11	
ACTION	9	2	4	3
ACTIVE	5	2	15	
ACTIVITIES	5	4	6	
ACTIVITY	5	4	11	
ACTUAL	31	3	8	3
ACTUALLY	31	4	9	3
ADD	5	1	7	
ADDED	14	2	8	
ADDITION	27	3	3	3
ADDITIONAL	27	4	2	3
ADDRESS	5	2	4	
ADDRESSED	5	2	11	
ADEQUATE	14	3	12	
ADJUSTMENT	19	3	10	3
ADMINISTRATION	16	5	7	3
ADMINISTRATIVE	16	5	13	
ADVANCE	5	2	8	
ADVANTAGE	21	3	6	1
ADVANTAGES	21	4	15	2

```
**************************************************************
```

Figure 1. Sample page of the dictionary.

```
        E D I T E D          T E X T          I M A G E

DEAR SIR:
      ****
YOUR LETTER OF MAY FIRST CAME TO ME THIS DAY . IT WILL BE / ONLY THREE
                                                     ****
DAYS BEFORE I CAN MAIL YOU THE TWO HUNDRED DAILY /01/ PAPERS FOR WHICH YOU
                                      *******
ASKED . IS THIS ALL RIGHT WITH YOU ? I WOULD / PUT A FAST SERVICE ON
                                              ****
THIS PACKAGE . THE COST WILL BE THREE DOLLARS /02/ FOR THE FIRST ONE
                                                              ***
HUNDRED , BUT ONLY TWO DOLLARS FOR THE REMAINING / ONE HUNDRED .
*******                                            *** *******
CORDIALLY ,


NUMBER OF TEXT CARDS READ ------------------------      7
NUMBER OF GOOD WORDS ON TEXT CARDS ---------------      60
NUMBER OF WORDS REJECTED ON TEXT CARDS -----------      8
NUMBER OF GOOD SYLLABLES ON TEXT CARDS -----------      74
SYLLABIC INTENSITY (GOOD SYLLABLES / GOOD WORDS) -   1.233
```

Figure 2. Computer output of edited text image showing rejected words.

```
        E D I T E D          T E X T          I M A G E

DEAR SIR :

: READ YOUR LETTER OF MAY FIRST THIS DAY . IT WILL / BE ONLY THREE

DAYS BEFORE I CAN MAIL YOU THE TWO DAILY /01/ PAPERS FOR WHICH YOU

ASKED . IS THIS ALL RIGHT WITH YOU ? I / WOULD PUT GOOD SERVICE ON

THIS PACKAGE . THE COST WILL BE THREE /02/ DOLLARS FOR THE FIRST ,

BUT ONLY TWO DOLLARS FOR THE / REMAINING .

CORDIALLY ,


NUMBER OF TEXT CARDS READ ------------------------      7
NUMBER OF GOOD WORDS ON TEXT CARDS ---------------      61
NUMBER OF WORDS REJECTED ON TEXT CARDS -----------      0
NUMBER OF GOOD SYLLABLES ON TEXT CARDS -----------      75
SYLLABIC INTENSITY (GOOD SYLLABLES / GOOD WORDS) -   1.229
```

Figure 3. Computer output of edited text image showing usable passage.

GROUP	FREQUENCY	PERCENT FREQUENCY
1	41	67.2
2	4	6.5
3	5	8.1
4	1	1.6
5	2	3.2
6	1	1.6
7	1	1.6
8	1	1.6
9	1	1.6
10	0	0.0
11	0	0.0
12	1	1.6
13	3	4.9
14	0	0.0
15	0	0.0
TOTAL	61	

Figure 4. Computer output of word frequency count by hundred groupings.

LESSON	FREQUENCY	PERCENT FREQUENCY
8	17	27.8
7	5	8.1
5	22	36.0
4	2	3.2
3	9	14.7
2	4	6.5
1	2	3.2
TOTAL	61	

Figure 5. Computer output of lesson frequency count.

```
LESSON  08        LESSON  05        LESSON  03
   BE                ASKED             DAYS
   BEFORE            BUT               DEAR
   CORDIALLY         CAN               I
   DAILY             FIRST             IT
   FOR               IS                PAPERS
   GOOD              LETTER            WILL
   ONLY              OF
   PUT               PACKAGE        LESSON  02
   THIS              SERVICE
   WHICH             SIR               MAIL
   WOULD             THE               READ
                     THREE             REMAINING
LESSON  07           WITH              RIGHT
                     YOU
   ALL               YOUR
   COST                             LESSON  01
   DOLLARS        LESSON  04
   ON                                 DAY
                     TWO               MAY
```

Figure 6. Computer output of word usage by lesson.

```
TYPE 1              THIS              TYPE 3
                    WHICH
   BE               WILL                 CORDIALLY
   BUT              WITH                 DAILY
   CAN              WOULD                ONLY
   FOR              YOU
   GOOD             YOUR
   I                                  TYPE 4
   IS
   IT                                    REMAINING
   OF            TYPE 2
   PUT
   THE              BEFORE
```

Figure 7. Computer output of word forms by type.

TYPE	FREQUENCY	PERCENT FREQUENCY
1	31	83.7
2	1	2.7
3	4	10.8
4	1	2.7

Figure 8. Computer output of word forms by count.

A Universal Word Game in BASIC

by Barney M. Milstein
Associate Professor of Literature
Stockton State College
Pomona, N. J.

This article describes an interactive paedagogical game written in BASIC for vocabulary building work in any natural language. Although the game as presented here is intended for antonym-matching, it can easily be modified to test definitions, either in the target natural language, or in the native language, as with remedial work. The version discussed below is for German; the program is named SPIEL1.

The same is played by presenting the student with three rounds of ten words each. Lexical items are ordered in each of three groups according to increasing difficulty. In order to advance a round, the student must match at least seven correct answers on the first attempt; otherwise he is ejected from the game at the end of the respective round. In case of errors, the correct answer is displayed for the student, and he must enter it before proceeding to the next item. At the end of three rounds, the student is given a 'rating' on a scale from 15 to 30. The parameters of the ratings, as well as those for advancing a round, are arbitrary and alterable at the will of the programmer.

Items are selected at random from a data array. In order to keep items from repeating, a flag is set on both the question and its antonym (i.e. the correct answer).

The reader is asked to consult the accompanying program listing for references to specific line numbers. The program as it appears here is implemented on the E. I. S. network in New Jersey.

Lines 70-280 contain instructions, and are self-explanatory. They should be modified in appropriate places for use with other languages, or with variations.

If the parameters for the ratings (lines 280-350) are altered, accompanying changes must be made in the conditions set in lines 790-860: these determine which message will be displayed to the student at the conclusion of the game.

Lines 360-380 are used in conjunction with the generation of a random number. In the CALL-OS system as used by E. I. S., the 'rnd' function can be provided with a 'throwaway' variable ('a'); this will produce a different sequence of random numbers if a different number for 'a' is entered each time the program is run.

The Dimension Statement is routine. In this case 216 items are present in the German array, with the variable 'w$' being the literal string. The variable 'f' is used to flag items for non-repetition.

Lines 410-440 initialize the three counters used in the game. C1 keeps count of correct answers in each round, and is again initialized at line 960. C2 keeps count of the absolute number of problems generated, and is used for going from one round to the next. C3 keeps a cumulative count of the total number matched correctly on the first try.

Lines 490-510 read in the literal items, which are stored as a data array of word pairs in lines 2000-4135. Care has been taken to keep all three sets of words equal in size, although this is not a strict necessity. In any case, the line numbering system used (2000-3000-4000) allows for expansion without the necessity for renumbering.

Line 520 is the beginning of the loop of ten problems per round. Since the absolute total of problems encountered is incremented in C2 (line 620), lines 530 and 540 determine from which group of items the test item will be selected. Thus, if C2 is less than 10, control passes to line 590, which sets a variable, 'z', equal to a random number between 1 and 72. If the student passes successfully through the first round, the condition set at 530 will be met, and control will pass to the number generator for the next round (570), and so on.

Lines 550, 570 and 590 generate random integers in the proper ranges for the three parts of the game. The number generated corresponds to the subscript of the literal variable 'w$', against which the student input ('x$' in lines 640 and 670) will be matched. The parameters of the generator are determined by the size of the array and the manner in which it is divided. In this case, the integers will be generated to fall between 1 and 72, 73 and 144 and 145 and 216. The random number actually generated by the function 'rnd' is between 0 and 1, thus necessitating some arithmetic to bring it to the proper value.

Lines 600 and 610 set a flag on the subscript variable 'z', sending control back to line 530 if that number is encountered a second time.

Line 615 displays to the student one of the 72 words in each main section. The 'correct answer' is a string corresponding to the other half of the word pair in the data array. Since the integer generated at random may be either odd or even, the correct answer matching 'x$' will be either 'w$(z+1)' (odd) or 'w$(z-1)' (even). By using the integer function ('int') to determine oddness or evenness of 'z' (line 630), control is branched to either 650 or 675 for a match test.

If a match is made on the first try a congratulatory message is displayed (line 680), counters 1 and 3 are incremented and the loop continues (line 742 is the bottom).

If a match is not made on the first attempt, the program branches to line 730, which prints the equivalent in the target language of "the answer is." The variable 'z' is again evaluated for evenness or oddness, and an appropriate branch to either 735 or 739 gives the student the correct answer, followed by a request to type it. Unless the student input ('t$') at this point matches, control branches back to 730 and the loop continues until a match is made.

The remainder of the program is taken up with evaluation by section and score, and is for the most part straightforward.

This program can be used for vocabulary games in any language. The data-read feature will easily handle an array of a few hundred items, but for larger item arrays it would probably be advisable to use a data file.

```
list spiell

spiell     10:16    09/25/74  wednesday

70 print 'welcome to spiell, the German word game.'
80 print 'do you want instructions?(yes/no)'
85 input a$
90 if a$= 'no' then 360
100 print 'in this game you will have to match a word'
110 print 'with its antonym or opposite meaning.'
120 print 'for example, if you are given "hot" you'
130 print 'are expected to type "cold." in'
140 print 'this game, the words are in german.'
150 print 'the entire game has three parts.'
160 print 'going from easy words to harder words.'
165 print 'some items are more than one word'
170 print 'on each part you will have to match seven out'
180 print 'of ten in order to go on to the next part.'
190 print 'if you fail to do this in the first or second parts'
200 print 'you will automatically be put out of the game.'
210 print 'the words are chosen at random from large'
220 print 'pools of lexical items.in some cases'
230 print 'a word or phrase may have more than one antonym,but'
240 print 'only one of them has been arbitrarily chosen'
250 print 'for the game.umlauts do not exist'
260 print 'in the system, so you are asked to type'
270 print 'the following for them:ae, oe, ue,aeu.'
271 print 'do not capitalize nouns.'
272 print 'questions and comments should be directed'
274 print 'to prof. barney milstein, stockton state'
276 print 'college, pomona, nj 08240.'
280 print 'the scale for the scores is as follows:'
290 print '          15-20-------student'
300 print '          21-22-------oberdummkopf'
310 print '          23-24-------dummkopf'
320 print '          25-26-------unterdummkopf'
330 print '          27-28-------klug'
340 print '          29      -------intelligent'
350 print '          30----------LEHRER!!!'
360 print 'give me a number to get me started,please'
365 input a
380 q = rnd(a)
400 dim w$(216),f(216)
410 c1=0
420 c2=0
430 c3=0
440 rem c1 ctr for corr ans;c2 for total in each section,
450 for l=1 to 216                c3 for tot crct.
460 f(1)=0
470 next l
480 rem f(1) is for flagging used words
490 for i= 1 to 216
500 read w$(i)
510 next i
520 for j= 1 to 10
530 if c2<10 then 590
540 if c2<20 then 570
550 z= int(144+(70*rnd+1))
560 go to 600
570 z = int(72+(70*rnd+1))
580 go to 600
590 z = int(70*rnd+1)
600 if f(z)=1 then530
610 f(z) = 1
615 print w$(z)
620 c2 =c2+1
625 rem test for odd or even z
630 if int(z/2)=z/2 then 670
640 input x$
645 f(z+1)=1
650 if x$<>w$(z+1) then 730
660 go to 680
670 input x$
674 f(z-1)=1
675 if x$<>w$(z-1) then 730
680 print 'gut!!'
690 c1=c1+1
710 c3=c3+1
720 go to 742
730 print 'die antwort ist: ';
733 if int(z/2) = (z/2) then 739
735 print w$(z+1);'--type it, please.'
736 input t$
737 if t$ = w$(z+1) then 742
738 go to 730
739 print w$(z-1);'--type it please.'
740 input t$
741 if t$ <> w$(z-1) then 730
742 next j
750 if z<= 72 then 870
760 if z<=144 then 925
770 print 'your score for all three parts is' ; c3
780 print 'your rating is'
790 if c3=30 then 1000
800 if c3 =29 then 1020
805 if c3>=27 then 1040
810 if c3>=25 then 1060
820 if c3>=23 then 1080
830 if c3>=21 then 1100
860 if c3<20 then 1120
870 if c1<7 then 5000
880 print 'you have done the first part'
890 print 'with' ; c1 ;'correct answers'
900 print 'you will now go on to the second part'
910 c1=0
920 go to 520
925 if c1<7 then 5000
930 print 'congratulations!!you have done the second part'
940 print 'with' ;c1; 'correctly answered'
950 print 'you will now go on to the third part.'
960 c1=0
970 go to 520
1000 print 'LEHRER!!!'
1010 go to 1140
1020 print 'intelligent'
1030 go to 1140
1040 print 'klug'
1050 go to 1170
1060 print 'unterdummkopf'
1070 go to 1170
1080 print 'dummkopf'
1090 go to 1170
1100 print 'oberdummkopf'
1110 go to 1170
1120 print 'student'
1130 go to 1170
1140 print 'this is not so bad'
1150 print 'come back and play again some time. Auf Wiedersehen!!!'
1160 go to5050
1170 print 'you can do better.come back and'
1180 print 'play again some time.auf Wiedersehen!!!'
1190 go to 5050
2000 data 'bekannt','unbekannt','gut','schlecht','krank','gesund'
2010 data 'lang','kurz','gross','klein','schwach','stark','arm','reich'
2020 data 'frueh','spaet','klug','dumm','leicht','schwer','immer','nie'
2030 data 'ohne','mit','heiss','kalt','vermeidlich','unvermeidlich'
2040 data 'nichts','alles','dunkel','hell','links','rechts','dick','duenn'
2050 data 'froh','traurig','suess','bitter','alt','jung','kuehl','warm'
2060 data 'letzt','erst','mehr','weniger','sicher','unsicher'
2100 data 'das ende','der anfang','fuehren','folgen','leer','voll'
2110 data 'hier','dort','rueckwaerts','vorwaerts','zuerst','zuletzt'
2120 data 'der frieden','der krieg','morgen','gestern','lieben','hassen'
2130 data 'das licht','die finsternis','der morgen','der abend','der tag'
2135 data 'die nacht'
3000 data 'hoch','niedrig','schoen','haesslich','faul','fleissig'
3010 data 'fuer','gegen','ueber','unter','vor','hinter','messbar'
3020 data 'unmessbar','viel','wenig','weich','hart','feucht','trocken'
3030 data 'sichtbar','unsichtbar','falsch','wahr','guenstig','unguenstig'
3040 data 'tapfer','feig','locker','fest','nackt','gekleidet','oft','selten'
3050 data 'offen','geschlossen','oben','unten','scharf','dumpf'
3060 data 'geschmacksvoll','geschmacklos','genau','ungefaehr','laut','leise'
3070 data 'moeglich','unmoeglich','weit','nah'
3100 data 'beginnen','enden','tot','am leben','sprechen','schweigen'
3110 data 'loben','tadeln','glauben','zweifeln','frei','gebunden'
3120 data 'der freund','der feind','freundlich','feindlich','woher','wohin'
3130 data 'verschwinden','erscheinen','ueberall','nirgendwo','niemand'
3135 data 'jedermann'
4000 data 'einfach','kompliziert','besonders','allgemein','sorgfaeltig'
4010 data 'schlampig','aeusserlich','innerlich','eng','breit'
4020 data 'genuegend','unzulaenglich','ausserordentlich','gewoehnlich'
4030 data 'winzig','riesig','gerade','krumm','staendig','unterbrochen'
4040 data 'himmlisch','irdisch','vorher','nachher','ledig','verheiratet'
4050 data 'wachen','schlafen','einschlafen','aufwachen','bejahen'
4060 data 'verneinen','aufmachen','zumachen','geben','nehmen'
4070 data 'flach','huegelig','mitternacht','mittag','bestehen','vergehen'
4080 data 'schliessen','oeffnen','sterben','geboren werden','sinnvoll'
4090 data 'sinnlos','vergessen','sich erinnern'
4100 data 'stolz','demutig','anzuenden','ausloeschen','erlauben','verbieten'
4110 data 'fuellen','leeren','loesen','binden','sinken','schwimmen'
4120 data 'wecken','einschlaefern','hinstellen','aufheben'
4125 data 'ablehnen','annehmen'
4130 data 'der vorteil','der nachteil','sich anziehen','sich ausziehen'
4135 data 'einpacken','auspacken'
5000 print 'you have gotten less than seven correct '
5005 if c2>10 then 5015
5010 print 'on the first part'
5012 go to 5020
5015 print 'on the second part'
5020 print 'go home and try again another day'
5030 print 'a u f'
5040 print 'w i e d e r s e h e n !!!'
5050 end
```

Dynamic Modelling Using FORTRAN IV

Jay Martin Anderson
Bryn Mawr College

Introduction

"Dynamic modelling," as used in this paper, means the construction of formal models of systems whose behavior in time is followed by computer simulation. Specifically, the paper will refer to the techniques of System Dynamics, as pioneered and developed by M. I. T. Professor Jay W. Forrester.[1,2] System Dynamics is a general theory of system structure which rests on four essential elements:

(1) The cause-and-effect links between elements of a system and the position of these elements within feedback loops are identified.

(2) The model is expressed in a formal, mathematical language in which the qualitative interactions identified in (1) are made quantitative.

(3) The behavior of the model is examined by computer simulation.

(4) The consequences of changing system structure are evaluated by iterating on steps (1) - (3) until a viable policy or set of policies for the system under study has evolved.

The integrity, if not the beauty, of System Dynamics has often been commented upon by Forrester[3] and his students and colleagues. Our purpose here is not to debate the merits of System Dynamics as a technique or theory, nor to expound its practice, but rather to focus on step (3) of the preceding four-step program: the computer simulation of System Dynamics models.

In recent years a number of System Dynamics models have reached the public eye, including Forrester's[4] and Meadows'[5] World models, and the several environmental models described in *Toward Global Equilibrium*.[3] These models are cast in the computer language DYNAMO[6], developed expressly for the purpose of serving the System Dynamics community. DYNAMO affords a one-to-one relationship between computer equations and System Dynamics concepts, assumes for itself the labor of arranging the equations in a computable order and providing printed or plotted output. DYNAMO is a compile-and-go processor which provides its own careful diagnostics, and is available for use in a limited number of computational environments from Pugh-Roberts Associates, 65 Rogers Street, Cambridge, Mass. 02142.

In spite of its simplicity and beauty, DYNAMO falls short in classroom situations for at least two reasons. First, it is not widely available, and, in all but the versions for IBM OS/360 and IBM CP/CMS on the 360/67, it is an expensive proprietary product. Second, because it is a compile-and-go processor, there is no opportunity to form load modules for repetitive classroom use; the cost of recompiling the source program must be borne at every use.

It is to these shortcomings that the present paper is addressed. A recipie is provided for translating System Dynamics models or existing DYNAMO programs into FORTRAN. In following this recipie, the FORTRAN programmer takes upon himself much of the effort that the DYNAMO processor does for the DYNAMO programmer. Nonetheless, the result is a program which is considerably more "transportable," and which can reside as a load module for frequent classroom execution.

It will be assumed that the reader is familiar with the elements of System Dynamics as contained in *Principles of Systems*[2]. The particular recipie presented here is cast in IBM FORTRAN IV(G1) but can easily be modified for other dialects. The recipie treats only a subset of DYNAMO, but a subset wide enough to accomodate, for example, the WORLD models.

The emphasis is on *recipie*: a method for formulating System Dynamics models in FORTRAN, but not a program nor a compiler nor a processor for so doing. The recipie admits some latitude, both in the use of particular ingredients and in the embellishments possible in a well-equipped kitchen.

One example of the recipie is presented here: Forrester's World Model.[4] Two other examples along with the technical appendices are available from the author. They are a model for "The Tragedy of the Commons" and a predator-prey model illustrating one of the concepts in *The Silent Spring*. These two have both been used in the undergraduate classroom.[7]

The Recipie

The purpose of the dynamic modelling program is to describe the behavior in time of generalized systems. Mathematically, this behavior is the result of integration of coupled differential equations. It is presumed that rates of change are sufficiently slow that integration may be accomplished by a simple coarse-grid approximation to the area under a curve comprised of straight line segments. Rates, auxiliary variables, and levels may be calculated; up to ten such quantities may be tabulated in printed form and up to five may be plotted, although the FORTRAN programmer may easily circumvent these arbitrary limits.

The main program includes seven sections. These are Specifications, Functions, Inputs, Initialization, Auxiliaries and Rates, Outputs, and Levels. This seven-part structure corresponds to DYNAMO's ability to order modelling equations. Within each part, the order of the equations must be carefully planned by the FORTRAN programmer.

Specifications and Functions. These sections may be thought of as essentially instructions to the FORTRAN compiler; the remaining five sections form the logical flow of the modelling program, as shown in Figure 1.

Input. This section reads control information for the simulation, as well as values of constants, table-functions, and initial values. Information for the plotter subroutine is also read at this point. Parameters of the model may be printed to help clarify and annotate the subsequent output.

Initialization. This section provides for starting the simulation clock, some housekeeping, and setting initial values of all levels.

Auxiliaries and Rates. In this section the computation of auxiliaries and rates from existing levels, and from previously calculated auxiliaries or rates, is carried out.

Output. Results of the simulation can be printed line by line as the simulation proceeds, but information for plotting is best saved until an entire page of graphical output has been accumulated. The arbitrary limits of ten printed and five plotted variables were chosen for simplicity in constructing a page-wide line of tabular information and for clarity in reading simultaneous plots. A print-plot subroutine which forms plots on a line-printer much like those formed by DYNAMO, is described in the Appendix. Clearly the FORTRAN programmer with more sophisticated graphical devices will wish to call upon these in writing output.

Levels. The integration is completed, and the clock and levels are updated. The details of the seven-step "recipie" are given in the appendix.

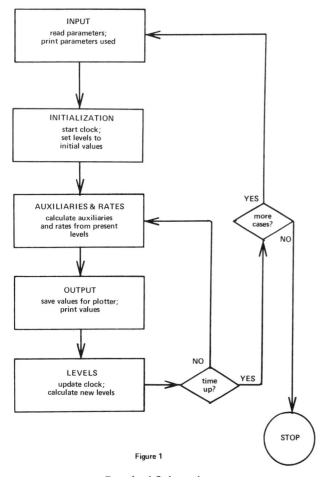

Figure 1

Required Subroutines

The recipie described briefly above and in detail in the Appendix requires additional subroutines to ease in writing DYNAMO-like programs. A limited subset of those provided for DYNAMO users might include CLIP, NOISE, RAMP, STEP, SWITCH, TABLE, and TABHL, as well as a simulation-plotter subroutine (SIMPLT). The Appendix includes source listings for the above.

It must be stressed that delays, which appear frequently in System Dynamics models, are not simply functions or subroutines, but "macros." Delays require integration, and therefore the programming of a delay requires insertion of FORTRAN source statements into several of the seven sections of the modelling program. An example, first- and third-order information delays (DYNAMO macros SMOOTH and DLINF3) are exhibited in the Appendix.

Output

The output of the program comprises three parts: a summary of parameters used in the model, a printed table, and a plot of various rates, levels, or auxiliaries as a function of time. The programmer may choose not to form a printed table or not to form a plot if he wishes, or to present the output in some other way. In the example, primary emphasis is placed upon a simple but crude print-plot, which should be within reach of all computer systems.

Example

The FORTRAN transcription of Forrester's World model, taken from his *World Dynamics* (reference 4) constitutes a simple and easily manageable program of just over a hundred lines. *World Dynamics* is ample documentation for the model. The source listing and "standard" simulation are shown here.

Appendices

Four appendices to this paper including a detailed explanation of the "Recipie," various subprograms, and three additional examples are available (free) direct from the author. The author has also offered to aid others in implementing these models, and will supply (at cost) card copies, source listings, and further documentation for each. Please write:

Jay Martin Anderson
Department of Chemistry
Bryn Mawr College
Bryn Mawr, Pennsylvania 19010

[1] Forrester, J. W., *Industrial Dynamics.* MIT Press, Cambridge, Mass. 1961.

[2] Forrester, J. W., *Principles of Systems.* Wright-Allen Press, Cambridge, Mass. 1968.

[3] See, for example, Forrester, J. W., "Counterintuitive Behavior of Social Systems." In *Toward Global Equilibrium: Collected Papers.* D. L. Meadows and D. H. Meadows, editors. Wright-Allen Press, Cambridge, Mass. 1973. First published in *Technology Review* 73(3): 3, January, 1971.

[4] Forrester, J. W., *World Dynamics.* Wright-Allen Press, Cambridge, Mass. 1971.

[5] Meadows, D. H., D. L. Meadows, J. Randers, and W. W. Behrens III. *The Limits to Growth.* Universe Books, New York. 1972.

[6] Pugh, A. L. III. *DYNAMO II Users' Manual.* 2nd edition. MIT Press, Cambridge, Mass. 1973.

[7] Anderson, J. M., "Computer Simulation in the Dynamics of Environmental Systems." In *Proceedings of the Fifth Conference on Computers in the Undergraduate Curricula.* Washington State University. Pullman, Washington. 1974.

PROGRAM LISTING

```
C   WORLD2
C   FROM WORLD DYNAMICS, BY J.W.FORRESTER (C) WRIGHT-ALLEN PRESS, 1971
C   FORTRAN IV(G1) TRANSCRIPTION, J.M.ANDERSON, SEPT 1974
C
C   1.   SPECIFICATIONS
      DIMENSION NAME(18),PP(51),PNR(51),FCI(51),PPOL(51),PQL(51)
      LOGICAL RPLOT/.TRUE./
      COMMON T,PP,PNR,PCI,PPOL,PQL
      REAL NR,NRUR,NRUN1,NREN,NRFR,MSL,NRMM,NRI,NRUN,LA
C   TABLE ENTRIES FOR TABLE LOOKUP FUNCTIONS
      REAL BRMMT(6)/1.2,1.,.85,.75,.7,.7/,NREMT(5)/0.,.15,.5,.85,1./,
     1 DRMMT(11)/3.,1.8,1.,.8,.7,.6,.53,.5,.5,.5,.5/,
     2 DRPMT(7)/.92,1.3,2.,3.2,4.8,6.8,9.2/,
     3 DRFMT(9)/30.,3.,2.,1.4,1.,.7,.6,.5,.5/,
     4 DRCMT(6),BRFMT(5)/0.,1.,1.6,1.9,2./,
     5 BRPMT(7)/1.02,.9,.7,.4,.25,.15,.1/,
     6 FCMT(6)/2.4,1.,.6,.4,.3,.2/,FPCIT(7)/.5,1.,1.4,1.7,1.9,2.05,2.2/,
     7 CIMI(6)/.1,1.,1.8,2.4,2.6,3./,FPMT(7)/1.02,.9,.65,.35,.2,.1,.05/,
     8 POLCMT(6)/.05,1.,3.,5.4,7.4,8./,
     9 POLATT(7)/.6,2.5,5.,8.,11.5,15.5,20./,CFIFRT(5)/1.,.6,.3,.15,.1/,
     A QLMT(6)/.2,1.,1.7,2.3,2.7,2.9/,QLFT(5)/0.,1.,1.8,2.4,2.7/,
     B GLCT(11)/2.,1.3,1.,.75,.55,.45,.38,.3,.25,.22,.2/,
     C QLPT(7)/1.04,.85,.6,.3,.15,.05,.02/,CIQRT(5)/.7,.8,1.,1.5,2./,
     D DRMMT(11)/0.,1.,1.8,2.4,2.9,3.3,3.6,3.8,3.9,3.95,4./
      NAMELIST /PARMS/ NRUN1,POLN1,DRCMT,BRCMT,CIGN1,BRN1,FC1,DRM1,NRI,
     1 CIDN1,YEAR
      DATA BRI,ECIRN,NRUN,DRN,LA,PDN,FC,FN,CIAFN,CIGN,CIDN,POLS,POLN,
     1 CIAFT,GLS /.04,1.,1.,.028,135.E6,26.5,1.,1.,.3,.05,.025,3.6E9,
     2 1.,.15,.1./
C   2.   FUNCTIONS
C   THERE ARE NONE
C
C   3.   INPUTS
      READ (5,1001) NAME
1001  FORMAT (18A4)
      READ (5,*) NUPL,NUPR,NU,NCPU
      NOCAL=NU*NCPU
      NUPT=NUPL*NCPU
      NUPR=NUPR*NCPU
      DT=1./FLOAT(NCPU)
      NCASE=0
1     READ (5,PARMS,END=100)
      NCASE=NCASE+1
      WRITE (6,1003) NAME,NCASE
1003  FORMAT ('1',18A4/' CASE ',I2/)
      WRITE (6,PARMS)
C
C   4.   INITIALIZATION
      NT=0
      P=1.65E9
      NR=NRI
      CI=0.4E9
      POL=0.2E9
      CIAF=0.2
2     NPL=0
C
C   5.   AUXILIARIES AND RATES
5     T=1900.+FLOAT(NT)/FLOAT(NCPU)
      CR=P/(LA*PDN)
      CIR=CI/P
      NRFR=NR/NRI
      CIRA=CIR*CIAF/CIAFN
      PCLR=POL/POLS
      NREM=TABLE(NREMT,NRFR,0.,1.,.25)
      ECIR=CIR*(1-CIAF)*NREM/(1-CIAFN)
      MSL=ECIR/ECIRN
      BRMM=TABHL(BRMMT,MSL,0.,5.,1.)
      DRMM=TABHL(DRMMT,MSL,0.,5.,.5)
      FCM=TABLE(FCMT,CR,0.,5.,1.)
```

```
      FPCI=TABEL(FPCIT,CIFA,0.,6.,1.)
      FPM=TABLE(FPMT,POLR,0.,60.,10.)
      FR=FPCI*FCM*FFM*CLIP(FC,FC1,YEAR,1)/FN
      DRPM=TABLE(DRPMT,FOLR,0.,60.,10.)
      DRFM=TABEL(DRFMT,FR,0.,2.,.25)
      DRCM=TABLE(DRCMT,CR,0.,5.,1.)
      BRCM=TABLE(BRCMT,CR,0.,5.,1.)
      BRFM=TABEL(BRFMT,FR,0.,4.,1.)
      BRPM=TABLE(BRPMT,POLR,0.,60.,10.)
      CIM=TABEL(CIMT,MSL,0.,5.,1.)
      POLCM=TABEL(POLCMT,CIF,0.,5.,1.)
      POLAT=TABLE(PCLATT,POLR,0.,60.,10.)
      CFIFR=TABEL(CFIFRT,FR,0.,2.,.5)
      QLM=TABEL(QLMT,MSL,0.,5.,1.)
      QLC=TABLE(QLCT,CR,0.,5.,.5)
      QLF=TABEL(QLFT,FR,0.,4.,1.)
      QLP=TABEL(QLPT,POLR,0.,60.,10.)
      NRMM=TABEL(NRMMT,MSL,0.,10.,1.)
      CIQR=TABEL(CIQRT,QLM/QLF,0.,2.,.5)
      BR=P*CLIP(BRN,BRN1,YEAR,T)*BRFM*BRMM*DRCM*BRPM
      NRUR=P*CLIP(NRUN,NRUN1,YEAR,T)*NRMM
      DR=P*CLIP(DRN,DRN1,YEAR,T)*DRMM*DFFM*DRFM*DRCM
      CIG=P*CIM*CLIF(CIGI,CIGN1,YEAR,T)
      CID=CI*CLIP(CIDN,CIDN1,YEAR,T)
      POLG=P*CLIF(POLN,POLN1,YEAR,T)*POLCM
      POLA=POL/POLAT
C
C  6.  OUTPUTS
      IF (MOD(NT,NUPT),NL,0) GO TO 20
      NPL=NPL+1
      PP(NPL)=P
      PNR(NPL)=NRFR
      PCI(NPL)=CI
      PPOL(NPL)=POLR
      PQL(NPL)=QLS*QLM*GL(*QLF*QLP
C  NOTE THAT A DYNAMO 'SUPPLEMENTARY' APPEARS ONLY IN THE OUTPUT SECTION
      IF (NPL,GE,51) GO TO 40
C
C  7.  LEVELS & FINISH
20    IF (NT,GE,NOCAL) GO TO 40
      P=P+DT*(BR-DR)
      NR=NR-DT*NRUR
      CI=CI+DT*(CIG-CID)
      POL=POL+DT*(POLG-POLA)
      CIAF=CIAF+DT*(CFIFR*CIQR-CIAF)/CIAFT
      NT=NT+1
      GO TO 5
40    CALL SIMPLT (5,NUPL,NPL,NAME,FPLOT)
      RPLOT=.FALSE.
      IF (NT-NOCAL) 2,1,1
100   STOP
      END
```

SAMPLE RUN

Sample run of Forrester's World-2 Model below shows input data and output plot. The following variables are used on the plot.

P POP, Population, billions of people
R NRFR, Natural resource fraction remaining, dimensionless
$ CAP, Capital stock, billions of dollars
* POLR, pollution relative to 1970, dimensionless
Q QL, Forrester's index of the Quality of Life, dimensionless

```
WORLD2 BY JWF

4 0 200 5

&PARMS NRUN1=1.,POLN1=1.,DRCMT=.9,1.,1.2,1.5,1.9,3.,

BRCMT=1.05,1.,.9,.7,.6,.55,CIGN1=.05,BRN1=.04,FC1=1.,

DRN1=.028,NRI=9.E11,CIDN1=.025,YEAR=1974.,&END

0.       1.      E+10P POP

0.       1.      RNRFR

0.       2.5     E+10$ CAP

0.       50.     *POLR

0.       5.      Q QL
```

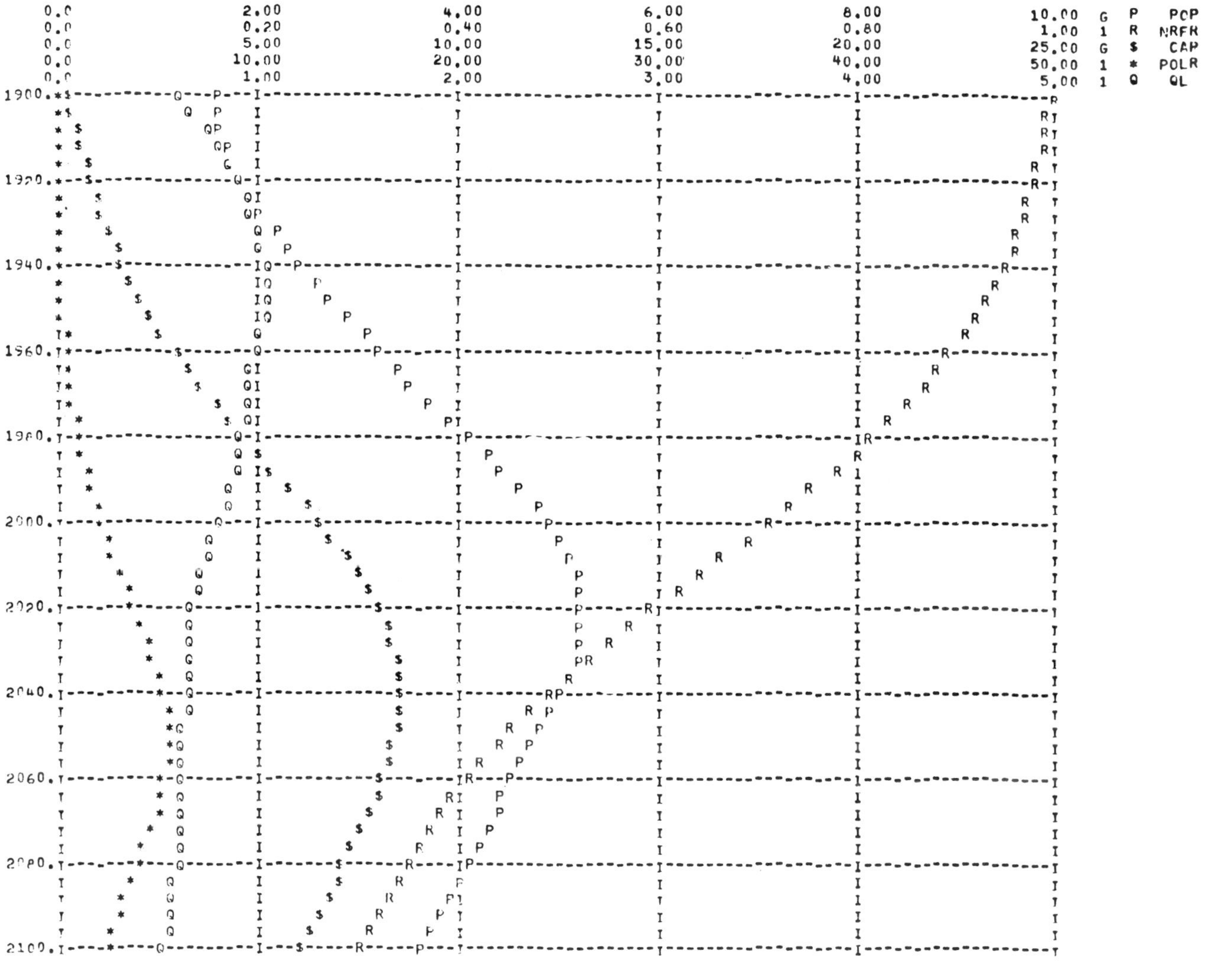

243

244

Computer Games

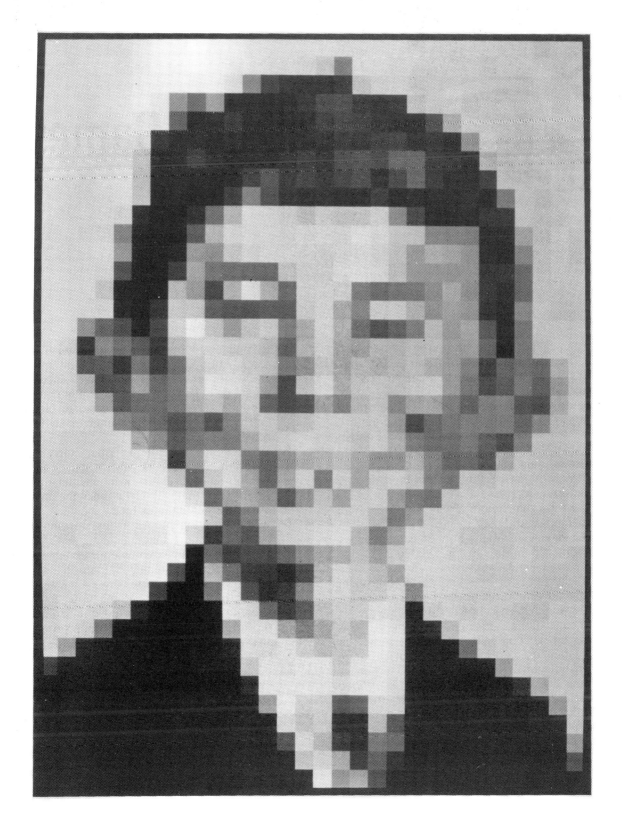

Call for Games

Do you have a favorite computer game? Why not share it with the readers of *Creative Computing*? Here's how to submit a game to us for publication:

1. Programs must be in BASIC, complete, debugged and with complete playing instructions for a beginning user. Watch English, grammar and spelling.
2. Please send us:
   A. Program listing (and paper tape, if possible)
   B. Two sample runs the way an AVERAGE person would play
   C. Brief verbal description of game, suggestions for modifications, related activities, etc.
   D. Description of any unusual computer or language features used. (Please try to use a standard version of BASIC).
   E. Your name, address, telephone, age, school or company affiliation, computer system used, original source of program (if not you).
3. Listing and runs must be on *white, unlined* paper. If you have lined paper, turn it around to the unlined side. We cannot publish material on yellow, pink, blue, or gray paper. Xerox, Ditto, or other copies are also unacceptable.
4. Listing and runs must be done with a *fresh black* ribbon. Not purple or blue and especially not a used ribbon. The Teletype ball must be clean, in good adjustment, and produce crisp copy. If necessary, clean the ball with a typewriter cleaner or stiff toothbrush.
5. If possible, submit a paper tape of the program. *Be sure* to wrap oiled paper tape (from Teletypes) in kitchen plastic wrap when you mail it. Otherwise the oil seeps out and smears the output.
6. Accompanying program descriptions should be typed double space.
7. If you want an acknowledgment that your contribution was received, include a stamped self-addressed envelope.
8. By submitting a program, you are giving *Creative Computing* the right to publish, reprint, distribute, or use your program in any other way. You will, of course, always be credited as the author.

HINT: Creative, original, interesting games are more likely to be published than new versions of old games. For example, we will absolutely *not* publish the following games (they are just too worn): Blackjack, Calendars, Craps, Football, Horse Race, Nim, Slot Machine, and Stock Market.

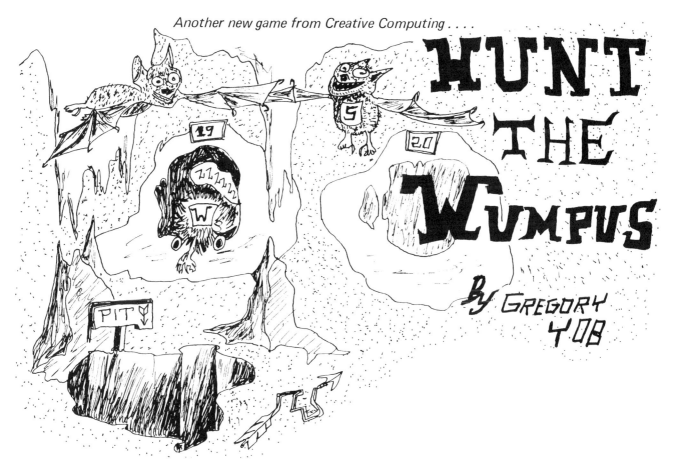

Another new game from Creative Computing . . . .

HUNT THE WUMPUS

By Gregory Yob

The Genesis of Wumpus

Two years ago I happened by People's Computer Company (PCC) and saw some of their computer games — such as Hurkle, Snark, and Mugwump. My reaction was: "EECH!!" Each of these games was based on a 10 x 10 grid in Cartesian co-ordinates and three of them was too much for me. I started to think along the lines of: "There has to be a hide and seek computer game without that (exp. deleted) grid!!" In fact, why not a topological computer game — Imagine a set of points connected in some way and the player moves about the set via the interconnections.

That afternoon in meditation the phrase "Hunt the Wumpus" arrived, and Wumpus was born. He's still a bit vague in physical detail as most dedicated Wumpus hunters know, but appearances are part of the game. (If you like, send me a picture of your version of a Wumpus. Perhaps friendly Dave, our editor, will publish the best one in *Creative Computing*.) The grid I chose was the vertices of a dodecahedron — simply because it's my favorite Platonic solid and once, ages ago, I made a kite shaped like one. The edges became the connecting tunnels between the caves which were the set of points for the game.

My basic idea at this time was for the player to approach the Wumpus, back off, and come up to him by going around the dodecahedron. To my knowledge, this has never happened . . . most players adopt other strategies rather than this cold-blooded approach.

Anyway . . . how to get the Wumpus! How about an arrow which could turn corners as it goes from room to room. Let the hunter tell the arrow where to go and let it fly. The shortest round trip without reversals is 5 caves — and thus the Crooked Arrow.

Hmmm . . . How does one sense the Wumpus? It's dark in yonder cave, and light would wake him up. If one got one cave away, the wumpus's distinct smell would serve as a warning. So far, so good . . . but Wumpus is still too easy, so let's find some appropriate hazards for the caves.

Bottomless pits were easy. Any imaginary cave would have a few of those around the place. Superbats were harder to come by. It took me a day or two to get that idea. The Superbats are a sort of rapid transit system gone a little batty (sorry about that one). They take you a random distance to a random cave and leave you there. If that's a pit or a Wumpus, well, you are in Fate's hands.

Around this time, I saw that Map-making would be a regular activity of Wumpus-hunters. I numbered the caves and made the scheme fixed in the hopes a practised player might notice this and make himself a permanent map of the caverns. (Another unrealised hope — as an exercise, make yourself such a map on a Squashed Dodecahedron).

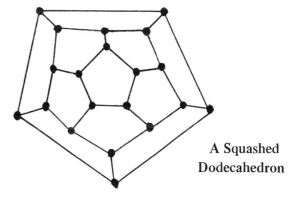

A Squashed Dodecahedron

To start the game fairly, Wumpus, Hazards, and Hunter are located on different points at the start of the game. Each game starts with random choices of location, but the hunter may restart with the same set-up if he chooses. This allows re-plays if the hunter, say, fell into a pit on the first move.

Wumpus was nearly done in my mind . . . (hint to a games-writer: Have a clear notion of your game before you start coding it. This saves MUCH confusion.) yet I felt it was a bit dull. Once you found the Wumpus all you had to do was shoot it. To fix this, the Wumpus was given a little life. If you shot an arrow or moved into his cave, he woke up and chose to move to a neighboring room or to the same room (one of 4 choices). If you and the Wumpus were in the same room after he moved, he ATE YOU UP!!

Around here I noticed that the pits and the bats didn't affect the Wumpus. To explain this, I added some color by making him heavy and with the legendary sucker feet. After all, evolution works in strange ways!! If you are a Wumpus fiend, make a version of Wumpus in which he avoids pits and superbats can carry him only one room (with the possibility of being dumped into your cave). This can be done by making the wumpus moving procedure a subroutine.

I wrote Wumpus and dropped it off at PCC. Then I went home and dreamed up Wumpus II which will be covered in the next issue of *Creative Computing*.

The Birth of Wumpus

Around a month later, I went to the Synergy conference at Stanford, where many of the far-out folk were gathered to share their visions of improving the world. PCC had a few terminals running in a conference room and I dropped by. To my vast surprise, all of the terminals were running Wumpus and scraps of paper on the floor with scrawled numbers and lines testified that much dedicated Wumpus-hunting was in progress. I had spawned a hit computer game!!!

Later, PCC published Wumpus in its newsletter (If you haven't seen it, write them for a subscription: P.O. Box 310, Menlo Park, Cal. 94025), and Wumpus appeared in all sorts of unlikely places. I have reports of Wumpus written in RPG, a listing of one in FORTRAN, a rumor of a system command of 'to Wumpus' on a large corporation's R&D computer system and have even seen an illustrated version for the Hazeltine CRT terminal!!

WUMPUS TAPES, ETC.

I can be found at:

Gregory Yob
PO Box 354
Palo Alto, Calif. 94301

Paper tapes of Wumpus, Wumpus 2 and Wumpus 3 are available and cost $5.00 each.

May your arrows remain straight. —Gregory Yob.

SAMPLE RUN

```
INSTRUCTIONS (Y-N)?Y
WELCOME TO 'HUNT THE WUMPUS'
  THE WUMPUS LIVES IN A CAVE OF 20 ROOMS. EACH ROOM
HAS 3 TUNNELS LEADING TO OTHER ROOMS. (LOOK AT A
DODECAHEDRON TO SEE HOW THIS WORKS-IF YOU DON'T KNOW
WHAT A DODECAHEDRON IS, ASK SOMEONE)

   HAZARDS:
BOTTOMLESS PITS - TWO ROOMS HAVE BOTTOMLESS PITS IN THEM
    IF YOU GO THERE, YOU FALL INTO THE PIT (& LOSE!)
SUPER BATS - TWO OTHER ROOMS HAVE SUPER BATS. IF YOU
    GO THERE, A BAT GRABS YOU AND TAKES YOU TO SOME OTHER
    ROOM AT RANDOM. (WHICH MIGHT BE TROUBLESOME)

   WUMPUS:
THE WUMPUS IS NOT BOTHERED BY THE HAZARDS (HE HAS SUCKER
FEET AND IS TOO BIG FOR A BAT TO LIFT). USUALLY
HE IS ASLEEP. TWO THINGS WAKE HIM UP: YOUR ENTERING
HIS ROOM OR YOUR SHOOTING AN ARROW.
    IF THE WUMPUS WAKES, HE MOVES (P=.75) ONE ROOM
OR STAYS STILL (P=.25). AFTER THAT, IF HE IS WHERE YOU
ARE, HE EATS YOU UP (& YOU LOSE!)

   YOU:
EACH TURN YOU MAY MOVE OR SHOOT A CROOKED ARROW
   MOVING: YOU CAN GO ONE ROOM (THRU ONE TUNNEL)
   ARROWS: YOU HAVE 5 ARROWS. YOU LOSE WHEN YOU RUN OUT.
   EACH ARROW CAN GO FROM 1 TO 5 ROOMS. YOU AIM BY TELLING
   THE COMPUTER THE ROOM#S YOU WANT THE ARROW TO GO TO.
   IF THE ARROW CAN'T GO THAT WAY(IE NO TUNNEL) IT MOVES
   AT RANDOM TO THE NEXT ROOM.
     IF THE ARROW HITS THE WUMPUS, YOU WIN.
     IF THE ARROW HITS YOU, YOU LOSE.

   WARNINGS:
   WHEN YOU ARE ONE ROOM AWAY FROM WUMPUS OR HAZARD,
   THE COMPUTER SAYS:
WUMPUS-  'I SMELL A WUMPUS'
BAT   -  'BATS NEARBY'
PIT   -  'I FEEL A DRAFT'
```

```
HUNT THE WUMPUS


BATS NEARBY!
YOU ARE IN ROOM   2
TUNNELS LEAD TO   1       3       10


SHOOT OR MOVE (S-M)?M
WHERE TO?1
ZAP--SUPER BAT SNATCH! ELSEWHEREVILLE FOR YOU!
YYYIIIIEEEE . . . FELL IN PIT
HA HA HA - YOU LOSE!
SAME SET-UP (Y-N)?Y
HUNT THE WUMPUS


BATS NEARBY!
YOU ARE IN ROOM   2
TUNNELS LEAD TO   1       3       10


SHOOT OR MOVE (S-M)?M
WHERE TO?3


YOU ARE IN ROOM   3
TUNNELS LEAD TO   2       4       12
```

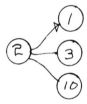

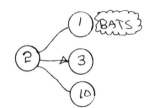

SUPER BATS PUT ME IN A PIT SOMEWHERES

more

248

```
SHOOT OR MOVE (S-M)?M
WHERE TO?4

YOU ARE IN ROOM  4
TUNNELS LEAD TO   3      5      14

SHOOT OR MOVE (S-M)?M
WHERE TO?5

BATS NEARBY!
YOU ARE IN ROOM  5
TUNNELS LEAD TO   1      4      6

SHOOT OR MOVE (S-M)?M
WHERE TO?6

I FEEL A DRAFT
YOU ARE IN ROOM  6
TUNNELS LEAD TO   5      7      15

SHOOT OR MOVE (S-M)?M
WHERE TO?7
YYYIIIIEEEE . . . FELL IN PIT
HA HA HA - YOU LOSE!
SAME SET-UP (Y-N)?Y
HUNT THE WUMPUS

BATS NEARBY!
YOU ARE IN ROOM  2
TUNNELS LEAD TO   1      3      10

SHOOT OR MOVE (S-M)?M
WHERE TO?10

BATS NEARBY!
YOU ARE IN ROOM  10
TUNNELS LEAD TO   2      9      11

SHOOT OR MOVE (S-M)?M
WHERE TO?11
ZAP--SUPER BAT SNATCH! ELSEWHEREVILLE FOR YOU!

YOU ARE IN ROOM  14
TUNNELS LEAD TO   4      13      15

SHOOT OR MOVE (S-M)?M
WHERE TO?15



I SMELL A WUMPUS!
YOU ARE IN ROOM  15
TUNNELS LEAD TO   6      14      16

SHOOT OR MOVE (S-M)?S
NO. OF ROOMS(1-5)?1
ROOM #?16
AHA! YOU GOT THE WUMPUS!
HEE HEE HEE - THE WUMPUS'LL GETCHA NEXT TIME!!
```

JUST KEEP ON TRUCKIN!

BLEW IT AGAIN!!.

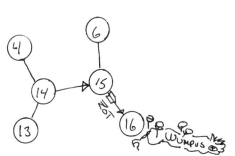

CAN YOU FIT THIS MAP INTO THE OTHER ONE ABOVE? FIGURE OUT HOW I KNEW THE WUMPUS WAS IN 16.

```
0010    REM- HUNT THE WUMPUS
0015    REM: BY GREGORY YOB
0020    PRINT "INSTRUCTIONS (Y-N)";
0030    INPUT I$
0040    IF I$="N" THEN 52
0050    GOSUB 1000
0052    REM- ANNOUNCE WUMPUSII FOR ALL AFICIONADOS ... ADDED BY DAVE
0054    PRINT
0056    PRINT "      ATTENTION ALL WUMPUS LOVERS!!!"
0058    PRINT "      THERE ARE NOW TWO ADDITIONS TO THE WUMPUS FAMILY";
0060    PRINT " OF PROGRAMS."
0062    PRINT
0064    PRINT "      WUMP2:  SOME DIFFERENT CAVE ARRANGEMENTS"
0066    PRINT "      WUMP3:  DIFFERENT HAZARDS"
0067    PRINT
0068    REM- SET UP CAVE (DODECAHEDRAL NODE LIST)
0070    DIM S(20,3)
0080    FOR J=1 TO 20
0090     FOR K=1 TO 3
0100      READ S(J,K)
0110     NEXT K
0120    NEXT J
0130    DATA 2,5,8,1,3,10,2,4,12,3,5,14,1,4,6
0140    DATA 5,7,15,6,8,17,1,7,9,8,10,18,2,9,11
0150    DATA 10,12,19,3,11,13,12,14,20,4,13,15,6,14,16
0160    DATA 15,17,20,7,16,18,9,17,19,11,18,20,13,16,19
0170    DEF FNA(X)=INT(20*RND(0))+1
0180    DEF FNB(X)=INT(3*RND(0))+1
0190    DEF FNC(X)=INT(4*RND(0))+1
0200    REM-LOCATE L ARRAY ITEMS
0210    REM-1-YOU, 2-WUMPUS,3&4-PITS,5&6-BATS
0220    DIM L(6)
0230    DIM M(6)
0240    FOR J=1 TO 6
0250     L(J)=FNA(0)
0260     M(J)=L(J)
0270    NEXT J
0280    REM-CHECK FOR CROSSOVERS (IE L(1)=L(2),ETC)
0290    FOR J=1 TO 6
0300     FOR K=J TO 6
0310      IF J=K THEN 330
0320      IF L(J)=L(K) THEN 240
0330     NEXT K
0340    NEXT J
0350    REM-SET# ARROWS
0360    A=5
0365    L=L(1)
0370    REM-RUN THE GAME
0375    PRINT "HUNT THE WUMPUS"
0380    REM-HAZARD WARNINGS & LOCATION
0390    GOSUB 2000
0400    REM-MOVE OR SHOOT
0410    GOSUB 2500
0420    GOTO 0 OF 440,480
0430    REM-SHOOT
0440    GOSUB 3000
0450    IF F=0 THEN 390
0460    GOTO 500
0470    REM-MOVE
0480    GOSUB 4000
0490    IF F=0 THEN 390
0500    IF F>0 THEN 550
0510    REM-LOSE
0520    PRINT "HA HA HA - YOU LOSE!"
0530    GOTO 560
0540    REM-WIN
0550    PRINT "HEE HEE HEE - THE WUMPUS'LL GETCHA NEXT TIME!!"
0560    FOR J=1 TO 6
0570     L(J)=M(J)
0580    NEXT J
0590    PRINT "SAME SET-UP (Y-N)";
0600    INPUT I$
0610    IF I$#"Y" THEN 240
0620    GOTO 360
1000    REM-INSTRUCTIONS
1010    PRINT "WELCOME TO 'HUNT THE WUMPUS'"
1020    PRINT " THE WUMPUS LIVES IN A CAVE OF 20 ROOMS. EACH ROOM"
1030    PRINT "HAS 3 TUNNELS LEADING TO OTHER ROOMS. (LOOK AT A"
1040    PRINT "DODECAHEDRON TO SEE HOW THIS WORKS-IF YOU DON'T KNOW"
1050    PRINT "WHAT A DODECAHEDRON IS, ASK SOMEONE)"
1060    PRINT
1070    PRINT "     HAZARDS:"
1080    PRINT " BOTTOMLESS PITS - TWO ROOMS HAVE BOTTOMLESS PITS IN THEM"
1090    PRINT "     IF YOU GO THERE, YOU FALL INTO THE PIT (& LOSE!)"
1100    PRINT " SUPER BATS - TWO OTHER ROOMS HAVE SUPER BATS. IF YOU"
1110    PRINT "     GO THERE, A BAT GRABS YOU AND TAKES YOU TO SOME OTHER"
1120    PRINT "     ROOM AT RANDOM. (WHICH MIGHT BE TROUBLESOME)"
1130    PRINT
1140    PRINT "     WUMPUS:"
1150    PRINT " THE WUMPUS IS NOT BOTHERED BY THE HAZARDS (HE HAS SUCKER"
1160    PRINT " FEET AND IS TOO BIG FOR A BAT TO LIFT).  USUALLY"
1170    PRINT " HE IS ASLEEP. TWO THINGS WAKE HIM UP: YOUR ENTERING"
1180    PRINT " HIS ROOM OR YOUR SHOOTING AN ARROW."
1190    PRINT "     IF THE WUMPUS WAKES, HE MOVES (P=.75) ONE ROOM"
1200    PRINT " OR STAYS STILL (P=.25). AFTER THAT, IF HE IS WHERE YOU"
1210    PRINT " ARE, HE EATS YOU UP (& YOU LOSE!)"
1220    PRINT
1230    PRINT "     YOU:"
1240    PRINT " EACH TURN YOU MAY MOVE OR SHOOT A CROOKED ARROW"
1250    PRINT "     MOVING: YOU CAN GO ONE ROOM (THRU ONE TUNNEL)"
1260    PRINT "     ARROWS: YOU HAVE 5 ARROWS. YOU LOSE WHEN YOU RUN OUT."
1270    PRINT "     EACH ARROW CAN GO FROM 1 TO 5 ROOMS. YOU AIM BY TELLING"
1280    PRINT "     THE COMPUTER THE ROOM#S YOU WANT THE ARROW TO GO TO."
1290    PRINT "     IF THE ARROG CAN'T GO DHAT WAY(IE NO TUNNEL) IT MOFES"
1300    PRINT "     AT RANDOM TO THE NEXT ROOM."
1310    PRINT "     IF THE ARROW HITS THE WUMPUS, YOU WIN."
1320    PRINT "     IF THE ARROW HITS YOU, YOU LOSE."
1330    PRINT
1340    PRINT "     WARNINGS:"
1350    PRINT "     WHEN YOU ARE ONE ROOM AWAY FROM WUMPUS OR HAZARD,"
1360    PRINT "     THE COMPUTER SAYS:"
1370    PRINT " WUMPUS-  'I SMELL A WUMPUS'"
1380    PRINT " BAT   -  'BATS NEARBY'"
1390    PRINT " PIT   -  'I FEEL A DRAFT'"
1400    PRINT ""
1410    RETURN
2000    REM-PRINT LOCATION & HAZARD WARNINGS
2010    PRINT
2020    FOR J=2 TO 6
2030     FOR K=1 TO 3
2040      IF S(L(1),K)#L(J) THEN 2110
2050      GOTO J-1 OF 2060,2080,2080,2100,2100
2060      PRINT "I SMELL A WUMPUS!"
2070      GOTO 2110
2080      PRINT "I FEEL A DRAFT"
2090      GOTO 2110
2100      PRINT "BATS NEARBY!"
2110     NEXT K
2120    NEXT J
2130    PRINT "YOU ARE IN ROOM "L(1)
2140    PRINT "TUNNELS LEAD TO "S(L,1);S(L,2);S(L,3)
2150    PRINT
2160    RETURN
2500    REM-CHOOSE OPTION
2510    PRINT "SHOOT OR MOVE (S-M)";
2520    INPUT I$
2530    IF I$#"S" THEN 2560
2540    O=1
2550    RETURN
2560    IF I$#"M" THEN 2510
2570    O=2
2580    RETURN
3000    REM-ARROW ROUTINE
3010    F=0
3020    REM-PATH OF ARROW
3030    DIM P(5)
3040    PRINT "NO. OF ROOMS(1-5)";
3050    INPUT J9
3060    IF J9<1 OR J9>5 THEN 3040
3070    FOR K=1 TO J9
3080     PRINT "ROOM #";
3090     INPUT P(K)
3095     IF K <= 2 THEN 3115
3100     IF P(K) <> P(K-2) THEN 3115
3105     PRINT "ARROWS AREN'T THAT CROOKED - TRY ANOTHER ROOM"
3110     GOTO 3080
3115    NEXT K
3120    REM-SHOOT ARROW
3130    L=L(1)
3140    FOR K=1 TO J9
3150     FOR K1=1 TO 3
3160      IF S(L,K1)=P(K) THEN 3295
3170     NEXT K1
3180     REM-NO TUNNEL FOR ARROW
3190     L=S(L,FNB(1))
3200     GOTO 3300
3210    NEXT K
3220    PRINT "MISSED"
3225    L=L(1)
3230    REM-MOVE WUMPUS
3240    GOSUB 3370
3250    REM-AMMO CHECK
3255    A=A-1
3260    IF A>0 THEN 3280
3270    F=-1
3280    RETURN
3290    REM-SEE IF ARROW IS AT L(1) OR L(2)
3295    L=P(K)
3300    IF L#L(2) THEN 3340
3310    PRINT "AHA! YOU GOT THE WUMPUS!"
3320    F=1
3330    RETURN
3340    IF L#L(1) THEN 3210
3350    PRINT "OUCH! ARROW GOT YOU!"
3360    GOTO 3270
3370    REM-MOVE WUMPUS ROUTINE
3380    K=FNC(0)
3390    IF K=4 THEN 3410
3400    L(2)=S(L(2),K)
3410    IF L(2)#L THEN 3440
3420    PRINT "TSK TSK TSK- WUMPUS GOT YOU!"
3430    F=-1
3440    RETURN
4000    REM- MOVE ROUTINE
4010    F=0
4020    PRINT "WHERE TO";
4030    INPUT L
4040    IF L<1 OR L>20 THEN 4020
4050    FOR K=1 TO 3
4060     REM- CHECK IF LEGAL MOVE
4070     IF S(L(1),K)=L THEN 4130
4080    NEXT K
4090    IF L=L(1) THEN 4130
4100    PRINT "NOT POSSIBLE -";
4110    GOTO 4020
4120    REM-CHECK FOR HAZARDS
4130    L(1)=L
4140    REM-WUMPUS
4150    IF L#L(2) THEN 4220
4160    PRINT "... OOPS! BUMPED A WUMPUS!"
4170    REM-MOVE WUMPUS
4180    GOSUB 3380
4190    IF F=0 THEN 4220
4200    RETURN
4210    REM-PIT
4220    IF L#L(3) AND L#L(4) THEN 4270
4230    PRINT "YYYIIIIEEEE . . . FELL IN PIT"
4240    F=-1
4250    RETURN
4260    REM-BATS
4270    IF L#L(5) AND L#L(6) THEN 4310
4280    PRINT "ZAP--SUPER BAT SNATCH! ELSEWHEREVILLE FOR YOU!"
4290    L=FNA(1)
4300    GOTO 4130
4310    RETURN
5000    END
```

A new computer game from CREATIVE COMPUTING Magazine......

DEPTH CHARGE

DESCRIPTION

In this program, you are captain of the destroyer, USS Digital. An enemy submarine has been causing trouble and your mission is to destroy it. You may select the size of the "cube" of water you wish to search in. The computer then determines how many depth charges you get to destroy the submarine.

Each depth charge is exploded by you specifying a trio of numbers; the first two are the surface coordinates, the third is the depth. After each depth charge, your sonar observer will tell you where the explosion was relative to the submarine.

PROGRAM AUTHOR

Dana Noftle (Age 18)
37 Mohawk Drive
Acton, MA 01720

USING THE PROGRAM

1. Type in the DEPTH CHARGE program on your computer. Convert it, if necessary, to your dialect of BASIC.

2. Divide into teams of 2 or 3 players and play the game. Try to come up with an optimal guessing strategy for a search area with a dimension of 10, of 100, of 1000.

3. Statement 30 sets the maximum number of trials allowed for search areas with different dimensions. Make a table like this:

SEARCH AREA SIZE	TRIALS ALLOWED
1	
2	
.	
.	
.	
100	

What does this tell you?

4. Modify the program to allow the submarine to move one grid point in any direction on each trial. It makes a more exciting game, but you'll have to allow additional trials to find the submarine. In this game, make TRIALS N a quantity to be input.

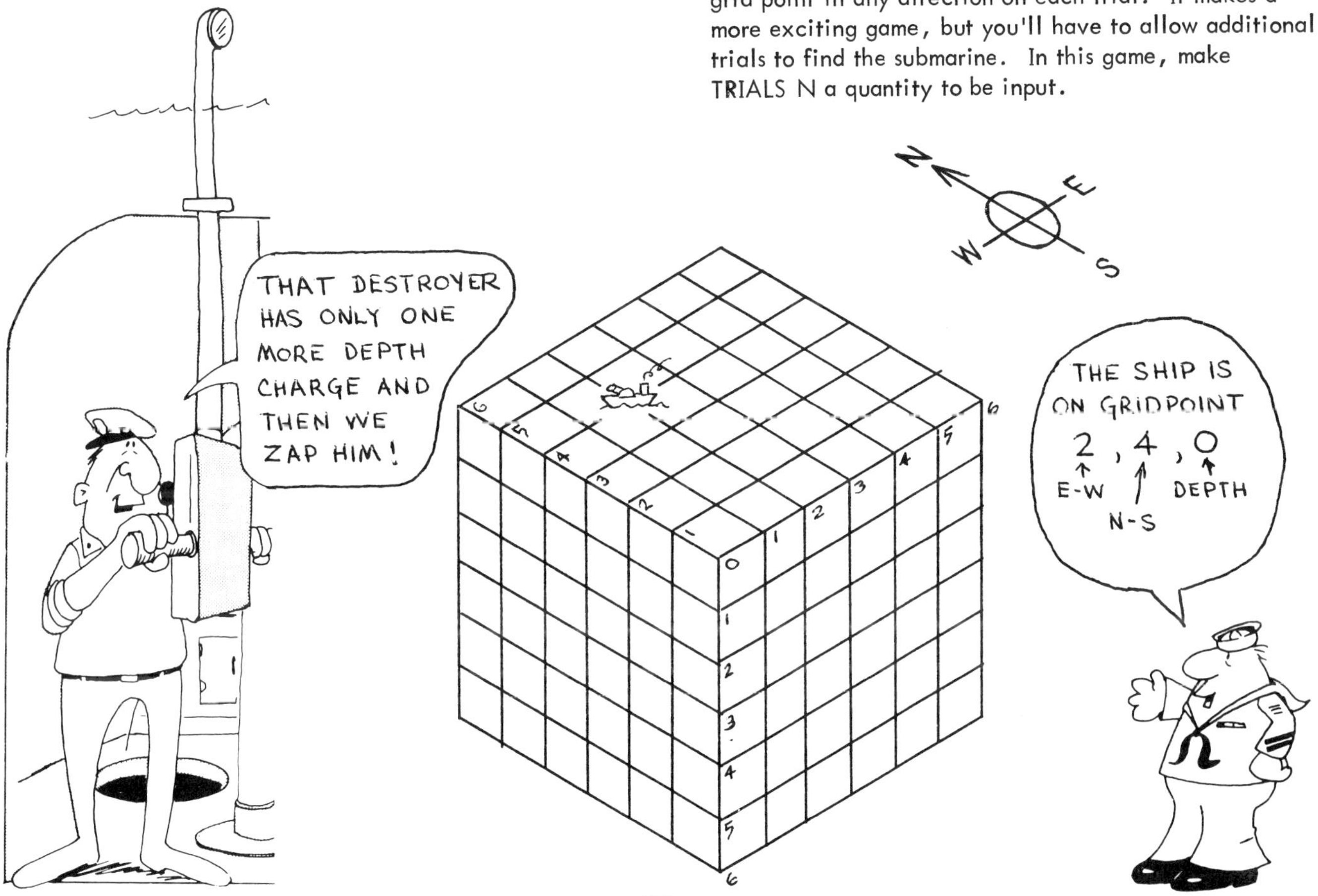

PROGRAM LISTING

```
LISTNH
10 PRINT "DEPTH CHARGE GAME" \ PRINT
20 INPUT "DIMENSION OF SEARCH AREA";G \ PRINT
30 N=INT(LOG(G)/LOG(2))+1 \ RANDOMIZE
40 PRINT "YOU ARE CAPTAIN OF THE DESTROYER USS DIGITAL."
50 PRINT "AN ENEMY SUB HAS BEEN CAUSING YOU TROUBLE; YOUR"
60 PRINT "MISSION IS TO DESTROY IT.  YOU HAVE"N"SHOTS."
70 PRINT "SPECIFY DEPTH CHARGE EXPLOSION POINT WITH A"
80 PRINT "TRIO OF NUMBERS -- THE FIRST TWO ARE THE"
90 PRINT "SURFACE COORDINATES; THE THIRD IS THE DEPTH "
100 PRINT \ PRINT "GOOD LUCK !" \ PRINT
110 A=INT(G*RND) \ B=INT(G*RND) \ C=INT(G*RND)
120 FOR D=1 TO N \ PRINT \ PRINT "TRIAL #"D, \ INPUT X,Y,Z
130 IF ABS(X-A)+ABS(Y-B)+ABS(Z-C)=0 THEN 300
140 GOSUB 500 \ PRINT \ NEXT D
200 PRINT \ PRINT "YOU HAVE BEEN TORPEDOED! ABANDON SHIP!"
210 PRINT "THE SUBMARINE WAS AT"A","B","C \ GOTO 400
300 PRINT \ PRINT "B O O M ! !  YOU FOUND IT IN"D"TRIES!"
400 PRINT \ PRINT \ INPUT "ANOTHER GAME (Y OR N)";A$
410 IF A$="Y" THEN 100
420 PRINT "OK.   HOPE YOU ENJOYED YOURSELF " \ GOTO 600
500 PRINT "SONAR REPORTS SHOT WAS ";
510 IF Y>B THEN PRINT "NORTH",
520 IF Y<B THEN PRINT "SOUTH",
530 IF X>A THEN PRINT "EAST";
540 IF X<A THEN PRINT "WEST";
550 IF Y<>B OR X<>A THEN PRINT " AND";
560 IF Z>C THEN PRINT " TOO LOW. "
570 IF Z<C THEN PRINT " TOO HIGH. "
580 IF Z=C THEN PRINT " DEPTH OK. "
590 RETURN
600 END
```

SAMPLE RUN

```
RUNNH
DEPTH CHARGE GAME

DIMENSION OF SEARCH AREA? 10

YOU ARE CAPTAIN OF THE DESTROYER USS DIGITAL.
AN ENEMY SUB HAS BEEN CAUSING YOU TROUBLE; YOUR
MISSION IS TO DESTROY IT.  YOU HAVE 4 SHOTS.
SPECIFY DEPTH CHARGE EXPLOSION POINT WITH A
TRIO OF NUMBERS -- THE FIRST TWO ARE THE
SURFACE COORDINATES; THE THIRD IS THE DEPTH.


GOOD LUCK



TRIAL # 1 ? 5,5,5
SONAR REPORTS SHOT WAS SOUTHEAST AND TOO HIGH.


TRIAL # 2 ? 3,7,7
SONAR REPORTS SHOT WAS SOUTHEAST AND DEPTH OK.


TRIAL # 3 ? 1,9,7
SONAR REPORTS SHOT WAS NORTHEAST AND DEPTH OK.


TRIAL # 4 ? 0,8,7

B O O M ! !  YOU FOUND IT IN 4 TRIES!
```

"I gather it chose his wife for him."

NOTONE -- A Challenge!

Something to ponder-- Determine the BEST strategy for playing the following game. If you think you have a good one, send it to Walter Koetke at Lexington High School, Lexington, Mass. 02173. If requested, he'll send you a punched paper tape of a program that plays the game reasonably well (not best). Tapes will only be sent to those submitting solutions with their request.

The game NOTONE is played with two players and a pair of dice. There are ten rounds in the game — one round consisting of one turn for each player. Players add the score they attain on each round, and the player with the highest score after ten rounds is the winner.

On each turn the player may roll the two dice from 1 to N times. If T_i is the total of the dice on the ith roll, then the player's score for the turn is $T_1 + T_2 + T_3 + ... + T_N$. However, and here's the catch, if any T_i is equal to T_1 then the turn is over and his score is 0 for that turn. After each roll that doesn't equal T_1, the player can decide whether to roll again or stop and score the number of points already obtained.

Creative Computing will print the best game submitted next issue.

NOT ONE

In the Nov-Dec 74 issue of *Creative Computing*, we challenged readers to write a good version of the game NOT ONE. Of the many versions received, the one printed below appears to be one of the best. It is by Robert Puopolo, Belmont Hill School, Belmont, Mass.

Complete playing instructions are given in the computer program itself. If you convert this to your version of BASIC, be alert for multiple statements on one line (separated by a colon) and extended IF statements (for example, IF-THEN-PRINT or IF-THEN-PRINT-ELSE-PRINT).

```
5 REM ROBERT PUOPOLO BELMONT HILL 6/25/74 "NOTONE"
7 PRINT:PRINT TAB(15);"NOTONE":PRINT
10 DIM T(50),R(10),C(10),L(12)
13 RANDOMIZE
15 INPUT "WOULD YOU LIKE THE INSTRUCTIONS";A$
20 IF A$="YES" THEN 35
25 IF A$="NO" THEN 100
30 PRINT:PRINT "ANSWER YES OR NO!!":PRINT:GOTO 15
35 PRINT:PRINT "THE GAME OF NOTONE IS PLAYED WITH"
40 PRINT "TWO PLAYERS AND A PAIR OF DICE. THERE ARE"
45 PRINT "TEN ROUNDS IN THE GAME. ONE ROUND CONSISTING"
50 PRINT "OF ONE TURN FOR EACH PLAYER. PLAYERS"
55 PRINT "(YOURSELF AND THE COMPUTER) ADD THE SCORE"
60 PRINT "THEY ATTAIN ON EACH ROUND, AND THE PLAYER"
62 PRINT "WITH THE HIGHEST SCORE AFTER TEN ROUNDS IS THE WINNER":PRINT
67 PRINT "ON EACH TURN THE PLAYER MAY ROLL THE TWO"
69 PRINT "DICE FROM 1 TO N TIMES. IF T1 IS THE TOTAL OF DICE ON"
72 PRINT "THE ITH ROLL, THEN THE PLAYERS SCORE FOR THE TURN IS"
75 PRINT "T(1)+T(2)+T(3)+........+T(N). HOWEVER,"
77 PRINT "AND HERE'S THE CATCH, IF ANY T(I)IS EQUAL TO T(1) THEN "
80 PRINT "THE TURN IS OVER AND HIS SCORE FOR THAT ROUND IS ZERO"
82 PRINT "AFTER EACH ROLL THAT DOESN'T EQUAL T(1), THE PLAYER CAN "
88 PRINT "DECIDE WHETHER TO ROLL AGAIN OR STOP AND"
90 PRINT "SCORE THE NUMBER OF POINTS ALREADY OBTAINED."
100 FOR T=1 TO 10:PRINT:PRINT "ROUND ",T
110 X=X+1:R1=INT(6*RND(X))+1
115 R2=INT(6*RND(X))+1:PRINT R1+R2
120 IF X>1 THEN 130
125 T(1)=R1+R2:GOTO 135
130 T(X)=R1+R2:IF T(1)=T(X) THEN
        PRINT "YOU GET A ZERO FOR THIS ROUND":X,T1=0:GOTO 200
135 T1=T1+T(X)
140 INPUT "ROLL AGAIN ";B$
145 IF B$="YES" THEN 110
150 IF B$="NO" THEN R(T)=T1:X,T1=0:T(A)=0 FOR A=1 TO 50:GOTO 200
160 PRINT:PRINT "ANSWER YES OR NO!!":PRINT:GOTO 140
200 PRINT:PRINT TAB(15%);"COMPUTERS MOVE":PRINT
201 RESTORE
202 R1=INT(6*RND(X))+1:R2=INT(6*RND(X))+1
204 READ L(D) FOR D=2 TO R1+R2
205 FOR C=1 TO L(D).IF C-1 THEN 215
210 R1=INT(6*RND(X))+1:R2=INT(6*RND(X))+1
215 PRINT "COMPUTER'S ROLL"C":";R1+R2
220 IF C>1 THEN 230
225 T(1)=R1+R2:GOTO 242
230 T(C)=R1+R2
235 IF T(C)=T(1) THEN PRINT "THE COMPUTER GETS A ZERO FOR THE TURN"
        :T1=0
        :GOTO 245
242 T1=T1+T(C):NEXT C
245 C(T)=T1:X,T1=0
250 C2=C2+C(T):C1=C1+R(T)
253 PRINT:T(B)=0 FOR B=1 TO 50
255 IF T=10 THEN PRINT "FINAL SCORE":PRINT
260 IF C2>C1 THEN PRINT "COMPUTER: ";C2,"YOU: ";C1 ELSE
        PRINT "YOU: ";C1,"COMPUTER: ";C2
300 NEXT T
305 DATA 18,18,9,9,6,6,6,9,9,18,18
310 PRINT:PRINT "SCORING SUMMARY":PRINT
315 PRINT TAB(17);"YOU":PRINT
320 PRINT E,R(E) FOR E=1 TO 10:PRINT:PRINT "TOTAL: ";C1:PRINT
325 PRINT TAB(17);"COMPUTER":PRINT
330 PRINT E,C(E) FOR E=1 TO 10:PRINT:PRINT "TOTAL: ";C2:PRINT
```

```
NOTONE

WOULD YOU LIKE THE INSTRUCTIONS? YES

THE GAME OF NOTONE IS PLAYED WITH
TWO PLAYERS AND A PAIR OF DICE. THERE ARE
TEN ROUNDS IN THE GAME. ONE ROUND CONSISTING
OF ONE TURN FOR EACH PLAYER. PLAYERS
(YOURSELF AND THE COMPUTER) ADD THE SCORE
THEY ATTAIN ON EACH ROUND, AND THE PLAYER
WITH THE HIGHEST SCORE AFTER TEN ROUNDS IS THE WINNER

ON EACH TURN THE PLAYER MAY ROLL THE TWO
DICE FROM 1 TO N TIMES. IF T1 IS THE TOTAL OF DICE ON
THE ITH ROLL, THEN THE PLAYERS SCORE FOR THE TURN IS
T(1)+T(2)+T(3)+........+T(N). HOWEVER,
AND HERE'S THE CATCH, IF ANY T(I)IS EQUAL TO T(1) THEN
THE TURN IS OVER AND HIS SCORE FOR THAT ROUND IS ZERO
AFTER EACH ROLL THAT DOESN'T EQUAL T(1), THE PLAYER CAN
DECIDE WHETHER TO ROLL AGAIN OR STOP AND
SCORE THE NUMBER OF POINTS ALREADY OBTAINED.

ROUND   1
 6
ROLL AGAIN ? YES
 4
ROLL AGAIN ? YES
 9
ROLL AGAIN ? YES
 7
ROLL AGAIN ? YES
 11
ROLL AGAIN ? NO

               COMPUTERS MOVE

COMPUTER'S ROLL 1 : 5
COMPUTER'S ROLL 2 : 7
COMPUTER'S ROLL 3 : 4
COMPUTER'S ROLL 4 : 6
COMPUTER'S ROLL 5 : 9
COMPUTER'S ROLL 6 : 5
THE COMPUTER GETS A ZERO FOR THE TURN

YOU:  37      COMPUTER:   0

ROUND   2
 3
ROLL AGAIN ? YES
 9
ROLL AGAIN ?

ANSWER YES OR NO!!

ROLL AGAIN ? YES
 9
ROLL AGAIN ? YES
 7
```

```
ROUND   10
 8
ROLL AGAIN ? YES
 6
ROLL AGAIN ? YES
 10
ROLL AGAIN ? YES
 5
ROLL AGAIN ? YES
 5
ROLL AGAIN ? NO

               COMPUTERS MOVE

COMPUTER'S ROLL 1  : 3
COMPUTER'S ROLL 2  : 4
COMPUTER'S ROLL 3  : 9
COMPUTER'S ROLL 4  : 10
COMPUTER'S ROLL 5  : 8
COMPUTER'S ROLL 6  : 8
COMPUTER'S ROLL 7  : 9
COMPUTER'S ROLL 8  : 7
COMPUTER'S ROLL 9  : 9
COMPUTER'S ROLL 10 : 8
COMPUTER'S ROLL 11 : 6
COMPUTER'S ROLL 12 : 3
THE COMPUTER GETS A ZERO FOR THE TURN

FINAL SCORE

YOU:   345     COMPUTER:   299
```

CIVIL WAR

GENERAL DESCRIPTION

The CIVIL program simulates 14 battles of the Civil War. For each battle, it specifies the number of men and amount of money available to each side and the rate of inflation affecting the value of money at that time. The program also determines the state of morale for the Confederate troops and whether they are on offense or defense.

The user of the program is always the Confederate Commander. He decides how much of the available money is to be spent on food, salaries and ammunition, and the strategy to be employed.

The CIVIL simulation makes a 'win or lose' determination based on the user's decisions, calculates the casualties and desertions for each side, and compares the casualties of the simulated battle with those of the actual battle. Whether you win or lose is a function of the simulated casualties for both sides and the morale factor.

FACTOR RELATIONSHIPS

The CIVIL program was developed by L. Cram, L. Goodie, and D. Hibbard, students at Lexington High School, Lexington, Massachusetts. Their description of some of the important features of the game follows:

1. *Men* — These amounts are based on actual figures from each battle in the Civil War. The number of troops the South has can vary greatly according to how well the operator of the computer plays. The two primary factors determining the number of men are morale and the amount of success you had from the last battle. If all of your men either die or desert, and this can happen, your army will be drastically diminished for the next battle.

2. *Money* — These amounts are not based on actual figures. They are probably nowhere near the actual figures but this does not make any difference since everything is relative in the program. Money is to be spent for food, salaries for your men, and ammunition and equipment, and can be saved from one battle for another.

3. *Inflation* — The percent of inflation fluctuates with your success in the previous battles. It determines the present value of your money and is used in calculating the effectiveness of your money.

4. *Morale* — The morale factor is determined from the amount of money spent on food and salaries and varies with your success.

5. *Strategy* — There are two sets of strategies, one for offense and one for defense. The computer will tell you which situation you are in, as determined from the actual Civil War battles. The computer, playing the part of the North, makes a random guess at your strategy and compares its guess to your actual strategy. Your success will depend upon how close the computer comes in its guess. Hence, the same decisions on two different runs of the same battle may have different results.

6. *Casualties* — Casualties are based on actual figures but vary according to how well the Southern army is managed. They tend to be very high if not enough money is spent on ammunition and equipment.

7. *Desertions* — Desertions tend to be very large if the morale factor is low.

8. *Percent of Casualties* — This is a comparison of your casualties and the casualties in the actual Civil War battles. It indicates how well you are waging your part of the war.

SAMPLE RUN

DO YOU WANT DESCRIPTIONS? YES

THIS IS A CIVIL WAR SIMULATION.
TO PLAY, TYPE A RESPONSE WHEN THE COMPUTER ASKS.
REMEMBER THAT ALL FACTORS ARE INTERRELATED AND THAT YOUR
RESPONSES COULD CHANGE HISTORY. FACTS AND FIGURES USED ARE
BASED ON THE ACTUAL OCCURRENCE. MOST BATTLES TEND TO RESULT
AS THEY DID IN THE CIVIL WAR, BUT IT ALL DEPENDS ON YOU!!

THE OBJECT OF THE GAME IS TO WIN AS MANY BATTLES AS POSSIBLE.

YOUR CHOICES FOR DEFENSIVE STRATEGY ARE:

    (1) ARTILLERY ATTACK
    (2) FORTIFICATION AGAINST FRONTAL ATTACK
    (3) FORTIFICATION AGAINST FLANKING MANEUVERS
    (4) FALLING BACK

YOUR CHOICES FOR OFFENSIVE STRATEGY ARE:

    (1) ARTILLERY ATTACK
    (2) FRONTAL ATTACK
    (3) FLANKING MANEUVERS
    (4) ENCIRCLEMENT

YOU MAY SURRENDER BY TYPING A '5' FOR YOUR STRATEGY.

YOU ARE THE CONFEDERACY. GOOD LUCK!

THIS IS THE BATTLE OF BULL RUN
JULY 21, 1861 GEN. BEAUREGARD COMMANDING THE SOUTH MET THE
UNION FORCES WITH GEN. MCDOWELL IN A PREMATURE BATTLE AT BULL
RUN. GEN. JACKSON HELPED PUSH BACK THE UNION ATTACK.

	CONFEDERACY	UNION
MEN	18000	18500
MONEY	$81000.	$83300.
INFLATION	25%	10%

HOW MUCH DO YOU WISH TO SPEND FOR
— FOOD.................?25000
— SALARIES...........?25000
— AMMUNITION.....?30000
(NOTE: Do not put commas in numbers.)

MORALE IS FAIR
YOU ARE ON THE DEFENSIVE

YOUR STRATEGY?4

	CONFEDERACY	UNION
CASUALTIES	1744	2596
DESERTIONS	10	46

YOUR CASUALTIES WERE 11% LESS THAN
THE ACTUAL CASUALTIES AT BULL RUN

YOU WIN BULL RUN

What would happen if you spent more on ammunition and less on food and salaries?

Do you remember who actually won Bull Run?

255

PROGRAM LISTING

```
1 LET L=0:LET W=0:LET R1=0:LET P1=0
2 LET Q1=0:LET M3=0:LET M4=0
3 LET P2=0:LET T1=0:LET T2=0
5 REMARKABLE PROGRAM BY L. CRAM , L. GOODIE , AND D. HIBBARD
6 PRINT "DO YOU WANT DESCRIPTIONS (0=YES, 1=NO)";
7 INPUT Z
9 FOR U=1 TO 6
10 PRINT
11 NEXT U
13 IF Z=1 THEN 100
15 PRINT "THIS IS A CIVIL WAR SIMULATION."
20 PRINT "TO PLAY, TYPE A RESPONSE WHEN THE COMPUTER ASKS."
30 PRINT "REMEMBER THAT ALL FACTORS ARE INTERRELATED AND THAT YOUR"
35 PRINT "RESPONSES COULD CHANGE HISTORY. FACTS AND FIGURES USED ARE"
40 PRINT "BASED ON THE ACTUAL OCCURENCE. MOST BATTLES TEND TO RESULT"
45 PRINT "AS THEY DID IN THE CIVIL WAR, BUT IT ALL DEPENDS ON YOU!!"
50 PRINT
51 PRINT "THE OBJECT OF THE GAME IS TO WIN AS MANY BATTLES AS POSSIBLE"
52 PRINT
55 PRINT "YOUR CHOICES FOR DEFENSIVE STRATEGY ARE:"
60 PRINT "        (1) ARTILLERY ATTACK"
65 PRINT "        (2) FORTIFICATION AGAINST FRONTAL ATTACK"
70 PRINT "        (3) FONTIFICATION AGAINST FLANKING MANUEVERS"
75 PRINT "        (4) FALLING BACK"
80 PRINT "YOUR CHOICES FOR OFFENSIVE STRATEGY ARE:"
85 PRINT "        (1) ARTILLERY ATTACK"
90 PRINT "        (2) FRONTAL ATTACK"
95 PRINT "        (3) FLANKING MANUEVERS"
96 PRINT "        (4) ENCIRCLEMENT"
97 PRINT "YOU MAY SURRENDER BY TYPING A '5' FOR YOUR STRATEGY."
98 PRINT
99 PRINT "YOU ARE THE CONFEDERACY.        GOOD LUCK!"
100 READ M1,M2,C1,C2,M,A,U
101 LET I1=10+(L-W)*2
102 LET I2=10+(W-L)*2
103 LET D1=100*INT((M1*(100-I1)/2000)*(1+(R1-Q1)/(R1+1))+0.5)
104 LET D2=100*INT(M2*(100-I2)/2000+0.5)
105 LET F1=5*M1/6
106 LET A1=Z
107 FOR U=1 TO 4
108 PRINT
109 NEXT U
110 PRINT "THIS IS THE BATTLE OF ";
115 GOSUB 800
120 PRINT " ","CONFEDERACY","  UNION"
130 PRINT "MEN"," ";INT(M1*(1+(P1-T1)/(M3+1))),"  ";
131 PRINT INT(M2*(1+(P2-T2)/(M4+1)))
140 PRINT "MONEY","$";D1,"$";D2
150 PRINT "INFLATION"," ";I1+15;"%","  ";I2;"%"
160 PRINT
170 PRINT "HOW MUCH DO YOU WISH TO SPEND FOR FOOD";
180 INPUT F
185 IF F<0 THEN 750
190 PRINT "HOW DO YOU WISH TO SPEND FOR SALARIES";
200 INPUT S
205 IF S<0 THEN 750
210 PRINT "HOW MUCH DO YOU WISH TO SPEND FOR AMMUNITION";
220 INPUT B
221 IF B<0 THEN 750
222 PRINT
224 IF F+S+B<=D1 THEN 230
226 PRINT "THINK AGAIN!   YOU HAVE ONLY $" D1
228 GOTO 160
230 LET O=((2+F*A2+S*A2)/F1*A2+1)
235 IF O<10 THEN 260
240 PRINT "MORALE IS HIGH"
250 GOTO 300
260 IF O<5 THEN 290
270 PRINT "MORALE IS FAIR"
280 GOTO 300
290 PRINT "MORALE IS POOR"
300 IF M<3 THEN 330
310 PRINT "YOU ARE ON THE OFFENSIVE"
320 GOTO 370
330 IF M<>1 THEN 360
340 PRINT "YOU ARE ON THE DEFENSIVE"
350 GOTO 370
360 PRINT "BOTH SIDES ARE ON THE OFFENSIVE"
370 PRINT
380 PRINT "YOUR STEGY";
390 INPUT Y
391 IF Y=5 THEN 1487
392 IF ABS(Y-3)<3 THEN 305
393 PRINT "YOU JERK!  USE THE OTHER SET OF STRATEGIES!!"
394 GOTO 370
395 PRINT
400 PRINT " ","CONFEDERACY","UNION"
410 LET C5=(2*C1/5)*(1+1/(2*(ABS(INT(4*RND(1)+1)-Y)+1)))
412 LET C5=INT(C5*(1+1/O)*(1.28+F1/(B+1))*0.5)
414 IF C5*100/O<M1*(1+(P1-T1)/(M3+1)) THEN 424
416 LET C5=INT(13*M1/20*(1+(P1-T1)/(M3+1)))
418 LET E=7*C5/13
420 LET U=1
422 GOTO 426
424 LET E=100/O
426 PRINT "CASUALTIES",C5,INT(17*C2*C1/(C5+20)+0.5)
430 PRINT "DESERTIONS",INT(E),INT(5*O)
432 PRINT
433 IF C5-C1>=0 THEN 439
435 PRINT "YOUR CASUALTIES WERE"INT(100*(C1-C5)/C1+0.5)"% LESS THAN"
437 GOTO 441
439 PRINT "YOUR CASUALTIES WERE"INT(100*(C5-C1)/C1+0.5)"% MORE THAN"
441 PRINT "THE ACTUAL CASUALTIES AT ";
443 LET A1=1
445 GO SUB800
450 IF U=1 THEN 470
460 IF C5*E<17*C2*C1/(C5+20)+5*O THEN 490
470 PRINT "YOU LOSE ";
471 LET L=L+1
480 GOTO 555
490 PRINT "YOU WIN ";
491 LET W=W+1
555 GOSUB 800
556 IF W=8 THEN 1490
580 LET T1=T1+C5+E
590 LET T2=T2+17*C2*C1/(C5+20)+5*O
600 LET P1=P1+C1
610 LET P2=P2+C2
620 LET Q1=Q1+(F+S+B)
630 LET R1=R1+M1*(100-I1)/20

635 LET M3=M3+M1
637 LET M4=M4+M2
650 IF A=14 THEN 1500
660 GOTO 100
670 DATA 18000,18500,1967,2708,1,1,0
672 DATA 40000,44894,10699,13047,3,2,0
674 DATA 95000,115000,20614,15849,3,3,0
676 DATA 54000,63000,10000,14000,2,4,0
678 DATA 40000,50000,10000,12000,3,5,0
680 DATA 75000,120000,5377,12653,1,6,0
682 DATA 38000,45000,11000,12000,1,7,0
684 DATA 32000,90000,13000,17197,2,8,0
686 DATA 50000,70000,12000,19000,1,9,0
688 DATA 72500,85000,20000,23000,3,10,0
690 DATA 66000,60000,18000,16000,2,11,0
692 DATA 37000,60000,6700,5800,2,12,0
694 DATA 62000,110000,17723,18000,2,13,0
696 DATA 65000,100000,8500,3700,1,14,0
750 PRINT "GO TO JAIL."
752 PRINT "GO DIRECTLY TO JAIL."
754 PRINT "DO NOT PASS GO."
756 PRINT "DO NOT COLLECT $200"
758 GOTO 107
800 IF A<>1 THEN 850
810 PRINT "BULL RUN"
820 IF A1=1 THEN 1480
830 PRINT"JULY 21,1861    GEN. BEAUREGARD COMMANDING THE SOUTH MET THE"
832 PRINT"UNION FORCES WITH GEN MCDOWLL IN A PREMATURE BATTLE AT BULL"
834 PRINT"RUN.  GEN. JACKSON HELPED PUSH BACK THE UNION ATTACK."
840 GO TO 1480
850 IF A<>2 THEN 900
860 PRINT "SHILOH"
870 IF A1=1 THEN 1480
880 PRINT"APRIL 6-7,1862    THE CONFEDERATE SURPRISE ATTACK AT SHILOH"
882 PRINT"FAILED DUE TO POOR ORGANIZATION."
890 GO TO 1480
900 IF A<>3 THEN 950
910 PRINT "SEVEN DAYS"
920 IF A1=1 THEN 1480
930 PRINT"JUNE 25-JULY 1,1862    GENERAL LEE (CSA) UPHELD THE OFFENSIVE"
932 PRINT"THROUGHOUT THE BATTLE AND FORCED GEN. MCCLELLAN AND THE UNION"
934 PRINT"FORCES AWAY FROM RICHMOND."
940 GO TO 1480
950 IF A<>4 THEN 1000
960 PRINT "THE SECOND BULL RUN"
970 IF A1=1 THEN 1480
980 PRINT"AUG 29-30,1862    THE COMBINED CONFEDERATE FORCES UNDER LEE AND"
982 PRINT"JACKSON DROVE THE UNION FORCES BACK INTO WASHINGTON."
990 GO TO 1480
1000 IF A<>5 THEN 1050
1010 PRINT "ANTIETAM"
1020 IF A1=1 THEN 1480
1030 PRINT"SEPT 17,1862    THE SOUTH FAILED TO INCORPORATE MARYLAND INTO"
1032 PRINT"THE CONFEDERACY."
1040 GO TO 1480
1050 IF A<>6 THEN 1100
1060 PRINT "FREDERICKSBURG"
1070 IF A1=1 THEN 1480
1080 PRINT"DEC 13,1862 THE CONFEDERACY UNDER LEE SUCESSFULLY REPULSED"
1082 PRINT"AN ATTACK BY THE UNION UNDER GEN. BURNSIDE."
1090 GOTO 1480
1100 IF A <>7 THEN 1150
1110 PRINT "MURFREESBORO"
1120 IF A1=1 THEN 1480
1130 PRINT"DEC 31,1862    THE SOUTH UNDER GEN. BRAGG WON A CLOSE BATTLE"
1140 GOTO 1480
1150 IF A<>8 THEN 1200
1160 PRINT "CHANCELLORSVILLE"
1170 IF A1=1 THEN 1480
1180 PRINT"MAY 1-6,1863    THE SOUTH HAD A COSTLY VICTORY AND LOST ONE"
1182 PRINT"OF THEIR OUTSTANDING GENERALS, 'STONEWALL' JACKSON."
1190 GOTO 1480
1200 IF A<>9 THEN 1250
1210 PRINT "VICKSBURG"
1220 IF A1=1 THEN 1480
1230 PRINT"JULY 4,1863    VICKSBURG WAS A COSTLY DEFEAT FOR THE SOUTH"
1232 PRINT"BECAUSE IT GAVE THE UNION ACCESS TO THE MISSISSIPPI."
1240 GOTO 1480
1250 IF A<>10 THEN 1300
1260 PRINT "GETTYSBURG"
1270 IF A1=1 THEN 1480
1280 PRINT"JUNE 30,1863    A SOUTHERN MISTAKE BY GEN. LEE AT GETTYSBURG"
1282 PRINT"COST THEM ONE OF THE MOST CRUCIAL BATTLES OF THR WAR."
1290 GOTO 1480
1300 IF A<>11 THEN 1350
1310 PRINT "CHICKAMAUGA"
1320 IF A1=1 THEN 1480
1330 PRINT"NOV 25,1863    AFTER THE SOUTH HAD SIEGED GEN. ROSENCRANS!"
1332 PRINT"ARMY FOR THREE MONTHS, GEN. GRANT BROKE THE SIEGE."
1340 GOTO 1480
1350 IF A<>12 THEN 1400
1360 PRINT "CHATTANOOGA"
1370 IF A1=1 THEN 1480
1380 PRINT"SEPT 15,1863    CONFUSION IN A FOREST NEAR CHICKAMAUGA LED"
1382 PRINT"TO A COSTLY SOUTHERN VICTORY."
1390 GOTO 1480
1400 IF A<>13 THEN 1450
1410 PRINT "SPOTSYLVANIA"
1420 IF A1=1 THEN 1480
1430 PRINT"MAY 5,1864    GRANT'S PLAN TO KEEP LEE ISOLATED BEGAN TO FAIL"
1432 PRINT"HERE, AND CONTINUED AT COLD HARBOR AND PETERSBURG."
1440 GOTO 1480
1450 PRINT "ATLANTA"
1460 IF A1=1 THEN 1480
1470 PRINT"AUGUST, 1864    SHERMAN AND THREE VETERAN ARMIES CONVERGED ON"
1472 PRINT"ATLANTA AND DEALT THE DEATH BLOW TO THE CONFEDERACY."
1480 PRINT
1485 RETURN
1487 PRINT "THE CONFEDERACY HAS SURRENDERED"
1488 GOTO 1500
1490 PRINT "THE UNION HAS SURRENDERED"
1500 PRINT
1510 PRINT "YOU HAVE WON" W; "BATTLES AND LOST" L; "BATTLES."
1515 IF Y=5 THEN 1550
1520 IF W<=L THEN 1550
1530 PRINT "THE CONFEDERACY HAS WON THE WAR"
1540 STOP
1550 PRINT "THE UNION HAS WON THE WAR"
1560 END
```

?᠎?᠎?¿?᠎? GUESS ?᠎?᠎?᠎?᠎?

GUESS is a simple introduction to the idea of a computer program and computer games. It also introduces the notions of comparison and searching a list.

Before playing GUESS on the computer, you may wish to play it in class at the chalkboard. One student is selected to be the computer. He is given the flowchart below and is asked to follow it and write on the chalkboard the statements in parentheses as well as each guess. Students take turns being the computer.

After playing the game manually, play GUESS on the computer. Divide the class into small teams of 2 or 3 members each. Have each team play 10 games on the computer and keep track of the number of guesses required to get each number. Compute the average guesses for each team and for the entire class. After playing the class should consider the following questions:

1. Why should it never take more than 7 guesses to find the number?

2. What was the average guesses for the class? How does this compare to the theoretical average (using the correct guessing strategy) of 5.3?

3. What are the maximum number of guesses required to find a mystery number between:

1 and 10	1 and 64
1 and 63	1 and 1000

FLOWCHART

PROGRAM LISTING

```
1  PRI "THIS IS A NUMBER GUESSING GAME.  I'LL THINK"
2  PRI "OF A NUMBER BETWEEN 1 AND ANY LIMIT YOU WANT."
3  PRI "THEN YOU HAVE TO GUESS WHAT IT IS."
4  PRI
5  PRI "WHAT LIMIT DO YOU WANT";
6  INPL
7  PRI
8  L1=INT(LOG(L)/LOG(2))+1
10 PRI"I'M THINKING OF A NUMBER BETWEEN 1 AND"L
11 G=1
14 PRI "NOW YOU TRY TO GUESS WHAT IT IS"
15 M=INT(L*RND(0))+1
20 INP N
21 IF N>0 THEN 25
22 GOSUB70
23 GOTO1
25 IF N=M THEN 50
30 G=G+1
31 IF N>M THEN 40
32 PRI "TOO LOW. GUESS AGAIN."
33 GOTO 20
40 PRI "TOO HIGH.  GUESS AGAIN "
42 GOTO 20
50 PRI "THAT'S IT!  YOU GOT IT IN"G"TRIES."
52 IF G<L1 THEN '58
54 IF G=L1 THEN 60
56 PRI"YOU SHOULD HAVE BEEN ABLE TO GET IT IN ONLY"L1"."
57 GOT 65
58 PRI"VERY ";
60 PRI"GOOD!
65 GOSUB70
66 GOTO10
70 FOR H=1 TO 5
71 PRI
72 NEXT H
73 RETURN
99 END
```

Note: BASIC statements in this program are abbreviated to their first 3 letters.

SAMPLE RUN

```
THIS IS A NUMBER GUESSING GAME.  I'LL THINK
OF A NUMBER BETWEEN 1 AND ANY LIMIT YOU WANT.
THEN YOU HAVE TO GUESS WHAT IT IS.

WHAT LIMIT DO YOU WANT? 100

I'M THINKING OF A NUMBER BETWEEN 1 AND 100
NOW YOU TRY TO GUESS WHAT IT IS
? 50
TOO HIGH.  GUESS AGAIN.
? 25
THAT'S IT!  YOU GOT IT IN 2 TRIES.
VERY GOOD!



I'M THINKING OF A NUMBER BETWEEN 1 AND 100
NOW YOU TRY TO GUESS WHAT IT IS
? 50
TOO HIGH.  GUESS AGAIN.
? 25
TOO LOW. GUESS AGAIN.
? 37
TOO HIGH.  GUESS AGAIN.
? 31
TOO HIGH.  GUESS AGAIN.
? 28
TOO LOW. GUESS AGAIN.
? 29
TOO LOW. GUESS AGAIN.
? 30
THAT'S IT!  YOU GOT IT IN 7 TRIES.
GOOD!
```

Another new game from Creative Computing . . . .

REVERSE

987654321   123456789

by Peter Sessions,
People's Computer Company,
Menlo Park, CA

Description

In the computer game REVERSE the player must arrange a list of numbers in numerical order from left to right. To move, you tell the computer how many numbers in the list (counting from the left) to reverse. For example, if the current list is:

2	3	4	5	1	6	7	8	9

and you reverse four numbers, the result will be:

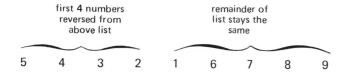

	first 4 numbers reversed from above list				remainder of list stays the same			
5	4	3	2	1	6	7	8	9

Now if you reverse five numbers, you win!

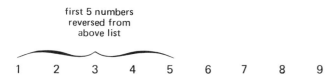

	first 5 numbers reversed from above list							
1	2	3	4	5	6	7	8	9

Playing Strategies

There are many ways to play the game; generally an approach can either be classified as *algorithmic* or *heuristic*. The game thus affords the player an opportunity to explore these concepts in a practical rather than a theoretical context.

An algorithmic approach is one that is described by means of a finite algorithm and guarantees a solution in a predictable number of moves. For example, an algorithmic approach to playing REVERSE would be to order the list from right to left starting with the highest value number and moving down. Using this strategy with a list of nine numbers, your first move would always be to get the 9 into position 1 (leftmost) and the second move would be to

reverse nine so the 9 was put into position 9 (rightmost). You would continue moving the 8 to position 1 and then to position 8, the 7, 6, 5 and so on until the list was ordered. This method guarantees a solution in 2N-3 moves (N numbers in the list). One could easily program a computer to play this strategy.

A heuristic approach to solving a problem can be thought of as a rule of thumb. Some rules of thumb are very good and lead to good solutions, others are not as good. Consequently, using a heuristic approach doesn't guarantee the best possible solution but for very complex problems (and even some simple ones) it may be a more efficient approach than a rigorous linear programming or mathematical method which guarantees a perfect solution.

The science of heuristic problem solving using the computer has become very advanced and is widely used for things like locating warehouses, railroad car routing and other problems involving hundreds of variables and many alternative solutions. Consider: a linear programming solution to routing a mixed load boxcar from Boston to receiving points in Hartford, Columbus, Atlanta, and Baton Rouge would take about 0.72 hours to run on a computer. The heuristic solution takes 0.002 seconds to run, yet it generally yields a solution within 5% of the linear programming (perfect) solution. Obviously, with millions of cars to be routed every day, the linear approach is not economically feasible.

The game of REVERSE lends itself very well to a heuristic approach. There are many possible solutions to each game. One is best, but the mathematics to determine this solution are quite complex and would be extremely time-consuming to calculate. (The simpler algorithmic approach above guarantees a solution, but it is far from optimal). A good heuristic approach which takes advantage of "partial orderings" in the list generally yields a solution within 1 or 2 moves of the perfect solution, i.e., within 10% to 20% of perfection.

Using a heuristic approach, your next move is dependent upon the way the list currently appears. No solution is guaranteed in a predictable number of moves, but if you are clever (and lucky?) you should come out ahead of the simple algorithmic approaches. For a list with nine numbers can you describe a heuristic strategy that wins the game in an average of 10 or fewer moves? You may well use more than one rule of thumb (heuristic).

PROGRAM LISTING

```
100 PRINT\PRINT "REVERSE -- A GAME OF SKILL"\PRINT
120 RANDOMIZE
130 DIM A(20)
140 REM *** N=NUMBER OF NUMBERS
150 N=9
160 INPUT "DO YOU WANT THE RULES (YES OR NO)";A$
180 IF A$="NO" THEN 210
190 GOSUB 710
200 REM *** MAKE A RANDOM LIST A(1) TO A(N)
210 A(1)=INT((N-1)*RND)+2
220 FOR K=2 TO N
230 A(K)=INT(N*RND)+1
240 FOR J=1 TO K-1
250 IF A(K)=A(J) THEN 230
260 NEXT J\NEXT K
280 REM *** PRINT ORIGINAL LIST AND START GAME
290 PRINT\PRINT "HERE WE GO ... THE LIST IS:"
310 T=0
320 GOSUB 610
330 INPUT "HOW MANY SHALL I REVERSE";R
350 IF R=0 THEN 520
360 IF R<=N THEN 390
370 PRINT "OOPS! TOO MANY - I CAN REVERSE AT MOST"N\GOTO 330
390 T=T+1
400 REM *** REVERSE R NUMBERS AND PRINT NEW LIST
410 FOR K=1 TO INT(R/2)
420 Z=A(K)
430 A(K)=A(R-K+1)
440 A(R-K+1)=Z
450 NEXT K
460 GOSUB 610
470 REM *** CHECK FOR A WIN
480 FOR K=1 TO N
490 IF A(K)<>K THEN 330
500 NEXT K
510 PRINT "YOU WON IT IN"T"MOVES !!!"\PRINT
530 INPUT "TRY AGAIN (YES OR NO)";A$
550 IF A$="YES" THEN 210
560 PRINT\PRINT "O.K.   HOPE YOU HAD FUN!!"\GOTO 999
600 REM *** SUBROUTINE TO PRINT LIST
610 PRINT\FOR K=1 TO N\PRINT A(K);\NEXT K
650 PRINT\RETURN
700 REM *** SUBROUTINE TO PRINT THE RULES
710 PRINT\PRINT "THIS IS THE GAME OF 'REVERSE'. TO WIN, ALL YOU HAVE"
720 PRINT "TO DO IS ARRANGE A LIST OF NUMBERS (1 THROUGH"N")"
730 PRINT "IN NUMERICAL ORDER FROM LEFT TO RIGHT. TO MOVE, YOU"
740 PRINT "TELL ME HOW MANY NUMBERS (COUNTING FROM THE LEFT) TO"
750 PRINT "REVERSE. FOR EXAMPLE, IF THE CURRENT LIST IS:"
760 PRINT\PRINT "2 3 4 5 1 6 7 8 9"
770 PRINT\PRINT "AND YOU REVERSE 4, THE RESULT WILL BE:"
780 PRINT\PRINT "5 4 3 2 1 6 7 8 9"
790 PRINT\PRINT "NOW, IF YOU REVERSE 5, YOU WIN!"
800 PRINT\PRINT "1 2 3 4 5 6 7 8 9"
810 PRINT "NO DOUBT YOU WILL LIKE THIS GAME OF SKILL, BUT"
820 PRINT "IF YOU WANT TO QUIT, REVERSE 0 (ZERO). "\PRINT\RETURN
999 END

READY
```

SAMPLE RUN

```
REVERSE -- A GAME OF SKILL

DO YOU WANT THE RULES (YES OR NO)? YES

THIS IS THE GAME OF 'REVERSE'. TO WIN, ALL YOU HAVE
TO DO IS ARRANGE A LIST OF NUMBERS (1 THROUGH 9 )
IN NUMERICAL ORDER FROM LEFT TO RIGHT. TO MOVE, YOU
TELL ME HOW MANY NUMBERS (COUNTING FROM THE LEFT) TO
REVERSE. FOR EXAMPLE, IF THE CURRENT LIST IS:

2 3 4 5 1 6 7 8 9

AND YOU REVERSE 4, THE RESULT WILL BE:

5 4 3 2 1 6 7 8 9

NOW, IF YOU REVERSE 5, YOU WIN!

1 2 3 4 5 6 7 8 9

NO DOUBT YOU WILL LIKE THIS GAME OF SKILL, BUT
IF YOU WANT TO QUIT, REVERSE 0 (ZERO).

HERE WE GO ... THE LIST IS:

 9 8 6 1 7 3 2 4 5

HOW MANY SHALL I REVERSE? 9

 5 4 2 3 7 1 6 8 9

HOW MANY SHALL I REVERSE? 4        HOW MANY SHALL I REVERSE? 7

 3 2 4 5 7 1 6 8 9                  6 7 1 5 4 3 2 8 9

HOW MANY SHALL I REVERSE? 2        HOW MANY SHALL I REVERSE? 2

 2 3 4 5 7 1 6 8 9                  7 6 1 5 4 3 2 8 9

HOW MANY SHALL I REVERSE? 6        HOW MANY SHALL I REVERSE? 7

 1 7 5 4 3 2 6 8 9                  2 3 4 5 1 6 7 8 9

HOW MANY SHALL I REVERSE? 2        HOW MANY SHALL I REVERSE? 4

 7 1 5 4 3 2 6 8 9                  5 4 3 2 1 6 7 8 9

HOW MANY SHALL I REVERSE? 6        HOW MANY SHALL I REVERSE? 5

 2 3 4 5 1 7 6 8 9                  1 2 3 4 5 6 7 8 9

                                   YOU WON IT IN 11 MOVES !!!
```

Another new game from Creative Computing . . . .

SCHMOO

by Frederick H. Bell
University of Pittsburgh

Computers, Coordinates, and Schmoos

This Module is a computer-based educational (and fun) game with instructions for its use. It is written in elementary BASIC and is compatible with nearly all BASIC interpreters.

Getting Ready

Before teaching this lesson load SPLAT2 into your computer system, debug it, and save it for future access.

Things to Know

You need to know a little bit about grids and angles. Like, (2,-3) means right 2 and down 3, and 237° is in the fourth (Whoops! That's third.) quadrant. Also, you should remember that the distance something travels through the air depends upon the angle at which it is thrown.

Review the Basics

Can you answer these questions? If not, hit the math books!

1. In each of the four quadrants, what are the signs of the x- and y- coordinates?
2. If 0° is the angle coinciding with the positive x- axis, what are the measures of angles whose terminal sides fall in Quadrant I? Quadrant II? Quadrant III, Quadrant IV?

Lines 5 to 70 explain how to play SPLAT2. This is a fun game to play in groups of two or three. If you're pretty good you can "splat the schmoo" in about eight tries; but don't cheat and use the formula. And don't expect me to tell you where it's hidden in the program!

More Things to Do

You might want to make a three dimensional game, SPLAT3 — with flying schmoos. The program shouldn't be too hard and it would be a really neat game. If you want to try something easier, fix SPLAT2 so that it requires initial velocities as well as angles. You could even make a low gravity, moon version of SPLAT2.

**Program Listing
Sample Output**

REMarks About BASIC
REMark Statements

REMember to REMind yourself when writing BASIC REMark statements to REMain imaginative. If you are not REMiss in this, you can REModel your programs into REMarkable masterpieces with no REMainder of your REMote past before you applied this REMedy and REMoved those old, dull REMark statements. REMit to this REMedial advice and you'll have no REMorse. Before long, you can be REMiniscent about your old programs containing REMinants of ordinary REMark statements.

10 REMARKABLE REMARKS BY DHA

```
5 PRINT"THIS IS A NEW SCHMOO GAME.  SCHMOOS"
10 PRINT"ARE IMAGINARY CREATURES WHO LOVE"
15 PRINT"BEING SPLATTED WITH JUICY MUD BALLS."
20 PRINT"YOU, BEING A SCHMOO LOVER, TRY TO"
25 PRINT"MAKE SCHMOOS HAPPY BY TOSSING MUD"
30 PRINT"BALLS AT THEM.  YOU HAVE A"
35 PRINT"MECHANICAL MUD SLINGER THAT WILL"
40 PRINT"SLING MUD TO A MAXIMUM DISTANCE"
45 PRINT"OF 46,500 INCHES.  YOUR JOB IS TO"
50 PRINT"SET THE MUD SLINGER AT THE CORRECT"
55 PRINT"ELEVATION (0 TO 90) AND THE CORRECT"
60 PRINT"DIRECTIONAL ANGLE (0 TO 360)TO SPLAT THE"
65 PRINT"SCHMOO.  A HIT WITHIN 100 INCHES OF"
70 PRINT"THE SCHMOO WILL SPLATTER HIM."
75 PRINT
90 PRINT
95 RANDOMIZE
100 K1 = 0
110 Z = INT(1+RND*4-1E-8)
120 ON Z GOTO 130,140,150,160
130 P = -1
135 Q = -1
138 GOTO 200
140 P = -1
145 Q = 1
148 GOTO 200
150 P = 1
155 Q = -1
158 GOTO 200
160 P = 1
165 Q = 1
200 X = (INT (26000*RND+5000))*P
210 Y = (INT(26000*RND+5000))*Q
220 S = 0
230 K1 = K1 +1
240 IF K1<2 GOTO 400
250 R = INT(7*RND) + 5
260 GOTO 400
300 PRINT "THE ELEVATION MUST BE BETWEEN 1 AND 90."
310 GOTO 500
320 PRINT"DIRECTIONAL ANGLE MUST BE FROM 0 TO 360."
340 GOTO 500
350 PRINT"*SCHMOO SPLATTED*";S;" MUD BALLS TOSSED."
351 PRINT
352 PRINT"I SEE ANOTHER SCHMOO.  TO SPLAT"
354 PRINT"HIM, TYPE MUD.  TO QUIT, TYPE QUIT."
356 PRINT
358 INPUT C$
360 IF C$ = "MUD" GOTO 110
361 STOP
362 PRINT"YOU MISSED THE SCHMOO AT (";X;",";Y;")."
364 PRINT"YOUR MUD HIT (";INT(X1);",";INT(Y1);")."
366 PRINT
370 IF K1<2 GOTO 500
380 IF S>=R GOTO 800
390 PRINT"SCHMOO MUD HIT ";R2;" INCHES FROM YOU."
395 GOTO 50U
400 PRINT
410 PRINT"COORDINATES OF SCHMOO ARE (";X;",";Y;")."
415 IF K1 <2 GOTO 420
417 PRINT"THE SCHMOO IS HAPPY TO BE SPLATTED."
418 PRINT"TO MAKE YOU HAPPY TOO,"
419 PRINT"HE WILL THROW MUD AT YOU."
420 PRINT
500 PRINT"MUD SLINGER ELEVATION";
502 INPUT B
504 PRINT"DIRECTIONAL ANGLE OF MUD SLINGER";
506 INPUT C
520 IF B = 90 GOTO 700
530 IF B >90 GOTO 300
540 IF B<1 GOTO 300
550 IF C<0 GOTO 320
560 IF C>(360-(1E-8)) GOTO 320
570 S = S+1
580 IF K1<2 GOTO 595
590 R2 = INT(ABS(300*RND*(11-2*S))+90)
595 J = 3.14159/180
596 D = ABS(INT(93000*SIN(B*J)*COS(B*J)))
610 X1 = D*COS(C*3.14159/180)
620 Y1 = D*SIN(C*3.14159/180)
630 D1 = SQR((X-X1)^2 + (Y-Y1)^2)
640 IF 100>=D1 GOTO 350
650 GOTO 362
700 PRINT"YOU DOPE!  YOU SPLATTED YOURSELF."
710 GOTO 900
800 PRINT"THE SCHMOO SPLATTED YOU!"
802 PRINT"CLEAN UP AND GOODBY!"
900 END
```

```
COORDINATES OF SCHMOO ARE ( 21065 - 5063 ).

MUD SLINGER ELEVATION ?10
DIRECTIONAL ANGLE OF MUD SLINGER ?23
YOU MISSED THE SCHMOO AT ( 21065 , 5063 ).
YOUR MUD HIT ( 14638 , 6213 ).

MUD SLINGER ELEVATION ?14
DIRECTIONAL ANGLE OF MUD SLINGER ?20
YOU MISSED THE SCHMOO AT ( 21065 , 5063 ).
YOUR MUD HIT ( 20513 , 7466 ).

MUD SLINGER ELEVATION ?13.5
DIRECTIONAL ANGLE OF MUD SLINGER ?18
YOU MISSED THE SCHMOO AT ( 21065 , 5063 ).
YOUR MUD HIT ( 20076 , 6523 ).

MUD SLINGER ELEVATION ?13.5
DIRECTIONAL ANGLE OF MUD SLINGER ?16
YOU MISSED THE SCHMOO AT ( 21065 , 5063 ).
YOUR MUD HIT ( 20292 , 5818 ).

MUD SLINGER ELEVATION ?13.5
DIRECTIONAL ANGLE OF MUD SLINGER ?15
YOU MISSED THE SCHMOO AT ( 21065 , 5063 ).
YOUR MUD HIT ( 20390 , 5463 ).

MUD SLINGER ELEVATION ?13.6
DIRECTIONAL ANGLE OF MUD SLINGER ?14
YOU MISSED THE SCHMOO AT ( 21065 , 5063 ).
YOUR MUD HIT ( 20623 , 5142 ).

MUD SLINGER ELEVATION ?13.7
DIRECTIONAL ANGLE OF MUD SLINGER ?13
YOU MISSED THE SCHMOO AT ( 21065 , 5063 ).
YOUR MUD HIT ( 20850 , 4813 ).

MUD SLINGER ELEVATION ?13.9
DIRECTIONAL ANGLE OF MUD SLINGER ?13
YOU MISSED THE SCHMOO AT ( 21065 , 5063 ).
YOUR MUD HIT ( 21130 , 4878 ).

MUD SLINGER ELEVATION ?13.9
DIRECTIONAL ANGLE OF MUD SLINGER ?13.5
*SCHMOO SPLATTED* 9  MUD BALLS TOSSED.

I SEE ANOTHER SCHMOO.  TO SPLAT
HIM, TYPE MUD.  TO QUIT, TYPE QUIT.

  ?MUD

COORDINATES OF SCHMOO ARE ( 15368 ,-16337 ).
THE SCHMOO IS HAPPY TO BE SPLATTED.
TO MAKE YOU HAPPY TOO,
HE WILL THROW MUD AT YOU.

MUD SLINGER ELEVATION ?15
DIRECTIONAL ANGLE OF MUD SLINGER ?316
YOU MISSED THE SCHMOO AT ( 15368 ,-16337 ).
YOUR MUD HIT ( 16723 ,-16151 ).

SCHMOO MUD HIT  1559  INCHES FROM YOU.
MUD SLINGER ELEVATION ?14.5
DIRECTIONAL ANGLE OF MUD SLINGER ?317
YOU MISSED THE SCHMOO AT ( 15368 ,-16337 ).
YOUR MUD HIT ( 16486 ,-15375 ).

SCHMOO MUD HIT  125  INCHES FROM YOU.
MUD SLINGER ELEVATION ?14.5
DIRECTIONAL ANGLE OF MUD SLINGER ?314
YOU MISSED THE SCHMOO AT ( 15368 ,-16337 ).
YOUR MUD HIT ( 15659 ,-16217 ).

SCHMOO MUD HIT  747  INCHES FROM YOU.
MUD SLINGER ELEVATION ?14.6
DIRECTIONAL ANGLE OF MUD SLINGER ?320
YOU MISSED THE SCHMOO AT ( 15368 ,-16337 ).
YOUR MUD HIT ( 17377 ,-14582 ).

SCHMOO MUD HIT  870  INCHES FROM YOU.
MUD SLINGER ELEVATION ?14.6
DIRECTIONAL ANGLE OF MUD SLINGER ?315
YOU MISSED THE SCHMOO AT ( 15368 ,-16337 ).
YOUR MUD HIT ( 16040 ,-16041 ).

SCHMOO MUD HIT  372  INCHES FROM YOU.
MUD SLINGER ELEVATION ?14.6
DIRECTIONAL ANGLE OF MUD SLINGER ?314.5
YOU MISSED THE SCHMOO AT ( 15368 ,-16337 ).
YOUR MUD HIT ( 15900 ,-16181 ).

THE SCHMOO SPLATTED YOU!
CLEAN UP AND GOODBY!
```

We didn't repeat the game instructions (Lines 5-70) here.

It may be easier with a diagram—

Why does the Schmoo throw mud at you this time??

BINARY

by Ted C. Park
Pacific Union College
Angwin, California

DESCRIPTION

This game tests your skills in binary-to-decimal and decimal-to binary conversion. You will be given twenty conversion trials. Numbers are chosen randomly and your score will be printed at the end. The answer to any conversion you miss will be displayed; if the next conversion is presented, you may assume you got the previous one correct.

SUGGESTED MODIFICATIONS

1. If your computer has an "ENTER" statement or some other sort of timed input, then fix-up this program to allow only a certain time for each conversion and then go on to the next one.
2. Allow the user to enter the range (number of bits) allowed for the binary numbers.
3. Being able to select the number of conversions of each type would be beneficial.
4. Extend this exercise to other bases!
5. Modify program to check for duplicate numbers.

LISTING

```
BINARY

100   DIM B$[2],B[5],I$[72]
110   B$="01"
120   T0=20
130   PRINT
140   PRINT
150   FOR I=1 TO 10
160   GOSUB 560
170   PRINT "BINARY:      ";
180   FOR J=1 TO 5
190   PRINT B$[B[J]+1,B[J]+1];
200   NEXT J
210   PRINT "     DECIMAL:    ";
220   INPUT A
230   IF A=D THEN 260
240   PRINT D
250   T0=T0-1
260   PRINT
270   NEXT I
280   PRINT
290   PRINT
300   FOR I=1 TO 10
310   GOSUB 560
320   PRINT "DECIMAL: ";D;
330   PRINT "      BINARY:     ";
340   I$="00000"
350   INPUT I$[6]
360   IF LEN(I$)>10 THEN 420
370   I$[11-LEN(I$)]=I$[6]
380   FOR J=1 TO 5
390   IF B$[B[J]+1,B[J]+1]#I$[J,J] THEN 420
400   NEXT J
410   GOTO 480
420   PRINT "  ";
430   FOR J=1 TO 5
440   PRINT B$[B[J]+1,B[J]+1];
450   NEXT J
460   PRINT
470   T0=T0-1
480   PRINT
490   NEXT I
500   PRINT
510   PRINT
520   PRINT "YOUR SCORE:";INT(T0/.2+.5);"%"
530   PRINT
540   PRINT
550   STOP
560   D=0
570   FOR J=1 TO 5
580   B[J]=INT(RND(0)+.5)
590   D=D*2+B[J]
600   NEXT J
610   RETURN
620   END
```

SAMPLE RUNS

```
RUN
BINARY


BINARY:      00111    DECIMAL:    ?14
7

BINARY:      11100    DECIMAL:    ?26
28

BINARY:      11000    DECIMAL:    ?24

BINARY:      10011    DECIMAL:    ?19

BINARY:      11100    DECIMAL:    ?28

BINARY:      01101    DECIMAL:    ?13

BINARY:      11010    DECIMAL:    ?26

BINARY:      10010    DECIMAL:    ?18

BINARY:      10000    DECIMAL:    ?16

BINARY:      10110    DECIMAL:    ?22


DECIMAL:  25     BINARY:    ?11001

DECIMAL:  3      BINARY:    ?11

DECIMAL:  7      BINARY:    ?111

DECIMAL:  8      BINARY:    ?1000

DECIMAL:  3      BINARY:    ?11

DECIMAL:  21     BINARY:    ?10101

DECIMAL:  15     BINARY:    ?1110
01111

DECIMAL:  4      BINARY:    ?100

DECIMAL:  8      BINARY:    ?1000

DECIMAL:  12     BINARY:    ?1100


YOUR SCORE: 85    %


DONE
```

261

Another new game from Creative Computing . . .

SEAWAR

DESCRIPTION

You are the commander of a fleet of ships operating in enemy territory. Your task force consists of 9 ships, and the enemy has 9 ships. Whoever sinks all of the opponent's ships first wins the campaign.

You, as the commander, must provide the angle of elevation at which the guns will be fired, neglecting air resistance. Your instruments will read the range to the target, and the initial velocity is held constant at about 675 meters per second. Since there is a 7 second time limit for entering the angle of elevation, you will have to act quickly!

PROGRAMMING NOTES

1. The program as listed will run on a Hewlett-Packard 2000F system, but it can be adapted to other computer systems using BASIC.
2. Statement 550 allows 7 seconds to input the angle of elevation. When the game is initially introduced, you may prefer to extend this time to 15-20 seconds.
3. Lines 210 and 1100 have the bell enclosed in the quotation marks.
4. The initial velocity may be varied by changing line 700.

SOURCE

The origin of SEAWAR is unknown. It was revised and submitted to us by David S. Paxton, Fairfax, Virginia. It was further revised and the writeup prepared by Mary T. Dobbs, Mathematics and Science Center, Glen Allen, Virginia.

USING THE PROGRAM

SEAWAR will help you learn about the paths of projectiles and what happens as the angle of elevation varies.

1. First, what do you think the path of the projectile looks like. Make a sketch. (If you're still not sure, do some research in the library — it will help you win the battle, commander!)
   a. What angle of elevation do you think will give the maximum range?
   b. What will happen if you fire the guns at 0°?
   c. What will happen to the projectile if you fire it straight up?
2. After becoming proficient at winning the battle, change the initial velocity of the projectile. How does this affect the range?
3. For a more sophisticated look at projectiles, check out these programs.
   "The Paris Gun," as listed and described in the Hewlett-Packard Users Group Newsletter, Nov-Dec 1974.
   **PRJTL, Huntington I Simulation Programs — PHYSICS, published by Digital Equipment Corporation.

```
RUN
SEAWAR                    SAMPLE RUN

YOU COMMAND A FLEET OF SHIPS OPERATING IN ENEMY TERRITORY!!!
DO YOU NEED INSTRUCTIONS ?YES
YOU TELL YOUR GUN CREWS THE ELEVATION TO SET THEIR GUNS.
ELEVATION IS IN DEGREES FROM 0 TO 360.
YOUR TASK FORCE CONSISTS OF 3 DESTROYERS, 2 CRUISERS,
2 BATTLESHIPS, AND 2 HEAVY AIRCRAFT CARRIERS.
THE ENEMY HAS 9 SHIPS FOR HIS DEFENSE.
IF YOU SUCCEED IN SINKING ALL HIS SHIPS BEFORE HE SINKS
YOURS, YOU HAVE WON.  HOWEVER, IF HE SINKS ALL YOUR SHIPS
BEFORE YOU HAVE DEFEATED HIM, YOU HAVE LOST!!
LET US BEGIN!!!

YOUR FLAGSHIP HAS DETECTED A U-BOAT APPROACHING AT 5 FATHOMS.
YOUR SUBMARINE DETECTION EQUIMENT READS THE RANGE TO THE TARGET
AS 23175 METERS.
THE U-BOAT HAS COMMENCED FIRING TORPEDOES AT YOUR SHIPS.
HIS FIRST TORPEDO EXPLODED  65 METERS BEHIND YOUR SHIP.
WHAT ELEVATION ** 13
-----FIRE!!!
DEPTH CHARGE EXPLODED 2792 METERS SHORT OF TARGET.
THE ENEMY TORPEDO EXPLODED  57 METERS IN FRONT OF YOUR
SHIP.
WHAT ELEVATION ** 15
-----FIRE!!!
DEPTH CHARGE EXPLODED RIGHT ON TOP OF THAT BABY!!!

TARGET DESTROYED!!!      *2 **  ROUNDS EXPENDED.
YOU HAVE LOST 0 SHIPS, AND THE ENEMY HAS LOST 1.

YOUR FLAGSHIP REPORTS THE SIGHTING OF AN ENEMY 210 MM SHORE GUN
YOUR INSTRUMENTS READ THE RANGE TO THE TARGET AS 22539
METERS.
THE ENEMY 210 MM SHORE GUN IS FIRING ON YOUR SHIPS!
HIS FIRST ROUND FELL 425 METERS SHORT.
WHAT ELEVATION **
             ADMIRAL !! YOU HAVE TO BE FAST IN THIS GAME!!
THE ENEMY 210 MM SHORE GUN SANK ONE OF YOUR DESTROYERS!!
WHAT ELEVATION ** 14
-----FIRE!!!
SHOT FELL   710 METERS SHORT OF TARGET.
THE ENEMY ROUND FELL 136 METERS SHORT.
WHAT ELEVATION ** 14.5
-----FIRE!!!
 ** BOOM **

TARGET DESTROYED!!!      *2 **  ROUNDS EXPENDED.
YOU HAVE LOST 1 SHIPS, AND THE ENEMY HAS LOST 2.

YOUR FLAGSHIP REPORTS THE SIGHTING OF AN ENEMY AIRCRAFT CARRIER
YOUR INSTRUMENTS READ THE RANGE TO THE TARGET AS 39604
METERS.
WHAT ELEVATION ** 29
-----FIRE!!!
SHOT FELL   171 METERS SHORT OF TARGET.
THE ENEMY ROUND FELL 263 METERS SHORT.
WHAT ELEVATION ** 29.3
-----FIRE!!!
 ** BOOM **

TARGET DESTROYED!!!      *2 **  ROUNDS EXPENDED.
YOU HAVE LOST 4 SHIPS, AND THE ENEMY HAS LOST 9.
      ******** PEACE *******


YOU FIRED 20 ROUNDS.  THE ENEMY FIRED 19 ROUNDS.
YOU HAVE DECIMATED THE ENEMY..........THAT'S NICE
THE BATTLE IS OVER.............YOU WIN!!!!
```

```
LIST
SEAWAR
10   PRINT "YOU COMMAND A FLEET OF SHIPS OPERATING IN ENEMY TERRITORY!!!"
20   PRINT "DO YOU NEED INSTRUCTIONS";
30   DIM Q$[12]
40   INPUT Q$
50   IF Q$="YES" THEN 90
60   IF Q$="NO" THEN 170
70   PRINT "INPUT 'YES' OR 'NO'"
80   GOTO 40
90   PRINT "YOU TELL YOUR GUN CREWS THE ELEVATION TO SET THEIR GUNS."
100  PRINT "ELEVATION IS IN DEGREES FROM 0 TO 360."
119  PRINT "YOUR TASK FORCE CONSISTS OF 3 DESTROYERS, 2 CRUISERS,"
120  PRINT "2 BATTLESHIPS, AND 2 HEAVY AIRCRAFT CARRIERS."
130  PRINT "THE ENEMY HAS 9 SHIPS FOR HIS DEFENSE."
140  PRINT "IF YOU SUCCEED IN SINKING ALL HIS SHIPS BEFORE HE SINKS"
150  PRINT "YOURS, YOU HAVE WON.  HOWEVER, IF HE SINKS ALL YOUR SHIPS"
160  PRINT "BEFORE YOU HAVE DEFEATED HIM, YOU HAVE LOST!!"
170  PRINT "LET US BEGIN!!!"
180  DIM Z$[20],D$[40],I$[10],P$[72],M$[40],N$[40]
190  A=O=S1=S2=P1=P2=P4=0
200  REM SELECTS NAME OF ENEMY SHIP
210  PRINT ""
220  READ Z$
230  A=A+1
240  GOTO 320
250  RESTORE
260  IF O=9 OR A=9 THEN 840
270  FOR X=1 TO A
280  READ Z$
290  NEXT X
300  READ Z$
310  A=A+1
315  REM SELECTS BATTLE MODE
320  IF Z$="AIRCRAFT CARRIER" THEN 390
330  IF Z$="U-BOAT" THEN 2000
340  IF Z$="TORPEDO BOAT" THEN 360
350  LET P=1
360  GOTO 400
390  RESTORE
399  REM BEGINS BATTLE WITH SIGHTING AND READING
400  PRINT
405  PRINT "YOUR FLAGSHIP REPORTS THE SIGHTING OF AN ENEMY ";Z$
410  T=43000.-30000*RND(RND(0)+(RND(0)*10)*.987654+102
420  IF T<10000 THEN 410
430  S=P2=0
440  T=INT(T)
450  IF Z$="U-BOAT" THEN 2030
460  PRINT  USING 470;T
470  IMAGE"YOUR INSTRUMENTS READ THE RANGE TO THE TARGET AS ",DDDDD
475  PRINT "METERS."
480  IF P=1 THEN 1480
490  IF S>4 THEN 510
500  GOTO 540
505  REM AFTER 5 TRYS BY US TARGET MOVES OUT OF RANGE
510  PRINT "ALL RIGHT, BAD SHOT, THE TARGET HAS MOVED OUT OF"
520  PRINT "RANGE !!!   LET'S TRY IT AGAIN !!!"
525  S1=S1+S
530  GOTO 320
535  REM INPUT ANGLE OF ELEVATION
540  PRINT "WHAT ELEVATION ** ";
550  ENTER 7,L,B
551  PRINT
560  IF L#-256 THEN 590
570  PRINT "         ADMIRAL !!  YOU HAVE TO BE FAST IN THIS GAME!!"
580  GOTO 1590
590  PRINT "-----FIRE!!!"
600  S=S+1
620  IF B>360 THEN 1410
630  IF B<0 THEN 750
640  IF B=0 THEN 770
650  IF B=90 THEN 980
660  IF B>330 THEN 770
670  IF B>180 THEN 1370
680  IF B>150 THEN 1300
690  IF B>90 THEN 1020
699  REM DISTANCE FROM TARGET CALCULATED
700  V1=675.285
705  E=INT(T-(V1^2/9.80665*SIN(2*B/57.3)))
710  IF ABS(E) <= 100 THEN 1050
720  IF E>100 THEN 1200
730  IF E<-100 THEN 1250
740  REM "GOOF"SHOTS
750  PRINT "GUN BACKFIRED, KILLING CREW!"
760  GOTO 820
770  PRINT "WHAT ARE YOU TRYING TO DO?  KILL SOME FISH?  THE SHELL"
780  PRINT "EXPLODED UNDER WATER FIFTY METERS FROM YOUR SHIP!!!"
790  GOTO 1590
820  PRINT "         ADMIRAL PLEASE !!!!"
830  GOTO 1590
839  REM PEACE AND WINNER
840  PRINT "        ******** PEACE ********"
850  PRINT
860  PRINT
870  PRINT
880  PRINT  USING 890;S1,S2
890  IMAGE "YOU FIRED ",DD," ROUNDS.  THE ENEMY FIRED ",DD," ROUNDS."
900  IF O=9 THEN 920
910  IF A=9 THEN 950
920  PRINT "ALL OF YOUR SHIPS HAVE BEEN SUNK.  SO SORRY"
930  PRINT "THE BATTLE IS OVER.............THE ENEMY WINS."
940  GOTO 2220
950  PRINT "YOU HAVE DECIMATED THE ENEMY.........THAT'S NICE"
960  PRINT "THE BATTLE IS OVER.............YOU WIN!!!!"
970  GOTO 2220
975  REM  "GOOF" SHOTS
980  PRINT "YOU IDIOT!! YOU SHOT STRAIGHT UP!!, AND THE SHELL"
990  PRINT "LANDED ON YOUR OWN GUN POSITION, DESTROYING IT!!!"
1000 GOTO 1590
1020 PRINT "HEY STUPID, YOU'RE FIRING ON YOU OWN SHIPS!!!"
1030 GOTO 1590
1040 REM ENEMY SHIP SUNK
1050 IF Z$="U-BOAT" THEN 1070
1060 GOTO 1090
1070 PRINT "DEPTH CHARGE EXPLODED RIGHT ON TOP OF THAT BABY!!!"

1080 GOTO 1100
1090 PRINT " ** BOOM ***"
1100 PRINT ""
1110 M$="TARGET DESTROYED!!!      ***"
1120 N$=" ** ROUNDS EXPENDED."
1130 PRINT  USING 1140;M$,S,N$
1140 IMAGE 26A,D,21A
1141 PRINT  USING 1142;O,A
1142 IMAGE "YOU HAVE LOST ",D," SHIPS, AND THE ENEMY HAS LOST ",D,"."
1150 S1=S1+S
1160 P=0
1190 GOTO 250
1200 IF Z$="U-BOAT" THEN 2130
1210 PRINT  USING 1220;ABS(E)
1220 IMAGE "SHOT FELL ",5D," METERS SHORT OF TARGET."
1230 GOTO 1590
1250 IF Z$="U-BOAT" THEN 2160
1260 PRINT  USING 1270;ABS(E)
1270 IMAGE "SHELL OVERSHOT TARGET BY ",6D," METERS."
1280 GOTO 1590
1300 REM "GOOF" SHOTS
1310 PRINT "  YOU SHOT A PROJECTILE, INTO THE AIR,"
1320 PRINT "  IT FELL TO THE WATER, YOU KNOW NOT WHERE."
1330 PRINT "BUT I DO, YOU IDIOT, YOU JUST SANK YOUR OWN FLEET TANKER!!"
1340 S1=S1+1
1350 IF P=1 THEN 1590
1360 GOTO 490
1370 PRINT "WHAT ARE YOU TRYING TO DO?? DRILL A NEW HATCH??  THE SHELL"
1380 PRINT "EXPLODED IN YOUR SHIP, DESTROYING IT!!!"
1385 O=O+1
1386 IF O=9 THEN 840
1390 IF P=1 THEN 1590
1400 GOTO 820
1410 PRINT "WHERE DID U LEARN TO TYPE? ";B;"DEGREES EXCEEDS 360 BY"
1420 PRINT B-360;" DEGREES."
1430 S1=S1+1
1440 IF P=1 THEN 1590
1450 GOTO 490
1480 PRINT "THE ENEMY ";Z$;" IS FIRING ON YOUR SHIPS!"
1490 P4=1234*RND(RND(0))+(RND(0)*10)
1500 IF P4>500 THEN 1490
1510 IF P2=1 THEN 1600
1520 IF INT(P4)<100 THEN 1800
1530 IF Z$="U-BOAT" THEN 2100
1540 PRINT  USING 1550;INT(P4)
1550 IMAGE"HIS FIRST ROUND FELL ",DDD," METERS SHORT."
1560 LET S2=S2+1
1570 GOTO 490
1590 IF P2=1 THEN 1490
1600 P1=1250*RND(RND(0))+(RND(0)*10)
1610 IF P1>P4 THEN 1600
1620 IF P1<(P4-400) THEN 1600
1630 IF P1<100 THEN 1710
1640 LET P4=P1
1650 S2=S2+1
1660 IF Z$="U-BOAT" THEN 2190
1670 PRINT  USING 1680;INT(P1)
1680 IMAGE"THE ENEMY ROUND FELL ",DDD," METERS SHORT."
1700 GOTO 490
1710 S2=S2+1
1720 LET P2=1
1730 GOSUB 1850
1750 PRINT "THE ENEMY ";Z$;" SANK ";D$
1760 O=O+1
1770 IF O=9 THEN 840
1780 IF D$="YOUR LAST BATTLESHIP!!" THEN 840
1790 GOTO 490
1800 P2=1
1810 GOSUB 1850
1820 PRINT "IN FACT, HE JUST SANK ";D$
1830 O=O+1
1840 GOTO 1770
1850 RESTORE
1860 FOR C=1 TO (9+O)
1870 READ D$
1880 NEXT C
1890 READ D$
1920 DATA "U-BOAT","210 MM SHORE GUN","70,000 TON CRUISER"
1930 DATA "BATTLESHIP","TORPEDO BOAT","HEAVY FRIGATE"
1940 DATA "E-TYPE DESTROYER","GUIDED-MISSILE SHIP","AIRCRAFT CARRIER"
1950 DATA "ONE OF YOUR DESTROYERS!!","YOUR HEAVY CRUISER!!"
1960 DATA "ANOTHER OF YOUR DESTROYERS!!","ONE OF YOUR BATTLESHIPS!!"
1970 DATA "YOUR LAST DESTROYER!!","YOUR AIRCRAFT CARRIER!!"
1975 DATA "YOUR LIGHT CRUISER!!","YOUR LAST AIRCRAFT CARRIER!!"
1980 DATA "YOUR LAST BATTLESHIP!!"
1990 RETURN
2000 PRINT "YOUR FLAGSHIP HAS DETECTED A U-BOAT APPROACHING AT 5 ";
2005 PRINT "FATHOMS."
2010 P=1
2020 GOTO 410
2030 PRINT "YOUR SUBMARINE DETECTION EQUIMENT READS THE RANGE TO THE";
2031 PRINT "TARGET"
2040 T=INT(T-1500)
2050 IF T<0 THEN 410
2060 PRINT  USING 2070;T
2070 IMAGE "AS ",5D," METERS."
2080 PRINT "THE U-BOAT HAS COMMENCED FIRING TORPEDOES AT YOUR SHIPS."
2090 GOTO 1490
2100 PRINT  USING 2110;(INT(P4)-50)
2110 IMAGE "HIS FIRST TORPEDO EXPLODED ",3D," METERS BEHIND YOUR SHIP."
2120 GOTO 1560
2130 PRINT  USING 2140;ABS(E)
2140 IMAGE"DEPTH CHARGE EXPLODED ",4D," METERS SHORT OF TARGET."
2150 GOTO 1590
2160 PRINT  USING 2170;ABS(E)
2170 IMAGE "DEPTH CHARGE EXPLODED ",4D," METERS AFT OF TARGET."
2180 GOTO 1590
2190 PRINT  USING 2200;(INT(P1)-50)
2200 IMAGE "THE ENEMY TORPEDO EXPLODED ",3D," METERS IN FRONT OF YOUR"
2201 PRINT "SHIP."
2210 GOTO 490
2220 END                    263
```

Another new game from Creative Computing . . .

LUNAR

by David Ahl

LUNAR, also known as ROCKET, APOLLO, LEM, etc. is, next to STAR TREK and SPACE WAR, the most popular computer game. It is certainly the most popular on smaller machines. (I remember a milestone of sorts when I managed to compress LUNAR to run on 4K PDP-8 BASIC while retaining full instructions and landing messages. I used every single character available.)

The version of LUNAR presented here was originally written in FOCAL by Jim Storer, a student at Lexington (Mass.) High School in the mid 60's. While everyone claims to be the original program author of LUNAR, I'm reasonably sure that Jim predates the others and therefore qualifies as the original, original author. I converted the program to BASIC in early 1970. It's a straight-forward version without side stabilization rockets or other goodies but, nevertheless, is quite a challenge to land successfully.

PLAYING THE GAME

Your mission is to achieve a soft landing of your LEM on the moon. You separate from the command ship 200 miles above the surface of the moon and, every 10 seconds, set the burn rate of your retro rockets to slow your craft. You may free fall (0 lbs./sec.) or burn at any rate between 8 lbs./sec. and 200 lbs./sec. Since ignition occurs at 8 lbs./sec., burn rates between 1 and 7 lbs./sec. may not be used. A negative burn rate automatically aborts your mission.

There are three popular ways to land:
1. Constant burn rate all the way down.
2. Free fall for a while, then maximum burn rate tapering off as you get close.
3. Gradually increase burn rate to a maximum, then taper off as you get close.

Recall from physics that Newton found the force of attraction (gravity) between two bodies varies directly with the mass of the bodies and inversely with the square of the distance between their centers. This may help you land successfully. Then again, it may not.

COMPUTER NOTES

Convert the program to your version of BASIC. Multiple statements on one line are separated by a colon (:). Everything else is standard.

Some computers produce an error calculating the expansions (Statements 910 and 920) when you get close to the moon and the numbers get very small. If yours does, substitute the expanded form. Here it is for Statement 910:

$$-Q*(1+Q*(1/2+Q*(1/3+Q*(1/4+Q/5))))$$

You should be able to figure out the other one yourself.

Would you like us to print the other versions of LUNAR in *Creative Computing*? If so, write and let me know—DHA.

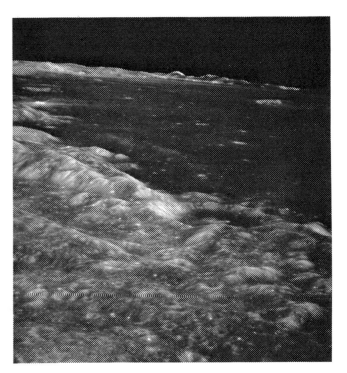

MAPPING THE MOON

This photograph pictures Mare Crisium, the large "flat" area near the eastern edge of the moon as seen from Earth. In the foreground is the mountainous terrain that forms the southern rim of Mare Crisium. Visible near the horizon, 285 miles across the mare, is its northern rim. Prominent at above right in the mare is the 24-mile-wide crater Picard. Photo was made from Apollo 10, the last flight before the lunar landing. (Photo Kodak)

SAMPLE RUN

```
RUNNH
LUNAR LANDING SIMULATION


CONTROL CALLING LUNAR MODULE..

YOU MAY SET THE FUEL RATE (K) TO ZERO OR ANY VALUE
BETWEEN 8 AND 200 LBS PER SECOND.   A NEGATIVE FUEL
RATE WILL ABORT THE MISSION.

YOU HAVE 16000 LBS OF FUEL.
ESTIMATED FREE FALL IMPACT TIME IS 120 SECONDS.
CAPSULE WEIGHT IS 32,500 LBS.

FIRST RADAR CHECK COMING UP...
BEGIN LANDING PROCEDURE

TIME(SECS)    HEIGHT(MI)    VELOCITY(MPH) FUEL(LBS)      FUEL RATE
0             120           3600          16000          K? 0
10            109.95        3636          16000          K? 0
20            99.8          3672          16000          K? 0
30            89.55         3708          16000          K? 0
40            79.2          3744          16000          K? 0
50            68.75         3780          16000          K? 0
60            58.2          3816          16000          K? 0
70            47.55         3852          16000          K? 200
80            37.3656       3476.43       14000          K? 200
90            28.2623       3072.94       12000          K? 200
100           20.3232       2637.46       10000          K? 200
110           13.644        2164.97       8000           K? 200
120           8.33572       1649.14       6000           K? 200
130           4.52958       1081.92       4000           K? 180
140           2.2887        522.398       2200           K? 90
150           1.22786       238.772       1300           K? 40
160           .718389       127.493       900            K? 20
170           .418089       88.5788       700            K? 22
180           .237646       41.1605       480            K? 14
190           .147722       23.5114       340            K? 10
200           .859622E-1    20.9169       240            K? 10
210           .317304E-1    18.0912       140            K? 12
ON THE MOON AT  218.451 SECS.
IMPACT VELOCITY OF  8.90172 M.P.H.
FUEL LEFT  38.5879 LBS.
VERY GOOD LANDING, NOT PERFECT YET.


TRY AGAIN (1 FOR YES, 0 FOR NO)? 0

CONTROL OUT

READY
```

PROGRAM LISTING

```
LISTNH
1 REM *** WRITTEN BY JIM STORER, LEXINGTON HS
2 REM *** CONVERTED FROM FOCAL TO BASIC BY  DAVID AHL, DIGITAL
10 PRINT "LUNAR LANDING SIMULATION":PRINT
20 PRINT:PRINT:PRINT "CONTROL CALLING LUNAR MODULE. ":PRINT
35PRINT"YOU MAY SET THE FUEL RATE (K) TO ZERO OR ANY VALUE"
40PRINT"BETWEEN 8 AND 200 LBS PER SECOND.  A NEGATIVE FUEL"
50 PRINT "RATE WILL ABORT THE MISSION.":PRINT
60PRINT"YOU HAVE 16000 LBS OF FUEL. "
70PRINT"ESTIMATED FREE FALL IMPACT TIME IS 120 SECONDS. "
80PRINT"CAPSULE WEIGHT IS 32,500 LBS. "
90 PRINT:PRINT "FIRST RADAR CHECK COMING UP... "
100 PRINT "BEGIN LANDING PROCEDURE":PRINT:PRINT
110PRINT"TIME(SECS)","HEIGHT(MI)","VELOCITY(MPH)","FUEL(LBS)","FUEL RATE"
120 LET L=0:LET A=120:LET V=1:LET M=32500:LET N=16500
170 LET G=.001:LET Z=1.8
210 PRINT INT(L+.5),A,V*3600,M-N,"K";
220 INPUT K
225 LET T=10
230 IF K<0 GO TO 590
235 IF K=0 GOTO 310
240 IF K<8 THEN 260
250 IF K<=200 GO TO 310
260 PRINT "NOT POSSIBLE",,,,"K";
270 INPUT K : GOTO 230
310 IF M-N-.001 <=0 GOTO410
320 IF T<.001 GOTO 210
330 LET S=T:IF N+S*K<=M GO TO 350
340 LET S=(M-N)/K
350 LET I0=1 : GOTO 900
360 IF I <= 0 GOT 0 710
370 IF V<=0 GO TO 380
375 IF J<0 GOTO 810
380 LET I0=1:GOTO600
410 PRINT"FUEL OUT AT ";L;"SECS. "
420 LET S=(-V+SQR(V*V+2*A*G))/G
430 LET V = V+G*S
440 LET L=L+S
510 PRINT"ON THE MOON AT ";L;"SECS. "
511 LET W = 3600*V
514 PRINT "IMPACT VELOCITY OF ";W;"M.P.H. "
520 PRINT "FUEL LEFT ";M-N;"LBS. "
530 IF W>1 GOTO 550
540 PRINT "PERFECT LANDING!  CONGRATULATIONS!!": GOTO 590
550 IF W >=10 THEN 560
552 PRINT "VERY GOOD LANDING, NOT PERFECT YET. ":GOTO590
560 IF W >= 25 THEN 570
562 PRINT "A FAIR LANDING, NO CRAFT DAMAGE. ":GOTO590
570 IF W >= 60 THEN580
572 PRINT "CRAFT DAMAGE.   HOPE YOUR OXYGEN HOLDS OUT UNTIL A"
574 PRINT "RESCUE MISSION ARRIVES!":GOTO 590
580 PRINT "SORRY, BUT THERE WERE NO SURVIVORS. "
585 PRINT "IN FACT YOU BLASTED A NEW LUNAR CRATER ";W*.277777;" FEET DEEP.
590 PRINT:PRINT:PRINT "TRY AGAIN (1 FOR YES, 0 FOR NO)";
592 INPUT R:IF R=1 THEN 90
595 PRINT : PRINT "CONTROL OUT" : GOTO 1800
600 LET L=L+S
610 LET T = T-S
620 LET M=M-S*K
630 LET A=I
640 LET V=J
650 IF I0=1 GO TO 310
660 IF I0=3 GO TO 850
710 IF S<.005 GO TO 510
720 LET S= 2*A/(V+SQR(V*V+2*A*(G-Z*K/M)))
730 LET I0=2 :GOTO 900
810 LET W=(1-M*G/(Z*K))/2
820 LET S=M*V/(Z*K*(W+SQR(W*W+V/Z)))+.05
825 LET I0=3 : GOTO 900
830 IF I<=0 THEN 710
840 GOTO 600
850 IF J>=0 THEN 310
860 IF V<=0 GO TO 310
870 GOTO 810
900 LET Q=S*K/M
905 IF Q<=0 THEN 1000
910 LET J=V+G*S+Z*(-Q*(1/2+Q*(1/3+Q*(1/4+Q*(1/5)))))
920 LET I=A-G*S*S/2-V*S+Z*S*(Q*(1/2+Q*(1/6+Q*(1/12+Q*(1/20+Q*(1/30))))))
930 IF I0=1 GOTO 360
940 IF I0=2 GOTO 600
950 IF I0=3 GOTO 830
1000 LET J=V+G*S
1010 LET I=A-G*S*S/2-V*S
1020 GOTO930
1800 END

READY
```

Appollo 14 Launch Control Center, Cape Kennedy, Florida

 ❧ LOVE ❧

by David H. Ahl

This program is designed to reproduce Robert Indiana's great work "Love" with a message of your choice up to 60 characters long.

The program was written in BASIC-PLUS for DEC's RSTS-11 family. You will probably have to change portions of it for your machine. Multiple statements on one line are separated by a backslash. The message is inputted as A$ in Statement 60. Statements 65-67 set the output device; eliminate them if the device is always a terminal. Statements 100-130 repeat the message A$ if it is less than 60 characters long and insert it in T$. Statements 210-400 actually print the design. The data statements are an alternating count of the numbers of characters printed and the number of blanks which form the design.

```
10 REMARKABLE PROGRAM BY DAVE AHL
20 PRINT "A TRIBUTE TO THE GREAT AMERICAN ARTIST, ROBERT INDIANA.
30 PRINT "HIS GREATEST WORK WILL BE REPRODUCED WITH A MESSAGE OF
40 PRINT "YOUR CHOICE UP TO 60 CHARACTERS.  IF YOU CAN'T THINK OF
50 PRINT "A MESSAGE, SIMPLY TYPE THE WORD 'LOVE'" \ PRINT
60 INPUT "YOUR MESSAGE PLEASE"AS \ L=LEN(AS)
65 INPUT "OUTPUT DEVICE (LP: OR KB:)";BS
66 IF BS="LP:" OR BS="KB:" THEN 67 ELSE PRINT "AGAIN" \ GOTO 65
67 OPEN BS FOR OUTPUT AS FILE 1
70 DIM TS(120) \ PRINT #1 FOR I=1 TO 10
100 FOR J=0 TO INT(60/L)
110 FOR I=1 TO L
120 TS(J*L+I)=MID(AS,I,1)
130 NEXT I \ NEXT J
140 C=0
200 A1=1 \ P=1 \ C=C+1 \ IF C=37 THEN 999
205 PRINT #1
210 READ A \ A1=A1+A \ IF P=1 THEN 300
240 PRINT #1," " FOR I=1 TO A \ P=1 \ GOTO 400
300 PRINT #1,TS(I); FOR I=A1-A TO A1-1 \ P=0
400 IF A1>60 THEN 200 ELSE 210
600 DATA 60,1,12,26,9,12,3,8,24,17,8,4,6,23,21,6,4,6,22,12,5,6,5
610 DATA 4,6,21,11,8,6,4,4,6,21,10,10,5,4,4,6,21,9,11,5,4
620 DATA 4,6,21,8,11,6,4,4,6,21,7,11,7,4,4,6,21,6,11,8,4
630 DATA 4,6,19,1,1,5,11,9,4,4,6,19,1,1,5,10,10,4,4,6,18,2,1,6,8,11,4
640 DATA 4,6,17,3,1,7,5,13,4,4,6,17,5,1,7,5,2,23,5,1,29,5,17,8
650 DATA 1,29,9,12,1,13,5,40,1,1,13,5,40,1,1,6,13,5,3,10,6,12,5,1
660 DATA 5,6,11,3,11,6,14,3,1,5,6,11,3,11,6,15,2,1
670 DATA 6,6,9,3,12,6,16,1,1,6,6,9,3,12,6,17,1,10
680 DATA 7,6,7,3,13,6,6,2,10,7,6,7,3,13,14,10,8,6,5,3,14,6,6,2,10
690 DATA 8,6,5,3,14,6,7,1,10,9,6,3,3,15,6,16,1,1
700 DATA 9,6,3,3,15,6,15,2,1,10,6,3,16,6,14,3,1,10,10,16,6,12,5,1
710 DATA 11,8,13,27,1,11,8,13,27,1,60
999 PRINT #1 FOR I=1 TO 10 \ CLOSE 1 \ END
```

GEOWAR

No writeup was included with this game except, of course, the instructions and remarks in the listing. The idea and approach came from Kenneth Janowiak, a teacher at St. Patrick HS, Chicago. Programming was done by Gary Lorenc, a former student. (See the review of GEOWAR on the facing page.)

PROGRAM LISTING

```
1 REM *** GEOWAR
2 REM *** WRITTEN BY GARY LORENC, IDEA BY KENNETH JANOWIAK
3 REM *** ST. PATRICK HS, 5900 W. BELMONT AVE., CHICAGO, ILL
4 REM *** UPDATED TO BASIC-PLUS BY DAVE AHL
5 PRINT"DO YOU WANT A DESCRIPTION OF THE GAME? (1=YES,0=NO) ";
6 INPUT I
7 IF I=0 THEN 46
8 PRINT
9 PRINT"    THE FIRST QUADRANT OF A REGULAR COORDINATE GRAPH WILL";
10 PRINT" SERVE AS"
11 PRINT"THE BATTLEFIELD.  FIVE ENEMY INSTALLATIONS ARE LOCATED ";
12 PRINT"WITHIN A"
13 PRINT"30 BY 30 UNIT AREA.  NO TARGET IS INSIDE THE 10 BY 10 ";
14 PRINT"UNIT AREA"
15 PRINT"ADJACENT TO THE ORIGIN, AS THIS IS THE LOCATION OF OUR ";
16 PRINT"BASE.  WHEN"
17 PRINT"THE MACHINE ASKS FOR THE DEGREE OF THE SHOT, RESPOND ";
18 PRINT"WITH A NUMBER"
19 PRINT"BETWEEN 1 AND 90."
20 PRINT
21 PRINT TAB(51),"SCARE**********"
22 PRINT"    1. A DIRECT HIT IS A HIT WITHIN 1 DEGREE OF";
23 PRINT TAB(51),"*          *"
24 PRINT"       THE TARGET.",TAB(51),"*  HIT******  *"
25 PRINT"    2. A HIT MUST PASS BETWEEN THE FIRST SET OF";
26 PRINT TAB(51),"*  *       *  *"
27 PRINT"       INTEGRAL POINTS NW AND SE OF THE TARGET.";
28 PRINT TAB(51),"*  *    D  *  *"
29 PRINT"    3. A SCARE MUST PASS BETWEEN THE NEXT SET OF";
30 PRINT TAB(51),"*  *       *  *"
31 PRINT"       INTEGRAL POINTS NW AND SE OF THE TARGET,";
32 PRINT TAB(51),"*  ******HIT  *"
33 PRINT"       AND CAUSES THE ENEMY TO RELOCATE A ";
34 PRINT TAB(51),"*          *"
35 PRINT"       MAXIMUM OF 1 UNIT IN ANY DIRECTION.";
36 PRINT TAB(51),"**********SCARE"
37 PRINT
38 PRINT
39 PRINT"    MISSILES HAVE INFINITE RANGE AND MAY HIT MORE THAN ";
40 PRINT"ONE TARGET."
41 PRINT"A MISSILE THAT NEARLY MISSES AN INSTALLATION (A SCARE) ";
42 PRINT"WILL BE"
43 PRINT"IMMEDIATELY SHOT DOWN.  ANY HITS BEFORE THIS TIME WILL ";
44 PRINT"NOT BE COUNTED"
45 PRINT"UNLESS A DIRECT HIT WAS MADE."
46 PRINT
47 PRINT
48 PRINT"READY TO GO? (1=YES,0=NO) ";
49 INPUT R2
50 IF R2=0 THEN 192
51 PRINT"GOOD LUCK!"
52 PRINT
53 DIM C(10),H(20),D(10),S(20),F(5)
54 DEF FNV(V1)=INT((180/3.14159)*ATN(V1)+.5)
55 X=250
56 X1=RND(X)
57 G2=0
58 S2=0
59 D2=0
60 H2=0
61 FOR K=1 TO 10
62 GO SUB 154
63 IF INT(K/2)<>K/2 THEN 70
64 IF C(K-1)>10 THEN 70
65 IF C(K)>10 THEN 70
66 FOR L=K-1 TO K
67 GOSUB 154
68 NEXT L
69 GO TO 63
70 NEXT K
71 S=0
72 FOR L=1 TO 5
73 D(L)=FNV(C(2*L)/C(2*L-1))
74 NEXT L
75 A=2
76 L1=10
77 T5=5
78 D5=0
79 H5=0
80 GO SUB 147
81 PRINT
82 PRINT"ENTER DEGREE OF SHOT ";
83 D1=0
84 H1=0
85 FOR Q=1 TO 5
86 F(Q)=20
87 NEXT Q
88 INPUT D
89 IF D>=90 THEN 81
90 IF D<0 THEN 177 ELSE IF D=0 THEN 192
91 S=S+1
92 FOR A=2 TO 10 STEP 2
93 IF D>S(A) THEN 103
94 IF D<S(A-1) THEN 103
95 IF D>H(A) THEN 105
96 IF D<H(A-1) THEN 105
97 IF D>D(A/2)+1 THEN 101
98 IF D<D(A/2)-1 THEN 101
99 D1=D1+1
100 GO TO 102
101 H1=H1+1
102 F(D1+H1)=A
103 NEXT A
104 GO TO 108
105 IF D1>0 THEN 118
106 GO SUB 138
107 GO TO 81
108 IF D1+H1<>0 THEN 112
109 IF T5=1 THEN 159
110 PRINT"NO LUCK -- TRY AGAIN."
111 GO TO 81
112 IF D1>0 THEN 118
113 IF H1>1 THEN 116
114 PRINT"**CONGRATULATIONS**    A HIT."
115 GO TO 124
116 PRINT"**CONGRATULATIONS**"H1" HITS."
117 GO TO 124
118 PRINT"****BULLS EYE**** "
119 IF D1>1 THEN 123
120 IF H1>0 THEN 123
121 PRINT" A DIRECT HIT!"
122 GO TO 124
123 PRINT D1+H1" HITS -- A DIRECT HIT ON"D1" OF THEM!"
124 T5=T5-(D1+H1)
125 D5=D5+D1
126 H5=H5+H1
127 IF T5=0 THEN 167
128 FOR J= 1 TO H1+D1
129 Z=F(J)
130 D(Z/2)=0
131 H(Z)=0
132 H(Z-1)=0
133 S(Z)=0
134 S(Z-1)=0
135 NEXT J
136 PRINT 5-T5" DOWN --"T5" TO GO."
137 GO TO 81
138 PRINT"A NEAR HIT.  ENEMY HAS RELOCATED."
139 FOR R=1 TO 2
140 X2=INT(RND(0)*100)
141 IF ABS(C(A-(R-1))-X2)>1 THEN 140
142 IF C(A-(R-1))<=2 THEN 140
143 C(A-(R-1))=X2
144 NEXT R
145 D(A/2)=FNV(C(A)/C(A-1))
146 L1=A
147 FOR I=A TO L1 STEP 2
148 H(I-1)=FNV((C(I)-1)/(C(I-1)+1))
149 H(I)=FNV((C(I)+1)/(C(I-1)-1))
150 S(I-1)=FNV((C(I)-2)/(C(I-1)+2))
151 S(I)=FNV((C(I)+2)/(C(I-1)-2))
152 NEXT I
153 RETURN
154 R=INT(RND(0)*100)
155 IF R>30 THEN 154
156 IF R<3 THEN 154
157 C(K)=R
158 RETURN
159 FOR Z1=1 TO 5
160 IF D(Z1)>1 THEN 162
161 NEXT Z1
162 IF D<D(Z1) THEN 165
163 PRINT"TOO HIGH -- TRY AGAIN."
164 GO TO 81
165 PRINT"TOO LOW -- TRY AGAIN."
166 GO TO 81
167 PRINT
168 PRINT"GAME TOTALS:"H5" HITS AND"D5" DIRECT HITS ON"S;"SHOTS."
169 PRINT
170 PRINT"READY FOR A NEW GAME? (1=YES,0=NO) ";
171 G2=G2+1
172 S2=S2+S
173 D2=D2+D5
174 H2=H2+H5
175 INPUT G
176 IF G=0 THEN 184
177 PRINT
178 PRINT
179 PRINT
180 PRINT"FIVE NEW INSTALLATIONS HAVE BEEN BUILT AT DIFFERENT ";
181 PRINT"LOCATIONS."
182 PRINT"GOOD LUCK!"
183 GO TO 61
184 PRINT
185 PRINT
186 PRINT "TOTALS FOR"G2"GAMES:"H2"HITS AND"D2
187 PRINT "DIRECT HITS ON"S2"SHOTS."
188 PRINT "AN AVERAGE OF"S2/(D2+H2)"SHOTS PER TARGET."
192 END
```

SAMPLE RUN

```
RUN
DO YOU WANT A DESCRIPTION OF THE GAME? (1-YES,0-NO) ?1

    THE FIRST QUADRANT OF A REGULAR COORDINATE GRAPH WILL SERVE AS
THE BATTLEFIELD.  FIVE ENEMY INSTALLATIONS ARE LOCATED WITHIN A
30 BY 30 UNIT AREA.  NO TARGET IS INSIDE THE 10 BY 10 UNIT AREA
ADJACENT TO THE ORIGIN, AS THIS IS THE LOCATION OF OUR BASE.  WHEN
THE MACHINE ASKS FOR THE DEGREE OF THE SHOT, RESPOND WITH A NUMBER
BETWEEN 1 AND 90.

                                          SCARE**********
    1. A DIRECT HIT IS A HIT WITHIN 1 DEGREE OF      *          *
       THE TARGET.                              *  HIT******  *
    2. A HIT MUST PASS BETWEEN THE FIRST SET OF *  *       *  *
       INTEGRAL POINTS NW AND SE OF THE TARGET. *  *    D  *  *
    3. A SCARE MUST PASS BETWEEN THE NEXT SET OF *  *       *  *
       INTEGRAL POINTS NW AND SE OF THE TARGET,  *  ******HIT  *
       AND CAUSES THE ENEMY TO RELOCATE A        *          *
       MAXIMUM OF 1 UNIT IN ANY DIRECTION.       **********SCARE


    MISSILES HAVE INFINITE RANGE AND MAY HIT MORE THAN ONE TARGET.
A MISSILE THAT NEARLY MISSES AN INSTALLATION (A SCARE) WILL BE
IMMEDIATELY SHOT DOWN.  ANY HITS BEFORE THIS TIME WILL NOT BE COUNTED
UNLESS A DIRECT HIT WAS MADE.
```

```
RLADY TO GO? (1-YES, 0-NO) !1
GOOD LUCK!

ENTER DEGREE OF SHOT !20
NO LUCK -- TRY AGAIN.

ENTER DEGREE OF SHOT !30
A NEAR HIT.  ENEMY HAS RELOCATED.

ENTER DEGREE OF SHOT !31
****BULLS EYE****    3  HITS -- A DIRECT HIT ON    2 OF THEM!
      3  DOWN --    2 TO GO.

ENTER DEGREE OF SHOT !40
NO LUCK -- TRY AGAIN.

ENTER DEGREE OF SHOT !50
NO LUCK -- TRY AGAIN.

ENTER DEGREE OF SHOT !60
****BULLS EYE****    2  HITS -- A DIRECT HIT ON    1 OF THEM!

GAME TOTALS:    2  HITS AND    3  DIRECT HITS ON    6 SHOTS.

READY FOR A NEW GAME? (1-YES, 0-NO) !1


FIVE NEW INSTALLATIONS HAVE BEEN BUILT AT DIFFERENT LOCATIONS.
GOOD LUCK!

ENTER DEGREE OF SHOT !45
A NEAR HIT.  ENEMY HAS RELOCATED.

ENTER DEGREE OF SHOT !44
A NEAR HIT.  ENEMY HAS RELOCATED.
```
```
ENTER DEGREE OF SHOT !31
A NEAR HIT.  ENEMY HAS RELOCATED.

ENTER DEGREE OF SHOT !30
****BULLS EYE****  A DIRECT HIT!
      2  DOWN --    3 TO GO.

ENTER DEGREE OF SHOT !25
A NEAR HIT.  ENEMY HAS RELOCATED.

ENTER DEGREE OF SHOT !26
A NEAR HIT.  ENEMY HAS RELOCATED.

ENTER DEGREE OF SHOT !27
**CONGRATULATIONS**   A HIT.
      3  DOWN --    2 TO GO.

ENTER DEGREE OF SHOT !65
**CONGRATULATIONS**   A HIT.
      4  DOWN --    1 TO GO.

ENTER DEGREE OF SHOT !50
TOO LOW -- TRY AGAIN.

ENTER DEGREE OF SHOT !70
TOO LOW -- TRY AGAIN.

ENTER DEGREE OF SHOT !80
**CONGRATULATIONS**   A HIT.

GAME TOTALS:    4  HITS AND    1  DIRECT HITS ON    29 SHOTS.

READY FOR A NEW GAME? (1-YES, 0-NO) !0

TOTALS FOR 2 GAMES:   6  HITS AND  4  DIRECT HITS ON  34 SHOTS
                      AN AVERAGE OF  3.40 SHOTS PER TARGET
```

(handwritten annotations) ← MULTIPLE HITS ARE POSSIBLE
← TOTALS FOR THE GAME (HARD TO BEAT IT!)
← HELP GIVEN ON LAST SHOTS "TOO HIGH" OR "TOO LOW"
← TOTALS FOR ALL GAMES & AVERAGE

REVIEW OF GEOWAR
by Gregory Yob

The editor of any publication has a dilemma. There's lots of material, but most of it is of low quality or presents the wrong viewpoint for his magazine. I am sure this is true of computer games as evidenced by the game of GEOWAR which was given to me by the editor of *Creative Computing.* As a dedicated games-lover, these comments are offered in the hopes for better games. In fact, please correspond with me if you share (or reject) my views.

Let's get down to business. GEOWAR is another of those "shoot the enemy with missiles (phasers, lasers, zap-beams, MIRVS, etc.)" games. In some ways I liked it; in most I didn't.

THE TECHNICAL LEVEL. Programming GEOWAR or an equivalent game requires a good knowledge of BASIC in many ways. Noted in the program were the uses of arrays, pointers, subroutines, library functions and a defined function. As a problem for a final exam (do the flowchart) GEOWAR is excellent. Writing and debugging GEOWAR is a fine term project for second-semester programming.

THE LEVEL OF CLARITY. The instructions for GEO-WAR are muddled a bit. It took me two readings to understand the first quadrant instead of the full 360 degrees was the playing area. I offer an improved diagram of the playing area (there wasn't any, a mortal

sin for tactical games) and a new version of the HIT-SCARE diagram (see figures). If you are to use a grid, show the points clearly!!! If your range of fire is limited, MAKE IT CLEAR!!! This is a usual case of pictures vs. kilowords.

TUTORIAL LEVEL. What does GEOWAR teach? Possibly about angles . . . Mostly it is a game of guessing. Guessing strategies are very clearly done in STARS. In a sense, GEOWAR is a five-number version of STARS. Regarding angles, STAR TREK is much more effective and lots of fun! I notice the games authors live in Chicago. A visit to Urbana and a tour of the games on PLATO is well worth the effort. I particularly suggest MOONWAR, CONQUEST, NOVA and ROSE. MOON-WAR is the most effective angle-teacher I have ever met. (All other games lovers should also try PLATO. Try DOGFIGHT!)

ESTHETIC AND PHILOSOPHICAL LEVEL. This is where I am most annoyed with GEOWAR. It's another hunt and kill game in an era where mutual co-operation in complex systems is a vital need. Missiles and cartesian grids are very common in computer games, and in writer's words, "the theme is a bit overdone". If we must teach of war, think about these situations:

a) an Army Artillery unit
b) a destroyer at sea
c) a jet in a dogfight
d) ICBMs (Minuteman, Polaris)

In each situation, the techniques and objectives differ. Hitting the target is only a small part of the game. Many neat games ideas can come of these situations viewed as part of a larger system, i.e., the artillery unit as part of supporting a commando unit.

WHAT I'D LIKE TO SEE:
1) Games using several players in different and mutually dependent roles.
2) Social, Economic and Ecological themes vs. War
3) An interesting field of play (as in HUNT THE WUMPUS) with variations and topography
4) The player's advantages to be the results of their actions. (the RND function is much over-used and often destroys the skill-learning aspects of a game)

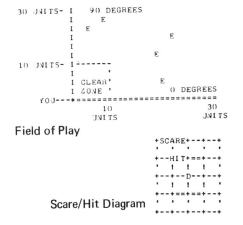

```
30 UNITS- I    90 DEGREES
          I       E
          I    E
          I                E
          I
          I                   E
10 UNITS- I--------
          I
          I
          I CLEAR           E
          I ZONE          0 DEGREES
  YOU---*=============================
             10              30
             UNITS           UNITS
```
Field of Play

```
        +SCARE+--+--+
        ' ' ' ' ' '
        +--HIT+==+--+
        ' ! ! ! '
        +--+--D--+--+
        ' ! ! ! '
        +--+==+==+--+
        ' ' ' ' ' '
        +--+--+--+--+
```
Scare/Hit Diagram

Another new game from Creative Computing . . .

SPLAT

OPEN A PARACHUTE AT THE LAST MOMENT
by John F. Yegge
Oak Ridge Associated Universities

SPLAT simulates a parachute jump in which you try to open your parachute at the last possible moment without going splat! You may select your own terminal velocity or let the computer do it for you. You may also select the acceleration due to gravity or, again, let the computer do it in which case you might wind up on any of the eight planets (out to Neptune), the moon, or sun.

The computer then tells you the height you're jumping from and asks for the seconds of free fall. It then divides your free fall time into eight intervals and gives you progress reports on your way down. The computer also keeps track of all prior jumps in the file PARACHUTE and lets you know how you compared with previous successful jumps. You can easily convert SPLAT to your version of BASIC by eliminating the file which keeps track of previous jumps although if you have file capabilities, use them — the game is that much more fun!

```
WELCOME TO 'SPLAT' -- THE GAME THAT SIMULATES A PARACHUTE
JUMP. TRY TO OPEN YOUR CHUTE AT THE LAST POSSIBLE
MOMENT WITHOUT GOING SPLAT.

  SELECT YOUR OWN TERMINAL VELOCITY (YES OR NO)? NO
OK.  TERMINAL VELOCITY = 796 MI/HR
WANT TO SELECT ACCELERATION DUE TO GRAVITY (YES OR NO)? NO
FINE. YOU'RE ON MERCURY. ACCELERATION=12.2FT/SEC/SEC

     ALTITUDE          = 9297 FT
     TERM.VELOCITY     = 1167.47 FT/SEC +-5%
     ACCELERATION      = 12.2 FT/SEC/SEC +-5%
SET THE TIMER FOR YOUR FREEFALL.
HOW MANY SECONDS? 8
HERE WE GO.

TIME (SEC)    DIST TO FALL (FT)
==========    =================
  0             9297
  1             9290.88
  2             9272.51
  3             9241.89
  4             9199.02
  5             9143.91
  6             9076.55
  7             8996.94
  8             8905.09
CHUTE OPEN
CONSERVATIVE AREN'T YOU?  YOU RANKED ONLY 9 IN THE
14 SUCCESSFUL JUMPS BEFORE YOURS.
DO YOU WANT TO PLAY AGAIN? YES

  SELECT YOUR OWN TERMINAL VELOCITY (YES OR NO)? NO
OK.  TERMINAL VELOCITY = 740 MI/HR
WANT TO SELECT ACCELERATION DUE TO GRAVITY (YES OR NO)? NO
THEN YOU'RE ON NEPTUNE. ACCELERATION=39.6FT/SEC/SEC

     ALTITUDE          = 5189 FT
     TERM.VELOCITY     = 1085.33 FT/SEC +-5%
     ACCELERATION      = 39.6 FT/SEC/SEC +-5%
SET THE TIMER FOR YOUR FREEFALL.
HOW MANY SECONDS? 18
HERE WE GO.

TIME (SEC)    DIST TO FALL (FT)
==========    =================
  0             5189
  2.25          5089.74
  4.5           4791.95
  6.75          4295.63
  9             3600.78
 11.25          2707.4
 13.5           1615.5
 15.75          325.072
 16.2678        SPLAT
MAY THE ANGEL OF HEAVEN LEAD YOU INTO PARADISE
I'LL GIVE YOU ANOTHER CHANCE.
DO YOU WANT TO PLAY AGAIN? YES
```

```
30 OPEN "PARXCHUTE" AS FILE 1%
40 DIM #1%,A(4000)
55 RANDOMIZE
95 PRINT "WELCOME TO !SPLAT! -- THE GAME THAT SIMULATES A PARACHUTE"
96 PRINT "JUMP.  TRY TO OPEN YOUR CHUTE AT THE LAST POSSIBLE"
97 PRINT "MOMENT WITHOUT GOING SPLAT."
118 PRINT\PRINT\D1=0\V=0\A=0\N=0\M=0\D1=INT(9001*RND(1)+1000)
119 PRINT " SELECT YOUR OWN TERMINAL VELOCITY (YES OR NO)"\INPUT A1$
120 IF A1$="NO" THEN 128 ELSE IF A1$="YES" THEN 123
121 PRINT "!YES! OR !NO! PLEASE"\INPUT A1$\GOTO 120
123 PRINT "WHAT TERMINAL VELOCITY (MI/HR)"\INPUT V1
125 V1=V1*(5280/3600)\V=V1+((V1*RND(0))/20)-((V1*RND(0))/20)\GOTO 135
128 V1=INT(1000*RND(0))
130 PRINT "OK.  TERMINAL VELOCITY ="V1"MI/HR"
131 V1=V1*(5280/3600)\V=V1+((V1*RND(0))/20)-((V1*RND(0))/20)
135  PRINT "WANT TO SELECT ACCELERATION DUE TO GRAVITY (YES OR NO)";
136 INPUT B1$
140 IF B1$="NO" THEN 150 ELSE IF B1$="YES" THEN 143
141 PRINT "!YES! OR !NO! PLEASE"\INPUT B1$\GOTO 140
143 PRINT "WHAT ACCELERATION (FT/SEC/SEC)"\INPUT A2
145 A=A2+((A2*RND(0))/20)-((A2*RND(0))/20)\GOTO 205
150 ON INT(1+(10*RND(0)))GOTO151,152,153,154,155,156,157,158,159,160
151 PRINT"FINE, YOU'RE ON MERCURY, ACCELERATION=12.2FT/SEC/SEC"\GOTO161
152 PRINT"ALRIGHT, YOU'RE ON VENUS, ACCELERATION=28.3 FT/SEC/SEC"\GOTO162
153 PRINT"THEN YOU'RE ON EARTH, ACCELERATION=32.16 FT/SEC/SEC"\GOTO 163
154 PRINT"FINE, YOU'RE ON THE MOON, ACCELERATION=5.15FT/SEC/SEC"\GOTO 164
155 PRINT"ALRIGHT, YOU'RE ON MARS, ACCELERATION=12.5FT/SEC/SEC"\GOTO 165
156 PRINT"THEN YOU'RE ON JUPITER, ACCELERATION=85.2FT/SEC/SEC"\GOTO 166
157 PRINT"FINE, YOU'RE ON SATURN, ACCELERATION=37.6FT/SEC/SEC"\GOTO 167
158 PRINT"ALRIGHT, YOU'RE ON URANUS, ACCELERATION=33.8FT/SEC/SEC"\GOTO 168
159 PRINT"THEN YOU'RE ON NEPTUNE, ACCELERATION=39.6FT/SEC/SEC"\GOTO 169
160 PRINT"FINE, YOU'RE ON THE SUN, ACCELERATION=896FT/SEC/SEC"\GOTO 170
161 A2=12.2\GOTO 145
162 A2=28.3\GOTO 145
163 A2=32.16\GOTO 145
164 A2=5.15\GOTO 145
165 A2=12.5\GOTO 145
166 A2=85.2\GOTO 145
167 A2=37.6\GOTO 145
168 A2=33.8 \GOTO 145
169 A2=39.6\GOTO 145
170 A2=896\GOTO 145
205 PRINT
206 PRINT "     ALTITUDE         ="D1"FT"
207 PRINT "     TERM.VELOCITY    ="V1"FT/SEC +-5%"
208 PRINT "     ACCELERATION     ="A2"FT/SEC/SEC +-5%"
210 PRINT "SET THE TIMER FOR YOUR FREEFALL."
211 PRINT "HOW MANY SECONDS"\INPUT T
215 PRINT "HERE WE GO."
217 PRINT
218 PRINT "TIME (SEC)","DIST TO FALL (FT)"
219 PRINT "==========","================="
300 FOR I=0 TO T STEP (T/8)
310 IF I>V/A GOTO 400
320 D=D1-((A/2)*I^2)
330 IF D<=0 GOTO 1000
340 PRINT I,D
350 NEXT I
360 GOTO 500
400 PRINT "TERMINAL VELOCITY REACHED AT T PLUS"V/A"SECONDS"
405 FOR I=I TO T STEP (T/8)
410 D=D1-((V^2/(2*A))+(V*(I-(V/A))))
420 IF D<=0 GOTO 1010
430 PRINT I,D
440 NEXT I
450 GOTO 500
500 PRINT "CHUTE OPEN"
510 K=0\K1=0
530 FOR I=1 TO 4000
550 IF A(I)=0 GOTO 620
560 K=K+1
570 IF D>=A(I) GOTO 600
580 K1=K1+1
600 NEXT I
620 A(I)=D
630 I=I-1
650 IF K-K1<=.1*K GOTO 700
660 IF K-K1<=.25*K GOTO 710
670 IF K-K1<=.5*K GOTO 720
680 IF K-K1<=.75*K GOTO 730
690 IF K-K1<=.9*K GOTO 740
695 GOTO 750
700 PRINT "WOW!  THAT'S SOME JUMPING.  OF THE"K"SUCCESSFUL JUMPS"
701 PRINT "BEFORE YOURS, ONLY"K-K1"OPENED THEIR CHUTES LOWER THAN"
702 PRINT "YOU DID."
703 GOTO 2000
710 PRINT "PRETTY GOOD! " K"SUCCESSFUL JUMPS PRECEDED YOURS AND ONLY"
711 PRINT K-K1"OF THEM GOT LOWER THAN YOU DID BEFORE THEIR CHUTES"
712 PRINT "OPENED." \GOTO 2000
720 PRINT "NOT BAD.  THERE HAVE BEEN"K"SUCCESSFUL JUMPS BEFORE YOURS."
721 PRINT"YOU WERE BEATEN OUT BY"K-K1"OF THEM."\GOTO 2000
730 PRINT "CONSERVATIVE AREN'T YOU?  YOU RANKED ONLY"K-K1"IN THE"
731 PRINT K"SUCCESSFUL JUMPS BEFORE YOURS."\GOTO 2000
740 PRINT "HUMPH!  DON'T YOU HAVE ANY SPORTING BLOOD?  THERE WERE"
741 PRINT K"SUCCESSFUL JUMPS BEFORE YOURS AND YOU CAME IN"K1"JUMPS"
742 PRINT "BETTER THAN THE WORST.  SHAPE UP!!!"\GOTO 2000
750 PRINT "HEY!  YOU PULLED THE RIP CORD MUCH TOO SOON.  "K"SUCCESSFUL"
751 PRINT "JUMPS BEFORE YOURS AND YOU CAME IN NUMBER"K-K1!  GET WITH IT!"
752 GOTO 2000
800 PRINT "REQUIESCAT IN PACE."\GOTO 1950
801 PRINT "MAY THE ANGEL OF HEAVEN LEAD YOU INTO PARADISE"\GOTO 1950
802 PRINT "REST IN PEACE"\GOTO 1950
803 PRINT "SON-OF-A-GUN."\GOTO 1950
804 PRINT "#$%&&%!$"\GOTO 1950
805 PRINT "A KICK IN THE PANTS IS A BOOST IF YOU'RE HEADED RIGHT"\GOTO 1950
806 PRINT "HMMM, SHOULD HAVE PICKED A SHORTER TIME."\GOTO 1950
807 PRINT "MUTTER, MUTTER, MUTTER."\GOTO 1950
808 PRINT "PUSHING UP DAISIES."\GOTO1950
809 PRINT "EASY COME, EASY GO."\GOTO 1950
1000 PRINT SQR(2*D1/A),"SPLAT"
1005 ON INT(1+(10*RND(0)))GOTO 800,801,802,803,804,805,806,807,808,809
1010 PRINT (V/A)+((D1-(V^2/(2*A)))/V),"SPLAT"
1020 GOTO 1005
1950 PRINT "I'LL GIVE YOU ANOTHER CHANCE."\GOTO 2000
2000 PRINT "DO YOU WANT TO PLAY AGAIN"\INPUT Z$
2001 IF Z$="YES" GOTO 118
2002 IF Z$="NO" GOTO 2005
2003 PRINT "YES OR NO"\GOTO 2000
2005 PRINT "PLEASE"\INPUT Z$\IF Z$="YES" THEN 118 ELSE 2007
2007 PRINT "SSSSSSSSSS."\GOTO 2046
2046 CLOSE 1%
9999 END
```

Another new game from Creative Computing . . .

ICBM

by Paul Calter
Vermont Technical College

Your radar station picks up an enemy ICBM heading your way, telling you its coordinates (in miles north and miles east of your location). You launch a surface-to-air missile (SAM) to intercept it.

Your only control over the SAM is that you can aim it in any direction, both at launch, and in mid-air. Using the coordinates of the ICBM as a guide, you INPUT the direction (measured CCW from North) in which you want the SAM to travel.

At the next radar scan one minute later, you are given the new coordinates of the ICBM, the coordinates of your SAM, and the distance between the two. You can now make corrections in the course of your SAM by entering a new direction.

You have no control over the altitude of your SAM, as it is assumed that it will seek the same altitude as the ICBM.

As the two missiles draw closer, you make adjustments in the direction of the SAM so as to intercept the ICBM. It's not easy to hit, because the ICBM is programmed to make evasive maneuvers, by taking random deviations from the straight line course to your location. Also, its speed is not known, although it does not vary after being randomly selected at the start of the run.

You can destroy the ICBM by coming within 5 miles of it, at which time your SAM's heat-seeking sensors will come into action and direct it to its target. If you overshoot the ICBM it's possible to turn the SAM around and chase the ICBM back towards your location. But be careful; you may get both missiles in your lap.

There is also some element of chance involved, as several accidents have been programmed to occur randomly. These can work for you or against you.

Some ways to improve and expand the program are:

1. Operator control over SAM speed: In the present version the speed of the SAM is randomly selected by the computer at the start of the run, and remains constant thereafter. This often results in overshooting the ICBM. Modify the program so that you can input a new speed (within limits) at the same time you input the new direction.

2. Three dimensional version: Have the computer print the *altitude* of the ICBM, as well as its coordinates. The operator will then have to INPUT the angle his SAM is to make with the horizontal, when entering the other quantities.

3. Extend to all Quadrants. In the present version, the ICBM approaches only from the Northeast. You can expand this to include approach from any compass direction.

This game is derived from a program submitted by Chris Falco, of Glen Ridge High School, NJ.

PROGRAM LISTING

```
100 RANDOMIZE
110 LET X1=0
120 LET Y1=0
130 LET X= INT (RND*800)+200
140 LET Y=INT(RND*800)+200
150 LET S=INT(RND*20+50)
160 LET S1=INT(RND*20+50)
170 PRINT"---------MISSLE----------        -------------SAM-------"
180 PRINT "MILES", "MILES", "MILES","MILES","HEADING"
190 PRINT "NORTH","EAST","NORTH","EAST","?"
200 PRINT "------------------------------------------------------------"
210 FOR N=1 TO 50
220 PRINT Y, X, Y1, X1,
230 IF X=0 THEN 550
240 INPUT T1
250 LET T1=T1/57.296
260 LET H=INT(RND*200+1)
270 IF H>4 THEN 290
280 ON H GO TO 470,490,510,530
290 LET X1=INT(X1+S1*SIN(T1))
300 LET Y1=INT(Y1+S1*COS(T1))
310 IF SQR(X1+2+Y1+2)>S THEN 350
320 LET X=0
330 LET Y=0
340 GO TO 430
350 LET R=SQR(X1+2+Y1+2)/1000
360 LET T=ATN(Y/X)
370 LET X=INT(X-S*COS(T)+RND*20*R)
380 LET Y=INT(Y-S*SIN(T)+RND*20*R)
390 LET D=SQR((X-X1)+2+(Y-Y1)+2)
400 IF D<=5 THEN 440
410 LET D=INT(D)
420 PRINT "ICBM & SAM NOW"; D; " MILES APART"
430 NEXT N
440 PRINT "CONGRATULATIONS!  YOUR SAM CAME WITHIN";D;"MILES OF"
450 PRINT "THE ICBM AND DESTROYED IT."
460 GO TO 560
470 PRINT "TOO BAD.  YOUR SAM FELL TO THE GROUND"
480 GO TO 560
490 PRINT"YOUR SAM EXPLODED IN MIDAIR"
500 GO TO 560
510 PRINT "GOOD LUCK-THE ICBM EXPLODED HARMLESSLY IN MID-AIR"
520 GO TO 560
530 PRINT "GOOD LUCK-THE ICBM TURNED OUT TO BE A FRIENDLY AIRCRAFT"
540 GO TO 560
550 PRINT "TOO BAD! THE ICBM JUST HIT YOUR LOCATION"
560 PRINT"DO YOU WANT TO PLAY MORE?  (Y OR N)"
570 INPUT A$
580 IF A$="Y" THEN 130
590 END
READY
```

SAMPLE RUN

ICBM   08 JAN 75

| ---------MISSLE---------- | | -------------SAM-------- | | |
MILES NORTH	MILES EAST	MILES NORTH	MILES EAST	HEADING ?
587	868	0	0	? 60
ICBM & SAM NOW 948 MILES APART				
565	832	29	50	? 60
ICBM & SAM NOW 859 MILES APART				
554	832	58	100	? 55
ICBM & SAM NOW 761 MILES APART				
525	773	91	147	? 60
ICBM & SAM NOW 667 MILES APART				
512	737	120	197	? 60
ICBM & SAM NOW 569 MILES APART				
493	701	149	247	? 55
ICBM & SAM NOW 470 MILES APART				
467	668	182	294	? 55
ICBM & SAM NOW 367 MILES APART				
436	635	215	341	? X55
ICBM & SAM NOW 371 MILES APART				
428	598	248	388	? 57
ICBM & SAM NOW 171 MILES APART				
392	565	279	436	? 57
ICBM & SAM NOW 76 MILES APART				
374	526	312	464	? 30
ICBM & SAM NOW 32 MILES APART				
346	483	360	512	? 225
ICBM & SAM NOW 21 MILES APART				
320	449	318	470	? 235
ICBM & SAM NOW 17 MILES APART				
295	408	284	422	? 245
ICBM & SAM NOW 12 MILES APART				
271	369	259	369	? 240
ICBM & SAM NOW 21 MILES APART				
242	335	229	318	? 60
ICBM & SAM NOW 82 MILES APART				
213	299	258	368	? 240
ICBM & SAM NOW 71 MILES APART				
182	262	228	317	? 235
ICBM & SAM NOW 64 MILES APART				
155	218	194	269	? 240
ICBM & SAM NOW 57 MILES APART				
126	175	164	218	? 240
ICBM & SAM NOW 49 MILES APART				
96	135	134	167	? 240
ICBM & SAM NOW 44 MILES APART				
67	92	104	116	? 220
ICBM & SAM NOW 37 MILES APART				
35	49	59	78	? 230

GOOD LUCK-THE ICBM TURNED OUT TO BE A FRIENDLY AIRCRAFT
DO YOU WANT TO PLAY MORE? (Y OR N)
? N

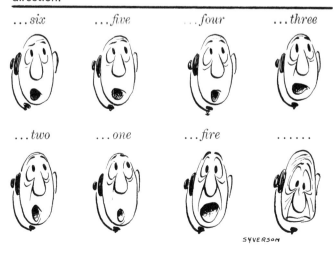

...six   ...five   ...four   ...three

...two   ...one   ...fire   ......

SYVERSON

269

RABBIT CHASE

by Ted C. Park
Pacific Union College
Angwin, California

DESCRIPTION

Seemingly, the purpose of this game is to chase-down and catch a rabbit. Now this rabbit is an elusive little devil — it can hop randomly in any direction. You can run at least as fast as the rabbit, maybe even faster (the computer will decide). You must get within 20 units of the rabbit to be able to catch him. Before each hop, the computer will print out your position, the rabbit's position, the direction the rabbit is going to jump, and your closest approach on the last hop. You are to tell the computer which direction you wish to run. All coordinates and directions are as a geometer would mark them on a standard Cartesian Coordinate System.

Really, the purpose of the game is to give you practice in using and visualizing an x-y coordinate plane.

USING THE PROGRAM

1. This program will run on most versions of BASIC, if your computer does not like it, convert it.
2. Consider the output and try to run the right direction.
3. Try to do all the figuring in your head. Using scratch paper is considered to be cheating (except for maybe the first time you play).

SUGGESTED MODIFICATIONS

1. Change the program so that you can choose your own speed.
2. The game is much more challenging when the "capture distance" can be varied. A distance of 50 units is a cinch, 15 units may make you wish for scratch paper, 5 units will require you to use a protracter and graph paper.
3. See if you can invent a way to extend this game to 3 dimensions! 4 dimensions!!! etc.!!!!!!
4. You might try limiting the total number of hops and/or having the computer give hints when requested.
5. If your BASIC supports a "print using" type of statement try rewriting the output section in a more clever manner.

SAMPLE RUN

```
SPEEDS (UNITS/HOP):
RABBIT - 140    YOU - 420

HOP#: 0001      DISTANCE TO RABBIT: 0445    CLOSEST APPROACH: 0445
RABBIT ---      POSITION: (-0180,-0407)     AND DIRECTION: 0153
YOU ------      POSITION: (+0000,+0000)     AND DIRECTION:?220

HOP#: 0002      DISTANCE TO RABBIT: 0075    CLOSEST APPROACH: 0075
RABBIT ---      POSITION: (-0305,-0343)     AND DIRECTION: 0189
YOU ------      POSITION: (-0322,-0270)     AND DIRECTION:?270

**********
* GOT YA *
**********
```

LISTING

```
CHASE

100  REM ( '.T' IS THE SQUARE OF THE CAPTURE DISTANCE )
105  LET T=400
110  REM
115  REM --  INITIALIZE VELOCITIES AND POSITIONS
120  REM
125  LET V1=INT(RND(0)*10+.5)*10+50
130  LET V2=(INT(RND(0)*2+.5)+1)*V1
135  LET X1=(INT(RND(0)*400)+100)*SGN(RND(0)-.5)
140  LET Y1=(INT(RND(0)*400)+100)*SGN(RND(0)-.5)
145  IF Y1=0 OR X1=0 THEN 135
150  LET X2=0
155  LET Y2=0
160  PRINT "SPEEDS (UNITS/HOP):"
165  PRINT "RABBIT -";V1,"YOU -";V2
170  PRINT
175  PRINT
180  PRINT
185  LET C=(X2-X1)↑2+(Y2-Y1)↑2
190  LET P1=3.14159/180
195  LET H=1
200  REM
205  REM --  PRINT OUT
210  REM
215  LET D1=INT(RND(0)*359)
220  PRINT "HOP#: ";
225  LET Z=H
230  GOSUB 545
235  PRINT "     DISTANCE TO RABBIT: ";
240  LET Z=SQR((X2-X1)↑2+(Y2-Y1)↑2)
245  GOSUB 545
250  PRINT "     CLOSEST APPROACH: ";
255  LET Z=SQR(C)
260  GOSUB 545
265  PRINT
270  PRINT "RABBIT ---       POSITION: (";
275  LET Z=X1
280  GOSUB 520
285  PRINT ",";
290  LET Z=Y1
295  GOSUB 520
300  PRINT ")       AND DIRECTION: ";
305  LET Z=D1
310  GOSUB 545
315  PRINT
320  PRINT "YOU ------       POSITION: (";
325  LET Z=X2
330  GOSUB 520
335  PRINT ",";
340  LET Z=Y2
345  GOSUB 520
350  PRINT ")       AND DIRECTION:";
355  INPUT D2
360  IF D2<0 OR D2 >= 360 THEN 355
365  PRINT
370  PRINT
375  REM
380  REM --  COMPUTE PATHS AND SEE IF THEY INTERSECT
385  REM
390  LET X3=V1*COS(D1*P1)/100
395  LET Y3=V1*SIN(D1*P1)/100
400  LET X4=V2*COS(D2*P1)/100
405  LET Y4=V2*SIN(D2*P1)/100
410  LET C=(X2-X1)↑2+(Y2-Y1)↑2
415  FOR I=1 TO 100
420  LET X1=X1+X3
425  LET Y1=Y1+Y3
430  LET X2=X2+X4
435  LET Y2=Y2+Y4
440  LET C=C MIN (X2-X1)↑2+(Y2-Y1)↑2
445  NEXT I
450  LET H=H+1
455  IF C>T THEN 215
460  PRINT
465  PRINT
470  PRINT "**********"
475  PRINT "* GOT YA *"
480  PRINT "**********"
485  PRINT
490  PRINT
495  PRINT
500  STOP
505  REM
510  REM --  CONVERTS NUMBERS TO STRINGS FOR CLEANER OUTPUT
515  REM
520  IF Z<0 THEN 535
525  PRINT "+";
530  GOTO 545
535  PRINT "-";
540  LET Z=-Z
545  LET Z=INT(Z+.5)
550  DIM S$(10)
555  LET S$="0123456789"
560  FOR I=1 TO 4
565  LET W=INT(Z/10↑(4-I))
570  PRINT S$(W+1,W+1);
575  LET Z=Z-W*10↑(4-I)
580  NEXT I
585  RETURN
590  END
```

Magic Square

We've all seen examples of magic squares. The most common one is a 3x3 square using the integers 1 through 9 in which the sum of each row, column and diagonal totals 15.

Here are a few manual games involving magic squares. Try them.

Complete this magic square to make the sums of the rows, columns, and diagonals the same.

This is a different kind of magic square. What are its characteristics?

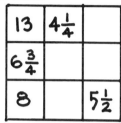

In the computer game of "Magic Square" the goal is to form a sum 15 magic square with you and the computer alternately filling in the integers between 1 and 9. If one player stumbles and puts a number in which causes the sum of a row, column, or diagonal to be something other than 15, he loses.

In forming a sum 15 magic square, there is only one fundamental solution. However, it can be rotated and reversed to form 8 solutions. Because the computer does not play a particularly creative game, all eight solutions cannot be obtained. How many can be?

Can you modify the computer program to play a more interesting game which permits all eight solutions? (Hint: Try randomizing the move position and number generators in Statements 400 and 410.)

Note: In converting "Magic Square" to your dialect of BASIC watch out for multiple statements on a line (indicated by a backslash) and compound IF statements.

by David H. Ahl

```
RUNNH
GAME OF MAGIC SQUARE BY DAVID AHL

PLAYERS ALTERNATELY CHOOSE AN INTEGER (1 TO 9)
THAT HAS NOT BEEN PREVIOUSLY USED AND PLACE IT
IN ANY UNFILLED CELL OF A TIC-TAC-TOE BOARD.
THE GOAL IS TO MAKE THE SUM OF EACH ROW, COLUMN,
AND DIAGONAL EQUAL TO 15.

THAT PLAYER LOSES WHO FIRST MAKES THE SUM OF THE
THREE FIGURES IN ANY ROW, COLUMN, OR DIAGONAL
SOMETHING OTHER THAN 15.

A TIE GAME DRAWS A MAGIC SQUARE!!

THE COMPUTER WILL ASK YOU ON EACH MOVE WHICH
CELL YOU WISH TO OCCUPY, AND THE NUMBER YOU WISH
TO PLACE IN THAT CELL.   YOUR INPUT SHOULD LOOK
LIKE '3,7' IF YOU WISHED TO PLACE A 7 IN CELL 3.

HERE ARE THE CELL NUMBERS:

1 2 3
4 5 6
7 8 9

YOUR MOVE -- CELL AND NUMBER? 2,6

   0  6  0
   0  0  0
   0  0  0

I MOVE TO CELL 1 WITH A 1

   1  6  0
   0  0  0
   0  0  0

YOUR MOVE -- CELL AND NUMBER? 4,7

   1  6  0
   7  0  0
   0  0  0

I MOVE TO CELL 3 WITH A 8

   1  6  8
   7  0  0
   0  0  0

YOUR MOVE -- CELL AND NUMBER? 7,4

   1  6  8
   7  0  0
   4  0  0

SORRY, YOU LOSE -- NICE TRY.

LET'S PLAY AGAIN...
```

```
20 PRINT "GAME OF MAGIC SQUARE BY DAVID AHL"\PRINT
25 PRINT "PLAYERS ALTERNATELY CHOOSE AN INTEGER (1 TO 9)"
30 PRINT "THAT HAS NOT BEEN PREVIOUSLY USED AND PLACE IT"
35 PRINT "IN ANY UNFILLED CELL OF A TIC-TAC-TOE BOARD."
40 PRINT "THE GOAL IS TO MAKE THE SUM OF EACH ROW, COLUMN,"
45 PRINT "AND DIAGONAL EQUAL TO 15."\PRINT
50 PRINT "THAT PLAYER LOSES WHO FIRST MAKES THE SUM OF THE"
55 PRINT "THREE FIGURES IN ANY ROW, COLUMN, OR DIAGONAL"
60 PRINT "SOMETHING OTHER THAN 15."\PRINT
62 PRINT "A TIE GAME DRAWS A MAGIC SQUARE!!"\PRINT
65 PRINT "THE COMPUTER WILL ASK YOU ON EACH MOVE WHICH"
70 PRINT "CELL YOU WISH TO OCCUPY, AND THE NUMBER YOU WISH"
75 PRINT "TO PLACE IN THAT CELL.  YOUR INPUT SHOULD LOOK"
80 PRINT "LIKE '3,7' IF YOU WISHED TO PLACE A 7 IN CELL 3."
85 PRINT\PRINT "HERE ARE THE CELL NUMBERS:"\PRINT
90 PRINT "1 2 3"\PRINT "4 5 6"\PRINT "7 8 9"
95 FOR I=1 TO 9\A(I)=0\B(I)=0\NEXT I\M=0\W=0
100 PRINT\INPUT "YOUR MOVE -- CELL AND NUMBER";I,N
105 IF I<1 OR I>9 OR N<1 OR N>9 THEN 130
110 IF A(I)=0 AND B(N)=0 THEN 150
130 PRINT "ILLEGAL MOVE ... AGAIN."\GOTO 100
150 A(I)=N\B(N)=1\M=M+1          !AN ACCEPTABLE MOVE
170 GOSUB 960                    !PRINT BOARD
180 GOSUB 800                    !A LOSING MOVE??
200 IF W=0 THEN 230              !GOOD MOVE, NO WINNER YET
210 PRINT "SORRY, YOU LOSE -- NICE TRY."\GOTO 560
230 IF M<5 THEN 400              !A TIE GAME?
240 PRINT "A TIE GAME -- BUT WE'VE DRAWN A MAGIC SQUARE!"\GOTO 560
400 FOR Q=1 TO 9                 !COMPUTER LOOKS FOR A GOOD MOVE
410 IF A(Q)>0 THEN 480           !CELL TAKEN??
420 FOR R=1 TO 9
430 IF B(R)>0 THEN 470           !NUMBER TAKEN??
435 A(Q)=R                       !TRY MAKING THE MOVE
440 GOSUB 800                    !IS THIS MOVE A LOSER?
450 IF W=0 THEN 500              !A GOOD MOVE!!
460 Q1=Q\R1=R\W=0\A(Q)=0         !RECORD BAD MOVE IN CASE NO GOOD ONE
470 NEXT R
480 NEXT Q
490 W=1\R=R1\Q=Q1\A(Q)=R         !IF GET HERE, COMPUTER HAS LOST
500 B(R)=1                       !COMPUTER MAKES ITS MOVE
520 PRINT "I MOVE TO CELL"Q"WITH A"R
530 GOSUB 960                    !PRINT BOARD
540 IF W=0 THEN 100              !THE GAME GOES ON....
550 PRINT "I LOSE -- YOU WIN!!"
560 PRINT\PRINT CHRS(7); FOR I=1 TO 15    !RINGS TELETYPE BELL
570 PRINT "LET'S PLAY AGAIN..."\GOTO 95
800 FOR X=1 TO 8                 !SUBROUTINE TO CHECK FOR LOSING MOVE
810 ON X GOTO 820,830,840,850,860,870,880,890
820 J=1\K=2\L=3\GOTO 900
830 K=4\L=7\GOTO 900
840 K=5\L=9\GOTO 900
850 J=4\L=6\GOTO 900
860 J=2\L=8\GOTO 900
870 J=3\L=7\GOTO 900
880 K=6\L=9\GOTO 900
890 J=7\K=8
900 IF A(J)=0 OR A(K)=0 OR A(L)=0 THEN 930
920 IF A(J)+A(K)+A(L)<>15 THEN 940
930 NEXT X
935 GOTO 950
940 W=1                          !A LOSER!!
950 RETURN
960 PRINT\PRINT A(1);A(2);A(3)   !SUBROUTINE TO PRINT BOARD
970 PRINT A(4);A(5);A(6)\PRINT A(7);A(8);A(9)\PRINT\RETURN
999 END
```

MADLIB ~ A GAME

Madlibs are a creation of Roger Price and were designed as a hilarious party game. In playing the game, the leader has a sheet of paper similar to the one below, with a short story written on it but with certain words missing. In turn, he asks each person in the room to supply one word, *before* reading the story. The first person may be asked for an adjective, the second for a noun, etc., until all the blanks are filled in. The leader then reads the story to the group in a hearty, booming voice.

FABLE

Once upon a time a_____dog got hold of a

                         adj.

_____bone. He was walking across a_____

   adj.   adj.

bridge and saw his_____reflection in the

                           adj.

water. "_____!" he said, "there is another

       exclamation

_____dog with another_____bone. I'll

   adj.   adj.

make a_____grab, take his and then I'll have two

          adj.

_____bones." With that the_____

   adj.   adj.

dog jumped into the water and_____drowned.

                           adverb

MORAL: A_____in the_____is worth

        noun   noun

two in the_____.

            noun

With Madlib, you can exercise some real creativity with synonyms. Consider: instead of saying "big" use another word like "huge," "tremendous," "enormous," "bulbous," "bulging," "massive," or "boundless."

Exercise 1

For each of the following words, write 10 synonyms. Use the most ludicrous synonyms you can think of. Try to do it by yourself, or use a dictionary or *Roget's Thesaurus*. Compare your word lists with those of other class members.

small   rough

old   ugly

witty   brain

Exercise 2

Play MADLIB on the computer. Set the tone of the finished story by using all ugly sounding words or all political words or all buzzwords from one profession. Compare your stories with those of other class members.

The MADLIB program was originally written by Henry Gallo, a high school student in Huntington, NY. It was extensively modified by David Ahl.

SAMPLE RUN

```
RUN MADLIB
MADLIB STORY-WRITER BY DAVE AHL BASED ON A PROGRAM
ORIGINALLY WRITTEN BY HENRY GALLO, JOHN GLENN HS.

O. K.   WE'RE GOING TO WRITE SOME MAD-LIB STORIES
TOGETHER.   YOU SUPPLY THE WORDS, I SUPPLY THE PLOT.

FIRST I NEED 11 ADJECTIVES.   ADJECTIVES MODIFY
A NOUN, E. G., RED, DIRTY, LARGE, ETC.
? HORRENDOUS
? UNUSUAL
? UGLY
? RANCID
? OVERFLOWING
? SMELLY
? IMPROPER
? DIRTY
? UNDIGESTED
? GROTESQUE
? FRANKFURTER

HOW ABOUT TWO FIRST NAMES OF MEN
? FRANK
? WOLFGANG
THE FIRST NAME OF A GIRL
? BERTHA
AND SOMEONE'S LAST NAME
? WASHINGTON
? GEOGRAPHICAL LOCATION
? ROXBURY SLUMS
? LIQUID
? MOXIE
AND FINALLY, AN EXCLAMATORY WORD OR TWO
? OH PSHAW

VERY GOOD!   WOULD YOU LIKE A NEWSPAPER AD (1),
A WESTERN (2), A STORY ABOUT THE ARMY (3), OR
A WATERBED (4).   WHICH ONE, 1, 2, 3, OR 4? 1


        DAILY GRUNT CLASSIFIEDS

FOR SALE: 1957 SEDAN.   THIS HORRENDOUS CAR IS IN A UNUSUAL
CONDITION.   IT WAS FORMERLY OWNED BY A UGLY SCHOOL TEACHER
WHO ALWAYS DROVE IT SLOVENLY.   THERE IS A RANCID GROUNDHOG IN
THE BACK SEAT.   IT HAS A CHROME BEER CAN ON THE HOOD, A OVERFLOWING
PAINT JOB, SMELLY TIRES AND THE BACK OPENS INTO A IMPROPER
GARBAGE CAN.   WILL CONSIDER TAKING A SLIGHTLY USED INSECT IN TRADE

LOST: IN THE VICINITY OF ROXBURY SLUMS, A DIRTY FRENCH
POODLE WITH UNDIGESTED HAIR AND A GROTESQUE TAIL.   IT ANSWERS
TO THE NAME OF BERTHA.   WHEN LAST SEEN IT WAS CARRYING A
AARDVARK IN ITS MOUTH.   A BLEEDING REWARD IS OFFERED.


        AN ADULT WESTERN

TEX WASHINGTON, THE MARSHALL OF FRANK CITY RODE INTO TOWN.   HE
SAT GREEDILY IN THE SADDLE, READY FOR TROUBLE.   HE KNEW THAT
HIS HORRENDOUS ENEMY, WOLFGANG THE KID WAS IN TOWN.   THE KID WAS
IN LOVE WITH TEX'S HORSE, BERTHA.   SUDDENLY THE KID CAME OUT
OF THE IMPROPER NUGGET SALOON.

'DRAW TEX,' HE YELLED HEAVENLY.

TEX REACHED FOR HIS INSECT, BUT BEFORE HE COULD GET IT
OUT OF HIS AARDVARK THE KID FIRED, HITTING TEX IN THE BELLY BUTTON
AND THE KNEECAP.

AS TEX FELL HE PULLED OUT HIS OWN DECTAPE AND SHOT THE KID
 17 TIMES IN THE PIGTAIL.   THE KID DROPPED IN A POOL
OF MOXIE.

'OH PSHAW,' TEX SAID, 'I HATED TO DO IT BUT
HE WAS ON THE WRONG SIDE OF THE FRANKFURTER.
```

```
10 PRINT "MADLIB STORY-WRITER BY DAVE AHL BASED ON A PROGRAM"
15 PRINT "ORIGINALLY WRITTEN BY HENRY GALLO, JOHN GLENN HS,":PRINT
20 DIM A$(11),B$(5),C$(10):RANDOMIZE
30 PRINT "O.K.  WE'RE GOING TO WRITE SOME MAD-LIB STORIES"
40 PRINT "TOGETHER.  YOU SUPPLY THE WORDS, I SUPPLY THE PLOT.":PRINT
60 PRINT "FIRST I NEED 11 ADJECTIVES.  ADJECTIVES MODIFY"
70 PRINT "A NOUN, E.G., RED, DIRTY, LARGE, ETC."
80 FOR I=1 TO 11:INPUT A$(I):NEXT I
90 PRINT:PRINT "NOW I NEED 5 ADVERBS.  THEY MODIFY VERBS"
100 PRINT "AND END IN 'LY' (SLOWLY, GREEDILY, ETC.)"
110 FOR I=1 TO 5:INPUT B$(I):NEXT I
120 PRINT:PRINT "O.K.  NOW 10 NOUNS, E.G., TELETYPE, INSECT, COAT, ETC."
130 FOR I=1 TO 10:INPUT C$(I):NEXT I
140 PRINT:INPUT "HOW ABOUT TWO FIRST NAMES OF MEN"D$:INPUT E$
160 INPUT "THE FIRST NAME OF A GIRL"F$
170 INPUT "AND SOMEONE'S LAST NAME"G$
180 INPUT "A GEOGRAPHICAL LOCATION"H$
190 INPUT "A LIQUID"I$
200 INPUT "AND FINALLY, AN EXCLAMATORY WORD OR TWO"J$:PRINT
220 PRINT "VERY GOOD!  WOULD YOU LIKE A NEWSPAPER AD (1),"
230 PRINT "A WESTERN (2), A STORY ABOUT THE ARMY (3), OR"
240 INPUT "A WATERBED (4).  WHICH ONE, 1, 2, 3, OR 4"N:PRINT
250 IF N>0 AND N<5 THEN 270
260 INPUT "COME ON NOW -- 1, 2, 3, OR 4"N:GOTO 250
270 PRINT FOR I=1 TO 6:ON N GOTO 300,400,500,600
300 PRINT "          DAILY GRUNT CLASSIFIEDS":PRINT
310 PRINT "FOR SALE: 1957 SEDAN.  THIS "A$(1)" CAR IS IN A "A$(2)
320 PRINT "CONDITION. IT WAS FORMERLY OWNED BY A "A$(3)" SCHOOL TEACHER"
330 PRINT "WHO ALWAYS DROVE IT "B$(1)". THERE IS A "A$(4)" "C$(1)" IN"
340 PRINT "THE BACK SEAT. IT HAS A CHROME "C$(2)" ON THE HOOD, A "A$(5)
350 PRINT "PAINT JOB, "A$(6)" TIRES AND THE BACK OPENS INTO A "A$(7)
360 PRINT C$(3)". WILL CONSIDER TAKING A SLIGHTLY USED "C$(4)" IN TRADE"
370 PRINT:PRINT "LOST: IN THE VICINITY OF "H$", A "A$(8)" FRENCH"
380 PRINT "POODLE WITH "A$(9)" HAIR AND A "A$(10)" TAIL. IT ANSWERS"
385 PRINT "TO THE NAME OF "F$". WHEN LAST SEEN IT WAS CARRYING A"
390 PRINT C$(5)" IN ITS MOUTH. A "A$(11)" REWARD IS OFFERED.":GOTO 700
400 PRINT "         AN ADULT WESTERN":PRINT
410 PRINT "TEX "G$", THE MARSHALL OF "D$" CITY RODE INTO TOWN. HE"
420 PRINT "SAT "B$(2)" IN THE SADDLE, READY FOR TROUBLE. HE KNEW THAT"
430 PRINT "HIS "A$(1)" ENEMY, "E$" THE KID WAS IN TOWN. THE KID WAS"
440 PRINT "IN LOVE WITH TEX'S HORSE, "F$".  SUDDENLY THE KID CAME OUT"
450 PRINT "OF THE "A$(7)" NUGGET SALOON.":PRINT
460 PRINT "'DRAW TEX,' HE YELLED "B$(3)".":PRINT
470 PRINT "TEX REACHED FOR HIS "C$(4)", BUT BEFORE HE COULD GET IT"
475 PRINT "OUT OF HIS "C$(5)" THE KID FIRED, HITTING TEX IN THE "C$(6)
480 PRINT "AND THE "C$(7)".":PRINT
485 PRINT "AS TEX FELL HE PULLED OUT HIS OWN "C$(8)" AND SHOT THE KID"
490 PRINT INT(50*RND+3)"TIMES IN THE "C$(9)". THE KID DROPPED IN A POOL"
492 PRINT "OF "I$".":PRINT:PRINT "'"J$",' TEX SAID, 'I HATED TO DO IT BUT"
495 PRINT "HE WAS ON THE WRONG SIDE OF THE "C$(10)".'":PRINT:GOTO 700
500 PRINT "IF YOU PLAN ON JOINING THE ARMY, HERE ARE SOME "A$(11)
510 PRINT "HINTS THAT WILL HELP YOU BECOME A "A$(10)" SOLDIER.":PRINT
520 PRINT "THE ARMY IS MADE UP OF OFFICERS, NON-COMS AND "C$(1)"S."
530 PRINT "YOU CAN RECOGNIZE AN OFFICER BY THE "C$(2)"S ON HIS"
540 PRINT "SHOULDERS AND THE FUNNY-LOOKING "C$(3)"S ON HIS CAP."
550 PRINT "WHEN YOU ADDRESS AN OFFICER, ALWAYS SAY "C$(4)" AND SAY IT"
555 PRINT B$(5)".  IF YOU GET A "A$(9)" HAIRCUT, KEEP YOUR "C$(5)"S"
560 PRINT "SHINED, AND SEE THAT YOUR "C$(6)" IS CLEAN AT ALL TIMES,"
565 PRINT "YOU WILL BE A CREDIT TO THE SLOGAN:":PRINT
570 PRINT "          THE ARMY BUILDS BETTER "C$(7)"S!":PRINT
575 PRINT "AT ROLL CALL, WHEN THE "A$(8)" SERGEANT CALLS YOUR NAME,"
580 PRINT "SHOUT '"J$"! LOUD AND CLEAR,":PRINT
585 PRINT "YOU WILL BECOME FAMILIAR WITH WEAPONS LIKE THE .30 CALIBRE"
590 PRINT C$(8)" AND THE AUTOMATIC "C$(9)".":PRINT
592 PRINT "FOLLOW THIS ADVICE AND YOU MAY WIN THE......"
595 PRINT "********* "A$(7)" CONDUCT "C$(10)" *********":GOTO 700
600 PRINT "BUST-A-BUTTON AND DUCK DEPT. STORE":PRINT"DIX HILLS, NEW YORK"
610 PRINT:PRINT "DEAR SIRS:":PRINT
620 PRINT "LAST WEEK I PURCHASED A "A$(2)" CONTOUR WATER BED IN YOUR"
630 PRINT "STORE. I GOT IT ESPECIALLY FOR MY "A$(4)" HUSBAND WHO SLEEPS"
640 PRINT "VERY "B$(1)" AND SAYS THAT "A$(6)" WATER BEDS THAT HAVE"
650 PRINT C$(1)"S IN THEM MAKE HIS "C$(3)" ACHE. WHEN THE BED"
655 PRINT "ARRIVED MY HUSBAND TESTED IT "B$(2)" AND SAID THE "A$(8)
660 PRINT C$(5)" WAS BENT AND KEPT PRESSING INTO HIS "C$(6)". HE SAYS"
665 PRINT "THIS COULD LEAD TO A "A$(10)" CONDITION OF THE "C$(8)".":PRINT
670 PRINT "I WOULD LIKE TO EXCHANGE THIS "A$(9)" BED FOR ONE THAT"
675 PRINT "WILL ALLOW MY HUSBAND TO SLEEP "B$(4)" AND WON'T MAKE"
680 PRINT "HIS "C$(10)" SORE.":PRINT:PRINT TAB(30)"YOURS "B$(5)","
690 PRINT TAB(30)F$" "G$:PRINT
700 PRINT FOR I=1 TO 6:INPUT "WANT ANOTHER STORY (YES OR NO)"Y$
710 IF Y$="NO" THEN 900
720 INPUT "WANT TO USE THE SAME WORDS (YES OR NO)"Y$:PRINT
730 IF Y$="YES" THEN 220 ELSE IF Y$="NO" THEN 60
740 INPUT "COME ON NOW -- 'YES' OR 'NO'"Y$:PRINT:GOTO 730
900 PRINT:PRINT "O.K.  SEE YOU AGAIN SOMETIME!"
999 END
```

Another new game from Creative Computing . . .

SUPER STAR TREK

History

by David Ahl

Many versions of Star Trek have been kicking around various college campuses since the late sixties. I recall playing one at Carnegie-Mellon Univ. in 1967 or 68, and a very different one at Berkeley. However, these were a far cry from the one written by Mike Mayfield of Centerline Engineering and/or Custom Data. This was written for an HP2000C and completed in October 1972. It became the "standard" Star Trek in February 1973 when it was put in the HP contributed program library and onto a number of HP Data Center machines.

In the summer of 1973, I converted the HP version to BASIC-PLUS for DEC's RSTS-11 compiler and added a few bits and pieces while I was at it. Mary Cole at DEC contributed enormously to this task too. Later that year I published it under the name SPACWR (Space War — in retrospect, an incorrect name) in my book *101 Basic Computer Games.* It is difficult today to find an interactive computer installation that does not have one of these versions of Star Trek available.

Of course, a program like Star Trek does not stay static for long. Of the many extensions I have seen, by far the best is by Bob Leedom of Westinghouse Defense and Electronic Systems Center. It's presented here as SUPER STAR TREK.

Quadrant Nomenclature

Recently, certain critics have professed confusion as to the origin of the "quadrant" nomenclature used on all standard CG (Cartesian Galactic) maps. Naturally, for anyone with the remotest knowledge of history, no explanation is necessary; however, the following synopsis should suffice for the critics:

As every schoolboy knows, most of the intelligent civilizations in the Milky Way had originated galactic designations of their own choosing well before the Third Magellanic Conference[*], at which the so-called "2^6 Agreement" was reached. In that historic document, the participant cultures agreed, in all two-dimensional representations of the galaxy, to specify 64 major subdivisions, ordered as an 8 x 8 matrix. This was partially in deference to the Earth culture (which had done much in the initial organization of the Federation), whose century-old galactic maps had always shown 16 major regions named after celestial landmarks of the Earth sky. Each of these regions was divided into four "quadrants," designated by ancient "Roman Numerals" (the origin of which has been lost).

To this day, the official logs of starships originating on near-Earth starbases still refer to the major galactic areas as "quadrants."

The relation between the Historical and Standard nomenclatures is shown in the simplified CG map below.

*Conference held at Federation Starbase 1, Stardates 1016-1021.

	1	2	3	4	5	6	7	8
1		ANTARES				SIRIUS		
	I	II	III	IV	I	II	III	IV
2		RIGEL				DENEB		
	I	II	III	IV	I	II	III	IV
3		PROCYON				CAPELLA		
	I	II	III	IV	I	II	III	IV
4		VEGA				BETELGEUSE		
	I	II	III	IV	I	II	III	IV
5		CANOPUS				ALDEBARAN		
	I	II	III	IV	I	II	III	IV
6		ALTAIR				REGULUS		
	I	II	III	IV	I	II	III	I
7		SAGITTARIUS				ARCTURUS		
	I	II	III	IV	I	II	III	IV
8		POLLUX				SPICA		
	I	II	III	IV	I	II	III	IV

Super STAR TREK Rules and Notes

by Robert Leedom and David Ahl

1. OBJECTIVE: You are Captain of the starship "Enterprise" with a mission to seek and destroy a fleet of Klingon warships (usually about 17) which are menacing the United Federation of Planets. You have a specified number of stardates in which to complete your mission. You also have two or three Federation starbases for resupplying your ship.

2. You will be assigned a starting position somewhere in the galaxy. The galaxy is divided into an 8 x 8 quadrant grid. The astronomical name of a quadrant is called out upon entry into a new region. (See "Quadrant Nomenclature.") Each quadrant is further divided into an 8 x 8 section grid.

3. On a section diagram, the following symbols are used:

<*>	Enterprise	>!<	Starbase
†††	Klingon	*	Star

4. You have eight commands available to you. (A detailed description of each command is given in the program instructions.)

NAV	Navigate the Starship by setting course and warp engine speed.
SRS	Short-range sensor scan (one quadrant)
LRS	Long-range sensor scan (9 quadrants)
PHA	Phaser control (energy gun)
TOR	Photon torpedo control
SHE	Shield control (protects against phaser fire)
DAM	Damage and state-of-repair report
COM	Call library computer

5. Library computer options are as follows (more complete descriptions are in program instructions):

0	Cumulative galactic record
1	Status report
2	Photon torpedo course data
3	Starbase navigation data
4	Direction/distance calculator
5	Quadrant nomenclature map

6. Certain reports on the ship's status are made by officers of the Enterprise who appeared on the original Roddenberry TV Show — Spock, Scott, Uhura, Chekov, etc.

7. Klingons are non-stationary within their quadrants. If you try to maneuver on them, they will move and fire on you.

8. Firing and damage notes:

A. Phaser fire diminishes with increased distance between combatants.
B. If a Klingon zaps you hard enough (relative to your shield strength) he will generally cause damage to some part of your ship with an appropriate "Damage Control" report resulting.

C. If you don't zap a Klingon hard enough (relative to his shield strength) you won't damage him at all. Your sensors will tell the story.
D. Damage control will let you know when out-of-commission devices have been completely repaired.

9. Your engines will automatically shut down if you should attempt to leave the galaxy, or if you should try to maneuver through a star, a starbase, or — heaven help you — a Klingon warship.

10. In a pinch, or if you should miscalculate slightly, some shield control energy will be automatically diverted to warp engine control (if your shields are operational!).

11. While you're docked at a Starbase, a team of technicians can repair your ship (if you're willing for them to spend the time required — and the repairmen *always* underestimate . . .).

12. If, to save maneuvering time toward the end of the game, you should cold-bloodedly destroy a Starbase, you get a nasty note from Starfleet Command. If you destroy your *last* Starbase, you lose the game! (For those who think this is too harsh a penalty, delete lines 5360 - 5390, and you'll just get a "you dumdum!"-type message on all future status reports.)

13. End game logic has been "cleaned up" in several spots, and it is possible to get a new command after successfully completing your mission (or, after resigning your old one).

14. For those of you with certain types of CRT/keyboards setups (e. g. Westinghouse 1600), a "bell" character is inserted at appropriate spots to cause the following items to flash on and off on the screen:

- The Phrase "*RED*" (as in Condition:Red)
- The character representing your present quadrant in the cumulative galactic record printout.

15. PROGRAMMING NOTES: This version of Star Trek was created for a Data General Nova 800 system with 32k of core. So that it will fit, the instructions are separated from the main program via a CHAIN. One minor problem: RANDOMIZE (Statement 160) should be moved after the return from the chained instructions, say to statement 245. It appears that the program should run in DEC BASIC-PLUS but it's going to be fun/trouble/challenging to convert it to DEC 8-family, HP, Honeywell, or other machines.

16. Paper tapes and other things. Neither *Creative Computing* nor Westinghouse are in the business of making and distributing paper tapes. Please DO NOT write either of us (Bob Leedom, David Ahl) asking for paper tapes. If you want to write us about other things try:

Robert C. Leedom   or   David H. Ahl
3429 Rollingview Ct.   *Creative Computing*
Ellicott City, Md. 21043

```
0010 REM INSTRUCTIONS FOR "STREK" GAME
0020 REM VERSION "STINST2" 12/8/74
0030 DIM A$[5]
0040 FOR I=1 TO 9
0050   ON I THEN GOSUB 0240, 0360, 0540, 0640, 0720, 0780, 0860, 0910, 0960
0060   PRINT
0070   PRINT "(TO CONTINUE, HIT 'RETURN')"
0080   PRINT
0090   INPUT A$
0100 NEXT I
0110 PRINT "1. WHEN YOU SEE 'COMMAND ?' PRINTED, ENTER ONE OF THE LEGAL"
0120 PRINT "   COMMANDS (NAV, SRS, LRS, PHA, TOR, SHE, DAM, COM, OR XXX)."
0130 PRINT "2. IF YOU SHOULD TYPE IN AN ILLEGAL COMMAND, YOU'LL GET A SHORT"
0140 PRINT "   LIST OF THE LEGAL COMMANDS PRINTED OUT."
0150 PRINT "3. SOME COMMANDS REQUIRE YOU TO ENTER DATA.  (FOR EXAMPLE, THE"
0160 PRINT "   'NAV' COMMAND COMES BACK WITH 'COURSE (1-9) ?'.)  IF YOU"
0170 PRINT "   TYPE IN ILLEGAL DATA (LIKE NEGATIVE NUMBERS), THAT COMMAND"
0180 PRINT "   WILL BE ABORTED."
0190 PRINT
0200 PRINT "HIT (CAR RET) TO CONTINUE."
0210 INPUT A$
0220 CHAIN "STREK" THEN GOTO 0250
0230 REM *** EXIT HERE ***
0240 PRINT
0250 PRINT "        INSTRUCTIONS FOR  ** STAR TREK **"
0260 PRINT
0270 PRINT "THE GALAXY IS DIVIDED INTO AN 8 X 8 QUADRANT GRID,"
0280 PRINT "AND EACH QUADRANT IS FURTHER DIVIDED INTO AN 8 X 8 SECTOR GRID."
0290 PRINT
0300 PRINT "  YOU WILL BE ASSIGNED A STARTING POINT SOMEWHERE IN THE GALAXY"
0310 PRINT "TO BEGIN A TOUR OF DUTY AS COMMANDER OF THE STARSHIP 'ENTERPRISE';"
0320 PRINT "YOUR MISSION: TO SEEK AND DESTROY THE FLEET OF KLINGON WARSHIPS"
0330 PRINT "WHICH ARE MENACING THE UNITED FEDERATION OF PLANETS."
0340 PRINT
0350 RETURN
0360 PRINT
0370 PRINT "YOU HAVE THE FOLLOWING COMMANDS AVAILABLE TO YOU AS"
0380 PRINT "CAPTAIN OF THE STARSHIP:"
0390 PRINT "'NAV' COMMAND = WARP ENGINE CONTROL --"
0400 PRINT "  COURSE IS IN A CIRCULAR NUMERICAL    4  3  2"
0410 PRINT "  VECTOR ARRANGEMENT AS SHOWN.          . . ."
0420 PRINT "  INTEGER AND REAL VALUES MAY BE        . . ."
0430 PRINT "  USED.  (THUS, COURSE 1.5 IS HALF-    5 ----- 1"
0440 PRINT "  WAY BETWEEN 1 AND 2.)                 . . ."
0450 PRINT "                                        . . ."
0460 PRINT "  VALUES MAY APPROACH 9.0, WHICH       6  7  8"
0470 PRINT "  ITSELF IS EQUIVALENT TO 1.0."
0480 PRINT "                                        COURSE"
0490 PRINT " ONE WARP FACTOR IS THE SIZE OF"
0500 PRINT " ONE QUADRANT.  THEREFORE, TO GET"
0510 PRINT " FROM QUADRANT 6.5 TO 5.5, YOU WOULD"
0520 PRINT " USE COURSE 3, WARP FACTOR 1."
0530 RETURN
0540 PRINT "'SRS' COMMAND = SHORT RANGE SENSOR SCAN"
0550 PRINT "  SHOWS YOU A SCAN OF YOUR PRESENT QUADRANT."
0560 PRINT "  SYMBOLOGY ON YOUR SENSOR SCREEN IS AS FOLLOWS:"
0570 PRINT "     <*> = YOUR STARSHIP'S POSITION"
0580 PRINT "     +++ = KLINGON BATTLE CRUISER"
0590 PRINT "     >!< = FEDERATION STARBASE (REFUEL/REPAIR/RE-ARM HERE!)"
0600 PRINT "      *  = STAR"
0610 PRINT "  A CONDENSED 'STATUS REPORT' WILL ALSO BE PRESENTED."
0620 PRINT
0630 RETURN
0640 PRINT "'LRS' COMMAND = LONG RANGE SENSOR SCAN"
0650 PRINT "  SHOWS CONDITIONS IN SPACE FOR ONE QUADRANT ON EACH SIDE"
0660 PRINT "  OF THE ENTERPRISE (WHICH IS IN THE MIDDLE OF THE SCAN)"
0670 PRINT "  THE SCAN IS CODED IN THE FORM '###', WHERE THE UNITS DIGIT"
0680 PRINT "  IS THE NUMBER OF STARS, TENS DIGIT IS THE NUMBER OF STARBASES,"
0690 PRINT "  AND HUNDREDS DIGIT IS THE NUMBER OF KLINGONS."
0700 PRINT "    EXAMPLE -- 207 = 2 KLINGONS, NO STARBASES, 7 STARS."
0710 RETURN
0720 PRINT "'PHA' COMMAND = PHASER CONTROL."
0730 PRINT "  ALLOWS YOU TO DESTROY THE KLINGON BATTLE CRUISERS BY"
0740 PRINT "  ZAPPING THEM WITH SUITABLY LARGE UNITS OF ENERGY TO"
0750 PRINT "  DEPLETE THEIR SHIELD POWER.  (REMEMBER, KLINGONS HAVE"
0760 PRINT "  PHASERS, TOO!)"
0770 RETURN
0780 PRINT "'TOR' COMMAND = PHOTON TORPEDO CONTROL."
0790 PRINT "  TORPEDO COURSE IS THE SAME AS USED IN WARP ENGINE CONTROL."
0800 PRINT "  IF YOU HIT THE KLINGON VESSEL, HE IS DESTROYED AND"
0810 PRINT "  CANNOT FIRE BACK AT YOU.  IF YOU MISS, YOU ARE SUBJECT TO"
0820 PRINT "  HIS PHASER FIRE."
0830 PRINT "    NOTE: THE LIBRARY-COMPUTER ('COM' COMMAND) HAS AN"
0840 PRINT "      OPTION TO COMPUTE TORPEDO TRAJECTORY FOR YOU (OPTION 2)."
0850 RETURN
0860 PRINT "'SHE' COMMAND = SHIELD CONTROL."
0870 PRINT "  DEFINES NUMBER OF ENERGY UNITS TO BE ASSIGNED TO SHIELDS."
0880 PRINT "  ENERGY IS TAKEN FROM TOTAL SHIP'S ENERGY.  NOTE THAT THE"
0890 PRINT "  TOTAL ENERGY INCLUDES SHIELD ENERGY."
0900 RETURN
0910 PRINT "'DAM' COMMAND = DAMAGE CONTROL REPORT"
0920 PRINT "  GIVES STATE OF REPAIR OF ALL DEVICES, WHERE A NEGATIVE"
0930 PRINT "  'STATE OF REPAIR' SHOWS THAT THE DEVICE IS TEMPORARILY"
0940 PRINT "  DAMAGED."
0950 RETURN
0960 PRINT "'COM' COMMAND = LIBRARY-COMPUTER"
0970 PRINT "  THE LIBRARY-COMPUTER CONTAINS SIX OPTIONS:"
0980 PRINT "  OPTION 0 = CUMULATIVE GALACTIC RECORD"
0990 PRINT "      WHICH SHOWS COMPUTER MEMORY OF THE RESULTS OF ALL PREVIOUS"
1000 PRINT "      LONG RANGE SENSOR SCANS."
1010 PRINT "  OPTION 1 = STATUS REPORT"
1020 PRINT "      WHICH SHOWS THE NUMBER OF KLINGONS, STARDATES, AND STARBASES"
1030 PRINT "      REMAINING IN THE GAME."
1040 PRINT "  OPTION 2 = PHOTON TORPEDO DATA"
1050 PRINT "      WHICH GIVES DIRECTIONS AND DISTANCE FROM THE ENTERPRISE"
1060 PRINT "      TO ALL KLINGONS IN YOUR QUADRANT"
1070 PRINT "  OPTION 3= STARBASE NAV DATA"
1080 PRINT "      WHICH GIVES DIRECTION AND DISTANCE TO ANY STARBASE"
1090 PRINT "      WITHIN YOUR QUADRANT"
1100 PRINT "  OPTION 4 = DIRECTION/DISTANCE CALCULATOR"
1110 PRINT "      WHICH ALLOWS YOU TO ENTER COORDINATES FOR"
1120 PRINT "      DIRECTION/DISTANCE CALCULATIONS."
1130 PRINT "  OPTION 5 = GALACTIC 'REGION NAME' MAP"
1140 PRINT "      WHICH PRINTS THE NAMES OF THE SIXTEEN MAJOR GALACTIC"
1150 PRINT "      REGIONS REFERRED TO IN THE GAME."
1160 RETURN
1170 END
```

```
0010 REM [VERSION "STREK7", 1/12/75  RCL]
0020 REM
0030 REM
0040 REM ***          *** STAR TREK ***          ***
0050 REM *** SIMULATION OF A MISSION OF THE STARSHIP ENTERPRISE,
0060 REM *** AS SEEN ON THE STAR TREK TV SHOW.
0070 REM *** ORIGINAL PROGRAM BY MIKE MAYFIELD; MODIFIED VERSION
0080 REM *** PUBLISHED IN DEC'S "101 BASIC GAMES", BY DAVE AHL.
0090 REM ***   MODIFICATIONS TO THE LATTER (PLUS DEBUGGING) BY
0100 REM ***     BOB LEEDOM -- APRIL & DECEMBER 1974,
0110 REM ***   WITH A LITTLE HELP FROM HIS FRIENDS . . .
0120 REM *** COMMENTS, EPITHETS, AND SUGGESTIONS SOLICITED --
0130 REM *** ADDRESS TO:   R.C.LEEDOM
0140 REM ***   WESTINGHOUSE DEFENSE & ELECTRONIC SYSTEMS CNTR.
0150 REM ***   BOX 746, M.S. 338   BALTIMORE, MD  21203
0160 RANDOMIZE
0170 PRINT TAB(15);"* * * STAR TREK * * *"
0180 PRINT
0190 PRINT "DO YOU NEED INSTRUCTIONS (YES/NO)";
0200 DIM A$[20]
0210 INPUT A$
0220 IF A$<>"YES" THEN GOTO 0240
0230 CHAIN "STINST"
0240 REM  PROGRAM BEGINS HERE . . . . .
0250 DIM Z$[72], Q$[72], R$[72], S$[72]
0260 DIM G1$[150], G2$[16], G3$[3], G4$[3]
0270 FOR I=1 TO 72
0280   LET Z$[I,I]=" "
0290   LET Q$[I,I]=" "
0300   LET R$[I,I]=" "
0310   LET S$[I,I]=" "
0320 NEXT I
0330 DIM G[8,8], C[9,2], K[3,3], N[3], Z[8,8]
0340 DIM O1$[40], C$[10]
0350 DIM A1$[20], T$[6]
0360 DIM D$[96], O3$[60]
0370 LET T=INT(RND(1)*20+20)*100
0380 LET T0=T
0390 LET T9=30
0400 LET D0=0
0410 LET E0=3000
0420 LET E=E0
0430 LET P=10
0440 LET P0=P
0450 LET S9=200
0460 LET S=0
0470 DEF FND(D)=SQR((K[I,1]-S1)^2+(K[I,2]-S2)^2)
0480 REM INITIALIZE ENTERPRISE'S POSITION
0490 LET Q1=INT(RND(1)*8+1)
0500 LET Q2=INT(RND(1)*8+1)
0510 LET S1=INT(RND(1)*8+1)
0520 LET S2=INT(RND(1)*8+1)
0530 MAT C=ZER
0540 LET C[3,1]=-1
0550 LET C[2,1]=-1
0560 LET C[4,1]=-1
0570 LET C[4,2]=-1
0580 LET C[5,2]=-1
0590 LET C[6,2]=-1
0600 LET C[1,2]=1
0610 LET C[2,2]=1
0620 LET C[6,1]=1
0630 LET C[7,1]=1
0640 LET C[8,1]=1
0650 LET C[8,2]=1
0660 LET C[9,2]=1
0670 DIM D[8]
0680 FOR I=1 TO 8
0690   LET D[I]=0
0700 NEXT I
0710 LET A1$="NSLPTSDCX"
0720 LET D$="WARP ENGINESS.R. SENSORSL.R. SENSORSPHASER CNTRL"
0730 LET D$=D$,"PHOTON TUBESDAMAGE CNTRLSHIELD CNTRLCOMPUTER"
0740 LET G4$="III"
0750 LET G1$="ANTARES.SIRIUS.RIGEL.DENEB.PROCYON.CAPELLA.VEGA."
0760 LET G1$=G1$,"BETELGEUSE.CANOPUS.ALDEBARAN.ALTAIR.REGULUS."
0770 LET G1$=G1$,"SAGITTARIUS.ARCTURUS.POLLUX.SPICA."
0780 LET B9=0
0790 LET K9=0
0800 LET A1$="NSLPTSDCX"
0810 REM  SET UP WHAT EXISTS IN GALAXY . . .
0820 FOR I=1 TO 8
0830   FOR J=1 TO 8
0840     LET R1=RND(1)
0850     IF R1>.98 THEN GOTO 0900
0860     IF R1>.95 THEN GOTO 0930
0870     IF R1>.8 THEN GOTO 0960
0880     LET K3=0
0890     GOTO 0980
0900     LET K3=3
0910     LET K9=K9+3
0920     GOTO 0980
0930     LET K3=2
0940     LET K9=K9+2
0950     GOTO 0980
0960     LET K3=1
0970     LET K9=K9+1
0980     LET R1=RND(1)
0990     IF R1>.96 THEN GOTO 1020
1000     LET B3=0
1010     GOTO 1040
1020     LET B3=1
1030     LET B9=B9+1
1040     LET S3=INT(RND(1)*8+1)
1050     LET G[I,J]=K3*100+B3*10+S3
1060     REM K3=#KLINGONS B3=#STARBASES S3=#STARS
1070     LET Z[I,J]=0
1080   NEXT J
1090 NEXT I
1100 LET K7=K9
1110 DIM X$[2], X0$[5]
1120 LET X$=""
1130 LET X0$=" IS "
1140 IF B9<>0 THEN GOTO 1200
1150 LET B9=1
1160 IF G[6,3]>=200 THEN GOTO 1190
1170 LET G[6,3]=G[6,3]+100
1180 LET K9=K9+1
1190 LET G[6,3]=G[6,3]+10
1200 IF B9=1 THEN GOTO 1230
1210 LET X$="S"
1220 LET X0$=" ARE "
1230 PRINT "YOUR ORDERS ARE AS FOLLOWS:"
1240 PRINT "   DESTROY THE"K9" KLINGON WARSHIPS WHICH HAVE INVADED"
1250 PRINT "  THE GALAXY BEFORE THEY CAN ATTACK FEDERATION HEADQUARTERS"
1260 PRINT "  ON STARDATE"T0+T9"; THIS GIVES YOU"T9" DAYS.  THERE"X0$
1270 PRINT " "B9" STARBASE"X$" IN THE GALAXY FOR RESUPPLYING YOUR SHIP."
1280 PRINT
1290 PRINT "HIT 'RETURN' WHEN READY TO ASSUME COMMAND ---"
```

```
1300 INPUT A$
1310 REM *** HERE ANY TIME ENTER NEW QUADRANT ...
1320 LET Z4=Q1
1330 LET Z5=Q2
1340 LET K3=0
1350 LET B3=0
1360 LET S3=0
1370 LET G5=0
1380 LET D4=.5*RND(1)
1390 IF Q1<1 THEN GOTO 1600
1400 IF Q1>8 THEN GOTO 1600
1410 IF Q2<1 THEN GOTO 1600
1420 IF Q2>8 THEN GOTO 1600
1430 GOSUB 9030
1440 PRINT
1450 IF T<>T0 THEN GOTO 1490
1460 PRINT "YOUR MISSION BEGINS WITH YOUR STARSHIP LOCATED"
1470 PRINT "IN THE GALACTIC QUADRANT, ´"G2$"´."
1480 GOTO 1500
1490 PRINT "NOW ENTERING "G2$" QUADRANT ... "
1500 PRINT
1510 LET X=G[Q1,Q2]*.01
1520 LET K3=INT(X)
1530 LET B3=INT((X-K3)*10)
1540 LET S3=G[Q1,Q2]-INT(G[Q1,Q2]*.1)*10
1550 IF K3=0 THEN GOTO 1590
1560 PRINT "COMBAT AREA      CONDITION RED"
1570 IF S>200 THEN GOTO 1590
1580 PRINT "  SHIELDS DANGEROUSLY LOW"
1590 MAT K=ZER
1600 LET I=1 TO 3
1610   LET K[I,3]=0
1620 NEXT I
1630 LET Q$=Z$
1640 LET R$=Z$
1650 LET S$=Z$[1,48]
1660 REM POSITION ENTERPRISE IN QUADRANT, THEN PLACE ´K3´ KLINGONS,
1670 REM    ´B3´ STARBASES, AND ´S3´ STARS ELSEWHERE.
1680 LET A$="<*>"
1690 LET Z1=S1
1700 LET Z2=S2
1710 GOSUB 8670
1720 FOR I=1 TO K3
1730   GOSUB 8590
1740   LET A$="+++"
1750   LET Z1=R1
1760   LET Z2=R2
1770   GOSUB 8670
1780   LET K[I,1]=R1
1790   LET K[I,2]=R2
1800   LET K[I,3]=S9
1810 NEXT I
1820 FOR I=1 TO B3
1830   GOSUB 8590
1840   LET A$=">!<"
1850   LET Z1=R1
1860   LET Z2=R2
1870   GOSUB 8670
1880   LET B4=Z1
1890   LET B5=Z2
1900 NEXT I
1910 FOR I=1 TO S3
1920   GOSUB 8590
1930   LET A$=" * "
1940   LET Z1=R1
1950   LET Z2=R2
1960   GOSUB 8670
1970 NEXT I
1980 GOSUB 6430
1990 IF S+E<=10 THEN GOTO 2020
2000 IF E>10 THEN GOTO 2060
2010 IF D[7]>=0 THEN GOTO 2060
2020 PRINT "<7>** FATAL ERROR **<7>   YOU´VE JUST STRANDED YOUR SHIP IN SPACE!!"
2030 PRINT "YOU HAVE INSUFFICIENT MANEUVERING ENERGY, AND SHIELD CONTROL"
2040 PRINT "IS PRESENTLY INCAPABLE OF CROSS-CIRCUITING TO ENGINE ROOM!!"
2050 GOTO 6260
2060 PRINT "COMMAND";
2070 INPUT A$
2080 FOR I=1 TO 9
2090   IF A$[1,1]<>A1$[I,I] THEN GOTO 2160
2100   IF I<>2 THEN GOTO 2140
2110   IF LEN(A$)<2 THEN GOTO 2140
2120   IF A$[2,2]="R" THEN GOTO 2140
2130   LET I=6
2140   ON I THEN GOTO 2300, 3850, 4000, 4260, 4700, 5530, 5690, 7290
2150   IF A$="XXX" THEN GOTO 6270
2160 NEXT I
2170 PRINT "ENTER ONE OF THE FOLLOWING:"
2180 PRINT "NAV (TO SET COURSE)"
2190 PRINT "SRS (FOR SHORT RANGE SENSOR SCAN)"
2200 PRINT "LRS (FOR LONG RANGE SENSOR SCAN)"
2210 PRINT "PHA (TO FIRE PHASERS)"
2220 PRINT "TOR (TO FIRE PHOTON TORPEDOES)"
2230 PRINT "SHE (TO RAISE OR LOWER SHIELDS)"
2240 PRINT "DAM (FOR DAMAGE CONTROL REPORT)"
2250 PRINT "COM (TO CALL ON LIBRARY-COMPUTER)"
2260 PRINT "XXX (TO RESIGN YOUR COMMAND)"
2270 PRINT
2280 GOTO 1990
2290 REM  COURSE CONTROL BEGINS HERE
2300 PRINT "COURSE (1-9)";
2310 INPUT C1
2320 IF C1>=1 THEN GOTO 2350
2330 PRINT " LT. SULU REPORTS, ´INCORRECT COURSE DATA, SIR!´"
2340 GOTO 1990
2350 IF C1<9 THEN GOTO 2380
2360 IF C1>9 THEN GOTO 2330
2370 LET C1=1
2380 PRINT "WARP FACTOR (0-8)";
2390 INPUT W1
2400 IF W1<=0 THEN GOTO 2420
2410 IF W1<=8 THEN GOTO 2450
2420 PRINT "  CHIEF ENGINEER SCOTT REPORTS ´THE ENGINES WON´T"
2430 PRINT "        TAKE WARP "W1"!´"
2440 GOTO 1990
2450 IF D[1]>=0 THEN GOTO 2490
2460 IF W1<=.2 THEN GOTO 2490
2470 PRINT "WARP ENGINES ARE DAMAGED.  MAXIMUM SPEED = WARP 0.2"
2480 GOTO 2300
2490 LET N=INT(W1*8+.5)
2500 IF E-N>=0 THEN GOTO 2590
2510 PRINT "ENGINEERING REPORTS ´INSUFFICIENT ENERGY AVAILABLE"
2520 PRINT "  FOR MANEUVERING AT WARP "W1"!´"
2530 IF S<N-E THEN GOTO 1990
2540 IF D[7]<0 THEN GOTO 1990
2550 PRINT "DEFLECTOR CONTROL ROOM ACKNOWLEGES"S" UNITS"
2560 PRINT "  OF ENERGY PRESENTLY DEPLOYED TO SHIELDS. "
2570 GOSUB 5530
2580 REM KLINGONS MOVE/FIRE ON MOVING STARSHIP ...
2590 FOR I=1 TO K3
2600   IF K[I,3]<=0 THEN GOTO 2700
2610   LET A$="   "
```

```
2620   LET Z1=K[I,1]
2630   LET Z2=K[I,2]
2640   GOSUB 8670
2650   GOSUB 8590
2660   LET K[I,1]=Z1
2670   LET K[I,2]=Z2
2680   LET A$="+++"
2690   GOSUB 8670
2700 NEXT I
2710 GOSUB 6000
2720 LET D1=0
2730 LET D6=W1
2740 IF W1<1 THEN GOTO 2770
2750 LET D6=1
2760 REM MAKE REPAIRS TO SHIP
2770 FOR I=1 TO 8
2780   IF D[I]>=0 THEN GOTO 2880
2790   LET D[I]=D[I]+D6
2800   IF D[I]<0 THEN GOTO 2880
2810   IF D1=1 THEN GOTO 2840
2820   LET D1=1
2830   PRINT "DAMAGE CONTROL REPORT:"
2840   PRINT  TAB(8);
2850   LET R1=I
2860   GOSUB 8790
2870   PRINT " REPAIR COMPLETED"
2880 NEXT I
2890 REM DAMAGE/IMPROVEMENT DURING SOME VES
2900 IF RND(1)>.2 THEN GOTO 3070
2910 LET R1=INT(RND(1)*8+1)
2920 IF RND(1)>=.6 THEN GOTO 3000
2930 LET D[R1]=D[R1]-(RND(1)*5+1)
2940 PRINT
2950 PRINT "DAMAGE CONTROL REPORT:";
2960 GOSUB 8790
2970 PRINT " DAMAGED"
2980 PRINT
2990 GOTO 3070
3000 LET D[R1]=D[R1]+(RND(1)*3+1)
3010 PRINT
3020 PRINT "DAMAGE CONTROL REPORT:";
3030 GOSUB 8790
3040 PRINT " STATE OF REPAIR IMPROVED"
3050 PRINT
3060 REM BEGIN MOVING STARSHIP **
3070 LET A$="   "
3080 LET Z1=INT(S1)
3090 LET Z2=INT(S2)
3100 GOSUB 8670
3110 LET X1=C[C1,1]+(C[C1+1,1]-C[C1,1])*(C1-INT(C1))
3120 LET X=S1
3130 LET Y=S2
3140 LET X2=C[C1,2]+(C[C1+1,2]-C[C1,2])*(C1-INT(C1))
3150 LET Q4=Q1
3160 LET Q5=Q2
3170 FOR I=1 TO N
3180   LET S1=S1+X1
3190   LET S2=S2+X2
3200   IF S1<1 THEN GOTO 3500
3210   IF S1>=9 THEN GOTO 3500
3220   IF S2<1 THEN GOTO 3500
3230   IF S2>=9 THEN GOTO 3500
3240   LET S8=INT(S1)*24+INT(S2)*3-26
3250   IF S8>72 THEN GOTO 3280
3260   IF Q$[S8,S8+2]="   " THEN GOTO 3360
3270   GOTO 3320
3280   IF S8>144 THEN GOTO 3310
3290   IF R$[S8-72,S8-70]="   " THEN GOTO 3360
3300   GOTO 3320
3310   IF S$[S8-144,S8-142]="   " THEN GOTO 3360
3320   LET S1=S1-X1
3330   LET S2=S2-X2
3340   PRINT "WARP ENGINES SHUT DOWN AT SECTOR "S1","S2" DUE TO BAD NAVIGATI
3350   GOTO 3370
3360 NEXT I
3370 LET A$="<*>"
3380 LET Z1=INT(S1)
3390 LET Z2=INT(S2)
3400 GOSUB 8670
3410 GOSUB 3910
3420 LET T8=1
3430 IF W1>=1 THEN GOTO 3450
3440 LET T8=.1*INT(10*W1)
3450 LET T=T+T8
3460 IF T>T0+T9 THEN GOTO 6220
3470 REM SEE IF DOCKED, THEN GET COMMAND
3480 GOTO 1980
3490 REM EXCEEDED QUADRANT LIMITS
3500 LET X=8*Q1+X+N*X1
3510 LET Y=8*Q2+Y+N*X2
3520 LET Q1=INT(X/8)
3530 LET Q2=INT(Y/8)
3540 LET S1=INT(X-Q1*8)
3550 LET S2=INT(Y-Q2*8)
3560 IF S1<>0 THEN GOTO 3590
3570 LET Q1=Q1-1
3580 LET S1=8
3590 IF S2<>0 THEN GOTO 3620
3600 LET Q2=Q2-1
3610 LET S2=8
3620 LET X5=0
3630 IF Q1>=1 THEN GOTO 3670
3640 LET X5=1
3650 LET Q1=1
3660 LET S1=1
3670 IF Q1<=8 THEN GOTO 3710
3680 LET X5=1
3690 LET Q1=8
3700 LET S1=8
3710 IF Q2>=1 THEN GOTO 3750
3720 LET X5=1
3730 LET Q2=1
3740 LET S2=1
3750 IF Q2<=8 THEN GOTO 3790
3760 LET X5=1
3770 LET Q2=8
3780 LET S2=8
3790 IF X5=0 THEN GOTO 3860
3800 PRINT "LT. UHURA REPORTS MESSAGE FROM STARFLEET COMMAND:"
3810 PRINT "  ´PERMISSION TO ATTEMPT CROSSING OF GALACTIC PERIMETER"
3820 PRINT "   IS HEREBY *DENIED*.   SHUT DOWN YOUR ENGINES. ´"
3830 PRINT "CHIEF ENGINEER SCOTT REPORTS ´WARP ENGINES SHUT DOWN"
3840 PRINT "     AT SECTOR "S1","S2" OF QUADRANT "Q1","Q2". ´"
3850 IF T>T0+T9 THEN GOTO 6220
3860 IF 8*Q1+Q2=8*Q4+Q5 THEN GOTO 3370
3870 LET T=T+1
3880 GOSUB 3910
3890 GOTO 1320
3900 REM MANEUVER ENERGY S/R ***
3910 LET E=E-N-10
3920 IF E>=0 THEN GOTO 3980
3930 PRINT "SHIELD CONTROL SUPPLIED ENERGY TO COMPLETE THE MANEUVER. "
```

278

```
3940 LET S=S+E
3950 LET E=0
3960 IF S>0 THEN GOTO 3980
3970 LET S=0
3980 RETURN
3990 REM L.R. SENSOR SCAN CODE ***
4000 IF D[3]>=0 THEN GOTO 4030
4010 PRINT "LONG RANGE SENSORS ARE INOPERABLE"
4020 GOTO 1990
4030 PRINT "LONG RANGE SENSOR SCAN FOR QUADRANT"Q1","Q2
4040 LET O1$="...................."
4050 PRINT O1$
4060 FOR I=Q1-1 TO Q1+1
4070    DIM N[3]
4080    FOR I1=1 TO 3
4090       LET N[I1]=0
4100    NEXT I1
4110    FOR J=Q2-1 TO Q2+1
4120       IF I<1 THEN GOTO 4180
4130       IF I>8 THEN GOTO 4180
4140       IF J<1 THEN GOTO 4180
4150       IF J>8 THEN GOTO 4180
4160       LET N[J-Q2+2]=G[I,J]
4170       LET Z[I,J]=G[I,J]
4180    NEXT J
4190    DIM P1$[20]
4200    LET P1$=": ### : ### : ### :"
4210    PRINT USING P1$,N[1],N[2],N[3]
4220    PRINT O1$
4230 NEXT I
4240 GOTO 1990
4250 REM *** PHASER CONTROL CODE BEGINS HERE
4260 IF K3>0 THEN GOTO 4300
4270 PRINT "SCIENCE OFFICER SPOCK REPORTS 'SENSORS SHOW"
4280 PRINT "  NO ENEMY SHIPS IN THIS QUADRANT.'"
4290 GOTO 1990
4300 IF D[4]>=0 THEN GOTO 4330
4310 PRINT "PHASERS INOPERATIVE"
4320 GOTO 1990
4330 IF D[8]>=0 THEN GOTO 4350
4340 PRINT "COMPUTER FAILURE HAMPERS ACCURACY"
4350 PRINT "PHASERS LOCKED ON TARGET; "
4360 PRINT "ENERGY AVAILABLE ="E
4370 PRINT "NUMBER OF UNITS TO FIRE:";
4380 INPUT X
4390 IF X<=0 THEN GOTO 1990
4400 IF E-X<0 THEN GOTO 4360
4410 LET E=E-X
4420 GOSUB 6000
4430 IF D[7]>=0 THEN GOTO 4450
4440 LET X=X*RND(1)
4450 LET H1=INT(X/K3)
4460 FOR I=1 TO 3
4470    IF K[I,3]<=0 THEN GOTO 4670
4480    LET H=INT((H1/FND(0))*(RND(1)+2))
4490    IF H>.15*K[I,3] THEN GOTO 4530
4500    PRINT "SENSORS SHOW NO DAMAGE"
4510    PRINT "   TO ENEMY AT "K[I,1]","K[I,2]
4520    GOTO 4670
4530    LET K[I,3]=K[I,3]-H
4540    PRINT H" UNIT HIT ON KLINGON AT SECTOR "K[I,1]","K[I,2]
4550    IF K[I,3]<=0 THEN GOTO 4580
4560    PRINT "   (SENSORS SHOW"K[I,3]" UNITS REMAINING)"
4570    GOTO 4670
4580    PRINT " *** KLINGON DESTROYED ***"
4590    LET K3=K3-1
4600    LET K9=K9-1
4610    LET A$="   "
4620    LET Z1=K[I,1]
4630    LET Z2=K[I,2]
4640    GOSUB 8670
4650    LET G[Q1,Q2]=K3*100+B3*10+S3
4660    IF K9<=0 THEN GOTO 6370
4670 NEXT I
4680 GOTO 1990
4690 REM PHOTON TORPEDO CODE BEGINS ***
4700 IF D[5]>=0 THEN GOTO 4730
4710 PRINT "PHOTON TUBES ARE NOT OPERATIONAL. "
4720 GOTO 1990
4730 IF P>0 THEN GOTO 4760
4740 PRINT "ALL PHOTON TORPEDOES EXPENDED"
4750 GOTO 1990
4760 PRINT "TORPEDO COURSE (1-9)";
4770 INPUT C1
4780 IF C1>=1 THEN GOTO 4810
4790 PRINT " ENSIGN CHEKOV REPORTS, 'INCORRECT COURSE DATA, SIR!'"
4800 GOTO 1990
4810 IF C1>9 THEN GOTO 4790
4820 IF C1<9 THEN GOTO 4850
4830 IF C1=9 THEN GOTO 4760
4840 LET C1=1
4850 LET X1=C[C1,1]+(C[C1+1,1]-C[C1,1])*(C1-INT(C1))
4860 LET X2=C[C1,2]+(C[C1+1,2]-C[C1,2])*(C1-INT(C1))
4870 LET E=E-2
4880 LET X=S1
4890 LET Y=S2
4900 LET P=P-1
4910 PRINT "TORPEDO TRACK:"
4920 LET X=X+X1
4930 LET Y=Y+X2
4940 LET X3=INT(X+.5)
4950 LET Y3=INT(Y+.5)
4960 IF X3<1 THEN GOTO 5490
4970 IF X3>9 THEN GOTO 5490
4980 IF Y3<1 THEN GOTO 5490
4990 IF Y3>9 THEN GOTO 5490
5000 PRINT "              "X3","Y3
5010 LET A$="    "
5020 LET Z1=X
5030 LET Z2=Y
5040 GOSUB 8830
5050 IF Z3<>0 THEN GOTO 4920
5060 LET A$="+++"
5070 LET Z1=X
5080 LET Z2=Y
5090 GOSUB 8830
5100 IF Z3=0 THEN GOTO 5210
5110 PRINT "*** KLINGON DESTROYED ***"
5120 LET K3=K3-1
5130 LET K9=K9-1
5140 IF K9<=0 THEN GOTO 6370
5150 FOR I=1 TO 3
5160    IF X3<>K[I,1] THEN GOTO 5180
5170    IF Y3=K[I,2] THEN GOTO 5190
5180 NEXT I
5190 LET K[I,3]=0
5200 GOTO 5430
5210 LET A$=" * "
5220 LET Z1=X
5230 LET Z2=Y
5240 GOSUB 8830
5250 IF Z3=0 THEN GOTO 5280
```

```
5260 PRINT "STAR AT"X3","Y3," ABSORBED TORPEDO ENERGY. "
5270 GOTO 5500
5280 LET A$=">!<"
5290 LET Z1=X
5300 LET Z2=Y
5310 GOSUB 8830
5320 IF Z3=0 THEN GOTO 4760
5330 PRINT "*** STARBASE DESTROYED ***"
5340 LET B3=B3-1
5350 LET B9=B9-1
5360 IF B9>0 THEN GOTO 5400
5370 PRINT "THAT DOES IT, CAPTAIN!!  YOU ARE HEREBY RELIEVED OF COMMAND"
5380 PRINT "   AND SENTENCED TO 99 STARDATES AT HARD LABOR ON CYGNUS 12!!"
5390 GOTO 6270
5400 PRINT "STARFLEET COMMAND REVIEWING YOUR RECORD TO CONSIDER"
5410 PRINT "   COURT MARTIAL!"
5420 LET D0=0
5430 LET A$="   "
5440 LET Z1=X
5450 LET Z2=Y
5460 GOSUB 8670
5470 LET G[Q1,Q2]=K3*100+B3*10+S3
5480 GOTO 5500
5490 PRINT "TORPEDO MISSED"
5500 GOSUB 6000
5510 GOTO 1990
5520 REM *** SHIELD CONTROL STARTS HERE
5530 IF D[7]>=0 THEN GOTO 5560
5540 PRINT "SHIELD CONTROL INOPERABLE"
5550 GOTO 1990
5560 PRINT "ENERGY AVAILABLE ="E+S". NUMBER OF UNITS TO SHIELDS:";
5570 INPUT X
5580 IF X>=0 THEN GOTO 5620
5590 IF S<>X THEN GOTO 5620
5600 PRINT "(SHIELDS UNCHANGED)"
5610 GOTO 1990
5620 IF E+S-X<0 THEN GOTO 5560
5630 LET E=E+S-X
5640 LET S=X
5650 PRINT "DEFLECTOR CONTROL ROOM REPORT:"
5660 PRINT "  'SHIELDS NOW AT "S" PER YOUR COMMAND'"
5670 GOTO 1990
5680 REM *** DAMAGE CONTROL STARTS HERE
5690 IF D[6]>=0 THEN GOTO 5910
5700 PRINT "DAMAGE CONTROL REPORT NOT AVAILABLE"
5710 IF D0=0 THEN GOTO 1990
5720 LET D3=0
5730 FOR I=1 TO 8
5740    IF D[I]>=0 THEN GOTO 5760
5750    LET D3=D3+.1
5760 NEXT I
5770 IF D3=0 THEN GOTO 1990
5780 LET D3=D3+D4
5790 IF D3<1 THEN GOTO 5810
5800 LET D3=.9
5810 PRINT "TECHNICIANS STANDING BY TO EFFECT REPAIRS TO YOUR SHIP;"
5820 PRINT "ESTIMATED TIME TO REPAIR: ";
5830 PRINT USING ". # STARDATES",D3
5840 PRINT "WILL YOU AUTHORIZE THE REPAIR ORDER (YES/NO)";
5850 INPUT A$
5860 IF A$<>"YES" THEN GOTO 1990
5870 FOR I=1 TO 8
5880    LET D[I]=0
5890 NEXT I
5900 LET T=T+D3+.1
5910 PRINT
5920 PRINT "DEVICE          STATE OF REPAIR"
5930 FOR R1=1 TO 8
5940    GOSUB 8790
5950    PRINT USING "  -##.##",D[R1]
5960 NEXT R1
5970 PRINT
5980 GOTO 5710
5990 REM "KLINGONS SHOOTING" CODE BEGINS ***
6000 IF K3<=0 THEN GOTO 6210
6010 IF D0=0 THEN GOTO 6040
6020 PRINT "STAR BASE SHIELDS PROTECT THE ENTERPRISE"
6030 GOTO 6210
6040 FOR I=1 TO 3
6050    IF K[I,3]<=0 THEN GOTO 6200
6060    LET H=INT((K[I,3]/FND(0))*(2+RND(1)))
6070    LET S=S-H
6080    PRINT H" UNIT HIT ON ENTERPRISE FROM SECTOR"K[I,1]","K[I,2]
6090    IF S<0 THEN GOTO 6240
6100    PRINT "     (SHIELDS DOWN TO"S" UNITS.)"
6110    IF H<20 THEN GOTO 6200
6120    IF RND(1)>.6 THEN GOTO 6200
6130    IF H/S<.02 THEN GOTO 6200
6140    LET D2=H/S+.5*RND(1)
6150    LET R1=INT(RND(1)*8+1)
6160    LET D[R1]=D[R1]-D2
6170    PRINT "DAMAGE CONTROL REPORTS '";
6180    GOSUB 8790
6190    PRINT "DAMAGED BY THE HIT!'"
6200 NEXT I
6210 RETURN
6220 PRINT "IT IS STARDATE "T
6230 GOTO 6270
6240 PRINT
6250 PRINT "THE ENTERPRISE HAS BEEN DESTROYED. THE FEDERATION WILL BE CONQUERED. "
6260 PRINT "IT IS STARDATE "T"."
6270 PRINT "THERE WERE "K9" KLINGON BATTLE CRUISERS LEFT AT"
6280 PRINT " THE END OF YOUR MISSION. "
6290 PRINT
6300 PRINT
6310 PRINT "THE FEDERATION IS IN NEED OF A NEW STARSHIP COMMANDER"
6320 PRINT "FOR A SIMILAR MISSION -- IF THERE IS A VOLUNTEER,"
6330 PRINT "LET HIM STEP FORWARD AND ENTER 'AYE'. "
6340 INPUT A$
6350 IF A$="AYE" THEN GOTO 0240
6360 GOTO 9250
6370 PRINT "CONGRATULATIONS, CAPTAIN! THE LAST KLINGON BATTLE CRUISER"
6380 PRINT "  MENACING THE FEDERATION HAS BEEN DESTROYED. "
6390 PRINT
6400 PRINT "YOUR EFFICIENCY RATING IS "((K7/(T-T0))*1000)". "
6410 GOTO 6290
6420 REM S.R. SENSOR SCAN & STARTUP SUBR. ***
6430 FOR I=S1-1 TO S1+1
6440    FOR J=S2-1 TO S2+1
6450       IF INT(I+.5)<1 THEN GOTO 6540
6460       IF INT(I+.5)>8 THEN GOTO 6540
6470       IF INT(J+.5)<1 THEN GOTO 6540
6480       IF INT(J+.5)>8 THEN GOTO 6540
6490       LET A$=">!<"
6500       LET Z1=I
6510       LET Z2=J
6520       GOSUB 8830
6530       IF Z3=1 THEN GOTO 6580
6540    NEXT J
6550 NEXT I
6560 LET D0=0
6570 GOTO 6650
```

```
6580 LET D0=1
6590 LET C$="DOCKED"
6600 LET E=3000
6610 LET P=10
6620 PRINT "SHIELDS DROPPED FOR DOCKING PURPOSES"
6630 LET S=0
6640 GOTO 6720
6650 IF K3>0 THEN GOTO 6690
6660 IF E<E0*.1 THEN GOTO 6710
6670 LET C$=" GREEN"
6680 GOTO 6720
6690 LET C$=" <7>*RED*<7>"
6700 GOTO 6720
6710 LET C$="YELLOW"
6720 IF D[2]>=0 THEN GOTO 6770
6730 PRINT
6740 PRINT "*** SHORT RANGE SENSORS ARE OUT ***"
6750 PRINT
6760 GOTO 7270
6770 LET O1$="---------------------------------"
6780 PRINT O1$
6790 DIM N5$[4]
6800 LET N5$="####"
6810 PRINT " ";
6820 FOR I=1 TO 22 STEP 3
6830   PRINT Q$[I,I+2]" ";
6840 NEXT I
6850 PRINT
6860 PRINT " ";
6870 FOR I=25 TO 46 STEP 3
6880   PRINT Q$[I,I+2]" ";
6890 NEXT I
6900 PRINT "        STARDATE        ";
6910 PRINT USING "####.#",T
6920 PRINT " ";
6930 FOR I=49 TO 70 STEP 3
6940   PRINT Q$[I,I+2]" ";
6950 NEXT I
6960 PRINT "       CONDITION      ";
6970 PRINT C$
6980 PRINT " ";
6990 FOR I=1 TO 22 STEP 3
7000   PRINT R$[I,I+2]" ";
7010 NEXT I
7020 PRINT "       QUADRANT      "Q1","Q2
7030 PRINT " ";
7040 FOR I=25 TO 46 STEP 3
7050   PRINT R$[I,I+2]" ";
7060 NEXT I
7070 PRINT "       SECTOR        "S1","S2
7080 PRINT " ";
7090 FOR I=49 TO 70 STEP 3
7100   PRINT R$[I,I+2]" ";
7110 NEXT I
7120 PRINT "       TOTAL ENERGY     ";
7130 PRINT USING N5$,E+S
7140 PRINT " ";
7150 FOR I=1 TO 22 STEP 3
7160   PRINT S$[I,I+2]" ";
7170 NEXT I
7180 PRINT "       PHOTON TORPEDOES ";
7190 PRINT USING N5$,P
7200 PRINT " ";
7210 FOR I=25 TO 46 STEP 3
7220   PRINT S$[I,I+2]" ";
7230 NEXT I
7240 PRINT "       SHIELDS          ";
7250 PRINT USING N5$,S
7260 PRINT O1$
7270 RETURN
7280 REM *** LIBRARY COMPUTER CODE BEGINS HERE
7290 IF D[8]>=0 THEN GOTO 7320
7300 PRINT "COMPUTER DISABLED"
7310 GOTO 1990
7320 PRINT "COMPUTER ACTIVE AND AWAITING COMMAND:";
7330 INPUT A
7340 IF A<0 THEN GOTO 1990
7350 PRINT
7360 LET H8=1
7370 IF A=0 THEN GOTO 7540
7380 ON A THEN GOTO 7900, 8070, 8500, 8150, 7400
7390 GOTO 7450
7400 REM *** SETUP TO CHANGE C.G. RECORD TO GALAXY MAP
7410 LET H8=0
7420 LET G5=1
7430 PRINT "                 THE GALAXY"
7440 GOTO 7550
7450 PRINT "FUNCTIONS AVAILABLE FROM LIBRARY-COMPUTER:"
7460 PRINT "   0 = CUMULATIVE GALACTIC RECORD"
7470 PRINT "   1 = STATUS REPORT"
7480 PRINT "   2 = PHOTON TORPEDO DATA"
7490 PRINT "   3 = STARBASE NAV DATA"
7500 PRINT "   4 = DIRECTION/DISTANCE CALCULATOR"
7510 PRINT "   5 = GALAXY 'REGION NAME' MAP"
7520 GOTO 7320
7530 REM *** CUM GALACTIC RECORD CODE BEGINS ***
7540 PRINT "COMPUTER RECORD OF GALAXY FOR QUADRANT "Q1","Q2":"
7550 PRINT "       1     2     3     4     5     6     7     8"
7560 LET O3$="     ----- ----- ----- ----- ----- ----- ----- -----"
7570 PRINT O3$
7580 DIM N1$[2],N2$[8],N$[5]
7590 FOR I=1 TO 8
7600   LET N1$="#"
7610   PRINT USING N1$,I;
7620   IF H8=0 THEN GOTO 7740
7630   FOR J=1 TO 8
7640     LET N2$="   ###"
7650     LET N$=""
7660     IF I<>Q1 THEN GOTO 7700
7670     IF J<>Q2 THEN GOTO 7700
7680     LET N$="<7>"
7690     PRINT N$;
7700     PRINT USING N2$,Z[I,J];
7710     PRINT N$;
7720   NEXT J
7730   GOTO 7850
7740   LET Z4=I
7750   LET Z5=1
7760   GOSUB 9030
7770   LET J0=INT(15-.5*LEN(G2$))
7780   PRINT TAB(J0);
7790   PRINT G2$;
7800   LET Z5=5
7810   GOSUB 9030
7820   LET J0=INT(39-.5*LEN(G2$))
7830   PRINT TAB(J0);
7840   PRINT G2$;
7850   PRINT
7860   PRINT O3$
7870 NEXT I
7880 GOTO 1990
7890 REM *** STATUS REPORT CODE BEGINS HERE ***
7900 PRINT "    STATUS REPORT:"
7910 LET X$=""
7920 IF K9=1 THEN GOTO 7940
7930 LET X$="S"
7940 PRINT K9" KLINGON"X$" LEFT"
7950 LET V5=(T0+T9)-T
7960 PRINT USING "MISSION MUST BE COMPLETED IN ##.# STARDATES",V5
7970 LET X$=""
7980 IF B9=1 THEN GOTO 8040
7990 LET X$="S"
8000 IF B9<>0 THEN GOTO 8040
8010 PRINT "YOUR STUPIDITY HAS LEFT YOU ON YOUR OWN IN"
8020 PRINT "   THE GALAXY -- YOU HAVE NO STARBASES LEFT!"
8030 GOTO 5690
8040 PRINT "THE FEDERATION IS MAINTAINING"B9" STARBASE"X$" IN THE GALAXY"
8050 GOTO 5690
8060 REM CODE FOR TORPEDO DATA, BASE NAV, D/D CALCULATOR ***
8070 LET H8=0
8080 FOR I=1 TO 3
8090   IF K[I,3]<=0 THEN GOTO 8480
8100   LET W1=K[I,1]
8110   LET X=K[I,2]
8120   LET C1=S1
8130   LET A=S2
8140   GOTO 8220
8150 PRINT "DIRECTION/DISTANCE CALCULATOR:"
8160 PRINT "YOU ARE AT QUADRANT ("Q1","Q2") SECTOR ("S1","S2")"
8170 PRINT "PLEASE ENTER --"
8180 PRINT "   INITIAL COORDINATES (X,Y)";
8190 INPUT C1,A
8200 PRINT "   FINAL COORDINATES (X,Y)";
8210 INPUT W1,X
8220 LET X=X-A
8230 LET A=C1-W1
8240 IF X<0 THEN GOTO 8350
8250 IF A<0 THEN GOTO 8410
8260 IF X>0 THEN GOTO 8280
8270 IF A=0 THEN GOTO 8370
8280 LET C1=1
8290 IF ABS(A)<=ABS(X) THEN GOTO 8330
8300 LET V5=C1+(((ABS(A)-ABS(X))+ABS(A))/ABS(A))
8310 PRINT "DIRECTION ="V5
8320 GOTO 8460
8330 PRINT "DIRECTION ="C1+(ABS(A)/ABS(X))
8340 GOTO 8460
8350 IF A>0 THEN GOTO 8390
8360 IF X=0 THEN GOTO 8410
8370 LET C1=5
8380 GOTO 8290
8390 LET C1=3
8400 GOTO 8420
8410 LET C1=7
8420 IF ABS(A)>=ABS(X) THEN GOTO 8450
8430 PRINT "DIRECTION ="C1+(((ABS(X)-ABS(A))+ABS(X))/ABS(X))
8440 GOTO 8460
8450 PRINT "DIRECTION ="C1+(ABS(X)/ABS(A))
8460 PRINT "DISTANCE ="SQR(X^2+A^2)
8470 IF H8=1 THEN GOTO 1990
8480 NEXT I
8490 GOTO 1990
8500 IF B3>0 THEN GOTO 8530
8510 PRINT "MR. SPOCK REPORTS, 'SENSORS SHOW NO STARBASES IN THIS QUADRANT.'"
8520 GOTO 1990
8530 PRINT "FROM ENTERPRISE TO STARBASE:"
8540 LET W1=B4
8550 LET X=B5
8560 GOTO 8120
8570 REM *** END OF LIBRARY-COMPUTER CODE
8580 REM S/R FINDS RANDOM HOLE IN QUADRANT
8590 LET R1=INT(RND(1)*8+1)
8600 LET R2=INT(RND(1)*8+1)
8610 LET A$="   "
8620 LET Z1=R1
8630 LET Z2=R2
8640 GOSUB 8830
8650 IF Z3=0 THEN GOTO 8590
8660 RETURN
8670 REM *** INSERTION IN STRING ARRAY FOR QUADRANT ***
8680 LET S8=INT(Z1+.5)*24+INT(Z2+.5)*3-26
8690 IF S8>72 THEN GOTO 8720
8700 LET Q$[S8,S8+2]=A$
8710 GOTO 8780
8720 IF S8>144 THEN GOTO 8760
8730 LET S8=S8-72
8740 LET R$[S8,S8+2]=A$
8750 GOTO 8780
8760 LET S8=S8-144
8770 LET S$[S8,S8+2]=A$
8780 RETURN
8790 REM *** PRINTS DEVICE NAME FROM ARRAY ***
8800 LET S8=R1*12-11
8810 PRINT D$[S8,S8+11],
8820 RETURN
8830 REM *** STRING COMPARISON IN QUADRANT ARRAY ***
8840 LET Z1=INT(Z1+.5)
8850 LET Z2=INT(Z2+.5)
8860 LET S8=Z1*24+Z2*3-26
8870 LET Z3=0
8880 IF S8>72 THEN GOTO 8920
8890 IF Q$[S8,S8+2]<>A$ THEN GOTO 9000
8900 LET Z3=1
8910 GOTO 9000
8920 IF S8>144 THEN GOTO 8970
8930 LET S8=S8-72
8940 IF R$[S8,S8+2]<>A$ THEN GOTO 9000
8950 LET Z3=1
8960 GOTO 9000
8970 LET S8=S8-144
8980 IF S$[S8,S8+2]<>A$ THEN GOTO 9000
8990 LET Z3=1
9000 RETURN
9010 REM ** S/R PRODUCES QUADRANT NAME IN G2$ FROM Z4,Z5(<=Q1,Q2)
9020 REM ** (CALL WITH G5=1 TO GET REGION NAME ONLY)
9030 LET L2=2
9040 IF Z5>=5 THEN GOTO 9060
9050 LET L2=1
9060 LET L3=2*(Z4-1)+L2
9070 LET I3=1
9080 LET I0=1
9090 FOR L=1 TO LEN(G1$)
9100   IF G1$[L,L]<>"." THEN GOTO 9140
9110   IF I3=L3 THEN GOTO 9150
9120   LET I0=L+1
9130   LET I3=I3+1
9140 NEXT L
9150 LET G2$=G1$[I0,L-1]
9160 IF G5=1 THEN GOTO 9240
9170 LET L3=25
9180 IF Z5<=4 THEN GOTO 9200
9190 LET L3=Z5-4
9200 LET G3$="IV"
9210 IF L3=4 THEN GOTO 9230
9220 LET G3$=G4$[1,L3]
9230 LET G2$=G2$," ",G3$
9240 RETURN
9250 STOP
9260 END
```

```
* RUN
              * * * STAR TREK * * *

DO YOU NEED INSTRUCTIONS (YES/NO) ? NO
YOUR ORDERS ARE AS FOLLOWS:
    DESTROY THE 16 KLINGON WARSHIPS WHICH HAVE INVADED
   THE GALAXY BEFORE THEY CAN ATTACK FEDERATION HEADQUARTERS
   ON STARDATE 2830; THIS GIVES YOU 30 DAYS.  THERE ARE
   3 STARBASES IN THE GALAXY FOR RESUPPLYING YOUR SHIP.

HIT 'RETURN' WHEN READY TO ASSUME COMMAND ---
?

YOUR MISSION BEGINS WITH YOUR STARSHIP LOCATED
IN THE GALACTIC QUADRANT, 'BETELGEUSE II'.

--------------------------------
    *      *       *              STARDATE      2800.0
 *      *     .  <*>    *          CONDITION     GREEN
                       *          QUADRANT       4, 6
        *                         SECTOR         3, 6
                                  TOTAL ENERGY   3000
                                  PHOTON TORPEDOES  10
                                  SHIELDS          0
--------------------------------
COMMAND ? LRS
LONG RANGE SENSOR SCAN FOR QUADRANT 4, 6
.................
: 7 : 1 : 8 :
.................
: 7 : 6 : 7 :
.................
: 6 : 8 : 8 :
.................
COMMAND ? NAV
COURSE (1-9) ? 7.7
WARP FACTOR (0-8) ? 3

NOW ENTERING ARCTURUS IV QUADRANT ...

--------------------------------
         *     *     *            STARDATE      2801.0
      <*>  *                      CONDITION     GREEN
        *                         QUADRANT       7, 8
        *                         SECTOR         3, 6
                                  TOTAL ENERGY   2966
        *          *              PHOTON TORPEDOES  10
                                  SHIELDS          0
--------------------------------
COMMAND ? LRS
LONG RANGE SENSOR SCAN FOR QUADRANT 7, 8
.................
: 4 : 2 : 0 :
.................
: 3 : 8 : 0 :
.................
: 4 : 106 : 0 :
.................
COMMAND ? SHE
ENERGY AVAILABLE = 2966. NUMBER OF UNITS TO SHIELDS: ? 1000
DEFLECTOR CONTROL ROOM REPORT:
   'SHIELDS NOW AT  1000 PER YOUR COMMAND'
COMMAND ? NAV
COURSE (1-9) ? 7
WARP FACTOR (0-8) ? 1.2

NOW ENTERING SPICA IV QUADRANT ...

COMBAT AREA      CONDITION RED
--------------------------------
       +++                        STARDATE      2802.0
        *                         CONDITION     *RED*
                                  QUADRANT       8, 8
       <*>                        SECTOR         5, 6
                                  TOTAL ENERGY   2946
   *                              PHOTON TORPEDOES  10
   *          *                   SHIELDS         1000
       *     *                   
--------------------------------
COMMAND ? COM
COMPUTER ACTIVE AND AWAITING COMMAND: ? 2

DIRECTION = 3.75
DISTANCE = 5
COMMAND ? TOR
TORPEDO COURSE (1-9) ? 3.75
TORPEDO TRACK:
        4, 5
        3, 5
        2, 4
        1, 3
*** KLINGON DESTROYED ***
COMMAND ? LRS
LONG RANGE SENSOR SCAN FOR QUADRANT 8, 8
.................
: 3 : 8 : 0 :
.................
: 4 : 6 : 0 :
.................
: 0 : 0 : 0 :
.................
COMMAND ? COM
COMPUTER ACTIVE AND AWAITING COMMAND: ? 0

COMPUTER RECORD OF GALAXY FOR QUADRANT 8, 8:
     1    2    3    4    5    6    7    8
   ---- ---- ---- ---- ---- ---- ---- ----
 1│  0    0    0    0    0    0    0    0
   ---- ---- ---- ---- ---- ---- ---- ----
 2│  0    0    0    0    0    0    0    0
   ---- ---- ---- ---- ---- ---- ---- ----
 3│  0    0    0    0    7    1    8    0
   ---- ---- ---- ---- ---- ---- ---- ----
 4│  0    0    0    3    7    6    7    0
   ---- ---- ---- ---- ---- ---- ---- ----
 5│  0    0    0    3    6    8    8    0
   ---- ---- ---- ---- ---- ---- ---- ----
 6│  0    0    0    0    0    0    4    2
   ---- ---- ---- ---- ---- ---- ---- ----
 7│  0    0    0    0    0    0    3    8
   ---- ---- ---- ---- ---- ---- ---- ----
 8│  0    0    0    0    0    0    4    6
   ---- ---- ---- ---- ---- ---- ---- ----
COMMAND ? NAV
COURSE (1-9) ? 5
WARP FACTOR (0-8) ? 3
```

```
COMMAND ? NAV
COURSE (1-9) ? 5
WARP FACTOR (0-8) ? .4
105 UNIT HIT ON ENTERPRISE FROM SECTOR 1, 1
  (SHIELDS DOWN TO 1258 UNITS.)
SHIELD CONTROL SUPPLIED ENERGY TO COMPLETE THE MANEUVER.
--------------------------------
  +++
                                  STARDATE      2817.2
       <*>                        CONDITION     *RED*
              *                   QUADRANT       2, 3
              *                   SECTOR         3, 3
                     *            TOTAL ENERGY   1255
                                  PHOTON TORPEDOES  5
                                  SHIELDS        1255
--------------------------------
COMMAND ? TOR
TORPEDO COURSE (1-9) ? 4
TORPEDO TRACK:
        2, 2
        1, 1
*** KLINGON DESTROYED ***
COMMAND ? LRS
LONG RANGE SENSOR SCAN FOR QUADRANT 2, 3
.................
: 12 : 8 : 5 :
.................
: 104 : 3 : 4 :
.................
: 7 : 5 : 6 :
.................
COMMAND ? NAV
COURSE (1-9) ? 4
WARP FACTOR (0-8) ? 1
ENGINEERING REPORTS 'INSUFFICIENT ENERGY AVAILABLE
   FOR MANEUVERING AT WARP 1!'
DEFLECTOR CONTROL ROOM ACKNOWLEGES 1255 UNITS
   OF ENERGY PRESENTLY DEPLOYED TO SHIELDS.
ENERGY AVAILABLE = 1253. NUMBER OF UNITS TO SHIELDS: ? 1100
DEFLECTOR CONTROL ROOM REPORT:
   'SHIELDS NOW AT  1100 PER YOUR COMMAND'
COMMAND ? NAV
COURSE (1-9) ? 4
WARP FACTOR (0-8) ? 1

NOW ENTERING ANTARES II QUADRANT ...
```

Space permits us to print only a small portion of the whole run; however, notes for the mission log are reproduced below.

✳   ✳   ✳
CAPTAIN'S NOTES — FOR MISSION LOG:

Stardate	*Remarks*
2804.0	—Bad news. 4 Stardates out, we've only got one Klingon to our credit so far, and our Warp Engines just went bad. Fortunately there's a Starbase nearby.
2805.2	—Sensor failure en route to Starbase — computer will have to help out on docking.
2806.2	—Repaired and ready to go.
2809.2	—Bad move! Tried to power up to Warp 5 without checking sensor readout — saved by auto-shut-down, but engines conked out again! Back to Altair III for repairs . . .
2815.5	—More bad luck — computer failure while moving into battle area, so I eyeballed the first torpedo shot. Missed! They fired back and further damaged the computer.
	Second shot put one of the three out, but as I maneuvered, they hit the computer again!
	One Klingon came up to meet me — finished him off with a photon torpedo.
	Phasers held up long enough to get the third one.
2815.8	—Condition yellow: too much energy deployed to shields. Will leave it this way until after the battle I expect in Rigel III.
2817.2	—While moving in for a better shot (since my computer can't help me aim), shield control had to help out on maneuvering energy. Fortunately, the enemy fought back without tactical movement.

Reviews

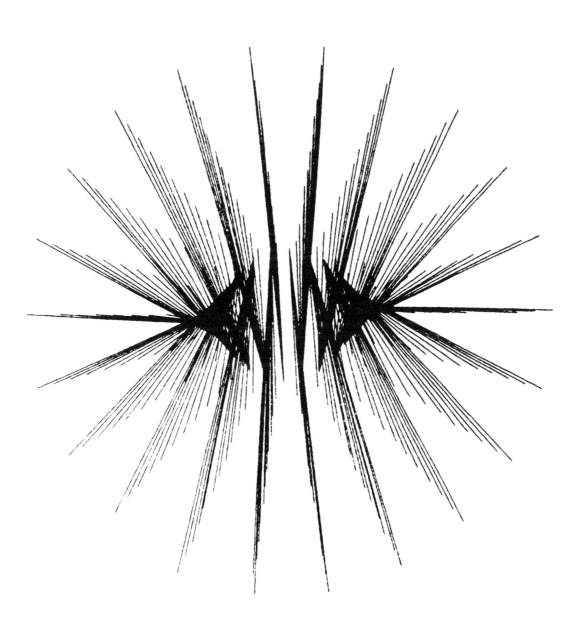

creative computing
LIBRARY

Four sets of books covering major topics in computer literacy.

COMPUTER GAMES

101 BASIC Computer Games- Dave Ahl
An anthology of games and simulations- from Acey-Deucey to Yahtzee, all in the BASIC language. Contains a complete listing and sample run of each game, plus a descriptive write-up. Large Format. 256 pp.   **$7.50**

What To Do After You Hit Return- Bob Albrecht
Another collection of games and simulations- all in BASIC- including number guessing games, word games, hide-and-seek games, pattern games, board games, business and social science simulations and science fiction games. Large format. 158 pp.   **$6.95**

Fun And Games With The Computer- Ted Sage
Teaches problem-solving, flow charting and computer programming (in BASIC) in the context of well-known games of chance and strategy. 351 pp.   **$5.95**

HAND CALCULATORS

Games, Tricks and Puzzles For A Hand Calculator- Wally Judd
This book is a necessity for anyone who owns or intends to buy a hand calculator, from the most sophisticated (the HP65 for example) to the basic "four banger". 110 pp.   **$2.95**

The Calculating Book- Jim Rogers
Discover where you can buy gas during the oil crisis. An anthology of games, puzzles, puns, magic tricks and math problems that can be performed or solved with the pocket calculator. 125 pp.   **$2.95**

150 Problems In Crypt-Arithmetic- Maxey Brooke
More grist for the calculator. 156 problems in which letters are substituted for numbers. Examine the number relations between the groups of symbols and solve the problem. 72 pp.   **$1.25**

Advanced Applications For Pocket Calculators- Jack Gilbert
This book shows what you can do with your calculator after you balance your checkbook. As much as 80 or 90 percent of the capacity of the calculator is not used, and this book shows you how to use it- step-by-step- regardless of type. Explores all functions of all existing calculators, and all scientific and business applications. 304 pp.   **$5.95**

COMPUTERS IN MATH

Problem Solving With The Computer- Ted Sage
Teaches problem solving, chart flowing, and computer programming (in BASIC) in the context of the traditional junior/senior high school curriculum precalculus math. 244 pp. **$4.95**

Problems For Computer Solution- Gruenberger & Jaffray
A collection of 92 problems in engineering, business, social science and mathematics. Oriented toward the FORTRAN language. 401 pp.   **$7.25**

My Computer Likes Me- Bob Albrecht
This workbook introduces the BASIC computer language to young or old. The teaching examples are drawn from population problems and demographic data. Large format. 64 pp.   **$2.19**

COMPUTERS IN SOCIETY

Electric Media- Les Brown and Sema Marks
How TV and computers affect individuals and society. Cable TV, air waves as public domain, popular and distorted views of the computer speed and storage capacities of computers, communicating with computers, artificial intelligence how computers learn, creative computers. Guest spots by Buzz Aldrin, Dick Cavett and Marshall McLuhan. 168 pp.   **$4.95**

Freedom's Edge- Milton Wessel
The computer threat to society. The author, an attorney, shows some of the ways in which the computer is changing our lives- or soon will be. Discusses the data bank, point-of-sale marketing and free competition, computer related crime, controlling the computer, etc. 137 pp.   **$4.95**

Computer Lib/Dream Machine- Ted Nelson
This book is devoted to the premise that everybody should understand computers. In a blithe manner the author covers interactive systems, terminals, computer languages, data structures, binary patterns, computer architecture, minicomputers, big computers, microprocessors, simulation, military uses of computers, computer companies, and much, much more. Large format. 127 pp.   **$7.00**

Computers in Society- Donald Spencer
How can the computer help the Businessman, artist, or sports announcer? This book examines a wide range of up to date applications of the computer to medicine, engineering, transportation, business, the arts, education, law, process control and many other areas. 208 pp. **$4.95**

CREATIVE COMPUTING Reviews

Creative Computing reviews books (fiction and non-fiction) related to computers, technology, and education; games; and other learning material.

Readers: Want to be a reviewer? Write directly to the Reviews Editor: Peter Kugel, School of Management, Boston College, Chestnut Hill, MA 02167.

Publishers: Send materials for review to the Reviews Editor.

Education and Ecstasy by George Leonard, $7.95, Delacorte Press, New York, 1968.

Workers developing educational materials using the computer can, and often do, simply start where they are, with whatever equipment they can acquire, and chip away at courses.

However, effective long-range plans must be much more systematic and detailed. We can often distinguish readily between short-range goals, what we are immediately trying to do with projects, and long-range goals. Long-range goals can be formulated only if we decide how the future *should* be shaped. Individuals with strong views about the future, with powerful ideas about what role computers should play in education twenty or twenty-five years from now, not only offer guidance, but may well influence the future; a prophecy of this kind can be a self-fulfilling prophecy.

Relatively few have attempted to view the future of computers in education. Developers who continue working where they are, with the equipment they have on hand, often become fierce defenders of that equipment, arguing its merits, rather than, perhaps more rationally, striving to improve it.

Science fiction has offered some views of a computerized future that mention educational aspects, in such works as Arthur Clark's *The City and the Stars*. Often the views presented in such literature are hostile. For example, the computer-teacher in Zamatien's *We* is not a positive thing, but aids in dehumanizing the society.

But George Leonard's book, *Education and Ecstasy*, shows a positive, and, I believe, extremely interesting view of the role computers may play in learning. This view is almost unknown to the developers of learning materials employing the computer, so I intend to review Leonard's picture of the future. This, like all predictions, must be taken with a grain of salt; Leonard suggests as much in the introduction to the two chapters of the book that will concern us. One of my knowledgeable friends has characterized the passages as romantic. I believe, nevertheless, that they do represent an interesting view of the future, even if time should prove them not accurate in *all* details.

Leonard's book combines two seemingly unrelated trends in modern society, the encounter group philosophy of such establishments as Esselin, and the technological, even Skinnerian, approaches to education, particularly those involving the computer. In earlier didactic chapters he brings these possibilities together while criticizing education as it exists today.

The main interest in *Education and Ecstasy*, to me, is in the chapters that portray a school of the year 2001. The description uses the fictional guise of a visit by parents to the school to watch the progress of their children. We get a panoramic view of the learning activity, and we see the overall "philosophy" underlying the school.

The learning structure pictured is completely dependent on the existence of the computer, and would be impossible without advanced technology. The computer technology depicted is graphic, employing large three-dimensional, color pictures, and sound, in addition to alphanumeric interactions.

The main arena for the knowledge-based forms of education is the Basics Dome. Students enter and leave freely; the entire school is unscheduled, stressing that students do not appear for "classes" at any particular time inasmuch as there *are* no classes!

The students are three to ten year olds. After age ten people are expected to know all the "basic" information, including calculus! Since the time is free, enormous thought has to be given to motivational issues, so that the students will *want* to do the necessary tasks, rather than be coerced to do them as is often the situation in schools today.

The educational view presented, the free learning view is a natural extension of the self-paced or Keller plan ideas that are now coming into practice, with much more emphasis given to complete freedom from scheduling, and with the material much more highly individualized than at present.

Students entering the Basics Dome see a circular ring of computer consoles around the outer wall. Each has a keyboard, allowing access to *all* human symbols, not just the restricted or full ASCII, or APL set, typical today. The technology for allowing access to all symbols is available and has been built into the PLATO system; but the standard terminals today deny us this feature. Each student has headphones for audio messages. The display is a large three-dimensional hologramic display in full color. The displays touch each other at the edges, so that the room has a continuous band of pictorial information. This touching is more than simply physical; the computer is clever enough to have the displays interact, and information may spread over more than one display, moving and contracting. Furthermore, displays will have in their intermediate areas related aspects of what students at each of the stations are doing.

Students are identified to the computer by means of an electronic identification device, which they attach to the chair. This device also does queueing. The computer has complete records of students' efforts, so whenever students resume work it is all ready. A session starts with review and then moves on to new items. The individual sessions shown are not long.

A sample session of language learning is sketched. As one would expect, this is difficult to do, and, while interesting, is perhaps one of the weaker features of the chapter. Writers about the future often have this problem. It is easier to imagine the overall structure than to delineate concrete details. This sketch is done much better in this book than in B. F. Skinner's *Walden II*, where a great discrepancy separates the glowing philosophy and the mundane details.

Graphics play a vital role. This trend is already established in contemporary education, but still is not as widely recognized as it should be. Almost all of the current major educational developmental projects in the United States are graphic based. I regard it as an historical accident that earlier terminals were nongraphic, forcing users of the computer in learning situations to begin with nonpictorial formats. The role of pictures is so important in all educational processes, in a variety of levels, that this seems to me to be an intolerable situation. Now that reasonably priced and highly reliable graphic terminals are available, I expect the situation to change. We could even argue that extensive nongraphic developmental work is a waste of time today. The future of computers in education will almost certainly be highly pictorial, allowing teachers to access to these important nonverbal learning techniques.

The learning environment in *Education and Ecstasy* is a computer-managed environment, with the computer knowing the educational progress of each student and making judgments based on this knowledge within the learning material. Each student is an individual with a highly individualized learning sequence. This is a long-standing goal for computers in education, even though it remains difficult to achieve in full-scale systems. We are now beginning to see systems that do this, systems where extensive memory of students' efforts and achievement both on and off the computer, is accessible to the program.

At least two aspects of the technology pictured are far beyond anything possible today (and probably beyond what will be available in 2001). The first, in active use in the school we visit, is the

use of brain wave information within the learning dialogs. The headset which brings the sound also picks up brain patterns, allowing the computer to determine what the student is absorbing, whether the material needs to be reviewed, whether the program can accelerate.

The second advanced technological innovation, more radical and "criticized" by the "conservative" school director, involves direct brain manipulation, bypassing the senses entirely. Naturally the details are vague and it is not clear if the criticism is tongue-in-cheek or is the usual resistance to new educational developments. Contemporary readers are almost certain to approach this with apprehension; such future possibilities have often been the subject of frightening fictional presentations, such as John Hershey's *The Child Buyer*. It seems unlikely that any such technique would be in use in just twenty-five years.

I hope I have encouraged at least some of you to read the book, which includes many more details.

How realistic is this view of the future? What alternate patterns are plausible? In discussions with friends, alternative views have been expressed, both the view that the picture presented is much too radical a change to occur in twenty-five years, and the view that changes will be much more drastic than those suggested. I don't know how to pick between these two positions! The notion that educational change occurs only slowly is ingrained, and does seem to have empirical basis. The vested interests in maintaining the system as it is are powerful. So desirable educational change is not rapid.

On the other hand, we are in a period of very rapid change in computer technology. Computers are becoming more economical while everything else is increasing in cost, promising that highly computerized educational systems *will* come into widespread use in the 80's and 90's. Economic considerations alone will be an important factor in pressing for such change, provided viable teaching materials can be developed in sufficient time.

This last factor, the existence of the pedagogical and programming skills discussed in *Education and Ecstasy*, is much more questionable than the hardware. None of our current computer-based education projects show such sophistication in computer use in educational situations, although many projects are striving to use computers more effectively. We still have a long way to go.

Even the hardware aspect is not entirely clear. The environment projected is a timesharing environment, with the central computer holding the record capabilities. There is probably local processing at the displays. Except for record keeping and large databases, future use may not be in the timesharing mode, but may tend toward sophisticated stand-alone machines. A striking aspect of recent technology has been the development of more and more compact computers. We have now many competing "computer-on-a-chip" assemblies which can be put together to form systems. This development of microcomputer technology will continue, with units becoming cheaper, faster, and easier to assemble for the purposes at hand.

To think of today's minis is misleading. The power of such systems in the near future will be more comparable to that of very large contemporary computers, even though these systems will be largely self-contained and stand-alone. Modern video-based technology will, I believe, have great ramifications too; it also suggests the possibility of very powerful local processing. The local processor can drive displays without timesharing limitations, and interactive computer graphics can overcome the limitations of a 1200 baud connection.

George Leonard's view of the future is only one of many. But such speculation, such description of ideal future conditions in a broad and sweeping sense, is important for developers of computer-based material. It is easy to become frozen in the hardware and technology available at the moment, and so waste years of time preparing materials that will only be obsolete when they are finished. Perhaps nowhere is the future shock phenomenon likely to be more important than in areas touched by the computer, because of the very rapid advances. Whether you accept George Leonard's view or not, or perhaps just deem it an interesting possibility, the need for long-range thinking and speculation about the future is important for all of us.

Alfred Bork
University of California – Irvine

* * *

MAN AND THE COMPUTER, John G. Kemeny, 151pp. $6.95, Charles Scribner's Sons, New York. 1972.

Although this book is based on a series of lectures delivered three years ago, it deserves a careful reading. It is written for the person unfamiliar with computers but could easily be read by computer professionals who need a new perspective of the computer. The author divides the book into two parts. The first part is a short history of computers and time-sharing plus speculation as to whether we should consider the computer a new species. The second part is a peek into 1990 to see how this relation between man and computer might develop.

From the development of stored programs with the leadership of John von Neumann, the computer exhibits characteristics of a species; i.e., metabolism, locomotion, reproduction, individuality, intelligence, and naturalness. However, this flies in the face of current acceptance of the definition of a "live species." The author, after a very clear explanation of Dartmouth Time Sharing, shows how the species of man and machine are coexisting. He then raises the question about this relationship — Is it symbiotic or parasitic? Humans fear that which they do not understand, and the computer professionals have not done a very good job of dispelling this fear. Symbiote or parasite — it is up to man to use "enough understanding and enough foresight" to "assure that the interaction between the two species will be totally beneficial to mankind."

1990 augurs widespread computer usage in business, education, and every day existence. With specific examples the author relates how the technology of 1971 could develop these relationships. Progress in computers has bounded forward with reduced costs in the use of microcomputers, computer terminals, and inter-computer communication. Project INTREX has demonstrated the possibility of storing vast amounts of information, but not

U.S. COLLEGE STUDENTS TAKING ASTROLOGY COURSES OUTNUMBER THOSE TAKING ASTROPHYSICS, BY 10-TO-1

economically yet. Hewlett-Packard has produced a personal programmable computer for under $800. Therefore, we humans need the help of a federally subsidized private agency to develop computer systems for public use. This agency could lead the way in controlling this "symbiotic evolution" so that we could experience a "new golden age for mankind."

Edgar T. Canty
Boston, MA.

* * *

Survival Printout, edited by Total Effect, Vintage Books, New York. 232 pg. Paperback. $1.95.

The Introduction of this book describes a dialogue in SEMANT between the editors (three professors of English who call their group Total Effect) and a Burroughs Illiac 4. By means of this dialogue, they claim that the computer actually chose the sixteen selections of science fact and science fiction that comprise the book.

The selections are divided into four groups. The first is called "Evolution/Identity" and the four short stories by Eiseley, Ballard, Bester, and Zelazny are speculations on man qua man. The first three delve into deep fantasy and bring tto the surface thoughts that we probably have all had during times of deep depression or extreme loneliness. For a Breath I Tarry by Roger Zelazny, the last selection in this group is by far the best and describes the thought process of a robot/computer attempting to achieve manhood. Absolutely fascinating!

The second section is called "Earth Probabilities". Arthur Clarke leads off with a factual article on the Social Consequences of Communications Satellites written in 1945 but timely today as it was then. The next two stories in this section by Silverberg and Lafferty describe living conditions in an urban city of the future and the reemergence of the streetcar. The last story is Harlan Ellison's I Have No Mouth and I Must Scream. It describes what happens when the remaining giant computers on the earth after a nuclear war get together to keep five human survivors living forever. It has been reprinted several places; however, if you haven't read it yet, you must! It's superb.

The third section "Ecosystems — Cellular and Solar" starts with a factual selection by Nigel Calder on exploding stars, black holes, pulsars, and other cosmic phenomena. An excellent introduction to the fundamentals of the universe. The other three stories in this section by Leiber, Delany, and Simak are good solid entertainment with a liberal sprinkling of naked truth among the fun and humor.

The last section "Time Space Travel" is probably the most speculative, dealing from several points of view with relativistic travel to other stars, galaxies, or galaxy clusters. It seems fairly clear that relativistic spaceflight is the way to go assuming a way can be found to propel the craft (anti-matter?) and protect the occupants. Cosmic radiation near the speed of light would have an intensity 100,000 times greater than that of sunlight at the earth's surface. Naturally in the three fiction selections by Smith, Heinlein, and Blish these problems have been overcome and we are fascinated with the paradoxes of time travel and the like.

Survival Printout is recommended for an entertaining, yet highly informative diversion from your computer.

David H. Ahl
Morristown, N. J.

Equations: The Game of Creative Mathematics, by Layman E. Allen. $6.50, WFF'N PROOF, 1490-SM South Blvd., Ann Arbor, MI 48104.

Instructional Math Play (IMP Kits: Simulations of Computer Assisted Instruction Programs, by Layman E. Allen and Jon K. Ross. $1.00 per kit, $15.00 for set of 21. WFF'N PROOF.

On-Words: The Game of Word Structures, By Layman E. Allen, Frederick L. Goodman, Doris J. Humphrey, and Joan K. Ross, $6.50, WFF 'N PROOF.

It is both convenient and natural to review these two games, and the associated instructional-simulation aids, as a single publication because they are, besides being designed by the same person or persons, very closely related in purpose, playing equipment, rules, and interest for the players.

EQUATIONS is played by two or more persons (or, as the IMP kits indicate, by a person and a computer program) with the objective of finding ways of expressing equations in simple arithmetic operations. One player defines a goal (one side of the equation) by selection of some of the numbers and operators provided by a roll of a dozen or more special dice. The players then try to come as close as possible to supplying a left-hand side, without actually doing so, by selecting one die at a time from the remaining dice. Getting too close to a solution, or preventing all solutions (by eliminating crucial dice from play) loses the game; successfully challenging an errant opponent wins.

The above description does not do full justice to the rules. Let me hasten to add that the actual rules supplied, including variants for those who find the standard rules too tame, covers forty (40) pages of printed text, so there is no way that a review can do justice to the rules. In fact, the standard rules, once understood, are not all that complex: rather, it is the presentation that is complex. This is the major problem with what are basically very interesting games: the statement of the rules is far too formal and complex.

The *IMP* kits contain a summary of the rules which is vastly easier to read and comprehend, and I would strongly recommend that anyone who buys *EQUATIONS* get some of the *IMP* kits as well. They provide solo practice as well as a clearer understanding of the rules (in Kit No. 1 only.) Once the rules have been assimilated, the game can be played by elementary school children (4th grade up) and will be enjoyed by many, I believe. The games have considerable popularity in some schools in which they are used.

My two boys (5th and 7th grades) found that they picked up new insights into arithmetic in their first attempts to play. However, they do not seem to be ready to accept the game as part of their regular selection (they are currently hung up on Cribbage.)

The play of *ON-WORDS* is similar: the goal is the length of a word, which is to be made up from a selection of the remaining cubes, which have letters on them. The general structure of the rules is identical, including, unfortunately, the complexity of the explanation. I find the game interesting and challenging, but an attempt to introduce it to a group of word-game enthusiast friends was met with furrowed eyebrows and eventual rejection. Maybe it's my poor powers of explanation, maybe they are just not ready for a game of this sophistication, but we did not get past the first game. It is a real pity that the author did not spend less time making the rules rigorous in favor of making them clear and concise.

L. D. Yarbrough
Lexington, Mass.

> "With regard to excellence, it is not enough to know, but we must try to have and use it."
> *Aristotle*

On-Sets (Game), by Layman E. Allen, Peter Kugel, and Martin F. Owens, $6.50, WFF'N PROOF, 1490 South Blvd., Ann Arbor, MI 48104.
Objectives:
After a student plays the game of ON-SETS he should know
1. what a set is.
2. the relationship between the names of a set and the number of things that are in the named set.
3. operations with sets such as union, intersection, complementation and difference.
4. what is meant by the universal set and the null set.
Evaluation:
There are many variations of the game; the simplest versions are for use in the primary grades. The game increases in complexity and should be suitable for use all the way up to the adult level. The instructions for the elementary versions are easy to follow, and this game can be used to effectively introduce concepts of set theory at an early age. The game is played by 2-3 children at any one time and should not take more than approximately 5-10 minutes to complete. It is, therefore, suitable for use in a classroom where a short time filler is needed to keep small groups of students occupied. This game is highly recommended for use at this level in the classroom.

The more advanced versions of this game are too complicated for general classroom use. It would be much simpler to explain set theory to the middle and high school student than the mechanics of this game. The rewards involved in playing the game do not warrant the time needed to explain the play of the game.

Ms. E. T. Rubin
Richmond, VA

* * *

Space Hop: A Game of the Planets by Helmut Wimmer. $12.95. Teaching Concepts, Inc., 230 Park Ave., New York, NY 10017.

"*Space Hop* is a valuable teaching tool in the form of a game which illustrates the scientific facts of our Solar System, its sun, moons, planets, comets and asteroids. One of a series of GAMES BY TEACHERS." (Publisher's description.)

This game is suggested as suitable for 9-to-adults, and that evaluation seems accurate. My two boys, 10 and 12, enjoy it thoroughly and like to show it off to their friends. The educational aspects are well planned and the competitive elements are just enough to make the game fun without introducing too many stress situations of the type likely to set siblings at each other's throats. In addition to coming away from the game with reinforced facts about the solar system (What was the first planet to be discovered by telescope? My mission is to go there . . .), they will subliminally pick up the concept of odd-even parity, and just may come away bemused by the peculiar topology of the "outer space" defined by the game.

I recommend the game for any group of "kids" with a scientific bent.

Lynn D. Yarbrough
Lexington, Mass.

* * *

BASIC in a Flash, by Earl Orf and Royce Helmbrecht. $1.50. The Math Group, Inc., 5625 Girard Ave. South, Minneapolis, MN 55419.

"This set of cards is designed to help students learn the meaning of symbols, commands, and statements used in the BASIC programming language. Terms are printed in red on one side and definitions in black on the other side. Many cards also contain examples showing how the term might be used. Blank cards are included to add your own terms. Could be used as flash cards or as a reference near the computer terminal." – Publisher's summary.

II *Cybernetic Frontiers*, Stewart Brand. 96 pgs. $2.00. Random House, Inc., 201 East 40th Street, New York 10022. 1974.

Stewart Brand, editor of The Last Whole Earth Catalog, examines two cybernetic frontiers in this book. The first frontier examined is the means by which the human mind processes and acts upon information. Instead of a straightforward discussion of this topic, Brand recounts a rambling dialogue between himself and Gregory Bateson, who is an anthropologist specializing in South Pacific natives. In the course of their conversation, both men present many unsupported personal hypotheses as undeniable facts. At one point Bateson confesses to an anti-experimental bias, while both Brand and Bateson state their belief in mysticism and usage of LSD as valid approaches to consciousness expansion. Their conclusions remain unconvincing when these factors are taken into account.

Unlike the first frontier, the second frontier described in the book makes fascinating and engrossing reading. In it Brand tells the story of a specific group of programmers and their recreation. The programmers were at MIT in the early 60's; their recreation was designing a computer game named Spacewar.

Brand's description of Spacewar is quite vivid. It is played with computer generated spacecraft displayed on a television screen. Players can control movement of their spacecraft on the screen via hand controls, while the computer figures in effects of acceleration and gravitational fields. Unfortunately there are no hard programming details, but there are numerous illustrations and interesting comments.

The reader follows the MIT group as Spacewar becomes only a pastime at first, then grows into an obsession and finally becomes a way of life. Through Spacewar, the programmers soon realize what "computer power to the people" could mean if it were to ever become a reality. Eventually the group dissolves and the members go their separate ways, all carrying the dream of "computer power to the people" around in their minds.

That was in the 60's. Today that dream has sprouted into half a dozen concrete realities which Brand examines in an Epilogue to his second frontier. Several individuals describe their work since Spacewar, including such things as storefront computer centers, personal TV scratchpads and marketing of educational computers. Many useful addresses are listed.

Despite its poor opening, this book is recommended to anyone wishing insight into the motivations of top programmers. It provokes the reader to imagine what the widespread use of computers could mean, and provides valuable reference material as well.

Ricky James Roberson
Cleveland, TN

*　*　*

The Use and Misuse of Computers in Education, by Allan B. Ellis. 226 pages. $12.95. McGraw Hill, 1974.

In chapter 1, the author describes commonly accepted definitions, attributes, and history of computers. He convincingly shows the short-comings of each of these. In chapter 2, he presents the best description of a Turing machine that I have read. He then defines a computer as a universal Turing machine. He ends Part I of the book discussing computing, iteration, semi-algorithms, algorithms, and heuristics, giving several interesting examples and analogies. This excellent presentation is marred by 2 gross errors in his iteration scheme for extracting square roots by Newton's method (square root of 1/4 is 17/16???). Regardless, these two chapters should be read by the computer novice, as well as by professionals teaching classes or writing books on computers.

The major premise of Part II is that education problems are the primary concern, and computerization is only of secondary importance (why computerize something that is educationally unsound?) In chapters 3 and 4, Ellis describes what has been done in education by Suppes at Stanford, Bitzer (PLATO) at Illinois, Papert (LOGO) at MIT, project LOCAL at Dartmouth, and other projects. He uses these projects to show potential dangers in computerizing education; but he does not accuse any of the projects as misusing the computer. Perhaps the word "Misuse" should not be in the title of the book. Anyone trying to computerize topics in teaching should read these two chapters.

Most of chapter 5 describes the history of the NESDEC-NEEDS project in Massachusetts. Most of the details seem irrelevant to the goals of this book.

Part III, starting with chapter 6, develops a case study of building a computer system, called ISVD, for providing guidance and counseling in schools. But the software developed could be used for other purposes, such as CAI (computer-assisted instruction), information retrieval, etc. Enroute, the author describes several computer programs for processing English words, phrases, and sentences, and programs for providing interaction with the time-share user, in English. I found this quite interesting. Anyone interested in CAI would find part III of interest to them. Chapter 8 presents a fictitious student using the system. ISVD really looks nice. But, as is typical of Ellis throughout the book, he ends the topic by showing ISVD's shortcomings.

The appendix introduces some hardware (some obsolete, probably because ISVD was implemented on the RCA Spectra 70/45 computer), as well as some brief theory on how the hardware works. Ellis makes several minor errors here, such as describing left-handed magnetic fields on page 209.

Over all, Ellis's book is a well-written thoroughly-documented criticism of current thought on computers and their use in education. But it is not an easy book to read. Rather, the book requires you to think skeptically as you read it, a reading technique most people are not used to.

James L. Boettler
Taladega, Alabama

*　*　*

Computers in the Classroom. Ed. by Joseph B. Margolin and Marion R. Misch. 382 pp. $14.00. Hayden Book Co., 50 Essex Street, Rochelle Park, New Jersey 07662. 1970.

A group of scientists and educators were briefed on the current state of computer technology. They then embarked on a week-long tour of five computer-assisted instruction centers across the country. Following this each member of the seminar prepared an article stating his views of the problems and issues facing education arising from this new technology.

The result is a very readable book which should be important reading for both the layman interested in education and the educator interested in the impact of computer technology on current education practices.

The book is organized into three parts. Part I focuses on the pre-seminar briefing in which government, academic, and business representatives spoke to the group on the major issues as they saw them. Part II details the traveling seminar and includes the participants' articles. Questions raised by the seminar participants in their articles are relevant to all areas of education today. Part III gives an excellent summary of the major issues raised as well as the predictions and recommendations of the panel members.

An extensive, if somewhat dated, bibliography is given at the end of the book.

Allan L. Forsythe

*　*　*

Learning for Tomorrow: The Role of the Future in Education, Alvin Toffler (Ed), 421 pp. $2.95. Vintage Books Div. of Random House, New York.

"All education springs from images of the future and all education creates images of the future." To support this thesis, editor Alvin Toffler (*Future Shock*) and eighteen leading psychologists, educators, futurists, social scientists, psychiatrists and humanists have joined together to put forth proposals for educational reform. With a dramatic call for "education in the future tense," they show why action learning, value clarification, racial and sexual equality, along with simulations, games, science fiction and other educational innovations need to be integrated and fused with a sense of "future – consciousness" if we are to design effective learning systems. This sense of "future – consciousness" must be developed early in the child's educational experience so that desirable futures can be planned for, and undesirable futures avoided. Teaching children to "model build", to see alternative solutions, to assume the responsibility for the implications of such alternatives, should be the primary role of education if we are to survive in a world bombarded with rapid technological innovations.

Each chapter is a self-contained unit, written by a different author on a different aspect of developing "a sense of the future". Yet, Toffler has done such a superb job of editing that the reader feels the continuity of a single authorship. The book is absorbing, developing a sense of urgency for some drastic change in our thinking on why we educate. It is also an eye opener, especially in the area of sexual and racial inequities. "Why Women See the Future Differently from Men" and "The Black Child's Image of the Future" should produce in the conscientious educator some sleepless nights.

This book is a must for all educators, instructors, and administrators alike. It provides challenging alternatives in approach to all areas of study. It has some vitally important things to say about the necessity for "real" change in our educational institutions as we encounter ever more rapid rates of technological change and accommodating changes in responding social structures.

Beginning where most proposals for education reform leave off, it demands change not merely in how, where and when we educate, but in WHY we educate.

J. Leone
THE Journal, Acton, MA

❋ ❋ ❋

Electric Media, by Les Brown and Sema Marks, 160 pp paper, $3.30. Harcourt Brace Jovanovich, 757 Third Ave., New York 10017.

Electric Media is one of six books in Harcourt Brace's "Making Contact" series. It is a book that is at once fascinating, educational, and stimulating. A remarkable combination. It is even more remarkable when you realize that the authors are describing on the printed page two media, television and computers, which go far beyond ink on paper. Yet Les Brown manages to plug in the reader with arresting discussions of America's adjustment to television (97% of households watch TV!), equal time/fairness/quality issues, viewing habits, connection into the world, public TV, and cable TV. Also in the TV section are interviews with Dick Cavett and Edwin (Buzz) Aldrin.

If the TV section of the book rates as excellent, Sema Marks' section on computers must be considered superlative! These 50 pages will do more to enhance public understanding, acceptance, and appreciation of computers than all the textbooks in print. Even old hand computer people will have their eyes opened here. You'll read about popular criticism of computers and what's wrong with it. You'll marvel to computers doing once impossible problems. You'll worry when the data bank privacy dragon rears its ugly head. And you'll go bananas when you read about Alan Kay's "Dynabook" project and sample the dialogue of ELIZA and ANIMAL. Closing out the book is a 1972 interview with Marshall McLuhan in which he states, "1984 really happened a long time ago." How true. And what do we do now?

(Although this is a Harcourt Brace book, my experience is that it's very hard to find. You can order it through Creative Computing Library Service – see ad – or from Harcourt Brace directly – ISBN 0-15-318734-4, $3.30 plus shipping. Teacher's Manual – ISBN 0-15-318736-0, $1.20.)

David H. Ahl

Computers and Young Children. Nuffield Foundation. John Wiley & Sons, Somerset, NJ, 1972.

How and what to teach children about computers is the subject of this latest Weaving Guide produced by the Nuffield Mathematics Project. The main parts of this book consist of information about preparing flowcharts and samples of simple flowcharts produced by children; suggestions for a classroom activity in which the children act as human computers; information about using and preparing punched cards to present the program to the computer; and the description of classes actually working with a computer. The elementary classroom teacher will gain much information about computers from reading this text. She also will find many practical suggestions for teaching children about computers.

Computer Poems, collected by Richard W. Bailey. Potagannissing Press, Ann Arbor, Mich., $2.25.

Computer Poems is an anthology of verse written by sixteen poet-programmers; selections range from clever computer-constructed pieces to poems that are amusing despite their origin. Although programming techniques are not discussed, this book will surely interest the computer buff and the layman alike.

Background Math for a Computer World, by Ruth Ashley. John Wiley & Sons, Inc., New York, 1973. $3.95.

A self-teaching guide to the fundamental mathematical knowledge required for further study of computer programming or computer science. Problems from a wide variety of math application areas exercise analytical talents and help to develop logical thought patterns. This is an excellent preview for further work with computers for the nontechnically oriented educator.

Computers, by Jane Jonas Srivastava. Thomas Y. Crowell Co., New York, 1972.

This book is part of the Young Math Books series, and is geared to the very young (primary age) child, with delightful drawings by Ruth and James McCrea.

After beginning with "A computer is a machine for counting," the book goes on to describe various uses of computers, as well as the functions of the five basic parts of digital computers. There is even a super flowchart for "counting giraffes met on the way to school."

The point is made that not only can a computer do a job very quickly, but it will do the same thing over and over, without getting bored and asking, "When's recess?"

Above four reviews by:
Peg Pulliam
Lexington, Mass.

❋ ❋ ❋

The Electronic Brain: How it Works, by Joseph J. Cook; 72 pp, $3.69; C. P. Putnam, 1969.

This book is written for students from grades five through eight, discusses the history, operation, and uses of computers. Unfortunately, the chapters are inconsistent in their approach, frequently omitting information necessary for the beginning student of computer science.

The chapter on the historical development of counting devices is both interesting and informative. It is a brief overview covering only the most important developments up to the MANIC – Mathematical Analyzer, Numerical Integrator, and Computer. Two chapters, "The Arithmetic of Electronic Computers" and "Inside the Electronic Brain" are written for those students who have a mastery of the decimal system and an aptitude for mathematics. All students, however, will understand and enjoy the chapters on present and future uses of the computer.

Although the format is academic and not catchy enough to generate immediate interest in the book, it should be in the school library as reference for those students who have an interest in learning about computers.

Flora Russ
Berkeley, California

BOOKS ON COMPUTER LITERACY

Peter Olivieri
Boston College

There are a great many textbooks, journals, articles, and publications that deal, on an instructional level, with the art and science of computing. However, these are often too technical for the casual reader, the individual who is merely seeking a brief introduction to what computers and computing is all about. These people have needs that I feel we all too often overlook. Providing the general public with more information about computers is something that we all should strive for. As computers become more commonplace, it is not unusual to find elementary school children (as early as Grade 3) being exposed to these machines. Materials need to be developed that provide a nontechnical, informative, and meaningful introduction to computers for people from age six to sixty. I have recently reviewed several such publications and present them here for addition to your memory banks should you have occasion to recommend something to a relative, friend, or acquaintance. This is by no means a collectively exhaustive list of all materials of this type, but rather a beginning.

THE STORY OF COMPUTERS. Donald Spencer. 64pp. Abacus Computer Corporation, Ormond Beach, Florida 32074. Paper. 1975. A nicely illustrated, clear, non-technical introduction to the world of computers. Geared for children in Grades four through nine. Recommended for your young children. Includes: What are computers? Who invented computers? What kinds of computers are there? How does a computer work? How do I tell a computer what to do? What are some useful computer terms?

COMPUTERS. William R. Corliss. 91pp. United States Atomic Energy Commission. Office of Information Services. Paper. 1973. A very readable book. Quite current (includes a section on optical reading of supermarket products). A little technical in parts (negligible). Includes: Calculating Prodigies. The Birth of Computers. Anatomy of a Computer. The Generation Gaps. Analog Computers. A Reading List. Selected Motion Pictures (too few of them).

THE FIRST BOOK OF INFORMATION SCIENCE. Joseph Becker. 91pp. United States Atomic Energy Commission. Office of Information Services. Paper. 1973. Not too much on computers. Excellent for the information on information sciences. Good photographs. Recommended for those with an interest in information and data. Includes: What is information? Storing and retrieving information. Putting information into a computer. Getting information from a computer. Communicating information. Finding information in microfilm. Future of information sciences. Epilogue. Glossary and a reading list.

COMPUTERS IN ACTION. Donald Spencer. 245pp. Hayden Book Company, New Jersey. Paper. 1974. A guide for the layman, businessman, high school student, teacher, or non-scientific college student. Excellent references at end of each chapter. Easy reading but not quick reading. Somewhat like a textbook. Actually teaches BASIC to the reader. Includes: The Computer Age, Computer Evolution, How Computers Work, Getting Information In and Out of the Computer, Computer Storage, Designing the Computer Program, The Language of the Computer, Introduction to Computer Programming.

UNDERSTANDING COMPUTERS. Thomas H. Crowley. 139pp. McGraw-Hill, New York. Paper. 1967. Written for high school teachers, business managers, and those with limited technical background who are interested in finding out what the computer business is all about. Not quick reading. A learning book rather than an information book. Somewhat outdated though not critically so. Strongly recommended for the serious layman. Includes: Introduction, Basic Computer Functions, What Is Being Processed? Interpretation of Symbols, Memory, Input-Output Operations, Symbol-Processing Operations, The Control Process, Stored Program Computers, Programming, Applications of Computers, Computer "Priests", What Does the Future Hold? 1984, Bibliography.

THE WAY THINGS WORK BOOK OF THE COMPUTER. Simon and Schuster. New York. 245pp. 1974. This is an illustrated encyclopedia of information science, cybernetics, and data processing. Very nicely illustrated. Clear, two-color charts and diagrams. Not light reading. Information packed. Some material a bit technical. Certainly recommended for your bookshelf. Might be geared more for the information or computer scientist, but there is enough here to satisfy many tastes. Only dissappointment was that it didn't go far enough in coverage. Another volume would be well received. Includes: Information and Documentation, Information and Cybernetics, Communication and Documentation, Statistics and Thermal Processes, Control, Self-correction and Automation, Information Theory, Redundancy, Cybernetics and Linguistics, Cybernetics and Physiology, Cybernetics and Psychology, Cybernetics and Biology, Cybernetics in Teaching, Cybernetics in Sociology, Cybernetics in Economics, Documentation, Number Systems, The Binary System, Binary Arithmetic, Logical Operations, Electromagnetic Switches, Electron Tubes, Semiconductor Logic Elements, Photo-electric Logic Elements, Fluidic Switches, Mechanical Storage Devices, Magnetic Storage Devices, Acoustic Data Storage Systems, Thin-Film Storage Devices, Analog Computation Principles, Data Processing Systems, Machine Languages and Symbolic Languages, Programming, Character Recognition, High Speed Printers and Filmsetting Techniques, Time Sharing Systems, Data Transmission, Process Computers, Data Banks, Artificial Intelligence.

✷ ✷ ✷

Computers: Tools for Today, by Claude J. DeRossi, $4.75; Children's Press, Chicago, IL, 1972.

Claude DeRossi has done an excellent job in presenting the intricacies of the computer world to the very young in his book entitled, *Computers: Tools For Today*. The book is written at a level understandable by students of the upper grades in elementary schools. The drawings by Margrit Fiddle together with the pictures are especially helpful in illustrating some of the concepts presented.

The objective of the book is to present a general picture of what computers are and what they can and cannot do. Some misconceptions concerning the capabilities of computers are discussed toward the beginning of the book, pointing out to the novice potential computer user that computers cannot solve all problems or answer all questions.

The book is well organized in that many facets of computers are discussed. The readers are introduced to computers by first discussing the history of computers. A couple of chapters discuss the capabilities and limitations of computers. Other chapters include the discussion of the following computer characteristics; input devices (punched cards and magnetic tape), how computers work (add), the numbering system of computers (binary system), and computer language (programs and how they are written including flow charts).

Joseph O. Garcia
Albuquerque, New Mexico

"He who has imagination without learning has wings and no feet."

Joseph Joubert

Computers and Society. Stanley Rothman and Charles Mosmann. 337 pp. Science Research Associates, Inc.

This textbook is designed for use in a one-term introductory course on computers and their impact on society. Considering the difficulties one faces in trying to decide what such a book should include, and the level at which it should be presented, the authors deserve considerable credit for doing as good a job as they have. But if I had to teach a course on computers and society, there are other books that I would be happier to teach it from. I would, I think, be hard to find the right kind of person to teach a course based on this book. The book is not technical enough for a technologist and not humane enough for a humanist.

The authors are clearly more at home with technical matters than they are with social implications. Part II, which explains what computers are, is very well done indeed. In the span of not much more than a hundred pages it explains a great deal about computers and explains it well. A student could find plenty to chew on here. Indeed, he may find too much.

But once the authors turn to the social implications of computers, the material gets pretty soggy. Part I is short and is intended, the Instructor's Guide tells us, to stimulate students. But one wonders what sort of student would be stimulated by such statements as "Morality may be viewed as a body of rules defining the individual's relationship to the social group," or "Can we have this freedom within our current system of government and law? Yes! The mechanisms to control technology and its employers are there."

Part III deals with the applications of computers and with the social implications of these applications. Part IV asks how we might control the use of computers and Part V speculates about the future. The book goes downhill as it gets less technical and focusses more on social implications. By the end of the course, the students are assumed to have scaled such heights of mediocrity that they are capable of devoting themselves to exercises like these: "How do you feel about the relative importance of work and leisure in your future life?" (Exercise 6, page 232) "Select a press release implicating the computer in a social mishap and analyze it for sensationalism or biased reporting." (Exercise 5, page 272) "Write an essay giving your opinion about whether research on computer learning should be pursued?" (Exercise 3, page 319). The teacher who likes to assign such exercises would probably like this book.

The job that the authors have tried to do is well worth doing and there will be some who find that the way they have done it in this book suits their tastes. However, I find this book too bland when it comes to social matters and possibly a bit too hard (considering the intended audience) when it comes to technical matters. The technical parts, though good, might be tough sledding because they cover so much in so few words. On the other hand, the non-technical parts are thin and seem intended to give the student the warm feeling of learning something or other without ever having worked very hard to learn it.

It may be that the job the authors have tried to do cannot be done to everyone's satisfaction. One cannot help thinking that mixing computer science and social science is a bit like mixing dill pickles with hot fudge sauce. Though the ingredients are tasty taken separately, they are not easy to mix well into a single course. The authors have tried to bring their ingredients together by eliminating some of the strong flavors of each. While it is true that they have done better in presenting the pickles of computer science than the hot fudge of social science, the mixture does not come off well as a single course. One feels the lack of a unifying concept. One cannot help but ask "Just what is the student of this textbook supposed to learn?"

Excluding the artwork, which has all the charm of a Bulgarian textbook on embalming, the book is attractively put together. it is amply illustrated and, considering how hard it is to illustrate any book about computers, the illustrations are very apt. The cartoons and illustrations

drawn from advertisements more than make up for the standard but rather dull, shots of equipment and installations.

The authors claim to have used this book successfully at the college level but it is written clearly enough to be usable in high schools too. The teacher who can provide the unifying concept that the book seems to lack, who can lead his students through the excellent, but difficult, technological parts and who can beef up the rather weak material on social implications will find many rewarding things in this text.

Peter Kugel
Boston, MA.

Getting Started in Classroom Computing. David H. Ahl. 29 pp. $1.50. Digital Equipment Corp., Maynard, Mass. 01754. 1974.

The six games in this booklet are to introduce the newcomer to using games and computers in the classroom. You don't need a computer to play the games but it's more fun. The games are described in the contents as:

Secret Codes — Introduction to the way punched cards and tapes work

Guess — Discover an efficient method of searching for a mystery number

Hurkle — An introduction to grids and coordinate systems

Bagels — An introduction to mathematical logic

Caves — Learn to creatively compare similarities and differences of objects

Each game has clear rules, a sample computer run, and ways to be used in the classroom.

I've had 7th and 8th graders play GUESS, HURKLE, and BAGELS — BAGELS is their special favorite and mine. I feel the games could easily be played and enjoyed by elementary students too. Easily read in one sitting, I recommend this booklet for the newcomer to games or computers. For the more advanced, I would suggest the companion books: *101 BASIC Computer Games* and *Understanding Mathematics and Logic Using BASIC Computer Games* by the same author.

Jim Albright
Springfield, OR

Hurkle

Computers and You, Kurt R. Stehling; 246 pp; $1.50. A Mentor Book (New American Library), 1301 Avenue of the Americas, New York, NY 10019; 1972.

In an easy-to-read book Kurt R. Stehling outlines the impact of the computer in several fields. The phenomenal growth and impact of computers and technology in education, transportation, medicine, weather, defense and space, business and commerce, the government and social uses is presented in separate chapters. The detail is sufficient to generate a certain amount of appreciation in addition to the acquisition of knowledge about computer uses. A general background and explanation of computers introduces the reader in a quiet way to this computer technology. A Glossary of Computer Terms is also included to help the novice reader with any unfamiliar terms or jargon.

The author expresses his ideas in a very readable fashion with parenthetical dry wit that is entertaining. Unfortunately, a sexist bias is evident in such references that equate a card punching phase with 200,000 woman days rather than worker days and a woman fumbling for change rather than a person. Such stereotyping is certainly unnecessary to accomplish the objective of the book.

The text can be easily read and enjoyed by an adult audience of general readers. Technical explanations are minimal and computer applications are explained in depth. It is an informative and enjoyable book to read.

Jane Donnelly Gawronski
San Diego, Calif.

✳ ✳ ✳

Computer-Assisted Instruction Project Final Report, by Alex Dunn and Jean Wastler. 507 pp., $12.50, Montgomery County Public Schools, Rockville, Maryland, 1972.

This is the final report of a three year computer-assisted instruction project in the Montgomery County Public School System, Montgomery County, Maryland. It provides those interested with the account of how a school system planned, developed, and implemented computer-assisted instruction.

The report includes a description of the instructional modules developed and used in the project. The documentation for each unit includes behavioral objectives, description of how the unit can be used, and the mode of presentation to the students. The units range from elementary school subjects such as operations with whole numbers through senior high school subjects such as trigonometry, chemistry, and physics. The text is illustrated with many flow-charts showing the instructional strategy of each unit and with sample computer print-outs showing the students' interaction with the computer.

This well written report also includes a description of the validation and evaluation of the project, a cost analysis of the operation, and a description of the computer system used.

This book should be recommended to administrators and supervisors who might be considering computer-assisted instruction as a means of using today's technology to individualize instruction.

Bruce W. De Young
Oakland, NJ

✳ ✳ ✳

Snobol: An Introduction To Programming, by Peter R. Newstead. 160 pp paper. $5.25. Hayden Book Co., 1975.

Every budding programmer deserves to have his mind blown periodically, to extend his view of what can be done with computers and how differently ideas can be expressed within a computer language framework. For anyone whose sole experience is with the usual algorithmic languages, e.g. BASIC, FORTRAN, COBOL, PL/I, or even Assembly languages, an introduction to the power of expression inherent in SNOBOL can be a refreshing experience. I feel that it should be more widely available than it is, even though SNOBOL4 is outnumbered in its implementations

by only a few of the above. It is wider in its applicability, especially for students who have not yet crystallized their occupational goals, than many of the others; yet most initial introductions into programming these days appear to be into BASIC.

The present book is designed to aid in teaching SNOBOL as a first language. Its treatment of computing in general is short and elementary and largely that of analogy. The teacher may have his own methods for this phase; chapter 1 is simply one point of view. The introduction to the language itself starts gently in chapter 2 and builds at a good pace, with lots of examples and exercises. Details of coding conventions and the intricacies of pattern matching follow in subsequent chapters. There is a good chapter on debugging and a chapter on user-defined functions which just skirts the edge of comprehensibility for a beginning programmer.

How good is the book? I think it will demand a good teacher with some experience and perhaps affection for the language, but it seems to be a good beginner's text. Any SNOBOL text is bound to have difficulty in competing with those by Griswold (the original SNOBOL author) et al: Griswold happens to be an excellent writer as well as authoritative. But the present book may be more useful as a beginner's text than some of the older books on the subject.

Lynn Yarbrough
Lexington, Mass.

✳ ✳ ✳

Business Data Processing I, by Robert Albrecht. Student workbook $2.00, Teacher's guide $1.50. Digital Equipment Corp., Maynard, MA 01754; 1974.

This is probably unlike most of the business data processing books you've seen. This one gets right into BASIC programming. The intent of this is to develop a series of programs to manipulate data. Working with subscripted variables, manipulating lists, and sorting lists are at the heart of this workbook. This treatment of subscripted variables is one of the best I've seen. A fresh writing style, plenty of annotated programs, drawings, and a host of both programming and non-programming exercises combine to make this a winner. The teacher's guide is but a collection of solutions. I would have liked to see teaching suggestions, alternate and additional exercises, more programming problems, etc., in such a guide. If you know this material, you don't really need the solution guide.

Joseph Kmoch
Milwaukee, WI

How To Survive in Your Native Land, James Herndon, 179 pp. $1.25, Bantam Books, New York, 1971

Contrary to the title, this book is not really a survival manual. In fact, it probably points out more pitfalls and reasons that most kids will have a hell of a time surviving in schools than it indicates solutions. The author, a junior high teacher for 10 years, found that an open approach worked for him but he's rather pessimistic whether it will be widely emulated. Indeed his own principal thinks it's maybe OK but can't really see what's wrong with Proven Establishment Methods. .

I could give you all the beautiful adjectives and superlatives and reasons you should read this book whether or not you're an advocate of open education. The main reason is that there's a damn important message about the nature of schools as an institution buried in the humor and poignancy and hope and pessimism. I'll let Herndon tell you about part of it. *"In all public schools in the United States* the percentage of kids who cannot really read the social studies textbook or the science textbook or the directions in the New Math book or the explanations in the transformational grammar book is extraordinarily high. Half the kids. The school tells everyone that reading is the key to success in school, and no doubt it is, a certain kind of reading anyway. Does the school then spend time and effort teaching those kids who can't read the texts how to read the texts? Shit no, man. Why mess up a situation made to order for failure? The school's purpose is not teaching. The school's purpose is to separate sheep from goats."

Whether you're a student, teacher, or whoever — skip a day of school and read this book. You'll be better off for it.

David H. Ahl

* * *

The Digital Villain: Notes on the Numerology, Parapsychology, and Metaphysics of the Computer. Robert Baer. 187pp. Addison-Wesley Publishing Company, Reading, Mass. Paper. 1972.

Don't let the title scare you off. This gets a four star rating for those who know all about computers, and a three star rating for those who do not. The author begins by saying that we invented computers to solve the problem. What seems to have happened is that computers have become the problem. Good references throughout. A most thought provoking book. Includes: The Semantics of Computer Science. Computer Pre-history: 1663 and all that. Turing's Mini Super-Computer. The Road to Bitsville. The Golden Bit. Games Computers Play. Playing the Game. Computer Pretense: the simulation extended. Tricks Computers Play. Artificial Intelligence and Intelligent Artifice. Rossum's Universal Robots: man as machine. The Desk Set: man vs. machine — the last victory. Billion Dollar Brain: the computer as espionage agent. Hour of the Robots: the computer as lover. The Tin Men: the computer as sportsman, moralist, and writer. Giles Goat-Boy: the computer as the military-scientific establishment. 2001: the computer as travelling companion. The Tale of the Big Computer: the computer as Chaucer or how the opposition sees man.

Peter Olivieri
Boston, Mass.

* * *

Databanks In A Free Society: Computers, Record-Keeping and Privacy, Westin and Baker, Report of the Project on Computer Databanks of the Computer Science and Engineering Board; National Academy of Sciences, New York: Quadrangle / The New York Times Book Co., 522 pp., $4.95, 1972.

This book is the report of a massive study, conducted between 1970 and 1972, on how databanks are actually being used in our society and, based on that, how use of databanks is likely to grow. Particular attention is paid to the area of civil liberties and privacy. Attention is focused on the question of whether advanced use of data processing has actually caused organizations to change their old policies and on whether present policies and legislation are adequate to ensure the rights of the people in the computer age.

A review of current data processing technology is included for those not already familiar with the area and the methodology of the study is clearly explained. Almost half the book is used to present the profiles of fourteen organizations which make extensive use of computer databanks, detailing how they make use of computers and how this use has changed their methods of operation. Included are such organizations as the Social Security Administration, the Bank of America, the Church of the Latter-day Saints and a municipal and a county government.

Following the profiles are presented the findings of the study. These cannot be adequately summarized and should be read by anyone seriously concerned with the area of the study. Many of the Project's findings are reassuring, but the report warns against being lulled into a false sense of complacency. Very real problems exist, primarily because our legal system has not moved with near the speed of computerization.

Although this book is hardly casual reading, it should not be missed by anyone concerned with the problems of databanks and privacy. As the first extensive study of its kind, it contains a wealth of information and will serve as a baseline against which future studies will be discussed.

John Lees
Rolla, MO

* * *

The Terminal Man by Michael Crichton. Alfred Knopf, Inc. New York, 1972. $6.95.

This novel combines authentic description with hair-raising suspense to open up for the reader a new area of modern science: surgical-computer mind control.

Psychosurgery is performed on a violent paranoid who has twice attempted to kill. A team of surgeons conducts a delicate operation, connecting 40 wires from the patient's brain to a microminiature computer implanted in his neck. It is the job of the computer to detect the start of a violent seizure and prevent it by stimulating a pleasure or calm node of the brain. The tension builds throughout the book from the initial conflict between the doctors to the final terrifying results when the patient escapes from the hospital before the computer program is tested.

Psychosurgery of the kind Crichton describes is already taking place in medical research centers today, thus making mind control a key scientific and moral issue of our time. Crichton takes it out of the realm of the abstract, and makes immediate its workings, its dangers, and its implications in a novel that provides urgent information and superb entertainment.

David H. Ahl
Morristown, NJ

* * *

The Electronic Criminals. Robert Farr. 194pp, $8.95. McGraw-Hill, New York, 1975.

Based on the author's experiences as a writer and as an expert in the field of computer fraud and industrial criminology, he details Ponzi schemes, technically sophisticated rip-offs, stock swindles, modern embezzlement methods, and out-and-out thefts using modern technology.

The Stanford Research Institute estimates that between 1967 and 1972 some 50,000 major crimes were committed worldwide with the technological assistance of computers, telecommunications devices, photocopy equipment, lasers, jet transportation, and so on. This broad spectrum of devices (with the exception of the jet aircraft) is covered in this book relegating computers, therefore, to a rather modest role.

From a sociological standpoint what is probably most interesting is the author's observation that such nefarious activities are a sign of the times. "More and more people freely admit, indeed positively boast, that they are not loyal to society and do not intend to serve its interests." This attitude is probably not new, but the openness in expressing it is. Indeed, for years our moral attitudes toward crime account for a peculiar ambivalence toward criminal behavior itself. On the one hand, it is feared, despised, and vigorously condemned. Yet it is also secretly admired, and we are always eager to hear the details of some outstanding criminal exploit. While not quite as lively as *The Godfather,* or *The Great Train Robbery, The Electronic Criminals* nevertheless will give you some insight into the emerging types of crimes, one of which almost assuredly by 2000 will have the title, "The Crime of the Century."

David H. Ahl
Morristown, NJ

* * *

Freedom's Edge: The Computer Threat To Society, by Milton R. Wessel, 137pp., $4.95. Addison-Wesley Publishing Company, 1974.

"A communications medium transmits messages. It also may affect the message itself.

"A computer system processes data. It also may affect the data itself. It is the theme of this book that when the computer's impact on the data is great enough, it changes the environment in which we live."

It is symptomatic that some people still insist that the time in which we are living be labeled "the atomic age" instead of "the computer age." Both technologies are approximately thirty years old, but while uses of atomic power are still almost nil, computers and data processing are so much a part of our world that we rarely even notice their existence. Therein lies a danger. Therein lies the threat to society.

In many ways computers are a unique invention; a general purpose invention. Computers do not simply affect one industry, nor one segment of society, nor one country. No aspect of our culture is left untouched: business, recreation, art, religion; they are all becoming computerized. Beside the influence of the computer, that of the omnipresent television set pales to insignificance. Perhaps in all of history only the invention of the printing press can compare in impact, and if you live in a large city you will find that the type in your daily newspaper is set by computer.

Milton Wessel is saying that we are right now tightrope walking on freedom's edge. The increase in use of computers is nothing short of phenomenal. In a very few years the pattern of the future will be set, and for the most

part *we do not realize what is happening to us.* Computer usage is so all-pervasive that only rarely does someone catch a glimpse of the whole picture and this is usually a trained professional, not the person in the street whose future is at stake.

Wessel's book is not technical in nature, but sociological. It is primarily a book of unanswered questions and very, very tentative suggestions. It is a quite readable book and assumes no technical expertise on the part of the reader. Wessel is himself not a computer professional but a lawyer. He has spent much time involved in the legal side-effects of a computerized society and much of what he has seen worries him.

Wessel is not opposed to computers. That is not the question at issue. Our modern lifestyle is absolutely dependent on the computer. Wessel is repeating a plea which has been raised many times in the past and is best summed up in the too often ignored motto of the Sierra Club: "Not blind opposition to progress, but opposition to blind progress." At this time the growing use of computers represents blind progress.

What we are blind to are the side-effects of computer usage. Most computer systems perform quite well the tasks they were designed to perform. But what else do they do? Wessel's point about a computer system affecting the very data it is processing is not a fear that some machiavellian computer is going to run amuck a la science fiction horror story. The point is that the very fact that the data is intended for computer processing will change that data; the manner in which it is collected, the manner in which it can be used, the manner in which it can interact with other data.

We have already seen this in the privacy issue; a data bank of personal information may have many uses other than the one for which it was explicitly designed. Other problems haunt the future. The computer credit card cashless society is almost upon us. It will be convenient. But it could also mean that a person cannot buy so much as a piece of bubble gum without that fact, and time and place of purchase, appearing in some data bank. Where were you at 7:23 p.m. the night of August 18, 1984? Hmmm, you were buying a copy of *Freedom's Edge.* Flag that person as a possible subversive!

Wessel gives many more examples, some less obvious, and raises many more questions, but they all boil down to one thing. When our society becomes one massive data processing system, will we be able to hold on to our individuality and our freedom? What if I do not *want* a computer credit card? Will I have a choice?

John Lees
Rolla, MO

* * *

Zen and the Art of Motorcycle Maintenance. Robert M. Pirsig. 406 pp. $2.25. Bantam Books, New York. 1974 (Paperback). Hardcover edition published by William Morrow & Co., Inc., New York. 1974. $7.95.

How, you might wonder, did a review of a book with a title like this get into *Creative Computing?* The reason is that this book has as much to say about computers as it does about either Zen Buddhism or motorcycle maintenance.

This is a novel, but is has more philosophical content than character development or plot. What it is primarily about is the relationship between people and machines. The main machine in the book is a motorcycle, but it could just as well be a computer. It is pretty obvious from reading the book that both Pirsig and his hero have dealt with computers, mainly from the technical writing end.

According to the author's view, there are two basic ways that humans understand their world and their machines. The "classical" way looks for the basic underlying forms while the "romantic" way looks mainly at the immediate appearances. Riding motorcycles is basically romantic and maintaining them is mainly classical. The romantic mode is "primarily inspirational, imaginative, creative. Intuitive feelings rather than facts predominate". The classical mode "proceeds by reason and by laws".

The main problem, as Pirsig sees it, is that these two modes of thought don't get along together. To the romantic, the classical mode seems "dull, awkward and ugly" and to the classical person, the romantic seems "frivolous, irrational, erratic, and untrustworthy,... shallow".

The big trouble arises because people tend "to think and feel exclusively in one mode or the other" and in doing so tend to misunderstand, not only each other, but one half of the world. If, suggests Pirsig, we could only go back and put both of these modes together, as they were before Plato and Aristotle broke them assunder to make Western Thinking and Western Civilization possible, we might be happier.

This book doesn't have much of a story line. A man and his son ride across the Western part of the U. S. on a motorcycle. The man has had a mental crack-up followed by electroshock therapy. Now he has trouble remembering his past, some of which he encounters along the way. That's about it at this level. But this is a book of ideas and, at this level, the three main characters are three basic ways of thinking about machines. In addition to the classical and romantic modes, there is the mode that looks, not just at the form and not just at the immediate appearance of things, but at something that Pirsig calls (misleadingly, I think) Quality. "The Quality he was talking about" writes Pirsig, "wasn't classic Quality or romantic Quality. It was beyond both of them". Frankly, it was beyond me too, but that probably is because I am hung up at the level of the classical-romantic dichotomy and can't get beyond it.

The second half of the book has this Quality as its major intellectual character and maybe this is why I found it so much less enjoyable than the first half. But Pirsig has more sensible things to say about the relationships between people and machines in the first half than a lot of books say in both halves. Don't let that title throw you.

Peter Kugel
Chestnut Hill, MA.

✳ ✳ ✳

The Eco-Spasm Report. By Alvin Toffler. $1.50 paper. Bantam Books, New York.

Despite the slightly erotic overtones of the title, our old friend of *Future Shock* fame is interested in economics rather than sex this time around. Toffler's book was written on his own authority at white heat in order to alert the reading public of the dire possibilities of the future. As he puts it in his wonderfully cliche-ridden style, "our world could end not with a bang or whimper but with an eco-spasm."

The eco-spasm evidently signifies the end of industrial society as we have known it, with a disintegration of our present economic organization regardless if it be capitalist or communist. Toffler visualizes our present recession and inflation as the warning symptoms of the emergence of a new post-industrial society evolving painfully into a super-industrial world which will still be technological but no longer industrial in its foundations. With the banking system falling apart and multinational corporations controlling ever increasing segments of the world economy, the specter of energy shortage arises to generate feelings of despair over the future. And indeed the situation is fraught with danger, but seer Toffler has the answers.

If the nations of the world will cooperate in creating transnational controls over global corporations and in acting to regulate energy shortages, a start toward a tolerable future can be made. Employment and economic policy making must take into account all facets of social change as well as the global effects of their decisions. But above all, Toffler stresses the need to convert participatory democracy into a reality in order to finally allow the peoples of the planet a meaningful voice in their destinies.

Toffler's book provides glib and often superficial answers to momentous questions, but if it sets people to thinking it may be a worthwhile contribution after all.

Norman Lederer
New York, NY

Computers In Society: The Wheres, Whys and Hows of Computer Use. Donald D. Spencer. 180pp. Hayden Book Company Incorporated, Rochelle Park, New Jersey.

Mr. Spencer, President of the Abacus Computer Corporation, presents a paperback describing basically what computers are, how and why they are being used, and what the future might bring. It is a non-technical treatment for the beginning student and layman of the applications of computers in a wide range of areas. None of the applications are in depth (but that is not the author's intent).

The main benefit to the reader is a description of what the computer does and can do in such areas as the Arts, Medicine, Law Enforcement, Business, Engineering, nd Education; what emerges is an appreciation for the impact of computers on society. The writing style is very readable — certainly non-technical; there is a conscious avoidance of jargon that plagues many areas (and especially alienates people to the computer profession). The illustrations are good. The plentiful cartoons are both amusing and pertinent to the text.

The book makes a point of a common fallacy of the media of blaming computers, rather than computer users, for "sensational" errors. Educating readers in this regard alone is a valuable contribution.

Appropriate for high school students, the book should be available to guidance counselors. Also as suggested reference material for beginning data processing students and as reading for computer appreciation courses. For these audiences, or for a layman seeking an overview, the book is highly recommended.

James A. Higgins
Binghamton, N. Y.

✳ ✳ ✳

Principles of Systems. Jay W. Forrester. 360 pp. $10.00 (paperback). Wright-Allen Press, Cambridge, Mass.
World Dynamics. Jay W. Forrester. 142 pp. $12.00. Wright-Allen Press, Cambridge, Mass. 1971.

It is the year 12,068 of the Galactic Era.

"...you will learn to apply psychohistory to all problems as a matter of course. — Observe." Seldon removed his calculator pad from the pouch at his belt. ... Red symbols glowed out from the gray.... "Put it into words. Forget the symbolism for a moment." "The Empire will vanish and all its good with it. Its accumulated knowledge will decay and the order it has imposed will vanish. Instellar wars will be endless; interstellar trade will decay; population will decline; worlds will lose touch with the main body of the Galaxy." ... "Enough. And what of the numerical probability of total destruction within five centuries?" ... "About 85%" ... "Not bad," said Seldon ...,"but not good. The actual figure is 92.5%"[1]

In 2024 AD the earth's population was just over seven billion and the quality of life was better than a hundred years previously. This was achieved through efforts in the midseventies to reduce the rate of pollution and the rate of natural resource usage while increasing both the rate of capital generation and the rate of food production. Unfortunately a catastrophe of unparalleled proportions occurred during the next thirty years. The population was decimated. By 2060 only a little over one billion people were still alive.

The first account is science fiction from Asimov's "Foundation". The second is a computer-generated prediction found in Forrester's "World Dynamics". Psychohistory is a figment of Asimov's imagination, but what of World Dynamics? Is it a powerful new tool to understanding or is it also science fiction?

The need for better tools to understand social, economic, business, and political systems has been evident for some time. When a law is passed, its actual effects are often quite different from the intended effects. After the initial novelty wears off, innovative programs in education are frequently found to be worse than the shortcomings they were designed to eliminate. Many public housing projects have deteriorated becoming more intolerable than the slums they replaced. In St. Louis it has even been necessary to demolish some of the worst after they were barely twenty years old. This situation is in stark contrast to that found in engineering and the natural sciences. As each Apollo flight blasted off to the moon, there was little real doubt that it would work. Although a hundred million dollar building or bridge may employ a new design, no one expects collapse. The few failures are the exception.

In the midfifties with the aid of a Ford Foundation grant, the Industrial Dynamics program was launched at MIT in order to reduce these disparities. The aim was the development of dynamic modeling techniques which would promote understanding and prediction in the social sciences. The first book evolving from this program, "Industrial Dynamics" by Jay W. Forrester, appeared in 1961. This was followed by several others, but it was not until the publication of Forrester's "World Dynamics" that the efforts were greeted by extensive coverage in the popular press. Most of the popular discussions actually centered on the book "The Limits to Growth" by Meadows, Meadows, Randers, and Behrens III which employed an improved version of the world dynamics model.

If one simply desires the results, then "The Limits to Growth" is the book to read. For those who want to understand the techniques, "World Dynamics" is the better book, though its model is more primitive. In the latter, knowledge of the systems dynamics approach is assumed. This background can best be acquired through "Principles of Systems".

"Principles of Systems" is an introduction to the terminology and techniques used to model dynamic systems. It begins by explaining the role of feedback loops in systems, and goes on in Chapter Two to discuss both positive and negative feedback loops of first and higher orders. These ideas are illustrated with a model explaining growth and saturation of sales. Unfortunately the model used is more complicated than it should be so early in the book.

In Chapter Three, the distinction between simulation and analytical solutions is made. Although it has been conceptually possible for many years to employ dynamic models in such areas as business, this has actually been attempted only since the development of economical computers. Without computers we must resort to hand simulations which are costly and lengthy or analytical solutions which can be hard to obtain.

In later chapters we learn general principles for developing dynamic models, the role of rates and levels, and the necessity of alternating rates and levels. The reader is shown how to express such models both as diagrams and as sets of equations.

Dynamic models are actually sets of coupled differential equations expressed in integral form. To solve these models we begin with the initial values of the variables. After choosing a suitable finite time interval, we evaluate the equations to obtain the values of the variables at the new time. This iteration continues until the behavior of the model is known during the relevant time span. Though the relationship between the dynamic models and differential equations is mentioned, the book is remiss in not including a chapter explaining how to translate between the two notations.

The flows within models are classified into conserved flows and information links. The importance of information as connecting tissue in systems is stressed. It is information which alters flow rates.

Numerous diagrams, graphs, and tables contained in the book do much to clarify the presentation. Over one half of the book is a workbook containing both problems and solutions. Many of the simulations are designed to be iterated by hand. The others are intended to be run on computer systems containing the DYNAMO compiler. Unfortunately, most people do not have easy access to such computers. Fortunately, it is fairly easy to translate the DYNAMO notation into computer languages such as BASIC. It would be helpful if the book included an explicit discussion of this procedure.[2] When undertaking such a task, it is important to write subroutines to carry out frequent calculations such as table interpolation and graphing.

The book was written for college students beginning their studies in the MIT systems dynamics program. It can be read profitably by anyone having at least a good understanding of high school algebra and familiarity with any of the popular programming languages.

This is a good introduction to modeling dynamic systems, but it can and should be updated as soon as possible. It has been around too many years as the second preliminary edition.

After reading "Principles of Systems", one is in a good position to understand "World Dynamics". "World Dynamics" is most useful if viewed not as a prediction of the future, but rather as an illustration of the procedure for constructing dynamic models. It is often surprising how few variables are required to simulate complicated systems. "World Dynamics" begins with a short discussion encouraging the use of models in understanding behavior. It then describes the actual model, and finally gives specific results.

The world model contains five levels: population, capital investment, natural resources, fraction of capital devoted to agriculture, pollution, and the rates controlling these levels. Since it is a highly aggregated model, factors such as geographical dispersion and transportation are not included. Although it is easy to offer suggestions for improving the model, such improvements also complicate the model. Once we understand modeling, it is always possible to construct more realistic models if we are seriously interested in the results.

Constituting over one fourth of the book, the third chapter, contains the dependence of the rates on the levels in both numerical and graphical form. The graphs are very helpful in visualizing these relationships.

The fourth chapter includes the actual results of the model. Most runs cover the time span from 1900 to 2100. The results are also displayed in graphical form. After exhibiting the basic model's behavior, a variety of alternative assumptions are explored. It is important to realize that this type of study does not give the best strategy, but illuminates the consequences of alternative strategies.

In the fifth chapter some obvious strategies are explored and are found wanting. Often strategies looking good in the short run have disastrous long term consequences.

For those seriously interested in dynamic models, appendices B and C are particularly helpful because they summarize the equations of the world model. These equations are designed to be run on a DYNAMO compiler, but, as previously mentioned, can be translated into BASIC or other languages with a modest effort. Such an effort probably gives a far better insight into the structure of dynamic models than simply running the model on a DYNAMO compiler.

The style is readable and the book is well laid out. There are a few minor errors. For example, the rate controlling the level capital-investment-in-agriculture fraction is missing from the complete system diagram. This book can be read and understood by anyone who has read "Principles of Systems".

Should these books be bought? Yes, even though they are slightly overpriced. As computers become cheaper and faster, we can expect greater use of dynamic models. These models will become a more integral part of the decision making process on all levels. Bad models will always give unreliable results even though they are computerized. Our best hope for preventing abuse of these models is an informed population understanding both their power and their limitations.

William H. Rybolt
Babson Park, MA.

[1] Asimov, Isaac, *Foundation*. Avon Books, New York, N. Y. 1971.
[2] Anderson, Jay Martin, *Dynamic Modelling Using FORTRAN IV*. In *Creative Computing*, May—June 1975, p. 59.

CREATIVE COMPUTING
Feature Review

34 Books on BASIC

Stephen Barrat Gray
Gray Engineering Consultants
260 Noroton Ave.
Darien, Conn. 06820

The first book about BASIC was published on the first day of 1966. Four years later only eight more on BASIC had been published, and there was little difficulty in choosing between them, especially since several weren't very well known.

As the use of BASIC grew, so did the number of books on the subject, until today there are nearly three dozen and, for several years, up until 1974, they were being published at the rate of one every two months.

Choosing a book on BASIC is not so easy now, whether for one's own reading or for class use. The task is only slightly simplified, and only for certain prospective users, by these 34 books falling into several categories: two are very simple, for children in the lower grades; six are limited in coverage, meant to give a solid foundation in elementary BASIC; and three use BASIC as part of a book (or set of books) on the larger subject of data-processing. But that still leaves 23 to pick from. Hopefully, this "group review" will make the choice a little simpler.

The Reason Why

This article had its origins several years ago while, in addition to being the corporate EDP communicator, I was managing a small time-sharing installation. Interested in learning all I could about BASIC, I began to collect the various books on the subject. After getting a dozen together, the feeling grew that a group review of all such books might be of interest to those looking for one or two that would best suit their needs.

This group review is not a scholarly dissertation, but hopes to be of help to those looking for a BASIC text for study or for use in the classroom. If it fails in this, then perhaps it can be considered as a reasonably accurate chronological bibliography of all the books in English on BASIC.

THE AUTHOR

Stephen B. Gray first became acquainted with data-processing as a field-service engineer with IBM, after which he wrote maintenance manuals for airline-reservation computers at Teleregister (now Bunker-Ramo). Five years as the computers editor of *Electronics* magazine at McGraw-Hill were followed by several at General Electric, supervising the writing of manuals for the 115 and 130 computers. He next became editor of John Diebold's *ADP Newsletter,* and then editor of American-Standard's corporate EDP newsletter and manager of their time-sharing installation. He is now an EDP consultant and writer, and is the editor of a technical consumer magazine. In 1966 he founded the Amateur Computer Society, and publishes its newsletter for an international membership of people who are building a digital computer as a hobby.

The Authors

These 34 books were written by at least 52 authors, nearly all of whom are college professors, or teachers in private schools. As for the others (at the time of the books' publication), Albrecht (14, 28 32) is with Dymax (part of the People's Computer Company), Barnett (23) is with TRW Systems, Farina (3 13) with General Electric, Keenan (12) with the National Science Foundation, Sack (27) is at Amdahl Corp., Smith (10 30) is with Control Data, and Spencer (6) is president of Abacus Computer Corp. No affiliation is given for Pavlovich (18) or for Stern & Stern (34). Two of the authors are students: Kaufman (33) and Tahan (18). The authors of two books are unknown: General Electric (15) and NCTM (4).

A few authors, including Farina (3 13) and Sack & Meadows (27) dive headlong into BASIC and shout "Come on in, the water's fine." The majority swim with varying degrees of enthusiasm in waters of various depths and temperatures. Some stand on dry land, point to the pool, and say "It's over there." Gruenberger (25) and Hare (8) say, in effect, that although BASIC may be fine for schoolchildren, there's nothing for a real man like the strong surf of FORTRAN.

The biggest problem for many authors is an apparent inability to put themselves in the reader's shoes, and write for the average beginner. All too often a program is presented without enough previous discussion of the statements and the programming techniques involved to allow the reader to readily understand the program. This "too much too soon" problem is severe enough in several books to make some average readers simply give up in bewilderment. Many of these books seem to have been written with the top student in mind, by authors who either don't realize that most readers are starting at zero, or who seem to assume that the reader is as smart as the writer. Three books in point are by Smith (10 30) and Gruenberger (25), who give the textual impression of being eccentric geniuses; under firm editorial control, their considerable talents could have produced outstanding books, rather than fascinating curiosities, best opened after mastering one or two less convoluted texts.

Some will argue that many of these books need to be used in a classroom, with a teacher to explain the hard parts and to fill in the gaps. Indeed, some of the texts seem written with the expectation that someone will be on hand to do just that.

The Writing

Nearly all the authors are ·in the academic world. No doubt several are brilliant in front of a class. But little of this brilliance appears in the rather pedestrian prose of most of these texts.

Although it can be argued that these works are not novels and thus there is no point in trying to achieve any particular literary style, nevertheless there is quite a difference in wading through the still waters of some authors' works, and in dipping into the sparkling brook of Farina's writing (3, 13), the careful detailed prose of Kemeny & Kurtz (2), the enthusiasm and flair of Dwyer & Kaufman (33), or the clear, flowing style of Sack & Meadows (27).

Feature Review of Books on Basic

	Title	Author	Publisher
1.	BASIC, Sixth Edition	Waite and Mather	University Press of N. E.
2.	BASIC Programming	Kemeny and Kurtz	Wiley
3.	Programming in BASIC	Farina	Prentice Hall
4.	Introduction to an Algorithmic Language (BASIC)	(no author)	NCTM
5.	Introduction to Computing Through BASIC Language	Nolan	Holt, Rinehart & Winston
6.	A Guide to BASIC Programming	Spencer	Addison-Wesley
7.	Problem-Solving With The Computer	Sage	Entelek
8.	Introduction to Programming: A BASIC Approach	Hare	Harcourt-Brace
9.	BASIC For Beginners	Gateley and Bitter	McGraw-Hill
10.	Discovering BASIC	Smith	Hayden
11.	Basic BASIC	Coan	Hayden
12.	Computer Science: BASIC Language Programming	Forsythe, et al.	Wiley
13.	Elementary BASIC With Applications	Farina	Prentice-Hall
14.	Teach Yourself BASIC	Albrecht	Tecnica
15.	Time Sharing's BASIC Language		General Electric
16.	BASIC Programming	Murrill and Smith	Intext
17.	BASIC: An Introduction to Computer Programming . . .	Sharpe and Jacob	Free Press
18.	Computer Programming in BASIC	Pavlovich and Tahan	Holden-Day
19.	An Introduction to the BASIC Language	Skelton	Holt, Rinehart & Winston
20.	Basic BASIC: Self-Instructional Manual	Peluso, et al.	Addison-Wesley
21.	BASIC Programming for Business	Sass	Allyn & Bacon
22.	Fundamental Programming Concepts	Gross and Brainerd	Harper & Rowe
23.	Programming Time-Shared Computers in BASIC	Barnett	Wiley
24.	Introducing BASIC	Blakeslee	Educomp
25.	Computing with the BASIC Language	Gruenberger	Canfield Press
26.	Business Programming with BASIC	Diehr	Wiley
27.	Entering BASIC	Sack and Meadows	SRA
28.	My Computer Likes Me	Albrecht	Dymax
29.	Elements of BASIC	Lewis and Blakeley	NCC
30.	A Visual Approach to BASIC	Smith	CDC
31.	BASIC, A Computer Programming Language . . .	Pegels	Holden-Day
32.	BASIC	Albrecht, Finkel & Brown	Wiley
33.	A Guided Tour of Computer Programming in BASIC	Dwyer and Kaufman	Houghton Mifflin
34.	Principles of Data Processing	Stern and Stern	Wiley

Review Copy Not Received —
	Interactive Computing in BASIC	Sanderson	Butterworth

Not Reviewed —
	BASIC In Ten Minutes	Hoitsma	Dartmouth
	School BASIC	Weissman	Dartmouth

The books are given an overall A-B-C-D rating. Ten are excellent, and rate an A. Ten more are very good, for a B. Another ten are average, C. Two are poor, getting a D. Two get split ratings: one gets an A for the first half of the book, a C for the second half; the other book rates a B+ for classroom use, but only a c- for the solitary reader.

Some authors chop their texts into very brief chapters, perhaps feeling that the reader's attention span may be very short for such material; Skelton (19), for example, has 12 chapters in 158 pages, with a 2½-page chapter on READ and DATA alone. Other cram quite a number of statements into each chapter, usually in related groups. Sass (21) has only nine chapters in 310 pages, and Barnett (23) has eight chapters in 366 pages.

Only eight of the books introduce string constants and variables at the same time as numeric constants and variables, rather than later in the text, or not at all.

Several of the authors are more terminal-oriented than others, and discuss the Teletype within the first half-dozen pages: Albrecht et al (32), Dymax (28), Pavlovich & Tahan (18), Pegels (31), Spencer (6) and Sass (21).

In ten of the books, INPUT is introduced before DATA, perhaps to emphasize the interactive nature of BASIC.

Several authors, or perhaps it was their publishers, have padded their books with a great deal of white space, blank pages, and meaningless appendixes. Several other authors, notably the anonymous ones of the 53-page NCTM booklet (4), have managed to cram more into each page than have the writers of many of the much longer books.

No Standardization

Comparing any two or three of these books with each other shows that there is no standardization in even the simplest features of BASIC. Most authors are divided between, for example, IF-THEN and IF/THEN; a couple use IF . . . THEN. Some authors write Basic, others BASIC. Waite & Mather (1) use the phrases "loop variable" and "running variable"; others call it the counter, index, control variable, index of a loop, or control identifier. Over half the books have no name for it at all, other than simply "I." Only Gross & Brainerd (22) distinguish between brackets and parentheses; Dwyer & Kaufman (33) also use both, but don't say why.

Three books mention one statement each that no others include: APPEND, PAUSE, and TYP.

The Programs

Most of the authors begin by presenting programs on a slow-and-easy basis, starting with no more than 2 to 5 lines, and building up from there. Kemeny & Kurtz (2) start with a 5-liner on page 1; NCTM (4) opens with a 2-liner. Gruenberger (25) is one of the few mavericks in this respect; he seems to believe in the sink-or-swim theory, and starts off with an 11-line program on page 2. Even though every line has a paragraph of explanation, the program is too difficult for many readers.

Farina, in his earlier book (3), is one of the few authors to keep all his programs short; the longest one contains 14 lines. The longest in NCTM (4) is 15 lines; in Peluso et al (2) it is 13, except for two longer ones; Stern & Stern (34) have only two over 15 lines; Gateley & Bitter (9), only two over 13 lines long. Even the 63-page Dymax (28) has programs 28 lines long.

A number of authors work their way up into some very long and overly complex programs, most of them too complicated for many beginners; these include Smith (10 30), Gross & Brainerd (22), Sharpe & Jacob (17), Nolan (5) and Hare (8).

Only a few authors go into the different levels of programming languages. Sack & Meadows (27) and Murrill & Smith (16) do a little, Hare (8) and Nolan (5) do more (2½ pages each), and Gross & Brainerd (22) do quite well by the subject, with 5½ pages.

Two authors discuss the history of time-sharing: Sass (21) and Spencer (6) take two pages each.

Sage (7) is the only author to use the expression "falling through" and to explain the principle thoroughly.

Most of the authors spread the teaching of the elements of BASIC over most of the length of their books. But there are some others who prefer to devote the major portion of their book to applications. For instance, Sage (7) has only 65 of 244 pages on the elements of BASIC; in Gross & Brainerd (22), BASIC is covered in the first 68 of the 304 pages; and Kemeny & Kurtz (2) spend only 43 of their 150 pages on the essentials.

There are a few contradictions between one book and another. For instance, Forsythe et al (12) have a section in the first chapter on testing a program, with a number of suggestions, including "When this experimental approach fails to reveal the trouble . . . . Another technique called *tracking* then becomes very helpful . . . . It is done by inserting PRINT statements at selected points in a program being tested." But Gruenberger (25) has a different viewpoint: "Warning: as a debugging tool, tracing is to be regarded as a last-ditch resort, and should never be used casually. Using a tool as crude as tracing for debugging is the mark of a poor programmer." That may well be true of an experienced programmer, but a beginner needs all the help he can get.

Only four texts show concern for the esthetics of programming. Blakeslee (24) puts it one way, "SERMON: Always remember the poor sucker who has to use the output of a program you write; keep it neat, keep it simple. That poor sucker could be you!" Gruenberger (25) notes that allowing a program to end in OUT OF DATA ON LINE XXX is "not the most graceful way to terminate a program." Sharpe & Jacob (17) say that a printout without headings is "hardly every elegant output." Waite & Mather (1), practical as always, not only note that a program ending in OUT OF DATA "does not yield an attractive printout," but add that it "prevents taking any action *after* the program discovers that it has run out of data."

Also in the realm of esthetics, although more on the side of readibility, are the suggestions in five of the books to use blank lines to "divide visually the major sections of a program," as Waite & Mather (1) put it. Seven books indent the statements inside a loop, between a FOR-NEXT pair.

Flowcharts, Indexes, and Tutorials

Not many authors are big on flowcharts; Kemeny & Kurtz (2), for instance, have only three in the whole book. Sage (7) and Smith (10) have flowcharts for every program example, and Peluso et al (2) have for most of their programs. Sass (21) has the most complex flowcharts, with Smith (10) not far behind. Others who make frequent use of flowcharts are Coan (11), Nolan (5), Lewis & Blakeley (29) and, above all, Forsythe et al (12), to whom flowcharting is everything.

Few authors seem to understand the art of indexmanship, as most have only a few pages; Barnett (23), for instance, has five pages of index. The one exception is Hare (8), whose index is a full 18 pages long. Four books have no index: Dymax (28), General Electric (15), NCTM (4) and Smith (10).

A few indexes must have been computer-generated, because they have some references to subjects that are mentioned only very briefly in the text, and which nobody would probably ever want to look up. The Gross & Brainerd (22) index lists "coconut" and "animal, carnivorous," while Kemeny & Kurtz (2) list "Oz, Land of."

Hare also has the longest glossary: 16 pages. Nolan (5) has 11½ pages, Sass (21) has 8, and Spencer (6) has five pages of glossary.

Seven of the books have authors who think enough of their programs to have separate indexes of them, by title and page number.

Most texts assume that the reader knows enough about the various areas of mathematics to need no tutoring, but several others devote sizable numbers of pages to teaching math, including nine pages on matrices and ten on trigonometry in Pavlovich and Tahan (18).

more

Exercises and Problems

All the books have exercises (some call them problems) that require writing programs, except for the General Electric programmed-instruction text (15). The "self-instruction" text by Peluso et al (20) has question-and-answer exercises, plus an appendix containing practice problems that require programs to be written. A few other texts require a minimum of program-writing. Skelton (19) has exercises that require modifying given programs and writing short subroutines. Waite & Mather (1), being a user's manual, has no problems or exercises of any kind.

There is a wide variety of ways of presenting problems and answers. Some books, such as Sharpe & Jacob (17) have problems at the end of each chapter, with all answers given. Sack & Meadows (27) give answers to selected problems at the end of each chapter. Kemeny & Kurtz (2) give no answers to the end-of-chapter problems.

Many authors provide exercises after each new idea (or group of new ideas); among these, Coan (11) gives answers to the even-numbered exercises, Sass (21) gives answers to selected ones, and Gross & Brainerd (22) give none.

A few books have only questions and answers, such as the General Electric text (15). There are very many Q&A in Stern & Stern (34) and all too many, 396 of them, in Diehr (26). Some readers like a good many questions, to help reinforce their learning; others will prefer more text or more programming problems and fewer questions.

Although most of the authors provide problems or exercises that are quite satisfactory, most of these are straightforward mathematics problems. This is fine for most readers, but for the younger ones, and perhaps also for those of us who get bored easily, several authors have out of their way to provide problems of unusual interest. Albrecht et al (32) have problems, for example, on generating "computer art," Barnett (23) on computing the (x y, z) position of a satellite, Dwyer & Kaufman (33) on an airline reservation system, and Kemeny & Kurtz (2) on writing four-part harmony for a given melody.

Handsome Is . . .

Not every good-looking BASIC book is also good reading. On one hand, the three handsomest single-volume works — Kemeny & Kurtz (2), Gateley & Bitter (9), and Barnett (23) — rate highly as useful taxes in addition to having excellent typography and layout. Also to be listed among the good-looking books are those by Sharpe & Jacobs (17), Pavlovich & Tahan (18), Gross & Brainerd (22), and Dwyer & Kaufman (33).

But the two handsome multiple-volume sets — Forsythe et al (12) and Stern & Stern (34) — have BASIC supplements that rate poorly, although Stern & Stern's main text and workbook give an excellent coverage of data processing.

Any bound book is difficult to use comfortably at the Teletype or other terminal. The first version of the earlier Smith book (10) was loose-leaf, so that individual pages (of heavy stock) could be removed for use at a terminal. The problem there, of course, was that those removable pages could be lost.

Most of the books use several type styles, but some overdo it, with up to seven in some cases, so that many pages are very distracting, as in the books by Ivan Flores. Hare (8), Murrill & Smith (16) and Albrecht et al (32) use up to seven typefaces on some pages, Spencer (6) has up to six, and Dymax (28) and Gruenberger (25) have as many as five. Dwyer & Kaufman (33) also use as many as seven, but in a way that isn't anywhere nearly as obtrusive as the others, which is one more tribute to the fine design of this book.

Half the authors show programs in Teletype originals (and many should have put a new ribbon on the machine); the rest use typed or machine-set examples. Two of the authors — Smith (10) and Coan (11) — give examples to problems requiring programs, in the back of the book, in Teletype originals reduced so greatly as to be eye-straining. Lewis & Blakeley (29), for some reason, show their Teletyped programs much smaller than necessary, even though there is plenty of room for them to be shown much bigger.

The size of each book is given because the number of pages alone is deceiving. Many of the smaller books contain over 300 pages, but contain less text than some larger books with many less pages. The most popular size is 6 by 9 inches, with 15 books at or near those dimensions. Second most popular is 8½ by 11 inches, with a dozen that size.

Eight of the authors are sinners in the eyes of Teletype Corp., because they write "teletype." No doubt all have been cautioned by Teletype's eagle-eyed legal department.

Personal Preferences

If I were limited to choosing only one book from these 34, it would be Kemeny & Kurtz (2), which is still the standard of excellence by which all the others must be judged. Waite & Mather (1) give all the nitty-gritty details. Then come, in order of preference, Barnett (23), Murrill & Smith (16), Dwyer & Kaufman (33), and Gross & Brainerd (22).

If a friend were to ask for a recommendation, it would be, again, Kemeny & Kurtz (2), if he wanted only to learn BASIC. For someone wanting to know about computers and BASIC, then it's Hare (8). If he wanted to learn about BASIC and business programming, I'd recommend Stern & Stern (34) for their main text and workbook, plus one of the five BASIC books listed above.

For any young person, or as a matter of fact for almost anybody, I'd recommend Dwyer & Kaufman (33), who do their best to make learning fun.

> For a future group review of books on applications of BASIC, I would appreciate information concerning such publications. This would include not only books such as Peckham's *Computers, BASIC and Physics*, but also applications books not oriented toward any particular language, but which could be used with BASIC, such as Gruenberger & Gaffrey's *Problems for Computer Solution*.
>
> Also appreciated is information about books on BASIC in languages other than English.

1. *BASIC, Sixth Edition*, edited by Stephen V. F. Waite and Diane G. Mather. In print Mar. 19, 1971, University Press of New England, Hanover, N. H., 183 pages, 8½ x 11, $4.00 (paperback).

The first BASIC user's manual, and still the best, although it describes an advanced version of BASIC. Rating: A

The first few editions of this user's manual were authored by John G. Kemeny and Thomas E. Kurtz, the originators of BASIC; the more recent editions carry the names of the editors.

According to Prof. Kurtz, the first draft of the BASIC instruction manual appeared in June 1964. The third edition was published on Jan. 1, 1966. ("Whatever happened to the second edition, I'll never know. I *think* we started counting editions with number three, and chose that number just to be on the safe side.") The date of the fourth edition is Jan. 1, 1968; Version I of the supplement, Feb. 28, 1969; Version II, April 3, 1969; the preliminary fifth edition, 1969, the fifth edition, 1970. The sixth edition, 1971; second printing, 1972.

According to the British book, *Specification for Standard BASIC*, by Bull, Freeman and Garland (National Computing Centre, London, 1973), "the first implementation was on a GE 265 system in 1964. The first issue of the programming manual from Dartmouth College (hitherto this and subsequent updates were the only definitive documents on BASIC) was in January 1965 . . . By January 1966, the third edition of the manual was published."

Of all the 34 books, this is the only user's manual on BASIC, with all the details, enough to satisfy the most inquisitive time-sharer. However, many of the advanced statements will be unknown and useless to any reader who does not have access to one of the five systems now using BASIC VI: Dartmouth, Annapolis (the Naval Academy), Computer Sharing Services in Denver, Grumman Data Systems on Long Island, and Polycom Systems in Toronto. Nevertheless, it is still valuable and fascinating, not only for its complete description of "standard" BASIC, but for showing us what can be done with some very interesting (and tantalizing) extensions to the standard language. It shows how extensive and powerful BASIC can be, especially when one reads the sections on FILES and segmentation.

The book is printed from typed originals, but is so crammed with valuable information that the reader easily overlooks the difficulty, if any, of reading typed pages. The programs are reproduced from Teletype originals.

There are ten chapters: introduction, BASIC primer (12 statements, loops), more about BASIC, files, segmentation, arrays, the TEACH system, debugging and compiling, error messages and other information (ASCII character set, accuracy and timing considerations), and a summary of BASIC.

The book starts right off with a 10-line program, a simple one on bank balance, with two and a half pages of explanation. There are four BANK programs, each one expanding and improving on the previous one, building up to a 33-line program by page 14. There are also five blank lines in BANK-4, "to divide visually the major sections of the program" and "greatly enhance the appearance and readibility of the program." Only four other books do this: Kemeny & Kurtz (2), Barnett (23), Diehr (26) and Dymax (28). Some program lines are indented, mostly those inside a loop.

The authors say "The technique of ending a program by having it run out of data is very simple and efficient. However, it does not yield an attractive printout and prevents taking any action *after* the program discovers that it has run out of data." Several other authors make note of the esthetic point, but none remark on the practical point.

The book abounds with unique nuggets that no other authors mention. "If the FROM, TO, and STEP elements of the FOR statement form an impossible combination . . . the body of the loop will not be performed and the computer will proceed immediately to the statement following the next." Another: "A step size of zero . . . in any loop where a positive step size is needed will cause an infinite loop."

The book is the only one that tells how to overprint, by using the carriage-return character, CH$(13).

There is a long, full and excellent description of FILES, 25 pages of it. There are 15 pages on error messages, some of which are very intriguing, such as ILLEGAL TREE CLIMBING, OUT OF ROOM, and UNDERFLOW.

As examples of the goodies available with this version of BASIC, there are eight special characters for defining PRINT USING fields or areas where variables are to be printed, and twelve commands for debugging, such as BREAK and TRACE.

The negative points are few and far between. Where every other system uses RESTORE, this one uses RESET. No examples are given to show the results of simple MAT operations. And no example is given of TEACH, an instructor's test program, although the chapter on the TEACH system is 4½ pages long. Very little information is given about RND, only three-quarters of a page.

This book, then, is excellent as a reference, or for reading if you want to know all there is to know about BASIC; BASIC VI, that is. Or to read after working with BASIC awhile, as this book will tell a beginner much more than he may want to know. The book covers (or so it seems) every last possible detail, and has a highly authoritative ring to it, which is only natural. Perhaps because of its extensive treatment of the language, the books, several authors and editors seem to have more of a sense of the "big picture" than all the others.

✳ ✳ ✳

BASIC: An Inttroduction to Computer Programming Using the BASIC Language, by William F. Sharpe. Pub. Aug. 1967, by The Free Press, div. of Macmillan, New York, N. Y., 137 pages, 6¾ x 10, paperback.
(Out of print, superseded by a revised edition, by Sharpe & Jacob (17).)

Sharpe published the first BASIC text. As he recounted recently, Sharpe had gotten an early user's manual and the specs from Dartmouth, and wrote a Fortran IV compiler for batch-mode BASIC, called UWBIC (University of Washington BASIC Interpretive Compiler). For a text to use in his classes, he wrote this book, and sent the manuscript to eight publishers. All eight said it was nice and well done, but only four showed an interest in publishing it. The other four said there was no market for a book on BASIC.

✳ ✳ ✳

2. *BASIC Programming,* by John G. Kemeny and Thomas E. Kurtz. Second edition pub. June 18, 1971 (first edition pub. Oct. 20, 1967), by John Wiley & Sons, New York, N. Y., 150 pages, 8½ x 11, $7.75 (paperback).
Not the first text, but the best, on almost all counts. Rating: A+

A winner when it first came out, often imitated but only partially equalled (and seldom, even that), this book has been improved and enlarged in its second edition.

The modest authors make no reference to having been the originators of BASIC, although the publisher does so on the back cover. Even though Kemeny and Kurtz may be said to have an inside track, the excellence of this book is due rather to the authors' "simple, gradual introduction to computer programming and to the use of time-sharing systems," as the back cover puts it, plus the most careful attention to every detail, covering all the bases and leaving as few questions unanswered as possible. Although there are many fine features, the outstanding one is the immense care taken to ensure that the reader will have a minimum of difficulty in learning BASIC.

Several BASIC books have summaries of the statements on the inside cover; this is the earliest of three with examples of each included.

The preface spells out the background requirements for the various portions of the book: chapters 8 to 12 and 18 "may be mastered with a background of three years of high school mathematics." Chapters 15 to 17 "consider three mathematical areas [statistics, vectors and matrices, calculus] that are normally taught at the college level."

The first chapter (numbered zero because it is new to this edition) is a simple introduction, with a few paragraphs on what is a computer, what is a program, what is BASIC, and how a computer is used.

The first page of Chapter One, on Elementary BASIC, presents a five-line program that divides one constant by another. This is explained in four paragraphs. The second program is 17 lines long, converts meters and centimeters to feet and inches. Over a page and a half of explanation follow (and these are large pages), covering every detail more thoroughly than any other author on any program in any of these books; the runner-up is the Waite & Mather book (1), which was originally written by Kemeny & Kurtz. This second program uses the INT statement, which most authors don't introduce until later; it is explained neatly and completely in four sentences.

There is a short summary at the end of each chapter, followed by a dozen or so exercises that are quite sensible, and some even include hints. But there are no answers.

After the elementary chapter is one on Time Sharing, covering What is Time Sharing, commands, interaction in

BASIC, editing and correcting. Two sentences describe the purpose of an executive program, while other authors usually make a big deal out of it (although very few others even mention it).

The subject of loops is considered important enough to be worth the entire third chapter, five pages. Here the book begins to get a little difficult for those who are not mathematically oriented, with a program that computes binomial coefficients. The authors "use the convention of indenting instructions between a FOR-NEXT pair," which only six other books do. "This clearly shows the scope of a loop. The convention is particularly useful when nested loops occur, such as the double loop in ROOTS." Double loops are then illustrated with a neat 9-line program.

Page 19 contains the only example in this book of an author tooting his own horn, ". . . and then determines the cell of the tally list N in a very ingenious way in line 150."

In the fourth chapter, on Lists and Tables, DIM is introduced very casually, without fanfare or a long-winded lead-in, as is often the case elsewhere.

In chapter five on Functions and Subroutines there are no individual examples, although there are several short programs that include six of the ten standard functions listed.

The unique and excellent method of demonstrating rounding-off goes through each part of the argument of the INT statement to show how it affects the number involved. This is not an easy concept for many readers to understand, yet the authors have managed to find what must be the simplest way of explaining it.

Page 29 contains one of the few chinks in the armor: a program not explained. The reader is expected to know Euclid's Algorithm for finding the greatest common divisor of two integers.

Page 36 contains the most complex program so far, an Eternal Calendar, 54 lines, but this is not impossible for one without a head for math to figure out.

The chapter on Debugging goes into tracing, and is the only book to describe both "full trace" and "selective trace."

Part Two, on applications, begins on page 47, with chapters on problems from elementary mathematics, number theory, simulation, games, business, files, text processing, statistics, vectors and matrices, calculus, and "special topics."

The chapter on number theory is where the book really begins to get difficult for all but math majors. The problem on the greatest common divisor isn't all that difficult, but the next one is, on modular arithmetic, using the Chinese remainder theorem. The rest of the chapter isn't any easier, with a counting problem (making change) being rather difficult, even with the explanation, which could be longer, but perhaps would have to be much too long for non-math-majors.

The next chapter, on simulation, eases off somewhat, and contains an explanation of RND that is simple and easy to grasp, and is better done than elsewhere. The chapter contains a baseball program that simulates the batting of one side in a nine-inning game; this is rather complex for all but the top-IQ types. The Knight's Tour problem is also rather difficult for a beginner's book.

With the chapter on Business Problems, the book goes back to something less than difficult. Many other authors would put those complex chapters (on number theory, simulation, and games) at the end of the book, so as not to discourage a reader who is only halfway through.

The chapter on Files is the only one among these books that distinguishes between Teletype files and numeric-and-string files, with a compact little table to summarize the differences.

The chapter on Statistics goes into contingency tables, using the chi-square test; both are introduced nicely, understandable even to those not majoring in mathematics, although there is no explanation of "number of degrees of freedom." The cahpter also contains a section giving A Ranking Procedure, with an explanation that is rather murky.

The text of the chapter on Vectors and Matrices is a little too loose to be readily understandable; the text accompanying the problem on electrical networks is not at all understandable to other than electrical engineers; the section on Markov Chains is not very well explained and both runs give data that is difficult to identify.

The chapter on Calculus is for math majors only, or for those with a knowledge of advanced math.

All the applications chapters contain, after the exercises at the end of each chapter, one or more projects that present more complex problems than do the exercises. These are all well thought out, and should provide the reader who has access to the terminal with a very thorough workout of his knowledge of the language, as well as, in many cases, his knowledge of (and aptitude for) mathematics.

The last section of the book is on Harmony in Music, giving a long program that writes four-part harmony for a given melody. The three projects for this chapter involve preparing a program to generate simple melodies randomly, generating poetry randomly, and devising programs to produce artistic patterns "on whatever plotting devices are available," with a number of helpful hints.

The program index at the end of the book is unique: for each of the 107 programs in the book, it gives the name, application, and page. The main index must have been computer-generated, as there are several trivial entries, including Ramanujan and "Oz, Land of."

As for drawbacks, the main one is that there are no answers to the exercises. The book contains only three flowcharts. The reader with only a modest mathematical background may have difficulty with the chapters on number theory, simulation, and games. REM is seldom used, although the authors say in a footnote that "REM statements are not always used in the programs in this book because all the programs are amply discussed in the text."

There are very few individual examples of statements and commands in this text; however, many sample programs make up for this by showing the statements and commands in use.

All in all, this is the best book on the subject at this level, even better in its second edition than the first.

The second edition inserts a five-line program as the first one in the book, before the 17-line one, to further simplify the beginning. These programs, and all the others in the book, were rerun for the second edition. A few blank lines have been added to separate groups of statements in programs not previously so treated.

The chapter on timesharing has been moved up from fifth to second place, and increased from two and a half pages to over four. Also added is a section on Commands in Time Sharing, and information on eight editing commands. The chapter on functions and subroutines has a new section on standard functions and multiple-line definitions.

The chapter on loops opens the same, but a new program has been inserted as the first one, on permutations and combinations. Several new exercises have been added at the end of the chapter, and some of the others have been reworded; this holds also for some other chapters.

The sixth chapter, on Alphabetic Information, is new to the second edition, and is all about strings. The first chapter on applications drops the section on Large-Number Arithmetic, which is a good idea, as it required a long and complex program. Replacing it is the Counting Problem, on making change, which is much easier to understand and to appreciate. The chapter on business problems adds a section on Critical Path Analysis.

The two new chapters in the applications part of the book are on Files and on Text Processing (line editing, character handling, constructing an index, codes).

The last chapter, Special Topics, eliminates the section on Teaching Machines, along with its teaching program. In its place is the complicated Marriage Rules in Primitive Societies, not as interesting but perhaps more indicative of what is being run on computers these days. The section on A Model From Ecology is the same, with one interesting change. In the first edition, the program output is a graph, plotted on a Teletype. In the second edition, the graph is made by an X-Y plotter. Three projects have been added at the end of this chapter, using the computer to generate melodies, poetry, and artistic patterns.

✳ ✳ ✳

3. *Programming in BASIC, The Time-Sharing Language*, by Mario V. Farina. Pub. Feb. 1968, by Prentice-Hall, Englewood Cliffs, N. J., 164 pages, 8½ x 11, $7.50 (paperback).

Slow but sure approach, in one of the best of the elementary texts. Rating: A

On one hand, the preface states that the book is intended for engineers and computer-programming students, as well as "programmers who need an easy-to-use language for checking out programs written in a more difficult programming language."

On the other hand, the book is designed like a primer, with short paragraphs of only one to three sentences, spaced a line apart, which spreads out the material and makes it so easy to read that this would be an excellent book for secondary schools.

The opening is on a high-school level: "Do you have problems? Do those problems involve repetitive calculations using a desk calculator or a slide rule? Why not have a computer help solve your problems? It's easy!"

The first program has five lines, multiplies one constant by another and adds a third to that. Widely spaced, the five lines take 1 5/8 inches of vertical space, the most "spaced-out" of any of these books. The programs are all in the same type as the text.

There are simple exercises at the end of each lesson, with "answers to selected exercises" at the back of the book.

The approach is slow but sure, with everything covered, leaving little if anything to the imagination. This is one of the best of the elementary BASIC texts, by a born teacher whose later book (13) has an even better style.

Each chapter takes quite a few pages to present a limited amount of material. Lesson 1 has a five-line program and a long explanation of it, then goes into legal names. Lesson 2, on What Is BASIC, is about writing equations, using LET. Lesson 3 goes into Teletype time-sharing, covering commands and shows a drawing of the keys and buttons of a model 33 Teletype. Lesson 4 is on flowcharting and is the longest chapter in the book, 14 pages that proceed very slowly and carefully, covering all the bases.

The style is conversational and light: "Of course, any names you choose would be OK, but names chosen should remind you what they stand for." There is a great deal of white space, such as half an inch of it above and below examples of program lines.

Lessons 5 through 11 are on: telling the computer about numbers, exponential notation, telling the computer what to do with numbers, built-in functions, making decisions, having the computer print out answers, and arrays and subscripts. Lessons 12, 13 and 14 are all on loops, a total of 24 pages.

Lesson 14, on Loops Within Loops, is 14 pages of the most explicit of all these books on this particular subject, and also goes into double-subscripted arrays, using the "loop-within-loop idea to set to 50 all elements of a double-subscripted array." This chapter is about as complicated as the book gets. Lesson 15, on Matrix Computations, has no examples of what MAT statements actually do to a matrix. This is the only chapter that could perhaps be improved, by having such examples, although their omission is in keeping with the secondary-school level of the text.

Lessons 16 through 18 are on home-made functions, subroutines, and INPUT. The lesson on Home-Made Functions, which is about DEF, shows how to use it to define hyperbolic sine and cosine, which is surprising in what up to this point was such a simple book.

Lesson 19, on Library, is about stored programs, and lists eleven that were among the 50 available on the General Electric system at the time of writing, including TRUINT*** and BLKJAK***.

Lessons 20 through 22 are on paper-tape usage, making corrections, and system commands and features.

Lesson 23, on Edit Commands, is on delete, extract, merge, weave and resequence. Lesson 24, on Extended BASIC Features, goes into strings, RANDOMIZE, multiple assignments with LET, TAB, MAT INPUT, passwords, etc.

Lesson 25 presents "A Program From Beginning to END," showing a 13-line program as typed in by the user, then the corrections made, the improvements and further errors and corrections, a total of six pages that are unique and valuable.

The Appendix gives a summary of BASIC statements.

One of the few drawbacks is that, although there are 43 programs in the book, there are no runs at all, except for the "Program From Beginning to End" in the last lesson, and three tiny, one-line printouts in the next-to-last chapter, on Extended BASIC Features. The reader may develop a somewhat constipated feeling, having to digest all these programs that have no output.

✳ ✳ ✳

4. *Introduction to An Algorithmic Language (BASIC)*. Pub. May 1, 1968 (third edition, 1972), by National Council of Teachers of Mathematics, 1906 Association Drive, Reston, Va. 22091, 53 pages, 6 x 9, $1.40 (paperback).

Excellent for what it sets out to do. Rating: B+

According to the introduction, "This booklet aims to help the mathematics teacher introduce computers through an easy, problem-oriented language." It achieves this goal, giving the essentials of BASIC in as little space as possible. It is a fine illustration of what can be done well in a minimum of space, packing much more information per page than many longer books, without skimping on detail.

The booklet starts right off on page 2 with a two-line program on squaring. The subsequent eight programs elaborate on that, all in Section I, on Introducing BASIC. In Section II, Sample Problems and Exercises, the first problem is on finding divisors of a positive integer, with three more programs that develop this further. The next program is on maximizing an area, with two elaborations; the last is on mean and standard deviation (this by page 32!), with one program 13 lines long. Each program introduces new concepts and statements, with an explanation of each program line where required.

There are three exercises at the end of the first section, and a total of eight within the second section. The answers are in the back of the booklet, in full; 8½ pages of answers for the eleven exercises, with 14 programs.

A short epilogue has a few words about other languages, and flowcharting.

Only nine statements are used (PRINT, END, READ, DATA, GO TO, INPUT, LET, IF-THEN, FOR-NEXT) and one system command, RUN. Nothing on REM, functions, matrices, arrays, lists, tables, etc.

If one must find fault, it is simply that this booklet is so well written that one wishes it were longer. Hence the highly subjective rating of B+. Many of those who find the booklet long enough would rate it A.

✳ ✳ ✳

"Like the Roman god Janus who faces both ways, BASIC faces the needs of those just entering the world of automated data processing as well as those departing for its more stratified plateaus."

From the preface to Entering BASIC, *by John Sack and Judith Meadows (27)*

To be continued next issue.

5. *Introduction to Computing Through The BASIC Language,* by Richard L. Nolan. Second edition pub. June 1974 (first edition pub. June 5, 1969), by Holt, Rinehart and Winston, New York, N. Y., 352 pages, 6 x 9, $9.00 (hardcover).

Some very good parts, but too disjointed, too many tangents. Rating: C

This review could have been rewritten to reflect the changes made in the recently-received second edition, but there are not many of significance, and it may be of interest to show how an author attempted to improve his text, but left the biggest fault untouched.

Although some of the changes are notable improvements, the allover effect is still the same, and so the one-line judgment and rating given for the first edition still apply to the second, except that the book might possibly rate a C+ now. The next dozen paragraphs refer to the first edition; the remaining ones delineate the changes, additions and deletions to the second.

The beginning is promising, with one of the most practical openings of all these books: the formula for calculating "the present worth of an investment for some number of years hence" is given. Then the author shows how the equivalent BASIC program line is almost the same. Four more lines are added to make the book's first program, which is then expanded upon so that several sets of constants can be used. These two programs and their explanations take up the first chapter, five pages.

But by page 13, the book begins to fall apart, with four pages that give a long table of nine BASIC definitions and twelve statements, with two or three examples of each. Too much is given in too short a space. This material should be spread out over a chapter or two, with much more text and also more examples.

Another "too much, too soon" item starts on page 19: three and a half pages of the error statements printed out by the batch-mode BASIC compiler (UWBIC) in response to 35 BASIC statements that contain one or more syntactical errors. If this is meant to show the wrong way of writing statements, there must be a better way of doing it.

Nolan goes into flowcharting early, and uses a good number of flowcharts in the text.

Page 47 starts a 69-line program, with a two-page flowchart, but there is no run to show what the program can do.

There are ten chapters: Introduction, Introduction to BASIC, BASIC Definitions, three chapters on 13 BASIC statements and the functions, Concept of a Computer (computer simulation model), Computer Hardware, Computer Software, Conclusion. There are five appendixes: time-sharing and batch-mode BASIC, techniques of flowcharting, matrices and MAT statements, additional BASIC statements (strings, computed GO TO, SGN, DEF, etc.), and some general application programs.

BASIC is covered in the first six chapters and 96 pages.

There are review questions and exercises at the end of each of these chapters (and of most of the others), with full answers and solutions at the end of the book.

Chapter 4 starts with a vocabulary and dryness that do not make this an easy book to read: "The syntactical relations and grammar discussed in the previous chapter provide the basis for developing a BASIC program. In this chapter, the response elicited from the computer by the REMARK, READ, DATA, END, LET, PRINT, and GO TO statements will be explained. This will be done in the context of the logic required to . . . ." The first example of each of these statement is in words, such as "READ variable, variable . . ., variable," after which actual examples are usually given. The first program in this chapter is a slight enlargement (via REMARK statements) of the very first program, which determines present worth. Memory cells are explained with a drawing of several mailboxes. The same program is used throughout the chapter, basically unchanged, to illustrate the use of the various statements. There are 18 excellent Review Questions and Exercises, seven of them requiring programs to be written.

Chapter 5 covers IF/THEN, FOR/NEXT, DIM, and STOP. The program on page 43 is actually only the second program in the book, if one discounts the several variations on the first one. This second program seems more complex than it really is, perhaps due to the nine REMARK statements in a program that has only six active lines plus two DATA statements. Again, the language is stiff and pedagogic, with words such as "concatenated." The third program (sorting, and counting in categories) is much too long so soon, unless the author's idea is to get the reader used to long programs. The principles could be explained with one or more much shorter programs; this one is 69 lines long (20 are REMARK lines), but without a run. A grade-sorting program is so long that the flowchart takes up three pages. The chapter contains too many programs without RUNs: ten of them, and only one with an output.

Chapter 6 is on functions and GOSUB/RETURN. A "nonsensical program" illustrates four stored functions, when several shorter, meaningful ones would be much better. RND is explained in one sentence: "The function returns a six-digit, uniformly distributed pseudo-random number between zero and one." The program using RND, concerning a silver miner's "grubstake," is explained in only five short sentences, leaving many readers still largely in the dark about RND. Perhaps as an exercise for the brighter students, the chapter ends with a time-sharing simulation program that computes a historical analysis of use (average wait, longest wait), with 76 lines and a 50-box flowchart three pages long.

Chapter 7 is Concept of a Computer, subtitled Computer Simulation Model. This goes into the writing of a BASIC program that will translate "Op-codes for machine-language programming system of model computer" (in machine language), so that programs can be written directly in the "pseudo-machine-language," as required in most of the exercises accompanying this chapter. A fascinating chapter, but this elementary book is not the place for it, not right after six introductory chapters on BASIC.

Chapter 9, on Computer Software, goes into the different levels of programming languages. There are some very good sections on system programmers, application programmers, and programming systems.

Appendix B, 20 pages on Techniques of Flowcharting, includes an entire page showing a table of USASI Working Groups, X3 Series. Why? The coverage of flowcharting is very thorough, although it is nearly all taken up with symbols and their meanings, and only two flowcharts are shown.

Appendix E covers Some General Application Programs: chi-square, T-test, correlation analysis, matrix inversion, linear programming, grade analysis. Much too much in an elementary text; the linear program is almost 300 lines long.

The Selected Bibliography lists 50 books and other publications, on a variety of computer subjects, from biomedical programs to business-data programming.

The last item in the book is a 12-page glossary. The inside covers contain a synopsis of BASIC definitions, functions and statements.

The preface calls this "an integrated approach to teaching computing." Disjointed is a better word, as there are too many tangents and space-fillers. The very simple is next to the very complex, all too dizzyingly often. There are some very good parts, making this a good source book for a teacher, or perhaps as a second or third book, or for browsing. But not as a first book, either for learning about BASIC or about computers, for the solitary reader.

The second edition is essentially the same as the first, except that it is now in hardcover instead of paperback, the entire book has been reset with different typefaces, and the text reworded and expanded (from 262 to 352 pages), with two new chapters (model building, programming languages), the appendix on flowcharting turned into a chapter, the three chapters on BASIC commands reworked into four chapters on BASIC statements, and two new appendixes added.

As an example of the rewording, the first sentence of the preface in the first edition is: "Computing no longer belongs to an 'esoteric cult.'" In the second edition: "Computing is no longer the sole province of an 'esoteric cult.'" And so on, with slightly different words but the same content, in the same paragraph groupings, for the rest of the chapter.

The first chapter was previously an "introduction" and was about the advantages of using computers, with some specific applications; now it is "problem solving and algorithms" and is mainly about defining the objective, formulating a solution, and carrying it out, with several examples, such as calculating the volume of a cube, preparing Boston baked beans, and preparing a payroll.

The second chapter, on flowcharting, was previously an appendix, and this time omits the entirely superfluous chart of USASI Working Groups, X3 Series. Previously, there were mostly symbols and only two flowcharts; now there are six flowcharts, for making Boston baked beans, digging a hole, determining whether a number is prime, etc.

Chapter 3, on BASIC elements, starts almost exactly the same as chapter 2 in the first edition. The first example is on interest; the second edition inserts a few sentences showing by exactly how much the principal would increase for several years, before presenting a formula for determining interest, along with a flowchart. The same programs are presented in both editions, with basically the same text.

Chapter 4, on concepts and definitions, is almost the same as before, bewildering to the beginner, with all the definitions and statements presented at once, along with the same 35 statements containing errors.

The three chapters on BASIC "commands" are turned into four chapters, by taking GOTO from one chapter and IF-THEN from another, to make a single new chapter. INPUT is added to the first of these four chapters, along with a small drawing to illustrate a data stack.

New page 52 shows that the second edition was designed with less care than the first. It is now crowded, with a typeface that seems rather loud when compared with the simpler and more elegant type of the first edition, page 30. However, the new type is larger, and thus easier to read.

A figure has been added in the section on PRINT, to show a page divided into five print zones, each 15 columns wide.

Two pages have been added to the FOR/NEXT section, to illustrate looping in greater detail, with a program that sums five numbers, and a table to show the "contents of memory cells during execution of FOR/NEXT loop." A second illustration has been added to show legal nested loops, and there is now one to show illegal nested loops.

The coverage of DIM is increased by two pages, by rewriting and expanding the text around the same programs and flowcharts, and adding a page with a chart that shows "contents of memory cells during execution of sort program." New pages 96 to 106 run exactly parallel with old pages 62 to 72, with the same figures, and almost the same text.

The random-number function is explained much better now, instead of with only sentence; three and a half pages have been added, with a coin-flipping simulation program and flowchart, a discussion of uniform distribution, etc.

Under GOSUB/RETURN, two figures have been added to show pictorially the use of subroutines and of nested subroutines.

The time-sharing simulation program is expanded, with a longer program and more complex flowchart, although the program is not nicely indented into related groups of lines as was the old one.

The new application chapter on model building is written in a stiff and highly formal manner. Two deterministic models are presented: automobile parts economic-order-quantity (with a 13-line program) and land investment (with a 25-line program not sufficiently explained by the three sentences discussing the fairly complex program and flowchart); this last is more confusing than a helpful example would be. The stochastic simulation models involve a queuing problem (at a car wash), decision trees (introducing a product), with long programs: 77 lines for car wash, with only two sentences of explanation and no flowchart; a long, seven-page explanation of the decision-tree problem, with three trees, a long flowchart with four subroutine charts, and a 115-line program, with only a paragraph of explanation.

The chapter on the computer simulation model is expanded by "specifying in BASIC the major parts of the computer model," and lengthening the program by adding DATA statements and showing an output of the program.

The chapter on computer software adds a flowchart showing the translation process, a table giving the IBM 360/370 Operating Systems Summary, and a table with the name and type of operating system used on twelve computers from eight manufacturers, from the Burroughs B 5500 to the Xerox Sigma 5/7. Much of this chapter has been rewritten, reshuffled, and expanded. Where the first edition was about system programmers, application programmers and the computer process, the second is about language processors, operating systems, and the technical services group, and covers system and application programmers in five sentences. Some material is repeated, with changes, such as the portion on programming systems. There is a completely new section, on control programs, service programs, and on the eight types of operating systems developed "to date." There is even a note on the "unbundling of IBM."

Chapter 13, on programming languages, is an enlargement of a portion of the old chapter on software. Only one figure is from the first edition, showing the levels of programming languages. The new material consists of a page each on FORTRAN, COBOL, PL/1, BASIC, ALGOL, and RPG. However, the only examples of these are in the figure taken from the first edition, which is a program showing a simple loop operation written in binary, hexadecimal, assembly language, and four of the high-level languages. The pages on the six languages are informative as to their origins, but tell much too little about the languages themselves.

Appendix A, on matrices, is exactly the same as previously, with the addition of a footnote stating that "the introduction to matrices is based on an unpublished paper written by David L. Smith, currently a lecturer at the University of Illinois."

Appendix B, on Additional BASIC Statements, covers some of the same areas as before; two of the programs that before had no output, now have one. There are now two pages on TAB and PRINT USING, with a program that is supposed to print HI three times (but somehow prints it five times), and a page on RESTORE.

The two new appendixes are on Using Files in BASIC, with five pages on creating and using files, three programs, and five-plus pages on Using BASIC on a Mini-Computer, with an 87-line program for the PDP-8/E that simulates the landing of a lunar rocket, although without output.

The last appendix, on Package Programs, presents four of the six programs from the first edition, dropping matrix inversion and grade analysis. The linear programming example uses the same objective function, subject to the same constraints, but the program is completely different, and produces a much shorter output, half a page instead of two pages.

The old Selected Bibliography was a single list, two pages long. The new one is over three pages long, with several publications for each chapter, except for chapters 3-8, for which there is one group of five books on BASIC, by Farina, Kemeny & Kurtz, Sass, Sharpe, and Spencer.

All these changes do little to help this become a unified text, with a feeling of overall cohesiveness between its various chapters. The disjointedness persists. The biggest fault is still the sudden and overwhelming presentation of the entire BASIC repertoire of characters, definitions, statements, and error messages, after only one short program has been given, thus putting a stone wall directly in the reader's path. However, the book no longer begins to fall apart apart by page 13; because of the added material, the collapse doesn't begin until page 32.

* * *

6. *A Guide to BASIC Programming: A Time-Sharing Language*, by Donald D. Spencer. Pub. Dec. 2, 1969, by Addison-Wesley, Reading, Mass., 216 pages 6½ x 9¼, $6.95 (paperback).

One of the better books, with an easily understood text, many examples, flowcharts throughout. Rating: B+

This book has many features to recommend it, and only a few drawbacks. There are many examples of each new statement, and many flowcharts, just about one for each program. Every chapter ends in exercises, although without answers.

Spencer is the only author other than Sass (21) to provide a short history of time-sharing, starting with the 1961 CTSS at MIT. The first chapter also presents a 15-line program for finding the roots of a quadratic equation, but with no explanation other than the mechanics of putting it into the system.

The second chapter, an Introduction to BASIC, is mainly about flowcharting. The next chapter, on Elements of BASIC, does get into the language, in a slow but sure way, using only REM and LET. The fourth chapter, on Reading and Printing, contains the first complete program, six lines on determining true annual interest rate, plus five more programs.

Chapter five begins to separate the men from the boys, or rather the high-school kids from the college students, with one example that uses the summation sigma. Another example goes off on a tangent by taking up three pages to discuss in detail the Newton-Raphson method for calculating square roots. Chapter six is on loops. Chapter seven, on Arrays and Subscripted Variables, contains another digression, a confusing one on the knight's tour. This may be a practical application of tables, but in a text as elementary as this, it's too much, adding little or nothing other than

confusion. The only point in including it seems to be the use of subscripted variables to indicate the path of the tour.

There is a fine chapter on matrices, 16 pages, taking the time to discuss the subject fully and carefully. Chapter 11 is Sample Programs For Study, selected from a variety of fields, with 17 problems on 45 pages, including Fibonacci numbers, coordinate geometry, greatest common divisor, compound interest, satellite orbit (two-dimensional), polynomial evaluation, generating prime numbers, maze-running, and magic-square generation. The last chapter, Problems For Reader Solution, has 23 problems, some with flowcharts (but none with solutions) including mortgage calculation, inventory turnover, number-base conversion, etc.

The section on references is unique: five pages that list 8 books on BASIC, 13 manufacturers' books on BASIC, 15 on other programming languages, 5 on programming and computers, etc.

There are five appendixes. The first is on BASIC implementations, a unique chart showing which of 96 statements are available on each of 14 different time-sharing systems. The second appendix is 7 pages on the ASR33 Teletype, followed by two pages on General Electric time sharing commands, then a five-page glossary, and a two-page true-false quiz on BASIC.

This is one of the better books, with an easily understood text, many examples, flowcharts throughout, and many programs. The drawbacks are few: no answers to the exercises, and wandering off twice (Newton-Raphson, knight's tour). The use of the summation sigma may actually bother only a few readers who haven't gotten that far in mathematics.

The typography is distracting, as the book is not well designed. There are too many typefaces; page 33, for instance, contains five different ones, making it a very busy page, with different fonts for the text, section headings, sample program lines, an actual program, and italics for formula constants.

* * *

7. *Problem-Solving With the Computer*, by Edwin R. Sage. Pub. 1969 by Entelek, Newburyport, Mass., 244 pages, 7 x 10, $4.95 (paperback).

Very slowly paced, aimed at secondary-school students. Rating: B

The first thing one might notice in this book is the very wide margin, almost three inches, which is used 47 times alongside programs and flowcharts. If the margin were reduced to just under an inch, the book could be made almost 30% narrower.

This is a high-school text, for grades 8 through 12. It teaches by giving a problem and then discussing the solution in detail. There is a flowchart for every demonstration problem.

There are eight chapters: BASIC Skills I, BASIC Skills II, A New Look at Numbers (rounding off, primes, random numbers, etc.), Algebra and the Computer, Geometry and the Computer, Data (FOR-NEXT, subscripts), Determinants, Approximations.

Sage is one of the very few to discuss debugging with the use of PRINT statements, and also by longhand, and in detail. He is also the only one to use the phrase "fall through," and to explain this highly important principle.

There are exercises after the introduction of every new idea, but without answers. These problems are all purely mathematical, and show little imagination. The one place where some imagination is used is in introducing flowcharts, where this is done for the steps involved in making a telephone call.

Some items are covered only as "Additional Facts" following the summaries at the ends of the chapters. This includes SQR and ABS, covered in one sentence each.

In the chapter on Geometry and the Computer, many problems are examined at length and in great detail. This is fine for the student who is weak in geometry, although it would bore one who isn't.

Although the beginning of the book is extremely slow, the last chapter, on approximations, is not slow and easy at all, and will be understood only by the bright students. The approximations are for sine and cosine, natural logarithms, slope of tangent line, and limits.

8. *Introduction to Programming: A BASIC Approach*, by Van Court Hare, Jr. Pub. May 25, 1970, by Harcourt, Brace & Jovanovich, New York, N. Y., 436 pages, 6 x 9, $10.95 (hardcover).

The only book to go extensively into computer hardware (120 pages) and also FORTRAN (60 pages). Fairly well done, with many interesting features. Rating: for the entire book: B+; for the BASIC portion only: B

The book gets a higher rating for its entirety than for the BASIC portion alone because of its uniqueness as a three-part text: hardware, BASIC, and FORTRAN.

The beginning chapters, on "the history and economics of computer development, the parts of a computer system, and the way in which computers handle data," go into just about the right amount of detail: enough to be informative, not so much as to be confusing and overly technical. The author goes into much more than technical developments; he tells how, for instance, Remington Rand had the "initial lead in manufacturing large-scale machines," but lost out to IBM.

The brief section on the development of programming languages is interesting and the only one in all these books. Hare is also the only author to quote from the Bible: "But let your communication be Yea, yea, Nay, nay; for whatsoever is more than these cometh of evil" (from Matthew 5:37, part of the Sermon on the Mount).

Hare is worldly as well as colloquial: he uses *Playboy* as an example of a publication, and writes of cores as "small donuts of magnetic material." And he has some interesting comments, such as on reliability: "If our automobiles and home television sets worked one millionth as reliably as computers do, there would be no local electronic or garage mechanic who could pay his rent; they would all be out of business."

Each chapter ends with problems, without answers.

Some of the sentences in the hardware portion of the book are so terse as to be confusing to the novice, such as "The output of the computer is often in excess of printing capability, and a number of printers may be used . . ." Another sentence that could use some more explanation is "The light pen is an outgrowth of friend-or-foe radar developments." An inquiring mind might want to know a little more than just that.

Around page 100 the author begins to slide slowly into BASIC, in a chapter on Programming Essentials, without going into any details of the language. The first exposure to a BASIC program is on page 128, with a five-liner on net pay, and three pages of explanation. Although many short programs are presented in the following three dozen pages, there is not one single run, not in the entire chapter on END, PRINT, READ, and DATA, nor in the chapter on LET and stored functions. Is this to get the reader to try these short programs on a terminal?

Not until page 164 is there a program of any substance: eight lines on summing the numbers from 1 to 10. Yet by page 174 there is a 32-line program, which, although simple, might not be understood, with so little preparation up to this point, except by the brighter readers and students. The program on page 176 is also presented without adequate preparation, as are several subsequent programs.

Sorting is covered only in problems at the end of a chapter, not in the preceding text. These are not problems, actually, but rather are presentations of three sorting programs.

Seven pages are devoted to matrices, with only one program on matrix operations, in a chapter on BASIC extensions, called Adult BASIC. The definition of matrix inversion is quite murky except to an expert on the subject, or to someone who has just taken a course on it.

Although the errors in the book are minor, they seem to stand out, perhaps because most of them are so obvious, such as (on page 289), "octal 4 is equal to 010." A few pages earlier, the text is careful to point out that in the preceding program, there is a leading space before a string variable in quotes. Yet in the program itself, there is no leading space in the referenced line.

Many of the programs are interesting, but many of them have too little explanation for a good understanding. An example is the program on page 296 for right-justifying the output, with only five explanatory sentences; enough for an experienced programmer, but too little for a beginner.

The portion on BASIC ends with a chapter of selected computer problems. They are all long and complex, much too much for the little preparation so far, on computer ciphering and deciphering, dating game, mazes and labyrinths. Very nice, but too hard, and with too little explanation. The author seems to assume top students who will dig hard into the problems and figure them out as a challenge.

Starting on page 233, Hare begins to work toward FORTRAN, saying it is more flexible, in a footnote. (This book has more footnotes than many scholarly monographs: 96 of them.) Hare seems more interested in the nitty-gritty of FORTRAN than of BASIC, where he seems more interested in applications. A FORTRAN program on cross-tabulation is explained in far greater detail than any of the BASIC programs.

There is some nice detail on the importance of rounding off in affecting close decisions, such as credit being accepted or rejected. However, FORTRAN is somehow made to seem hellishly complex, which to some it may well be.

There are 18 chapters: From Loom to Electron; Bistable Devices and Binary Codes; Input/Output Devices; Memory Devices; Data and Programs in Memory; Programming Essentials; Getting the Computer to Work; END, PRINT, READ, and DATA; LET and Stored Functions; REM, GO TO, IF-THEN, and INPUT; FOR-NEXT, Subscripted Variables, and DIM; Subroutines and Their Use; A Baker's Dozen (13 problems with computer solutions); Extensions of the BASIC Language; Selected Computer Problems; Extending What You Have Learned (data format, introduction to FORTRAN); and two chapters on Thirteen FORTRAN Translations (of the BASIC programs in chapter 13).

The first appendix is unique: a side-by-side comparison of the individual features and statements of BASIC and FORTRAN, nine pages worth.

Hare has the longest glossary of all these authors: 16 pages. Nolan (5) has 11½, Sass (21) has 8, and Spencer (6) has 5 pages.

The author goes into great detail in some places, such as explaining why most systems require RUBOUT at the end of each line on paper tape when punching, and also the reason for typing TAPE before inputting tape; no other author explains these two things. Yet when it comes to the chapter involving PRINT, there are no examples of the various PRINT options. Nor is there a single printout in the chapter on LET and stored functions. The reader finds himself saying "Show me!" Thus this is an uneven book, with too much detail in many places where it isn't really necessary, and not enough in all too many instances.

The book is set in a sans-serif type. Some programs are set in boldface, others are Teletype originals in various reductions from full-size to quite small; the mixture produces many odd-looking pages.

This book may be suitable for class use where the problems will be worked, but not for reading only. The author seems to be writing on a programmer-to-programmer level.

9. *BASIC For Beginners*, by Wilson Y. Gateley and Gary G. Bitter. Pub. June 25, 1970, by McGraw-Hill, New York, N. Y., 152 pages, 5½ x 8, $5.50 (paperback).

Very good for its limited coverage. Rating: B+

Two striking features of this book are its pleasing design and handsome typeface; this is one of the best looking books. All the programs and program-line examples are in an easily-read sans-serif type.

"This book is a descendant of one written during the Spring of 1968 for the purpose of providing a self-instructional manual for students at Colorado College." It doesn't actually get into BASIC until page 40. First comes a nice introduction consisting of a chapter on The Beginning (programming, computers, languages) and one on Using the Terminal (33 and 35 Teletypes, system commands, paper tapes, correcting errors). The actual text on BASIC runs up to page 117, a total of 78 pages, covering 26 statements. GOSUB and RETURN are not covered "because of our feeling that the subroutine concept, although admittedly of great usefulness in complicated programs, is of little value in most beginner's programs and is more likely to confuse than to help the novice."

There are eight chapters: The Beginning; Using the Terminal; A Start At BASIC; BASIC Control Statements; Loops and Arrays; Library Functions and DEF; Input, Printing and String Data; The End and The Beginning.

There are questions at the end of each chapter, followed by the answers, and then by several exercises, without answers. Each exercise requires writing and running a program to solve the given problem.

The start is slow and conversational, with much "you" and "we," and the coverage is quite thorough. The examples (other than program lines) are not set apart from the text, as in most other books, but are included within the body of the text: "Thus X, B, C1 and N9 are legal variables, but 9N, BX, and X23 are not." This makes the reading flow somewhat more easily than in the books that give a larger number of examples and set them apart, but some may prefer more examples over easier reading.

A unique feature is Chapter 8 on The End and The

Beginning, which is four brief pages on various subjects not covered in the previous chapters, such as editing commands, MAT statements, data files, and FORTRAN.

There are three appendixes. The first is a table of the differences between 15 time-sharing systems as to 13 features and limitations, such as maximum number of digits in a constant, whether variable initialization to zero is automatic, etc. The second appendix shows how a simple four-line program that calculates several combinations of two constants will look if run on 14 different systems. Actually, one or two of the runs, within the main text, would suffice. The third appendix consists of additional exercises, providing two problems in each of 13 disciplines, from algebra ("write a program which will carry out synthetic division") to political science ("write a computer program which . . . computes both the Democratic percentage vote and the Republican . . ."); answers are provided for these exercises.

This is one of seven books that give statements and functions on the inside covers, for ready reference.

There are not as many examples as the other texts give, such as for constants, variables, formulas, etc. And there are only nine complete programs in the entire book, although there are 14 more programs in the questions at the end of the chapters.

The first program in the book is a four-liner that prints several combinations of two assigned constants, and which is explained briefly, on page 23 of the chapter, Using the Terminal, which is long before BASIC is actually taught, starting on page 46. The second program is not in the chapter on A Start At BASIC, but actually appears in the questions at the end of that chapter, on page 56.

The language of the text is a little too involved at times, due mainly to the constant use of "you" and "we," which makes for involved phrases and sentences.

On the whole, a nice little book, with its limitations due mainly to its brevity: 78 pages plus wraparound.

10. *Discovering BASIC: A Problem Solving Approach*, by Robert E. Smith. Pub. Aug. 27, 1970, by Hayden Book Co., New York, N. Y., 203 pages, 5½ x 8¼, $7.95 (hardcover), $5.95 (paperback).

Only for the hardworking and conscientious student. Must be used with a terminal. Rating: As a second or third book, B+; as a first book, C−

This is a bound version of the author's looseleaf, ringbound "BASIC Ideas," published in 1969 by International Timesharing Corp. in Minneapolis, Minn., at $5.95. The idea of the original edition was that the pages could be removed from the binder and easily placed at or on the terminal, which is difficult or impossible with a bound book. The bound edition is identical in content with the looseleaf one.

The book is in two distinct parts. The first 95 pages consist of 41 lessons. The book teaches by asking the reader to run a given program on the computer, and builds the text around such programs, most of which are given with little or no explanation as to how they work, other than the accompanying flowcharts. The reader must figure out a great deal by himself, and is not given adequate preparation in many cases. A program for building magic squares is given as early as page 16, 20 lines long, with a skeletal flowchart and no explanation of what a magic square is, much less some explanation of how the program works.

A time-sharing terminal is essential because most of the lessons present a program and a flowchart, without any explanation or REM statements, only an exhortation to "Try it!" So if the program runs, the reader has an answer, but he probably won't understand how or why. This must be the "problem-solving approach" denoted by the book's subtitle. If so, it's a misnomer, as the computer solves the problems, not the reader. Of course, a bright reader could probably figure out what's going on, but should a programming book be written only for the top five percent (or less) of the population?

There are four review tests within the first 95 pages, and they are scored by running given programs, with one's answers put into the DATA statements. There are no explanations whatsoever as to how these scoring programs work; this too is left as an exercise for the student.

The writing style is not at all smooth, with such cute phrases as "by tags we mean the cute little messages . . ."

Many statements are presented without explanation of any kind, such as RND in the magic-square program. The REM statement gets only 26 words of explanation. The few times a reader is asked to write a program, in the 41 lessons, he usually has not been given enough information beforehand to be able to do so, and since most of the programs are given in the text, he has had very little experience in writing programs — he's been running the author's programs nearly all the time.

In a program that determines the highest common factor, there is no explanation that program lines 45 to 55 exchange the values of X and Y, one of the crucial parts of the program.

Page 34 gives an uncompleted program, the reader being expected to fill in the missing seven lines. Some readers may learn from this type of teaching, but not many.

A program on page 66 contains a command that no other author mentions: PAUSE.

The second part of the book consists of 50 review problems, each with a short description of the problem, and a flowchart. The reader is expected to write programs that solve a great variety of problems, such as radix sorting, simulating a dice game, rank correlation, annuity interest, linear correlation, etc. A couple of the problems have complete or partial programs. The reader could learn much more if the programs required were simpler to write, and if he had to write his own flowcharts. As it is, many of the 50 review problems leave too much to the imagination. Review problem 6 is on a chi-square test, without bothering to explain what a chi-square test is. But a full 50-line program is given.

There is no index.

The last 39 pages contain program solutions to problems in the text, photographically reduced to the eye-straining dimension of 22 characters per horizontal inch.

A reader *can* learn from this book if he will conscientiously dig his way through the lessons and programs. The question is, will he do this, or get bored early, and start to skip pages? For the very bright, with highly inquisitive minds, there is something to be mined here — the hard way. For the rest, meaning the majority, the book as a first text is much too difficult.

The back cover notes that the author's books on computer programming "are distinguished by his originality of presentation and his ability to clarify computer languages." That latter claim may well be true of the author's FORTRAN and COBOL books, but not of this one.

11. *Basic BASIC: An Introduction to Computer Programming in BASIC Language*, by James S. Coan. Pub. Sept. 11, 1970, by Hayden Book Co., New York, N. Y., 256 pages, 6 x 9, $8.25 (hardcover), $6.50 (paperback).

Despite some drawbacks, a useful and helpful book. Rating: B+

There are many good points to this book, some of them unique. The statements, with brief explanations, are presented in boxes, and so stand out loud and clear. Some other authors intimidate the reader by presenting long and complex programs much too early; early in his book, Coan gets the reader used to the sight of long programs, but they are relatively simple ones. The 50-line program on page 36 is easy to understand; it has many explanatory PRINT lines and concerns various ways of printing the items in a list. This is in the chapter on Loops And Lists, which starts out, like the other chapters, with short programs (6 lines here) and builds up to larger ones.

There are 13 chapters: Introduction to BASIC, Writing a Program, Loops And Lists, Computer Functions, Elementary Data Processing, Introduction to INPUT and RESTORE, Specific Applications (Euclidian algorithm, change of base, looking at integers digit by digit), The Quadratic Function, Trigonometry, Complex Numbers, Polynomials, MAT Instructions, Elementary Probability. There are seven appendixes: Storing Programs on Paper Tape, Error Diagnosis, Special Formatting Functions (TAB, IMAGE), Summary of Flowchart Shapes, Summary of Statements in BASIC, Index of Programs in Text, Answers to Even-Numbered Problems.

There are problems for each section within a chapter. Some problems are check-marked to indicate that they are the more difficult ones.

Some fairly complex programs are presented, such as the one on page 85 on questionnaire analysis, which very few authors get into. A few pages later, the author mixes two programs (two-way temperature conversion) and calls one or the other with 0 or 1, a unique program in these books. Not only is Coan the only author to go into complex numbers, he has an eight-page chapter on the subject. He is also the only one to give programs for synthetic division, integral zeros, real zeros, complex zeros, and the Descartes rule of signs, in a chapter on polynomials. And there is a fine seven-page appendix on Error Diagnosis, explaining the three types of errors in detail.

The items on the minus side of the ledger may not bother every reader, but can be annoying to some. The type is small and uncomfortable to read; the back-of-the-book answers to problems are tiny photoreductions of Teletype output, 27 miniscule characters to the horizontal inch.

The writing style is odd, as though it were a transcription of classroom lectures, quite prosaic and showing little imagination. For example the definition of IF-THEN is "XXX IF YYYYY THEN ZZZ. If YYYYYY is true, transfer to line ZZZ. If YYYYY is false, pass to the next line after XXX." Not very helpful.

Some features of BASIC are given very short shrift. The explanation of the E format for exponentiation takes all of one sentence, and there is none at all for negative E.

Some parts of the book, such as the portion on testing integers for divisibility, on page 102, contain mathematical manipulations that would be hard for many to follow without a teacher for guidance.

The final chapter, on Elementary Probability, is one that only the top students may understand. The chapter contains a teaser, in showing a RUN that gives all the four-letter combinations of the word FLAG, but not the program itself. The excuse given is that "the techniques required for this vary so greatly from system to system that we will not present the program, but only the RUN."

Most of these drawbacks can easily be ignored by the reader who is after the many excellent parts of this book, which in a future edition may become an outstanding one.

12. *Computer Science: A Primer*, by Alexandra I. Forsythe, Thomas A. Keenan, Elliott I. Organick, and Warren Stenberg. Pub. Sept. 25, 1969, by John Wiley & Sons, New York, N. Y., 403 pages, 6¼ x 9¼, $11.00 (hardcover).

Computer Science: A First Course, by Forsythe et al. Pub. Oct. 31, 1969, 553 pages, 6½ x 9½, $14.25 (hardcover).

Computer Science: BASIC Language Programming, by Forsythe et al. Pub. Nov. 13, 1970, 124 pages, 6½ x 9½, $5.50 (paperback).

For the reader who wants to learn all about flowcharts, the rating is A. For learning about BASIC, the rating is D

This handsome set of books is dedicated to the proposition that thou shalt worship the flowchart as thy god. And because of the great emphasis on flowcharts, less BASIC is taught than in many shorter books.

The BASIC supplement is meant to be used in parallel with either the First Course or the Primer. The only difference between these two is that the Primer does not include the last five chapters, which is Part III, on Nonnumerical Applications. The Primer is said to be perhaps "more suitable for a short course or for one that concentrates exclusively on numerical computation."

According to the introduction, "To increase the applicability of this book, the specific syntactic details of computer language have been separated from the main flow-chart text into a language supplement. The flow-chart language used in the main textbook deals only with concepts of central interest to all programming languages ... The great reward to the student from this separation of main concepts from syntactic details is the universal applicability of flow-chart language, which he learns first." Then, later, "Beginning with Chapter 2, any corresponding chapter can be read, section by section, along with the main language." Programming language texts are available for BASIC, FORTRAN, PL/1, and APL; they are "especially useful because they are designed to dovetail, section for section, with the principal chapters of the basic text. The study of a computer programming language ... from one of these supplements will help the student to convert the abstract algorithmic solutions of the problems from the basic text into actual solutions on the computer that is available to him."

The First Course starts with an algorithm for "the everyday process of changing a flat tire," presents a flowchart for it, then improves it in several steps. The exercise for this part of the book is to prepare a flowchart representing a recipe for making "Rocky Road" cookies. Then comes a numerical algorithm on the Fibonacci sequence, two pages, with flowchart.

Page 11 presents a Model of a Computer, with window boxes for memory, and three workers: master computer and two assistants, the assigner and the reader. Six pages translate the words of the Fibonacci sequence into "formal flow-chart language."

Page 23 starts the presentation of SAMOS, a prototype computer (the acronym is not explained), and several of its instructions: LDA, BMI, WWD, and BRU.

The portion on rounding uses CHOP, which takes the whole part of the number.

Chapter 3, Additional Flow-Chart Concepts, begins a really heavy diet of flowcharts. Chapter 4, Looping, is 65 pages long, with 44 flowcharts and 26 partial flowcharts.

Chapter 6, Functions and Procedures, represents the SQR subroutine as a sealed brick chamber with a funnel on top and a window on the side; a similar concept is used to explain MIN, SORT, and COMPEQUAL.

Part III starts with a chapter on Trees, going into tree searches, the four-color problem, etc. The next chapter, Compiling, covers Polish strings as applied to the prototype SAMOS machine, translating from infix to postfix, and flowcharting the translation process.

Chapter 12, Lists and Strings: Their Storage Structures and Uses, covers editing, string manipulation, string operations in the flowchart language, and unknowns in pattern-match operations.

Chapter 13, More Aspects of Compiling, starts with

"Transformation of Postfix Strings to SAMOS Machine Code," then goes into "Conversion from Symbolic to Actual SAMOS."

The appendix is 27 pages on SAMOS, going into its 11 basic instructions, some illustrative problems, indexing, table lookup, and subprograms.

There are exercises throughout each chapter, after each section, without answers.

The BASIC supplement notes that in both the Primer and First Course, "flow charts are painstakingly introduced and built up feature by feature ... Designed for use with either of the above-mentioned texts, this book bridges the narrow gap between the flow chart language and BASIC."

Part I, on BASIC concepts, has five chapters: Algorithms and Computers, The BASIC Language, Additional BASIC Concepts, Looping, and Approximations. Part II, on numerical applications, has one chapter, Functions and Procedures (functions, subroutines, symbol manipulation).

The first program generates a Fibonacci sequence, with the Teletyped program lines laid out in parallel with their corresponding boxes in the flowchart. The flowchart is in the same elegant style as in the parent text, with shaded boxes, and lettering that imitates Teletype print.

As in the parent texts, there are several sets of exercises in each chapter.

The style is often stilted, as on page 9: "Exercise a vigilant awareness toward these potential sources of error, and never assume you have solved all of the difficulties the first time." Sounds rather Victorian.

Chapter Two, BASIC Language Elements, is a jumbling together of all the elements without sufficient explanation or examples. Predefined functions are covered in a single short paragraph, accompanied by a table of eleven functions. The explanation of E notation is all too skimpy.

The section on RESTORE gives a good simile for the data pointer: a "moving finger." The next page has a program that computes the volumes of five boxes, given length, width and height; six of these dimensions are negative. What sort of boxes are these?

The section on Rounding explains that although INT(X) is the same as the CHOP(X) mentioned in the parent text for positive arguments, it differs for negative arguments. This is the first of several problems that come up when translating from the flowchart language to BASIC, and which do not help the cause of having to learn an intermediate language.

A program on page 43 contains the funniest line in any of these books: REM A TWO MILLION DOLLAR COMPUTER USED FOR TALLYING. What isn't so funny is that the program has no safeguard against inputting a grade over the highest possible score. So if a grade of 152 is entered, the program jumps to print 0 STUDENTS TOOK THE TEST.

These authors are the only ones to recommend tracing with a printout that includes line numbers.

The book is handsomely produced, with shaded boxes in the flowcharts, and shaded lines in programs for those lines that require explanation.

Another translation problem comes up on page 72: "The iteration box has a nearly perfect parallel in Basic called the FOR statement." Nearly? This is explained on page 95: "The iteration box of the flow chart has the violation of the condition ABS(T) A as a criterion for escaping from the loop. The FOR statement of Basic cannot incorporate this kind of criterion." Page 89 has a third problem, noting that the MAT READ statement "does not have the same generality as the flow chart notation."

There is, of course, a great deal to be said in favor of learning to flowchart accurately. Yet so much emphasis is laid on flowcharting here that BASIC almost gets lost in the shuffle. So much effort has been spent in setting up the form, that content has been neglected in the BASIC supplement. The main advantage of these texts is that one learns thoroughly, not BASIC, but flowcharting. And the main advantage of the two-text system seems to be, not to the reader, but to the authors and publishers. If nothing else were available, this system might seem admirable, but there are better and more interesting books that teach BASIC, and more of it, from a single text, without requiring the reader to switch back and forth between two books.

For schools, there may be much value in these three books. But the solitary reader may not enjoy having to study an artificial language and an imaginary computer to such depths. The whole idea of learning a flowchart language as an intermediate step is like having to learn Esperanto before being allowed to go on to a living language.

✻ ✻ ✻

13. *Elementary BASIC With Applications*, by Mario V. Farina. Pub. Dec. 8, 1972, by Prentice-Hall, Englewood Cliffs, N. J., 309 pages, 6 x 9, $8.95 (hardcover), $5.95 (paperback, out of print).

Well written by a born teacher who moves along quickly but covers every point. Rating: A

The free-flowing, conversational writing style makes this a pleasure to read. The author is a born teacher who anticipates the reader's questions.

There are 24 chapters, covering such basic areas as loops, reading data, printing headings and labels, making decisions, flowcharting, lists, random numbers, alphanumeric manipulations, and applications such as finding areas under curves, random motion in two directions, plotting, and file maintenance.

Each chapter ends with a "mini-lesson" that recaps what was learned in the lesson, and a set of exercises (with answers at the back of the book).

A unique and appealing feature is the presenting of an example program, and *then* explaining the point it demonstrates, thus giving the reader a chance to figure out for himself what's going on, if he can.

The book begins to get difficult at page 105, with list-searching by the binary method, but the author later explains everything in detail.

The writing is informal, with "OK" used often.

Farina is imaginative: the random-walk problem is presented on the basis of a wandering drunk. He is the only one to go into such areas of string manipulation as foreign-language translation, in addition to cryptography.

Early in the book, on page 30, the author stresses the advantage of program efficiency: after pointing out that a certain program could be run faster by computing and assigning a name to a certain function, he says, ". . . we save the computer some effort in computing. Saving the computer effort, saves money. It's a small point, but it is the awareness of cost-saving techniques like this which differentiate between a mediocre programmer and a good one." No other author makes this point.

There are only a few minor errors in this book. Some readers may object to the text being typewritten, which is not as easy to read as a typeset book. And it does take a while to get used to the flowcharts being laid out horizontally. The chapter on tape sorting, although only five pages long, seems somewhat extraneous, especially since the method given is described as inefficient, and no program is included. The only real objection is to the total lack of REM statements — there isn't one in the book.

✻ ✻ ✻

14. *Teach Yourself BASIC*, by Robert L. Albrecht. Pub. 1970 by Tecnica Education Corp., 1864 S. State St., Suite 100, Salt Lake City, Utah 84115. Vol. I, 64 pages; Vol. II, 64 pages, 8½ x 11, $1.95 (paperback) each, plus 15¢ each for shipping and handling.

Fine for someone wanting or needing a slow start on a minimum amount of BASIC. Rating: B

These two booklets were first published by a company of the same name in San Carlos, Calif., whose publications were later taken over by a Utah organization formed for the purpose.

Presenting BASIC at about the lowest possible level, these booklets proceed quite slowly, emphasizing each point. Only 13 statements are covered in Volume I (from PRINT to SQR), and 9 in Volume II (from IF-THEN to DIM).

The first program is on page 5, a simple two-liner using only PRINT and END. No new statements are used for the next 15 pages, after which LET is introduced, and that holds the stage for the following seven pages, until INPUT.

Yet despite such limited coverage and the slow pace, there is much here to hold the interest of the school-age reader. The author chooses a simple yet ingenious method for demonstrating elementary FOR-NEXT loops, by using them to print computer-art patterns. This is picked up again in Volume II, with a whole chapter on patterns, a graphic and interesting way of demonstrating INPUT and TAB statements.

Instead of printing H or T for the output of a coin-flipping program, the author's program prints out either asterisks or spaces in small rectangular patterns, producing an output much more pleasing than HTHHHTTT . . . .

Poll-taking is on the popular level: Snoopy or the Red Baron for President? Trix, Total, Cheerios or No Opinion for the preferred breakfast cereal?

The last program is the only one the average might have trouble with, a 38-liner on the game of "23 matches." Only the bright readers may be able to get much out of this program, but in any case it's the last one.

There are only two drawbacks. One is that the reader may wish to go further, but he won't find another text that teaches BASIC in such a slow, relaxed and interesting manner; the closest is Dwyer & Kaufman (33). The second is that the exercises at the ends of each chapter include programs for the reader to write, but there are no answers.

There are seven chapters in the first booklet, with catchy, pop-style headings: Getting Started, Moving On (PRINT, floating point, exponents), Gathering Speed (variables), Feeding the Beast (INPUT, GO TO, READ, DATA), You Can Count On It (loops), Encore (FOR-NEXT), Function Junction (INT, SQR). In the second booklet, eight chapters: Finding Your Way (flowcharts), Decisions (IF), Patterns (computer graphics), Meandering (random numbers), Little Boxes (subscripts), Snoopy and the Red Baron, The People's Poll, Kaleidoscope (coin-tossing, dice, Nim, rounding, trig functions).

The contents of these two booklets appeared later, in almost identical form, as the first chapter in the Digital Equipment Corp. "Edusystem Handbook," which is part of the PDP-8 handbook series. DEC has added pages on RESTORE, subroutines, "miscellaneous math" (LOG, EXP, ABS, SGN), and programmer-defined functions. For the most part, the Tecnica and DEC texts run in parallel, line for line. The Tecnica booklets are set entirely from type; the DEC book uses the actual Teletype output where applicable.

15. *Time Sharing's BASIC Language*. Pub. 1970, by General Electric Training and Education Programs, Bldg. 23, Rm. 290, 1 River Rd., Schenectady, N. Y. 12345, 250 pages, 8½ x 11, $6.95 (paperback).

A programmed instruction text of average value. Rating: C

This is the only programmed instruction text in the group. "Information is presented in frames — easily assimilated units of information. You test yourself on the information in each frame before you go on to the next," and so on, for 6½ pages of introduction on just how to use a programmed instruction text. Unlike the more complex PI texts, this one does not ask the reader to skip to one place or another, depending on which answer he gives to a question, so that if he answers incorrectly he will be given additional material on that subject, before getting back on the track again. The reader of this book simply continues straight through.

However, there are seven pre-tests throughout the book, each with up to a dozen questions that, if all are answered correctly, allow the reader to skip over the following chapter. Thus a highly informed reader could read only the seven pages of pre-tests and finish the book in minutes, if he felt like playing such a game. For the less well informed, the pre-tests indicate to which frames a reader should turn for help on each question missed.

The book insists that the reader write the answers on a separate sheet of paper. "It's part of the learning process, according to current learning theory and experimental evidence. To get the most you can out of this book, you *must* write the answers."

Questions are asked on almost every page; the answers, in the right-hand column, are to be covered up with the provided cardboard mask until the reader has answered the question in his head. To keep the reader from glancing at an answer on an opposite page, only the right-hand page is used; after 121 pages, there is this note: "For next frame, turn the page, then turn the book upside down and continue."

This method of programmed instruction seems to require much white space; the actual text takes up only about 50 percent (or less) of the page.

There are seven sections: Time-Sharing Computer Systems, Remote Terminal Familiarization, BASIC System Commands, BASIC Program Statements, Paper Tape, Advanced BASIC (editing commands, functions), Matrices. A "Comprehensive Exam" of 28 questions completes the main text. There is an appendix on error messages, and another on BASIC limitations (due to limited storage).

The book starts off very simply, with a two-line program using PRINT and END, and proceeds very slowly.

Nearly every point is gone over several times; there are six pages on E-notation and decimals. The first program of any real complexity is on page 193, and consists of 20 lines that demonstrate the use of lists, tables and loops in computing total sales for several salesmen. The program is explained briefly but adequately. The next long program, on page 200, has 32 lines that compute the greatest common divisor, but with very little explanation.

For a book that starts off so slowly, this one goes much too fast at the finish; the last program manipulates a Hilbert matrix without even bothering to explain what a Hilbert matrix is, or what it can be used for. The last section is on matrices, with such an emphasis that one can only conclude the authors are terribly fond of matrices.

This is one of three books (the others are Gross & Brainerd (22) and Farina (3)) to note that only program lines should be punched in paper tape: "do not allow the program name, date, etc., to be punched. Otherwise this information will enter as unnumbered program statements which will result in an error output when you try to run the program."

The biggest fault of this book, aside from its insipid text and the fact that it doesn't require the reader to write a single program, is its lack of an index.

✳ ✳ ✳

16. *BASIC Programming*, by Paul W. Murrill and Cecil W. Smith. Pub. April 5, 1971, by Intext Educational Publishers, Scranton, Pa., 154 pages, 8½ x 11, $6.00 (paperback).

Straightforward, thorough, simple, and good. Rating: A

This book is very well designed, with much thought given to readibility. Programs and runs are in Teletype originals; all statements and program lines in text are in boldface type.

There are eight chapters: Introduction to Digital Computers, Simple Programs (using six statements), Transfer of Control, Loops, Arrays, Input/Output, Functions and Subroutines, MAT Statements. The three appendixes are: Intrinsic Functions, Flow-Chart Symbols, and Solutions to Selected Exercises.

The exercises at the end of each chapter are outstanding in quantity, quality, and variety. They are taken from various fields, such as mathematics, finance, engineering, etc. The chapter on loops, for instance, includes 20 excellent exercises, covering 10 pages and involving interest, factorials, capital recovery, depreciation, evaluating series, finding roots, evaluating integrals (three methods), and ends with one on solving higher-order differential equations.

The text coverage is thorough, and includes many small points that other authors skip over. The authors note, for example, that "it is possible to transfer to a REM statement, but this is effectively the same as transferring to the first executable statement following the REM statement."

This is a college-level text: "most of the problems . . . can be comprehended by a college freshman or even a senior high school student." Most of the problems, yes, but there are many, such as the problem using a fourth-order Runge-Kutta to solve a differential equation, that would certainly mystify most college freshmen, and many college seniors. The book would certainly be useful to many high-school students, if there is an instructor on hand to clarify the difficult points.

The authors are the only ones to note, "for the student who is concerned about programming in the most efficient manner," that execution of B*B is somewhat faster than that of B↑2. Smith (30) notes that "if the exponent is small – 2 or 3 – it is customary to use the asterisk," but gives no reason for doing so.

One must dig to find something negative to say about this work. The authors recommend using a zero as the flag for the last DATA item (they are not alone in doing so) and although they do say it should be used only when the programmer knows that none of the data items is zero, it would be better not to take chances, and to use a very large or very small number. The section on files is very short, only 3½ pages. The authors explain this brevity by noting that "Unfortunately, the versions of BASIC for different systems seem to differ more in regard to the features pertaining to files than in any other respect. We shall consequently have to discuss in terms of generalities to some extent." These two points, on zero flag and files, are trivial in comparison with the many good points of this excellent text.

✳ ✳ ✳

17. *BASIC: An Introduction to Computer Programming Using the BASIC Language,* by William F. Sharpe and Nancy L. Jacob. Pub. May 1971 by The Free Press, div. of Macmillan, New York, N. Y., 177 pages, 6½ x 10, $7.95 (hardcover), $3.95 (paperback).

Starts out fine, well written, but gets much too hard except for top students. Rating: for the first seven chapters, A; for the remainder, C

This is a revised edition of Sharpe's August 1967 book with the same title, same publisher, 137 pages. The first seven chapters are essentially the same; a few paragraphs have been added, several paragraphs reworded, some problems added, a different printer used for the terminal output, and the word "labels" changed to "strings."

After chapter seven, the earlier book had four appendixes: the Dartmouth/GE system, the UWBIC system, "some useful programs" (critical path, grading, questionnaire analysis, regression and correlation, simultaneous linear equations, subroutines for automatic file maintenance), and a summary of the language.

The revised edition eliminates all four appendixes, substitutes a chapter on conversational programming and five on extended BASIC, and adds an index. All or most of the new material was apparently written by Jacob.

There are eight chapters in Part I on Essential BASIC: Introduction, Getting Started, Conditional Transfers, Reading and Printing, Loops, Lists and Tables, Functions and Subroutines, and Conversational Programming. Part II, on Extended BASIC, has five chapters: More on Strings, String Applications, Matrix Commands, Programmer-Defined Functions, and Additional Features (ON-GOTO, RESTORE, TAB, expanded IF, files).

The problems at the end of each chapter are immediately followed by the answers in full. These problems are not all as simple as they may look at first.

One first impression is that much thought has been given to readability. The programs and runs are all printed by Teletype on shaded backgrounds to set them off, certain program lines are indented, and two hyphens are used between REMARK and the remark itself. The flowcharts are elegant, with shadow-lines that give a three-dimensional effect.

The authors start right off, on page 7, with "here is an extremely simple program," and they present one with 21 lines. However, it really is simple, and five pages are taken to explain it in detail.

Here is another book concerned with the appearance of output; a printout without headings is called "hardly very elegant output."

The second program, also simple, is 42 lines long, and uses 20 REMARK lines, 8 of them blank. This is one of four books to use blank REMARK lines, and to indent certain program lines, mainly loops. It is also the only book to explain why variables should be initialized to zero, and one of the few to discuss minor print zones.

The chapter is Reading and Printing is excellent, with fine problems; the chapter has nice and explicit detail work, going into all the odds and ends.

The first half of the book is well written, in an easy, comfortable style, seeming to catch every little important detail. There are some curious omissions: no examples of switch sorting, nor of lists or tables. There are very few program runs in the book – only eleven. At times the book seems aimed at math majors: standard deviation is explained in one sentence in a footnote. Page 40 starts a complete withholding program of 50 lines which, although straightforward, requires so many inequality statements that it may be quite confusing so early in the text; this is a little too soon to separate the men from the boys. The last program in this first half is for playing roulette, and although it has many explanatory remarks, it is still very hard to follow for a beginner with no teacher to turn to.

The general picture changes from page 83 on. In the chapter on Conversational Programming, there is a program of four lines, another of 13 lines, and then a whopper, 136 lines, for playing blackjack, taking up, with its explanation, almost half the chapter. An interesting program, but why hit the reader over the head with such a long one only halfway through the text?

There are few useful applications other than a financial language called FL-1, which gets into more mathematics than many readers may be able to understand or care for. This language takes up the entire chapter on String Applications, and may be appreciated only by the top-ranking math students. They might also go for the program that generates 1,000 random normally-distributed numbers, but the average reader probably would not.

The imbalance resulting from the inclusion of these fancy mathematical programs is not realized until the section on files, which covers only four pages. A better balance might be more on files and less on higher math.

Although Part II on Extended BASIC "is designed for those persons with deeper interests and/or the need to use computers for more complex tasks," the text might appeal to a much wider audience if it didn't require a knowledge (or appreciation) of statistics, and use simpler programs in several instances.

✳ ✳ ✳

18. *Computer Programming in BASIC*, by Joseph P. Pavlovich and Thomas E. Tahan. Pub. June 24, 1971, by Holden-Day, San Francisco, Calif., 345 pages, 6 x 9, $8.95 (paperback).

Generally quite good, with many examples, much detail, and a nice variety. Rating: B

A somewhat mixed bag, although mostly on the plus side of the ledger. The back cover says that, for the reader, this book "acquaints him generally with the use of computers in a time-sharing environment as well as in a batch-processing environment." Yet the word "batch" isn't used in the book once. The book is said to "teach by example"; yes, it does, with nice long comments on the various parts of each program, and with many examples. The back cover also says the book is "designed not only for the experienced programmer, but also more especially for the beginning program." A neat trick if true, but it isn't.

A very neat format, with all program examples in Teletype originals, set off by horizontal lines across the page, above and below each program and its output. There are many of these examples. The authors go into many areas, such as exponential notation, in great detail.

There are eleven chapters, each divided into sections: time-sharing; Teletype; PRINT, arithmetic operation, corrections, LET, READ and DATA, INPUT; built-in functions, numbers in BASIC; flowcharts, IF-THEN, alphanumeric data and string variables, GO TO, loops, FOR-NEXT, DIM; GOSUB-RETURN, MAT, CHANGE, defining functions; debugging, solutions of triangles, graphs, real zeroes; matrices; statistical program, area under a curve; summary of BASIC statements; system commands. There are excellent exercises at the end of most of these sections, although without answers. Each chapter ends with a summary of what the reader has learned.

The seven appendixes give a variety of programs (and runs) in seven categories: algebra (15 programs), geometry (3), trig (1), analytic geometry (2), calculus (4), probability (1), special (4). The last of the specials is a 130-line program that prints "A Meaningless Technical Report" by randomly combining phrases used in the aerospace industry.

Two ingenious lines in the dice-game program are all that's needed to take care of the five combinations that win or lose on the first roll:

410 IF (R-7)*(R-11)=0 THEN 490
420 IF (R-2)*(R-12)=0 THEN 530

(Kemeny & Kurtz (2) do it with a single ON-GOTO statement using 11 branches; Smith (10) uses four IF statements).

The authors are among the very few to note that quote marks around a space in a PRINT statement will skip a column, in some systems.

The RESTORE statement is explained too soon, on page 38, with an example of no significant value. And instead of explaining built-in functions simply, as almost all other authors do, these define it in all too stiff and formal mathematical terms, using words such as "domain," "range" and "set." Fine for those familiar with set theory; Greek to the rest.

Although a great variety of flowcharting symbols is used in these books, this is the only one to use a triangle — for a starting or stopping point (Peluso et al (20) use it for an entry point) — even though it is the ANSI symbol for off-line storage.

Multiline function definitions are presented as though available on any BASIC time-sharing system, instead of only a few. And although the section on this subject contains some clever programs, they are difficult to understand, even with the explanations.

Ten pages are taken up with a long tutorial on trigonometry, leading up to one big program that solves any triangle, given a side and any two other parts. And there are nine pages of tutorial on matrices, a total of 19 pages that might have been better spent teaching BASIC.

By page 180, the book has gotten quite complex for a non-mathematician, with a program for finding real zeros of a function, which requires very close attention to be able to follow, and is very difficult to do so.

* * *

19. *An Introduction to the BASIC Language*, by John E. Skelton. Pub. Aug. 17, 1971, by Rinehart and Winston, New York, N. Y., 158 pages, 6 x 9, $3.95 (paperback).

Although fairly well written, there is too much padding and too little coverage of some areas. Rate: C

The preface notes that this slim paperback is an introductory text "intended for use at the high-school junior or senior or the college freshman level . . . . The text is not intended to be an exhaustive treatment of the BASIC language; in fact some features of the language (such as MAT) have been left out."

Not for lack of space, surely. There are many blank pages between chapters, and a whole page is used up for each chapter number and title. Some 20 percent of the book (over 30 pages) is blank or almost-blank pages, which could have been used to better advantage, such as providing more examples, of which there are all too few. And there is too little on lists and tables, only 2½ pages, to be really worthwhile. An entire chapter is devoted to READ and DATA, a full 2½ pages, with no mention of RESTORE.

There are ten chapters: The Problem-Solving Process; Computation: LET; Input/Output: INPUT and PRINT; Control Statements: GO TO, IF and END; Lists and Tables: DIM; Computing the Values of Polynomials (algorithms, flowcharts); Loops: FOR and NEXT; READ and DATA; Functions and Subroutines: DEF and GOSUB; Some More Programming Techniques. The exercises at the end of each chapter are few, without answers.

The real padding is in the eight appendixes, 42 pages showing how eight different time-sharing systems operate. Seven of these are accompanied by exactly the same photograph of an ASR33 Teletype, taken from a low angle so that only the tape unit shows clearly.

The writing style is rather dull. The first sentence is enough to put one off: "It is a well-known mathematical fact that any integer can be expressed as the product of prime numbers." And the text is not always easy to follow. The FOR statement is introduced this way: "The general form of the FOR statement is: LN FOR CV = EX1 TO EX2 STEP EX3, and corresponding to this statement somewhat later, LN NEXT CV." A practical example would be much better.

There are some nice things to be said about this book. Although some authors do mention that a flowchart should be checked out by hand calculations, Skelton is the only one to show exactly how this is done, several times, by giving a table of, for instance, "Calculations to Check Flowchart of Figure 1-1." There is a good section on number representation, and a detailed discussion of rounding.

This, then, is a 62-page book stretched out to 158 with many blank pages, 42 pages of not-too-useful appendixes, and a few exercises. Not quite cricket, really.

* * *

20. *Basic BASIC Programming: Self-Instructional Manual and Text*, by Anthony P. Peluso, Charles R. Bauer, and Dalward J. Debruzzi. Pub. Sept. 13, 1972, by Addison-Wesley, Reading, Mass., 274 pages, 8½ x 11, $7.50 (paperback).

An excellent book, very thorough in imparting information. Rating: A

There are many excellent features in this book, and very few drawbacks. The self-instructional feature involves blanks or questions, following short portions of text called "frames." The reader is asked to place a shield over the page to cover the correct responses which follow the blanks or questions immediately, just below a dotted line across the page, which indicates that a response is required. There are tests throughout the book, at the end of each chapter, plus five tests within Chapter Two. All answers are at the back of the book.

There are twelve chapters: Introduction to Computers, Fundamentals of BASIC, Input/Output (PRINT, END, READ, DATA), Branching, Looping, Program Preparation and Processing (including flowcharting), Advanced Looping, Advanced Branching, Advanced Input/Output, Special Functions and Subroutines, Arrays, Matrices. There are eight appendixes: Practice Problems, Hints to Practice Problems, Error Messages, Errors While the Program is in Progress, Control Commands, Limitations on BASIC, Sample Programs, Solutions to Exercises and Answers to Tests.

The best feature of this book is its thoroughness. It starts out slow and easy, goes a little faster starting with Chapter Four, but remains relatively slow. There are over ten pages on the order of operations. The first complete program is on page 52, four lines long. The IF-THEN statement is covered so completely that even the slowest learner should be able to understand it. The chapter on Advanced Branching is excellent, covering some areas that few other BASIC authors do. In these pages is one of the few full and excellent explanations of the DEF statement. Arrays are gone into fully, with many detailed examples. Appendix I contains 25 practice problems; "A few of these problems require a knowledge of first-year high school algebra, but most problems require no mathematical training." Appendix VII contains ten sample programs, with flowcharts, input listing and output, on interest, largest and smallest numbers in an array, averages, etc. Simple but instructive.

Another unique feature is that by page 25 the reader is writing program statements based on word descriptions of the desired function.

The entire book is typewritten, except for some Teletype output after page 106, and is double-spaced, so it could be half as long, although not as easy to read. The self-instruction part of the book uses very little extra white space, in comparison with, for example, the General Electric book (15).

The authors use a zero as the final data element to "provide a means of terminating execution of the program." Only three other books use a zero; most prefer either something like 99999, or a very large number such as 1E20, because zero could in some cases be a valid data element. There isn't much on matrices; 13 pages cover both arrays and matrices, with only one example of manipulation: addition of matrices. However, the slighting of this area may be understandable in light of the back-cover note that this is "written for beginning students with little or no background in the computer field." Although some statements are thoroughly covered, there are only two pages on GOSUB and RETURN. Appendix II contains Hints to Practice Problems to help solve those on the preceding pages, but without answers to any of the 25.

All in all, a very satisfying text, written by people who not only have teaching experience, but who know how a teaching text should be written. Some 40 BASIC statements are covered (of which 11 are for matrices, 9 are built-in functions, and two are logic operators for "advanced branching").

✳ ✳ ✳

21. *BASIC Programming for Business*, by Joseph C. Sass. Pub. Nov. 1, 1971, by Allyn and Bacon, Boston, Mass., 310 pages, 5¾ x 8¾, $7.95 (paperback).

Several unique and outstanding features, but sticking to a rigid method causes serious problems. Rating: B

This book has many things going for it. It is small and convenient to hold, well designed in both layout and typography. There are two unique features of great merit. The first is the use of examples of every statement: a set of proper ones, and another set of statements illustrating common errors occuring with that statement. The second outstanding feature is the use of a column of description alongside the example statements, explaining each one, not in the following text, but right up where it can be read with the statement, right where it is most needed.

There are nine chapters: Introduction; BASIC Commands; INPUT, READ-DATA, and REMARK; Transfer Commands; FOR-NEXT Loops and Arrays; Additional Features; Matrix Commands; Files; Samples With Solutions and Additional Problems. There are appendixes on error messages, correcting errors, system commands, terminal operation, and an eight-page glossary.

The text combines three kinds of type. The main body is in a sans-serif font, while the word BASIC, and all statements, whether in the text or in example groupings, are in serif type. The programs themselves are Teletype originals, reduced (when required) to a maximum 4½-inch width.

The main programs are based on two problems, bank deposit and salesmen's pay, which start small, and are expanded upon in each new chapter.

Each chapter is divided into sections; each important section is followed by exercises that pertain only to the preceding material. Answers are provided for selected exercises.

But all these fine features are not put to the best use, and the resulting book does not live up to its initial promise.

The bank deposit and salesmen's pay examples, although standard types, tend to become dull after the reader has seen them so many times, getting longer and longer as they get more complex. There are 15 of the bank problems and 12 pay problems. Although, for instance, the BANK10 program has some quite different statements than BANK09, these differences are not explained very well. And what is said, is confusing. The buildup of a simple program into more and more complex ones begins to bog down on page 119, due to their own weight, complexity, and single-mindedness. Shorter programs could have been used much more effectively to highlight the new types of statements used. BANK 10 could have been made much more understandable with the use of some examples at vital points in the discussion, but the author's rigid format, which puts examples only in groups that are not related to any of the programs, does not allow using examples where they are most needed.

The writing is another drawback; in many places it is pedantic and dull. On page 2: "The user has access to the computer by means of a typewriter-like device called a remote terminal. . . ." Even worse is on page 4: "One of the most popular terminals being used to utilize the time sharing computer. . . ." There is much excess verbiage, as on page 2: "The memory unit performs the function of retaining or storing for later use the data or information that is transmitted to the computer by the input function." On page 12: "The purpose of flowcharting is fourfold."

Sass is the only one to trace, although briefly, the origins of BASIC, from MIT down through JOSS. Also unique is the only illustration in all 34 books that graphically shows what Teletype print fields are. Also unique: three different ways of writing the first program, to show the reader that "there are many different, but all correct, solutions to the same problem when writing programs." Sass is one of the few authors to use string variables right from the beginning; page 15, in this case.

Although there are many exercises, and they are well placed in the book, the answers at the end of the book are to only a select few, usually only the first and third ones. Fine for school use, but hard on the lone reader.

Sorting by the "copy method" is explained only by a flowchart, without any accompanying, amplifying text.

The book doesn't live up to its title. There is nothing on business programs until page 189, other than the deposit and pay programs, which are standard in many programming texts. The first business program is on page 189, on production management, illustrating the use of matrix statements, just to solve two equations in two unknowns. Chapter 9, beginning on page 223, contains seven business problems, which is about all the claim this book has to being business-oriented, other than that item on page 189. The seven problems are on: "switch method" of sorting, sort using a key, marketing simulation, depreciation of an asset, interest, inventory simulation, and production simulation, a total of 29 pages. Two of the programs, marketing simulation and depreciation, need explanations, but don't get them. The "switch method" of sorting is not properly described: it is said to be done "by swapping locations with *another* value." The swapping is of *adjacent* pairs.

Appendix B shows a six-line program as run on twelve different systems. There is very little difference in the twelve runs, so why take up a dozen pages with them? The stated reason: ". . . to illustrate the slight differences in sign-on and sign-off procedures for different commercial sharing vendors." Fascinating.

creative computing
catalogue

Are you interested in one of these?

Then you'll need some of these!

Here's an unretouched memo from our Publisher to our Editor. You'll find it interesting!

```
                         MEMO

         To: Steve Gray

         From: Dave Ahl

         Subj: Editorial direction


         The comments from our readership survey and "meet the publisher
         sessions" at 3 recent conferences indicate that people would like
         to the see the following stuff in Creative.

         First of all, readers are looking to us for applications and
         software. They want, and we must provide, complete nuts and bolts
         how-to material. No gee-whiz success stories, but stuff that is
         complete, thorough, and that can be understood and built by a
         knowledgable beginner. I don't want to get into home-brew CPUs,
         but if an application requires a piece of hardware not commer-
         cially available, I want complete schematics and construction
         details. Same with software -- I'd like to focus on high-level
         langauges, but if it's necessary for an application, we should
         provide machine code programs or subroutines.

         Readers seem to like our diversity; hence we should endeavour
         to maintain our broad scope in educational and recreational com-
         puting. Specific articles that we should shoot to run in the
         next 12 months include:

            1. File catalog and retrieval system. Generalized so can
         be used for books, magazines, LP records and tapes, antiques,
         coins, household inventory (for insurance), etc. Maybe two ver-
         sions -- one for cassette, one for floppy.

            2. Text editing system(s). One use is for writing and edit-
         ing letters and reports (both for kids in school and adults).
         The other use we should hit is for responding to correspondence
         by using canned letters and paragraphs.

            3. Computer assisted instruction. A non-trivial drill and
         practice/tutorial system with full individualized record-keeping
         for mathematics and language arts for a fairly small micro.

            4. Small business customer records system.

            5. Kinetic and/or video art system. Must go beyond TV Dazzler

            6. External device interfacing (A/D, D/A, sensors) tutorial.

            7. A complete series on speech synthesis, speech recognition,
         and music synthesis.

            8. A very thorough product-by-product comparison of all high-
         level mini and micro software. Let's start with Basic interpreters

         I have lots more -- let's get together when I get back next week
         and map out the next issue in detail. By the way, I just got in
         some Fabulous new Basic games -- let's talk about possibly run-
         ing the in optical bar code along with the listings.  Till then.
```

You should subscribe to
creative computing
today! Here's why —

Creative Computing will help you decide which computer is best for you.

Creative's no-nonsense equipment profiles arm you with the facts before you talk to the vendor or dealer. Whether you're interested in a microcomputer kit, a mini, terminal, or programmable calculator, you'll find the evaluative information you need in *Creative*. Indeed, one wise hardware decision could save you the cost of a lifetime subscription!

Creative Computing discusses computer applications in non-technical, understandable language.

Business people who want to know what's going on in the EDP department, students who want to learn about microprocessors, hobbyists looking to make good use of home computers, or anyone concerned about the effect of the computer on society will find these and many, many more mind-expanding topics covered on the pages of *Creative*.

Creative Computing covers computer education in depth.

After all, that's where we got our start and so we continue to present four or five major learning activities every issue. If you're a teacher, *Creative* will save you hours of preparation time. If you're a student, you'll be way ahead of your class with *Creative*. And if you've already graduated, you can bone up on what you missed.

Creative Computing carries outstanding fiction every issue.

One of the best ways of exploring future scenarios of computer usage is through fiction, so *Creative* seeks out material from the best authors — Isaac Asimov, Frederik Pohl, Arthur C. Clarke to name just a few, as well as many others who are destined to be the best of the next generation.

Creative Computing's book reviews are honest and timely.

We're not owned by a big book publisher to whom we owe loyalty, nor do we depend upon advertising for our revenue. Hence, not only do our reviews pull no punches, but we also rank order similar books (like all 34 books on the BASIC language which we reviewed last year). *Creative* reviews virtually every computer book of interest to educators, hobbyists, and general laypeople, even including vendor manuals and government pamphlets.

An extensive resource section will save you time and money.

Every issue of *Creative* carries 40 or more short resource reviews evaluating periodicals, booklets, hardware, terminals, couplers, peripherals, software packages, organizations, dealers, and much more. Every entry has a brief description, evaluation, and the name, address, and phone number of the vendor. You'll save valuable time seeking out this information, much of which you'd possibly never come across.

Creative Computing will provide hours of mind-expanding entertainment, even if you don't have a computer.

Creative Computing carries 10 or 12 pages of games and puzzles every issue. Most of the puzzles don't need a computer or calculator to solve; some do. Naturally, the 4 or 5 new computer games (in Basic, Fortran, and APL) in every issue require access to a computer.

Creative Computing gives you things to actually do with a computer.

Home computer kit, mini, timesharing terminal — whatever your access to computer power, *Creative* provides thoroughly documented programs with complete listings and sample runs that you can use with minimum effort. Games, simulations, CAI, computer art — whether education or recreation is your bag, you'll find programs which you can use in *Creative*.

A no-compromise policy of editorial excellence means every issue is of value to you.

We firmly intend to be around a long time and we believe the way to do that is to publish only material of the very highest quality. We believe our readers are among the most astute, intelligent, and active people in the world. You can't afford to waste time reading imprecise, opinionated, or wordy articles and you won't find any in *Creative*.

The price is right — only $21 for 3 years.

That same $21 will buy you a pair of Star Trek walkie talkies, six direct dialed 10 minute calls between New York and Boston, 3 tankfulls of gas, or 10 cocktails at a Hilton hotel. Wouldn't you rather have 18 issues of Creative Computing each containing over 85 pages of solid editorial material (including advertising, over 100 pages per issue). Count the editorial pages in *any other* hobbyist or special interest magazine and compare it to *Creative*. *Any other*. 1 year subscription $8. Lifetime $300.

NO RISK GUARANTEE
You may cancel your subscription at any time for any reason and we will refund the balance without question.

David H. Ahl, Publisher

FOR FASTER RESPONSE
800-631-8112
(In NJ, call 201-540-0445)

SUBSCRIPTION ORDER FORM

Type	Term	USA		Foreign Surface		Foreign Air	
Individual	1-Year	☐	$ 8	☐	$12	☐	$20
	3-Year	☐	21	☐	33	☐	57
	Lifetime	☐	300	☐	400	☐	600
Institutional	1-Year	☐	15	☐	15	☐	23
	3-Year	☐	40	☐	40	☐	60

☐ New   ☐ Renewal

☐ Cash, check, or M.O. enclosed

☐ BankAmericard   Card No. _____

☐ Master Charge   Expiration date _____

☐ Please bill me ($1.00 billing fee will be added)

Name _____

Address _____

City _____ State _____ Zip _____

Send to: Creative Computing, **ATTN:** Cindy
P.O. Box 789-M, Morristown, NJ 07960

The Best of **creative computing** Volume 2

NEW!

This fascinating 336-page book contains the best of the articles, fiction, foolishness, puzzles, programs, games, and reviews from Volume 2 issues of *Creative Computing* magazine. The contents are enormously diverse with something for everyone. Fifteen new computer games are described with complete listings and sample runs for each; 67 pages are devoted to puzzles, problems, programs, and things to actually do. Frederik Pohl drops in for a visit along with 10 other super storytellers. And much more! The staggering diversity of the book can really only be grasped by examining the contents, or better yet, the book itself. Price is $8.95

NOTE: Reviews marked with a † are longer feature reviews.

For FAST service, use your bank card and our toll-free order hot line

800-631-8112
(In NJ, call 201-540-0445)

COMPUTER RAGE is a fascinating new board game based on a large-scale multi-processing computer system. The object is to move your three programs from input to output. Moves are determined by the roll of 3 binary dice. Hazards include priority interrupts, program bugs, decision symbols which alter your path, power failures, and restricted use input and output channels. Notes are included for using the game in school. Ages 10-adult; 2-4 players. COMPUTER RAGE comes with a colorful board, 12 program playing pieces, 3 binary dice, 38 interrupt cards. Orders must be prepaid. Only $8.95 postpaid ($10 outside of USA). Creative Computing, P.O. Box 789-M, Morristown, NJ 07960, ATTN: Cindy

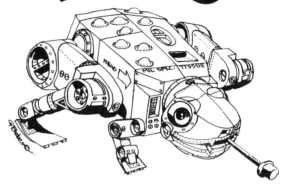

BIONIC TOAD FOR CHILDREN

The same super bionic toad design (riveted on warts and all) as on our best-selling adult T-shirt. Deep purple design on light blue shirt. Children's sizes S (6-8), M (10-12), L (14-16) and, of course, adult men's sizes too S,M,L,XL. One price for all: $4.50 postpaid in USA, $5.50 to foreign addresses. Creative Computing, P.O. Box 789-M, Morristown, NJ 07960. Attn: Cindy

101 BASIC Computer Games is the most popular book of computer games in the world. Every program in the book has been thoroughly tested and appears with a complete listing, sample run, and descriptive write-up. All you need add is a BASIC-speaking computer and you're set to go.

101 BASIC Computer Games. Edited by David H. Ahl. 248 pages. 8½x11 paperbound. $7.50

THE BEST OF BYTE — VOL. 1

The Best of Byte - Volume 1 is a 384-page blockbuster of a book which contains the majority of material from the first 12 issues of Byte magazine. 146 pages are devoted to "Hardware" and are cram full of how-to articles on everything from TV displays to joysticks to cassette interfaces. The section on computer kits describes building 7 major kits. But hardware without software might as well be a boat anchor, so there are 125 pages of "Software and Applications" ranging from on-line debuggers to games to a complete small business accounting system. A section on "Theory" examines the how and why behind the circuits and programs, and a final section "Opinion" looks at where this explosive new hobby is heading.

The Best of Byte - Volume 1 is edited by Carl Helmers and David Ahl and published by Creative Computing Press. Price in the US is $11.95 plus $1.00 shipping and handling ($12.95 total); foreign orders add $1.00 ($13.95 total). Orders from individuals must be prepaid. Creative Computing Press, Attn. Cindy., P.O. Box 789-M, Morristown, NJ 07960. Allow 8 weeks for delivery.

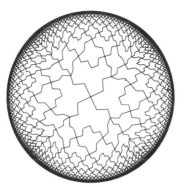

ARTIST AND COMPUTER is a unique new art book that covers a multitude of computer uses and the very latest techniques. In its pages, 35 artists who work with computers explain how the computer can be programmed either to actualize the artist's concept (such as the visualization of fabric before it is woven) or to produce finished pieces. Illustrated with more than 160 examples of computer art, 9 of them in full color. ARTIST AND COMPUTER will fascinate and inspire anyone who is interested in art or computer technology. Size 8½" x 11".

ARTIST AND COMPUTER

Edited by RUTH LEAVITT

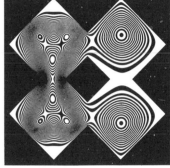

132 pages, soft cover $4.95
Cloth cover $10.00

STAR TREK COMPUTER IMAGES

Mr. Spock Poster. Large (17" x 23") computer image on heavy poster stock. A digital scanning densitometer transformed each 50 micron square point on the negative into a line printer character (using two overprintings). $1.50 postpaid.

Set of 7 Computer Images. Kirk, Spock, McCoy, Sulu, Scott, Uhrura, and the Enterprise. On heavy poster stock. 8½ x 11. $1.50 per set postpaid.

Hundreds and hundreds of cartoons about computers, robots, calculators, AI, and much more.

THE COLOSSAL COMPUTER CARTOON BOOK

128 big pages! Paperbound.

Only $4.95

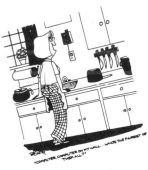

BOOKS BOOKS BOOKS

Computer Games

101 Basic Computer Games

David H. Ahl. An anthology of games and simulations—from Acey-Deucey to Yahtzee, all in the BASIC language. Contains a complete listing, sample run, plus a descriptive write-up of each game. Our most popular book! Large format, 248 pp. $7.50 [6C]

What to Do After You Hit Return

Another collection of games and simulations—all in BASIC—including number guessing games, word games, hide-and-seek games, pattern games, board games, business and social science simulations and science fiction games. Large format. 158 pp. $8.00 [8A]

Games & Puzzles Magazine

The only magazine in the world devoted to games and puzzles of every kind — mathematical, problematical, crosswords, chess, gomoko, checkers, backgammon, wargames, card games, board games, reviews, competitions, and more. Monthly. 1-Year sub'n $12.00 [3A]

The Star Trek Star Fleet Technical Manual

Franz Joseph. This important resource book is packed with the data you need to create or modify STAR TREK computer games (see 2 above), including all Starship operating characteristics, and defense and weapon systems; standard orbits; velocity/time relationship; space warp technology; Milky Way galaxy charts; Federation charts; Federation codes; etc., etc. A national best seller. Large format, vinyl binder. 180 pp. $6.95 [8C]

Fun & Games with the Computer

Ted Sage. "This book is designed as a text for a one-semester course in computer programming using the BASIC language. The programs used as illustrations and exercises are games rather than mathematical algorithms, in order to make the book appealing and accessible to more students. The text is well written, with many excellent sample programs. Highly recommended." — *The Mathematics Teacher* 351 pp. $6.95 [8B]

Game Playing With the Computer, 2nd Ed.

Donald Spencer. Over 70 games, puzzles, and mathematical recreations for the computer. Over 25 games in BASIC and FORTRAN are included complete with descriptions, flowcharts, and output. Also includes a fascinating account of the history of game-playing machines, right up to today's computer war games. Lots of "how-to" information for applying mathematical concepts to writing your own games. 320 pp. 1976 $16.95 [8S]

Hand Calculators

Games, Tricks and Puzzles For A Hand Calculator

Wally Judd. This book is a necessity for anyone who owns or intends to buy a hand calculator, from the most sophisticated (the HP65, for example) to the basic "four banger." 110 pp. $2.95 [8D]

Games With The Pocket Calculator

Sivasailam Thiagarajan and Harold Stolovitch. A big step beyond tricks and puzzles with the hand calculator, the two dozen games of chance and strategy in this clever new book involve two or more players in conflict and competition. A single inexpensive four-banger is all you need to play. Large format. 50 pp. $2.00 [8H]

Advanced Applications for Pocket Calculators

Jack Gilbert. Emphasizes new and unique applications that go way beyond manufacturer instruction manuals. Shows how to do scientific calculations with a basic 4-banger. Also covers scientific, programmable and advanced business calculators. Hundreds of examples and tables. 304 pp. 1975 $5.95 [8G]

All 3 New!

Problem Solving

How to Solve Problems

Wayne Wickelgren. This helpful book analyzes and systematizes some of the basic methods of solving mathematical problems. Illustrative examples include chess problems, logical puzzles, railroad switching problems and ones from science and engineering. For each, the author provides hints for the reader to tackle the problem, and then a complete solution is given. Want to solve a complex problem with a computer? Begin here. 1974. 262 pp. $6.50 [7Y].

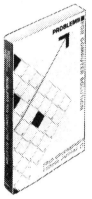

Problems For Computer Solution

Gruenberger & Jaffray. A collection of 92 problems in engineering, business, social science and mathematics. The problems are presented in depth and cover a wide range of difficulty. Oriented to Fortran but good for any language. A classic. 401 pp. $8.95 [7A]

Problem Solving With The Computer

Ted Sage. This text is designed to be used in a one-semester course in computer programming. It teaches BASIC in the context of the traditional high school mathematics curriculum. There are 40 carefully graded problems dealing with many of the more familiar topics of algebra and geometry. Probably the most widely adopted computer text. 244 pp. $6.95 [8J]

LOOK!

Problem Solving: The Computer Approach

LaFave, Milbrandt, and Garth. Describes the process of thinking through the steps needed to solve a problem, flowcharting the steps, coding in a computer language, development of appropriate test data, and manual checking. 176 pp. 1973 $11.65 [8U]

Prices subject to change without notice.

Programming

The Art of Computer Programming

Donald Knuth. The purpose of this series is to provide a unified, readable, and theoretically sound summary of the present knowledge concerning computer programming techniques, together with their historical development. For the sake of clarity, many carefully checked computer procedures are expressed both in formal and informal language. A classic series. Vol. 1: Fundamental Algorithms, 634 pp. $20.95 [7R]. Vol. 2: Seminumerical Algorithms, 624 pp. $20.95 [7S]. Vol. 3: Sorting and Searching, 722 pp. $20.95 [7T].

A Guided Tour of Computer Programming In Basic

Tom Dwyer and Michael Kaufman. "This is a fine book, mainly for young people, but of value for everyone, full of detail, many examples (including programs for hotel and airline reservations systems, and payroll), with much thought having been given to the use of graphics in teaching. This is the best of the introductory texts on BASIC." — *Creative Computing* Large format. 156 pp. $4.80 [8L]

Computer Algorithms and Flowcharting

G. Silver and J. Silver. A straightforward approach to analyzing problems and structuring solutions suitable for the computer. Branching, counters, loops, and other important concepts are presented in easily-grasped modular units in the text. 176 pp. 1975 $8.95[8W]

A Simplified Guide to Fortran Programming

Daniel McCracken. A thorough first text in Fortran. Covers all basic statements and quickly gets into case studies ranging from simple (printing columns) to challenging (craps games simulation). 278 pp. $8.75 [7F]

Instant BASIC

Jerald Brown. A self-teaching guide to BASIC for the beginners. Designed to be used with a personal microcomputer running Altair BASIC or a terminal running DEC BASIC-PLUS. Self-tests, practical demonstrations, and practice problems assure fast effective learning. Large format. 1977. $6.00 [7L]

NEW!

Computer Science: A First Course, 2nd Ed.

A.I. Forsythe, T.A. Keenan, E.I. Organick and *W. Stenberg.* An improved version of an extremely complete and well-prepared volume, this is ideal for self-study or daily reference on the job. Covering all topics in greater depth — and, of course, now providing more up-to-date information — it gives you the material you need on algorithms, data structures, programming, and computer architecture.

In addition, you'll discover extensions and applications of basic concepts in special areas. Further help is provided by the numerous tables, flowcharts, and data structure diagrams, plus a common base flowchart language for use in top-down structured programming and adaptable to a wide variety of problem application areas. 880 pp. (1975) $16.95 [7D]

My Computer Likes Me

This entertaining self-teaching workbook introduces the BASIC language to young or old. Problems and examples are drawn from population problems and demographic data. A nice, easy start into BASIC. Large format. 60 pp. 1973. $2.00 [8K]

Some Common BASIC Programs

Adam Osborne. An ideal workbook to accompany an elementary BASIC programming course. Contains 76 general purpose practical BASIC programs. The listings are extensively commented. A restricted subset of BASIC was used to insure maximum transferability. 1977. $7.50 [7M]

BASIC Programming 2nd Ed

Kemeny and Kurtz. "A simple gradual introduction to computer programming and time-sharing systems. The best text on BASIC on almost all counts. Rating: A+" - *Creative Computing.* 150 pp. $8.50 [7E]

Programming Proverbs

Henry Ledgard. Features 26 ingenious proverbs to strengthen your powers of program organization and logical thinking. Complete explanation of each proverb including examples of its use or lack of it. Guaranteed improvement of your programming clarity, accuracy, and style. 144 pp. 1975. $6.50 Please specify sample programs in FORTRAN [8Y]. Sample programs in PL/I, ALGOL and other languages [8X].

BASIC

Albrecht, Finkel, and Brown. A self-teaching guide to BASIC written in an informal, easy-going manner. Every difficult point is explained in great detail. 324 pp. $4.95 [7G]

ANS COBOL

Ruth Ashley. An excellent self-teaching book for people without previous programming experience and with no access to a terminal. The author anticipates common errors of first-time COBOL users and gives extra help to readers through these parts. 242 pp. $4.95 [7H]

The Calculus With Analytic Geometry Handbook

Jason Taylor. Ideal for a HS or college introductory calculus course or for self-learning. Five chapters include: analytic geometry; functions and derivatives; integration techniques; vectors and functions of more than one variable; and sequences and series. Widely acclaimed by educators, this book is fast becoming the *standard calculus reference text.* Handy reference for scientists, engineers, and mathematicians too. Large format. 68 pp. 1976. $2.95 [7Q]

Understanding Solid State Electronics

An excellent tutorial introduction to transistor and diode circuitry. Used at the TI Learning Center, this book was written for the person who needs to understand electronics but can't devote years to the study. 242 pp. $2.95 [9A]

Microprocessors

A collection of articles from *Electronics* magazine. The book is in three parts: device technology; designing with microprocessors; and applications. 160 pp. 1975 $13.50 [9J]

Microprocessors: Technology, Architecture and Applications

Daniel R. McGlynn. This introduction to the microprocessor defines and describes the related computer structures and electronic semi-conductor processes. Treats both hardware and software, giving an overview of commercially available microprocessors, and helps the user to determine the best one for him/her. 240 pp. $12.00 [7C]

Software Design for Microprocessors

Wester and Simpson. A complete stand-alone guide for beginner or professional which presents the basics of microprocessor machine code and assembly language. The first chapter starts with basic terms, then gets into machine architecture with a detailed look at instructions and addressing. Succeeding chapters present the process of generating software, designing a simple demonstration machine as well as four comprehensive sample problems. 350 pp. 1976 $12.95 [9D]

Building Your Own

Microcomputer Handbook

Charles J. Sippl. A comprehensive microcomputer reference guide for designers, users, students, and hobbyists. Covers microcomputer design; software and programming techniques; available products, kits, and development systems; comparison of micros, minis and standard systems; and applications including use in control systems, businesses, banks, factories, and homes. A vital reference. 480 pp. 1977. $19.95 [7N]

Build Your Own Working Robot

David Heiserman. Complete plans, schematics and logic circuits for building a robot. Not a project for novices, this robot is a sophisticated experiment in cybernetics. You build him in phases and watch his capabilities increase and his personality develop. Phase I is leash led, Phase II has a basic brain, while Phase III responds and makes decisions. 238 pp. 1976 $5.95 [9M]

Introduction To Microcomputers: Basic Concepts

Adam Osborne. This book became a leading text in colleges and universities just a few months after release. The book assumes no prior knowledge of computers; therefore, computer concepts are described, beginning with first principles, binary arithmetic and boolean algebra. The book covers in depth memory organization, the microprocessor CPU, I/O logic, programming, and then discusses a hypothetical instruction set. 304 pp. (1976) $7.50 [9k]

An Introduction to Microcomputers — Vol. 2: Some Real Products (2nd Edition)

Adam Osborne. Covers over 20 real microprocessors (4, 8, and 16 bit) in considerable detail. For example, 19 timing diagrams are presented for using the 8080A call instruction as an interrupt response. Also covers major chip slice products. 304 pp. 1977. $15.00 [9L]

Computing Milieu

PCC's Reference Book of Personal and Home Computing

Ever try to find the address of a manufacturer of a cassette interface that a friend told you about 2 weeks ago? Frustrating isn't it? This book will go a long way towards ending that frustration with its comprehensive list of manufacturers, stores, and products. Also contains survey articles on software, hardware, kits, and applications as well as an index of articles from various hobbyist magazines. Several bibliographies too. 1977. $4.95 [7P]

Computer Lib/ Dream Machine

Ted Nelson. This book is devoted to the premise that everybody should understand computers. In a blithe manner the author covers interactive systems, terminals, computer languages, data structures, binary patterns, computer architecture, mini-computers, big computers, microprocessors, simulation, military uses of computers, computer companies, and much, much more. Whole earth catalog style and size. A doozy! 127 pp. $7.00 [8P]

Computer Power and Human Reason

Joseph Weizenbaum. In this major new book, a distinguished computer scientist sounds the warning against the dangerous tendency to view computers and humans as merely two different kinds of "thinking machines." Weizenbaum explains exactly how the computer works and how it is being wrongly substituted for human choices. 300 pp. $9.95 [8R]

The Underground Buying Guide

Dennis A. King. The Guide is written for hams, CBers, Experimenters, and Computer Hobbyists. It lists a wide range of parts, supplies, and services categorized by firms, products, and geographic location and completely cross-referenced. Covers 250 product categories and 650 firms from tiny to huge. 200 pp. 1977. $5.95 [7K]

⭒LOOK !

Freedom's Edge

Milton Wessel. The computer threat to society. The author, an attorney, shows some of the ways in which the computer is changing our lives—or soon will be. Discusses the data bank, point-of-sale marketing and free competition, computer related crime, controlling the computer, etc. 137 pp. $5.95 [8N]

Computers in Society

Donald Spencer. How can the computer help the businessman, artist, or sports announcer? This book examines a wide range of up to date applications of the computer to medicine, engineering, transportation, business, the arts, education, law, process control, and many other areas. 208 pp. $5.50 [8Q]

The Thinking Computer

Bertram Raphael. This book is a lucid introduction to artificial intelligence with a minimum of technical jargon. It discusses the progress of AI, research goals, and the current approaches for making the computer more intelligent. 1976. 321 pp. $6.95 [7X].

Texas Instruments Data Books

Linear and Interface Circuits Data Book

Contains full specs and data on linear (72000 series) and interface (75000 series) logic gates and circuits. 688 pp. $3.95 [9G]

Semiconductor Memory Data Book

Contains complete data on practically every random access (RAM) and read only (ROM) semiconductor memory. 272 pp. $2.95 [9H]

Transistor and Diode Data Book

Describes the characteristics of over 800 transistors and 500 silicon diodes most widely used in switching and amplifying applications. Covers low-power (1 watt or less) semiconductors. You'd expect a big, comprehensive data book from one of the pioneers in the field and this is it. 1248 pp. $4.95 [9B]

Power Semiconductor Handbook

Covers high-power transistors and related switching devices. Want your computer to control some external device? Then this is the book. 800 pp. $3.95 [9C]

TTL Data Book

Presents detailed specifications of most 7400 series TTL logic devices. This is the industry standard data book for design engineers, hobbyists, educators, or anyone working with TTL. 640 pp. $4.95 [9E]

326

CREATIVE COMPUTING ORDER FORM

A Name and Address

Sold to -

Name _____

Address _____
_____

City _____ State _____ Zip _____

Ship to (if different from "Sold to") -

Name _____

Address _____
_____

City _____ State _____ Zip _____

B Creative Computing Subscriptions

Bi-monthly	USA	Foreign Surface	Foreign Air
Individual 1-Year	☐ $8	☐ $12	☐ $20
Individual 3-Year	☐ 21	☐ 33	☐ 57
Individual Lifetime	☐ 300	☐ 400	☐ 600
Institutional 1-Year	☐ 15	☐ 15	☐ 23
Institutional 3-Year	☐ 40	☐ 40	☐ 60

☐ New ☐ Gift (Put your name in "sold to"and
☐ Renewal   recipients in "ship to")

C Back Issues (when available)

Quantity	Vol./No. or Cover Date	Price Ea.*	Total
_____	_____	$1.75	____
_____	_____	1.75	____
_____	_____	1.75	____
_____	_____	1.75	____
_____	_____	1.75	____

*Foreign price $2.50 each   Total ____

D Books and Merchandise

Quantity	Cat. No.	Title	Price Ea.	Total
CREATIVE COMPUTING PRESS BOOKS -				
_____	6A	Best of Creative Computing - Vol. 1	$8.95	____
_____	6B	Best of Creative Computing - Vol. 2	8.95	____
_____	6F	Best of Byte - Vol. 1	11.95	____
_____	6C	101 BASIC Computer Games	7.50	____
_____	6D	Artist and Computer	4.95	____
_____	6G	The Colossal Computer Cartoon Book	4.95	____
_____	6H	Amazing, Thrilling, Fantastic Computer Stories	5.95	____
_____	6Z	Computer Rage (board game)	8.95	____

OTHER BOOKS AND MERCHANDISE

_____	_____	_____	_____	____
_____	_____	_____	_____	____
_____	_____	_____	_____	____
_____	_____	_____	_____	____
_____	_____	_____	_____	____
_____	_____	_____	_____	____
_____	_____	_____	_____	____

Prices subject to change without notice.

Shipping and handling (USA: 1 book $1.00, 2 or more $2.00;
Foreign: $1.25 per book)   ____

Total ____

E Total Order

Part B   _____
Part C   _____
Part D   _____

New Jersey residents add 5% sales tax _____

Billing Fee $1.00 (book orders from   _____
individuals must be prepaid)

Grand Total   _____

You can speed your order by calling us and charging your bank
card. Dial **800-631-8112** (In NJ, dial 201-540-0445).

☐ Cash, check, or M.O. enclosed
☐ BankAmericard ⎫ Card No. _____
☐ Master Charge ⎭ Expiration date _____
☐ Bill me ($1.00 billing fee. Book orders from individuals and all
   foreign orders must be prepaid.)

Return form to: CREATIVE COMPUTING, P.O. Box 789-M, Morristown, New Jersey 07960 Attn: Cindy

It's Easy to Order

1. Fill out the front of the form completely.
2. Tear out form and fold on scored lines.
3. If you are paying by a bank card, tape the form closed, put on a first class stamp and mail.
4. If you enclose payment, enclose form and payment in an envelope and mail.

Thank you!

FOLD HERE

Place
first class
stamp here.

creative computing

P.O. Box 789-M
Morristown, NJ 07960

Attn: Cindy

FOLD HERE

Save Time With Our Toll-Free Number

Any products in this catalog section can be ordered by calling us direct and charging your Visa/BankAmericard or Master Charge.

800-631-8112
(In New Jersey, call 201-540-0445)